America's
TEST KITCHEN

ADDITIONAL COOKBOOKS AND DVD SETS AVAILABLE FROM THE PUBLISHER OF COOK'S COUNTRY INCLUDE:

The *America's Test Kitchen* Family Cookbook
The Best of *America's Test Kitchen* 2007
Cook's Country 2005 Annual Edition

THE BEST RECIPE SERIES

The Best 30-Minute Recipe
The Best Light Recipe
The *Cook's Illustrated* Guide to Grilling and Barbecue
Best American Side Dishes
Cover & Bake
The New Best Recipe
Steaks, Chops, Roasts, and Ribs
Baking Illustrated
Restaurant Favorites at Home
Perfect Vegetables
The Quick Recipe
Italian Classics
The Best American Classics
The Best Soups & Stews

THE AMERICA'S TEST KITCHEN SERIES

(companion cookbooks and DVD sets to our hit public television series)

Test Kitchen Favorites: 2007 season companion cookbook
Cooking at Home with *America's Test Kitchen:* 2006 season companion cookbook
America's Test Kitchen Live! 2005 season companion cookbook
Inside *America's Test Kitchen:* 2004 season companion cookbook
Here in *America's Test Kitchen:* 2003 season companion cookbook
The *America's Test Kitchen* Cookbook: 2002 season companion cookbook
The *America's Test Kitchen* 2006 season 4-DVD boxed set
The *America's Test Kitchen* 2005 season 4-DVD boxed set
The *America's Test Kitchen* 2004 season 4-DVD boxed set
The *America's Test Kitchen* 2003 season 4-DVD boxed set
The *America's Test Kitchen* 2002 season 4-DVD boxed set
The *America's Test Kitchen* 2001 season 2-DVD boxed set

ADDITIONAL BOOKS FROM THE EDITORS OF COOK'S ILLUSTRATED MAGAZINE INCLUDE:

The Cook's Bible
The *Cook's Illustrated* Complete Book of Pasta and Noodles
The Kitchen Detective
834 Kitchen Quick Tips
1993–2006 *Cook's Illustrated* Master Index
Cook's Illustrated Annual Editions from each year of publication (1993–2006)

To order any of our cookbooks listed above, give us a call at 800-611-0759 inside the U.S., or at 515-246-6911 if calling from outside the U.S.
You can order subscriptions, gift subscriptions, and any of our books by visiting our online store at www.cookscountry.com

$35.00

Published by America's Test Kitchen, 17 Station Street, Brookline, MA 02445
ISBN-13: 978-1-933615-13-4 ISSN: 1552-1990

To get home delivery of *Cook's Country,* call 800-526-8447 inside the U.S., or 515-247-7571 if calling from outside the U.S., or subscribe online at www.cookscountry.com.

2006 Recipe Index

RC = Recipe card
IBC = Inside back cover

C

Q

R

Y

Z

Cook's Country

FEBRUARY/MARCH 2006

Hearty Vegetable Soup
In Just 30 Minutes

Texas BBQ Brisket
Smoky Flavor from Your Oven

Stuffed Chicken Breasts
Quick Filling, Crunchy Coating

RATING NONSTICK SKILLETS
$10 Pan Beats Competition

FREEZER ENCHILADAS
Just Bake and Serve

DEVIL'S FOOD CUPCAKES
6 Decorating Ideas

SLOW-COOKER BOLOGNESE
Easy, Rich, and Meaty Sauce

GREEN BEANS PARMESAN
Crispy Topping, Tender Beans

CINNAMON ROLL MAKEOVER
Lighter, Quicker, Better

GLAZED PORK TENDERLOIN
Spicy Glaze Keeps Meat Moist

CRISPY POTATO PANCAKES
Frozen Secret to Fast Recipe

Our Pasta Casserole Contest Winner!
Vanessa Bryce of Dallas, Texas, won first place with a recipe that uses baked vermicelli as the crust for a meaty, cheesy filling. See page 4 for her **Spaghetti Pie.**

$4.95 U.S./$6.95 CANADA
0 3>
0 74470 05251 7

Cook's Country

Dear Country Cook,

I grew up sugaring at Charlie Bentley's saphouse, just off the road to the gravel pit. I still remember slipping off the galvanized covers and carrying the heavy buckets to the 250-gallon container on the wagon. Some days we hitched up the team, Duke and Dan, to pull the sap, and other times we used the rusted International Scout. After hours of collecting, my flannel shirt and gloves were soaking wet. That's when I headed for the saphouse.

Inside, it was dark and smelled like a pancake breakfast, and I could see that Fred Woodcock was in charge of the boiling. (He's buried up in the cemetery with the things he loved best carved into his tombstone: his dog, a plate of doughnuts, and a can of beer.) Today, we use a special glass densimeter to determine when the syrup is ready, but in those days Fred simply relied on a skimmer, letting the hot syrup drip off the edge until it curled and dripped just right.

Even though our family still sugars in March, I look back on those days and think not of the syrup or the homemade snow cones but the sense of common purpose. We all did our part, from 8-year-olds to grandparents. It's funny how the sweetest memories come from our hardest labors.

Christopher Kimball
Founder and Editor, Cook's Country Magazine

Winter Treat Vermont farmer Harold Eastman of Quechee Fells Farm pours hot farm-made maple syrup onto cold snow to make a New England treat known as sugar-on-snow, 1950. (Photo by John Titchen/Three Lions/Getty Images)

"Home on the Range"

FEBRUARY/MARCH 2006

Cook's Country

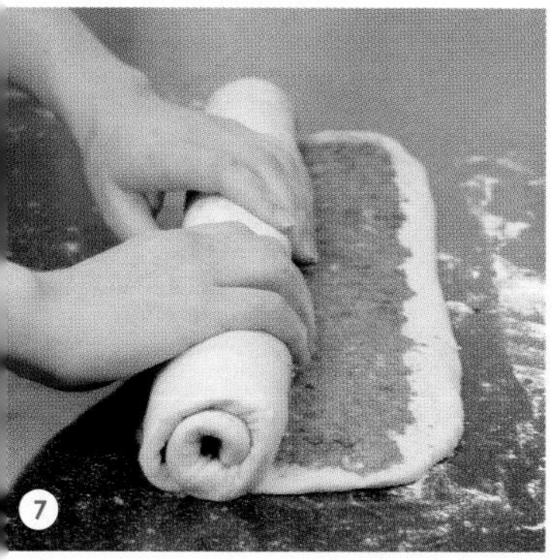

departments

features

in every issue

Founder and Editor Christopher Kimball
Executive Editor Jack Bishop
Senior Editor Bridget Lancaster
Test Kitchen Director Erin McMurrer
Copy Chief India Koopman
Associate Editors Keri Fisher, Eva Katz
Assistant Editor Melissa Baldino
Test Cooks Stephanie Alleyne, Katie Henderson, Jeremy Sauer
Assistant Test Cooks Meredith Butcher, Cali Rich
Kitchen Assistant Nadia Domeq
Recipe Tester Barbara Akins

Design Director Amy Klee
Marketing Designer Julie Bozzo
Designer Heather Barrett
Staff Photographer Daniel J. van Ackere

Production Director Guy Rochford
Project Manager Anne Francis
Production Assistants Jeanette McCarthy, Christian Steinmetz, Matthew Warnick
Systems Administrator Richard Cassidy
Internet Technology Director Aaron Shuman
Web Producer Lauren Record

Chief Financial Officer Sharyn Chabot
Controller Mandy Shito
Staff Accountant Maya Santoso
Office Manager Saudiyah Abdul-Rahim
Receptionist Henrietta Murray
Publicity Deborah Broide

Vice President Marketing David Mack
Circulation Director Bill Tine
Fulfillment Manager Carrie Horan
Circulation Assistant Elizabeth Dayton
Products Director Steven Browall
Direct Mail Director Adam Perry
Customer Service Manager Jacqueline Valerio
Customer Service Representative Julie Gardner
E-Commerce Marketing Manager Hugh Buchan

Vice President Sales Demee Gambulos
Marketing Assistant Connie Forbes

Editorial Office: 17 Station Street, Brookline, MA 02445; 617-232-1000; fax 617-232-1572
Subscription inquiries: 800-526-8447
Postmaster: Send all new orders, subscription inquiries, and change-of-address notices to Cook's Country, P.O. Box 8382, Red Oak, IA 51591-1382

ON THE COVER: PHOTOGRAPHY: Peter Howard Smith/StockFood. ILLUSTRATION: John Burgoyne.
IN THIS ISSUE: COLOR FOOD PHOTOGRAPHY: Keller + Keller. STYLING: Mary Jane Sawyer, Marie Piraino. ILLUSTRATION: Lisa Parett.

Cook's Country magazine (ISSN 1552-1990), number 7, is published bimonthly by Boston Common Press Limited Partnership, 17 Station Street, Brookline, MA, 02445.

Application to mail at periodical postage rates pending at Boston, Mass., and additional mailing offices. POSTMASTER: Send address changes to Cook's Country, P.O. Box 8382, Red Oak, IA 51591-1382. For subscription and gift subscription orders, subscription inquiries, or change-of-address notices, call 800-526-8447 in the U.S. or 515-247-7571 from outside the U.S., or write us at Cook's Country, P.O. Box 8382, Red Oak, IA 51591-1382. PRINTED IN THE USA

Visit us at www.cookscountry.com!
Go online to ask questions, share kitchen tips, and enter recipe contests. You can also take a sneak peek at what we've got cooking for upcoming issues.

Kitchen Shortcuts

READERS SHARE CLEVER TIPS FOR EVERYDAY COOKING CHALLENGES

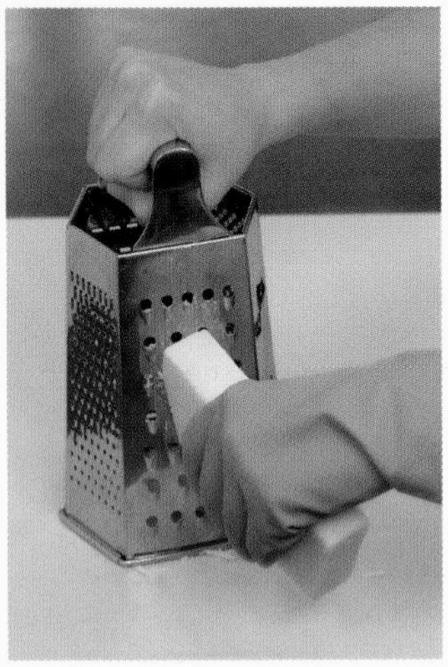

Safe Grating

When grating cheese or vegetables with a box grater, I wear a clean dishwashing glove. It keeps my knuckles from getting scraped if I get too close to the grater, and it helps me keep a grip on the food. When I'm finished, I just wash my hands with the glove still on to remove any residue.

Laura K. Valangeon
Dayton, Ohio

Degrease with a Turkey Baster

To remove the grease from the skillet after browning ground beef, I push all the meat to one side, tilt the pan to let the grease run to the empty side, and use my turkey baster to remove it.

Jennifer Hatridge
Brunswick, Maine

Bigger Is Better

Funneling Preserves

Spooning preserves into canning jars is a messy process. I thought to cut the bottom off an old funnel so that it just fit the mouth of the jar. After sterilizing the funnel, I placed it atop the jar and easily spooned in the hot preserves. The lids sealed better on clean rims, and cleanup was a cinch: I just rinsed out the funnel.

Dick Mazziotti
Luray, Va.

Steady as She Goes

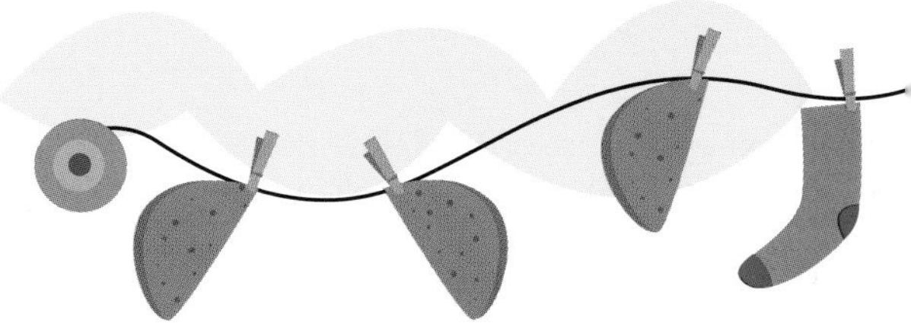

FILLING TACO SHELLS NEATLY

To make sure crispy taco shells stay upright when I'm filling them, I use plastic clothespins to hold three shells together in one unit. The shells don't fall over while I'm filling them, and the toppings stay in place. When it's time to clean up, the clothespins go right in the dishwasher.

Todd Giese Brooklyn, N.Y.

QUICK STIR-IN IDEAS

For a delicious, make-at-home cherry cola, add maraschino cherry juice to your favorite brand. And, for a change of pace from everyday oatmeal, add a heaping spoonful of Ovaltine to the milk.

Joan Nesmith
Williams, Minn.

NO-MESS HONEY

To keep honey from dripping all over the place when you're cooking, run hot water over a metal measuring spoon; the honey slips right off the hot spoon, with no sticky drips. This tip also works if you want to sweeten a cup of tea—just dip your spoon in the hot tea before dipping it into the honey jar.

Millie Barnes
Via e-mail

EASY-MAKE DOUGH

When I make bread or any yeast-risen dough, I do it from start to finish in an upside-down Tupperware-style cake keeper. I tilt it to one side to combine the warm water, yeast, and sugar and then add the remaining ingredients. I knead the dough in the container and cover it loosely with the lid (actually the bottom) while the dough rises. No more messy countertops, and the straight sides make it easy to judge when the dough has doubled in size.

Jane Howell
Aurora, Ill.

NEW USE FOR OLD WINE BOTTLES

Instead of paying for decorative bottles for my oil and vinegar, I use empty wine bottles. After washing them and letting them dry, I fill them with olive oil or vinegar and top them with plastic liquor pourers for handy use. They work (and look) great!

Gordon Dunham
Saratoga, Calif.

ERASABLE LABELS

Labeling leftovers isn't so easy, especially if you're like me and you use Rubbermaid containers. Felt tip markers stain the containers, and using labels is a pain. Now I use vis-à-vis markers (for dry-erase boards); the ink can be wiped off with nothing more than a damp paper towel. I've tied a vis-à-vis to the refrigerator door, and everything that goes in the fridge gets a quick label.

Ben Thompson
Los Angeles, Calif.

WASH AND CHOP

To wash and chop parsley simultaneously, discard the large stems and place the leaves in a blender. Add cold water until the blender is about two-thirds full, then blend in short bursts until the parsley is roughly chopped. Let the parsley sit in the water for a minute so that the dirt sinks to the bottom and then remove the chopped parsley with a slotted spoon and press it dry between a few layers of paper towels.

Stacy Vezos
Ft. Lauderdale, Fla.

INSTANT COLESLAW

When entertaining, I use a whole head of cabbage as a "dip bowl." I cut a slice off the bottom of the cabbage to make it level and use a paring knife to carve out the inside. Then I fill it with dip and surround it with a mixture of chopped veggies or chips. When the party's over, I chop up the cabbage with the remaining dip and get instant coleslaw!

Fay Abrahamsson
Guilford, Conn.

NO MORE TORN TOAST

To avoid tearing my morning toast when attempting to spread it with cold butter, I simply melt a tablespoon or two in the microwave while the bread is toasting. Once the toast is done, I give it a quick brush with the melted butter. This gives me perfect, evenly buttered toast every time.

Rita Curtis
Brownstown, Pa.

If you'd like to submit a tip, please send a letter to Kitchen Shortcuts, Cook's Country, P.O. Box 470739, Brookline, MA 02447. Or e-mail us at shortcuts@bcpress.com. Include your name, address, and phone number. If we publish your tip, you will receive a free one-year subscription to *Cook's Country*.

A VERY A-PEEL-ING TIP

For an easy way to remove the skins from garlic, put the cloves in a zipper-lock plastic bag and pound them with a mallet. Remove the crushed cloves and then discard the bag, skins and all! There's no mess, and it saves a boatload of time.

Constance S. Munoz
Tacoma, Wash.

FIRE AND ICE CREAM CAKE

Here's a great way to cut frozen ice cream cake or even cheesecake. Turn a gas burner to medium-low heat. Hold the blade of the slicing knife over the flame for a few seconds, then cut into the cake. Wipe the knife clean with a paper towel and hold the blade over the flame again before making another cut.

Rosemary Schaumburg
Larkspur, Colo.

SEASONING CHECK FOR RAW MEAT

Whenever I want to taste the seasoning for something that I don't want to eat raw, like meat loaf, I pinch off a few tablespoons of the raw mixture and cook it in the microwave for a few minutes. It doesn't necessarily taste the same as it would when cooked in the oven, but it's close enough for me to tell whether the seasonings need to be adjusted.

Sue Epstein
Atlanta, Ga.

EASY SAUSAGE SEASONING

I make Italian sausage quite often and like to mix the seasonings into the ground pork with a potato masher. It works quite well and requires little cleanup.

Lynn Anderson
Hayden Lake, Idaho

ROLLING 'CAN'

We're in between homes right now, and my rolling pin ended up in storage instead of the kitchen. Unfortunately, I didn't find this out until after I had my pie dough ready to roll out. As a last resort, I pulled out a can of Pam, washed it off, and rolled away. To my surprise, it worked really well.

Carla Luan
Houston, Texas

BAG YOUR BLENDER

To keep food particles from getting trapped in and around the buttons on my blender, I cover them with a plastic sandwich bag and secure it with transparent tape. When the bag gets worn out, I just throw it away and replace it with another.

Lois Miller
Modesto, Calif.

COOLING DOWN OATMEAL

When my boys want oatmeal, they want it ASAP and at a palatable temperature. (No time to wait for it too cool down!) Here's what to do if you, too, want to get it on the table quick and "cooled": Microwave the desired amount of oatmeal with a lesser amount of water. It will be a globby mess at first, but don't worry, just add flavorings (brown sugar, cinnamon, and so forth), then add one to three small ice cubes, stirring as they melt. As the ice melts, the oatmeal will thin out and cool down to a ready-to-eat temperature. No more complaints about scorched tongues.

Rebecca Cagle
Belton, Texas

FLEXIBLE FUNNEL

My flexible cutting mat is one of the most versatile tools in my kitchen. I use it to funnel chopped vegetables directly into a pan or bottle (when I chop garlic for salad dressing), but it's also great when transferring dry items such as breakfast cereal, flour, or sugar into storage jars. I just roll the mat into a funnel shape and then transfer the item quickly and neatly.

Kim Anasoulis
Honolulu, Hawaii

SIFT AWAY

Sifting flour can be a messy experience. To cut down on cleanup, I place a paper plate under the measuring cup so that when I sift, the extra falls on the plate. Afterward, I can easily fold the plate and pour the extra flour back into the canister.

Floris Hills
Owasso, Okla.

Color-Coded Eggs

EASY EGG ID

To keep track of hard-boiled eggs in the fridge, I add a few drops of food coloring to the boiling water. My family knows that the tinted eggs are ready for eating.

Alison Rempel Los Altos, Calif.

Hole in One

Instead of draining tomatoes and other canned foods in a strainer, which I then have to wash, I punch a hole in the top of the can with a church-key can opener. It's easy and efficient.

Rosalyn Beaver
Memphis, Tenn.

Chopsticks as Space Savers

Whenever I'm cooking foods that require lots of advance preparation, I find myself struggling to find shelf space in the fridge. Then I thought to set wooden skewers across the dishes so I can stack them. Last week I put several skewers on top of a 13 by 9-inch baking dish and then stacked a smaller baking dish on top. Using another couple of skewers, I stacked a dinner plate on top of that—all on the bottom shelf of my small fridge.

Sam Tutterow
Edina, Minn.

Core Technique

Tomato Baller

When coring and seeding plum tomatoes, I use a melon baller. It's just the right size to fit down into the tomato, and it's quick, too!

Sue Warner
Raleigh, N.C.

Easy Lid Storage

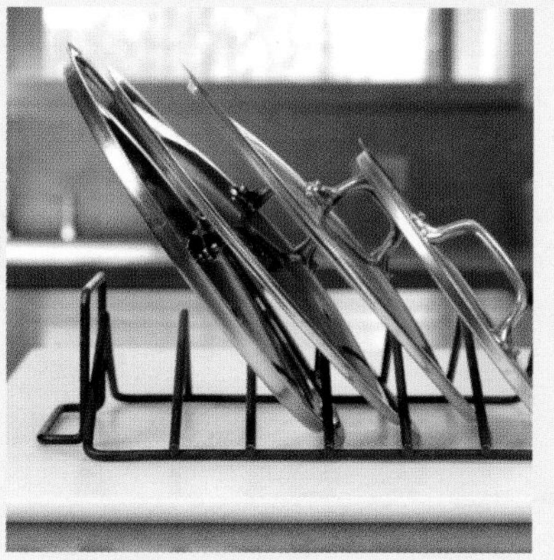

I could never keep track of pot lids until I started "filing" them in the slats of an upside-down V-rack. Storing the lids in the V-rack saves space, too.

Ashley Dombkowski
San Francisco, Calif.

A Creative Spaghetti Pie Is Crowned Contest Winner

Our $500 Grand-Prize Winner!

Vanessa Bryce Dallas, Texas

What's the secret to a successful pasta casserole? According to Vanessa Bryce, originality is key—and our test kitchen tasters heartily agree. Vanessa told us that her recipe was a kind of wedding present from her mother-in-law—a surefire way to keep her future husband happy. She serves this spaghetti pie as an alternative to lasagna (it's a lot simpler) and rounds out the meal with salad and garlic bread. "I can't remember how many times I've written this recipe on a card for friends," she said. We're pleased to share it with a whole new group of friends.

SPAGHETTI PIE SERVES 6 TO 8

To keep the vermicelli from flying all over the kitchen, wrap the noodles in a clean dish towel before attempting to break them into shorter lengths.

Pasta Crust

- Salt
- 4 ounces vermicelli, broken into 2-inch pieces
- 1 garlic clove, minced
- 2 tablespoons unsalted butter
- 1 cup grated Parmesan cheese
- 1 large egg, beaten
- 1 tablespoon minced fresh basil

Filling

- 2 teaspoons vegetable oil
- 1 small onion, chopped fine
- 1/2 pound 90 percent lean ground beef
- 1 (15-ounce) can tomato sauce
- 3 tablespoons tomato paste
- 1 teaspoon sugar
- 1 tablespoon minced fresh basil
- Salt and pepper
- 1 cup whole milk ricotta cheese
- 1 large egg
- 1 teaspoon dried oregano
- 1 1/2 cups shredded whole milk mozzarella cheese

1. For the crust: Adjust oven rack to lowest position and heat oven to 350 degrees. Bring 2 quarts water to boil in large saucepan. Add 1 teaspoon salt and vermicelli and cook until al dente. Drain well.

2. Combine cooked vermicelli, garlic, butter, Parmesan, egg, and basil in medium bowl. Press mixture into deep 10-inch pie plate. Bake until crust has set, 15 to 20 minutes. Cool while making filling.

3. For the filling: Heat oil in large skillet over medium heat until shimmering. Add onion and cook until softened, about 4 minutes. Add beef and cook until lightly browned, 6 to 8 minutes. Drain off any excess fat. Stir in tomato sauce, tomato paste, and sugar and simmer until thickened, about 3 minutes. Stir in basil and season with salt and pepper.

4. Stir ricotta, egg, and oregano together in small bowl. Spread ricotta mixture over pasta crust. Top with meat sauce and sprinkle with mozzarella. Bake until golden brown on top, about 25 minutes. Cool 15 minutes. Slice into wedges and serve.

This 'pie' has a crisp pasta crust that holds layers of herb-flavored ricotta cheese, meaty tomato sauce, and mozzarella.

Judy Wilson Sun City West, Ariz.

Jacqueline McComas Paoli, Pa.

James Hayes Ridgecrest, Calif.

CHICKEN NOODLE CASSEROLE SERVES 8 TO 10

Judy writes: "This is pure comfort food. Sometimes I roast a chicken just to have this casserole the next day." Use leftover roasted or poached chicken in this recipe or buy a rotisserie-cooked bird at the supermarket.

Topping

- 2 tablespoons unsalted butter, melted
- 1 cup fresh bread crumbs
- 1/2 cup grated Parmesan cheese
- 1 tablespoon chopped fresh parsley

Filling

- Salt
- 12 ounces egg noodles
- 6 tablespoons unsalted butter
- 1/2 small onion, chopped fine
- 1 pound white mushrooms, cleaned and sliced thin
- Pepper
- 1/4 cup all-purpose flour
- 2 garlic cloves, minced
- 3 cups low-sodium chicken broth
- 3 tablespoons dry sherry
- 2 cups sour cream
- 4 cups cubed leftover chicken
- 1 tablespoon chopped fresh parsley
- 2 teaspoons chopped fresh thyme
- 1/4 teaspoon nutmeg

1. For the topping: Mix melted butter, bread crumbs, Parmesan, and parsley together in bowl.

2. For the filling: Adjust oven rack to middle position and heat oven to 350 degrees. Bring 4 quarts water to boil in Dutch oven. Add 1 tablespoon salt and noodles and cook until nearly tender. Drain and set aside in colander.

3. Melt 2 tablespoons butter in now-empty Dutch oven over medium heat. Add onion and cook until lightly browned, about 5 minutes. Add mushrooms, ½ teaspoon salt, and ¼ teaspoon pepper and cook until mushrooms begin to brown, about 7 minutes.

4. Stir in remaining 4 tablespoons butter until melted. Add flour and stir until lightly browned, about 2 minutes. Add garlic and cook until fragrant, about 30 seconds. Gradually whisk in broth, sherry, and sour cream, and cook, not letting mixture boil, until thickened, 5 to 7 minutes. Stir in chicken, noodles, parsley, thyme, and nutmeg and season with salt and pepper.

5. Transfer mixture to 3-quart baking dish. Top with bread-crumb mixture and bake until browned and bubbly, about 30 minutes. Cool 5 minutes. Serve.

PASTA CASSEROLE WITH BACON, ASPARAGUS, AND TOMATO SERVES 6 TO 8

Jacqueline writes: "My family says this tastes like breakfast in a casserole." Because this dish goes under the broiler, it cannot be prepared in a Pyrex casserole dish.

Topping

- 2 tablespoons unsalted butter, melted
- 1/2 cup fresh bread crumbs
- 1/2 cup lightly crushed corn flakes

Filling

- Salt
- 1 cup elbow macaroni
- 4 asparagus spears, cut into 1/2-inch pieces
- 6 slices bacon, chopped
- 1/2 small onion, chopped fine
- 3 tablespoons unsalted butter
- 3 tablespoons all-purpose flour
- 1 1/4 cups evaporated milk
- 1 1/4 cups low-sodium chicken broth
- 1/2 cup shredded Monterey Jack cheese
- 1/2 cup shredded cheddar cheese
- 1/4 teaspoon pepper
- 2 large egg yolks
- 1 tomato, seeded and chopped fine
- 1 tablespoon minced chives

1. For the topping: Adjust oven rack to upper-middle position and heat broiler. Mix melted butter with bread crumbs and corn flakes in bowl.

2. For the filling: Bring 2 quarts water to boil in large saucepan. Add 1 teaspoon salt and macaroni and cook until tender. Add asparagus and cook 1 minute more. Drain and set aside in colander.

3. Cook bacon in Dutch oven over medium heat until crisp, about 8 minutes. Transfer bacon to plate lined with paper towel. Pour off all but 1 teaspoon bacon grease. Add onion to pot and cook until softened, about 3 minutes. Add butter and heat until foaming. Add flour, stirring constantly until light brown, about 2 minutes. Gradually whisk in evaporated milk and broth. Bring to boil over medium-high heat, then reduce to simmer, whisking constantly until mixture thickens slightly, about 5 minutes. Stir in cheeses, ½ teaspoon salt, and pepper.

4. Off heat, whisk in yolks. Return macaroni, asparagus, and bacon to pot and stir in tomato and chives.

5. Transfer mixture to 2-quart broilersafe casserole dish and sprinkle with topping. Broil until golden brown, 3 to 5 minutes. Cool 5 minutes. Serve.

SMOKIN' MAC 'N' CHEESE SERVES 8 TO 10

James writes: "This recipe is moderately spicy but very tasty. I like to serve it with a fresh vegetable salad, whole grain bread, and a frosted mug of beer."

Topping

- 1 cup fresh bread crumbs
- 2 tablespoons unsalted butter, melted
- 1 garlic clove, minced
- 1/4 teaspoon salt
- 1/4 teaspoon pepper
- 1/8 teaspoon cayenne pepper

Filling

- Salt
- 1 pound elbow macaroni
- 3 tablespoons unsalted butter
- 3 tablespoons all-purpose flour
- 3 cups heavy cream
- 2 cups whole milk
- 2 cups shredded Monterey Jack cheese
- 2 cups shredded cheddar cheese
- 1 canned chipotle chile in adobo sauce, minced
- 1/4 cup canned sliced green chiles, minced
- Pepper

1. For the topping: Combine bread crumbs, melted butter, garlic, salt, pepper, and cayenne in bowl.

2. For the filling: Adjust oven rack to middle position and heat oven to 350 degrees. Bring 4 quarts water to boil in Dutch oven. Add 1 tablespoon salt and macaroni and cook until nearly tender. Drain macaroni and set aside in colander.

3. Melt butter in now-empty Dutch oven over medium-high heat. Add flour and whisk constantly until mixture is light brown, 2 to 3 minutes. Gradually whisk in cream and milk. Bring to boil, then reduce heat and simmer, whisking constantly, until mixture is slightly thickened, 5 to 7 minutes. Stir in macaroni, cheeses, and chiles and season with salt and pepper.

4. Transfer to 2-quart baking dish and top with bread-crumb mixture. Bake until golden brown and bubbly, about 30 minutes. Cool 5 minutes. Serve.

We want your chicken soup recipes for an upcoming contest. Please submit entries by March 31, 2006. Write to us at Recipe Contest, Cook's Country, P.O. Box 470739, Brookline, MA 02447, or e-mail us at recipecontest@bcpress.com. Include your name, address, and daytime phone number, and tell us what makes your recipe special. The grand-prize winner will receive $500. All entries become the property of *Cook's Country*. For more information on this and other contests, go to www.cookscountry.com.

Ask Cook's Country

WE TRY TO ANSWER ANY QUESTION YOU THROW AT US!

YELLOW VERSUS WHITE ONIONS

Aside from color, what's the difference between yellow onions and white onions?

Rebecca Molanphy Maple Grove, Minn.

In our recipes, unless otherwise specified, we use yellow onions, the kind that comes in 5-pound bags at the supermarket. But your question intrigued us, so we decided to hold a blind tasting of yellow and regular white onions (not sweet onions, which are also often white). We tried both kinds raw in *pico de gallo* (an onion relish), cooked in a simple tomato sauce, and slowly caramelized. Of a dozen tasters, more than half confessed that they could not detect a difference in the preparations; the others tasted only minor variations in sweetness and pungency. Our recommendation? Go ahead and use white and yellow onions interchangeably in any recipe that calls for "onions."

USING DRIED HERBS

During the times of year that some fresh herbs are not available, I find myself with the dried supermarket stuff. How do I know how much of a dried herb to substitute when a recipe calls for fresh?

'noodletrail' Via e-mail

We are not fans of most dried herbs, which have a dusty, stale quality than can ruin a dish. In fact, in a comparison tasting of nine common herbs, we found only oregano, rosemary, sage, and thyme to be usable in dried form, and then only in slow-cooked soups and stews rather than quick-cooked sauces and dressings. The other dried herbs we tried—basil, dill, chives, parsley, and tarragon—were unpalatable in all applications. Because fresh herbs are mostly water, their dried counterparts have a more concentrated flavor. If you have to substitute dried herbs for fresh, use only half the amount called for and stick with long-cooking recipes.

THE BEST WAY TO ROAST GARLIC

How do you roast garlic so that it's sweet, tender, and easily spread on crusty bread?

Gary Bacchetti Boston, N.Y.

We love the smooth texture and sweet, rich flavor of roasted garlic spread on a piece of bread, mashed into potatoes, stirred into soups, and blended into salad dressings. Our research turned up a number of different methods for "roasting" garlic, including baking, steaming, and even microwaving. With the exception of the microwave, which turned out bland, pallid garlic, all the methods we tried worked. But we had the most flavorful results with the garlic we roasted uncovered rather than wrapped in foil, a common suggestion. The uncovered garlic not only mellowed and softened but caramelized as well, thus developing even more flavor.

Here's how to do it: Remove the papery outer layers from one head of garlic and cut off ½ inch from the top (not the end with the little roots). Drizzle the cut portion with 2 teaspoons olive oil and sprinkle with a little salt. Roast on a baking sheet or small baking dish at 400 degrees until soft and golden, 30 to 40 minutes, depending on the size of the head.

To remove the cooled garlic from the skin, use your fingers or a pair of tongs to gently squeeze the root end; the cloves should slip out easily. Any stubborn cloves that remain can be squeezed out individually. Mash the garlic with a fork to form a paste. Use it immediately or cover tightly and refrigerate up to one week.

EASIER FLIPPING?

My husband, the king of grilled sandwiches in our house, is enthralled by the Grip 'n Flip commercials. Looks pretty silly to me, but he won't stop talking about it! Have you tried it? If it makes him happy enough to make me another grilled cheese sandwich, I might break down and buy it for him.

Kara Watson Via e-mail

The Grip 'n Flip is a plastic utensil that is a cross between a spatula and a pair of tongs. One arm is a flat spatula, the other a U-shaped, two-pronged fork. Our first tests focused on the Grip 'n Flip's purported ability to flip fried eggs. The U-shaped arm is designed to fit snugly on either side of the yolk, supposedly to allow easy flipping and to prevent breaking the yolk. Unfortunately, it failed on both counts; limited maneuverability and awkward design resulted in torn eggs and many a broken yolk. We then tried the Grip 'n Flip on grilled cheese sandwiches and were pleasantly surprised. In fact, we loved it. We were able to flip the sandwiches neatly and easily with just one hand rather than having to hold the sandwich together with one hand and flip it with the other. The Grip 'n Flip also worked as promised on bacon, allowing us to turn three slices at a time. While the $19.95 price tag is a little steep, it's certainly worthwhile if it will get more grilled cheese sandwiches out of your husband. Available at www.gripnflip.com.

Though the Grip 'n Flip failed to produce intact eggs over easy, it did successfully grip—and flip—grilled cheese sandwiches.

MESS-FREE SLOW COOKING

I recently saw Reynolds Slow Cooker Liners at the supermarket and wondered if you had tried them. I use my slow cooker at least once a week.

Brian Chang Narberth, Pa.

Having spent far too much time scrubbing remnants of 10-hour chili out of our slow cooker, we were excited to try these new liners, which are bags that fit much like garbage bags, coming up over the rim of the pot to be secured. The bags look like plastic, but they are actually made from nylon resins, the same materials used to make oven bags, so they are food- and heatsafe. After trying them, we can gladly say goodbye to our dishpan hands. Even with some serious digging with a ladle, the bags stayed intact throughout the cooking and serving process. Best of all, cleanup was as easy as promised. We just gathered the top of the bag and tossed the whole thing in the trash. Though not all slow-cooker dishes leave a mess behind—after a simple beef stew, for example, the crock will need only a quick wash—we'll keep some of these bags on hand for those slow-cooker favorites that require serious scrubbing, such as chili, baked beans, or the meaty pasta sauce on page 8.

These new bags from Reynolds make slow-cooker cleanup a breeze.

'SHAKE 'N BAKE' CHICKEN?

My family loves your Quick and Crunchy Pork Chops (April/May 2005), and we all thought the coating would be good on chicken cutlets. What do you think?

Lucille Yip Lahaina, Hawaii

We thought it sounded good, too, so we headed to the kitchen and found that you can substitute boneless, skinless chicken breasts for the pork chops in the recipe with a few small changes: Chicken breasts are thicker at one end, so you'll have to pound them to an even thickness to ensure even cooking. They're also bigger than pork chops, so you'll have only enough coating for three chicken breasts (the recipe doubles easily). Finally, the proper internal temperature for a chicken breast is 165 degrees. The chicken breasts should reach this temperature after 20 to 25 minutes in a preheated 425-degree oven. Go to www.cookscountry.com for our Quick and Crunchy Chicken Cutlets recipe.

To ask us a cooking question, write to Ask Cook's Country, P. O. Box 470739, Brookline, MA 02447. If you prefer e-mail, write to askcookscountry@bcpress.com. See if you can stump us!

Recipe Makeover CINNAMON ROLLS

Weighing in at 400-plus calories per roll and requiring up to four hours of preparation time, cinnamon rolls are one recipe in dire need of a makeover.

These sweet rolls are so good no one will suspect they are low in fat.

Cinnamon rolls are made with buttery yeast dough, a swirl of buttery cinnamon filling, and then finished with a thick cream cheese frosting that is enriched with more butter. With so much butter, what's not to love? How about the 16 grams of fat and 430 calories in just one roll? Or maybe the 5 A.M. wake-up call necessary to get the test kitchen's favorite cinnamon rolls to the breakfast table on time? My goals were formidable: to trim fat and time.

Most "quick" cinnamon roll recipes replace the yeast dough with biscuit dough leavened with baking powder and/or baking soda. But when I tried to trim butter from this quick dough, I hit a wall. Lean biscuit-style rolls were dry and crumbly, not soft and chewy, like the real thing. No matter how hard I tried, the baking-powder-biscuit approach just fell short. Switching gears, I returned to the more traditional yeasted rolls and tested several adventurous low-fat recipes. My tasters were not impressed by rolls made with odd butter substitutes, including applesauce, cottage cheese, and mashed potatoes. They may have been low-fat rolls, but that's largely because nobody was eating them.

Disappointed, I returned to the test kitchen's favorite high-fat, time-intensive recipe and looked for places to trim fat and time. The stick of butter in the rich dough was a good place to start. I tried dough made with water, skim milk, maple syrup (for extra moisture), and 2 tablespoons of melted butter. To my surprise, this dough made rolls that were soft and pillowy. True, the dough itself was not nearly as flavorful as the original dough, but I hoped that with the filling and icing, no one would notice.

Although the typical cinnamon-sugar filling contains up to 6 tablespoons of butter, I found that I could use far less. As long as the filling was made with more brown sugar than white sugar (the former is more moist and helps ensure that the filling is plenty gooey when baked), just 1 tablespoon of melted butter would hold it together.

The creamy blanket of frosting is traditionally made with butter, cream cheese, and confectioners' sugar. The butter was easy enough to trim, but most recipes rely on an entire package of cream cheese. I tried replacing the cream cheese with buttermilk, but the glaze was thin and unsatisfying. When I tried nonfat cream cheese, tasters turned up their noses at the grainy texture of the glaze. Why ruin perfectly good buns, they asked? I eventually settled on light cream cheese (nearly as good as the full-fat stuff) and used far less than the typical recipe (just one-quarter of a package). To make the cream cheese go further, I stretched it with skim milk.

Most yeasted dough recipes require two lengthy rises, especially necessary with a heavy, butter-enriched dough. My leaner dough was already rising relatively quickly, and I sped up the process by putting it in a warm oven; now the first rise took only 10 minutes. Once shaped and filled, the rolls doubled in size in about half an hour and then baked up in just 20 to 25 minutes. These rolls were now ready to eat about 90 minutes after I started—not bad for a recipe that usually takes three to four hours.

Enjoyed warm from the oven (the way all cinnamon rolls are best eaten), these rolls amazed tasters, who couldn't believe I had shaved 150 calories, 12½ grams of fat, and more than two hours from our favorite recipe. Did I mention that we now have a new favorite cinnamon roll? **–Katie Henderson**

LOW-FAT CINNAMON ROLLS

MAKES 12 ROLLS

Depending on the humidity, the dough may need up to 1/4 cup extra flour, as directed in step 2.

Dough

- **1 1/3 cups warm skim milk (110 degrees)**
- **3 tablespoons maple syrup**
- **2 tablespoons unsalted butter, melted**
- **3 1/2 cups all-purpose flour, plus extra for work surface**
- **1 package rapid-rise or instant yeast**
- **1 teaspoon salt**

Filling

- **1/2 cup packed dark brown sugar**
- **1/4 cup granulated sugar**
- **2 teaspoons cinnamon**
- **1/8 teaspoon salt**
- **1 tablespoon unsalted butter, melted**

Icing

- **1 cup confectioners' sugar**
- **4 tablespoons light cream cheese**
- **1 tablespoon skim milk**
- **1/2 teaspoon vanilla extract**

1. For the dough: Adjust oven rack to middle position and heat oven to 200 degrees. When oven reaches 200 degrees, turn it off. Lightly grease large bowl with nonstick cooking spray. Coat 13 by 9-inch baking dish with cooking spray.

2. Mix milk, syrup, and melted butter together in large measuring cup. Mix flour, yeast, and salt together in bowl of standing mixer fitted with dough hook. Turn machine to low and slowly add

(continued on page 8)

Know-How
MAKING CINNAMON ROLLS

1. Pat the sugar mixture into the dough, leaving a 1/2-inch border along the top edge. **2.** Carefully roll the dough into a cylinder, moistening the border with water to seal the dough. **3.** Cut the cylinder in half, then in half again (making 4 pieces). Cut each piece into three pieces, yielding 12 rolls.

And the Numbers . . .

All nutritional information is for a single serving (one roll).

TRADITIONAL CINNAMON ROLL
CALORIES: **430**
FAT: **16g**
SATURATED FAT: **11g**

COOK'S COUNTRY LOW-FAT CINNAMON ROLL
CALORIES: **280**
FAT: **3.5g**
SATURATED FAT: **2.5g**

Cinnamon Rolls

continued from page 7

milk mixture. After dough comes together, increase speed to medium and mix until shiny and smooth, 4 to 6 minutes. (Dough will be sticky; if it seems too wet and is not forming ball, add up to ¼ cup more flour as needed and knead dough 2 minutes more.) Turn dough onto heavily floured work surface, shape into ball, and place in greased bowl. Cover and rest in warm oven for 10 minutes.

3. For the filling: While dough is resting, mix sugars, cinnamon, salt, and melted butter in medium bowl until incorporated.

4. To make the rolls: On lightly floured work surface, roll dough into 18 by 12-inch rectangle with long side facing you. Sprinkle sugar mixture over dough, leaving ½ inch border along top edge, then lightly press sugar into dough (see photo 1 on page 7). Starting at edge nearest you, roll up dough (photo 2). Brush border with water, then press dough to seal.

5. Using chef's knife, slice dough into 12 rounds (photo 3), then place in prepared pan with cut side up. Cover pan with plastic wrap coated with cooking spray and return to warm oven until rolls have nearly doubled in size, 30 to 40 minutes.

6. Remove pan from oven and heat oven to 350 degrees (rolls will continue to rise on counter as you wait for oven to heat). Remove plastic wrap and bake until rolls are deep brown and filling is melted, 20 to 25 minutes, rotating pan front to back halfway through baking.

7. For the icing: While rolls are baking, whisk confectioners' sugar, cream cheese, milk, and vanilla together in small bowl until smooth. Remove pan from oven, turn rolls out onto rack, and flip them right side up. Cool 10 minutes, then spread icing over rolls. Serve hot or warm.

Don't Have a Mixer?

In step 2, mix flour, yeast, and salt together in large bowl. Make well in flour, then add milk mixture to well. Stir until dough becomes shaggy and difficult to stir. Turn out onto heavily floured work surface and knead until dough forms cohesive ball and is smooth, about 10 minutes. Proceed as directed.

Slow Cooking MEATY TOMATO SAUCE

You can make a big batch of this hearty sauce in your slow cooker—if you know one simple trick.

As a slow-simmering pasta sauce, Bolognese would seem ideally suited to the slow cooker. So why do most recipes fail?

Meaty Bolognese is my favorite pasta sauce. As the ingredients simmer away, tough ground meat is transformed into a silky sauce with complex flavors. Great Bolognese is darn near magic. But I rarely make it. Why? Well, this sauce is a time killer. First there's the softening of vegetables, the browning of ground beef, and the gradual addition of liquids—milk, wine, and canned tomatoes. Then there's the painfully slow simmering—three or more hours—during which frequent stirring and constant attention to the heat level are required.

Could I adapt this classic Italian recipe for the slow cooker? Research uncovered a few recipes. One simply threw all the ingredients in the slow cooker and let them cook. Hours later, my family dined on waterlogged hamburger soup. The problem was clear. With its tight-fitting lid, a slow cooker does not allow evaporation, a key element in Bolognese sauce.

To get around this hurdle, one recipe simmered the liquids on the stovetop before adding them to the slow cooker, but simmering milk with acidic wine and tomatoes just made a curdled mess. Another recipe suggested using less liquid—tablespoons rather than cups—so there would be no need for evaporation. Several hours later, this sauce looked the part, but the rich flavor that comes from simmering large amounts of liquid down to a concentrated base was absent.

I went back to the drawing board. Softening the vegetables (onions, carrots, celery, and garlic) on the stovetop was a must. Next, I browned the ground meat (meat-loaf mix had proved the most tasty, but a combination of ground chuck and pork also worked well) and reduced the milk over the meat (keeping the milk away from the acidic liquids seemed wise). I then transferred everything to the slow cooker, added the wine and tomatoes, and cracked the lid to allow for evaporation. So far so good, but the temperature plummeted to an unsafe 120 degrees.

Then it hit me. I had assumed that the low setting on my slow cooker would work best. After all, "slow and low" is the mantra for this sauce when made on the stovetop. But when I switched the cooker to high, the mixture bubbled away and remained at a safe 190 to 200 degrees, even with the lid off, which allowed for maximum evaporation. Eight hours later, I had a tender, silky, and robust Bolognese sauce.

I think this slow-cooker recipe rivals any prepared by the traditional method—and it's ideally suited to a super-sized batch, so I could freeze the leftovers and enjoy Bolognese in minutes. Now that's my idea of good slow cooking. **–Bridget Lancaster**

SLOW-COOKER BOLOGNESE SAUCE

MAKES 12 CUPS, ENOUGH TO SAUCE 4 POUNDS OF PASTA

Because steam rises from the sauce as it cooks, it's best to place the slow cooker on a counter with no cabinetry overhead. If you need more than the 7 or 8 hours of cooking time called for in the recipe, in step 3 set the lid halfway off the cooker rather than removing it, then simmer the sauce for 10 to 11 hours. Freeze leftover sauce in airtight containers for up to 2 months.

- 3 tablespoons unsalted butter
- 1/2 small onion, chopped fine
- 1 small carrot, peeled and chopped fine
- 1/2 rib celery, chopped fine
- 3 garlic cloves, minced
- 3 tablespoons tomato paste
- 3 pounds meat-loaf mix or 1 1/2 pounds ground chuck and 1 1/2 pounds ground pork
- Salt and pepper
- 3 cups whole milk
- 3 cups dry white wine
- 2 (28-ounce) cans whole tomatoes, ground in blender until smooth
- 1 teaspoon chopped fresh thyme

1. Heat butter in Dutch oven over medium-high heat until foaming. Add onion, carrot, and celery and cook until softened but not colored, about 6 minutes. Add garlic and tomato paste and cook until fragrant, about 1 minute. Add meat, 1 teaspoon salt, and ½ teaspoon pepper and cook, breaking up meat, until crumbled into tiny pieces and lightly browned, about 5 minutes.

2. Add milk, bring to vigorous simmer, and cook until milk evaporates and only clear fat remains, 10 to 15 minutes. Add wine, tomatoes, and thyme; cover and bring to boil. Transfer mixture to slow cooker, cover, set temperature to high, and bring to boil.

3. Once mixture comes to boil, remove lid and simmer until sauce is very thick, 7 to 8 hours. Season with salt and pepper. Serve.

Make Ahead

This recipe can be partially made the night before so that it's ready to place in the slow cooker in the morning. Complete steps 1 and 2 and refrigerate the mixture in the Dutch oven. The next morning, bring the mixture back to a boil, transfer it to the slow cooker, and proceed as directed.

War rationing led to the creation of some unusual recipes, including a delicious—and super-easy—chocolate cake with an odd name.

As the test kitchen's resident history buff, I spend a lot time reading old recipes, and cakes are almost always the most interesting of the lot. I've stumbled across Coca-Cola cake, tomato-soup cake, and flowerpot cake, but it was wacky cake that really caught my attention. Evidently, this cake didn't earn its name for some weird flavor combination; it is described as a chocolate cake. I read that it was developed during the war, but which war? To get some answers, I spent several days searching the Internet and combing through vintage cookbooks at a local university library. Here's what I discovered.

During World War I, "make-do" cake recipes were popular. At various times, butter, granulated sugar, milk, and eggs were in short supply. For instance, in 1914, Procter and Gamble, the original maker of Crisco, offered a recipe for butterless, milkless, eggless cake. This yellow cake derived most of its sweetness from dried fruit, with a little help from brown sugar. The recipe was renamed Depression cake after the stock market crash of 1929.

During World War II, American women revived and improved upon the make-do cake recipes their mothers had used a generation earlier. Several sources suggested that wacky cake was invented during the 1940s, but I couldn't understand how it earned its name until I read a recipe in *The* Time *Reader's Book of Recipes,* a collection of reader recipes compiled by the editors of *Time* magazine in 1949.

Mrs. Donald Adam of Detroit, Mich., submitted this strange recipe, which called for mixing the dry ingredients—flour, cocoa powder, sugar, salt, and baking soda—right in the baking pan. If that wasn't strange enough, three holes—two small and one large—were made in the dry mix. Into the large hole went melted vegetable shortening, while vanilla and vinegar were placed in the smaller holes. Cold water was poured over everything, then the whole mess was stirred and popped into the oven.

Back in the test kitchen, I followed the instructions, and right before my eyes the batter began to bubble and rise—even before it hit the oven. It was the easiest cake I'd ever made. And it was surprisingly good. A nice chocolate flavor and an incredibly moist crumb made even the pickiest of my test kitchen colleagues take notice.

How does this strange recipe work? Without eggs, this cake depends on the last-minute reaction of vinegar and baking soda to lift the thick batter. The three holes ensure that the dry ingredients (including the baking soda) remain dry until the last possible second. Mixing in the pan might seem like a gimmick, but when I combined the ingredients in a bowl and scraped the batter into a pan, the cake did not rise as well. The lift provided by the baking soda and vinegar reaction is fleeting, and the recipe's odd mixing method ensures that the batter gets into the oven quickly.

The 1949 recipe I had found needed little improvement. To simplify things, I replaced the melted shortening with vegetable oil, and to boost the chocolate flavor I added another tablespoon of cocoa. The cake was a bit sweet, so I trimmed a little sugar, and, because several tasters complained about a slight "soapy" flavor, I decreased the baking soda.

On a whim, I decided to try this cake with more "modern" ingredients. I replaced the oil with melted butter and used milk instead of water. This cake was less chocolaty and more crumbly; I honestly felt that the original was better. Hard times gave rise to a not-so-wacky recipe that still deserves a place in the American kitchen. **–Bridget Lancaster**

There's nothing crazy about this super-simple chocolate cake.

WACKY CAKE

SERVES 6 TO 8

See page 29 for information on natural cocoa powder. This moist cake gets even better when served with vanilla ice cream or a dollop of whipped cream.

- **1½ cups all-purpose flour**
- **¾ cup sugar**
- **¼ cup natural cocoa powder**
- **¾ teaspoon baking soda**
- **½ teaspoon salt**
- **5 tablespoons vegetable oil**
- **1 tablespoon distilled white vinegar**
- **1 teaspoon vanilla extract**
- **1 cup water**
- **Confectioners' sugar**

1. Adjust oven rack to middle position and heat oven to 350 degrees. Coat 8-inch-square baking pan with nonstick cooking spray.

2. Whisk flour, sugar, cocoa, baking soda, and salt together in pan. As shown in photo 1, make 1 large and 2 small craters in dry ingredients. Add oil to large crater and vinegar and vanilla separately to remaining small craters. Pour water into pan (photo 2), and mix until just a few streaks of flour remain (photo 3). Immediately put pan in oven.

3. Bake until toothpick inserted in center of cake comes out with a few moist crumbs attached, about 30 minutes. Cool in pan, then dust with confectioners' sugar. (If tightly wrapped, cake will keep for 3 days at room temperature.)

WORLD WAR II POSTER During World Wars I and II, American cooks were encouraged to prepare "make-do" recipes with rationed ingredients.

Know-How
A WACKY MIXING METHOD

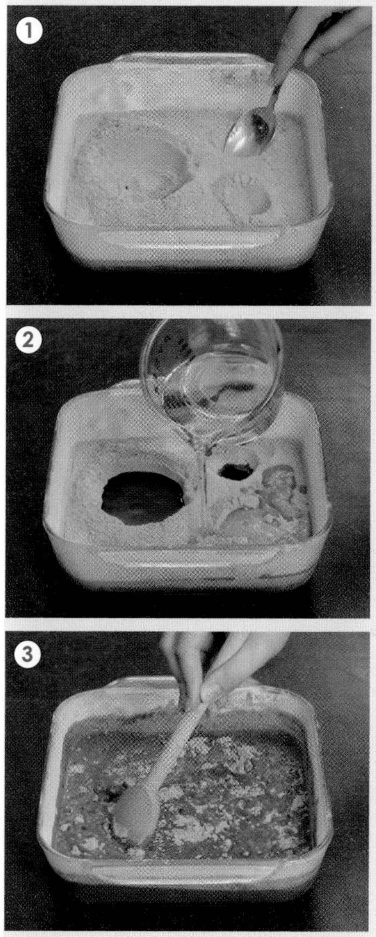

1. Using a spoon, make 1 large and 2 small craters in the dry mix. **2.** Pour the vegetable oil into the large crater, then the vinegar and vanilla into the smaller craters. Pour the water over all the ingredients. **3.** Using a wooden spoon or spatula, mix the batter, taking care not to overmix; the batter should still contain a few streaks of flour.

The Best Shepherd's Pie

Shepherd's pie can be wonderful comfort food, but it's often bland and mushy. Can you come up with a really meaty version, like what you'd find in a good pub? –Marybeth Highton, Virginia Beach, Va.

To pack long-cooked flavor into a quick ground-meat filling, we added soy sauce, tomato paste, and beer.

Know-How

APPLYING THE POTATO TOPPING

When applying the mashed potato topping, you want to seal in the filling to keep it from bubbling over the sides of the pan. Use a rubber spatula to scrape small piles of potato around the edge of the dish. Dollop more potato into the center of the dish and then spread the potato until a smooth, seamless layer covers all of the filling and is flush with the edge of the pan.

Shepherd's pie was originally made from leftover roast lamb mixed with leftover gravy and topped with mashed potatoes. A well-loved staple of the British diet, the dish eventually came to be made with ground lamb rather than the trimmings from a roast so it could be made anytime. On this side of the Atlantic, where most people don't have much taste for lamb, the ground lamb has been traded for ground beef. The result often tastes like boiled hamburger or a bland Sloppy Joe. Putting some meaty flavor back into this retread seemed like a good idea.

After browning onions and carrots, I cooked the ground beef (85 percent lean was the best choice) and added the Worcestershire sauce called for in many recipes. I was sure this was the key to better flavor. Not so. While the Worcestershire made the filling taste beefier, it also added some unpleasant sour notes. I wondered if soy sauce—also known to enhance meat flavor—could pinch-hit. Odd as it may seem, soy sauce worked well, without calling attention to itself.

In the test kitchen, we often use tomato paste to add depth to stews and sauces. Just a tablespoon did the trick. For the liquid ingredient, tasters preferred chicken broth over what they called the "tinny" flavor of beef broth.

Given the popularity of shepherd's pie as pub food, I wasn't surprised to find recipes that called for a pint of beer. Guinness, my favorite pub beer, was too bitter. Most mild lagers and ales were fine, but it was an unlikely choice, O'Doul's nonalcoholic amber beer, that tasters deemed their favorite. Its sweet, malty flavor may not be terribly satisfying at a pub, but it worked perfectly in this dish. A splash of cream kept the meat from toughening as it simmered.

The only thing missing was the crown of mashed potatoes. Regular mashed potatoes turned to mush when placed on top of the saucy filling. A stiff mash—with less butter and cream—was needed. Brushing the potatoes with beaten egg helped create a beautiful golden brown crust, as did a quick run under the broiler after the pie had baked for 15 minutes.

–Katie Henderson

Make Ahead

Make the filling through step 2, but do not add the peas. Store in an airtight container in the refrigerator for up to two days. When ready to proceed, reheat the filling in a large saucepan, stir in the peas, and transfer to a broilersafe 2-quart casserole. Proceed with the recipe from step 3.

SHEPHERD'S PIE

SERVES 6 TO 8

Although just about any mild beer will work in this recipe, we particularly enjoyed the sweet flavor of O'Doul's nonalcoholic amber.

Filling

- 2 tablespoons unsalted butter
- 1 large onion, chopped fine
- 2 medium carrots, peeled and chopped fine
- 2 pounds 85 percent lean ground beef
- Salt and pepper
- 5 tablespoons all-purpose flour
- 1 tablespoon tomato paste
- 1/4 cup heavy cream
- 1 3/4 cups low-sodium chicken broth
- 3/4 cup beer (see note above)
- 2 tablespoons soy sauce
- 2 teaspoons minced fresh thyme
- 1 cup frozen peas

Topping

- 2 1/2 pounds russet potatoes, peeled and cut into 2-inch pieces
- Salt
- 2 tablespoons unsalted butter, melted
- 1/3 cup heavy cream, warmed
- Pepper
- 1 large egg, beaten

1. For the filling: Heat butter in large skillet over medium-high heat until foaming. Add onion and carrots and cook until soft, about 8 minutes. Add meat, ½ teaspoon salt, and ½ teaspoon pepper and cook, breaking up meat into small pieces with wooden spoon, until browned, about 12 minutes. Add flour and tomato paste and cook until paste begins to darken, about 1 minute.

2. Add cream and cook until it spatters, about 1 minute. Add broth, beer, soy sauce, and thyme and simmer over medium heat, stirring frequently, until mixture is thick but still saucy, 15 to 20 minutes. Remove from heat, stir in peas, adjust seasonings, and transfer to broilersafe 2-quart casserole dish.

3. For the topping: Adjust oven rack to upper-middle position and heat oven to 375 degrees. Bring potatoes, ½ teaspoon salt, and water to cover to boil in large saucepan over high heat. Reduce heat to medium-low and simmer until tender, 15 to 20 minutes. Drain potatoes, return to saucepan, and mash potatoes with butter and cream until smooth. Season with salt and pepper.

4. Spread potatoes over filling, using spatula to smooth top (see photo at left). Brush with egg and drag fork across top to make ridges. Bake until filling is bubbling, about 15 minutes. Turn on broiler and cook until top is golden brown, 3 to 5 minutes. Remove from oven and cool 10 minutes. Serve.

Sugar-Glazed Roasted Carrots

What's the best way to caramelize carrots in the oven?

Let's face it. Carrots are not the sexiest vegetable in the produce aisle, but at this time of year, they are reliable. When roasted, they can make an excellent side dish. The perfect roast carrots are tender and sweet, with a caramelized crust. High heat and sugar are the usual means of coaxing this kind of browning out of carrots, but it's a high-wire act. Carrots can go from crunchy and pale to mealy and charred in a matter of minutes.

My first decision took place in the produce aisle. Although baby carrots require no preparation (just open the bag and dump into a pan), the results I got with them were disappointing. After 10 minutes in the oven, they were shriveled and soggy. Maybe the pool of water in most bags of baby carrots was the culprit. In any case, these carrots are often bland and woody. It was worth taking an extra 10 minutes to peel and cut grown-up-sized carrots myself.

When I tested roasting times and temperatures, I found that shorter and hotter were better. When cooked for a long time in a moderate oven, the carrots ended up soggy and overcooked before any real caramelization could occur. I had the best results in a very hot oven set to 475 degrees. Heating the baking sheet before adding the carrots jump-started the browning process. In less than 20 minutes, the carrots were perfectly cooked.

Carrots tossed in butter browned a bit better than those tossed in oil, but the addition of sugar—just 1 tablespoon for 1½ pounds of carrots—made a big difference. Granulated sugar was up to the job, but I got really dramatic results when I tried dark brown sugar.

After peeling my weight in carrots, I had finally developed a reliable recipe. Best of all, it was quick and easily adapted to flavor variations. Carrots were never so appealing.

–Meredith Butcher

Twenty minutes in a very hot oven can turn humble carrots into an interesting side dish.

SUGAR-GLAZED ROASTED CARROTS SERVES 4 TO 6

For instructions on how to cut the carrots, see page 29. If the carrots have very narrow tips, trim the thin ends; they scorch easily.

- **1½ pounds medium carrots, peeled and cut into 2 by ½-inch pieces**
- **2 tablespoons unsalted butter, melted**
- **1 tablespoon dark brown sugar**
- **½ teaspoon salt**
- **½ teaspoon pepper**

1. Adjust oven rack to middle position and heat oven to 475 degrees. Heat rimmed baking sheet in oven for 10 minutes.

2. Toss carrots, melted butter, sugar, salt, and pepper in medium bowl until thoroughly combined. Remove pan from oven and place carrots in single layer on hot baking sheet. Roast until carrots are beginning to brown on bottom, about 15 minutes.

3. Remove pan from oven, toss carrots to redistribute, and continue to roast until tender and deep amber in color, about 3 minutes. Serve.

MAPLE-NUT CARROTS

Combine 2 tablespoons maple syrup, ½ teaspoon vanilla extract, ¼ teaspoon chili powder, and ½ cup toasted and chopped walnuts in bowl. Follow recipe for Sugar-Glazed Roasted Carrots, adding maple mixture when carrots are tossed in step 3.

SPICY ASIAN CARROTS

Combine 1 tablespoon soy sauce, 1 teaspoon toasted sesame oil, 1 tablespoon toasted sesame seeds, ½ teaspoon red pepper flakes, and 2 scallions, cut into ½-inch lengths, in bowl. Follow recipe for Sugar-Glazed Roasted Carrots, adding soy mixture when carrots are tossed in step 3.

HERB-GARDEN CARROTS

Follow recipe for Sugar-Glazed Roasted Carrots, adding 1 teaspoon minced fresh tarragon and 1 teaspoon minced fresh parsley when carrots are tossed in step 3.

SPICED MOROCCAN CARROTS

Combine 2 tablespoons orange juice, ¼ teaspoon cumin, ⅛ teaspoon cinnamon, and ⅛ teaspoon cayenne pepper in bowl. Follow recipe for Sugar-Glazed Roasted Carrots, adding spice mixture when carrots are tossed in step 3.

FOOD HISTORY: *The history of carrots dates back 5,000 years. Early carrots were purple, black, white, red, yellow, and green—but not orange. The first orange carrots were developed in Holland in the 16th century in tribute to Prince William of Orange, known as the key founder of Dutch independence from Spain.*

Reader Mailbag

Thanks for the Memories: LITTLE-BITTY PANCAKES

Terri Kovach, Monroe, Mich.: "Pancakes were always a treat at our house and always accompanied by a game my father used to play with my five sisters and me. When he passed out the pancakes, there was always the anticipation of who was going to get the 'special' ones, the tiny, little-bitty pancakes formed by a drop or two of batter on the griddle. He would say, 'And for *you*,' as he placed little pancakes in the middle of an empty breakfast plate. Then, a moment of silence would pass, and that day's honoree would feign sadness over her puny meal. We would all laugh and my dad would offer up the real pancakes to fill the plate. My father passed away 35 years ago, but I still remember this breakfast-table ceremony."

Birthday Cake on Fire!

Carolynn Hayman, Ann Arbor, Mich.: "For my daughter Anna's ninth birthday we threw a *Series of Unfortunate Events* party. She decided to make a birthday cake 'on fire.' We used spray food coloring to get the fiery look, and we put marshmallows, charred with our crème brûlée torch, around the bottom of the cake."

Universal Language

Ann Mailly, Santa Clara, Calif.: "My husband and I recently visited his family in Aquaviva della Fonti, Italy. They taught me how to make *panzerotti*, which resemble deep-fried calzones. Although I don't speak Italian, we were able to communicate in the kitchen. It was an experience that I will always cherish. I am on the right in this picture, with family matriarch Giuseppina Tricarico in the middle and Eugenia Mailly, my mother-in-law, on the left."

Thanks for the Memories: A PRAYER WITH WAFFLES

Camille Brennecke Falconnier, House Springs, Mo.

"Pajama clad and still groggy, my six younger brothers and sisters and I would stumble into the kitchen every Saturday morning, beckoned by the sweet toasty smell of Daddy's waffles. Dad would proudly place three huge platters on the table, stacked to what seemed like 50 waffles high. We would sing the 'Johnny Appleseed Prayer' and bedeck the waffles with butter, maple syrup, grandma's homemade red plum jam, peanut butter, or sugar."

Johnny Appleseed Prayer

Oh, the Lord's been good to me,
And so I thank the Lord,
For giving me the things I need,
The sun and the rain and the apple seed.
The Lord's been good to me.
Amen, Amen, Amen, Amen, Amen.

For Your Convenience: Chicken Pot Pie

Is quick chicken pot pie worth eating?

Traditional recipes for from-scratch chicken pot pie call for poaching a stewing hen, straining broth, preparing vegetables, making sauce, and mixing and rolling out a topping. Simply put, traditional pot pie—no matter how good—is not appropriate for weeknight cooking. But given how much I like pot pie (and who doesn't?), I wondered if convenience products could do some of the work.

I prepared half a dozen quick recipes for my test kitchen colleagues, and we critiqued every element. Rotisserie chicken from the supermarket was pretty good—its roasted flavor was actually better than the watery meat from a poached stewing hen. The frozen vegetables were overcooked, but that could be remedied. The sauce from every recipe, however, was terrible, and the super-sweet refrigerator biscuits had an artificial butter flavor that reminded everyone of movie-theater popcorn.

To fix the dull, stodgy sauce, I decided to lose the cream of mushroom soup used in most quick recipes and streamline a traditional recipe. Sautéing minced onion and celery added depth of flavor (other ingredients were superfluous), but my real discovery was a toasted roux. Instead of just sprinkling some flour into the pan to thicken the sauce, I let the flour cook until it turned light brown. The toasted roux added tons of flavor in just six minutes.

After testing seven brands of refrigerator biscuits (see page 29), I changed my opinion about this product. The best ones had a decent buttery flavor, and sprinkling them with salt tempered their sweetness. Baking the biscuits separately (while the filling cooked on the stovetop) saved time and kept the bottoms of the biscuits from becoming soggy. My final recipe took just 30 minutes to prepare—start to finish—and I'm not sure I'll ever poach a stewing hen again.

–Eva Katz

A fast homemade sauce is the key to this 30-minute recipe.

QUICK CHICKEN POT PIE

SERVES 6 TO 8

Serve this pot pie right out of the skillet or transfer the mixture to a large pie plate and top with the baked biscuits.

- 1 package refrigerator biscuits (see page 29)
- Salt
- 4 tablespoons unsalted butter
- 1 medium onion, minced
- 1 celery rib, chopped fine
- 1/4 cup all-purpose flour
- 1/8 teaspoon cayenne pepper
- 2 3/4 cups low-sodium chicken broth
- 1/2 cup heavy cream
- 2 teaspoons chopped fresh thyme
- 1 (10-ounce) package frozen peas and carrots
- 1 rotisserie chicken, skin discarded, meat shredded into large pieces (4 cups)
- 4 teaspoons lemon juice
- Pepper

1. Remove biscuits from package, place on baking sheet, and sprinkle with salt. Bake according to package instructions.

2. Meanwhile, melt butter in large skillet over medium heat. Add onion and celery and cook until soft, about 4 minutes. Stir in flour and cayenne and cook, stirring constantly, until mixture is light brown, about 6 minutes. Slowly whisk in broth, cream, and thyme and simmer until thickened, about 5 minutes. Stir in vegetables, chicken, and lemon juice and simmer until heated through, 2 to 3 minutes. Season with salt and pepper. Top with biscuits and serve.

Spicy Glazed Pork Tenderloin

I love grilled pork tenderloin with a spicy glaze and would like to reproduce it indoors for a winter fix. I've tried broiling, but the meat was pale and dry. Am I barking up the wrong tree?
–Barbara Cuppman, Boulder, Colo.

Skillet glazing adds flavor to mild pork tenderloin and ensures that this lean cut remains moist as it cooks.

Pork tenderloins are small, thin, cylindrical cuts that cook fast. The key is to develop a flavorful browned crust before the interior overcooks and dries out, not an uncommon outcome given modern pork's lack of fat. (See "Pretty in Pink," below.) Because a grill puts out such intense heat, it is ideally suited to this process. When I tried to replicate these results in a hot oven (I tried both roasting and broiling), the browning was spotty at best. Broiling had an additional problem. I had to go in and out of the oven to turn the meat every three or four minutes until all four sides had browned. I thought maybe the stovetop would be better for this job.

I seared two tenderloins in a hot skillet and was impressed with the evenly browned crust that formed. Clearly, direct contact between the meat and the hot pan was the closest I could get to replicating the intense heat of the grill. Unfortunately, I now had a new problem—the roast was browned before the meat was cooked through.

When this happens on the grill, you just slide the meat to a cooler spot on the grate. When this happens on the stovetop, you have to move the meat to the oven. Wanting to keep this recipe simple, however, I simply reduced the heat to medium and added the glaze. As the glaze thickened, the tenderloins gently cooked through in about 10 minutes and remained remarkably moist.

I turned my attention to perfecting the spicy glaze, which I wanted to be sweet and sour as well as packed with heat. For the sweetness, brown sugar and smoky molasses did the job. For the sourness, lime juice and pineapple juice were far better than all the other juices and vinegars I tried. Cayenne ensured steady and direct heat, while a jalapeño added freshness. A little cumin complemented the others flavors. Nothing quite rivals meat cooked on the grill, but my recipe comes close. **–Eva Katz**

SPICY GLAZED PORK TENDERLOINS SERVES 4

See page 28 for tips on buying tenderloins.

- **1/2 cup pineapple juice**
- **1/4 cup juice from 2 limes**
- **1/3 cup packed light brown sugar**
- **1 tablespoon molasses**
- **1 teaspoon ground cumin**
- **1/2 teaspoon cayenne pepper**
- **1 jalapeño chile, seeded and minced**
- **2 pork tenderloins (12 to 16 ounces each), trimmed of silver skin (see photo at right)**
- **Salt and pepper**
- **2 teaspoons vegetable oil**

1. Stir pineapple juice, lime juice, brown sugar, molasses, cumin, cayenne, and jalapeño in small bowl. Pat tenderloins dry with paper towels and season with salt and pepper.

2. Heat oil in large nonstick skillet over medium-high heat until just smoking. Cook tenderloins, turning until browned on all sides, 5 to 8 minutes total. Reduce heat to medium, add lime juice mixture, and cook, rolling tenderloins to coat, until mixture is thick and syrupy and internal temperature of tenderloins registers 140 degrees on instant-read thermometer, 9 to 11 minutes.

3. Transfer tenderloins to cutting board, tent loosely with foil, and let rest until internal temperature rises to 150 degrees, about 10 minutes. Cut tenderloins crosswise into ½-inch-thick slices, arrange on platter, and pour glaze in pan over slices. Serve.

Secret Step
REMOVING THE SILVER SKIN

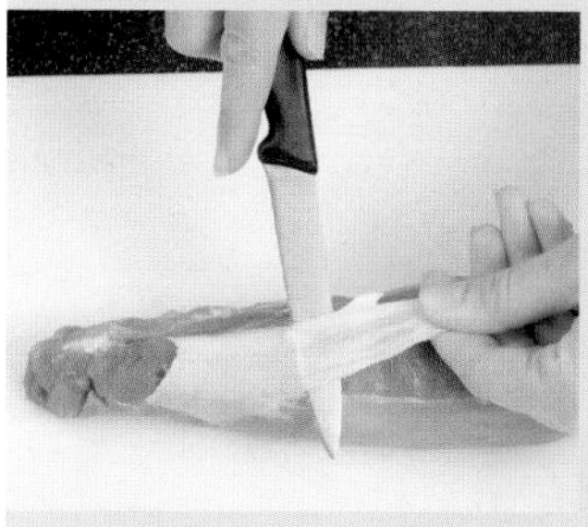

The silver skin is a thin, translucent membrane that covers parts of the tenderloin. It is pretty tough and should be removed before cooking. Slip a knife under the silver skin, angle it slightly upward, and use a gentle back-and-forth motion to remove the silver skin.

Pretty in Pink

The pork of yesteryear was always cooked till gray, but that pork was a lot fattier than what's on the market today. Selective breeding has made today's pork much leaner, and if you cook it till gray, the meat will be dry and tough. We think the leanest cuts—like tenderloin—are best cooked to 150 degrees. At this point, the meat will still have a tinge of pink in the center.

What about trichinosis? Better farming practices have all but eliminated the trichina parasite from American-raised pork. According to the Centers for Disease Control and Prevention, the number of trichinosis cases averages 12 per year—and most of those cases have been linked to wild game, not commercially raised pork. Also, the trichina parasite is killed when the temperature of the meat rises to 137 degrees, so cooking pork to 150 degrees should do the job.

Pink pork isn't completely without risk. All meat (including beef) may be subject to cross-contamination with several pathogens, such as salmonella. This can happen during processing, at the supermarket, or in your home. To reduce this risk, some food safety experts recommend cooking all meat to 160 degrees—that is, until it is well done. But if you think it's worth taking the small risk to enjoy a rosy steak, you might as well to do the same with pork.

Diner Home Fries at Home

What's the best way to make diner-style home fries—the kind with a thick, crunchy crust and creamy interior? –John Forrest Sanders, New York, N.Y.

Any decent grill cook can turn a pile of cubed potatoes into perfectly crisp, impeccably seasoned home-fried potatoes—or so it would seem. While the well-seasoned, flat griddle at the diner certainly helps, the real secret is precooking the potatoes. Having worked as a cook, I know that most restaurants use leftover roasted or boiled potatoes (preferably medium-starch potatoes that hold their shape well) to make their home fries. But who has precooked potatoes at home? Skip this step and you'll end up with a greasy mound of crunchy potatoes. So why on earth are they called home fries when they are so impractical to make at home?

Because I don't want to get up at the crack of dawn to boil or roast potatoes, I turned to the quickest cooker in the kitchen: the microwave. In the past, I've microwaved diced potatoes with a bit of oil, but in this application I found the flavor of the oil distracting. A touch of butter added a rich, nutty taste to the slightly sweet potatoes, and after just five minutes in the microwave the potatoes were parcooked and ready for the skillet.

I decided to use a nonstick skillet so that I could "home-fry" the potatoes without using an excess of butter. Unfortunately, the potatoes weren't developing the thick crust I wanted. I tried turning the heat up and down, but neither helped much. To replicate the heavy cast-iron tool used in many diners to press the potatoes flat against the griddle, I slid my heaviest pot (a Dutch oven) on top of the potatoes as they cooked. The weight of the Dutch oven kept the potatoes in constant contact with the hot skillet, producing a thick and even crust—but what a mess.

Setting the Dutch oven aside, I tried packing the potatoes down with my spatula (to approximate the effect of the Dutch oven) and let them cook undisturbed. After five minutes, the potatoes were beginning to develop a golden brown crust, so I tossed them around, packed them down again, and waited some more. After repeating this process a few more times, the potatoes were evenly browned and extra-crusty.

The last step was flavoring. Sautéed onion was a must, but when the onions were cooked with the potatoes, their moisture caused the home fries to lose their cherished crust. To keep the potatoes crispy, I browned the onions separately and added them to the pan just before the potatoes were finished. Taking a trick from my local diner, I tried sprinkling the home fries with a bit of garlic salt just before serving. Its deep, savory flavor nicely balanced the sweetness of the onion and potatoes. Finally, I had hassle-free home fries worthy of their name. **–Jeremy Sauer**

SHORT-ORDER HOME FRIES SERVES 4

Although we prefer the sweetness of Yukon Gold potatoes, other medium-starch or waxy potatoes, such as all-purpose or red-skinned potatoes, can be substituted. If you want to spice things up, add a pinch of cayenne pepper.

- **1½ pounds Yukon Gold potatoes (4 medium), scrubbed and cut into ¾-inch pieces**
- **4 tablespoons unsalted butter**
- **1 onion, chopped fine**
- **½ teaspoon garlic salt**
- **½ teaspoon salt**
- **Pepper**

A nonstick skillet turns precooked potatoes (steamed for five minutes in a microwave) into crunchy, crusty home fries.

1. Arrange potatoes in large microwave-safe bowl, top with 1 tablespoon butter, and cover tightly with plastic wrap. Microwave on high until edges of potatoes begin to soften, 5 to 7 minutes, shaking bowl (without removing plastic) to redistribute potatoes halfway through cooking.

2. Meanwhile, melt 1 tablespoon butter in large nonstick skillet over medium heat. Add onion and cook until softened and golden brown, about 8 minutes. Transfer to small bowl.

3. Melt remaining 2 tablespoons butter in now-empty skillet over medium heat. Add potatoes and pack down with spatula. Cook, without moving, until underside of potatoes is brown, 5 to 7 minutes. Turn potatoes, pack down again, and continue to cook until well browned and crisp, 5 to 7 minutes. Reduce heat to medium-low and continue cooking, stirring potatoes every few minutes, until crusty, 9 to 12 minutes. Stir in onion, garlic salt, salt, and pepper to taste. Serve.

GREEK-DINER-STYLE HOME FRIES

Add 2 minced garlic cloves, 1 tablespoon fresh lemon juice, and ½ teaspoon dried oregano to potatoes along with onion in step 3. Omit garlic salt.

HOME FRIES WITH FRESH HERBS

In step 3, add 1 teaspoon each chopped fresh basil, parsley, thyme, and tarragon along with onion.

The Golden Starches

High-starch/low-moisture potatoes, such as russets, may be great for baking and mashing, but when it comes to home fries, they are not the best choice. The fluffy flesh of these potatoes breaks down in the skillet, leaving nothing but a greasy pool of spuds. For tender tubers that retain their texture, we prefer medium-starch or waxy varieties, such as Yukon Gold, all-purpose, and red potatoes. They hold their shape in the skillet, develop a great crust, and fry up to a beautiful golden brown.

RUSSET POTATOES
A falling-apart mess

YUKON GOLD POTATOES
Intact, crisp, and browned

FOOD FACT: *In 2002, mozzarella surpassed cheddar to become America's most popular cheese. Annual per capita consumption of mozzarella is now almost 10 pounds. Cheddar remains in second place, followed by cream cheese and Swiss cheese.*

INSIDE THE TEST KITCHEN:

The Cheese Dilemma

Test cook Jeremy Sauer liked the creamy flavor of fresh mozzarella in these stuffed chicken breasts, but he couldn't resist the convenience or superior meltability of the shrink-wrapped mozzarella sold in supermarkets. His solution—to mix a little heavy cream with shrink-wrapped cheese that he shredded himself—offers the best of both worlds.

Cheesy Basil-Stuffed Chicken Breasts

A cheesy stuffing turns boring chicken cutlets into something my family can get excited about, but it's so much work. Can you help?

–Erin Gasparini, Wethersfield, Conn.

I have always had a soft spot for stuffed chicken breasts, but not for all the work they can entail. Pounding and rolling chicken breasts into pretty little pinwheels is great for when the in-laws are coming, but for everyday eating I prefer a simpler approach. I just cut a pocket in the thick part of the chicken breast, spoon in a filling, and thread the opening shut with a skewer or toothpick. This way, I get a nice little hiding place for a cheesy stuffing—minus the hassle.

For the filling, I've always been partial to mozzarella for its terrifically gooey texture, but which kind is best? My tasters liked the pronounced milky flavor of fresh mozzarella, but it didn't melt as well as block mozzarella. For the best of both worlds, I added a touch of cream to the plain old block mozzarella. It infused the supermarket cheese with a dairy-fresh flavor to go along with its superb meltability. The flavors of basil, garlic, lemon juice, and black pepper complemented the cheese nicely.

In my opinion, stuffed chicken needs a crunchy breadcrumb coating—as long as the coating stays put and doesn't fall off in the baking dish. To help the bread crumbs adhere, I brushed the chicken with mayonnaise (stickier than the other options I tried, including butter) before sprinkling it with crumbs. After 30 minutes in a 425-degree oven, the chicken was cooked, the cheese melted, and the bread crumbs crisped.

My dish was pretty good, but tasters in the kitchen decided that they wanted tomato sauce, too. I eventually came up with a simpler solution. I just nestled halved cherry tomatoes around the chicken breasts as they cooked. Once roasted, the sweet-tart tomatoes served as both sauce and vegetable side dish. I now had dinner ready in less than an hour from start to finish. **–Jeremy Sauer**

Our method for stuffing chicken breasts is so simple you'll have time to add a crunchy topping and juicy cherry tomato sauce.

CHEESY BASIL-STUFFED CHICKEN BREASTS SERVES 4

Avoid thin chicken breasts for this recipe; they are difficult to stuff without tearing. Whole-milk block mozzarella will provide the creamiest filling; preshredded or part-skim mozzarella will also work, but the filling will be grainy. To make fresh bread crumbs, process 2 slices of hearty white sandwich bread in the food processor.

- 1 cup shredded mozzarella cheese (see note above)
- 1/4 cup minced fresh basil
- 2 tablespoons heavy cream
- 1 tablespoon fresh lemon juice
- 3 garlic cloves, minced
- Salt and pepper
- 4 boneless, skinless chicken breasts (6 to 8 ounces each)
- 3 tablespoons mayonnaise
- 1 cup fresh bread crumbs
- 2 tablespoons extra-virgin olive oil
- 1 pint cherry tomatoes, halved

1. Adjust oven rack to middle position and heat oven to 425 degrees. Combine cheese, 2 tablespoons basil, cream, lemon juice, 2 teaspoons garlic, ½ teaspoon salt, and pepper to taste in medium bowl.

2. Cut pocket in chicken breasts, stuff with cheese mixture, and seal (see photos 1 through 3 at right). Transfer stuffed breasts to 13 by 9-inch baking dish and spread tops evenly with mayonnaise.

3. Combine bread crumbs, remaining garlic, remaining 2 tablespoons basil, and 1 tablespoon oil. Sprinkle crumb mixture over chicken, pressing lightly to adhere.

4. Toss tomatoes with remaining tablespoon oil, ½ teaspoon salt, and pepper to taste. Arrange in baking dish around chicken. Bake until crumbs are golden brown and thickest part of chicken registers 160 degrees on instant-read thermometer, about 25 minutes. Serve.

How to STUFF CHICKEN BREASTS

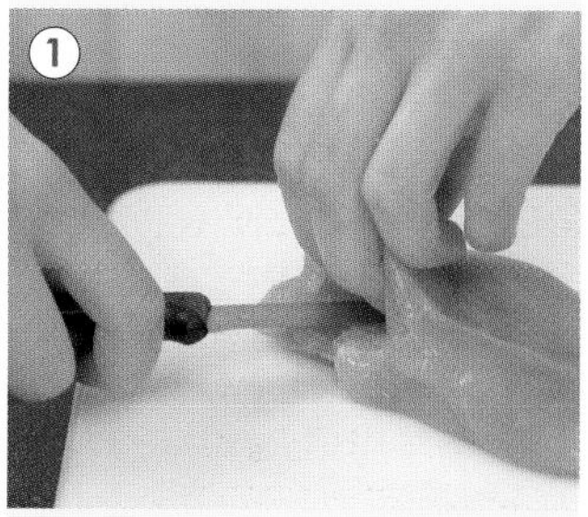

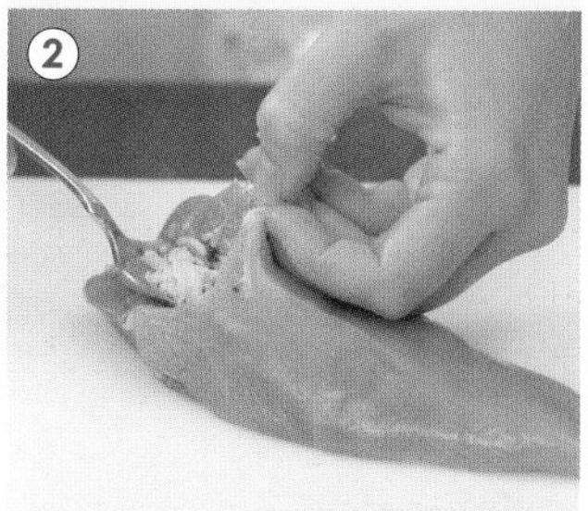

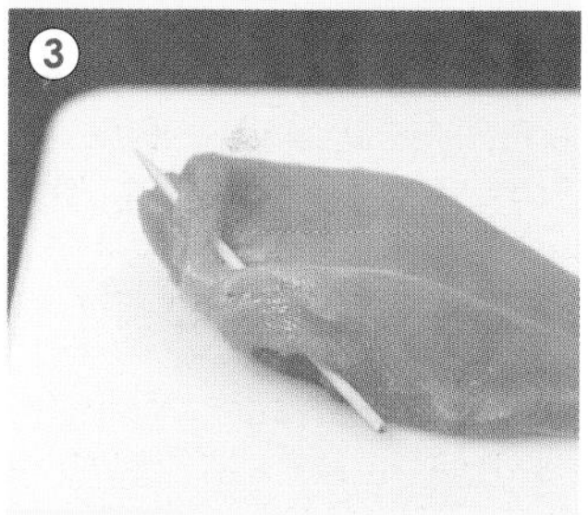

1. Working carefully, use a sharp paring knife to cut a pocket in the thickest area of the chicken breast. Gently work the knife back and forth until the pocket extends down into most of the breast. **2.** Use a small spoon to scoop one-quarter of the filling into each chicken breast. **3.** Seal in the filling by threading a toothpick or wooden skewer through the chicken about 1/4 inch from the opening.

I'm Looking for a Recipe

READERS HELP READERS FIND RECIPES

We've Got Mail

Lots of readers submitted recipes in response to the request for *chrusciki* (October/November 2005 issue). We really liked the letter and recipe sent by Jill Sawyer (at right). For the test kitchen's notes on this recipe (with more details on cooking times and procedures), go to **www.cookscountry.com** and click **Looking for a Recipe**. You'll find dozens more recipes submitted by readers who responded to recipe requests in other issues of *Cook's Country*.

CHRUSCIKI **Jill Sawyer** Dallas, Texas

When I saw the chrusciki request, I thought of my grandmother, Sophie Dombrowski, the daughter of Polish immigrants, who lived in Milwaukee. In an effort to find this recipe, I searched in some of the community cookbooks my grandmother had given me. I found a recipe and, lo and behold, it was my grandmother who had submitted it! Her version of these crisp, deep-fried cookies does not include rum, but it is, I hope, close enough.

- **4 large eggs, lightly beaten**
- **8 tablespoons unsalted butter, melted and cooled**
- **1 cup heavy cream**
- **Confectioners' sugar**
- **5 cups all-purpose flour**
- **1 1/2 quarts vegetable oil**

INSTRUCTIONS: **1.** Whisk together eggs, butter, cream, and 1/4 cup sugar. Gradually add flour and beat until dough is satiny and smooth, about 4 minutes with standing mixer. **2.** Divide dough into 4 pieces. On lightly floured surface, roll out each piece 1/8 inch thick. Cut into 1-inch-wide strips, then cut each strip crosswise into 4-inch pieces. Cut 1-inch hole in center of each strip and pull one side of strip through hole, making bow tie. Repeat with remaining dough. **3.** Heat oil in large Dutch oven to 360 degrees. Fry cookies in batches until golden brown on both sides, 2 to 3 minutes. Remove with slotted spoon and drain on paper towels. Place on serving plate and sprinkle heavily with confectioners' sugar.

Chocolate Rice Cake

My mother, who was from the town of Fiume (now Rijeka) in Croatia, used to make a chocolate rice cake. She cooked rice in chocolate milk, then mixed it with flour and dried fruit before baking it. She passed away in 1968 and I never got the recipe. It was called *koff de risi* (my spelling may be wrong).

Mario Properz
St. Andrews, Australia

Green Bell Pepper Jelly

When I was young, my mother used to make jelly in the summer with fresh green bell peppers. We used it as a condiment for most of our grilled beef dinners. I am looking to recapture that part of my youth. Most of the recipes I have seen call for jalapeño or other hot peppers. The recipe I am looking for uses only sweet green peppers.

Jill Firse
Belleville, Ill.

Hungarian Hurka

I'm looking for a Hungarian recipe called *hurka*. I grew up in Cleveland, where this type of sausage is common, but, since moving to New York State many years ago, I haven't been able to find it. I've had to rely on buying it whenever I go back to Ohio to visit family. The sausage contains pork, pork liver, rice, and marjoram.

Marty Pavelka
Rochester, N.Y.

Boston Cream Loaf Candy

My mother-in-law used to make wonderful Boston cream loaf candy. It had a creamy texture but did not have maraschino cherries, as most recipes for this candy do. I am trying to put together a recipe book for my family, and I was distressed when I could not find this one.

Leona Julian
San Marios, Texas

Italian Bread

When we lived in Connecticut, it was easy to find this wonderful Italian bread made with bits of crispy pork. The best was at Di Sorbo's Bakery in New Haven. I may be wrong about the spelling, but it sounds like *chickla* when pronounced correctly.

Diana Kulaga
Port St. Lucie, Fla.

Dried Fig Candy

Every year when her fig tree was loaded with fruit, my grandmother would make candy. She would dry whole figs, but I am not sure if she soaked them in anything. The end product was like a whole dried fig with sugar on it.

Laurie Wall
Alpine, Calif.

Purple Potato Salad

Forty years ago, when my grandfather died, a neighbor brought us the most beautiful potato salad. It was purple, with sliced boiled eggs mixed in. The yellow and white of the eggs really stood out against the purple potatoes. It may be a southern recipe, as my grandfather lived in Shady Valley, Tenn.

Mary McBride
Cedar Rapids, Iowa

Nesselrode Pie

My grandmother used to make something called Nesselrode pie. From what I know, it was made with classic Bavarian cream, chestnut puree, rum, and something called Raffetto's Nesselro fruits. Does anyone have a recipe for this pie, possibly one without rum?

Robin Johnson
Los Angeles, Calif.

Peach Cobbler Cheesecake

I was at a luncheon in Las Vegas and was served a peach cobbler cheesecake for dessert. Do you know of such a recipe?

Sylvia Sulmar
Lost Angeles, Calif.

Oatmeal 'Mexican Wedding Cake' Cookies

I am looking for a recipe that was very popular in the late 1950s and 1960s. This cookie was similar to a pecan dainty, Mexican wedding cake, and Russian tea cake, but instead of nuts it was made with oatmeal, and the cookie melted in your mouth. Like these other cookies, it was rolled in powdered sugar.

Louise Morris
Lago Vista, Texas

Orange Block Cake

Years ago, I had a recipe book called *Old Southern Receipts* that was printed around 1910. It contained a recipe for something called orange block cake that was particularly fabulous. It was a sheet cake covered with a thick boiled frosting, and the whole thing was flavored with lemons and oranges. Served chilled on a hot day, it was just the best thing in the world! I don't have the book anymore, but I would love to find that recipe again.

Steve Gentis
Seattle, Wash.

German Cheese Buttons

My mother-in-law used to make a German recipe called cheese buttons. It was cottage cheese wrapped in a pasta-like dough and lightly simmered.

Ann Logan
Via e-mail

Chocolate Chip Microwave Cake

I am looking for a quick but delicious chocolate chip cake recipe that was printed on the back of the 24-ounce bag of Nestlé Toll House chips in the early 1990s. It was so easy to make. You would mix up the ingredients, bake it in the microwave, and spread the remaining chips on the hot cake to melt. We usually put it together just before we ate and enjoyed it when dinner was over.

Carol Waterbury
Waco, Texas

Burdock's Fish and Chips

My wife and I enjoyed the best fish and chips in Ireland at Leo Burdock's behind Dublin Castle. We have tried many times to duplicate Burdock's fried fish here at home and have failed miserably. It is somewhat inconvenient to travel 5,000 miles for our fish and chips fix!

Marv Soloff
Clifton, N.J.

Crispy Bran Muffin Tops

I love bran muffins with tops that are crusty, crispy, thin, and spread out. I've had muffins with tops like this, but none of the places that sell "muffin tops" exclusively seem to get it right. I've tried recipes from many cookbooks, but none were satisfactory and most of them simply produced thinner muffins without much of a top.

R. Fiske
Hopedale, Mass.

Are you looking for a special recipe? Let other readers of this magazine help. Just send us your requests, and we will print as many of them as we can. Write to Looking for a Recipe, Cook's Country, P.O. Box 470739, Brookline, MA, 02447, or e-mail us at lookingforarecipe@bcpress.com. If you can help with one of the above requests, contact us at the same postal or e-mail address. We will post responses to recipe requests on www.cookscountry.com.

Find the Rooster! A tiny version of this rooster has been hidden somewhere in the pages of this issue. If you find it, write to us with its location (plus your name and address), and you will be entered into a random drawing. The first winning entry drawn will receive the Cuisinart nonstick skillet (our test winner—see page 31), and the next five winners will each receive a free one-year subscription to *Cook's Country*. To enter the contest, write to us at Rooster, Cook's Country, P.O. Box 470739, Brookline, MA 02447, or e-mail us at rooster@bcpress.com. Entries are due by March 31, 2006.

Did you find the rooster in the October/November 2005 issue? It was hidden in the photo of the Cream Sauce with Sausage and Peas on page 5. Lenda Burns of Huntington, W.V., spotted it and won a Krups Universal Grill and Panini Maker.

Quick Cooking

MUSTARD PORK CHOPS WITH CRISPY CABBAGE

Quick Cooking

SKILLET SAUSAGE AND PEPPERS

Quick Cooking

SESAME-GINGER SHRIMP

Quick Cooking

ANTIPASTO SALAD

SKILLET SAUSAGE AND PEPPERS SERVES 4

Serve the sausages, peppers, and onions on Italian sub rolls or with mashed potatoes.

- 1 tablespoon olive oil
- 8 sweet Italian sausages (about 1 1/2 pounds)
- 1 large onion, halved and sliced thin
- 1 large red bell pepper, seeded and cut into thin strips
- 1 large yellow bell pepper, seeded and cut into thin strips
- 2 garlic cloves, minced
- 2 tablespoons tomato paste
- 1/2 cup dry white wine
- 1/2 cup water
- 1/2 teaspoon dried oregano
- 1 tablespoon balsamic vinegar

1. Heat oil in large skillet over medium heat until shimmering. Prick sausages with fork in several places, add to skillet, and cook until browned on all sides, about 10 minutes. Transfer to large bowl and pour off all but 1 tablespoon fat from skillet. When cool enough to handle, cut sausages in half diagonally and set aside in bowl.

2. Add onion and peppers to skillet and cook until peppers are beginning to wilt, about 5 minutes. Add garlic and tomato paste and cook until fragrant, about 1 minute. Add wine, water, oregano, sausages, and any accumulated juices. Cover and cook until sausages are cooked through, about 5 minutes. Add vinegar and cook, uncovered, until sauce has thickened, 1 to 2 minutes. Serve.

MUSTARD PORK CHOPS WITH CRISPY CABBAGE

SERVES 4 TO 6

For this dish, buy pork chops about 1/4 inch thick.

- 1/2 large head green cabbage, cut into 1-inch wedges (core left intact)
- 3 tablespoons unsalted butter, 2 tablespoons melted
- Salt and pepper
- 6 thin bone-in pork chops (about 1 1/2 pounds), trimmed of excess fat
- 2 teaspoons vegetable oil
- 1 cup low-sodium chicken broth
- 1/4 cup heavy cream
- 2 1/2 tablespoons grainy mustard

1. Adjust oven rack to upper-middle position and heat oven to 450 degrees. Place cabbage on baking sheet, drizzle with melted butter, and sprinkle with salt and pepper. Roast until cabbage is browned around edges, 20 to 25 minutes.

2. Meanwhile, pat pork chops dry with paper towels and season with salt and pepper. Heat oil and remaining 1 tablespoon butter in large skillet over high heat until foaming subsides. Cook 3 chops until well browned on both sides, 1 1/2 to 2 minutes per side. Transfer chops to serving plate and cover tightly with foil. Repeat with remaining chops.

3. Discard fat in pan. Add broth and bring to boil, scraping up browned bits with wooden spoon. Reduce heat to medium and simmer until thickened, 4 to 6 minutes. Add pork chops and accumulated juices to skillet. Add cream and simmer until thickened, 2 to 3 minutes. Stir in mustard and season with salt and pepper. Pour sauce over chops and serve with cabbage.

ANTIPASTO SALAD SERVES 4

If you have homemade pesto on hand, by all means use it. Otherwise, store-bought pesto is fine for this recipe. We prefer the kind found in the refrigerated section of the supermarket (usually next to the fresh pasta).

- 2 cups grape or cherry tomatoes, halved
- 1/2 pound mini mozzarella balls, drained and halved
- 4 tablespoons extra-virgin olive oil
- Salt and pepper
- 1/4 cup prepared pesto
- 2 1/2 tablespoons red wine vinegar
- 1 package romaine hearts (3 heads), torn into bite-sized pieces (about 14 cups loosely packed)
- 1/2 cup loosely packed torn fresh basil
- 8 thin slices prosciutto
- 8 thin slices capicola or salami

1. Toss tomatoes, mozzarella, and 1 tablespoon oil together in medium bowl and season with salt and pepper.

2. Whisk pesto, vinegar, and remaining 3 tablespoons oil together in large bowl. Add romaine hearts and basil, toss to combine, and season with salt and pepper.

3. Divide salad among 4 plates and drape 2 slices of each meat over greens. Mound portion of tomato-mozzarella mixture on top. Serve.

SESAME-GINGER SHRIMP SERVES 4

Toast the sesame seeds in a small skillet over medium heat until fragrant, about 3 minutes. Serve this dish with rice.

- 1 pound extra-large shrimp (21 to 25 count), peeled and deveined
- 4 teaspoons soy sauce
- 2 garlic cloves, minced
- 1 (1/2-inch) piece fresh ginger, peeled and minced
- 1/4 teaspoon red pepper flakes
- 2 tablespoons plus 1 teaspoon peanut oil or vegetable oil
- 1/2 cup water
- 1 tablespoon toasted sesame oil
- 1 tablespoon oyster sauce
- 1 teaspoon cornstarch
- 1 red bell pepper, seeded and cut into thin, 2-inch-long strips
- 5 scallions, white and light green parts, cut into 2-inch pieces
- 1 teaspoon lemon juice
- 1 tablespoon sesame seeds, toasted

1. Toss shrimp and 2 teaspoons soy sauce in medium bowl. Combine garlic, ginger, pepper flakes, and 1 teaspoon peanut oil in small bowl. Stir water, sesame oil, oyster sauce, remaining 2 teaspoons soy sauce, and cornstarch together in measuring cup.

2. Heat 1 tablespoon peanut oil in large nonstick skillet over high heat until smoking. Add bell pepper and scallions and cook until browned in spots, about 5 minutes. Transfer to bowl. Add remaining tablespoon peanut oil and shrimp to empty skillet and cook, tossing until just opaque, about 30 seconds. Push shrimp to sides of skillet, add garlic mixture to center of pan, and mash with spoon until fragrant, 10 to 15 seconds. Stir mixture into shrimp. Add water mixture and cook until thickened, 60 to 90 seconds. Return vegetables to pan, add lemon juice, and toss until heated through. Transfer to platter and sprinkle with sesame seeds. Serve.

Quick Cooking

CREAMY BROCCOLI-PARMESAN FETTUCCINE

Quick Cooking

SKILLET FLANK STEAK WITH SPICY RED PEPPER SAUCE

Quick Cooking

MEXICAN CHICKEN SOUP

Quick Cooking

SPINACH, POTATO, AND BACON FRITTATA

SKILLET FLANK STEAK WITH SPICY RED PEPPER SAUCE SERVES 4

Toast the almonds in a small skillet over medium heat until lightly colored and fragrant, about 4 minutes.

- 1 slice hearty white sandwich bread
- 2 tablespoons slivered almonds, toasted
- 1 cup drained jarred roasted red peppers
- 1 plum tomato, seeded and chopped
- 1 garlic clove, minced
- 1 tablespoon extra-virgin olive oil
- 2 teaspoons red wine vinegar
- $^1/_8$ teaspoon cayenne pepper
- Salt
- 2 tablespoons vegetable oil
- 1 flank steak (about $1^1/_2$ pounds)
- Pepper

1. Toast bread in toaster on lowest setting until surface is dry but not browned. Remove crust and cut bread into rough $^1/_2$-inch pieces. Process bread and almonds in food processor until finely ground. Add red peppers, tomato, garlic, olive oil, vinegar, cayenne, and $^1/_2$ teaspoon salt and pulse, scraping down sides of bowl as necessary, until mixture has texture similar to mayonnaise. Adjust seasoning with salt and transfer to small serving bowl.

2. Heat vegetable oil in large, heavy-bottomed skillet over medium-high heat until smoking. Season steak with salt and pepper and cook, without moving, 5 to 6 minutes, until well browned on first side. Turn steak over and repeat on second side. Transfer to large plate, tent with foil, and let rest for 5 minutes. Cut steak in thin slices on bias against grain. Serve with sauce.

CREAMY BROCCOLI-PARMESAN FETTUCCINE

SERVES 4 TO 6

You can substitute two 9-ounce packages of fresh fettuccine for the dried. If using fresh pasta, increase the reserved pasta water to 1 cup.

- 2 tablespoons unsalted butter
- 1 tablespoon olive oil
- 1 large head broccoli, florets cut into 1-inch pieces, stalks peeled and cut into $^1/_4$-inch pieces
- Salt
- 4 garlic cloves, minced
- $1^1/_2$ cups heavy cream
- $^1/_8$ teaspoon red pepper flakes
- 1 pound dried fettuccine
- 2 teaspoons grated zest and 5 teaspoons juice from 2 lemons
- $^3/_4$ cup grated Parmesan cheese

1. Bring 4 quarts water to boil in large pot over high heat. Meanwhile, heat butter and oil in large nonstick skillet over medium-high heat until butter is foaming. Add broccoli, season with salt, and cook until browned in spots and just tender, about 5 minutes. Add garlic and stir until fragrant, about 30 seconds. Add 1 cup cream and red pepper flakes and bring to boil. Reduce heat to low and gently simmer until broccoli is tender (sauce will still be a bit thin), 6 to 7 minutes.

2. Meanwhile, add 1 tablespoon salt and pasta to boiling water and cook until al dente. Reserve $^1/_2$ cup pasta cooking water, then drain pasta and return to pot. Add broccoli sauce and remaining $^1/_2$ cup cream to pot with pasta and simmer over medium heat, tossing constantly, until sauce has thickened, 1 to 2 minutes. Stir in lemon zest, lemon juice, and Parmesan and toss until cheese has melted, adding reserved pasta water as needed to adjust consistency of sauce. Adjust salt to taste and serve.

SPINACH, POTATO, AND BACON FRITTATA SERVES 4

This hearty Italian open-faced omelet can be served hot or warm.

- 10 large eggs
- 3 tablespoons half-and-half
- Salt and pepper
- $^1/_2$ cup crumbled goat cheese
- 1 (6-ounce) bag baby spinach
- $^3/_4$ pound Yukon gold potatoes, peeled and cut into $^1/_2$-inch pieces
- 6 slices bacon, cut crosswise into $^1/_4$-inch strips

1. Adjust oven rack about 5 inches from heating element and set oven to broil. Whisk eggs, half-and-half, $^1/_4$ teaspoon salt, and $^1/_4$ teaspoon pepper together in bowl until combined. Stir in $^1/_4$ cup cheese.

2. Microwave spinach in large microwave-safe bowl, covered with plastic wrap, on high power until wilted, about 90 seconds. Transfer spinach to clean dish towel and squeeze out excess liquid. Microwave potatoes in now-empty bowl, covered with plastic wrap, on high power until tender, about 5 minutes.

3. Meanwhile, fry bacon in medium nonstick ovensafe skillet over medium heat until crisp, about 6 minutes. Transfer bacon to plate lined with paper towel and pour off all but 1 tablespoon fat from skillet. Add potatoes to skillet and cook until golden brown, about 5 minutes. Add spinach, bacon, and egg mixture and cook, using rubber spatula to stir and scrape bottom of skillet, until large curds form but eggs are still very wet, about 2 minutes. Shake skillet to distribute eggs evenly and cook, without stirring, until bottom is set, about 30 seconds. Sprinkle remaining cheese over top.

4. Broil until surface is spotty brown, 3 to 4 minutes (eggs should be slightly wet and runny inside). Remove from oven and let stand 5 minutes to finish cooking. Slide frittata onto platter and cut into wedges. Serve.

MEXICAN CHICKEN SOUP SERVES 6 TO 8

Garnish the soup with avocado, Monterey Jack cheese, and cilantro. You can temper the heat of this spicy soup by reducing the amount of adobo sauce.

- 6 cups low-sodium chicken broth
- 6 boneless, skinless chicken thighs (about $1^1/_2$ pounds)
- 1 large onion, quartered
- 4 garlic cloves, peeled
- 10 sprigs cilantro
- Salt
- 1 (14.5-ounce) can whole tomatoes in juice, drained, with juice reserved
- $^1/_2$ jalapeño chile, seeds and ribs removed
- 1 canned chipotle chile in adobo sauce, plus 1 tablespoon sauce
- 1 tablespoon vegetable oil
- 2 cups frozen corn kernels
- 2 (14-ounce) cans kidney beans, drained and rinsed
- 2 tablespoons lime juice

1. Bring 4 cups broth, chicken, 2 onion quarters, 2 garlic cloves, cilantro, and $^1/_2$ teaspoon salt to boil in large skillet over high heat. Cover and cook over low heat until chicken is cooked through, 8 to 10 minutes. Transfer chicken to large plate.

2. Puree tomatoes, remaining 2 onion quarters, remaining 2 garlic cloves, jalapeño, chipotle, and adobo sauce in blender until smooth.

3. Heat oil in Dutch oven over high heat until shimmering. Add tomato mixture and $^1/_8$ teaspoon salt and cook until darkened in color, 8 to 10 minutes. Strain broth directly into pot with tomato puree (discard solids). Add remaining 2 cups broth, reserved tomato juice, corn, and beans and simmer to blend flavors, about 5 minutes. Shred or dice chicken into bite-sized pieces and add to soup. Stir in lime juice and season with salt and pepper. Serve.

Hearty Vegetable Soup

My family loves thick, hearty vegetable soup, the kind that really sticks to your ribs. What's the best way to make this kind of soup with a minimum of fuss? –Amy Lockhost, Pomona, N.Y.

A brothy soup with bits of vegetables is fine the rest of the year, but in the dead of winter I want a soup thick enough to stick to my spoon and my ribs. Long simmering of starchy root vegetables (especially potatoes) or dried beans is the most common way to create a really hearty soup. But is it the only way?

Some recipes speed up the process by pureeing part of the soup once the vegetables are tender. I found this technique added more body to the soup and helped infuse the broth with more vegetable flavor, but the soup was still not hearty enough. A selection of winter vegetables (my tasters liked carrots, parsnips, and onions) and the starchiest potatoes (russets instead of waxy red potatoes) helped, too, but the soup still wasn't ready for main-course status

Maybe pureeing a starchy ingredient with part of the soup would make it thicker. My first thought was canned beans, but my tasters were unimpressed, calling the soup "mealy," with an easily identifiable "grainy bean texture." Tasters also rejected cooked rice, which gave the soup an overwhelming rice flavor and unappealing viscous texture.

The surprise solution was plain old sandwich bread, lightly toasted to remove moisture and to help the slices dissolve in the blender. The bread gave the soup an almost creamy consistency (several tasters insisted I had sneaked in some heavy cream) and did not interfere with the vegetable flavor.

I now had a rich, hearty vegetable soup that cooked in less than 30 minutes, but it needed some color and variety in texture. A little fresh spinach and either frozen lima beans or peas helped, as did herbs. Cannellini beans (not pureed this time) were also a nice addition. Tasters wanted a little acidity to finish the soup, and slightly sweet balsamic vinegar was preferred to other vinegars or lemon juice. In the end, I had a vegetable soup with a hearty slow-cooked texture but without the slow cooking—and it was as easy as sliced bread. **–Keri Fisher**

HEARTY VEGETABLE SOUP

SERVES 6 TO 8

This soup won't freeze very well, but leftovers can be refrigerated for two or three days.

- **2 tablespoons vegetable oil**
- **3 large carrots, peeled and cut into 3/4-inch pieces**
- **2 large parsnips, peeled and cut into 3/4-inch pieces**
- **2 small onions, peeled and cut into 1/2-inch pieces**
- **6 garlic cloves, minced**
- **8 cups low-sodium chicken broth**
- **2 medium russet potatoes, peeled and cut into 1-inch pieces**
- **2 teaspoons minced fresh thyme**
- **1 sprig fresh rosemary**
- **1 bay leaf**
- **2 slices hearty white sandwich bread, lightly toasted**
- **2 cups curly spinach, stemmed and chopped**
- **1 (14.5-ounce) can cannellini beans, drained and rinsed**
- **1 (10-ounce) package frozen baby lima beans or peas**
- **Balsamic vinegar**
- **Salt and pepper**

1. Heat oil in large heavy-bottomed pot over medium-high heat until shimmering. Add carrots, parsnips, and onions and cook until lightly browned and softened, 5 to 7 minutes. Add garlic and cook until fragrant, about 30 seconds. Add broth, potatoes, thyme, rosemary, and bay leaf and bring to boil. Reduce heat to low, cover, and simmer until vegetables are soft, about 15 minutes.

2. Remove and discard rosemary and bay leaf. Transfer 3 cups solids, 1 cup broth, and bread to blender and puree until smooth. Stir puree back into pot, add spinach, cannellini beans, and lima beans and cook over medium heat until spinach is tender and beans are heated through, about 8 minutes. Stir in 1 tablespoon vinegar and season with salt and pepper to taste. Serve, passing extra vinegar at table.

A splash of balsamic vinegar is the finishing touch for this hearty but surprisingly quick soup.

Kitchen Tip
TAMING ROSEMARY

Rosemary's piney flavor can easily overpower a soup, making it taste medicinal and harsh. But a little woodsy rosemary is a great accent in many winter soups. To keep the rosemary in check, we simmer the whole sprig in the soup to extract its flavor. After about 15 minutes, once the rosemary has lightly perfumed the broth, we remove it from the pot and discard it.

Chicken Enchiladas from Your Freezer

I love chicken enchiladas but can't find an easy recipe for weeknight meals. It is always such a production. Any suggestions?
–Tiffany Stephens, Longview, Wash.

Saucy and cheesy, chicken enchiladas are just the thing I want to tuck into after a long day at work. The problem is that by the time they come out of the oven I'm half asleep, having slaved over a long list of steps: browning onions, toasting spices, cooking chicken, making sauce, straining, shredding, dipping, filling, rolling, baking—the work seems endless. My goal was simple: Streamline this recipe and make it freezer-worthy, so I could have enchiladas whenever the mood struck.

Our test kitchen already had a favorite recipe for enchiladas, so I made them and froze them, waited several days, then thawed them in the baking dish and popped the whole thing into the oven. The tortillas had turned into cornmeal mush, and what little sauce the tortillas hadn't absorbed was burned onto the bottom of the baking dish. In addition, the recipe itself was complicated and time-consuming. I definitely had my work cut out for me.

I started with the sauce. Instead of browning onions, roasting fresh tomatoes, and toasting spices, I found I could simply puree the sauce ingredients (canned tomato sauce, garlic, cumin, onion, and coriander) in a blender and then concentrate the flavors by simmering everything for 10 minutes in a saucepan. Smoky chipotle chiles were a key discovery; they added deep, complex flavor, and all I had to do was open a can.

As for the filling, most recipes poach, braise, or roast chicken with pungent spices. Rotisserie (or leftover) chicken was the obvious way to streamline this process, but how would I add spice flavor? A little of my sauce (no more than ¾ cup or the tortillas became soggy) did the trick. To enrich the filling further, I took some of the cheese generally reserved for the top of the enchiladas and added it to the filling.

The traditional method of dipping each corn tortilla in oil and sauce so that it becomes soft enough to fill and roll is tedious. Even more important, tortillas treated this way turn to mush once frozen, thawed, and baked. After trial and error, I found that a light coating of cooking spray and 2 minutes in a moderate oven softened the tortillas just enough for rolling while also helping to prevent sogginess.

After many disastrous attempts, I realized that tortillas would survive the freezing process only if completely unsauced. So, after chilling down the filled enchiladas, I wrapped them in bundles—well protected with plastic wrap and foil—and froze the sauce separately. Essentially, I now had an enchilada "kit" in the freezer.

Deciding on the best assembly procedure for this kit was key. If sauced before they went into the oven, the enchiladas acted liked a sponge. But if I baked the enchiladas without sauce, the tortillas dried out. For the second time, the solution was cooking spray. Coating the filled tortillas with cooking spray and baking the enchiladas "naked" for 20 minutes before slathering on the sauce allowed the tortillas to crisp before they absorbed any sauce.

These enchiladas were very good, but who would have thought that accidentally omitting a step would take them from good to great? With no time left in the workday to wait for the enchiladas to thaw, I put them right in the oven, stone-cold frozen. I couldn't believe it. These enchiladas had the best texture yet, soft but still toothsome. Once I thought about what had happened, it made sense. Thawing allows the enchiladas to absorb moisture as they soften. Not given the chance, these straight-from-the-freezer enchiladas were hot and cheesy on the inside but nowhere near mushy.

I can't say that these enchiladas are labor-free. But with a little bit of advance preparation, they're ready to eat just about half an hour after I walk in the door. **–Cali Rich**

How to FREEZE AND BAKE ENCHILADAS

1. Tightly wrap the chilled enchiladas in bundles of five, first in plastic and then in foil. The sauce should be frozen separately. **2.** Arrange the frozen enchiladas in a single layer in a greased baking dish and coat the tops with cooking spray. **3.** Pour the defrosted sauce over the enchiladas after they have baked for about 20 minutes (and the tortillas are starting to flake).

Taking the enchiladas straight from freezer to oven saves time and prevents soggy tortillas.

FREEZER CHICKEN ENCHILADAS SERVES 4 TO 6

Use leftover cooked chicken or a store-bought rotisserie chicken in this recipe. Note that you won't need 1½ cups of the cheese until you bake the enchiladas. Serve with avocado, pickled jalapeños, shredded lettuce, and/or sour cream.

- 1 (29-ounce) can tomato sauce
- ½ medium onion, chopped
- 3 garlic cloves, minced
- 1 canned chipotle chile in adobo sauce
- 1 teaspoon cumin
- 1 teaspoon coriander
- ¼ teaspoon salt
- ½ cup low-sodium chicken broth
- 1 tablespoon vegetable oil
- 3 cups shredded cooked chicken
- 2½ cups shredded Monterey Jack cheese
- ⅓ cup chopped fresh cilantro
- 2 tablespoons minced canned pickled jalapeños
- 10 (6-inch) corn tortillas
- Cooking spray

1. To make ahead: Blend tomato sauce, onion, garlic, chipotle, cumin, coriander, salt, and broth in blender until smooth. Heat oil in large nonstick skillet over medium heat until shimmering. Add tomato mixture, bring to boil, reduce heat to medium-low, and simmer until mixture is reduced to 3½ cups, 8 to 10 minutes. Transfer to bowl and refrigerate until cool, about 1 hour.

2. Adjust oven rack to middle position and heat oven to 300 degrees. Toss ¾ cup sauce with chicken, 1 cup cheese, cilantro, and jalepeños.

3. Place 5 tortillas on baking sheet and lightly coat both sides with cooking spray. Bake tortillas until just pliable, about 2 minutes. Working quickly, transfer one tortilla at a time to work surface, fill with ⅓ cup chicken mixture, and roll tightly. Transfer, seam side down, to large plate. Repeat warming and rolling process with remaining 5 tortillas. Place plate in freezer until enchiladas are frozen, at least 1 hour.

4. Place remaining sauce in freezersafe container and press 2 layers of plastic wrap directly onto surface of sauce. Tightly wrap enchiladas in bundles of 5, first in plastic and then in foil. Freeze for up to 2 months.

5. When ready to serve: Adjust oven rack to middle position and heat oven to 350 degrees. Defrost enchilada sauce in microwave on defrost setting, about 12 minutes.

6. Coat 13 by 9-inch baking dish with cooking spray. Arrange frozen enchiladas in single layer in baking dish and coat tops with cooking spray. Bake until tops of tortillas are just beginning to flake, about 20 minutes. Remove dish from oven, top enchiladas with 1½ cups sauce, and bake 10 minutes longer. Sprinkle enchiladas with remaining 1½ cups cheese and bake until cheese melts and center of casserole is hot and bubbling, 3 to 5 minutes. Serve, passing remaining sauce and garnishes (see note above) at table.

Taste Test: ENCHILADA SAUCE

Curious as to how canned enchilada sauces would stack up against our homemade version, we tried six supermarket brands: Old El Paso, La Victoria, Hatch, La Preferida, Comida Mexicana, and Las Palmas. None could compete with our recipe. Tasters compared one sauce to "canned tomato soup" and another to "spicy Chef Boyardee." Some comments were even more scathing, likening the supermarket sauces to "burnt coffee grounds" and "salty and bitter tomato paste." If you're taking the time to make our enchiladas, why spoil their flavor with a subpar sauce? Ours can be ready in less than 15 minutes. **–Cali Rich**

ne of these sauces compare vith our 15-minute recipe.

On the Side: Green Beans Parmesan

For something different, cook green beans in a garlicky tomato sauce and then sprinkle them with cheesy bread crumbs.

How do you add cheese, tomato sauce, and crisp bread crumbs to a favorite green vegetable?

Whether it's served up with chicken or eggplant, I like the combination of gooey cheese, garlicky tomato sauce, and crisp bread crumbs that defines the "Parmesan" treatment. Being partial to green beans, I wondered how they would respond to these flavors.

Boiling the beans and then simmering them in tomato sauce was a bust; the beans became waterlogged and tasted washed out. To help the beans soak up the flavors of the tomato sauce, I decided to cook them raw right in the sauce. The results were pretty good, but I wondered if browning the beans first (a trick I'd seen in other green bean recipes) would improve their flavor. Sure enough, sautéing the beans gave them a nice bronzed color and toasted flavor. I added the sauce, slid the cover on the skillet, and simmered the beans until they were tender.

The most convenient choice for the sauce was canned diced tomatoes, which I doctored with onion and garlic sautéed in the skillet before the tomatoes went in. After sampling this more finished version of the sauce, I realized the acidity of the tomatoes was coming on too strong (not a problem when making this dish with the more robust eggplant or chicken). Replacing the tomato juices (I had strained out the solids) with plain water was an improvement, but chicken broth was even better.

To finish the dish, I stirred in ½ cup of grated Parmesan, but my tasters wanted more cheese. Increasing the Parmesan, known more for its flavor than its meltability, left the beans with unsightly half-melted clumps of cheese. I was stumped until I remembered the bread crumbs I'd wanted to use for the topping. After sautéing a cup of fresh bread crumbs in the skillet, I simply transferred them to a bowl and tossed them with extra Parmesan and a bit of basil.

Now I had what I wanted: green beans given the "Parmesan treatment," and all made in one skillet. **–Cali Rich**

GREEN BEANS PARMESAN SERVES 6 TO 8

Water can be used in place of the chicken broth, but the flavor won't be as good. To make fresh bread crumbs, process 2 slices of hearty white sandwich bread in a food processor.

- 2 tablespoons unsalted butter
- 1 cup fresh bread crumbs
- ¾ cup grated Parmesan cheese
- 1 tablespoon chopped fresh basil
- 2 tablespoons olive oil
- 1 small onion, chopped fine
- Salt
- 2 garlic cloves, minced
- 1 (14.5-ounce) can diced tomatoes, drained
- 1 pound green beans, ends trimmed
- ⅓ cup low-sodium chicken broth
- Pepper

1. Melt butter in large skillet over medium heat. Stir in bread crumbs and cook, tossing often, until golden brown, 3 to 5 minutes. Transfer to medium bowl and toss with ¼ cup Parmesan and basil.

2. Wipe out skillet, add 1 tablespoon oil, and heat over medium heat until shimmering. Add onion and ¼ teaspoon salt and cook until soft and golden, 3 to 5 minutes. Add garlic and cook until fragrant, about 1 minute. Add tomatoes and cook until liquid evaporates, about 3 minutes. Transfer to small bowl.

3. Wipe out skillet again and heat remaining tablespoon oil over medium-high heat until just smoking. Add green beans and ½ teaspoon salt and cook, turning beans several times, until browned in spots, about 8 minutes. Reduce heat to medium-low and stir in tomato mixture and broth. Cover and cook until beans are just tender, about 5 minutes. Remove lid and cook until liquid evaporates, 1 to 2 minutes.

4. Off heat, toss in remaining ½ cup Parmesan and adjust seasonings with salt and pepper. Transfer to serving dish and top with bread crumbs. Serve.

Easier Than You Think: Crispy Potato Pancakes

Frozen hash browns and oven-frying can make potato pancakes fast and hassle-free, but what about crispy?

How to Make POTATO PANCAKES IN A HURRY

Shape potato mixture into 10 equal-sized balls, then drop onto a hot, oiled baking sheet. Use a greased metal spatula to press each ball into a pancake.

FROZEN HASH BROWNS
A cool way to make quick potato pancakes.

The combination of lacy, golden brown exterior and creamy interior boasted by the best potato pancakes is hard to beat. Traditional potato pancakes are made with grated potatoes (squeezed dry to remove excess moisture), eggs, onions, and a dry binder (usually flour or matzo meal). Formed into flat disks, they are fried in a pan of hot oil until golden brown. You can fry only a few pancakes at a time, so keeping the first batches hot while making more is always a challenge. No wonder most cooks save potato pancakes for special occasions.

Could I make this recipe suitable for a weeknight dinner by using frozen hash-brown potatoes? (They've been shredded and squeezed dry, which is half the work.) After my first tests, I had my doubts: Microwave-thawed hash browns made for tough, bland pancakes. For my next test, I tried adding butter (for flavor as well as moisture) and was pleasantly surprised by the improvement. Because I was not grating potatoes, the idea of grating onions (the usual procedure in most recipes) seemed silly. Minced raw onions were too crunchy, but scallions provided the same flavor without any textural distraction.

A single egg helped bind the potatoes and scallions, but I needed a dry binder, too. Flour gave the pancakes a pasty texture. Matzo meal worked fine, but not everyone has this ingredient on hand. Cornstarch worked just as well and is a staple in most kitchens.

Now that I had simplified my ingredient list, I needed a method to match. Instead of pan-frying, I wanted to oven-fry my pancakes in a single batch on an oiled baking sheet. Preheating the oiled baking sheet turned out to be essential—without this step the pancakes were not sufficiently crisp. Going one step further, I coated each potato ball with cooking spray before pressing it into a 1/2-inch-thick disk on the hot baking sheet. The light, even coating of fat provided by the spray helped the pancakes to develop the texture and color characteristic of pan-frying. Tasters marveled at the creamy interior and extra-crispy exterior of my pancakes—and no one guessed I had started with frozen hash browns. **–Meredith Butcher**

Do you love potato pancakes but hate shredding potatoes and frying them? We have a solution.

WHAT READERS ARE SAYING: Potato Pancakes

Traditional potato pancakes are pretty finicky. If you don't handle every step in the process just so, the results are unappetizing, as these readers will attest.

Marcia Pearson, Washington, D.C.: Several years ago, I tried to make potato pancakes (twice) and each time it was a disaster! I think that I grated the potatoes too large and did not squeeze out enough of the potato water. So when I tried to mix in the eggs and flour, the potatoes were turning brown and the mixture was soupy! I fried some of them, but they tasted funny.

Molly Hislop, Norcross, Ga.: I have attempted to make potato pancakes several times, and they've never turned out as good as my mother's. They were too starchy, too underdone on the inside, and sort of fell apart.

Elizabeth Ellers, Leesburg, Va.: Sometimes my potato pancakes come out just right, but more often the potatoes turn gray after grating, the outside burns before the interior is cooked through, or the added onions burn.

CRISPY POTATO PANCAKES SERVES 4

At the supermarket, you can find frozen shredded hash browns near the frozen french fries. Serve these crisp pancakes with sour cream and/or applesauce.

- **2 tablespoons vegetable oil**
- **5 cups frozen shredded hash-brown potatoes**
- **4 tablespoons unsalted butter**
- **1 large egg**
- **2 scallions, chopped fine**
- **1 tablespoon cornstarch**
- **1/2 teaspoon salt**
- **1/2 teaspoon pepper**
- **Cooking spray**

1. Adjust oven rack to upper-middle position and heat oven to 475 degrees. Coat rimmed baking sheet with vegetable oil.

2. Place hash browns and butter in large microwave-safe bowl. Cover tightly with plastic wrap and microwave on high power until butter is melted and hash browns are defrosted, about 5 minutes. Remove plastic wrap, stir well, and let cool.

3. Whisk egg, scallions, cornstarch, salt, and pepper together in medium bowl until thoroughly combined. Add to hash-brown mixture and stir until incorporated. Divide mixture into 10 equal-sized balls and set aside on large plate.

4. Place oiled baking sheet in oven and heat until oil is just beginning to smoke, about 6 minutes. Remove baking sheet from oven and, working quickly, place potato balls on hot baking sheet. Spray each ball with cooking spray, then press each one into ½-inch-thick disk using metal spatula (spray back of spatula with cooking spray if potato balls start to stick). Bake until potato pancakes are golden brown on bottom, about 10 minutes. Flip pancakes over, press down using metal spatula, and bake until crisp and golden brown on second side, about 8 minutes more. Place pancakes on plate lined with paper towels and let drain briefly. Serve.

Texas-Style BBQ Brisket Indoors

I love Texas-style barbecued brisket, but given the cold, snowy winters here in Vermont, I'd rather not spend all day tending a fire outdoors. Can you make BBQ brisket in the oven? –Doug Bloomberg, Colchester, Vt.

Most Texans will tell you that the secret to blue-ribbon brisket is hours and hours of slow, smoky heat. The low heat (between 200 and 300 degrees) converts collagen (the connective tissue that makes brisket tough) to gelatin, leaving the meat tender. Exposing the meat to smoke for hours creates a distinct barbecue flavor, and it's hard to imagine getting that out of an oven. But I figured it was worth a try. I've tried barbecuing in the snow, and it isn't much fun.

Approximating the temperature of the grill was easy—I just had to set my oven—but capturing the smoky flavor of the grill was another story. Traditional Texas recipes for brisket start by rubbing the meat with spices, and I saw no reason to deviate from this plan. I wrapped the meat in foil (to keep it from drying out in the oven), and it emerged tender and flavorful—but not smoky.

To add a smoky flavor, some recipes resort to oven-smoking, a technique involving some form of wood product (sawdust or cedar planks, for instance) and a hot sheet pan, but I was looking for something a little less complicated. I tried both marinating the brisket with chipotle chiles (smoked jalapeños) and drizzling it with liquid smoke, but neither one really got much smoky flavor into the meat.

I was stumped until I thought about my favorite bean recipes, which rely on smoked meats (ham hocks, smoked sausage, or bacon) to add smoky flavor. Bacon seemed like the easiest choice, so I added a few slices to the foil packet with the brisket. I detected a faint whiff of smoke in the meat, so I kept at it. In the end, I found that poking the brisket all over with a fork before wrapping it with a pound (yes, 1 pound) of bacon produced a noticeably sweet-smoky flavor. In the heat of the oven, the bacon fat rendered and dripped into the holes in the meat, seasoning the brisket throughout.

When it's too cold to barbecue outside, you can still add smoky flavor to brisket by using your oven—and bacon.

Because I was cooking the brisket wrapped in bacon and in foil, the exterior was pretty pale. I missed the deeply caramelized, almost crisp crust that graces true barbecued brisket. To remedy this problem, at the end of cooking I removed the bacon, flipped the brisket fat side up, and ran it under the broiler for a couple of minutes. The fat browned nicely, but the meat was still too pale.

Looking at the bacon that I'd removed from the brisket, I got an idea. Using the bacon and the juices from the brisket, I made a quick barbecue sauce and brushed it over the top of the brisket before running it under the broiler again. This time the sauce glazed the top of the brisket, turning it a rich mahogany color that would fool even the most ardent barbecue fan. –Jeremy Sauer

OVEN-BARBECUED BEEF BRISKET SERVES 8 TO 10

Our own Smoky Bacon BBQ Sauce (below) is our first choice, but feel free to use 3 1/2 cups of store-bought sauce. If you do use another sauce, skip steps 3 and 4 and go directly to step 5. See page 28 for tips on buying brisket.

Brisket

- 1/3 cup All-Purpose BBQ Rub (see recipe on page 22)
- 1 brisket roast (4 to 5 pounds), fat trimmed to 1/4 inch thick
- 1 pound bacon

Smoky Bacon BBQ Sauce

- Bacon from cooked brisket
- 1 onion, chopped fine
- 1/2 cup cider vinegar
- 1/3 cup packed dark brown sugar
- 1–2 cups low-sodium chicken broth
- 1/2 cup ketchup
- 1 canned chipotle chile in adobo sauce, minced

1. For the brisket: Adjust oven rack to upper-middle position and heat oven to 275 degrees. Massage dry rub into meat and poke all over with fork (see photo 1, below). Arrange half of bacon strips, overlapping slightly, crosswise

(continued on page 22)

Know-How COAXING BBQ FLAVOR FROM YOUR OVEN

1. Massage the dry rub into the meat and poke all over with a fork. **2.** Arrange half of the bacon strips, overlapping slightly, crosswise on the bottom of a broilersafe 13 by 9-inch baking dish. Place the brisket, fat side down, in the bacon-lined pan, and place the remaining strips of bacon on top.

Texas-Style BBQ Brisket Indoors

continued from page 21

on bottom of broilersafe 13 by 9-inch baking dish. Place brisket, fat side down, in bacon-lined pan and place remaining bacon strips on top, tucking ends of strips underneath brisket (see photo 2 on page 21). Cover pan with foil and roast until fork inserted into brisket can be removed with no resistance, about 4 hours.

2. Remove pan from oven and carefully flip brisket fat side up. Replace foil and return brisket to oven. Turn off heat and allow brisket to rest in warm oven for 1 hour.

3. For the sauce: Pour accumulated juices into 1-quart measuring cup and set aside. Remove bacon from brisket, chop into small pieces, and heat in medium saucepan over medium heat until fat has rendered, about 5 minutes. Add onion and cook until softened, about 5 minutes. Off heat, add vinegar and sugar and stir to combine. Return to medium heat and reduce to syrupy consistency, about 5 minutes

4. Meanwhile, skim fat from reserved juices and discard fat. Add enough chicken broth to juices to make 3 cups. Add to saucepan and reduce until mixture in saucepan measures 3 cups, about 8 minutes. Off heat, stir in ketchup and chipotle. Strain through fine-mesh strainer, if desired.

5. Turn oven to broil. Brush brisket with 1 cup sauce and broil until top is lightly charred and fat is crisped, 5 to 7 minutes. Transfer to cutting board and slice across grain into ¼-inch slices. Serve with remaining sauce.

ALL-PURPOSE BBQ RUB

MAKES ABOUT ⅓ CUP

This recipe can be doubled or tripled. Store the extra in an airtight container for up to 1 month.

- 4 teaspoons brown sugar
- 4 teaspoons paprika
- 2 teaspoons dry mustard
- 2 teaspoons black pepper
- 2 teaspoons salt
- 1 teaspoon onion powder
- 1 teaspoon garlic powder
- 1 teaspoon cumin
- ¼ teaspoon cayenne

Combine ingredients in bowl, breaking up any lumps of sugar.

Make Ahead

Follow recipe through step 1. In step 2, place the brisket fat side up on aluminum foil and wrap tightly; reserve juices in an airtight container. Refrigerate for up to 3 days. When ready to proceed, remove the bacon from the brisket, rewrap the brisket in foil, and cook for 1 hour in a 350-degree oven. Proceed with the recipe from step 3. In step 5, remove the foil from the brisket and proceed as directed.

The American Table: Barbecue Roots

We readily concede that "barbecuing" in the oven is something of a heresy. But our method does share something in common with the earliest barbecue recipes. Many sources say that modern barbecue is a direct descendent of Mexican *barbacoa*, a traditional cooking technique in which tough cuts of meat are wrapped in leaves from a maguey plant or banana tree and buried in a shallow pit filled with hot coals. Our oven-barbecued brisket trades aluminum foil for leaves and an oven for a hole in the ground, but the concept (tightly wrapped meat cooked slowly in a moderately hot enclosed space) is the same. **–J.S.**

Photo courtesy of UTSA Institute of Texan Cultures

Regional Favorites: Red Beans and Rice

New Orleans native Louis Armstrong loved this Louisiana dish so much that he signed his letters "Red beans and ricely yours."

Serve our recipe over hot white rice and pass hot sauce at the table.

Louisiana is home to two great cuisines, Creole and Cajun. A blend of French, Spanish, and African influences, Creole cooking is fairly refined and relies on many classic French techniques and ingredients. The Cajun people trace their roots back to France, but they spent nearly 150 years in Canada developing a unique culture of their own. Exiled from Acadia (modern-day Nova Scotia), these people found a home in sparsely populated areas along the Louisiana coast. Their cooking style was more rustic and often quite spicy. Because of their close proximity, it was inevitable that these two distinct styles of cooking would influence each other. Red beans and rice is a prime example.

Originally, red beans and rice was a Creole dish served on wash Mondays. The hambone left over from Sunday night's dinner and red beans were slowly simmered in a pot on the back burner while the women of the house washed and line-dried clothing. The marrow from the cracked bone flavored the beans and the broth, which slowly thickened over hours of simmering. Eventually, andouille, a heavily spiced and smoked Cajun pork sausage, became part of the standard recipe. The combination of pork products created a rich dish that became a meal when served over rice.

In my attempt to replicate red beans and rice in the test kitchen, I ran into a few obstacles. Realizing that most home cooks do not have a leftover hambone in their refrigerator, I started with a ham hock in its place. Although some tasters enjoyed the flavor, others found it too salty and smoky, masking the essence of the beans. Bacon, which has a similar but milder flavor profile, was an easy compromise everyone could agree on. Traditional recipes use water as the cooking liquid, but without bones my beans and rice were a bit bland. Replacing the water with chicken broth made the beans taste too "chickeny"; chicken broth cut with water was just right.

Great-tasting andouille can be hard to find in some parts of the country. If you have access to the real stuff, use it; otherwise, smoky kielbasa is a good alternative. Adding the sausage in the last half-hour of cooking keeps it from overpowering the beans or becoming too tough. Spooned over hot white rice and seasoned with a couple splashes of hot pepper sauce, this Louisiana classic is good enough to eat any day of the week. **–Meredith Butcher**

RED BEANS AND RICE SERVES 8 TO 10

Andouille is the traditional sausage for this dish, but we also had good results with kielbasa.

- 4 slices bacon, chopped medium
- 1 small onion, chopped fine
- 1 green bell pepper, chopped fine
- 1 celery rib, chopped fine
- 4 garlic cloves, minced
- Pepper
- 1 teaspoon minced fresh oregano
- 1 teaspoon minced fresh thyme
- ½ teaspoon cayenne pepper
- 4 bay leaves
- Salt
- 1 pound dried red kidney beans, rinsed and picked over
- 7 cups low-sodium chicken broth
- 7 cups water
- ½ pound andouille sausage or kielbasa, halved lengthwise and cut into ¼-inch half-moons
- 6 cups cooked long-grain rice (from 3 cups raw rice)
- Hot pepper sauce

1. Cook bacon in large Dutch oven over medium heat until lightly browned and fat has rendered, about 7 minutes. Add onion, bell pepper, and celery and cook, stirring frequently, until softened, about 8 minutes. Stir in garlic and cook until fragrant, about 30 seconds. Add 1 teaspoon pepper, oregano, thyme, cayenne, bay leaves, ½ teaspoon salt, beans, broth, and water, and bring to boil over high heat. Reduce heat to maintain vigorous simmer (mixture will be steaming and several bubbles should be breaking the surface) and cook, uncovered, stirring occasionally, until beans are soft and liquid thickens, 2 to 2½ hours.

2. Stir in sausage and cook until liquid is thick and creamy, about 30 minutes. Season with salt and pepper. Serve over hot cooked rice with hot pepper sauce, if desired. (Leftover beans can be refrigerated in airtight container for several days.)

Getting to Know Dried Beans

Dried beans come in all shapes, sizes, and, yes, flavors. To better understand what each bean really tastes like, we boiled 16 varieties, from supermarket staples to obscure heirlooms, and sampled them unadorned (read our comments below). For information about cooking beans, see page 28.

Black

INKY AND EARTHY

Also known as turtle beans, these medium-small, ink-black beans have a "rich," "earthy" flavor and hold their shape well, making them perfect for salads, salsas, and rice dishes.

COOKING TIME: 1 1/2 hours

Pinto

REFRIED FAVORITE

These mottled pink and beige beans are most commonly featured in Mexican cuisine. They are medium-sized and have a mild "peppery" flavor and "custardy" texture.

COOKING TIME: 1 1/2 hours

Kidney

CURVED AND CREAMY

Named for their gently curved kidney shape, these assertive beans have a slight "metallic" flavor. Although their skin is quite tough, the inside becomes creamy when fully cooked.

COOKING TIME: 1 1/2 hours

Chickpea

NUTTY AND CRUNCHY

Called *garbanzos* in Spain and *ceci* in Italy, these yellowish, pockmarked beans have a firm, "almost crunchy" texture and a distinct, "nutty" flavor.

COOKING TIME: 2 hours

Lima

LIKE BUTTER

These medium-large beans are named for their Peruvian hometown. Referred to as butter beans in the Southern United States, they possess a "super-creamy" interior and a sweet, "mineral-like" flavor."

COOKING TIME: 1 1/2 hours

Black-Eyed Pea

LUCKY LEGUME

Black-eyed peas have a firm texture and a "peanutty" flavor with a "smoky aftertaste." Famously featured in Hoppin' John, black-eyed peas are said to bring good luck if eaten on New Year's Day.

COOKING TIME: 2 hours

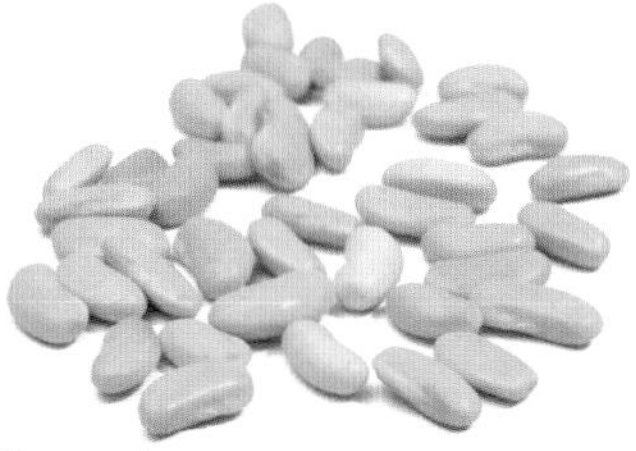

Flageolet

FRENCH FAVORITE

These tiny, capsule-like French beans are an elegant "sea foam" color. They hold their shape well, exhibiting a pleasant, "waxy" texture. Their flavor is "herbaceous" and a bit like "popcorn."

COOKING TIME: 1 hour

Navy

YANKEE DOODLE DANDY

These small, ivory-white beans are so named because they've been a staple on U.S. naval vessels for nearly 200 years. Their "crumbly texture" and mild sweetness are most often featured in Boston baked beans.

COOKING TIME: 2 hours

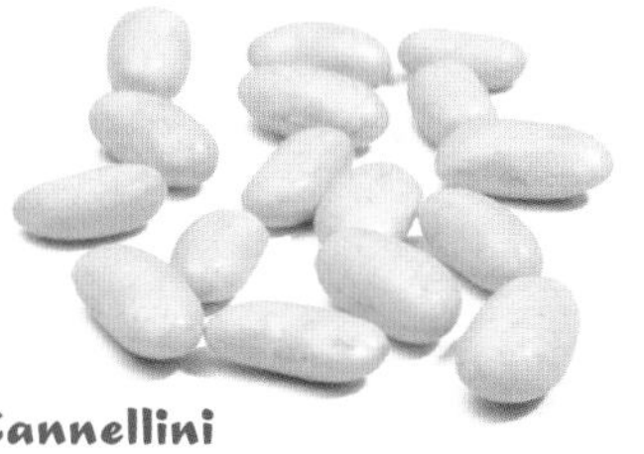

Cannellini

CREAMY AND MILD

These white beans are cousins of the kidney bean. A favorite in Italy, cannellini beans are "very creamy" and "thin skinned," with a mild flavor reminiscent of "mashed potatoes."

COOKING TIME: 1 1/2 hours

Borlotti

SPECKLED AND FRECKLED

Also called cranberry beans, these medium-sized beans are cousins to pinto beans. They have a "soft, starchy texture" and a "mild nuttiness."

COOKING TIME: 1 1/2 hours

Gigante

GENTLE GIANT

These huge, flat beans look like a giant version of lima beans. Given their size, they are surprisingly "silky" in texture and have a "buttery" flavor. Often used in Greek appetizer plates.

COOKING TIME: 2 hours

Scarlet Runner

BOLD AND BEAUTIFUL

These beans are large, plump, and kidney shaped, but it's their splotchy black and scarlet color that really defines them. Their texture is starchy and firm, and they taste like "roasted chestnuts."

COOKING TIME: 2 to 3 hours

Soybean

BEAN OF ALL TRADES

These yellowish, spherical beans have a "crisp" texture and a nutty, mildly "fishy" flavor. This staple of Asian cuisine has spawned many popular cooking products, including soy sauce, tofu, tempeh, soymilk, and miso paste.

COOKING TIME: 2 1/2 hours

Anasazi

NATIVE AMERICAN

This clay-red and beige heirloom bean is named after the ancient inhabitants of what is now the American Southwest. An ancestor of the pinto bean, the anasazi bean has a "dense, starchy" texture and a "yeasty" flavor.

COOKING TIME: 1 1/2 hours

Butterscotch

BUTTERY SWEET

Also called yellow-eye beans, these medium-sized heirloom beans have a distinct bronze marking in their center. They are soft skinned, with a "slightly granular" texture and a flavor reminiscent of "sweet potatoes."

COOKING TIME: 1 1/2 hours

Calypso

EBONY AND IVORY

Also called yin-yang or orca beans for their striking black-and-white pattern, these medium-large heirloom beans are closely related to cannellini beans. They are "very soft and creamy," with a complex "metallic-fruity aftertaste."

COOKING TIME: 1 hour

Stuffed French Toast

The crisp exterior on this French toast contrasts perfectly with the sweet cream cheese filling.

We often order stuffed French toast when we go out for brunch and would like to make it at home. Do you have a good recipe?

–William and Megan Bromley, Philadelphia, Pa.

Good stuffed French toast marries a creamy filling with a really crisp exterior. It's this contrast in textures that makes stuffed French toast different from ordinary French toast. To "stuff" the French toast, a filling is spread between two slices of regular sandwich bread (the moist filling acting as a seal). The stuffed sandwiches are then dipped in an egg-based batter and cooked in butter, much like regular French toast.

The cookbooks I consulted offered two options for the stuffing: jam or sweetened cream cheese. Tasters overwhelmingly preferred the latter, with many likening it to the filling in a cheese Danish. As a bonus, the sweetened cream cheese was better than the jam at holding the bread slices together.

I wasn't ready to give up on the jam altogether, however. After more testing, I found that a small amount of jam combined with the cream cheese was a great way to add different flavors. Blueberry jam was a big hit, as was apricot (especially when combined with a bit of almond extract). Apple jelly didn't win much support, though richly flavored apple butter provided a homey apple pie version. My favorite variation, though unorthodox, was chocolate chip; the chips melted into the cream cheese, making the filling taste just like chocolate cheesecake (you'll probably want to skip the maple syrup on that variation).

Satisfied with the stuffing, it was time to focus on the "toast." The typical egg and milk batter used with regular French toast wasn't producing the kind of crisp exterior I envisioned. I found recipes that called for everything from a thick pancake batter to a heavy, cream-based dip, but none gave me a really crisp exterior to contrast with the soft filling.

After yet another failed test, a fellow cook suggested tempura batter. Though I was initially skeptical, her idea made sense. A tempura batter is a thin mixture made with flour, egg, and either sparkling water or beer. Although it traditionally provides a thin, super-crisp coating for seafood and vegetables, why not try it as dip for French toast?

Beer was certainly not on the menu for breakfast (not at work, anyway), so I combined a mixture of sparkling water, flour, and egg. This was perfect; the bread fried up to a crisp golden brown and provided the perfect contrast with the creamy stuffing. I wondered, though, if I really needed the sparkling water. It turns out that I didn't; the lacy texture that sparkling water provides wasn't crucial to my recipe, and cold tap water served to create the same great crisp texture. **–Keri Fisher**

STUFFED FRENCH TOAST

SERVES 4

We like large loaves of sandwich bread for this recipe, with slices about 5 inches by 4 inches. If you use the smaller, standard-sized sandwich bread, you won't need all of the filling.

- 6 **ounces cream cheese, softened**
- 3 **tablespoons sugar**
- $1/4$ **teaspoon cinnamon**
- 8 **slices good-quality sandwich bread**
- 1 **large egg**
- 1 **cup cold water**
- $1/2$ **cup all-purpose flour**
- 1 **teaspoon vanilla extract**
- 4 **tablespoons unsalted butter**
- **Maple syrup for serving**

1. Combine cream cheese, sugar, and cinnamon in medium bowl. Spread on 4 bread slices. Top with remaining bread slices, pressing down gently, forming 4 sandwiches.

2. Combine egg, water, flour, and vanilla in shallow pie plate. Melt 2 tablespoons butter in large nonstick skillet over medium heat. Dip both sides of 2 sandwiches in batter and place in skillet. Cook until deep golden brown on both sides, about 3 minutes per side. Repeat with remaining butter and bread.

3. Cut into triangles and serve immediately with maple syrup.

The American Table: What's So French about French Toast?

Just as french fries are not exclusively "French," French toast is made around the world. The first written recipe for bread soaked in milk and beaten eggs and fried in oil appears in the writings of Apicius, ancient Rome's leading food writer, who lived in the first century A.D. From China to Europe, most cultures now have recipes that soak leftover bread in dairy and/or eggs and then fry it up for breakfast (or dessert). In England, this dish is known as poor knights of Windsor or simply poor knights, which is comparable to this recipe's name in Denmark (*arme riddere*), Germany (*arme ritter*), and Sweden (*fattiga riddare*). Even here in the United States, before the term "French" toast came into vogue in the late 19th century, this dish was known variously as Spanish, German, American, cream, or nun's toast. **–K.F.**

Fun Flavors

BLUEBERRY COBBLER FRENCH TOAST

Reduce cream cheese to 4 ounces and substitute 2 tablespoons blueberry jam for 2 tablespoons of the sugar.

APPLE PIE FRENCH TOAST

Reduce cream cheese to 4 ounces and substitute 3 tablespoons apple butter for $1\frac{1}{2}$ tablespoons of the sugar.

APRICOT-ALMOND FRENCH TOAST

Reduce cream cheese to 4 ounces and substitute 2 tablespoons apricot jam for 2 tablespoons of the sugar and $1/8$ teaspoon almond extract for the cinnamon.

CHOCOLATE CHIP FRENCH TOAST

Reduce cream cheese to 4 ounces and substitute $1/4$ cup semisweet chocolate chips for $1\frac{1}{2}$ tablespoons of the sugar. Omit cinnamon.

FOOD FACT: *Although there are dozens of lemon varieties, just two—Eureka and Lisbon—show up in supermarkets. Trendy, mild-tasting Meyer lemons are likely a cross between a lemon and an orange or a mandarin.*

Creamy Lemon Squares

Most lemon squares aren't lemony enough for me. I want a recipe that tastes like real lemons. –Westelle Griswa, Clovis, Calif.

With their thin smear of timidly flavored filling, most lemon squares seem designed to please people who like the shortbread crust more than the lemon filling. But if I want shortbread, I'll make shortbread. If I want lemon squares, I want a thick, creamy topping with a bold—though not mouth-puckering—lemon flavor.

Most recipes mix lemon juice, sugar, and eggs, pour this mixture over a prebaked crust, and then continue baking until the filling has set. Unfortunately, I found that these easy recipes produce a lemon layer that's thin and rubbery. A better option is to cook the filling ingredients into a thick curd. Once poured onto the crust and popped into the oven, the curd bakes up creamy and rich.

A combination of yolks and whole eggs is necessary to give the curd its structure and creaminess, whole eggs providing the former and yolks the latter. For a curd that was solid enough to hold its shape but was plenty creamy as well, the winning combination was 4 whole eggs and 3 egg yolks. For even more creaminess, I finished the curd with 2 tablespoons each of heavy cream and butter.

For serious lemon flavor, I learned that it's essential to use both juice and zest. Many recipes rely on juice alone, but its flavor fades in the oven. The zest has the stronger, brighter lemon flavor. My tasters weren't wild about the stringy bits of zest in their lemon squares, though, and I easily eliminated them by straining the cooked curd.

The shortbread crust is nothing more than flour, confectioners' sugar, and butter. To support a thick layer of lemon curd, the crust has to be sturdier than most. A few extra tablespoons of butter ensured a firm crust that didn't crumble under the thick lemon topping.

My lemon squares are not the lightest you'll ever find, but each creamy bite is packed with serious lemon flavor. As one of my kitchen colleagues joked, only lemon lovers need apply.

–Keri Fisher

A crisp, buttery shortbread crust supports our extra-lemony, extra-creamy filling.

No Food Processor?

To make the crust without a food processor, grate the cold butter (do not cut it in 12 pieces) on the large holes of a box grater and toss into the flour, sugar, and salt mixture. Using a fork, press the butter into the mixture until it is the texture of coarse meal. Proceed to press and bake the crust as directed.

LEMON SQUARES

MAKES 9

Crust

- 1 1/4 cups all-purpose flour
- 1/2 cup confectioners' sugar
- Pinch salt
- 12 tablespoons (1 1/2 sticks) cold unsalted butter, cut into 12 pieces

Filling

- 4 large eggs
- 3 large egg yolks
- 1 cup granulated sugar
- Pinch salt
- 1 tablespoon grated zest plus 2/3 cup juice from 4 lemons
- 2 tablespoons unsalted butter, cut into 2 pieces
- 2 tablespoons heavy cream
- Confectioners' sugar

1. For the crust: Adjust rack to middle position and heat oven to 350 degrees. Line 8-inch-square baking pan with aluminum foil, leaving overhang on all sides.

2. Pulse flour, sugar, and salt in food processor 2 to 3 times. Add butter and pulse until mixture resembles coarse meal (some pea-sized pieces of butter will remain) and will stick together if squeezed into ball, about fifteen 1-second pulses. Sprinkle dough into prepared pan and press in even layer. Bake until light golden brown, 15 to 20 minutes.

3. For the filling: While crust is cooling, whisk eggs, yolks, sugar, and salt together in saucepan. Add zest and juice and cook over medium-low heat, stirring constantly, until thickened and pudding-like, 8 to 10 minutes. Press through fine-mesh strainer into medium bowl. Stir in butter and cream.

4. Pour filling over crust and tilt to spread evenly. Bake until filling is set, about 15 minutes. Cool to room temperature, at least 1 hour, then, using foil overhang, lift bars from pan and cut into 9 squares. Dust with confectioners' sugar just before serving. (Squares will keep in airtight container in refrigerator for 3 days. Redust with confectioners' sugar before serving.)

How to Make LEMON SQUARES

1. Sprinkle the crust crumbs into the pan and press down gently with a measuring cup to form an even layer. **2.** The lemon curd is done when dragging a finger through the curd on the back of a spoon leaves an empty trail behind. **3.** Press the curd through a fine-mesh strainer to remove the lemon zest. **4.** After pouring the hot curd into the pan, tilt to ensure an even layer.

Devil's Food Cupcakes

Devil's food is my favorite chocolate cake, but when I use my recipe for cupcakes they end up crumbling in my hand and all over my shirt. Can you help? –Dawn Mitchell, Baltimore, Md.

Our Devil's Food Cupcakes work equally well with white or dark chocolate frosting.

When properly prepared, devil's food cake has an intense chocolate flavor and a delicate, almost velvety crumb. While that works well in a layer cake bound by frosting on all sides and eaten on a plate with a fork, it's a messy experience when translated to a cupcake. I know because the test kitchen baked several cake recipes into little cupcakes. What a mess. Chocolate crumbs covered our faces, clothes, and even the floor.

Before tackling the crumbly problem, I wanted to choose a color. Some bakers believe devil's food cake should be jet black—a color produced by Dutch-processed cocoa. Others say this cake should have a reddish tint, which is supplied by natural cocoa, such as the widely available Hershey's. I think devil's food should be reddish. Because natural cocoa isn't quite as flavorful as Dutch-processed, my chocolate selection would be very important. Bittersweet was good but a bit "too adult" for some tasters. (I also worried that kids—the target audience for any cupcake—would find the flavor too intense.) Milk chocolate was too timid and unsweetened chocolate too sour. Semisweet was the best choice.

To enhance the chocolate flavor further, I used boiling water, often added to devil's food cake recipes to melt the chocolate and dissolve the cocoa. The reason this "blooming" method works is simple: The boiling water melts the cocoa butter (the fat) that surrounds the potent cocoa solids and helps to release flavor. I also added a little espresso powder to the mix to boost the chocolate's intensity.

Brown sugar is a key ingredient in devil's food cake, helping to ensure moistness. Unfortunately, it also contributes to the crumbly problem. Using a mix of half granulated and half brown sugar yielded a moist cupcake that was less crumbly. Sour cream (not milk or buttermilk) gives devil's food a fine, delicate texture—sometimes too delicate, so I cut back a bit on this ingredient. One last change finally solved the case of the crumbly cupcake. Eggs give baked goods structure. An extra egg made my cupcakes sturdy enough to eat without the usual lapful of crumbs.

All that was left to do was to top these little devils. A frosting with an emphasis on chocolate (rather than butter) was tasters' favorite; also liked was a white chocolate frosting and a fluffy whipped version.

So now you can have your cupcake and eat it, too, without worrying that it will fall apart on the way to your mouth.

–Katie Henderson

DEVIL'S FOOD CUPCAKES

MAKES 24

If you don't have bar or block chocolate on hand, use semisweet chips in the cake and frosting. See page 29 for information on natural cocoa. If you like, you can cut this recipe in half to prepare 12 cupcakes.

- **2/3 cup boiling water**
- **2/3 cup natural cocoa powder**
- **4 ounces semisweet chocolate, chopped**
- **2 tablespoons instant espresso powder or instant coffee**
- **4 large eggs**
- **2/3 cup sour cream**
- **2 teaspoons vanilla extract**
- **1 1/2 cups all-purpose flour**
- **1 teaspoon baking soda**
- **1/2 teaspoon salt**
- **3/4 cup granulated sugar**
- **3/4 cup packed light brown sugar**
- **16 tablespoons (2 sticks) unsalted butter, softened but still cool**

1. Adjust rack to lower-middle position and heat oven to 350 degrees. Line 2 standard muffin tins with cupcake liners.

2. Whisk boiling water, cocoa, chocolate, and espresso powder together in small bowl. Whisk eggs, sour cream, and vanilla together in medium bowl until well combined.

3. With electric mixer on low speed, combine flour, baking soda, salt, granulated sugar, and brown sugar in large bowl until blended. Add butter and mix on low until incorporated, about 1 minute. Add egg mixture in 2 additions, then beat at medium speed, scraping down

DECORATING IDEAS

What's a cupcake without decorations? Here are some easy ways to dress up our Devil's Food Cupcakes.

SWEET ROSE

Laura DeNeui of Los Angeles, Calif., arranges Hershey's Milk Chocolate Swoops, cut in halves and in quarters, in a circular pattern to mimic rose petals.

BAKED ALASKA

Hollow out the top of each cupcake. Fill with strawberry ice cream and freeze. When ready to serve, top the cupcakes with meringue and broil.

ROCKY ROAD

Press mini marshmallows into the frosting, then paint the top with melted chocolate. Sprinkle with coarsely chopped dry-roasted peanuts.

CHOCOLATE-DIPPED STRAWBERRY

Add 1 tablespoon strawberry liqueur to the frosting and top with a chocolate-dipped strawberry.

HUGS AND KISSES

Fill cupcake liners partway with batter, add dark Hershey's Kiss, add more batter, and bake. Top with White Chocolate Hug and Mini Kisses.

LOCO COCO

Shingle frosting with toasted shaved coconut to make each cupcake look like a tropical hut.

sides of bowl as needed, until combined, about 1 minute.

4. Add chocolate mixture and beat at medium speed until incorporated, about 1 minute. Divide batter evenly among 24 cupcake liners. Bake until skewer or toothpick inserted in cupcake comes out with a few moist crumbs attached, about 20 minutes. Cool cupcakes in muffin tins for 10 minutes before removing and cooling completely on wire rack. Frost, using one of following recipes.

DARK CHOCOLATE FROSTING

MAKES ABOUT 3 CUPS, ENOUGH TO FROST 24 CUPCAKES

Semisweet chips also work well in this recipe.

- **12 ounces semisweet chocolate, chopped**
- **1 tablespoon corn syrup**
- **Pinch salt**
- **1/2 cup heavy cream**
- **1/2 cup confectioners' sugar**
- **8 tablespoons (1 stick) cold unsalted butter, cut into 1/2-inch pieces**

1. Place chocolate, corn syrup, and salt in food processor. Bring cream to boil in small saucepan. With machine running, add hot cream in steady stream and blend until chocolate melts, about 1 minute. Stop food processor, add confectioners' sugar, and process until sugar is incorporated, about 30 seconds. With machine still running, add butter, one piece at a time, and process until completely smooth, about 1 minute.

2. Transfer frosting to medium bowl and refrigerate, stirring frequently, until cooled and very thick, at least 30 minutes. (A spoon should be able to stand up in frosting.)

WHITE CHOCOLATE FROSTING

MAKES ABOUT 3 CUPS, ENOUGH TO FROST 24 CUPCAKES

White chocolate chips also work well in this recipe.

- **12 ounces white chocolate, chopped**
- **1 tablespoon corn syrup**
- **1 teaspoon vanilla extract**
- **Pinch salt**
- **1/2 cup heavy cream**
- **1/4 cup confectioners' sugar**
- **4 tablespoons cold unsalted butter, cut into 1/2-inch pieces**

1. Place chocolate, corn syrup, vanilla, and salt in food processor. Bring cream to boil in small saucepan. With machine running, add hot cream in steady stream and blend until chocolate melts, about 1 minute. Stop food processor, add confectioners' sugar, and process until sugar is incorporated, about 30 seconds. With machine still running, add butter, one piece at a time, and process until completely smooth, about 1 minute.

2. Transfer frosting to medium bowl and refrigerate, stirring frequently, until cooled and very thick, at least 30 minutes. (A spoon should be able to stand up in frosting.)

WHIPPED FROSTING

Both of the frosting recipes above produce a silky, creamy frosting. If you want a fluffier consistency, beat the cooled frosting with an electric mixer at medium speed for about 2 minutes. We especially like the white version when whipped.

Make Ahead

Unfrosted cupcakes can be stored in an airtight container at room temperature for up to 3 days. (They also can be individually wrapped in plastic and frozen in a zipper-lock bag for up to 1 month.) The frostings can be refrigerated for up to 5 days; see page 29 for tips on softening them to the correct consistency. Once frosted, the cupcakes are best eaten within a day, but leftovers will keep in the refrigerator for several days.

Food Gifts: Valentine's Candies

Three easy recipes are a sweet way to say you care.

Yes, you can buy expensive candy for your sweetheart, but why not make your own? These three recipes are very simple—no melting of sugar and no candy thermometer needed. Just start with good-quality chocolate and add some creative embellishments for homemade candy that looks and tastes like it came in a fancy box. **–Lauren Chattman**

Surprise someone you love with no-fuss homemade candies. From left to right: Milk Chocolate Truffle Hearts, Chocolate Caramel Chews, and White Chocolate Nonpareils.

MILK CHOCOLATE TRUFFLE HEARTS

MAKES ABOUT 35

You will need a small heart-shaped cookie cutter (measuring 1 to 1 1/2 inches across) for this recipe. Look for one in cookware shops or order it by mail (see page 28). Roll leftover teaspoonfuls of firm chocolate mixture into balls and coat in extra cocoa powder or chopped nuts for quick truffles.

- **8 ounces milk chocolate, chopped fine**
- **4 ounces bittersweet chocolate, chopped fine**
- **2 tablespoons unsalted butter**
- **3/4 cup heavy cream**
- **2 tablespoons cocoa powder**

1. Line 9-inch-square baking pan with aluminum foil so that foil covers bottom and sides of pan and overhangs edges by at least 1 inch.

2. Place chocolates and butter in large heatproof bowl. Bring cream just to boil in small saucepan. Whisk hot cream into chocolate and butter until smooth. Scrape mixture into prepared pan, smooth into even layer, and refrigerate until set, about 1 hour.

3. Cover plate with foil or parchment paper. Using foil overhang as handles, lift chocolate mixture out of pan and transfer to cutting board. Using 1- to 1 1/2-inch heart-shaped cookie cutter, cut and lift out 30 to 35 hearts and place on prepared plate. Sift cocoa powder over hearts. Transfer to airtight container, placing candies between sheets of parchment paper, and refrigerate for up to 1 week.

CHOCOLATE CARAMEL CHEWS

MAKES 24 CANDIES

Let the chilled candies soften at room temperature for at least 15 minutes before serving.

- **1/2 cup pecans, walnuts, or almonds, chopped fine**
- **24 soft caramel candies, unwrapped**
- **4 ounces semisweet or bittersweet chocolate, melted**

1. Cover large plate with parchment paper. Place nuts in shallow bowl.

2. Drop caramel into bowl with melted chocolate and, using fork, turn until covered completely with chocolate. Using fork, transfer caramel to parchment-lined plate and sprinkle nuts on top. Repeat with remaining caramels. Refrigerate candies until firm, about 15 minutes. Transfer to airtight container and refrigerate for up to 3 days.

WHITE CHOCOLATE NONPAREILS

MAKES ABOUT 50

Pink and red nonpareils are sold in many supermarkets during the Valentine's season. For mail-order information, see page 28.

- **1/2 pound white chocolate, melted and cooled slightly**
- **2 tablespoons pink and/or red nonpareils**

1. Line baking sheet with parchment paper. Scrape melted chocolate into 1-quart zipper-lock plastic bag, press out air, and seal tightly. Cut small hole in one corner of bag. Pipe quarter-sized circles of chocolate onto lined baking sheet.

2. Sprinkle chocolate circles heavily with nonpareils. Let stand until hardened, about 30 minutes. Transfer to airtight container and store at room temperature for up to 1 week.

Notes from Our Test Kitchen

TIPS, TECHNIQUES, AND TOOLS FOR BETTER COOKING

< Making Meringue THE "CRUNCH" IN OUR STRAWBERRY CAKE

A crisp layer of baked meringue is the secret ingredient in our **Strawberry Crunch Cake** (see inside back cover). Although a baked meringue might sound fancy, it's made with just three ingredients—egg whites, cream of tartar (to help stabilize the egg foam), and sugar—and requires only 5 minutes of hands-on work. For our cake recipe, beat 2 large egg whites and 1/4 teaspoon cream of tartar with an electric mixer set to medium-high speed until frothy. Add 1/2 cup sugar, a tablespoon at a time, continuing to beat until the whites hold stiff peaks, 1 to 2 minutes. At left, Cali demonstrates how to spread the meringue into a round. Once baked and cooled (instructions are provided below), the meringue can be stored in an airtight container for up to one day before the cake is assembled.

1. Draw an 8-inch circle on a piece of parchment (tracing around the circumference of an 8-inch cake pan makes this easier), then flip the parchment over onto a rimmed baking sheet so that the tracing faces down.
2. Using a rubber spatula, spread the meringue out to the edges of the traced circle and smooth out the top. Bake the meringue on the middle rack of a 250-degree oven until completely dry, about 50 minutes. Then turn off the oven and let the meringue cool completely in the oven, about 2 hours.

Bean Basics

Canned beans are convenient, but in many recipes (particularly those with long cooking times) we prefer to use dried beans. Here's how we ensure perfectly cooked beans every time.

• **Soaking Controversy:** Presoaking beans can knock 30 minutes or so off of their cooking time, but, despite what many cookbooks say, it is not a necessary step. What is necessary, however, is picking through the beans before cooking to check for loose stones. Just one small stone is enough to spoil an otherwise perfectly good bowl of **Red Beans and Rice** (page 22). To spot and remove stones before cooking, spread the beans on a white plate or a cutting board.

• **Water, Water Everywhere:** For evenly cooked beans, use 5 quarts of water per pound of dried beans. This gives the beans plenty of room and ensures that the water will not boil off as they cook.

• **Salting Myth:** Many recipes say not to salt beans until the last minute, but, in our opinion, that's too little too late and a surefire recipe for bland beans. Go ahead and add 2½ teaspoons of salt (less if there are other salty ingredients, like chicken broth, in the pot) to the water along with the beans. As the beans cook they absorb the salted water and become more flavorful.

• **Simmering Down:** Once you've brought the beans and water up to a boil, reduce the heat and cook the beans at a gentle simmer. A rolling boil will cook the beans unevenly and cause them to split open.

• **Easy Does It:** When it's time to take the beans out of the pot, we usually scoop out a few just to make sure they are all evenly cooked. If most of the beans are perfectly cooked but a few are lagging behind, don't turn up the heat. Instead, cover the pot and set it aside for a few minutes to let gentle residual heat soften the remaining beans without overcooking the others.

–Jeremy Sauer

Butcher Shop: Which Brisket Is Best?

Because whole beef briskets can weigh well over 10 pounds, they are typically butchered and sold as two separate cuts—"point" and "flat." The flat cut, the most common in grocery stores, is leaner and thinner, with a rectangular shape and an exterior fat cap. The point cut has an irregular shape and contains large interior fat pockets. Many pitmasters prefer the point cut, believing that its higher fat content keeps the brisket moist over long periods of cooking. For our **Oven-Barbecued Beef Brisket** (page 21), we prefer the flat cut, finding that its external fat cap helps to keep the meat plenty moist. Whichever cut you choose, be sure to purchase a brisket of roughly 4 to 5 pounds that still has a good amount of fat attached. It's better to trim the fat yourself (we like to leave about 1/4 inch of fat) than to have the butcher rob your brisket of its moisture. Some butchers cut brisket into small 2- to 3-pound roasts. If this is all that you can find, you can substitute two of the smaller cuts; the cooking time may vary slightly. **–Jeremy Sauer**

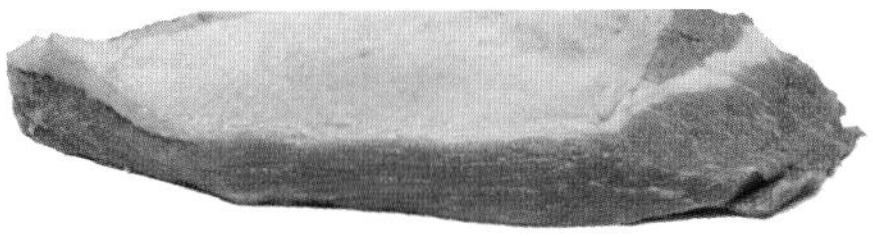

FLAT CUT
The fat cap on this cut keeps the heat plenty moist.

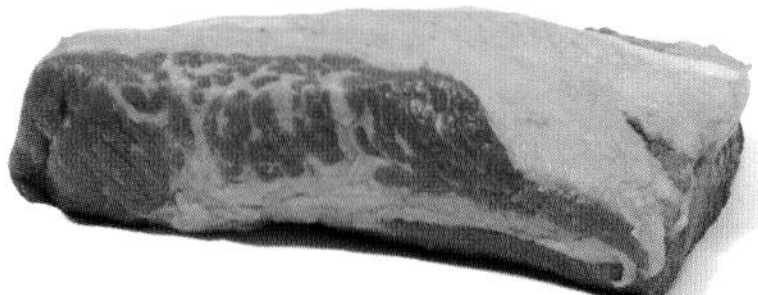

POINT CUT
Although this cut is very moist, most supermarkets don't carry it.

Hearts and Sprinkles

Ready to make **White Chocolate Nonpareils** (page 27) but you're fresh out of red and pink nonpareils? If you're having trouble locating these colored candies in the baking aisle at your local supermarket, head for your local craft store. Many of these stores have a candy-making supply section and carry sprinkles, jimmies, and nonpareils of all shapes, sizes, and colors. If you can't get to a craft store, go online to the Wilton Store (www.wilton.com) and purchase a set of Nonpareils 6-Mix Sprinkle Assortment (item #710-4125) for $4.99. The set contains pink, orange, green, red, yellow, and purple nonpareils.

Wilton is also a sure bet for finding heart-shaped cookie cutters in just about any size, including a 1½-inch cutter, which can be used to make our **Milk Chocolate Truffle Hearts** (page 27). This small cutter comes in a set of six called the Hearts Nesting Cutter Set (item #2304-115) for $2.99.

–Bridget Lancaster

Pork Tenderloin

Pork tenderloins are almost always sold in pairs in vacuum-sealed packages. After buying dozens of packages for our **Spicy Glazed Pork Tenderloins** (page 13), we found that the average tenderloin weighs 12 to 16 ounces. However, we did find some packages with larger tenderloins (up to 1½ pounds) or with two tenderloins of dramatically different sizes. Larger loins are fine for grilling but hard to fit in a skillet. When shopping, pay attention to the total weight of the two tenderloins (which should be 1½ to 2 pounds) and squeeze the package to see if the tenderloins feel similar in size.

–Eva Katz

Shopping with the Test Kitchen
Cocoa Powder

Two types of cocoa powder are available in supermarkets: regular (or natural) cocoa and Dutch-processed cocoa. To make all cocoa powder, manufacturers remove most of the fat from unsweetened chocolate and then pulverize the chocolate. When Dutch-processed cocoa powder is made, the chocolate is treated with an alkaline solution to make it less bitter. Dutch-processed cocoa powder is darker than natural cocoa and produces baked goods that are very brown, almost black. In contrast, natural cocoa is redder and more astringent.

When making hot cocoa, we prefer the less bitter flavor of Dutch-processed cocoa. In baking, however, the sugar, butter, and other ingredients temper some of the bitterness in natural cocoa, and its strong flavor translates as intensity.

THE NATURAL

Familiar Hershey's is the most commonly available brand of natural cocoa and is the cocoa we use in the test kitchen. Hershey's also makes Dutch-processed cocoa powder, as do most European chocolate companies. It's important to shop carefully, as natural and Dutch-processed cocoa can react differently in recipes with baking soda and baking powder and don't always produce similar results. If you have any doubts, read the ingredient list, which will indicate if the cocoa has been "Dutch-processed" or "treated with alkali."

Bring Home the Biscuits

Our **Quick Chicken Pot Pie** (page 12) calls for store-bought refrigerator biscuits, but we found that not all brands are created equal. Pillsbury has cornered the market on refrigerator biscuits, but they sell several dozen varieties with a confusing array of names. We tasted seven Pillsbury biscuits. While put off by the artificial flavors and gummy textures in several samples, we found three good choices. Golden Homestyle Buttermilk Biscuits and Golden Layers Flaky Biscuits were our top favorites. Reduced Fat Buttermilk Grands! Biscuits also received good scores and are a decent backup if your supermarket doesn't stock either of the "golden" varieties. **–Eva Katz**

BISCUITS RISE TO THE TOP
Pillsbury Golden Homestyle Buttermilk Biscuits (above) were a test kitchen favorite in a taste test.

Kitchen Tips Chocolate Frosting

FROSTING IN THE FRIDGE

The super-chocolaty frostings that top our **Devil's Food Cupcakes** (page 26) can be prepared days in advance and refrigerated until the day you make the cupcakes. But chilled frosting will be too stiff to spread over these tender cupcakes. To soften cold frosting, transfer it to a microwave-safe bowl and microwave on the lowest setting for 20 seconds. Stir to check the consistency. If it is still too stiff to spread, continue to microwave on the lowest setting for 10-second intervals. **–Katie Henderson**

LEFTOVER FROSTING

During development of our cupcakes, the test kitchen's refrigerators were filled with leftover bowls of frosting. One thrifty test cook decided to roll balls of chilled frosting into quick truffles. Rolled again in either cocoa powder or finely chopped nuts, these candies were pretty enough to take to a party. **–K.H.**

Making Sense of Mozzarella

Most supermarkets offer a variety of mozzarella choices that can be divided into two basic categories: high moisture (or fresh) and low moisture. Fresh mozzarella comes in many sizes and is usually packed in brine. Its soft texture and milky flavor are best appreciated within a day or two of purchase, as it can quickly sour. Low-moisture mozzarella typically comes shrink-wrapped in a large block or preshredded in a resealable bag. This cheese, which was essentially developed for the U.S. pizza industry (hence its alias, "pizza cheese"), is less perishable and melts into beautifully gooey strands.

Because fresh mozzarella is more expensive, we tend to save it for eating raw—usually with tomatoes, basil, and good olive oil—and use the low-moisture cheese for our **Cheesy Basil-Stuffed Chicken Breasts** (page 15) as well as lasagna, pizza, and (a test kitchen favorite) fried mozzarella sticks.

–Jeremy Sauer

Straight-Sided Squares

To produce **Lemon Squares** (page 25) with neat and trim edges, we like to use a straight-sided, 8-inch-square pan; rounded pans yield rounded edges that must be trimmed from the bars. In the test kitchen, we rely on the Calphalon Commercial Bakeware 8-Inch Square Cake Pan, available at Amazon.com for $17.99. **–Keri Fisher**

Easy Mexican Cheese

The refrigerator section of our local supermarket practically overflows with varieties of preshredded cheese, but the flavorful combination known as Mexican cheese blend (a mix of three or four cheeses, often Monterey Jack, cheddar, queso quesadilla, and asadero) recently caught our attention. It's perfect in many Mexican dishes, including our **Freezer Chicken Enchiladas** (page 19). Don't confuse this blend with taco cheese blend, which includes both cheese (often cheddar, Colby, and Monterey Jack) and spices (usually chili powder, garlic powder, and cumin). We found these added seasonings to be redundant in most recipes.

–Stephanie Alleyne

Mexican cheese blend is both tasty and convenient.

Kitchen Know-How The Final Cut

To ensure even cooking, our Sugar-Glazed Roasted Carrots recipe (page 11) calls for cutting each carrot into 2 inch by 1/2-inch pieces—not necessarily an easy task given that carrots vary in thickness from end to end. Here's how to produce pieces that are evenly sized.

1. Cut a peeled carrot into thirds, with each piece measuring roughly 2 inches long.

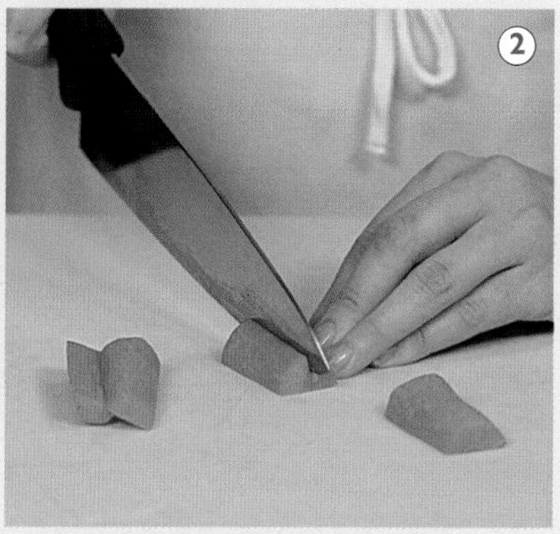

2. Cut each piece in half or quarters lengthwise to yield pieces that are 1/2 inch thick.

Food Shopping

SANDWICH BREAD: Which Slice Is Best?

With all the hype about artisanal bread, the sliced stuff in the plastic bags doesn't get much attention these days, but it should. In my house, we still go through a loaf or two of sandwich bread every week. So why not buy the best? We gathered eight leading brands of white sandwich bread, in country styles with larger slices whenever possible, and held a blind tasting.

For our first test, tasters sampled the bread plain. Because some of the breads are not available in large slices, I cut the samples into pieces so tasters would focus on taste and texture, not size. Tasters weren't fooled. They gave top marks to the hearty texture of Arnold Country Classics and Pepperidge Farm Farmhouse. These brands also have larger-than-usual slices—1½ ounces each versus 1 ounce for the competition.

Tasters detected big flavor differences, too. Top-rated Arnold and Pepperidge Farm were deemed the "sweetest" breads in the lineup. There were many complaints about "sour" and "off" notes in the lower-rated brands. It turns out that some of these brands contain vinegar (often added to increase shelf life). Lower-rated breads also contain almost twice as many ingredients as our top-rated breads, with many more additives and preservatives, which may also explain the unpleasant aftertaste.

I then asked tasters to try the breads in grilled cheese sandwiches. Though volunteers for this tasting were plentiful, clear winners were not—all the breads were pretty good. In short, once you slather your bread with butter and load it up with cheese, it gets very hard to tell one brand from another.

For our final test, I prepared simple croutons seasoned only with olive oil and salt. Again, Arnold and Pepperidge Farm swept the tasting. They were consistently ranked as crunchier than the other brands.

Based on our tests, we recommend Arnold Country Classics and Pepperidge Farm Farmhouse. Their hearty texture and slightly sweet (not sour) flavor put them a cut above the competition. The breads are listed in order of preference. **–Keri Fisher**

Top Picks

1

2

1. **ARNOLD Country Classics White**
$3.19 for 24 ounces
"This is what I expect from sandwich bread," wrote one taster of our top-rated brand. Others agreed, praising its "perfect structure" and "subtle sweetness."

2. **PEPPERIDGE FARM Farmhouse Hearty White**
$2.50 for 24 ounces
Tasters deemed this top-rated bread "well balanced," "likeable," and "flavorful (for white bread!)," with a "familiar" taste that was "not overly sweet—just enough."

Don't Bother

3. **WONDER Country White** **$2.69 for 24 ounces**
This upscale version of the bread many of us grew up with was panned as "rather dry and cardboard-like," with a "blah" flavor and "slightly sour aftertaste."

4. **SUNBEAM Giant White** **$2.39 for 22 ounces**
Described as "classic packaged American white bread," this "squishy" bread had a "strong sour flavor" and a "texture like cotton candy" that turned off tasters.

5. **FREIHOFER'S Country White** **$2.69 for 24 ounces**
There were few fans of this bread, which was described as "tasteless," "too soft," and "borderline gummy."

6. **J. J. NISSEN ButterTop White** **$2.39 for 20 ounces**
"Who calls this fluff 'bread'?" asked one taster of this "really soft and spongy" bread with "nonexistent" flavor. More "like eating air" than bread, said another.

7. **HOME PRIDE Butter Top White** **$2.39 for 20 ounces**
Tasters found this "plasterboard sample" to be so "coarse and dry" that it would be "great for exfoliating your feet"; otherwise, a "waste of flour."

8. **COUNTRY KITCHEN Giant White** **$2.49 for 22 ounces**
This "gutless" bread was deemed "ridiculously soft and bland," with a "plasticky" flavor that "tastes like additives."

3

4

5

6

7

8

Taste Test Bread Crumbs

When a recipe calls for bread crumbs, you have more choices than you might think. Besides supermarket bread crumbs (both plain and Italian-seasoned), there is the option of homemade bread crumbs, made from grinding bread in the food processor. And should you use those fresh crumbs as is or toast them first in the oven? Finally, many chefs rave about panko, large, flaky Japanese-style crumbs, now available in many supermarkets as well as gourmet stores.

Bread crumbs have three basic uses in the kitchen: coating, binding, and topping. To find out which crumb was best suited to each culinary task, we prepared batches of breaded chicken cutlets, meat loaf, and buttery crumb-topped macaroni and cheese, using each type of bread crumb and holding a blind tasting to see what tasters preferred.

Tasters overwhelmingly preferred the fresh toasted bread crumbs in every application, praising their crisp texture and toasty flavor. Supermarket crumbs were similarly panned in every application for their gritty, sandy texture. Fresh (untoasted) crumbs and panko were suitable for some tasks but not others. Crumbs are listed below in order of preference, with tasters' comments. **–K.F.**

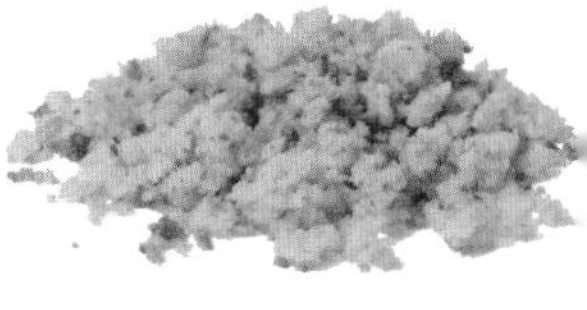

Fresh Toasted
Our favorite crumb gave macaroni and cheese a "nice and crunchy" topping and yielded breaded chicken cutlets with "great crunch" and "nice flavor."

Fresh (Untoasted)
These crumbs were too soft for coating chicken cutlets but were good as a binder in meat loaf. Once buttered and broiled on top of macaroni and cheese, fresh crumbs were praised for being "very crunchy," with "good flavor."

Panko
These large, flaky crumbs are perfect when you want big crunch. Tasters touted their "crispy" texture on chicken cutlets but dismissed the meatloaf as "pasty" and "gummy."

Plain Packaged
Consistently described as "stale" and "sandy," these store-bought crumbs provided a passable crust on chicken cutlets, but tasters rejected their "gritty" texture in meat loaf and on macaroni and cheese.

Italian Packaged
As bad as the plain crumbs were, the crumbs with Italian seasonings were even worse. The "artificial," "bad oregano flavor" was overwhelming.

Equipment Roundup

NONSTICK SKILLETS: Can You Get a Good 12-Inch Pan for $50 or Less?

You can spend upward of $150 on a large nonstick skillet. But for that kind of money, we want a pan that will last a lifetime. The trouble is that nonstick coatings peel and chip. We think it makes more sense to buy a reasonably priced pan (under $50) so it won't be so hard to part ways when the time comes. To find the best option, we gathered nine 12-inch nonstick skillets ranging in price from $8.99 to $49.99 and prepared omelets, cooked onions, and seared salmon, all the while judging the usability of each pan. The pans are listed in order of preference at right. Here are some key findings from our tests.

GETTING A HANDLE ON IT: Though all the pans sported a similar dark nonstick interior and all food released easily, other design features varied greatly. Exterior materials ranged from stainless steel and copper to enamel and anodized aluminum, though this didn't prove to be a factor in performance. Handle styles, on the other hand, could make or break the pan. We had two criteria: comfort and stability. In terms of comfort, we looked for handles that fit well in the hand and didn't get too hot during cooking. As for stability, we found welded or riveted handles to be sturdier than those that were simply screwed on (a flaw in the Innova and T-fal pans).

BOTTOMS UP: Sure, they're all 12-inch skillets (manufacturers measure pans across the top), but the cooking surface is considerably smaller. The diameter of the bottom of our top-rated skillet, the Cuisinart, was more than 2 inches larger than that of the low-rated Innova pan. That extra space means less crowding in the pan and more even cooking.

IF YOU CAN'T STAND THE HEAT: All of the pans produced good omelets, although several struggled with the salmon test, which was conducted over higher heat. The best pans turned out fish with beautiful brown crusts; the worst pans produced blackened or unevenly cooked salmon.

LOW AND SLOW: The ability to maintain even heat during prolonged cooking is a must. To measure this trait, we cooked diced onions in each pan for 10 minutes over medium heat. Our goal: soft, evenly cooked, golden brown onions with no signs of charring. More often than not, we got dark brown onions, indicating a faster cooking speed, or, even worse, onions that were browned on the edges yet still crunchy in the middle.

SUMMING UP: The $9 Wearever (available at hardware stores and Amazon.com) was a far better option than some pans that cost up to five times as much. Because testers put a premium on cooking space, however, the heavy-duty Cuisinart pan (also available at Amazon.com) earned the top slot—but only by a hair.

–Keri Fisher

Recommended

CUISINART Chef's Classic Nonstick Hard Anodized Omelet Pan

Price: $41.95
Bottom Diameter: 10 1/2"
Weight: 3 lb 6.8 oz

Comments: With the largest cooking area of all the skillets, this pan impressed us with its sturdiness and heft. Salmon was beautifully and evenly browned, though onions cooked at a moderately fast pace.

WEAREVER Collections Premium Nonstick Aluminum Skillet

Price: $8.99
Bottom Diameter: 10"
Weight: 2 lb 14.9 oz

Comments: Though not as heavy as some of the other top finishers, this pan was sturdy, comfortable, and well designed, with a sleek look reminiscent of more expensive skillets. The spacious pan held heat well, giving salmon a beautiful golden brown crust. The onions did cook a bit fast, though.

FARBERWARE Millennium Soft Touch Stainless Steel Omelet Pan

Price: $39.95
Bottom Diameter: 9 1/2"
Weight: 3 lb 13.3 oz

Comments: Its rubber-coated handle was comfortable and stayed cool through most tests, though the bare metal closest to the pan got hot toward the end of the salmon test. Onions were beautifully cooked, though salmon was somewhat unevenly browned.

KITCHENAID Gourmet Essentials Nonstick French Skillet

Price: $39.95
Bottom Diameter: 9"
Weight: 3 lb 9.6 oz

Comments: Heavy and sturdy, with solid riveted handles, this skillet impressed us with excellent crust formation on the salmon, though the onions were unevenly cooked. The rubber-coated handle is comfortable, and the grip opposite the main handle is a nice touch.

SIMPLY CALPHALON Stainless Omelet Pan with Nonstick Interior

Price: $49.99
Bottom Diameter: 8 3/4"
Weight: 3 lb 11.8 oz

Comments: Though a bit oddly shaped, the contoured metal handle stayed cool through all of our cooking tests. Onions cooked unevenly, though salmon developed a nice brown crust. We wish this smallish pan was a little bit bigger.

Recommended with Reservations

REVERE Copper Ellipse Nonstick Skillet

Price: $49.49
Bottom Diameter: 9 3/4"
Weight: 3 lb 13.4 oz

Comments: This pan aced every cooking test, but the hollow metal handle got very hot during cooking. Some complained about the weight of this heavy pan, too. If you're strong and don't mind having to use a potholder, this is the pan to get.

Not Recommended

CIRCULON 2 Nonstick French Skillet

Price: $49.99
Bottom Diameter: 9 1/4"
Weight: 2 lb 14.5 oz

Comments: It wasn't the strange circular ridges inside of the pan (hence the name) that turned us off, it was the burnt onions and charred salmon. This lightweight pan simply couldn't compare with other pans that cost much less.

INNOVA Kitchen Basics Stainless Steel Frypan with Nonstick Interior

Price: $39.99
Bottom Diameter: 8 1/4"
Weight: 2 lb 2.2 oz

Comments: Omelets were unevenly browned and onions and salmon charred to an even black. The flimsy design, including a screwed-on plastic handle that got uncomfortably warm during cooking, inspired little confidence.

T-FAL Initiatives 12.5" Nonstick Sauté Pan

Price: $17.99
Bottom Diameter: 10 1/4"
Weight: 1 lb 15 oz

Comments: The lightest pan in the group, the T-fal produced slightly charred onions and burned one side of the salmon. The screwed-on handle only accentuated the flimsiness of the pan, and we found the "Thermo-Spot" heat indicator, which changes color when the pan is hot, to be utterly useless.

Gadgets & Gear Universal Handle Cover

Because several skillets were downgraded for scorching-hot handles, we decided to test the HotHandle Silicone Cookware Handle Holder ($6.99), which promises to keep your hands cool no matter how hot a handle gets. While this gadget fit just about every pot and pan in the test kitchen, it didn't fit any of them well. For instance, the narrow handle of the Simply Calphalon omelet pan got lost in the roomy silicone cover, making it very hard to get a good grip to lift the pan. We'll stick with potholders for our hot handles. **–K.F.**

When Things Go Wrong in the Kitchen

READERS SHARE FUNNY STORIES ABOUT COOKING MISHAPS

A STINGING SALAD

I had prepared a special dinner to celebrate two occasions: a dear friend's first visit to our new Texas home and the completion of the major job of remodeling our kitchen. The meal turned out so perfectly that I was already secretly congratulating myself as I served the last course, a gorgeous summer salad. My husband ceremoniously poured the dressing as I began to toss the salad. Then I screamed and all eyes gazed widely at the spectacle in the bowl. There, on top, glistening with oil and vinegar, was a full-grown scorpion! Needless to say, the salad was discarded, but over the years, the scorpion story has been served up many, many times.

Vickie Lynn Buttery Christoval, Texas

ST. PATRICK'S DAY SURPRISE

When I was 11 or 12 years old, I decided to make a cake to celebrate St. Patrick's Day. I reckoned it would be a nice surprise for my parents, who had gone out shopping, leaving me in the care of my grandparents. Grandpa was down in the basement playing our old piano, and Grandma was resting upstairs. As the cake cooled, I worked on the chocolate frosting. I added a few drops of green food coloring, but it wasn't turning green. A few more drops, still brown. Perplexed, I poured the whole bottle into the frosting and frosted the cake. Having smelled the cake, my grandfather came upstairs and cut himself a piece. As he was eating, my parents came home. They were so pleased that I had made such a nice cake, until Grandpa lifted his head to speak and we saw that his false teeth had turned green!

Aviva Rothschild Aurora, Colo.

SURPRISING PIE

I wanted to impress my boyfriend, Dave, with a fabulous meal, and I knew that he liked strawberry-rhubarb pie. I had never tasted rhubarb, let alone cooked with it, so I called my sister, who said it was "red and green, like celery." After much toiling, the pie looked great. As Dave ate my pie he smiled, and he even said it tasted good. I was thrilled! The next day my sister came over to see how the big dinner had gone, so I offered her a piece of the pie. After one bite she cringed. She opened my refrigerator, grabbed the stalk of "rhubarb," and proclaimed, "Jackie, this is Swiss chard, not rhubarb!" I was mortified. My boyfriend later confessed that the pie was terrible, but he didn't want to hurt my feelings. He and I have been married for more than 10 years now, and every time I make strawberry-rhubarb pie, he double-checks the ingredients!

Jacquelyn Buige Raco Royersford, Pa.

A CAKE THAT SMELLED LIKE BODY LOTION

I decided to try out a low-fat zucchini-chocolate Bundt cake for a friend who had lost 100 pounds. I gathered all the ingredients, handed my boyfriend the zucchinis, a grater, and a plate, and sent him to the family room while I worked on the batter in the kitchen. It wasn't long before I started hearing comments from the family room like, "Wow, I didn't know there would be so much water" and "This zucchini smells like your body lotion!" My boyfriend was utterly unfamiliar with baking, so I rolled my eyes and pressed on. He came back to the kitchen with a plate full of very, very wet shredded zucchini. There was so much moisture that I cut down on the amount of oil.

To my surprise, the baked cake looked absolutely picture perfect. But after my first bite, I knew something was wrong. I thought, "The cake does smell like body lotion, my cucumber lotion!" Later, I confessed my major blunder to my boyfriend: I had used cucumbers instead of zucchini. Not only did he laugh it off, but he insisted on finishing the cake over the next few days! What else could I do but marry him?

Olivia Darzell-Karp Citrus Heights, Calif.

IS IT SPICY YET?

I had just moved to Dallas and decided to make chili for the first time. I found a recipe that called for 6 tablespoons of chili powder, but I ran out after just 2 tablespoons. Fortunately, someone had given me a welcome gift that included Tabasco sauce, something I had never tasted before. I proceeded to add 4 tablespoons of Tabasco sauce—and then 2 extra tablespoons, since I was sure that chili powder was hotter than Tabasco.

When my guests arrived, they insisted that I come out of the kitchen to chat while my friend David prepared the drinks. They were all Dallas natives and assumed I wouldn't have any idea how to cook chili—I was from up North. They conspired to have David add a can of jalapeños to the chili without my knowing. When I tasted the chili, my eyes started tearing and I ran to the bathroom to take out my contact lenses. When I came back, I offered to cook hot dogs for everyone, but, to my surprise, my friends absolutely loved the chili. Several people were already having seconds. I was the only one who ended up eating a hot dog!

Diane Bick Mountain View, Calif.

AN ILL-TEMPERED PAN

Several years ago, I was making roast beef and Yorkshire pudding. As always, I had the batter cooling in the refrigerator and the hot suet melting in my old Pyrex glass pan on the stovetop. I added the cold batter to the hot fat and the thing exploded like a grenade, sending shards of glass and thick Yorkshire batter ricocheting around the kitchen. Luckily, I was alone in the kitchen at the time. And although I was covered with batter and had slivers of glass stuck in my hair and on my clothes, I was unhurt. Later I learned that Pyrex glass pans "lose their temper" after years of use. Don't we all? (*Note from the editors:* Even new Pyrex pans can "lose their temper" when placed on a hot burner—in short, don't try this at home.)

Ricky Baldwin Westport, Conn.

A LITTLE ELBOW GREASE

My husband believes this story is commonplace, but I am betting it's not. When we were first married, I cooked all the meals and he would clean up. One evening, after using my brand new nonstick grill pan for the first time, I left to do some shopping while he washed the dishes. When I returned, he apologetically told me that he had been unable to clean all of the "black stuff" from one pan no matter how hard he scrubbed. He even had the blisters to prove it. Believe it or not, he had diligently scrubbed all but a few specks of the nonstick coating from that brand new pan, which was now gleaming silver. Please let me know that you have never heard this one before so I can prove my husband wrong!

Claudia Peano Park Ridge, Ill.

Send us your funniest kitchen disaster stories. Please write to us at Kitchen Disasters, Cook's Country, P.O. Box 470739, Brookline, MA 02447. If you'd like to use e-mail, write to us at kitchendisasters@bcpress.com. If we publish your story, you'll receive a complimentary one-year subscription to *Cook's Country*.

The Great American Cake

Strawberry Crunch Cake

Strawberries are the unofficial fruit for Valentine's Day, and this dessert—with tender yellow cake, sweet whipped cream, and crunchy baked meringue—shows them at their very best.

To make this cake you'll need:

- **2 quarts strawberries, hulled and sliced thin**
- **3 tablespoons granulated sugar**
- **2 cups heavy cream**
- **1 baked 8-inch yellow cake round***
- **1 baked 8-inch meringue round** **(see page 28)**
- **12 whole strawberries for garnish**
- **Confectioners' sugar for dusting**

For the filling: Toss sliced berries and 2 tablespoons sugar in bowl and stir occasionally until sugar dissolves, about 15 minutes. Beat cream and remaining 1 tablespoon sugar with electric mixer at medium-high speed until cream just holds stiff peaks, 2 to 3 minutes.

To assemble: Slice cake horizontally into two layers. Place one layer, cut side up, on serving plate. Spread with $1\frac{1}{2}$ cups whipped cream. Arrange half of sliced berries on cream, then top with meringue. Arrange remaining sliced berries on meringue, spread $1\frac{1}{2}$ cups whipped cream over berries, then top with remaining cake layer, cut side down. Spoon remaining 1 cup whipped cream on top of cake and arrange whole berries. Dust with confectioners' sugar.

* Go to www.cookscountry.com for a yellow cake recipe—or use your own.

Recipe Index

RC = Recipe Card

Cook's Country

APRIL/MAY 2006

Herbed Roast Pork
With Old-Fashioned Flavor

Chicken Noodle Soup
Best Broth, Tender Meat

Roast Potatoes
Crispy and Garlicky

PASTA PRIMAVERA
Without the Fuss

LEMON POUND CAKE
Sour Cream Makes It Moist

ROASTED ASPARAGUS
High Heat, Big Flavor

CHICKEN AND RICE
Complete Supper in a Skillet

FUDGY BROWNIES
Secrets to Less Fat, More Flavor

PARING KNIVES
$5 Model Dices Competition

TASTING MILK CHOCOLATE
Brands with Big Flavor Win

PEPPERONI PAN PIZZA
Secrets to Restaurant-Style Deep-Dish Crust

Our Creative Sandwich Contest Winner!

Rebecca Williams of Goldsboro, N.C., won first place with a recipe that combines an Italian mozzarella, tomato, and basil salad with an American sandwich classic. See page 4 for her **Caprese BLT.**

$4.95 U.S./$6.95 CANADA

Cook's Country

Dear Country Cook,

Old photographs lie. When the people in them are wearing bobby socks, saddle shoes, and a dress while working on a farm, it's easy to miss the greater truth. Where did all those eggs come from? There is no henhouse visible (it looks like this girl is coming back from the horse barn) and she is carrying a whole lot of eggs.

But old photos do contain a truth of sorts. They tell us that there is something universal and satisfying about chores. They convey the pure joy of the ordinary. They show us that hard work, sometimes even suffering, is intimately connected to happiness. And, most of all, that all those who lived before us are counting on us not to let them down.

I just ran across a 1905 photo of Charlie Bentley's father when he was a young man. I knew Charlie's father well and even attended his funeral back in the sixties. In those days, I also worked on Charlie's dairy farm. I have lived most of my life trying to live up to Charlie's hardscrabble expectations. Work hard. Don't complain. Be useful. Looking at that old photo, I can see that this is not just a matter between Charlie and me. It is a case of being accountable to the many generations of Bentleys who came before.

Christopher Kimball
Founder and Editor, *Cook's Country* Magazine

Francis Larson collecting eggs on her Iowa farm, 1948. (Photo: Bob Landry/Time Life Pictures/Getty Images.)

APRIL/MAY 2006

Cook's Country

departments

features

in every issue

Editorial Office: 17 Station Street, Brookline, MA 02445; 617-232-1000; fax 617-232-1572
Subscription inquiries: Cook's Country, P.O. Box 8382, Red Oak, IA 51591-1382
800-526-8447

ON THE COVER: PHOTOGRAPHY: StockFood/Studio Adna. ILLUSTRATION: John Burgoyne.
IN THIS ISSUE: COLOR FOOD PHOTOGRAPHY: Keller + Keller. STYLING: Mary Jane Sawyer, Marie Piraino. ILLUSTRATION: Lisa Parett.

Cook's Country magazine (ISSN 1552-1990), number 8, is published bimonthly by Boston Common Press Limited Partnership, 17 Station Street, Brookline, MA, 02445. Copyright 2006 Boston Common Press Limited Partnership. Application to mail at periodical postage rates pending at Boston, Mass., and additional mailing offices. POSTMASTER: Send address changes to Cook's Country, P.O. Box 8382, Red Oak, IA 51591-1382. For subscription and gift subscription orders, subscription inquiries, or change-of-address notices, call 800-526-8447 in the U.S. or 515-247-7571 from outside the U.S., or write us at Cook's Country, P.O. Box 8382, Red Oak, IA 51591-1382.
PRINTED IN THE USA

Visit us at www.cookscountry.com!
Go online to ask questions, share kitchen tips, and enter recipe contests. You can also take a sneak peek at what we've got cooking for upcoming issues.

Kitchen Shortcuts

READERS SHARE CLEVER TIPS FOR EVERYDAY COOKING CHALLENGES

Keep Your Balance

Clip Your Lids

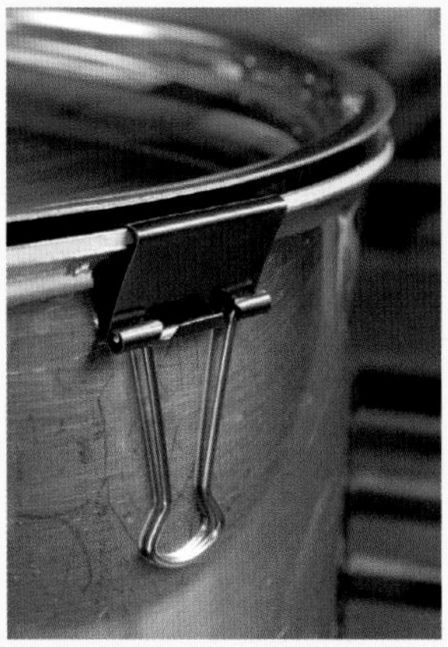

The binder clips sold in stationery stores are great for keeping pot lids slightly ajar during cooking. Simply clamp them on the side of your pot, and when you put the lid on it will be slightly elevated. No more rattling tops—this works much better than trying to balance the lid on the pot.

Linda De Mayo
Ballston Spa, N.Y.

Organizing Grocery Bags

I used to have a messy pile of plastic grocery bags underneath my sink. Now, when I get home from the grocery store, I push the clean bags into an empty tissue box, which keeps them nice and tidy and ready for the picking. When I need a bag, I reach for the box.

Helen Joy Steiner
Santa Rosa, Calif.

Roll Over Herbs

Chopping a big batch of herbs, such as parsley or cilantro, can be a chore, and a food processor can reduce them to mush. Then I thought to use the super-sharp blade on my largest pizza wheel. It easily slices mounds of herbs without crushing them, and it gives me more control than a knife.

John Bliss
Chicago, Ill.

Bye-Bye Moisture

FISH BLOW-DRIED, THEN FRIED

When my mom fries fish, she uses a blow-dryer to remove moisture from the skin. That way, when she puts it in the pan, the oil doesn't pop and splatter onto the stovetop, and she doesn't have to worry about getting burned.

Vivian Zhou Irvine, Calif.

CLEANER MUSHROOMS

I clean mushrooms by putting them in a large zipper-lock plastic bag filled halfway with water. I seal the bag, shake it, rinse, and repeat. The mushrooms absorb hardly any water, and it's 10 times faster than brushing each one clean.

Lily Starr
Potomac, Md.

REFRESHING BREAD

If you have a loaf of unsliced bread that's a little stale, don't throw it out. Instead, splash a little water on your hands and then pat the loaf all over to dampen it. Place it in a 350-degree oven for about 10 minutes, or until it is dry. Not only will your home smell like you just baked the bread from scratch, but the bread will taste that way, too. This works especially well with baguettes and rustic-style breads.

Davida Skigen
Chicago, Ill.

EASY SPINACH SQUEEZE

I came up with a shortcut to drain frozen spinach of all its extra liquid without taking the trouble to use a colander or squeeze it dry in a kitchen towel. I just thaw the spinach in its packaging, then snip off a corner of the box and squeeze out the water. It's less messy and more efficient.

Joyce Herring
Memphis, Tenn.

A BERRY COOL TIP

I freeze blueberries, raspberries, and blackberries during the summer months, when they are inexpensive. Come winter, when I make hot oatmeal, I throw in a few frozen berries to help cool it off. It's a healthy way to sweeten and cool your breakfast.

Wendy J. Beyer
Whitehouse Station, N.J.

DISPOSABLE CUTTING BOARD

If you're in a pinch and don't have the time or space to pull out your cutting board, try using a disposable plastic or heavy paper plate instead. They're great for small jobs like cutting tomatoes, slicing cake, and coring bell peppers—and they're easily disposed of when you're done.

Dawn Bagnetto
Wichita Falls, Texas

KEEPING AVOCADOS GREEN

To keep avocado halves from discoloring, spray the exposed surface lightly with a cooking spray, such as PAM. This works even better than lemon juice, and it doesn't add any flavor!

Melissa Charron
Washington, D.C.

SALAD IN A BAG

When I bring salad to a party, I don't want to dress it until the last minute. Instead of carting my Tupperware around (and then leaving it behind) or having to ask the host for a bowl, I pack the salad in one of those huge zipper-lock bags. Then I add the dressing, give the bag a quick shake, and the salad is ready to go.

Heidi Sekowski
Glen Ellyn, Ill.

NO-SPILL TACO TIP

Tacos are a weeknight staple at our house, but keeping the loose and crumbly meat mixture in the shells and tortillas can be a challenge, especially for children. I solved the problem by stirring a few spoonfuls of store-bought refried beans into the taco meat. Now the filling has the perfect consistency and stays put in the shells.

Nicole Somerville
Port Orchard, Wash.

FLASH-CARD SHOPPING

Index cards (3 by 5 inches) come in handy for making grocery lists. They're small enough to fit in a purse or the palm of your hand while you shop.

Adrianne Johnson
Topeka, Kan.

If you'd like to submit a tip, please send a letter to Kitchen Shortcuts, Cook's Country, P.O. Box 470739, Brookline, MA 02447. Or e-mail us at shortcuts@bcpress.com. Include your name, address, and phone number. If we publish your tip, you will receive a one-year subscription to *Cook's Country*.

SAVIN' BACON
My family doesn't eat much bacon, so it's always a struggle to use a whole pound before it goes bad. To make sure this doesn't happen, I lay out a long piece of plastic wrap, place one slice of bacon at the end of the wrap, and fold it over just to cover the slice. I then place a second piece of bacon on the wrap and fold the wrap over again to cover it. I continue "jellyroll" style until I run out of bacon, then I freeze the stack. Whenever I need a couple of strips, I unroll the plastic wrap and take out the pieces I need. You don't even need to defrost them before cooking!

Susan P. Love
Circleville, Ohio

'COFFEE' CAKE LINER
I've found that cakes will slip right out of their pans if I line them with a flattened "round-shaped" coffee filter (#4). Try it!

Adele Haas
Tonawanda, N.Y.

SIFT AWAY
Sifting flour can be a messy experience. To cut down on cleanup, I place a paper plate under my measuring cup. When I sift into the cup, the extra flour falls on the plate. Afterward, I can easily fold the plate and pour the extra flour back into my flour canister.

Floris Hills
Owasso, Okla.

BRUSH HOUR
I keep an inexpensive toothbrush near the kitchen sink to aid in the cleaning of graters, sieves, and so on. I also find that the tip of a toothpick comes in handy to gently clean small, hard-to-reach areas of tools such as a garlic press and an immersion blender.

Linda Rosenjack
Aurora, Ohio

CUT SPONGE PRICES IN HALF
I've always used scrubber sponges in the kitchen instead of dishcloths because I like the rough side for many cleaning tasks. Unfortunately, these sponges have to be replaced regularly. A couple of years ago, I started cutting the sponges in half. This has not only been a money-saver, but I now prefer the smaller sponge. It is much easier to handle when I need to get into corners or the bottoms of wine or cordial glasses that I don't trust to the dishwasher.

Judith Troka
Merrillville, Ind.

A HANDY SCRAPER
I've found that the lids of plastic tubs containing margarine, sour cream, ice cream, and the like make handy—and cheap—pot and bowl scrapers. Just cut the hard rims off the lids; the remaining pliable circle of plastic works perfectly.

Rosemary Eng
North Vancouver, B.C., Canada

BIODEGRADABLE BOWLS
The hollowed-out halves of grapefruits, oranges, lemons, and limes make pretty individual dishes for ice cream, sherbet, or fruit salad—and there are no dishes to wash! Sometimes I even bring them on picnics. They're biodegradable, so I don't have to carry dirty dishes back home.

Karen Ann Bland
Gove, Kan.

QUICK-FIX POTATO RICER
If you find yourself without a ricer for mashed potatoes, you can push the potatoes through the large holes of a colander.

Nitza E. Villalobo
Chicago, Ill.

A SHARP IDEA!
Out of bamboo skewers? Just use a pencil sharpener on take-out chopsticks to make disposable barbecue skewers.

Chris Butler
Keller, Texas

HEAT CONTROL
Several hot sauces that I've bought recently pack a really big kick. A few drops too many and the taste goes from spicy to too hot to eat. Ruining a whole pot of chili is a real downer, so now I keep an eyedropper in my drawer along with the measuring spoons. This way, I can add exactly the right amount for the perfect level of heat.

Pam Hansberger
Norwalk, Ohio

Cheap and Breathable Bags
Instead of buying the more expensive perforated zipper-lock bags designed for storing vegetables, I use regular bags and prick tiny holes in them with an instant-read thermometer, a skewer, or a corn-cob holder.

Dagmar Harrison
Morgantown, W.V.

Use Ice Cubes to Remove Fat
My father-in-law taught me years ago the best way to defat drippings. Just pour everything—juices, drippings, fat—while still hot into a large Pyrex measuring cup. Put in four or five large ice cubes (enough to cover the entire surface of the cup), and, after a few minutes, give the cubes a gentle stir—they'll be covered with congealed fat. Use a slotted spoon to remove the fat-coated cubes.

Robert C. Shoemaker
Claremont, N.H.

No-Fuss Lemon Juice
Want fresh lemon juice without any seeds? Cut the lemon in quarters and place the quantity you need in a plastic sandwich bag. Squeeze the lemon quarters in the bag, then use scissors to snip a tiny hole (smaller than the seeds) in a bottom corner of the bag. The juice comes out easily and the seeds and spent lemon pieces stay in the bag, ready to be thrown into the trash.

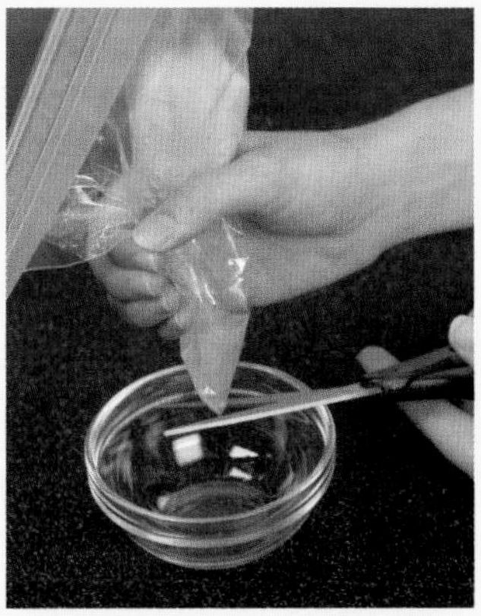

Alan Hobson,
Wichita, Kan.

Neat Treats

When I make Rice Krispies Treats, I find that my meat pounder (the one with the heavy, round metal disk) works beautifully. I brush the base liberally with butter to make sure it won't stick and then run it back and forth over the top of the treats until they're completely flat and smooth.

Mary A. Bantle
La Crosse, Wis.

Sweet Idea
JUST A SPOONFUL OF SUGAR
Whenever I chop onions or garlic, my hands stay stinky for what seems like days. Here's my tip to get rid of the smell. Simply wet your hands with warm water and then sprinkle them with a tablespoon of granulated sugar. Rub the sugar into your hands for a minute or so (it's great for exfoliating, too) and then rinse. Works every time!

Christy Durham Forsyth, Mont.

An Italian Salad Inspires an Award-Winning Sandwich

Basil mayonnaise and fresh mozzarella cheese give the classic BLT an Italian twist.

Our $500 Grand-Prize Winner!

Rebecca Williams
Goldsboro, N.C.

Rebecca Williams usually makes authentic Mexican fare (her roots are in Texas), but her husband, Russell, can't get enough of her Caprese BLT. The couple were on a trip to Italy when they first tasted Caprese salad, which inspired Rebecca to create this sandwich, now a household favorite. "A Caprese is usually served with just a few basil leaves," Rebecca told us, "but I wanted my sandwich to have more of an herb kick. My overgrown basil plant needed a trim, and making a mayonnaise seemed like a great way to use the surplus. But my husband's favorite addition to this recipe was the bacon." Part of being a great cook is improvising, and Rebecca definitely has this talent. "When my husband was stationed in Germany, we had access to so many interesting ingredients. That experience definitely made me take more risks in the kitchen. I'll try anything at least once!" Russell is now stationed with the Air Force in Baghdad. Rebecca told us that she made Russell's day with her news about winning this recipe contest.

CAPRESE BLT

SERVES 4 TO 6

Many supermarket bakeries carry ciabatta. An Italian loaf can be used instead, but be sure to discard the interior of the bread, as directed.

- **2 medium tomatoes, sliced thin**
- **Salt**
- **1 tablespoon extra-virgin olive oil**
- **1 tablespoon balsamic vinegar**
- **1 loaf ciabatta**
- **1⅓ cups packed fresh basil**
- **⅓ cup mayonnaise**
- **2 teaspoons lemon juice**
- **1 garlic clove, minced**
- **⅛ teaspoon hot sauce**
- **8 slices bacon, cooked until crisp, drained, and crumbled**
- **4 romaine lettuce leaves**
- **8 ounces fresh mozzarella, sliced thin**

1. Place tomato slices on several layers of paper towels and sprinkle with ½ teaspoon salt. Let sit for 15 minutes, then press with additional paper towels to extract excess moisture. Mix oil and vinegar together in small bowl. Slice bread in half horizontally and use fingers to remove and discard all but ½ inch of interior crumb.

2. Puree 1 cup basil, mayonnaise, lemon juice, garlic, hot sauce, and ¼ teaspoon salt in blender or food processor until smooth, stopping to scrape down sides several times. Spread basil mayonnaise on both cut sides of bread. Sprinkle bacon on bottom half of bread and place romaine on top of bacon. Shingle tomatoes and mozzarella alternately over romaine and drizzle with oil and vinegar mixture. Place remaining ⅓ cup basil in single layer on top and replace top half of bread. Cut crosswise into 2-inch sandwiches. Serve.

Dan Barnhardt
Atlanta, Ga.

Edith Smith
Scotch Plains, N.J.

Mara Elliott
Delmar, N.Y.

Alanna Taylor-Tobin
San Francisco, Calif.

EASY PO' BOYS SERVES 4

Dan writes: "Having spent a lot of time in New Orleans, I decided to make my favorite sandwich, the po' boy. But I didn't want to fry shrimp, so I made a quick shrimp salad and topped it with buttered bread crumbs for crunch."

- **4 (6-inch) sub rolls**
- **3 tablespoons unsalted butter**
- **2 slices bacon, cooked until crisp, drained, and crumbled**
- **3 tablespoons chopped scallions**
- **1/4 cup ketchup**
- **1/4 cup mayonnaise**
- **1 teaspoon prepared horseradish**
- **1/4 teaspoon hot sauce**
- **9 ounces cooked and peeled shrimp, chopped**
- **3 cups watercress, stemmed**

1. Adjust oven rack to middle position and heat oven to 400 degrees. Cut thin slice from top of each roll and reserve; pull out all but 1/2 inch of interior crumb and reserve. Melt butter in skillet. Brush hollowed-out rolls with 2 tablespoons butter and toast on baking sheet in oven until light golden, about 5 minutes.

2. Pulse reserved bread in food processor to fine crumbs. Add 1 cup crumbs to skillet with remaining butter and cook over medium heat, stirring occasionally, until golden brown, about 5 minutes. Transfer to bowl and toss with bacon and 1 tablespoon scallions.

3. Whisk ketchup, mayonnaise, horseradish, and hot sauce together in medium bowl. Stir in shrimp and remaining 2 tablespoons scallions. Line each bun with watercress and top with shrimp mixture. Sprinkle bread crumbs over shrimp. Serve.

ANTIPASTO MELTS SERVES 4

Edith writes: "Antipasto salad is one of my signature dishes that my family always asks for. I thought I would add a twist by turning it into a cooked sandwich. Now I'm getting requests for my sandwich!" You'll need oversized slices from a large loaf of peasant bread to support the substantial ingredients in this eat-with-a-fork sandwich. Look for tapenade (a puree of black olives) in the Italian section of your local market.

- **3 tablespoons extra-virgin olive oil**
- **1 tablespoon black olive tapenade**
- **4 (1/2-inch-thick) slices from large crusty peasant loaf**
- **16 slices Genoa salami**
- **8 slices capicola**
- **4 very thin slices red onion**
- **4 slices mozzarella cheese**
- **4 slices provolone cheese**
- **2 cups baby spinach**
- **1 tablespoon balsamic vinegar**

1. Position oven rack 6 inches from broiler element and heat broiler. Mix 2 tablespoons oil and tapenade in small bowl and spread mixture onto tops of bread slices. Place bread on baking sheet and broil until lightly toasted, about 2 minutes.

2. Remove from oven and layer each slice bread with 2 slices salami, 2 slices capicola, 2 more slices salami, 1 slice red onion, 1 slice mozzarella, and 1 slice provolone. Broil until cheese is melted and beginning to brown, about 2 minutes.

3. Toss spinach, remaining 1 tablespoon oil, and vinegar together in medium bowl. Divide spinach evenly on top of each sandwich. Serve.

COBB CLUB SANDWICHES
SERVES 4

Mara writes: "Cobb is my favorite salad, but it isn't always transportable. This sandwich is a great way to carry the flavors I love out to a picnic or ballgame."

- **1 medium tomato, sliced thin**
- **1/2 teaspoon salt**
- **2/3 cup mayonnaise**
- **3 tablespoons crumbled blue cheese**
- **12 slices hearty white sandwich bread, toasted**
- **2 large eggs, hard-cooked, peeled, and sliced thin**
- **1 ripe avocado, pitted, peeled and sliced thin**
- **8 slices bacon, cooked until crisp and drained**
- **3 cooked boneless, skinless chicken breasts, cooled and sliced thin**

1. Place tomato slices on several layers of paper towels and sprinkle with salt. Let sit for 15 minutes, then press with additional paper towels to extract excess moisture.

2. Using fork, mash 1/3 cup mayonnaise and blue cheese together in small bowl until smooth.

3. Spread blue cheese mixture on 8 slices toast. Spread 3 tablespoons mayonnaise on remaining 4 slices toast. Place 4 cheese-coated toasts on work surface. Layer each with sliced tomato, egg, and avocado. Place plain mayonnaise-coated toasts, mayonnaise side down, over avocado; spread tops of toast with remaining mayonnaise. Continue layering with 2 strips bacon and sliced chicken. Top with remaining blue cheese–coated toasts, facing down. Cut each sandwich into triangles. Serve.

ELEGANT EGGS ON TOAST
SERVES 4

Alanna writes: "This sandwich mingles the spicy bite of fresh arugula with the sumptuous texture of eggs and smoked salmon. It makes an elegant weekend breakfast."

- **8 large eggs**
- **1/2 cup whole milk**
- **1/2 teaspoon salt**
- **1/8 teaspoon pepper**
- **1 tablespoon unsalted butter**
- **1/4 cup minced chives**
- **4 ounces goat cheese**
- **8 slices pumpernickel bread, toasted**
- **1 1/3 cups fresh arugula leaves**
- **4 slices smoked salmon**

1. Beat eggs, milk, salt, and pepper in bowl until uniformly yellow. Meanwhile, heat butter in medium nonstick skillet over high heat until foam subsides. Pour in egg mixture and, using rubber spatula, push eggs from one side of pan to other side, lifting and folding eggs until they form single mound but remain shiny and wet, 1 1/2 to 2 minutes. Transfer to medium bowl and toss with chives.

2. Spread cheese on 4 slices toast, then layer each with arugula and 1 slice salmon. Spoon eggs over salmon and top with remaining 4 slices toast. Serve.

We are looking for holiday cookie recipes for an upcoming contest. Please submit entries by May 31, 2006. Write to us at Recipe Contest, Cook's Country, P.O. Box 470739, Brookline, MA 02447, or e-mail us at recipecontest@bcpress.com. Include your name, address, and daytime phone number, and tell us what makes your recipe special. The grand-prize winner will receive $500. All entries become the property of *Cook's Country*. Visit our Web site at www.cookscountry.com for more information on this and other contests.

Ask Cook's Country

WE TRY TO ANSWER ANY QUESTION YOU THROW AT US!

Which nuts taste best with basil pesto?

NUTS FOR PESTO

I like pesto but am not a big fan of pine nuts. Have you tried other nuts? I was thinking about using pistachios.

Eric Pauls St. Louis, Mo.

We raided the nut aisle and prepared batches of pesto with walnuts, almonds, pecans, pistachios, sunflower seeds, cashews, hazelnuts, and peanuts. We also prepared a batch without nuts and had tasters sample each pesto. "Mild and balanced" walnuts and "buttery" pecans were favored by all tasters. Sunflower seeds were dismissed as "too strong" and too much "like rabbit food." The pesto made with peanuts was panned for being "too peanutty" and tasting like "basil peanut butter." Other strong-flavored nuts tended to overpower the basil flavor of the pesto, getting mixed reviews: Cashews were deemed "acceptable but weird," hazelnuts "slightly strong but pleasant," pistachios "OK but not great," and almonds "good" but too strong, making the pesto "taste like almonds and nothing else." Most tasters found the pesto made without nuts to be "thin and oily," without "the balance" provided by the nuts. Our advice? Stick to mild, neutral nuts that will let the flavor of the basil shine. That includes pine nuts, walnuts, and pecans.

TO REFREEZE, OR NOT TO REFREEZE

I took some ground beef out of the freezer for dinner but then never used it. Can I refreeze it?

Traci Ward Framingham, Mass.

According to the U.S. Department of Agriculture, as long as the meat was thawed properly in the refrigerator and not at room temperature, it is safe to refreeze it. The danger of thawing frozen meat at room temperature is that it may sit in the danger zone of 40 to 140 degrees Fahrenheit, which is the optimum environment for bacteria growth. In addition to the safety issue is the question of quality. When meat is frozen, the liquid within the cells expands, which can damage the cell walls. When the meat is thawed, the liquid seeps out, leaving the meat more prone to drying out as it cooks. The more times this process is repeated, the more likely the quality of the meat will deteriorate. To find out just how bad this deterioration is, we prepared burgers with two batches of ground beef, one frozen and then thawed in the refrigerator just once and one refrozen and thawed a second time. Tasters noted the difference immediately, calling the refrozen batch "a little tough and springy," "grainy," and "a little drier" than the batch that had been frozen only once. Our advice? Skip the refreezing.

COCOA POWDER OR UNSWEETENED CHOCOLATE

I notice that some cookbooks recommend cocoa powder for brownies but most tend to recommend unsweetened chocolate. Which do you prefer? Also, if a recipe calls for one, can I safely use the other? If yes, is there a conversion factor I can use?

'rmoe' Via e-mail

Cocoa powder is unsweetened chocolate from which 76 to 90 percent of the cocoa butter has been removed. It is generally called for when a big hit of chocolate flavor is desired without any additional fat, usually in recipes that already contain a lot of butter, such as cakes and cookies. Some cocoas are packaged with instructions indicating that 3 tablespoons of cocoa powder combined with 1 tablespoon of vegetable oil can be substituted for 1 ounce of unsweetened chocolate. To find out if this substitution works, we prepared batches of brownies made with the 6 ounces of unsweetened chocolate called for in the recipe and with the cocoa and oil substitution. To our surprise, tasters found no textural differences between the two batches, and even the author of the recipe conceded that both batches were acceptable.

TESTING SILICONE BAKEWARE

What do you think of silicone muffin pans? I've gotten mixed reviews from friends.

Dana Thompson Gresham, Ore.

We prepared batches of blueberry muffins in standard metal and silicone muffin tins. Makers of silicone bakeware may tout the flexibility of their products, but we found it to be more hindrance than help. The floppy muffin pan had to be steadied on a metal sheet pan, which slowed the cooking time and inhibited browning. In fact, the muffins from the silicone pan turned an unsightly shade of white even on the sides, with none of the characteristic browning we like in a muffin. Because the muffins must be literally peeled from the pan, they must be cooled completely before removal. That meant a difference of 40 minutes between when we could eat the muffins from the standard tin (nice and warm) and when we could eat those from the silicone pan. We'll continue to stick with our metal muffin tins.

Muffins baked in a silicone pan pale in comparison with those baked in a traditional metal pan.

CANNED MILK PRIMER

What's the difference between sweetened condensed milk and evaporated milk? Can I substitute either of them for fresh milk in a recipe?

Drew Michaels Westin, Fla.

Both sweetened condensed milk and evaporated milk consist of milk from which 60 percent of the water has been removed. The only difference between the two is that sweetened condensed milk, as its name suggests, is highly sweetened, consisting of 40 to 45 percent sugar. This makes it popular for use in sweet custards and puddings. Evaporated milk, which is commonly used in savory custards or cream sauces in which excess moisture is unwanted, can be substituted for regular milk in recipes by adding an equal amount of water (1 cup evaporated milk plus 1 cup water equals 2 cups whole milk). Because of its high sugar content, sweetened condensed milk cannot be substituted for either evaporated or regular milk.

Which product can replace fresh milk in a pinch?

FREEZING CREAM CHEESE

Does cream cheese freeze well? We use a fair amount of it, and our local market sometimes sells it on a deep discount.

Kati Wood Southfield, Mich.

With fresh bagels as bait, we lured 10 tasters into the test kitchen to sample fresh and thawed frozen cream cheese. The previously frozen cream cheese was described as "chalky," "broken and curdled," and "watery." We then tried the frozen cream cheese in cheesecake. Tasters again described it as "grainy," "dry," "crumbly," and "awful." When cream cheese is frozen, the water in it turns to ice, expanding and breaking apart the cream cheese. When the cream cheese is thawed, the ice melts and the water drains away, leaving the cream cheese dry. The obvious verdict: No matter how deep the discount, buy only the cream cheese you need.

To ask us a cooking question, write to Ask Cook's Country, P. O. Box 470739, Brookline, MA 02447. If you prefer e-mail, write to askcookscountry@bcpress.com. See if you can stump us!

Lost Recipes GRASSHOPPER PIE

Save the ice cream for sundaes. A true grasshopper pie should have a creamy, billowy chiffon filling.

I've had grasshopper pie twice in my lifetime. Years ago, at a diner, I spied a Kelly-green pie in its chocolate-cookie crust and had to try it. It was the fluffiest, creamiest pie I had ever eaten, with enough mint and chocolate flavor to shame a Peppermint Pattie.

I'd forgotten about that pie until recently, when I saw grasshopper pie on another diner menu. When the slice I'd ordered arrived at the table, it had the chocolate crust I remembered, but in place of the fluffy mint filling there was mint chocolate chip ice cream. Complaining under my breath (as I ate the whole thing), I was determined to revisit the classic version of this recipe, the one that had caught my attention the first time.

The pie takes its name from a cocktail, the grasshopper, which was invented at Tujague's Restaurant in New Orleans near the end of Prohibition. This bright green drink is a mix of heavy cream, white crème de cacao (a clear version of the dark chocolate cordial), and green crème de menthe (a mint cordial) that is shaken with ice and strained into a cocktail glass. Grasshopper pie was born during the 1950s, when chiffon pies were the rage. These fluffy pies start with a flavored gelatin base and then fold in whipped egg whites and/or whipped cream.

I found a classic Knox Gelatine recipe reprinted in Jean Anderson's *The American Century Cookbook* (1997). The gelatin was softened and dissolved in water, then mixed with green crème de menthe and white crème de cacao. After it firmed up a bit, in went stiffly beaten egg whites and whipped cream. It was light and fluffy and darn good, but not perfect. The whipped egg whites made this pie a little less creamy than I had hoped, but I managed to polish off a few slices anyway.

I finally found a near-perfect recipe in *Gourmet* magazine's *Menu Cookbook* (1963). It, too, started with gelatin, this time softened in heavy cream instead of water. After the liqueurs were added and the mixture set up, only whipped cream was folded in—no egg whites. Soft and super-minty, it was the closest thing yet to that grasshopper pie I had eaten years ago.

Because I still wanted the pie to be a bit creamier and also taller, I increased the whipped cream. Where I made my big breakthrough, however, was the crust. I kept the melted butter, but rather than using the traditional ground chocolate wafers, I tried Mint 'n Creme Oreo Cookies, basically a "Double Stuffed" Oreo flavored with mint. They worked like a charm, and now both the filling and the crust were flavored with both chocolate and mint. A new cookie made this old recipe even better than I had thought possible.

–Bridget Lancaster

Replacing the beaten egg whites called for in most recipes with additional whipped cream helped us create an extra-fluffy filling.

GRASSHOPPER PIE SERVES 8

For tips on making a crumb crust, see page 28. To garnish the pie with chocolate curls, see page 29.

Crust

- **16 Mint 'n Creme Oreo Cookies (with filling), broken into rough pieces**
- **3 tablespoons unsalted butter, melted and cooled**

Filling

- **3 large egg yolks**
- **1 envelope unflavored gelatin**
- **1/2 cup sugar**
- **2 cups heavy cream**
- **Pinch salt**
- **1/4 cup green crème de menthe**
- **1/4 cup white crème de cacao**

1. For the crust: Adjust oven rack to middle position and heat oven to 350 degrees. Grind cookies in food processor to fine crumbs. Transfer to bowl, drizzle with butter, and toss well. Press crumbs evenly into bottom and sides of 9-inch pie plate and refrigerate crust until firm, about 20 minutes. Bake until set, 8 to 10 minutes. Cool completely on wire rack.

2. For the filling: Beat egg yolks in medium bowl. Combine gelatin, sugar, ½ cup cream, and salt in medium saucepan and let sit until gelatin softens, about 5 minutes. Cook over medium heat until gelatin dissolves and mixture is very hot but not boiling, about 2 minutes. Whisking vigorously, slowly add gelatin mixture to egg yolks. Return mixture to saucepan and cook, stirring constantly, until slightly thickened, about 2 minutes. Remove from heat and add crème de menthe and crème de cacao. Pour into clean bowl and refrigerate, stirring occasionally, until wobbly but not set, about 20 minutes.

3. Beat remaining 1½ cups cream with electric mixer to stiff peaks. Whisk 1 cup whipped cream into gelatin mixture until completely incorporated. Using rubber spatula, fold gelatin mixture into remaining whipped cream until no streaks of white remain. Scrape mixture into cooled pie shell, smooth top, and refrigerate until firm, at least 6 hours or preferably overnight. (The pie will keep tightly wrapped in refrigerator for up to 2 days.) Serve, topped with chocolate curls, if desired.

NOT JUST FOR COCKTAILS
In the 1950s and 1960s, liqueur makers, such as Hiram Walker, developed numerous recipes that showcased their products in desserts—everything from chantilly mousse (promoted in the above pamphlet) to grasshopper pie. Unfortunately, the Hiram Walker recipe for grasshopper pie that we tasted relied on melted marshmallows, which gave the filling an unpleasant grainy texture.

Move Over, Peppermint Pattie

Our grasshopper pie gets its mint and chocolate flavor from several sources. The filling gets a serious mint-chocolate punch from the cordials green crème de menthe and white crème de cacao, and the crust gets the same from Mint 'n Creme Oreo Cookies.

TRADITIONAL FLAVORS
Grasshopper pie filling is traditionally flavored with both mint and chocolate liqueurs.

NEW IDEA
Rather than the classic chocolate-cookie crumb crust, we like one made with minty Oreo cookies.

Recipe Makeover FUDGY BROWNIES

It's easy to make an uninspired, cakey low-fat brownie, but what about a fudgy one worth eating?

I have tried many recipes for "healthy" brownies, but it usually takes just one bite for me to regret the effort. Either the texture is incredibly dry or the chocolate flavor is anemic. The best of the lot are usually cakey and spongy, which is OK if what you want is a flat piece of chocolate cake but not if you want a real brownie, which should be moist, fudgy, and packed with chocolate flavor.

Fudgy brownies tend to rely on a generous amount of butter (usually an entire stick) and unsweetened chocolate (at least 2 ounces, often more). Many low-fat brownie recipes call for "alternative" ingredients such as applesauce, prune puree, or even yogurt, but the test kitchen's opinion of these stand-ins was unanimously negative.

Applesauce masked the chocolate flavor and gave the brownies a texture that reminded me of an oily sponge. Prune puree yielded flavorless hockey pucks. Although yogurt produced a pleasing texture, tasters turned up their noses at the tart flavor. I decided to stick with the test kitchen's favorite recipe for fudgy brownies and see where I might trim calories and fat.

Cocoa powder, which is unsweetened chocolate with most of the fat removed, is a common ingredient in many low-fat chocolate recipes. Replacing all of the chocolate with cocoa powder is a mistake—the result was a very dry texture. Replacing all but 2 ounces was a vastly better approach. I also found that Dutch-processed brands contributed more flavor than "natural" cocoas. The last trick was to use bittersweet chocolate, which has less fat per ounce (by about 5 grams) than unsweetened chocolate.

It was time to confront the real problem with low-fat brownies: the butter. Leave it out and you might as well throw the brownies in the trash. But to make a significant dent in the calorie and fat count, I couldn't add more than 2 tablespoons—far less than the usual stick—and that meant dry, cakey brownies. I would have to find another source of moisture to make my brownies more gooey. A squirt of chocolate syrup (such as Hershey's), which contains no fat and plenty of chocolate flavor, helped things along, but it wasn't enough.

In my research, I ran across several low-fat chocolate cake recipes that called for nonfat sour cream. Could it help my brownies? After my first test, I would have said no. The brownies were still too dry. Then, in place of the nonfat sour cream, I tried low fat, which has only about one-third the fat of the regular stuff. These brownies were much better, not just moist and fudgy but also more tender. That's because the acidity in sour cream has a tenderizing effect on baked goods.

I had trimmed more than half the calories and two-thirds of the fat from my favorite fudgy brownie recipe. And my low-fat brownies were good enough to merit a second, even a third bite—with no regrets. **–Meredith Butcher**

No, you're not dreaming. These low-fat brownies sacrifice neither chocolate flavor nor moist texture.

And the Numbers . . .

All nutritional information is for a single serving (one brownie).

TRADITIONAL FUDGY BROWNIES
CALORIES: **220**
FAT: **12g**
SATURATED FAT: **7g**

COOK'S COUNTRY FUDGY LOW-FAT BROWNIES
CALORIES: **110**
FAT: **4.5g**
SATURATED FAT: **1.5g**

FUDGY LOW-FAT BROWNIES

MAKES 16 BROWNIES

Melt the chocolate and butter together in a bowl set over a pan of simmering water or in a microwave set to 50 percent power. For a truly fudgy consistency, don't overbake the brownies; as soon as a toothpick inserted into the center comes out with sticky crumbs attached, the brownies are done. If the toothpick emerges with no crumbs, the brownies will be cakey.

- 3/4 cup all-purpose flour
- 1/3 cup Dutch-processed cocoa powder
- 1/2 teaspoon baking powder
- 1/4 teaspoon salt
- 2 ounces bittersweet chocolate, chopped
- 2 tablespoons unsalted butter
- 2 tablespoons low-fat sour cream
- 1 tablespoon chocolate syrup
- 2 teaspoons vanilla extract
- 1 large egg plus 1 large egg white
- 1 cup sugar

1. Adjust oven rack to middle position and heat oven to 350 degrees. Fold two 12-inch pieces foil lengthwise so each measures 7 inches wide. Fit 1 sheet into 8-inch-square baking dish, pushing foil into corners and up sides of pan (overhang will help in removal of brownies). Repeat with second sheet, placing in pan perpendicular to first sheet. Spray foil with cooking spray.

2. Whisk flour, cocoa, baking powder, and salt together in medium bowl. Melt bittersweet chocolate and butter in large bowl until smooth (see note at left). Cool 2 to 3 minutes, then whisk in sour cream, chocolate syrup, vanilla, egg, egg white, and sugar. Using rubber spatula, fold dry ingredients into chocolate mixture until combined.

3. Pour batter into pan, spread into corners, and level surface with spatula. Bake until slightly puffed and toothpick inserted in center comes out with a few sticky crumbs attached, 20 to 25 minutes. Cool brownies completely in pan on wire rack, at least 1 hour. Remove brownies from pan using foil handles. Cut into 2-inch squares and serve. To keep brownies moist, do not cut until ready to serve. (Brownies can be wrapped in plastic and refrigerated for 3 days.)

Sour Cream in Brownies?

We found that an unlikely ingredient—low-fat sour cream—helped keep our brownies fudgy even though they contain very little butter.

Slow Cooking COUNTRY CAPTAIN CHICKEN

This Southern stew should be tender and spicy, but a slow cooker can make the meat stringy and the sauce bland.

My slow cooker is high up on the list of things I would take to the proverbial desert island. OK, I know that most desert islands don't have electricity, but that gives you an idea of how much I depend on my slow cooker—at least once a week—to prepare long-simmering meat dishes such as chili, stew, and pot roast. I've seen many slow-cooker recipes for chicken, but I've had my doubts about them; cooking chicken for hours on end usually produces stringy, bland results.

I decided to cast aside my doubts and try one of my favorite—and most flavorful—chicken dishes in my slow cooker. I thought the fragrant stew known as country captain, rich with mango, raisins, tomatoes, and curry, would have flavors bold enough to withstand hours in a slow cooker.

My first thought was to dismiss the host of "dump-and-cook" country captain recipes typical of slow-cooker manuals. From past experience, I knew that browning the chicken and vegetables would be essential to building flavor.

My next task was to decide between white and dark meat. Tasters rejected all the stews made with breast meat (dry as dust no matter what I tried), but the thigh meat was very moist and meaty. Thighs are sold in two forms—boneless, skinless and bone-in, skin-on. Without skin to protect the meat during browning, the boneless, skinless thighs turned tough and stringy. The stews made with bone-in, skin-on thighs had moist, tender meat and a richer overall flavor. To avoid a mouthful of rubbery chicken skin, I removed it after browning without sacrificing any flavor.

Unlike tough cuts of meat, which typically need as many as 12 hours to become tender, chicken will overcook—even in a slow cooker. Many recipes called for eight hours of cooking on the low setting, but this left me with chicken so soft it literally fell off the bone. I found that six hours was a much better option, making this recipe more suitable to a day when you're around the house as opposed to a workday.

Although the chicken tasted great, the long, slow cooking was taking a toll on the seasonings; the curry flavor had faded, and not a hint of sweetness remained in the raisins and mango. Bumping up the curry to a whopping 2 tablespoons was an easy fix, but I had to be really creative about the fruit. Simmering it for six hours left it bloated and bland. I could have added the fruit near the end of the cooking time, but I didn't want to fuss with the slow cooker as the chicken cooked. On a whim, I swapped the mango and raisins for a jar of mango chutney, which added just the right amount of sweet-tart flavor.

With a bowl of steamed rice and the full array of country captain garnishes (nuts, coconut, fruit) before me, I was more than ready to dig into this new addition to my slow-cooker repertoire.

–Stephanie Alleyne

This Georgia chicken stew is traditionally garnished with toasted nuts, shredded coconut, and diced fresh fruit—and always served with rice.

SLOW-COOKER COUNTRY CAPTAIN CHICKEN SERVES 6 TO 8

Basic curry powder turns bitter after six hours in a slow cooker, so stick with Madras curry powder (see page 29). By tradition, this dish can be garnished with any or all of the following: sliced toasted almonds, shredded coconut, diced Granny Smith apples, and diced banana. Steamed long-grain rice is a must. Unlike beef, which can be browned and chilled the night before it goes into the slow cooker, once the chicken is browned it should be cooked right away.

- **8 bone-in, skin-on chicken thighs (about 4 pounds), excess fat trimmed**
- **Salt and pepper**
- **1 tablespoon vegetable oil**
- **2 onions, chopped coarse**
- **1 green bell pepper, seeded and chopped coarse**
- **1 cup low-sodium chicken broth**
- **1 (14.5-ounce) can diced tomatoes**
- **5 tablespoons tomato paste**
- **1 (9-ounce) jar chutney, such as Major Grey's**
- **4 garlic cloves, minced**
- **2 tablespoons Madras curry powder**
- **1½ teaspoons paprika**
- **1 teaspoon dried thyme**
- **¼ teaspoon cayenne**

1. Season chicken with salt and pepper. Heat oil in large skillet over medium-high heat until shimmering. Add chicken and brown on both sides, about 10 minutes. Slightly cool chicken on plate, remove and discard skin, and transfer chicken to slow-cooker insert.

2. Discard all but 1 tablespoon fat from skillet and return pan to medium-high heat. Add onions, bell pepper, and ½ teaspoon salt and cook until vegetables soften, about 5 minutes. Add broth, tomatoes, and tomato paste and, using wooden spoon, scrape up browned bits from pan bottom. Simmer until thick and smooth, about 2 minutes. Off heat, stir in chutney, garlic, curry powder, paprika, thyme, and cayenne. Pour mixture into slow-cooker insert, submerging chicken in sauce.

3. Cover and cook on low until chicken is tender, about 6 hours. Turn off slow cooker, remove lid, and gently stir sauce to recombine. Replace lid and let stand for about 15 minutes to thicken sauce before serving.

DOUBLE DUTY
Made from mangos and raisins, jarred chutney not only makes a great substitute for the real thing (the fruit doesn't fare well in the slow cooker), it also helps to thicken the sauce.

The American Table: A Georgia Classic

Although some sources claim this recipe was invented in the American South, most food historians believe this vibrant stew was introduced to the residents of Savannah by British sea captains who had traveled along the spice route during the late 18th or early 19th century. In any case, the dish has its roots in India. The first printed recipe I could find appeared in *Miss Leslie's New Cookery Book* (1857), and from the 20th century onward country captain became a staple in many Southern and all-purpose cookbooks, including the original *Joy of Cooking* (1931). President Franklin D. Roosevelt is said to have been a fan of this dish, having enjoyed it during his frequent visits to Warm Springs, Ga., for rest and recuperation. **–S.A.**

Foolproof Deviled Eggs

I really like deviled eggs but hate the greenish tinge that the yolks sometimes get. What am I doing wrong? –Susanna Huber, via e-mail

Perfect deviled eggs start with a foolproof cooking method and end with a filling that has carefully balanced sweet, tart, and spicy flavors.

Sometimes the simplest recipes are the trickiest to execute, and I've made more than my fair share of deviled eggs with greenish yolks and bland fillings. I wanted to bulletproof this recipe, and I figured I would start with the most difficult task: hard-cooking the eggs.

There's no way to watch the egg cook under its shell, and the test kitchen's fail-safe tool for checking doneness—the instant-read thermometer—isn't an option. Most recipes simmer the eggs for a specified period, but they tend to turn out greenish eggs that look like something out of Dr. Seuss. After some research, I learned that the green color appears when the iron in the yolk reacts with the sulfur in the white to produce ferrous sulfide. Prolonged heating is the culprit.

This led me to wonder if all those not-so-foolproof recipes were falling down over the definition of "simmer." I found that eggs cooked for 15 minutes at a hard simmer (might as well call it a boil) overcook, while those cooked for 15 minutes at a gentle simmer don't. To remove the guesswork, in the test kitchen we start the eggs in cold water, bring the water to a boil, then turn off the heat and put the cover on the pan. The residual heat cooks the eggs, which are done in exactly 10 minutes. Plunging the eggs into ice water stops the cooking process and prevents the green ring from forming.

With the eggs cooked, it was time to mash the yolks and season them with the usual suspects: mayonnaise, vinegar, and mustard. Plain mayonnaise is too bland, but Miracle Whip (called for in many recipes) has an odd sweet-tart flavor that tasters did not love. Instead, mixing a little sour cream with plain mayonnaise added that much-needed punch.

As for mustard, plain yellow was too bland, but Dijon was too potent; spicy brown mustard (like Gulden's) was a good compromise. Fancier recipes use cider vinegar or even balsamic vinegar, but I found that plain old distilled white vinegar produced quite enough pucker without adding any distracting flavors. Now my deviled eggs were truly foolproof.

–Meredith Butcher

DEVILED EGGS

MAKES 1 DOZEN FILLED HALVES

To center the yolks, turn the carton of eggs on its side in the refrigerator the day before you plan to cook the eggs (see page 28 for details). You'll find tips for peeling hard-cooked eggs on page 29.

- **6 large eggs**
- **2 tablespoons mayonnaise**
- **1 tablespoon sour cream**
- **1/2 teaspoon distilled white vinegar**
- **1/2 teaspoon spicy brown mustard (such as Gulden's)**
- **1/4 teaspoon sugar**
- **1/8 teaspoon salt**
- **1/8 teaspoon pepper**

1. Place eggs in medium saucepan, cover with 1 inch of water, and bring to boil over high heat. Remove pan from heat, cover, and let stand 10 minutes. Meanwhile, fill medium bowl with 1 quart water and 1 dozen ice cubes. Pour off water from saucepan and gently shake pan back and forth to crack shells. Transfer eggs to ice water with slotted spoon and let cool 5 minutes.

2. Peel eggs and slice in half lengthwise. Transfer yolks to fine-mesh sieve and use spatula to press them through sieve and into bowl. Add remaining ingredients, mashing mixture against sides of bowl until smooth.

3. Arrange whites on serving platter and fill with yolk mixture, mounding filling about ½ inch above whites. Serve immediately.

How to FILL DEVILED EGGS

Getting the filling into the cooked egg white can be a messy ordeal. A pastry bag fitted with a large star tip makes beautiful deviled eggs, but who has this sort of equipment at home? We found that you can "pipe" the filling through a large plastic storage bag. Force the egg yolk mixture into one corner of the bag and twist the bag to keep the filling in the corner. Using scissors, snip off about 1/2 inch of the corner of the bag. Squeeze the bag to pipe the filling through the hole into the egg whites.

Make Ahead

You can make the deviled eggs up to 2 days ahead. Wrap the peeled egg-white halves tightly with a double layer of plastic wrap and place the filling in a zipper-lock plastic bag (squeezing out all the air). Refrigerate until ready to fill and serve.

Reader Recipes

Although paprika is the most common garnish for deviled eggs, several readers wrote to us with more creative ideas.

THAI DELIGHT
Kathleen Hulsy
Biddeford, Maine
Top eggs with a mixture of chopped cilantro, sliced cooked shrimp, and minced fresh ginger.

IT'S ITALIAN
Robyn Cavallaro
Easton, Pa.
Top eggs with red pepper flakes, capers, and minced fresh parsley.

CHICKEN COOP
Michaela Rosenthal
Woodland Hills, Calif.
Blot sun-dried tomatoes dry on paper towels and then mince. Top eggs with a mixture of sun-dried tomatoes and chopped cooked chicken and sprinkle with smoked paprika.

FIESTA
Angela Buchanan
Boulder, Colo.
Stir 1 teaspoon adobo sauce from canned chipotle chiles into yolk mixture. Sprinkle eggs with crumbled cooked bacon and finely chopped scallions.

Easy Pasta Primavera

I like to order pasta primavera at Italian restaurants, but when I try to make it at home the sink fills up with pots and pans. Is there a simpler way? After all, it's just noodles and vegetables. –Judith Crawford, Las Vegas, Nev.

There's a reason why pasta primavera—a mixture of vegetables, cream sauce, tomato sauce, and pasta—is a restaurant classic. The average recipe requires two hours, six pots, eight vegetables, and some fancy knife work best left to the pros. What's more, the vegetables have to be cooked twice, first blanched in water to set their color and then sautéed in butter. The results are great, but this elaborate procedure seems worth the effort only if you're getting $20 per bowl.

My first task was to trim the ingredient list, and the vegetables were the obvious target. After dismissing fennel and broccoli (too overpowering), artichokes (too fussy), and snow peas (better in a stir-fry), I settled on asparagus, zucchini, and frozen peas. This list is pretty subjective (I rejected green beans because I don't really like them), but my tasters were happy, and the prep work these three vegetables require is minimal.

I wanted to limit my recipe to two pans and just one cooking method for the vegetables, either boiling or sautéing. This effort met with failure after failure. I tried browning the vegetables in a skillet and then adding them to the pasta (too crispy), sautéing and then finishing them in the cream sauce (limp and lifeless), and boiling them in the pot of water I would eventually use to cook the pasta (fishing around the pot for cooked vegetables was a bore).

I wondered if I could simply cook the vegetables in the pot as the pasta cooked. Once the pasta was nearly done, I put the slowest-cooking vegetable, the asparagus, in the pot. Next came the zucchini and, last, the peas. The pasta and vegetables now finished cooking at the same time. All I had to do was drain the pot and marry them to the sauce.

In the original recipe, two separate sauces—a garlicky mushroom and tomato sauce and a creamy cheese sauce—are combined with the pasta and vegetables at the last minute. I wanted to collapse these two sauces (each made in a separate pan) into one sauce made in one pan. After browning mushrooms and onions in butter, I added garlic, tomatoes, and cream. The sauce seemed a bit thin and the flavors were flat. Grated Parmesan added body and fresh basil and lemon juice brightened the taste.

In the end, my recipe for pasta primavera called for just two pots, 30 minutes, and a staff of one. And it cost a whole lot less than $20 per bowl.

–Katie Henderson

This bowl of pasta might look fancy, but it can be on the table in about half an hour.

PASTA PRIMAVERA

SERVES 4

The test kitchen prefers the hearty strands of egg-enriched fettuccine usually sold in 12-ounce boxes (see page 28). We found that you need to salt the water used to cook the pasta and vegetables quite heavily to make sure they emerge nicely seasoned.

- 2 tablespoons unsalted butter
- 1 small onion, chopped fine
- 8 ounces white mushrooms, quartered
- Salt and pepper
- 2 garlic cloves, minced
- 1 (14.5-ounce) can diced tomatoes, drained
- 1 cup heavy cream
- 12 ounces egg-enriched dried fettuccine (see note above)
- 1 pound asparagus, tough ends discarded, spears cut diagonally into 1-inch pieces
- 1 medium zucchini, cut into ½-inch dice
- 1 cup frozen peas
- ½ cup grated Parmesan cheese, plus extra for serving
- 1½ tablespoons lemon juice
- ¼ cup thinly sliced basil

1. Bring 4 quarts water to boil in large pot for cooking pasta. Meanwhile, melt butter in large skillet over medium heat until foaming. Add onion, mushrooms, ½ teaspoon salt, and ½ teaspoon pepper and cook until soft and browned, about 8 minutes. Add garlic and cook until fragrant, about 1 minute. Stir in tomatoes and cream, increase heat to high, bring to boil, and remove pan from heat.

2. As sauce cooks, add 2 tablespoons salt and pasta to boiling water and cook until just beginning to soften, about 6 minutes. Add asparagus to pot and cook for 1 minute. Add zucchini and cook for 2 minutes. Add peas and cook until pasta is al dente, about 1 minute.

3. Drain pasta and vegetables and return to pot. Toss in cream sauce, cheese, lemon juice, and basil and season with salt and pepper. Serve, passing extra cheese at table.

Old-Fashioned Roast Pork

Having grown up in Kansas City, my grandmother always served pork roast for Sunday dinner. I remember the meat was really succulent, with a rich, full pork flavor. I've tried to re-create her recipe, but my pork loin turns out fairly bland. Can you help? –Cathy Kurtz, Superior, Colo.

Secrets to OLD-FASHIONED FLAVOR

Boneless pork shoulder, or Boston butt, costs as little as $1.50 per pound, but it takes some work to transform this cheap cut into a memorable meal. This roast is usually sold in netting. Once you remove the netting at home, the roast will open up and you can start its transformation.

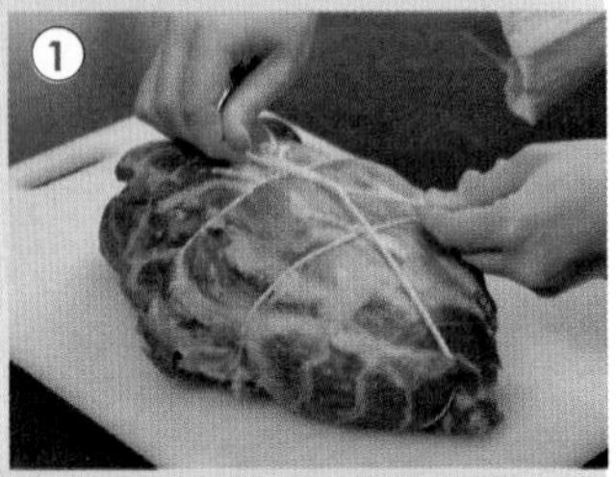

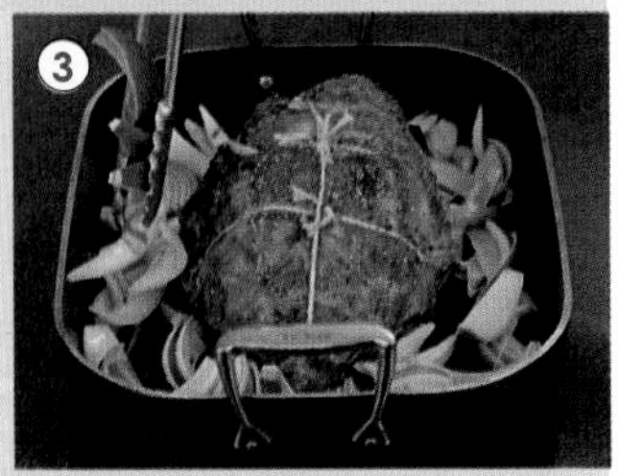

1. TRIM AND TIE
Trim any excess fat, leaving behind an 1/8-inch-thick layer. Tie the trimmed roast tightly into a uniform shape, with 3 pieces of butcher's twine running around the width of the roast and one piece running around its length.

2. RUB WITH HERBS
Rub a mixture of rosemary, sage, fennel seeds, garlic, salt, and pepper over the roast.

3. COOK FOR A LONG TIME
Roast the pork for 3 hours, add onion wedges, and continue to roast until the meat is extremely tender, 3 1/2 to 4 hours more.

The pork your grandmother cooked had much more fat than the "other white meat" now available in supermarkets. Pork today is about 30 percent lower in fat than it was 20 years ago. Fat gives meat flavor and keeps it moist during cooking; with so little fat, typical supermarket pork tends to be bland and dry. Although a good sauce can help, today's pork loin will never be as flavorful or succulent as your grandmother's.

Because the loin is especially lean, my first thought was to try roasting a fattier cut (it's possible that your grandmother was on this track as well). The obvious choice was pork shoulder, the classic roast for barbecued pulled pork. The shoulder is nice and fatty, so the meat is especially flavorful and moist. And the $10 price tag for a large roast that can feed eight people is hard to resist. Could I just "barbecue" this cut indoors, without the usual spices or smoke, and make something appropriate for Sunday dinner?

My first task was to choose a specific roast. A pork shoulder is massive, weighing between 14 and 20 pounds. Because of its size, supermarkets cut the shoulder in half to make it more manageable. The upper portion is sold as either a pork shoulder roast or a Boston butt and weighs 6 to 8 pounds. The lower portion is called the picnic roast and runs about the same size. In side-by-side tests, we preferred the richer flavor and slightly more tender texture of the Boston butt.

Following the lead of barbecue pitmasters, I roasted a dozen Boston butts using different combinations of temperature and time. I found that seven hours (yes, seven hours) in a 300-degree oven produced meat that was nearly perfect. The connective tissue melted and converted to gelatin, making the meat very tender, while the melting fat kept the meat moist. The results I got when I tried to speed up the process by using a hotter oven simply were not as good. The only problem was that the roast could not be carved into neat slices. What I had was more like shreds and chunks, and it was hard to resist the urge to cover them up with barbecue sauce. But I wanted neat slices that I could place on a serving platter.

I tried letting the roast rest longer than the usual 20 or 30 minutes, but even an hour wasn't sufficient. The roast still wouldn't carve neatly and still shed a lot of juice. In frustration, I ended up refrigerating one of my unsliced roasts at the end of a long day in the test kitchen. The next morning, I sliced the cold roast effortlessly into clean slices, poured a bit of liquid over the meat, and warmed the meat in the oven. The roast not only looked better in neat slices but tasted better, too, because the juices had become completely redistributed throughout the meat; nothing was lost to the cutting board. OK—maybe your grandmother didn't have to roast her pork on one day and serve it on the next, but this isn't your grandmother's pork. This meat is so juicy and succulent it's definitely worth the wait.

Now that I had my roasting technique, I turned my attention to flavoring the roast. I

Our pork roasts for almost seven hours and requires an overnight stay in the fridge to facilitate carving—but it's worth the wait.

INSIDE THE TEST KITCHEN: Chill, Then Slice

Shredded pork shoulder is great off the barbecue, but we wanted intact, company-friendly slices of pork that could be served for a Sunday or holiday dinner. Author Eva Katz found that if she cut into the pork immediately after roasting, it fell apart into shreds. To avoid this problem, she chilled the cooked pork roast overnight in the refrigerator, making the job of cutting thin slices the next day incredibly easy.

thought garlic and herbs would be a good match, and tasters agreed, favoring garlic, rosemary, sage, and fennel seeds.

Because I was using liquid to moisten the slices of meat as they reheated, I developed a simple sauce that could be used both to flavor the meat as it reheated and to serve at the table. A classic combination of onions and apples was a nice counterpoint to the rich flavors of the meat. Clearly, the shoulder is the best choice you can make to get old-time flavor out of today's "other white meat." **–Eva Katz**

OLD-FASHIONED ROAST PORK SERVES 6 TO 8, WITH ENOUGH LEFTOVERS FOR 4 CUBAN SANDWICHES

A heavy, deep-sided (3-inch) roasting pan is the best choice for this recipe, but a shallow broiler pan also works well. If you plan to make the Cuban sandwiches (see recipe at right), slice off and reserve a half-pound piece of the roast at the beginning of step 4; if wrapped tightly, it will keep in the refrigerator for several days.

- **1 (6-pound) boneless pork shoulder roast (Boston butt)**
- **3 garlic cloves, minced**
- **2 teaspoons freshly cracked pepper**
- **1 1/2 teaspoons salt**
- **1 tablespoon chopped fresh rosemary**
- **1 tablespoon chopped fresh sage**
- **1 tablespoon fennel seeds, roughly chopped**
- **2 large red onions, cut into 1-inch wedges**
- **1 tablespoon vegetable oil (if necessary)**
- **1 cup apple cider**
- **1/4 cup apple jelly**
- **2 tablespoons cider vinegar**

1. Adjust oven rack to lower-middle position and heat oven to 300 degrees. Trim outer fat from pork, leaving 1/8-inch-thick layer. Combine garlic, pepper, salt, rosemary, sage, and fennel seeds in small bowl. Following photos on page 12, tie pork roast tightly into uniform shape. Rub with herb mixture.

2. Transfer to roasting pan and cook 3 hours. Scatter onion wedges around meat, tossing onions in pan drippings to coat. (If roast has not produced any juices, toss onions with oil.) Continue roasting until meat is extremely tender and skewer inserted into center meets no resistance, 3 1/2 to 4 hours. (Check pan juices every hour to make sure they have not evaporated. If necessary, add 2 cups water to pan and stir browned bits into water.)

3. Transfer roast to large baking dish, place onions in medium bowl, and pour pan drippings into liquid measuring cup, adding enough water to measure 1 1/2 cups. Allow all to cool 30 minutes, cover with plastic wrap, and refrigerate overnight.

4. One hour before serving, adjust oven rack to middle position and heat oven to 300 degrees. Cut cold meat into 1/4-inch slices and overlap in large baking dish. Spoon fat layer off drippings (discard fat) and transfer drippings and reserved onions to medium saucepan. Add cider, jelly, and vinegar and bring to boil over medium-high heat, then reduce to simmer. Spoon 1/2 cup simmering sauce over pork slices and cover baking dish with foil. Place in oven and heat until very hot, 30 to 40 minutes. Meanwhile, continue reducing sauce until dark and thickened, 10 to 15 minutes (reheat mixture just before serving pork). Serve pork, spooning onion mixture over meat or passing at table.

What to Do with Leftover Roast Pork: Cuban Sandwiches

How do you re-create this sandwich-shop special at home—without a sandwich press?

Made with a combination of roast pork, ham, Swiss cheese, and pickles, and sometimes mustard and mayonnaise, south Florida's most popular sandwich, the Cubano, is brushed with melted butter, pressed, and grilled. The bread should be golden brown and crisp and the filling hot, its ingredients melded together.

Cubanos are traditionally made with Cuban bread; submarine shaped and often made with lard, this bread browns and crisps beautifully. In hopes of finding a suitable substitute, I tested every type of sub roll and baguette-style bread sold in local supermarkets. Unfortunately, they were either too dense and bready, even when compressed, or too light and airy, in which case they turned crackery when pressed and grilled.

Forgoing the traditional shape, I tried round rolls and had more success. The best was the slightly sweet potato roll, which crisped up beautifully while still maintaining some of its thick, bready chew. The sandwiches were so popular in the test kitchen that tasters actually looked forward to these "leftovers."

–Eva Katz

Roast pork lives again in this classic sandwich from south Florida.

No Press, No Problem

Cubanos are traditionally cooked under a heavy cast-iron sandwich press that heats the sandwich from the top as it compresses the contents.
To get the effects of a press, we weight the sandwiches with a preheated Dutch oven.

CUBAN SANDWICHES SERVES 4

To ensure very thin slices of pork, slice the leftover roast straight from the refrigerator. Arnold or Freihofer's potato rolls are our first choices for this recipe, but Kaiser rolls can be used as a substitute.

- **1/3 cup diced dill pickles**
- **1/3 cup diced jarred banana peppers (see page 29)**
- **4 potato sandwich rolls**
- **2 tablespoons mayonnaise**
- **1 1/2 tablespoons yellow mustard, such as French's**
- **1/4 pound thinly sliced baked ham, preferably Virginia or Black Forest**
- **1/2 pound cold roast pork, sliced thin**
- **1/4 pound thinly sliced Swiss cheese**
- **3 tablespoons unsalted butter, melted**

1. Combine pickles and peppers in small bowl. Split rolls in half; spread top half with mayonnaise and bottom half with mustard. Layer ham, roast pork, pickle mixture, and cheese onto bottom half, finishing with cheese on top. Set tops of rolls in place and press down to flatten sandwiches.

2. Heat large nonstick skillet over medium-low heat for 4 minutes. Meanwhile, heat large pot or Dutch oven over medium-low heat for 4 minutes. Brush tops of sandwiches with melted butter and place in skillet buttered side down. Brush bottoms of rolls with remaining butter and use preheated pot to compress sandwiches for 15 to 20 seconds (see photo at left). Cook (keeping pot on sandwiches but not pressing down) until first side is golden brown, 3 to 5 minutes. Remove pot, flip sandwiches over, replace pot on top of sandwiches, and cook until golden brown, 3 to 4 minutes. Serve immediately.

FOOD FACT: *Asparagus is a member of the lily family. Like other members of this family, it is a perennial that will produce "flowers" (the edible spears) once a year, often for several decades. But don't expect instant gratification with this vegetable. The seeds are usually started in a greenhouse, and it takes one year for the plant to produce spears.*

Roasted Asparagus

A super-hot oven coaxes maximum flavor from this spring staple.

A garlicky marinade seasons this asparagus, which is roasted along with yellow peppers and shallots.

No matter how you cook it, asparagus almost always looks good. Making it taste good is another story. Most cooks boil or steam asparagus, methods that are apt to wash away its sweet, nutty flavor. I wanted to try roasting, a dry-heat cooking method likely to enhance rather than diminish the essential flavor of this popular vegetable.

Maximizing the flavor of asparagus, I discovered, requires more than baking at modest temperatures—it has to sizzle. When I roasted asparagus in a moderate oven, it ended up wizened. I had better results with a quick blast in 450-degree heat. During my tests, I kept raising the rack until I reached the highest (and hottest) place in the oven. At first, I was afraid the delicate tips would scorch, but instead they caramelized and turned crispy.

I had the best luck with a heavy-duty rimmed baking sheet (a roomy broiler pan works in a pinch), which gets very hot, very quickly. A pan with a shallow rim is also important. When I used a roasting pan with deeper sides, the moisture shed by the asparagus did not evaporate as quickly and the spears steamed.

Having nailed my technique, I wanted to add some other flavors—and vegetables—to make things more interesting. A garlicky marinade seasoned the asparagus perfectly. As for vegetables, I had good results with mushrooms, bell peppers, cherry tomatoes, shallots, and sweet onion, all of which cooked at the same rate as the asparagus. Some acidity (in the form of lemon juice or vinegar) punched up the flavors. Here at last was asparagus that tasted as good as it looked.

–Stephanie Alleyne

ROASTED ASPARAGUS WITH PEPPERS AND SHALLOTS SERVES 4

- 3 tablespoons olive oil
- 2 garlic cloves, minced
- 1 teaspoon chopped fresh thyme
- Salt and pepper
- 1 pound medium asparagus, tough ends trimmed
- 1 yellow or red bell pepper, sliced thin
- 4 shallots, sliced thin
- 1 tablespoon red wine vinegar

1. Adjust oven rack to upper position and heat oven to 450 degrees. Stir oil, garlic, thyme, ½ teaspoon salt, and ¼ teaspoon pepper together in large bowl. Spread asparagus across rimmed baking sheet or broiler pan; drizzle with half of garlic mixture and toss to coat. Rearrange asparagus in single layer. Combine bell pepper and shallots with remaining garlic mixture in bowl and toss to coat. Scatter pepper and shallots evenly over asparagus.

2. Roast until asparagus begins to soften and turns bright green with some dark brown edges, about 10 minutes. Drizzle with vinegar and continue roasting until asparagus is softened and bell pepper and shallots are just beginning to turn golden brown around edges, about 5 minutes. Toss vegetables, season with salt and pepper, and transfer to platter. Serve.

ROASTED ASPARAGUS WITH MUSHROOMS

SERVES 4

Use a vegetable peeler to remove paper-thin shavings from a block of Parmesan.

- 3 tablespoons olive oil
- 2 garlic cloves, minced
- ½ teaspoon chopped fresh thyme
- Salt and pepper
- 1 pound medium asparagus, tough ends trimmed
- 10 ounces white mushrooms, stemmed and quartered
- 1 tablespoon lemon juice
- ½ cup shaved Parmesan cheese

1. Adjust oven rack to upper position and heat oven to 450 degrees. Stir oil, garlic, thyme, ½ teaspoon salt, and ¼ teaspoon pepper together in large bowl. Spread asparagus across rimmed baking sheet or broiler pan; drizzle with half of garlic mixture and toss to coat. Rearrange asparagus in single layer. Combine mushrooms with remaining garlic mixture and toss to coat. Scatter mushrooms over asparagus.

2. Roast until asparagus begins to soften and turns bright green with some dark brown edges, about 10 minutes. Drizzle with lemon juice and continue roasting until asparagus is softened and mushrooms are deeply browned, about 5 minutes. Toss vegetables, season with salt and pepper, transfer to platter, and sprinkle with Parmesan. Serve.

ROASTED ASPARAGUS WITH SWEET ONION

SERVES 4

Any sweet onion (see page 23) will work in this recipe.

- 3 tablespoons olive oil
- 1 tablespoon honey
- 2 garlic cloves, minced
- Salt and pepper
- 1 pound medium asparagus, tough ends trimmed
- ½ Vidalia onion, sliced thin
- 1 tablespoon balsamic vinegar

1. Adjust oven rack to upper position and heat oven to 450 degrees. Stir oil, honey, garlic, ½ teaspoon salt, and ¼ teaspoon pepper together in large bowl. Spread asparagus across rimmed baking sheet or broiler pan; drizzle with half of garlic mixture and toss to coat. Rearrange asparagus in single layer. Combine onion with remaining garlic mixture in bowl and toss to coat. Scatter onion evenly over asparagus.

2. Roast until asparagus begins to soften and turns bright green with some dark brown edges, about 10 minutes. Drizzle with vinegar and continue roasting until asparagus is softened and onion just begins to turn golden brown around edges, about 5 minutes. Toss vegetables, season with salt and pepper, and transfer to platter. Serve.

ROASTED ASPARAGUS WITH MEDITERRANEAN FLAVORS SERVES 4

- 3 tablespoons olive oil
- 2 garlic cloves, minced
- 2 tablespoons chopped fresh parsley
- Salt and pepper
- 1 pound medium asparagus, tough ends trimmed
- 2 cups grape or cherry tomatoes, halved
- ½ cup kalamata olives, pitted and chopped coarse
- 1 tablespoon lemon juice

1. Adjust oven rack to upper position and heat oven to 450 degrees. Stir oil, garlic, parsley, ½ teaspoon salt, and ¼ teaspoon pepper together in large bowl. Spread asparagus across rimmed baking sheet or broiler pan; drizzle with half of garlic mixture and toss to coat. Rearrange asparagus in single layer. Combine tomatoes and olives with remaining garlic mixture in bowl and toss to coat. Scatter tomatoes and olives evenly over asparagus.

2. Roast until asparagus begins to soften and turns bright green with some dark brown edges, about 10 minutes. Drizzle with lemon juice and continue roasting until asparagus is softened and tomatoes begin to release their juices, about 5 minutes. Toss vegetables, season with salt and pepper, and transfer to platter. Serve.

Getting this rice dish off the stovetop—and into the oven—allows heat to attack the pot from all sides, not just the bottom. The result is perfectly cooked jambalaya.

Perfect Shrimp Jambalaya

I'm a New Orleans native, but jambalaya has never been a favorite with me. It's usually a gummy glob of overcooked mush—it's very hard to get the rice cooked properly. Can you help? –Holly Collins, Ashland City, Tenn.

Packed to the gills with shrimp, sausage, rice, and vegetables, jambalaya is the cream of the one-pot crop. But what makes it so attractive—its hodgepodge of textures and flavors—is also what makes it such a challenge to prepare. Whether the rice is too crunchy, the shrimp is too chewy, or everything is just plain overcooked, it can be tough to juggle all these ingredients in just one pot.

After experimenting with various cooking techniques, I found that the ingredients had to be cooked in stages to ensure that each would have optimal flavor and texture. I first rendered the sausage (andouille was tasters' favorite for its smoky, spicy kick) to release its flavorful fat. With the browned sausage set aside, I added onion, bell pepper, and celery as well as garlic to the pot. Once they released their aromas and softened, I added rice and then stirred in tomato paste, diced tomatoes, herbs, and chicken broth. Going against the advice in many recipes, I added the shrimp last to keep them from overcooking. So far so good, except for the flavor of the shrimp. They tasted as bland and boiled as cocktail shrimp, and they contributed no flavor to the dish.

To develop more seafood flavor, I started by replacing the chicken broth with bottled clam juice. My tasters loved its subtle but sweet brininess. Still, the shrimp themselves remained awfully boring. To pump up their flavor, I tried browning them in the rendered sausage fat. When I added the shrimp to the jambalaya just prior to serving, their flavor was much improved, but they were a little rubbery. After a couple more fruitless tests, a colleague suggested searing the shrimp prior to peeling them. This made sense—restaurant chefs often use flavorful shrimp shells to make stock—and it turned out to be the perfect solution. The shells gave the jambalaya a more complex shrimp flavor, and they kept the flesh of the shrimp from scorching in the pan.

–Jeremy Sauer

SHRIMP JAMBALAYA

SERVES 4 TO 6

When shopping, look for shrimp that are still in their shells. If you cannot find andouille sausage, substitute an equal amount of chorizo.

- **2 teaspoons vegetable oil**
- **8 ounces andouille sausage, halved lengthwise, then cut into 1/4-inch half-moons**
- **1 pound large (31 to 40 per pound) shell-on shrimp**
- **1 onion, chopped fine**
- **1 celery rib, chopped fine**
- **1 green bell pepper, chopped fine**
- **5 garlic cloves, minced**
- **1 1/2 cups long-grain white rice**
- **1 tablespoon tomato paste**
- **1 teaspoon salt**
- **1/2 teaspoon minced fresh thyme**
- **1 (14.5-ounce) can diced tomatoes, drained, with 1/4 cup juice reserved**
- **2 (8-ounce) bottles clam juice**
- **1 bay leaf**
- **2 scallions, sliced thin**

1. Adjust oven rack to middle position and heat oven to 325 degrees.

2. Heat oil in Dutch oven over medium-high heat until shimmering. Add sausage and cook until browned, 3 to 5 minutes. Using slotted spoon, transfer sausage to plate lined with paper towel. Add shrimp to pot and cook until shells are lightly browned on both sides, about 1 minute per side. Transfer shrimp to large bowl and refrigerate.

3. Reduce heat to medium and add onion, celery, bell pepper, and garlic to pot. Cook, stirring occasionally, until vegetables have softened, 5 to 10 minutes. Add rice, tomato paste, salt, and thyme and cook until rice is coated with fat, about 1 minute. Stir in tomatoes, reserved tomato juice, clam juice, bay leaf, and sausage. Place square of aluminum foil directly on surface of rice. Bring to boil, cover pot, transfer to oven, and bake until rice is almost tender and most of liquid is absorbed, about 20 minutes.

4. Meanwhile, peel shrimp (devein if desired) and discard shells. Remove pot from oven, lift off aluminum foil, and gently stir in peeled shrimp and any accumulated juices. Replace foil and lid, return to oven, and cook until rice is fully tender and shrimp are cooked through, about 5 minutes. Remove from oven, discard foil and bay leaf, and fold in scallions. Serve.

Foiled Again!

Baking the jambalaya in the oven ensures that the rice won't scorch, as often happens when this dish is prepared on top of the stove. A great form of insurance against any persistently crunchy grains of rice is a sheet of aluminum foil, placed directly on the surface of the rice (and pressed against the sides of the pot) before the jambalaya goes into the oven. The foil holds in steam and heat, ensuring that every grain of rice cooks perfectly. And, whatever you do, don't stir the rice as it cooks—this will only make it gluey.

I'm Looking for a Recipe

READERS HELP READERS FIND RECIPES

We've Got Mail

Several readers sent us recipes in response to the request for Australian oat cookies (October/November 2005 issue). We really liked the letter and recipe sent by Alison White (at right). For the test kitchen's notes on this recipe (with more details on cooking times and procedures), go to **www.cookscountry.com** and click **Looking for a Recipe.** You'll find dozens more recipes submitted by readers who responded to recipe requests in other issues of *Cook's Country.*

ANZAC BISCUITS **Alison White** Fayetteville, N.C.

The Australian oat cookie recipe requested in the October/November 2005 issue sounds like ANZAC biscuits. I grew up in New Zealand, and these cookies were a staple in our home. They date back to WWI, when wives and mothers shipped them overseas to their loved ones. (ANZAC stands for Australian New Zealand Army Corps.) When my husband was deployed to Iraq, I made them for him, as any good New Zealand wife would.

- 3/4 **cup flour**
- 3/4 **cup sugar**
- 1 **cup unsweetened coconut**
- 1 **cup rolled oats**
- 7 **tablespoons butter**
- 1 **tablespoon golden syrup***
- 1/2 **teaspoon baking soda**
- 2 **tablespoons boiling water**

INSTRUCTIONS: Mix flour, sugar, coconut, and oats together. Melt butter and golden syrup in medium pot. Dissolve baking soda in boiling water and add to butter and golden syrup. Remove from heat and add dry ingredients. Place spoonfuls on greased tray. Bake for 15 to 20 minutes at 350 degrees.

*Note: Light corn syrup can be used in place of golden syrup.

Potluck Pie

I used to attend a monthly church potluck, where all the women would try to outdo each other. At every single potluck, someone would bring a fluffy lemon or pineapple dessert with a graham cracker crust and crumbs sprinkled on the top. I think these desserts were made with Jell-O or marshmallows. I'm not sure if there was whipped cream, but I do know the desserts had to be refrigerated. My mother-in-law is 91, and I'd like to surprise her with a blast from the past. I think it would cheer her up immensely.

Arlene Calkins
Salt Lake City, Utah

Honeycomb Cake

I'm looking for a recipe called honeycomb cake for a friend. It's flavored with honey and has a texture similar to a honeycomb. She said it's a Jewish recipe, and I have looked through dozens of Jewish cookbooks and even Jewish cooking Web sites without any luck.

Emily Whitfield
Chaffee, Mo.

Sweet Potato Pudding

When I was growing up, my grandmother made sweet potato pudding every Thanksgiving. She cooked it in an 8-inch-square glass pan, and the servings were cut into squares the thickness of brownies. It was similar to sweet potato pie in taste, maybe a little sweeter. There was no crust, but the bottom and edges were a little thicker than the rest of it. It was so good! I'd love to serve sweet potato pudding to my family next Thanksgiving.

Laurel Uhlar
Norfolk, Va.

Bolo Bread

Many years ago (I am now 85), my mother made a sweet bread called bolo bread. It was baked in a Turk's head pan and was made with cinnamon, sugar, and nuts.

Ed Plummer
Via e-mail

Frosted Ginger Cookies

I live in Kansas City, and there is an ice cream shop called Murray's in Westport that makes these delicious ginger cookies that are soft and have a brown sugar, cream cheese, and maple frosting. I used to buy them once a week when I was pregnant. Now, two children later, I rarely get there—and they are quite pricey. I would like to make them at home.

Susan Black
Leawood, Kan.

Potato Rolls

My mother passed away last year and I cannot find her recipe for potato rolls. Those rolls were so delicious. Does anyone have a recipe? All I remember is standing by the oven as a kid with a knife and butter, waiting for those rolls to come out of the oven.

Carol Walker
Philadelphia, Pa.

A Taste of Yugoslavia

I have been looking for a recipe for *leskovačka mućkalica* for the past 15 years. We were in Yugoslavia in 1991. It seemed to be the national dish, as it appeared on every menu. It is a spicy pork or veal stew with tomatoes and onions and a little sour cream on top. It was fabulous, and I'm dying to get the recipe. I've spent hours looking for it on the Internet to no avail.

Linda Walker
Ojai, Calif.

Potato Candy

My grandmother, long gone now, used to make a candy with potatoes back when she lived on a farm in Emporia, Kan. My dad said you'd never know this candy came from potatoes. I'd love to surprise him with a batch, but I don't know where to begin as it seems like this recipe has become extinct. I was hoping someone could help.

Monique Cuvelier
Burlington, Mass.

Old-Fashioned Buckwheat Cakes

I grew up on a farm in Pennsylvania in the late 1930s. It was a rare morning that we didn't have what I now call old-fashioned buckwheat cakes. There are a few restaurants in northeastern Pennsylvania that still serve the real thing, but they guard the recipes with their lives.

Howard Cain
Via e-mail

1950s Butter Cake

My grandmother used to make a delicious cake that was dense and very yellow. It had a wonderful crunchy, buttery topping that must have been made with granulated sugar and butter, crumbled together. There were no flavorings, except perhaps a little vanilla. We went through all her recipes (she called them "receipts," in the old-fashioned way!) after she passed away but could never find this one.

Barbara Boissonnas
St. Charles, Ill.

The Continental Sandwich

There used to be a small chain restaurant called Mr. Steak that served a sandwich called The Continental. It consisted of two beef patties with a mushroom-cheese sauce inside. I think the cheese was Swiss. The sandwich was served on grilled pumpernickel bread.

Eva Kinstle
Ames, Iowa

Grandma's Serbian Cookies

My grandmother was of Serbian descent, but I remember that she often used Polish and other Slavic recipes. She used to make cut-out butter cookies. There were six egg yolks in the dough, and she would use the six egg whites in a meringue topping and sprinkle a few ground walnuts on top for decoration. I fondly remember everyone loving these cookies because they were not too sweet but very rich.

Jan A. Moore
Austin, Texas

White Steamed Cherry Pudding

I'm 73 now, but when I was a kid our family had a favorite dessert: white steamed sweet cherry pudding served with a sweet custard sauce. The sauce isn't a problem, but my two sisters and I cannot find a copy of the original recipe for the pudding. The finished product is white and similar to a cake in texture, although firm, like most steamed puddings.

Pete Schuyler
Sarasota, Fla.

Key Lime Pie

Years ago, the Key Largo Restaurant in Key Largo, Fla., made a Key lime pie that had 13 eggs in it. It was the most delicious pie I have ever had. It did not have canned or condensed milk. The restaurant has been out of business for 30 or 40 years now. The chef gave me the recipe for his wonderful pie, but I lost it.

Tommie D. Campbell
Beaver Creek, Colo.

Are you looking for a special recipe? Let other readers of this magazine help. Just send us your requests, and we will print as many of them as we can. Write to Looking for a Recipe, Cook's Country, P.O. Box 470739, Brookline, MA, 02447, or lookingforarecipe@bcpress.com. If you can help with one of the above requests, contact us at the same postal or e-mail address. We will post the responses on www.cookscountry.com.

Find the Rooster!

A tiny version of this rooster has been hidden somewhere in the pages of this issue. If you find it, write to us with its location (plus your name and address), and you will be entered into a random drawing. The first winning entry drawn will receive the Forschner paring knife (our test winner—see page 31), and the next five winners will each receive a free one-year subscription to *Cook's Country*. To enter the contest, write to us at Rooster, Cook's Country, P.O. Box 470739, Brookline, MA 02447, or e-mail us at rooster@bcpress.com. Entries are due May 31, 2006.

Did you find the rooster in the December/January 2006 issue? It was hidden in the pear salad photo on page 21. Ann Mantooth of Knoxville, Tenn., spotted it and won a Farberware toaster.

Quick Cooking

SKILLET STRATA WITH ASPARAGUS AND BOURSIN

Quick Cooking

FRIED RICE WITH HAM AND PEAS

Quick Cooking

LEMON CHICKEN AND RICE SOUP

Quick Cooking

STEAK TIPS WITH MUSHROOMS, GARLIC, AND THYME

FRIED RICE WITH HAM AND PEAS

SERVES 4 TO 6

For more information about Uncle Ben's Ready Rice, see page 28. You can also use 4 cups of leftover rice.

- **3 tablespoons oyster sauce**
- **2 tablespoons soy sauce**
- **3 tablespoons peanut or vegetable oil**
- **3 large eggs, beaten lightly**
- **1 cup frozen peas, thawed**
- **1/2 pound thick-sliced baked ham, cut into 1/4-inch pieces**
- **2 garlic cloves, minced**
- **2 (8.8-ounce) packages Uncle Ben's Whole Grain Brown Ready Rice**
- **1 1/2 cups bean sprouts**
- **5 medium scallions, sliced thin**

1. Combine oyster and soy sauces in small bowl; set aside. Heat 1 1/2 teaspoons oil in large nonstick skillet over medium heat until just smoking. Swirl to coat pan bottom, add eggs and cook, without stirring, until just set, about 20 seconds. Scramble and break eggs into small pieces and cook, stirring constantly, until cooked through but not browned, about 1 minute. Transfer to small bowl.

2. Increase heat to high and heat remaining 2 1/2 tablespoons oil until just smoking. Swirl to coat pan bottom, add peas and ham and cook, stirring constantly, for 30 seconds (watch for splattering). Stir in garlic and cook until fragrant, about 30 seconds. Add rice and oyster sauce mixture and cook, stirring constantly and breaking up rice clumps, until heated through, about 3 minutes. Add eggs, bean sprouts, and scallions and cook, stirring constantly, until heated through, about 1 minute. Serve.

SKILLET STRATA WITH ASPARAGUS AND BOURSIN

SERVES 4

Be careful not to brown the onions too quickly—they will continue to brown as they cook with the bread.

- **1 pound asparagus, tough ends snapped off, spears cut diagonally into 1-inch pieces**
- **6 large eggs**
- **1 1/4 cups milk**
- **Pepper**
- **4 tablespoons unsalted butter**
- **1 small onion, minced**
- **Salt**
- **4 slices hearty white sandwich bread, cut into 1-inch squares**
- **3/4 cup Boursin cheese, crumbled**

1. Adjust oven rack to middle position and heat oven to 400 degrees. Toss asparagus with 2 tablespoons water in microwave-safe bowl. Cover with plastic wrap and microwave on high power until crisp-tender, about 2 minutes. Drain. Whisk eggs, milk, and 1/4 teaspoon pepper together in large bowl.

2. Melt butter in large nonstick ovensafe skillet over medium-high heat. When butter foams, swirl to coat skillet and add onion and 1/2 teaspoon salt. Cook until onion is soft, about 3 minutes. Add bread and cook, stirring frequently, until bread and onion are lightly browned, about 3 minutes. Off heat, stir in asparagus and egg mixture until well incorporated. Scatter cheese on top and bake until top is puffed and edges have pulled away from sides of pan, 15 to 20 minutes. Serve.

STEAK TIPS WITH MUSHROOMS, GARLIC, AND THYME

SERVES 4

Steak tips are sold as whole steaks, cubes, and strips. For this recipe, use strips and cut them into 6- to 8-inch-long pieces, if necessary.

- **2 tablespoons vegetable oil**
- **10 ounces white mushrooms, halved or quartered if large**
- **4 garlic cloves, sliced thin**
- **1 1/2 pounds sirloin steak tips (see above note), patted dry**
- **Salt and pepper**
- **1/4 cup brandy**
- **3/4 cup low-sodium chicken broth**
- **2 teaspoons roughly chopped fresh thyme**
- **2 teaspoons Dijon mustard**
- **1 tablespoon unsalted butter**

1. Heat 1 tablespoon oil in large nonstick skillet over high heat until just smoking. Cook mushrooms, stirring occasionally, until browned in spots, 5 to 6 minutes. Reduce heat to medium and push mushrooms to sides of pan. Add 1 teaspoon oil and garlic to clearing in center of pan and stir until garlic is browned and crisp, about 30 seconds. Stir garlic into mushrooms, cook for 30 seconds, then transfer mixture to serving platter.

2. Increase heat to high, add remaining 2 teaspoons oil to skillet, and season steak with salt and pepper. Place steak in pan so pieces are not touching. Reduce heat to medium-high and cook until well browned, 3 to 5 minutes per side. Transfer steak to platter and tent loosely with foil.

3. Combine brandy and broth in small bowl. Add to pan along with thyme and mushroom mixture. Using wooden spoon, scrape browned bits from bottom of pan. Simmer until thickened, 5 to 7 minutes. Add accumulated beef juices back to pan, whisk in mustard and butter, and season with pepper. Pour mushrooms and sauce over meat. Serve.

LEMON CHICKEN AND RICE SOUP

SERVES 4

To avoid scrambling the eggs, add the hot broth to the egg yolks slowly.

- **6 cups low-sodium chicken broth**
- **1 tablespoon vegetable oil**
- **2 boneless, skinless chicken breasts (6 to 8 ounces each), patted dry**
- **Salt and pepper**
- **1 medium onion, minced**
- **2 medium carrots, peeled and sliced into 1/4 -inch rounds**
- **1 teaspoon minced fresh thyme**
- **3/4 cup long-grain rice**
- **2 tablespoons minced fresh parsley**
- **3 tablespoons lemon juice**
- **4 large egg yolks**

1. Bring broth to boil in large saucepan over high heat. Cover and set aside. Heat oil in Dutch oven over medium-high heat until just smoking. Season chicken with salt and pepper and cook until lightly browned on both sides, about 2 minutes per side. Transfer to plate. Lower heat to medium-low, add onion, and cook until lightly browned, 3 to 5 minutes. Stir in hot broth, using wooden spoon to scrape browned bits from pan. Add carrots, thyme, rice, and chicken. Cover and simmer over low heat until chicken is cooked through, about 10 minutes.

2. Transfer chicken to cutting board and continue simmering soup, covered, until rice is tender, about 10 minutes. Cut chicken into bite-sized pieces. Off heat, stir in chicken and parsley.

3. Whisk lemon juice and yolks together in bowl. Whisking constantly, gradually ladle 1 cup hot soup into egg mixture, then stir egg mixture back into soup. Reheat over low heat for 1 minute. Season with salt and pepper. Serve.

Quick Cooking

ASIAN SPINACH AND SHRIMP SALAD WITH SESAME DRESSING

Quick Cooking

SKILLET CHICKEN AND POTATOES

Quick Cooking

SEARED SALMON WITH BALSAMIC GLAZE

Quick Cooking

PASTA WITH CHICKEN AND ARTICHOKES

SKILLET CHICKEN AND POTATOES

SERVES 4

If you prefer, substitute fresh thyme or oregano for the sage.

- **1 pound small red potatoes, halved**
- **3 tablespoons olive oil**
- **1/4 cup all-purpose flour**
- **4 boneless, skinless chicken cutlets (6 to 7 ounces each), trimmed**
- **Salt and pepper**
- **2 tablespoons unsalted butter**
- **3/4 cup low-sodium chicken broth**
- **1 tablespoon chopped fresh sage**
- **2 tablespoons lemon juice**

1. Toss potatoes and 1 tablespoon oil together in microwave-safe bowl. Cover with plastic wrap and microwave on high power until tender, 4 to 5 minutes, tossing potatoes halfway through cooking.

2. Place flour in shallow dish. Season chicken with salt and pepper, dredge in flour, and shake to remove excess. Melt 1 tablespoon butter with remaining 2 tablespoons oil in large skillet over medium-high heat. When foam subsides, cook chicken until browned on both sides, 3 to 5 minutes per side. Transfer to plate, leaving fat in skillet, and cover chicken with foil.

3. Reduce heat to medium, add potatoes, cut side down, and cook until browned, 4 to 5 minutes. Transfer to platter. Add broth, sage, and lemon juice and, using wooden spoon, scrape browned bits from skillet. Return chicken and accumulated juices to pan and simmer until sauce is slightly thickened and chicken is cooked through, about 5 minutes. Transfer chicken to platter with potatoes. Whisk remaining tablespoon butter into sauce, season with salt and pepper, and pour sauce over chicken and potatoes. Serve.

ASIAN SPINACH AND SHRIMP SALAD WITH SESAME DRESSING

SERVES 4

Depending on how juicy the oranges are, you may need 2 oranges to yield 1/2 cup of squeezed juice.

- **1/2 cup juice plus 1 teaspoon grated zest from 1 orange (see above note)**
- **12 cups lightly packed baby spinach**
- **2 teaspoons minced fresh ginger**
- **3 tablespoons rice vinegar**
- **1 teaspoon honey**
- **3 tablespoons vegetable oil**
- **2 tablespoons toasted sesame oil**
- **Salt and pepper**
- **1 pound cooked and peeled medium shrimp**
- **2 oranges, peeled and segmented**
- **1/2 cup chopped scallions**

1. Bring orange juice to boil in small saucepan over medium-high heat and simmer until reduced to about 1 tablespoon, about 6 minutes. Meanwhile, place spinach in large bowl and set aside.

2. Whisk reduced orange juice, zest, ginger, vinegar, and honey together in small bowl. Whisk in vegetable and sesame oils and season with salt and pepper.

3. Toss shrimp, orange segments, and scallions with 2 tablespoons dressing in bowl and season with salt and pepper. Toss spinach with remaining dressing and season with salt and pepper. Divide spinach among individual plates and top with shrimp and oranges. Serve.

PASTA WITH CHICKEN AND ARTICHOKES

SERVES 4

The brined artichokes add a lot of salty flavor, so be judicious when seasoning.

- **4 tablespoons unsalted butter**
- **1 pound boneless, skinless chicken breasts, cut into 1/4-inch slices**
- **1 (14-ounce) can artichoke hearts packed in brine, rinsed, dried on paper towels, and each cut into 6 wedges**
- **6 garlic cloves, minced**
- **2 teaspoons all-purpose flour**
- **1 1/4 cups low-sodium chicken broth**
- **1 cup grated Parmesan cheese**
- **3 tablespoons lemon juice**
- **1/4 cup minced fresh parsley**
- **1/2 pound bow-tie pasta**
- **Salt and pepper**

1. Bring 2 quarts water to boil in pot for cooking pasta. Meanwhile, melt 1 tablespoon butter in large nonstick skillet over high heat until foaming subsides. Cook chicken in single layer without stirring for 1 minute, then stir and cook until no longer pink, about 2 minutes. Transfer to bowl.

2. Lower heat to medium and melt 1 tablespoon butter in pan. Cook artichokes until lightly browned, about 2 minutes. Add garlic and cook until fragrant, about 30 seconds. Add flour and cook for 30 seconds. Add broth and simmer until slightly thickened, 5 to 7 minutes. Stir in remaining 2 tablespoons butter, Parmesan, lemon juice, parsley, and chicken and cook until chicken is cooked through, about 1 minute.

3. As sauce cooks, add pasta and 2 teaspoons salt to boiling water and cook until al dente. Reserving 1/2 cup cooking water, drain pasta, then return to pot. Toss with chicken and sauce, moistening with reserved water as needed. Season with salt and pepper. Serve.

SEARED SALMON WITH BALSAMIC GLAZE

SERVES 4

For a complete meal, serve the salmon with steamed broccoli and rice.

- **1/4 cup balsamic vinegar**
- **1/4 cup orange juice**
- **2 tablespoons honey**
- **1/8 teaspoon red pepper flakes**
- **1 (5-inch) sprig rosemary**
- **2 teaspoons vegetable oil**
- **4 skin-on salmon fillets, 6 ounces each, 1 to 1 1/4 inches thick**
- **Salt and pepper**
- **2 tablespoons unsalted butter**

1. Whisk vinegar, juice, honey, and pepper flakes together in small bowl, then add rosemary. Heat oil in large nonstick skillet over medium-high heat until smoking. Season salmon with salt and pepper and cook, skin side up, without moving, until well browned, 4 to 5 minutes. Flip fish skin side down and cook until all but very center of fish is opaque, 2 to 3 minutes. Transfer to platter and tent with foil.

2. Wipe out pan with paper towels and lower heat to medium. Carefully pour balsamic mixture into pan (it will splatter). Simmer until thick and syrupy, about 5 minutes. Remove rosemary sprig. Whisk in butter, season sauce with salt and pepper, and pour over salmon. Serve.

Classic Lemon Pound Cake

What's the secret to moist, tender, lemony pound cake? Mine comes out tough and dry, with almost no lemon flavor.

–Julia McAneny, Waltham, Mass.

For potent lemon flavor, add lemon zest to the cake batter, brush the just-baked cake with lemon syrup, and then spread the cooled cake with lemon glaze.

Pound cake has been around for a long time (it was popular in Colonial America), but that doesn't mean that most recipes for it are reliable. It often turns out heavy, leaden, and dry, when it should be rich, buttery, and moist.

The easily memorized ingredient list (1 pound each of butter, sugar, eggs, and flour) and instructions (beat softened butter and sugar until fluffy, add eggs, and finish with flour) probably explain its longevity. Since pound cake predates the widespread availability of chemical leaveners by about 150 years, traditional recipes don't contain baking powder. As a result, the only air in the batter comes from creaming the butter and sugar. If the butter is too warm or too cold (and there's little margin for error), the cake turns out not airy and tender but dense and tough.

Several years ago, the test kitchen developed a recipe that skirted this problem by using melted butter and the whirring action of the food processor to ensure its even incorporation. But not everyone has a big food processor. Could I devise a less radical solution to make this recipe more reliable—one that would employ an electric mixer and the classic mixing method?

To lighten the load, many modern recipes add baking powder. Some of the recipes I tested went overboard, and their texture was like that of a fluffy layer cake. In the end, I found that a half-teaspoon of baking powder was enough to lighten the texture. The crumb was still fine and compact, but it wasn't quite so leaden.

I realized I needed to try something a bit bolder, and I wondered if a dairy ingredient (usually not part of the pound cake formula) would help. Milk turned the cake springy and layer-cake-like, while cream cheese imparted an odd flavor that reminded tasters of a breakfast Danish. Sour cream, however, transformed the cake, making the crumb tender and moist. Creaming the butter and sugar was still an important step, but the recipe was no longer so fickle.

It was time to introduce lemon into the equation. Lemon juice was losing most of its punch in the oven, so I determined that a mix of juice and zest was a must. Beating the zest with the sugar helped to release its flavorful oils. But even hefty amounts of juice and zest got me only so far. Some recipes resort to lemon extract, but this gave the cake an artificial flavor. Lemon syrup (nothing more than lemon juice simmered with sugar), brushed over the cake once it emerged from the oven, was a better option. I added another blast of lemon by replacing the usual milk in the white glaze spread over the cooled cake with lemon juice.

–Stephanie Alleyne

LEMON POUND CAKE

SERVES 8

For best results, the butter should be between 65 and 70 degrees—it should give slightly when pressed with your finger but still hold its shape. You will need three lemons for this recipe. To double the recipe and make two cakes, see page 29.

Cake

- **16 tablespoons (2 sticks) unsalted butter, softened but still cool, plus extra for greasing pan**
- **1 3/4 cups all-purpose flour, plus extra for dusting pan**
- **1/2 teaspoon baking powder**
- **1/2 teaspoon salt**
- **1/4 cup sour cream**
- **1 1/2 tablespoons lemon juice**
- **1 1/2 tablespoons grated lemon zest**
- **1 cup plus 2 tablespoons granulated sugar**
- **5 large eggs, at room temperature, beaten**

Syrup

- **1/4 cup granulated sugar**
- **1/4 cup lemon juice**

Glaze

- **1/2 cup confectioners' sugar, sifted**
- **1 tablespoon lemon juice**

1. For the cake: Adjust oven rack to middle position and heat oven to 325 degrees. Grease 9 by 5-inch loaf pan with butter; dust pan with flour, then tap out excess. Sift flour, baking powder, and salt into bowl. Stir sour cream and lemon juice together in second bowl.

2. Using fingers, toss lemon zest and sugar together in large bowl until clumps are gone. Add butter and beat with electric mixer at medium-high speed until smooth and light, about 3 minutes. Scrape down sides of bowl. Add beaten eggs in three additions, mixing until smooth and scraping down bowl after each addition (mixture will begin to look curdled). With mixer on low, add one-third of flour mixture, followed by half of sour cream mixture, stopping as necessary to scrape down bowl. Repeat, ending with flour mixture. Scrape down bowl, then mix on low until smooth, about 30 seconds. Use rubber spatula to give batter final stir.

3. Pour batter into pan and smooth top. Gently tap pan on counter to release air bubbles. Bake until golden brown and toothpick inserted into center comes out with a few crumbs attached, 55 to 70 minutes.

4. For the syrup: While cake bakes, stir sugar and lemon juice together in saucepan over medium-high heat until sugar dissolves. Simmer for 2 minutes, remove from heat, and set aside.

5. Cool cake in pan on cooling rack for 10 minutes, then turn out onto rack. Brush top and sides of still-warm cake with syrup and cool completely, about 2 hours.

6. For the glaze: Whisk confectioners' sugar and lemon juice in bowl until smooth. Spread glaze over cake, allowing some to drip down sides. Let glaze set for at least 15 minutes before serving.

Make Ahead

The test kitchen found this cake to be more moist the day after it was baked. In fact, when tightly wrapped, the cake will stay fresh up to 5 days. This cake also freezes well. Apply syrup, let cool, and wrap, unglazed, in two layers of plastic wrap and freeze in a zipper-lock plastic bag for up to 1 month. When ready to serve, defrost the cake, still wrapped, at room temperature, then remove the plastic wrap and proceed with the recipe from step 6.

The Best Chicken Noodle Soup

My chicken soup often turns out watery, and the meat is stringy and dry. I want a rich-tasting broth and tender meat. Otherwise, I might as well open a can. –Yun Cheng, San Francisco, Calif.

Know-How

DEGREASING CHICKEN BROTH

Chicken thighs give the broth flavor—but also fat. Removing the skin after browning the thighs helps cut down on the greasiness, but some fat will still float to the surface as the broth cools. Here's how to remove it.

1. Place a single paper towel on the surface of the slightly cooled broth. **2.** Gather the corners of the paper towel and lift the towel out of the broth, allowing excess broth to drip back into the bowl. Repeat with additional paper towels until all surface fat has been removed.

A bowl of homemade soup might not cure the common cold, but it will make you feel better.

Few kitchen failures are more disappointing than bad homemade chicken noodle soup. Since making soup from scratch takes a lot more effort than opening a can of Campbell's, it's awfully deflating when the chicken turns out tough and dry and the broth is only one step up from dishwater.

First, some basic chicken facts. The breast meat doesn't add much flavor to the broth, and it cooks in a flash. Most of the flavor comes from the dark meat and bones—and it takes time for them to give up their essence to the broth (and in that time the white meat overcooks).

During early tests, I found that most tasters didn't care for dark meat in the finished soup; they wanted tender chunks of white meat. With this in mind, I decided to try making the broth with dark meat, removing it, and then quickly poaching the white meat in the broth to finish the soup. My job was made that much easier when I realized I didn't have to cut up a whole chicken myself but could simply buy chicken parts.

My first thought was to brown the dark meat so that it would release its flavor more quickly. Instead of simply poaching the meat in water (which takes two to three hours), I browned the chicken, poured off the excess grease, then added water, salt, and bay leaves. After 45 minutes of simmering, my broth was plenty strong, and the dark meat had held up to the cooking—it was still moist and tender enough to use in chicken salad or even soup, if you're a fan of dark meat.

I conducted a side-by-side tasting of broths made with just wings, just drumsticks, and just thighs. The broth made with the thighs had the cleanest, most intense chicken flavor, although, like the other two, it was too greasy. This was easily remedied by removing the skin after browning the thighs and quickly degreasing the broth with paper towels.

Next I began to tinker with the addition of white meat. I found that raw boneless, skinless breasts could be poached in the simmering broth during the last 15 minutes of cooking. They could then be removed from the broth, cooled, shredded, and added back to the soup during the last minutes of cooking to reheat.

With the main components of the soup—the broth and the meat—taken care of, all I had to do was put the supporting elements together. Because I'd gone to a fair amount of trouble to create a great broth and tender meat, I did not want to overwhelm them with too many other ingredients. Tasters liked onion, carrot, and celery, and I found that sautéing the vegetables in a thin film of oil (rather than just poaching them in the broth) intensified their flavor. I let the vegetables finish cooking in the broth (simmering them for about 15 minutes), along with some chopped fresh thyme, to meld all the flavors.

When I cooked the noodles in a separate pot of boiling water and then added them to the soup, they were terribly bland. The noodles were best cooked right in broth, where they soaked up chicken flavor. Once the noodles are cooked, however, the soup must be served immediately. When I tried refrigerating leftovers, the noodles became bloated and mushy.

Taking up several fellow cooks on the same suggestion, I finished my soup with a handful of fresh parsley and then watched with satisfaction as they emptied their bowls. No truly homemade soup is quick, but this recipe is pretty easy to follow, and the results are much better than anything that comes out of a can.

–Cali Rich

CHICKEN NOODLE SOUP

SERVES 8 TO 10

The thighs are used to flavor the broth; once the broth is strained, shred the thigh meat and reserve it for a salad or pot pie. If you prefer dark meat in your soup, you can omit the chicken breasts and add the shredded thigh meat to the soup instead.

Broth

- **12 bone-in, skin-on chicken thighs (about 4 pounds)**
- **Salt and pepper**
- **1 tablespoon vegetable oil**
- **1 medium onion, chopped**
- **3 quarts water**
- **2 bay leaves**
- **2 large boneless, skinless chicken breasts (about 1 pound)**

Soup

- **1 tablespoon vegetable oil**
- **1 medium onion, chopped fine**
- **1 carrot, sliced thin**
- **1 celery rib, halved lengthwise, then sliced thin**
- **2 teaspoons minced fresh thyme**
- **6 ounces wide egg noodles**
- **1/4 cup minced fresh parsley**
- **Salt and pepper**

1. For the broth: Pat thighs dry with paper towels and season with salt and pepper. Heat oil in large Dutch oven over medium-high heat until smoking. Cook half of thighs skin side down until deep golden brown, about 6 minutes. Turn thighs and lightly brown second side, about 2 minutes. Transfer to strainer-lined large bowl. Repeat with remaining thighs and transfer to strainer; discard fat in bowl. Pour off fat from pot, add onion, and cook over medium heat until just softened, about 3 minutes. Meanwhile, remove and discard skin from thighs. Add thighs, water, bay leaves, and 1 tablespoon salt to pot. Cover and simmer for 30 minutes. Add chicken breasts and continue simmering until broth is rich and flavorful, about 15 minutes.

2. Strain broth into large container, let stand at least 10 minutes, then remove fat from surface (see photos on page 18). Meanwhile, transfer chicken to cutting board to cool. Once cooled, remove thigh meat from bones, shred, and reserve for another use (can refrigerate for up to 2 days or freeze for up to 1 month). Shred breast meat and reserve for soup.

3. For the soup: Heat oil in now-empty Dutch oven over medium-high heat until shimmering. Add onion, carrot, and celery and cook until onion has softened, 3 to 4 minutes. Stir in thyme and broth and simmer until vegetables are tender, about 15 minutes. Add noodles and shredded breast meat and simmer until noodles are just tender, about 5 minutes. Off heat, stir in parsley and season with salt and pepper. Serve.

Make Ahead

The broth (and shredded breast meat) for this soup can be refrigerated for up to 2 days or frozen for up to 1 month before being used to make soup. To avoid soggy noodles and vegetables, finish the soup (step 3 in the recipe) just before you plan on serving it.

Regional Favorites: Green Goddess Dressing

This California classic should balance color and consistency with intense herb flavor.

Green goddess is a thick, creamy salad dressing made with mayonnaise and fresh herbs. Drizzled over a wedge of crisp lettuce, it offers a potent first taste of spring. This recipe first appeared in 1923 on the menu of San Francisco's Palace Hotel, created by the hotel chef in honor of British actor George Arliss, who was staying at the hotel while starring in a play titled *Green Goddess*.

Contemporary versions of this recipe are thick, more like mayonnaise than salad dressing. My tasters rejected them as well as versions made with avocado, an ingredient not found in the original recipe but now common. The avocado made the dressing green (many of my early test recipes were too white), but it also bullied the other flavors and turned the dressing into a dip.

Some recipes add a dairy ingredient to thin out the stiff mayonnaise. Milk and cream made the dressing too runny. Buttermilk reminded my tasters of ranch dressing, and yogurt was much too tart. In the end, sour cream gave the dressing the proper texture and added a subtle tang.

As the name implies, "green goddess" contains multiple herbs, tarragon being the most prominent. To my amazement, the milder, mellower flavor of dried tarragon was preferable to the strong, grassy flavor of fresh. To help wake up the flavor of the dried tarragon, I found it best to soak it for 15 minutes; otherwise, it was too tame. Tasters also liked fresh parsley and chives, a bit of lemon juice, garlic, and anchovies, which gave the dressing some kick.

My dressing tasted great, but it wasn't really "green." I solved the problem by breaking with tradition. Rather than stirring the ingredients by hand, I used a blender, which broke down the herbs more thoroughly than a knife and turned the dressing bright green. And because the ingredients were pureed into tiny bits, their flavors were more vibrant, too. After an hour in the refrigerator, where the flavors could meld, my version of this California classic was ready to pour over lettuce and become a smash hit. **–Eva Katz**

Lose the avocado (a modern addition that makes this dressing too thick) and rely instead on herbs for color and flavor.

GREEN GODDESS DRESSING

MAKE ABOUT 1 1/4 CUPS, ENOUGH FOR 6 WEDGES OF LETTUCE

To appreciate the full flavor of this rich dressing, drizzle it over chilled wedges of mild iceberg lettuce or leaves of romaine lettuce. A blender yields a brighter, slightly more flavorful dressing, but a food processor will work, too.

- **2 teaspoons dried tarragon**
- **1 tablespoon lemon juice**
- **1 tablespoon water**
- **3/4 cup mayonnaise**
- **1/4 cup sour cream**
- **1/4 cup roughly chopped fresh parsley**
- **1 medium garlic clove, chopped**
- **1 anchovy fillet, rinsed and dried**
- **1/4 cup chopped chives**
- **Salt and pepper**

1. Combine tarragon, lemon juice, and water in small bowl and let sit for 15 minutes.

2. Blend tarragon mixture, mayonnaise, sour cream, parsley, garlic, and anchovy in blender until smooth, scraping down sides as necessary. Transfer to medium bowl, stir in chives, and season with salt and pepper. Chill until flavors meld, about 1 hour. (Dressing can be covered and refrigerated for up to 1 day.)

Spaghetti and Meatball Soup

Could we take the flavors of spaghetti and meatballs and turn them into a quick soup?

Spaghetti and meatballs are a family favorite for everyone except the cook. It takes a lot of work to make tomato sauce, shape and fry meatballs, cook pasta, and then wash all those bowls and pots. Could I reproduce the flavors of this dish in a single pot, minimizing the number of ingredients and the hassle? I thought a quick tomato soup (in which I simmered the meatballs and pasta) might answer the call.

For the soup, I followed the outlines of my favorite simple tomato soup recipe, sautéing onions, carrots, and garlic in olive oil and then simmering them in chicken broth and canned tomatoes. Once the solids were tender, I strained them out and processed them in a blender with just a splash of the soup liquid to eliminate the need for multiple batches of pureeing.

For the meatballs, I took a very simple approach. Instead of mixing the meat with a laundry list of seasonings and binders, I substituted pesto (yes, store-bought is OK). Pesto has many of the same ingredients that are typically added to meatballs—cheese, herbs, and garlic—but requires no mincing or grating. I also switched the traditional ground beef to ground chicken, which made the flavor of the pesto more pronounced, made the meatballs lighter, and made the soup less greasy. And you can forget about taking the trouble to brown the meatballs; they can poach directly in the soup.

Spaghetti, even when broken into small pieces, is too difficult to scoop up with a spoon. *Ditalini*, a small tubular pasta, is a better alternative. If the pasta sits in the soup too long, it absorbs excess liquid and makes the broth too thick. If you're not eating the soup right away, or if you won't finish the pot in one sitting, it's best to cook the pasta separately and add it to the soup just before serving. **–Eva Katz**

SPAGHETTI AND MEATBALL SOUP

SERVES 6

Use any small, bite-sized pasta in this recipe.

- 1 **tablespoon olive oil**
- 1 **red onion, chopped coarse**
- 1 **carrot, peeled and chopped coarse**
- 3 **garlic cloves, minced**
- 5 **cups low-sodium chicken broth**
- 2 **(28-ounce) cans diced tomatoes**
- 1/2 **pound ground chicken**
- 1/3 **cup pesto, plus extra for serving**
- 1/3 **cup plain bread crumbs**
- **Salt and pepper**
- 2 **cups ditalini pasta**
- **Grated Parmesan cheese**

1. Heat oil in Dutch oven over medium heat until shimmering. Add onion and carrot and cook until onion is soft, about 5 minutes. Add garlic and cook until fragrant, about 1 minute. Stir in broth and tomatoes. Bring to boil, reduce heat, cover, and simmer until carrot softens, 15 to 20 minutes.

2. Meanwhile, mix chicken, pesto, bread crumbs, ¼ teaspoon salt, and ⅛ teaspoon pepper together in large bowl. Use heaping teaspoon to form mixture into forty ¾-inch meatballs.

3. Strain soup into large bowl and rinse out pot. Transfer solids in strainer to blender with 1 cup strained liquid and puree until smooth. Return pureed mixture and remaining strained liquid to pot and heat until simmering. Season with salt and pepper.

4. Add pasta and meatballs and simmer until pasta is al dente and meatballs are cooked through, 12 to 15 minutes. Ladle soup into bowls and serve with dollops of additional pesto and grated Parmesan.

Recipe Revival: Pepper Steak

This 1960s favorite has been relegated to the frozen food aisle, but it's easily made at home from scratch.

Some dishes are meant to stay buried deep in our past, but I'm not convinced that pepper steak is one of them. Not to be confused with steak au poivre, the bistro classic with the peppercorn coating, pepper steak marries beef with bell peppers, onions, and tomatoes in a savory brown sauce that includes soy sauce. This dish emerged in the early 1960s, just as Americans began to take an interest in Asian cooking. With recognizably American ingredients, it gave many of us our first taste of "Chinese" food. I thought this utterly simple dish was ready for a revival.

Too bad most of the recipes I tried yielded tough meat and bitter peppers. Stir-frying the beef and getting it out of the pan to build the sauce was key. Older recipes just left the meat in the pan to simmer its way to toughness. Flank steak worked well, but my tasters preferred the slightly richer flavor of sirloin steak tips.

While most vegetables benefit from a quick stir-fry to retain their crunch, my tasters rejected the strong bitter flavor of undercooked green peppers. After stir-frying the peppers until lightly browned, I added a little beef broth to the skillet and put the lid on. After two minutes, the peppers were tender and their flavor was less harsh and metallic, but they still had a bitter edge. Replacing some of the green peppers with red peppers solved the bitterness problem and improved the appearance of the dish as well.

For the sauce, I used a base of beef broth and sherry thickened with a little cornstarch. This gave the sauce a perfect consistency and sheen. The last step was to warm the final traditional ingredient, diced canned tomatoes, in the sauce. **–Keri Fisher**

PEPPER STEAK **SERVES 4**

Serve the pepper steak over buttered egg noodles or rice.

- 2 **tablespoons soy sauce, plus extra for passing at table**
- 1 **pound sirloin steak tips, sliced very thin against the grain**
- 1 **cup plus 2 tablespoons low-sodium beef broth**
- 2 **tablespoons dry sherry**
- 4 **teaspoons cornstarch**
- 2 **tablespoons vegetable oil**
- 1 **medium red bell pepper, sliced thin**
- 1 **medium green bell pepper, sliced thin**
- 1 **medium onion, halved and sliced thin**
- 3 **garlic cloves, minced**
- 1/2 **cup canned diced tomatoes, drained**
- **Salt and pepper**

1. Toss soy sauce and steak in medium bowl. Cover with plastic wrap and refrigerate while preparing other ingredients. Whisk 1 cup beef broth, sherry, and cornstarch together in medium bowl.

2. Heat 2 teaspoons oil in large nonstick skillet over medium-high heat until shimmering. Add half of beef and cook, turning once, until browned at edges, about 2 minutes. Transfer to clean plate. Add 2 teaspoons oil to pan, repeat with remaining beef, and transfer to plate.

3. Add remaining 2 teaspoons oil to pan and heat until shimmering. Add peppers, onion, and garlic and cook until just beginning to brown, about 4 minutes. Add remaining 2 tablespoons broth, reduce heat to low, cover, and cook until peppers are soft, about 2 minutes.

4. Return beef to pan along with cornstarch mixture. Increase heat to high and simmer until sauce is thickened, about 2 minutes. Stir in tomatoes and season with salt and pepper. Serve immediately, passing extra soy sauce at table.

Pepperoni Pan Pizza

I have longed to duplicate Pizza Hut's wonderful pan pizza crust. Nobody makes a crust as good as theirs. Can you tell me how to make it at home? –Eileen Eck, Edna, Kan.

Our pan pizza is better than takeout and almost as quick.

Great pan pizza—named for the pan in which the dough is risen and cooked—has an irresistible crust that's crispy on the bottom and soft and chewy in the middle. The generous amount of oil first poured into the pan creates the crisp bottom; the soft interior is harder to figure out.

Pan pizza isn't something you find in most cookbooks, so I turned to the Internet. After a few clicks, I found a Web site that claimed to reveal the secret Pizza Hut formula. I doubted the recipe was authentic, but I decided to try it because it included a novel ingredient: powdered milk.

Classic pizza dough contains flour, yeast, water, and olive oil, but never milk. I knew, though, that many tender yeast breads are made with milk. Could powdered milk be the key to soft pizza dough?

This dough was tender, with just the right chew. Because most cooks don't have powdered milk on hand, I wondered if fresh milk would work. It did. In fact, the texture of the crust was even better. Whole milk was fine, but dough made with skim milk rose better and baked up especially soft and light.

All-purpose flour, which yields softer baked goods than bread flour, was the right choice, as was a healthy dose of olive oil (2 tablespoons). Although sugar is not traditional in pizza, my tasters thought a little (just 2 teaspoons) made the dough taste better, and I knew that sugar gives yeast a nice jumpstart. To deliver my pan pizzas to the table in record time, I used a warm, turned-off oven to help the dough rise faster. Thirty minutes later, I had dough that was ready to shape.

After producing some less-than-stellar crusts, I discovered it was important not to overwork the dough. Beating the dough into submission with a rolling pin caused it to tear or snap back like a rubber band. In the end, I developed the following hybrid method: I used a rolling pin for the first (and easy) part of the process and then stretched the dough over the tops of my knuckles to finish the job—gently.

With my dough nice and tender, it was time to fine-tune the crispness factor. Three tablespoons of oil in each pan delivered maximum crispness without greasiness. After trying various oven temperatures, I settled on 400 degrees as the best compromise between a crisp bottom and scorched toppings.

Everything was perfect—except for the grease on top of my pies. When just plopped onto the pizza and baked, the pepperoni floated in pools of orange grease. My first thought was to fry it, just as I'd do with bacon. But this made the pepperoni too crisp and turned it an ugly shade of brown. A colleague suggested the microwave. Layered between paper towels, the pepperoni slices emerged pliable and brightly colored, while the paper towels were soaked with orange fat—the microwave had done its job.

From beginning to end, this pizza can be made in 90 minutes. Not as quick as delivery, but less greasy and with the same great crust. **–Katie Henderson**

PEPPERONI PAN PIZZA

MAKES TWO 9-INCH PIZZAS, SERVING 4 TO 6

Dough

- 1/2 cup olive oil
- 3/4 cup plus 2 tablespoons skim milk, warmed to 110 degrees
- 2 teaspoons sugar
- 2 1/3 cups all-purpose flour, plus extra for counter
- 1 package instant yeast
- 1/2 teaspoon salt

Topping

- 1 (3.5-ounce) package sliced pepperoni
- 1 1/3 cups plain tomato sauce (see recipe on page 28)
- 3 cups shredded part-skim mozzarella cheese

1. To make the dough: Adjust oven rack to lowest position and heat oven to 200 degrees. When oven reaches 200 degrees, turn it off. Lightly grease large bowl with cooking spray. Coat each of two 9-inch cake pans with 3 tablespoons oil.

2. Mix milk, sugar, and remaining 2 tablespoons oil in measuring cup. Mix flour, yeast, and salt in standing mixer fitted

(continued on page 22)

How to Make PAN PIZZA

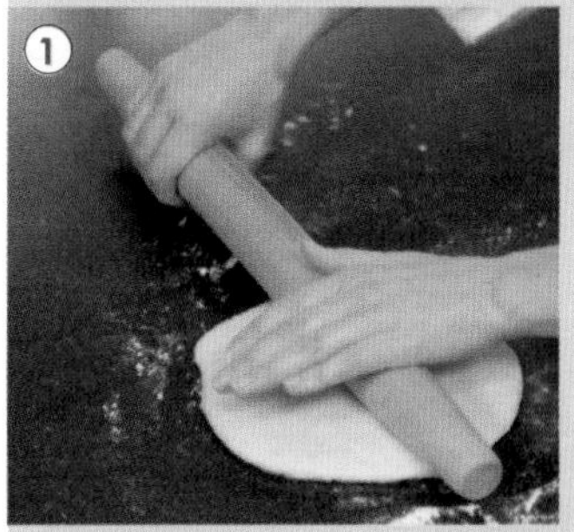

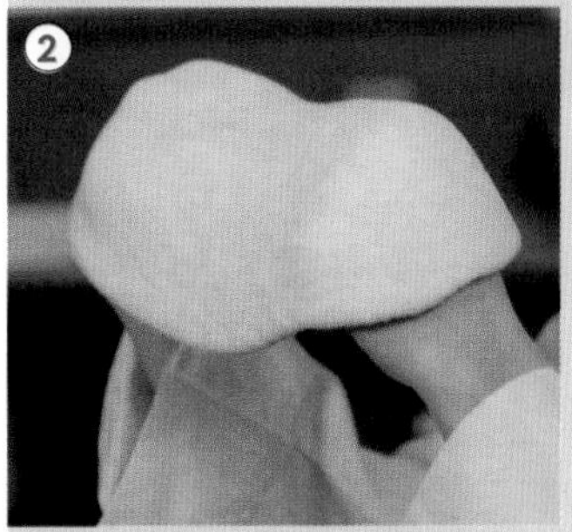

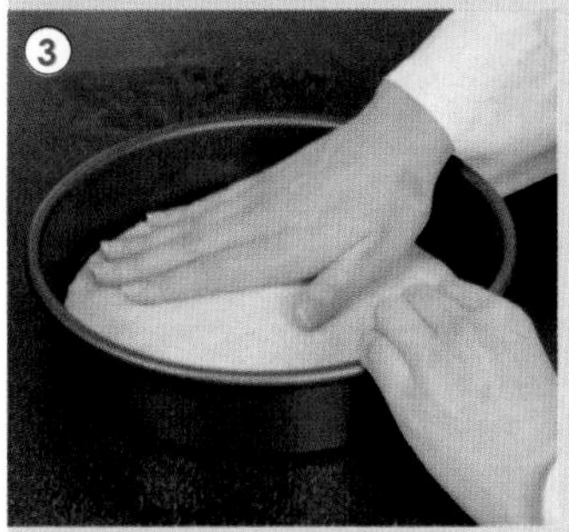

1. Roll the dough outward from the center in all directions to form a 7-inch circle.
2. With the dough draped over your knuckles, gently stretch it, using the weight of the dough to make a 9 1/2-inch circle that is slightly thinner at the center.
3. Place the dough in the oiled cake pan and gently push it to the edge, taking care not to let too much oil spill over the top.

The Amazing Shrinking Pepperoni

Microwaving pepperoni eliminates the possibility that it will turn your pizza into a grease trap. You can see how much fat is rendered in only 30 seconds by comparing the size of the slices before and after microwaving.

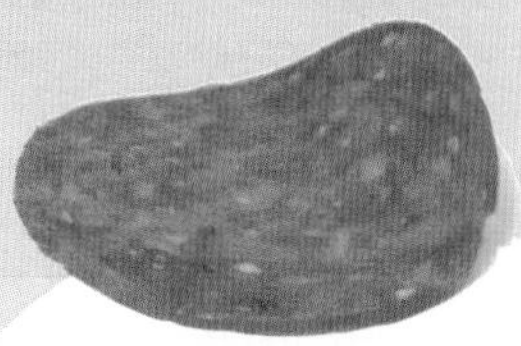

BEFORE

AFTER

Pepperoni Pizza

continued from page 21

with dough hook. Turn machine to low and slowly add milk mixture. After dough comes together, increase speed to medium-low and mix until dough is shiny and smooth, about 5 minutes. Turn dough onto lightly floured counter, gently shape into ball, and place in greased bowl. Cover with plastic wrap and place in warm oven until doubled in size, about 30 minutes.

3. To shape and top the dough: Transfer dough to lightly floured counter, divide in half, and lightly roll each half into ball. Working with 1 dough ball at a time and following photos on page 21, roll and shape dough into 9½-inch round and press into oiled pan. Cover with plastic wrap and set in warm spot (not in oven) until puffy and slightly risen, about 20 minutes. Meanwhile, heat oven to 400 degrees.

4. While dough rises, put half of pepperoni in single layer on microwave-safe plate lined with 2 paper towels. Cover with 2 more paper towels and microwave on high for 30 seconds. Discard towels and set pepperoni aside; repeat with new paper towels and remaining pepperoni.

5. Remove plastic wrap from dough. Ladle ⅔ cup sauce on each round, leaving ½-inch border around edges. Sprinkle each with 1½ cups cheese and top with pepperoni. Bake until cheese is melted and pepperoni is browning around edges, about 20 minutes. Remove from oven; let pizzas rest in pans for 1 minute. Using spatula, transfer pizzas to cutting board and cut each into 8 wedges. Serve.

Pizza Dough without a Mixer

In step 2, mix the flour, yeast, and salt together in a large bowl. Make a well in the flour, then pour the milk mixture into the well. Using a wooden spoon, stir until the dough becomes shaggy and difficult to stir. Turn out onto a heavily floured work surface and knead, incorporating any shaggy scraps. Knead until the dough is smooth, about 10 minutes. Shape into a ball and proceed as directed.

Oven-Fried Onion Rings

Can an oven produce onion rings with deep-fried flavor?

What could be better with a burger or steak than crispy, crunchy onion rings that you don't have to fry?

Oven-fried onion ring recipes promise to eliminate the mess associated with deep-frying, but they don't really work—at least none of the recipes I've tried. With the oven, I have gotten dehydrated onion rings, tough onion rings, and soggy onion rings but have never come close to the deep-fried crunch and flavor of the real thing.

Deep-fried onion rings start with sliced onions that are dunked in a thick batter, usually made with flour, egg, and liquid. When fried, the batter forms a crisp shell that helps the onions steam and become tender. When I tried it in the oven, however, the batter slid off the rings and stuck to the baking sheet instead.

Dredging the onion rings in flour first helped—the batter now had something to cling to. As for what went into the batter, I dismissed milk (too thin) and mayonnaise (too thick) before hitting on the right combination of buttermilk, egg, and flour. This batter was pretty good, but I wanted more crunch and thought an additional crumb coating might help.

Tossing my batter-dipped onion rings with bread crumbs was a step in the right direction, but my tasters wanted even more crunch. At the local supermarket, I bought anything that looked like it might make a good crumb coating, including cornmeal, corn flakes, Melba toast, Weetabix cereal, Ritz crackers, and saltines. Back in the test kitchen, only the saltines were met with even a lukewarm reception; their salty kick was well liked, but the crumbs were too powdery.

I headed back to the market and searched for less obvious options. If I wanted deep-fried flavor, then what about mixing the saltines with potato chips? This worked far better than I expected. It was almost impossible to tell that these super-crunchy onion rings had come out of the oven.

For four to six servings of rings made from two large onions, 6 tablespoons of vegetable oil was just right, giving the rings a good sear without making them too oily. Admittedly, these onion rings, like many oven-fried recipes, are not low in fat, but that was not my goal. I wanted deep-fried flavor without the mess or the smell—and this recipe delivers on both counts. **–Cali Rich**

OVEN-FRIED ONION RINGS

MAKES 24 RINGS, SERVING 4 TO 6

Slice the onions into ½-inch-thick rounds, separate the rings, and discard any rings smaller than 2 inches in diameter.

- **½ cup all-purpose flour**
- **1 large egg, at room temperature**
- **½ cup buttermilk, at room temperature**
- **¼ teaspoon cayenne**
- **Salt and pepper**
- **30 saltines**
- **4 cups kettle-cooked potato chips**
- **2 large yellow onions, cut into 24 large rings (see note above)**
- **6 tablespoons vegetable oil**

1. Adjust oven racks to lower-middle and upper-middle positions and heat oven to 450 degrees. Place ¼ cup flour in shallow baking dish. Beat egg and buttermilk in bowl. Whisk remaining flour, cayenne, ½ teaspoon salt, and ¼ teaspoon pepper into buttermilk mixture. Pulse saltines and chips together in food processor until finely ground; place in separate shallow baking dish.

2. Working one at a time, dredge each onion ring in flour, shaking off excess. Dip in buttermilk mixture, allowing excess to drip back into bowl, then drop into crumb coating, turning ring to coat evenly. Transfer to large plate.

3. Pour 3 tablespoons oil onto each of two rimmed baking sheets. Place in oven and heat until just smoking, about 8 minutes. Carefully tilt heated sheets to coat evenly with oil, then arrange onion rings on sheets. Bake, flipping onion rings over and switching and rotating position of baking sheets halfway through baking, until golden brown on both sides, about 15 minutes. Briefly drain onion rings on paper towels. Serve immediately.

Make Ahead

The onion rings can be breaded in advance and refrigerated for up to an hour. Let them sit at room temperature for 30 minutes before baking; if baked straight from the fridge, the onions will not soften properly and will remain crunchy.

Deep-Fried Coating without the Deep Fryer

Our oven-fried onion rings are so crisp and crunchy that you'd swear they came straight from the fryer. The secret is a coating made with kettle-cooked potato chips and saltines ground to fine crumbs.

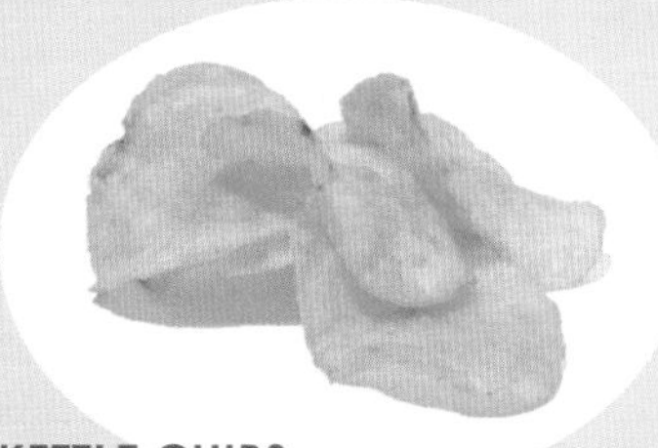

KETTLE CHIPS
When crumbled, these chips produce a golden brown crust that almost seems deep-fried.

SALTINES
Crushed crackers add a nice salty kick and absorb excess grease from the potato chips

Getting to Know the Onion Family

We gathered 15 members of the onion family (technically called alliums) and tasted them raw to best appreciate their flavor and potency. As the tasting notes below demonstrate, they are surprisingly different.

Texas 1015
LONE STAR SWEETIE

This extra-large, extra-sweet variety was developed at Texas A&M University; the name also reflects its optimal planting date: October 15. This "very sweet" and "juicy" onion resembles watermelon in taste and texture.

Yellow Globe
OLD FAITHFUL

The most common supermarket onion ranges in color from light yellow to deep orange. Despite displaying a "watered-down" onion flavor, it retains a "strong," "hot" bite.

White Globe
PRETTY BORING

Ranging from stark white to ivory in color, this large, thin-skinned onion is more style than substance. The "mildly sweet but boring" flavor is punctuated by a "bitter," "sulfurous" aftertaste.

Cipolline
SWEET AND SQUAT

Popular in Italy, these small onions have a high moisture content. They have a "mildly sweet," "winey" flavor with a "slight peppery burn." Great in stews and braises.

Pearl
STICK TO FROZEN

These tiny onions are densely planted to stunt their growth. Their "extremely mild" flavor and "crunchy" texture remind us of Chinese cabbage. Because they are so hard to peel, buy frozen (which come peeled).

Boiling
STEW-PENDOUS

Slightly larger than pearl onions, these white onions are common additions to stewed dishes. Their flavor is mild and "washed out," with a "slight burn." Their "mealy" texture improves with cooking.

Red Globe
HOT TO TROT

This large onion boasts a "sweet," "peppery" flavor as well as "biting heat." Good for cooking (although the flavor dulls), salads, or salsas.

Walla Walla
SWEET SWEET

This sweet onion originated in Italy but is named for its primary area of cultivation, Walla Walla, Wash. Large and spherical in shape, its flavor is "sugary," with a "mild garlic aroma" and "bitter finish."

Vidalia
GEORGIA BORN

This pale yellow, slightly squat onion hails from Vidalia, Ga. It has a "crunchy" texture and a "sweet," "bright" flavor with "very little bite." Best used raw.

Shallot
FRENCH CONNECTION

Shallots have the same papery skins as onions but are often composed of multiple cloves. A staple of French cuisine, shallots offer a complex, subtle "mineral-like," "sweet" flavor with a "good punch of acidity."

Scallion
EARTHY AND GREEN

Scallions have an "earthy," "almost nutty" flavor, similar to chives but much stronger and capable of withstanding some cooking. Both the white bulb and green leaves are edible.

Chives
SNIP TO IT

Considered more herb than vegetable, chives are mild tasting, with a "newly cut grass" flavor, "garlicky" aftertaste, and "crisp" texture. Best used raw.

Garlic
HEAD OF THE CLASS

Garlic has long been considered medicine, aphrodisiac, and even vampire repellent. Its flavor is "pungent" and "sweet-hot," with an "intoxicating" aroma.

Elephant Garlic
GREAT PRETENDER

Unlike true garlic, elephant garlic is actually a type of leek. Its gigantic cloves, which can weigh up to 1 ounce each, have a "subdued" flavor and a "bitter," "yeasty" finish.

Leek
THE BIG BOY

Leeks can grow to more than 2 feet in length, but only the white and light green parts are suitable for eating. They are "vegetal and fibrous," with a potent, "earthy" flavor. Grown in sandy soil, leeks must be washed well and are almost always cooked.

FOOD FACT: *Garlic has been used for thousands of years to fight disease—everything from snake bites to hypertension. In 1858, Louis Pasteur documented garlic's ability to kill bacteria; during World War II, garlic was used on the battlefield to treat open wounds and prevent gangrene.*

Crispy Roasted Garlic Potatoes

I love crisp roasted garlic potatoes, but mine often turn out greasy, soggy, and so garlicky that they give me instant indigestion.

—Miranda Dunning, Oshkosh, Wis.

A hot baking sheet and a dusting of cornstarch create roasted potatoes that are seriously crisp.

Like you, I've always thought that good roasted garlic potatoes are pretty hard to beat. Also like you, I was tired of turning out greasy spuds with a vicious garlic bite. To me, the ultimate roasted garlic potato has a crispy golden shell containing a delicate creamy interior. And every bite should provide a hit of garlic flavor, but without a trace of harshness or bitterness.

It all starts with choosing the right kind of potato, and I favored waxy red, whose high moisture content would ensure a creamy interior. A rimmed baking sheet allowed the potatoes to brown better than a high-sided roasting pan (which inhibits evaporation), and preheating the baking sheet helped jump-start the browning process and improved crispness. Using a preheated pan also reduced sticking, letting me use just 3 tablespoons of oil. So far so good, but the potatoes still weren't really crisp.

After several more rounds of fruitless testing and research, I remembered that a recent test kitchen recipe used cornstarch to crisp the skin on roast chicken. Adapting this idea to my recipe, I tossed the cut potatoes with a tablespoon of cornstarch—a strange idea at best—and it turned my potatoes seriously crisp, even crunchy! (Cornstarch works this magic by absorbing moisture released from the potatoes during cooking, before it has the chance to turn the exteriors soggy.) Now I had the crunch, so it was on to garlic flavor.

My first thought was to toss roasted garlic with the roasted potatoes. Although the flavor was good, the extra moisture from the roasted garlic turned my once-crispy potatoes soggy. If roasted garlic didn't work, then what about fresh? Thrown in with the potatoes at the outset, the sticky fresh garlic clumped, creating a full blast of burnt garlic flavor. I had better success mixing already-roasted potatoes with a little garlic butter as soon as they came out of the oven. The garlic was evenly dispersed, and the residual heat from the potatoes mellowed any harsh garlic overtones.

My tasters wanted still more garlic flavor, but adding more than a single clove to the garlic butter was overkill. That's when a colleague suggested garlic powder. I was skeptical (garlic powder doesn't have much flavor, does it?), but I sprinkled a little on the potatoes before roasting them. Boy, was I surprised. Unlike fresh garlic, garlic powder could handle the heat of the oven and actually developed a deep, roasted flavor. **–Katie Henderson**

ROASTED GARLIC POTATOES SERVES 4

- **2 pounds large red potatoes, scrubbed, dried, and each cut into 8 wedges**
- **1 tablespoon cornstarch**
- **1/2 teaspoon garlic powder**
- **Salt and pepper**
- **3 tablespoons vegetable oil**
- **1 tablespoon unsalted butter, softened**
- **1 large garlic clove, minced**
- **1 teaspoon minced fresh parsley**
- **1/8 teaspoon grated lemon zest**

1. Adjust oven rack to upper-middle position, place rimmed baking sheet on rack, and heat oven to 450 degrees.

2. Meanwhile, toss potatoes, cornstarch, garlic powder, 3/4 teaspoon salt, and 1/4 teaspoon pepper together in large bowl. Carefully remove preheated baking sheet from oven, add oil, and tilt baking sheet to evenly coat with oil. Place potatoes, cut side down in single layer, on baking sheet. Roast until browned around edges, about 30 minutes.

3. While potatoes roast, mix butter, garlic, parsley, and zest together in medium bowl. Remove baking sheet from oven and, using metal spatula, turn potatoes skin side down. Roast until potatoes are crisp and deep golden brown, 10 to 15 minutes.

4. Transfer potatoes to bowl with butter and toss until evenly coated. Season with salt and pepper. Serve.

On the Mild Side

For a rich garlic flavor without any harshness or bitterness, we tossed the potatoes with garlic powder before roasting them. Unlike fresh garlic, the powder will not burn in the oven and has a gentle flavor besides. For a hit of fresh garlic, we tossed the roasted potatoes with garlic butter—made with a single minced clove—just before serving.

GARLIC POWDER

Skillet Supper: Fiesta Chicken and Rice

Cooking chicken and rice in the same pan sounds appealing, but not if the chicken is rubbery, the rice is mushy, and the flavor is bland.

Even if you get the basics right, chicken and rice can be pretty bland and boring. With its tomato, spices, onion, and bell pepper, Mexican rice is one of my favorite side dishes. Could I take the flavors in this classic Mexican recipe and use them to jazz up a common American weeknight supper?

My first task was to make good chicken and rice. The cause of the soupy, blown-out rice was easily diagnosed: The instructions on many packages of rice are wrong! Rather than adding 2 cups of liquid for every cup of rice, it's best to use just 1 1/2 cups of liquid.

Many Mexican rice recipes call for frying the rice in oil to give it a toasty flavor. Was it worth adding this step to my recipe? My tasters said yes. The rice tasted better and the grains cooked up less gluey and more separate. To ensure even cooking of the rice, I found it necessary to stir it halfway through the cooking time. Otherwise, a few stray grains would not soften properly.

To keep things simple, I chose boneless, skinless breasts over bone-in parts. When I just slid the raw chicken into the skillet with the rice, it emerged rubbery and pale. Browning the chicken before adding it to the rice improved its flavor and appearance.

My tasters wanted cheese (totally untraditional, but delicious anyway), so I added some at the very end of cooking, off the heat. You can bring the skillet right to the table, along with the usual Mexican condiments, for a weeknight meal that will be anything but boring.

–Stephanie Alleyne

This Mexican-inspired casserole is cooked—and served—all in one skillet.

FIESTA CHICKEN AND RICE

SERVES 4

This dish is good on its own but even better with some accompaniments. Test kitchen favorites include warm flour tortillas, sliced avocado, minced jalapeños or a few dashes of hot sauce, sour cream, chopped cilantro, and lime wedges.

- 4 boneless, skinless chicken breasts (about 1 1/2 pounds)
- Salt and pepper
- 1/4 cup vegetable oil
- 1 cup long-grain rice
- 1 onion, chopped medium
- 4 garlic cloves, minced
- 1 teaspoon dried oregano
- 1 teaspoon chili powder
- 1/8 teaspoon cayenne pepper
- 1 (14.5-ounce) can diced tomatoes, drained
- 1 green bell pepper, chopped medium
- 1 1/4 cups low-sodium chicken broth
- 1 cup shredded Mexican-style cheese
- 4 scallions, sliced thin

1. Season chicken liberally with salt and pepper. Heat oil in large, heavy skillet over medium-high heat until shimmering. Cook chicken until golden brown on one side, about 4 minutes. Transfer chicken to large plate, leaving fat in pan.

2. Add rice, onion, and 1/2 teaspoon salt to skillet and cook, stirring frequently, until grains are sizzling and toasted and onion begins to soften, about 3 minutes (reduce heat if rice browns too quickly). Stir in garlic, oregano, chili powder, and cayenne and cook until fragrant, about 15 seconds. Stir in tomatoes, green pepper, and broth and bring to boil, scraping up any browned bits. Nestle chicken, browned side up, into rice and pour in any juices accumulated on plate. Cover skillet, reduce heat to low, and cook until chicken is cooked through, about 12 minutes.

3. Working quickly, transfer chicken to cutting board and cover loosely with foil. Stir rice, replace cover, and continue cooking until rice is tender and liquid is absorbed, about 12 minutes. Slice chicken breasts into 1/2-inch pieces.

4. Remove skillet from heat. Arrange sliced chicken on top of rice and sprinkle with cheese and scallions. Cover and let stand until cheese is melted, about 5 minutes. Serve.

Reader Mailbag

Photo from the inside front cover of our April/May 2005 issue.

Ice Cream, Then and Now

Rick Budde and Penny Harris, Novato, Calif. The 1941 photo of two boys in your April/May 2005 issue reminded us of a photo of our grandsons, Raynan and Tony. We took it a couple of years ago, when they were 5 and 3 years old.

Thanks for the Memories:

PILFERED PEARS

Laurel Green, Albuquerque, N.M.

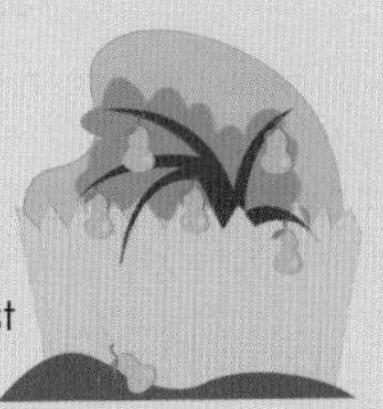

I've never liked pears very much, so I suppose it's hard to understand why I pilfered my neighbor's pears last summer. No, I didn't climb over the fence and sneak into his yard under the cover of darkness to fill my basket with ill-gotten fruit. The pears are what my mother called a windfall—they fell to the ground from tree branches hanging over my side of our adjoining property.

I never took much notice of my neighbor's rotting windfall pears before. But last summer, they somehow sparked a long-dormant gene, the one that probably kicks in at about age 60 in most of us, when the children are grown and the first grandchild is taller than we are, when the realization sinks in that there is less time left to pick and save and store away.

My pear pilfering brought to mind a comment I once heard from a female character on a television show. She said the moment she first realized she had arrived at middle age was when she went to put on her coat and was shocked to see it was not her hand, but her mother's, that emerged through the sleeve opening. I suspect that the hands probing the dense honeysuckle vines along my neighbor's fence for pears were not mine but my mother's.

Be Careful When You Measure

Sheree Slagle, Berwyn, Neb.

One morning, my daughter Alissa and I started making a big batch of cinnamon rolls for one of her 4-H projects. As she was measuring out the ingredients, she incorrectly added 3 tablespoons, instead of 3 teaspoons, of salt to the batter. Being a thrifty person, I hated to waste all that batter, so we increased the other ingredients to compensate for the excess salt. Alissa ended up kneading this gigantic mound of dough and we made 24 dozen cinnamon rolls! We froze lots of them and gave many away. Alissa also had a great topic for her 4-H speech: "Be Careful When You Measure!"

Stuffed Turkey Breast

I'd like to know how to make a stuffed turkey breast that looks good, tastes good, and doesn't dry out in the oven. I think it would be a great change from the usual whole roast turkey. –Andrea Vorvick, Tigard, Ore.

While I can't imagine Thanksgiving without a 20-pound stuffed turkey, this recipe gets dusted off only once a year. But boneless, skinless turkey breast, now widely available in supermarkets, weighs just 3 to 4 pounds and is a top contender for a family meal: It's easily stuffed and won't leave behind a week's worth of leftovers. Being without skin, bones, or dark meat, however, this ultra-lean cut often ends up flavorless, overcooked, and utterly dry.

When it comes to flavor, most recipes go wrong by depending on a bland bread stuffing. This type of stuffing is fine for a whole bird, in which the drippings from the turkey carcass help season the stuffing, but for a boneless, skinless breast the opposite is true: The stuffing, not the turkey, must provide the flavor.

I took a more aggressive route by substituting potent vegetable- and cheese-based fillings for the plain bread stuffing. My best attempts relied on relatively moist vegetables—mushrooms and spinach—and assertively flavored ingredients such as garlic, hard cheeses, and fresh herbs. When paired with the turkey, these concentrated stuffings seasoned the typically bland white meat from the inside out.

The stuffings remedied the lack of flavor but not the lack of moisture in the meat. The solution, I hoped, could be found in the cooking method.

Most recipes call for searing the turkey breast in a hot skillet before transferring it to the oven. This method produced a bronzed bird in record time, but searing really dried out the exterior. High-temperature roasting also produced an even brown color, but by the time the turkey was cooked to its core, the outside was, yet again, dry and stringy. In the end, I found that the only way to guarantee juicy turkey was to keep the oven temperature at 325 degrees. The problem? My tasters were now turned off by the turkey's pallid and flavorless exterior, with some wondering if it had been poached rather than roasted.

Then one test cook suggested coating the turkey with a light sprinkling of sugar, thinking that the sugar would encourage browning. I doubted this would work in such a cool oven, but I was wrong. The sugared turkey displayed a golden exterior, but, even better, it was the tastiest bird yet! Similar to salt, the sugar had enhanced the natural flavor of the turkey. For yet more flavor, I also sprinkled the roast with salt and a generous amount of freshly ground black pepper. My stuffed turkey breast was now as moist and flavorful as a bone-in bird—and it was a whole lot easier to manage.

–Jeremy Sauer

A turkey breast can be butterflied, stuffed, rolled, and roasted. When sliced, this method yields spirals of turkey and filling that are attractive and flavorful.

Make Ahead

Once stuffed and tied, the turkey breast can be held in the refrigerator for up to 2 days before roasting. Or just make either stuffing in advance. Both will keep in the refrigerator for up to 3 days.

STUFFED TURKEY BREAST SERVES 6 TO 8

Before stuffing the turkey, make sure the stuffing is completely chilled. Some stores only sell boneless turkey breasts with the skin still attached; the skin can be removed easily with a paring knife. This recipe calls for one turkey breast half. Don't buy an entire breast with two lobes of meat—it's too large for this recipe.

- **1 boneless, skinless turkey breast (3 to 4 pounds)**
- **2 cups stuffing (at right)**
- **2 tablespoons vegetable oil**
- **1 tablespoon sugar**
- **2 teaspoons pepper**
- **1 teaspoon salt**

1. Adjust oven rack to middle position and heat oven to 325 degrees. Following photos on page 28, butterfly turkey, cover with plastic wrap, and pound lightly with meat mallet until about ½ inch thick. Spread stuffing in even layer over turkey. Starting with short side nearest you, roll up turkey and tie at 1-inch intervals.

2. Rub turkey with oil and sprinkle evenly with sugar, pepper, and salt. Place on wire rack set over rimmed baking sheet and roast, turning every 30 minutes, until internal temperature reaches 160 degrees on instant-read thermometer, about 2 hours. Transfer turkey to cutting board, cover loosely with foil, and let rest for 15 minutes. Remove twine and slice crosswise into ½-inch-thick slices. Serve.

extra stuff

MUSHROOM-MARSALA STUFFING

MAKES ABOUT 2 CUPS

To avoid flare-ups, make sure to remove the pan from the heat before adding the marsala.

- **2 tablespoons unsalted butter**
- **1 onion, minced**
- **1 pound white mushrooms, chopped fine**
- **2 garlic cloves, minced**
- **2 teaspoons minced fresh thyme**
- **1/4 cup marsala**
- **1 cup grated Parmesan cheese**
- **2 tablespoons minced fresh parsley**
- **Salt and pepper**

Melt butter in large skillet over medium-high heat until foaming. Add onion and cook until softened, about 5 minutes. Reduce heat to medium, add mushrooms and cook until liquid has evaporated, 10 to 15 minutes. Add garlic and thyme and cook until fragrant, 30 seconds. Off heat, stir in marsala. Return to heat and cook until mushrooms are dry and golden brown, about 5 minutes. Remove from heat and cool 10 minutes. Stir in Parmesan, parsley, and salt and pepper to taste. Refrigerate until ready to use.

LEMONY SPINACH AND FONTINA STUFFING

MAKES ABOUT 2 CUPS

Soggy spinach can make for a watery filling, so wring out excess moisture in a kitchen towel (or try the kitchen shortcut on page 2).

- **2 tablespoons extra-virgin olive oil**
- **1 onion, minced**
- **1 (8-ounce) package frozen spinach, thawed, squeezed dry, and chopped**
- **3 garlic cloves, minced**
- **1/4 teaspoon grated lemon zest**
- **2 cups grated fontina cheese**
- **Salt and pepper**

Heat oil in large skillet over medium-high heat until shimmering. Add onion and cook until softened, about 5 minutes. Stir in spinach, garlic, and zest and cook until fragrant, 30 seconds. Remove from heat and cool 10 minutes. Stir in fontina and salt and pepper to taste. Refrigerate until ready to use.

Bake-Sale Favorites: Peanut Blossom Cookies

Could we improve upon this classic 1950s cookie?

Finely ground peanuts pump up the flavor in these cookies, and an unlikely baking method keeps the Kisses from gushing.

When Freda Smith entered her peanut blossoms in the 1957 Pillsbury Bake-Off, little did she know that she had created a cookie sensation that would endure for nearly five decades. This Gibsonburg, Ohio, native may not have won the $25,000 first prize (although as a runner-up her winnings included a General Electric stove), but her peanut blossoms, chocolate-kissed peanut butter cookies, quickly eclipsed that year's winner, a recipe for walnut-flavored butter cookies called accordion treats.

Since Freda's recipe is where it all began, I used it as a starting point to create my own version. Although her recipe produced a good cookie, my tasters wanted more peanut flavor. Freda's recipe calls for creamy peanut butter. Cookies made with chunky peanut butter received praise for their strong peanut flavor, but tasters disliked their craggy texture and appearance. I decided to stick with creamy peanut butter and try replacing some of the flour with ground peanuts. Sure enough, finely ground peanuts added a deep peanut flavor to the cookies without compromising their texture.

The cookies were almost perfect, but I was frustrated by one thing: the Hershey's Kiss. Every recipe that I found called for the Kisses to be pressed into the cookies immediately after baking. But I found that the residual heat in the cookies softened the Kisses so much that they took at least four hours to firm up again. If I took a bite any sooner, a squirt of chocolate would drip down my chin.

After a bit of tinkering, I found an unlikely solution to the problem of gushing Kisses. Strangely enough, placing the chocolates on the cookies during the last two minutes of baking helped them to firm up more quickly. Why? It turns out that a little direct heat stabilizes and sets the exterior of the chocolate; the Kisses handled this way were firm enough to eat after just two hours on a cooling rack.

–Cali Rich

PEANUT BLOSSOM COOKIES

MAKES ABOUT 8 DOZEN

Any Hershey's Chocolate Kiss—dark, milk, white, or "Hugs"—works in this recipe (see page 28 for a tempting new Kiss). For best results, the cookies should be baked on the middle rack, one baking sheet at a time. This recipe can be cut in half.

- **2 3/4 cups all-purpose flour**
- **1/2 teaspoon salt**
- **1/2 teaspoon baking soda**
- **1/2 teaspoon baking powder**
- **1 cup roasted, salted peanuts**
- **16 tablespoons (2 sticks) unsalted butter, softened but still cool**
- **3/4 cup packed dark brown sugar**
- **3/4 cup granulated sugar**
- **1 cup creamy peanut butter**
- **2 large eggs, at room temperature**
- **2 teaspoons vanilla extract**
- **96 Hershey's Chocolate Kisses (from two 1-pound bags), wrappers removed**

1. Adjust oven rack to middle position and heat oven to 350 degrees. Line two baking sheets with parchment paper.

2. Whisk 1¾ cups flour, salt, baking soda, and baking powder together in medium bowl. Process remaining 1 cup flour and peanuts in food processor until ground, about fifteen 1-second pulses, then stir into flour mixture.

3. Beat butter and sugars together in large bowl with electric mixer at medium-high speed until fluffy, about 3 minutes. Add peanut butter and continue to beat until combined. Add eggs, one at a time, beating after each addition, until incorporated, about 30 seconds, then beat in vanilla, stopping to scrape down sides of bowl, if necessary. Reduce speed to low, add flour mixture in two batches, and mix until incorporated. Cover bowl and refrigerate dough until stiff, about 30 minutes.

4. Roll 1-inch balls of dough and space 2 inches apart on baking sheet. Bake until just set and beginning to crack, 9 to 11 minutes, rotating baking sheet from front to back halfway through baking (while cookies are baking, place additional balls of dough on second baking sheet). Working quickly, remove baking sheet from oven and firmly press one Kiss in center of each cookie. Return baking sheet to oven and bake until lightly golden, about 2 minutes. Transfer baking sheet to wire rack to cool for 5 minutes, then transfer cookies directly to wire rack to finish cooling. Repeat rolling and baking remaining cookies. Cool completely. (Cookies will be cool enough to eat after about 30 minutes, but Kisses will take 2 hours to set completely.)

The American Table: First Kiss

Hershey's Kisses date back to 1907. Each candy was originally hand-wrapped in silver foil. In 1921, Hershey's switched over to an automatic wrapping machine and added the trademark paper "plume." Production was halted from 1942 to 1949 owing to the rationing of silver foil during and immediately after World War II. Today, Hershey's manufactures 80 million Kisses every day at factories in Hershey, Pa., and Oakdale, Calif.

Notes from Our Test Kitchen

TIPS, TECHNIQUES, AND TOOLS FOR BETTER COOKING

Kitchen Creations
Pizza Sauce

You can use a plain jarred tomato sauce (nothing too flavorful) when making our **Pepperoni Pan Pizza** (page 21), but making homemade sauce isn't much harder than opening the lid on the store-bought stuff. When it comes to pizza sauce, you want something thick, and that means starting with smooth canned crushed tomatoes rather than whole or diced. As for the seasonings, all that's needed is garlic, olive oil, salt, and pepper to complement the pepperoni, which should be the star of this recipe.

BASIC PIZZA SAUCE
MAKES 2²/₃ CUPS

This recipe makes enough for four pan pizzas, so you will need only half when making the Pepperoni Pan Pizza on page 21. Freeze the remaining sauce for future pizza making.

- 1 **tablespoon olive oil**
- 2 **garlic cloves, minced**
- 1 **(28-ounce) can crushed tomatoes**
- **Salt and pepper**

Cook oil and garlic in medium saucepan over low heat until fragrant, about 2 minutes. Add tomatoes, increase heat to medium, and cook until slightly thickened, 10 to 15 minutes. Season with salt and pepper.

Primo Pasta for Primavera

As a rule, we think fresh pasta does a better job of absorbing creamy sauces than dried pasta. But for our **Pasta Primavera** (page 11), we found that fresh fettuccine was too soft and wilted under the weight of all those vegetables. Regular dried pasta wasn't much better—the noodles were chewy, and the sauce slid right off. We had the best results with dried egg-enriched fettuccine. These noodles are substantial enough to stand up to the vegetables yet also possess the eggy richness and cream-absorbing ability of fresh pasta. Dried egg-enriched fettuccine (we particularly like Ronzoni) is sold in 12-ounce packages, perfect for four people.

–Katie Henderson

Perfectly Centered Yolks

Throughout testing of my **Deviled Eggs** (page 10), I noticed a lot of inconsistency in the location of the yolks. Sometimes they were in the center, sometimes so close to the edge that the whites ripped as soon as I tried to extract the yolk. I surfed the Web for ideas on how to center my yolks and found dozens of bizarre tips, everything from spinning eggs like a top on the counter (definitely messy, as one or two eggs will topple onto the floor) to spinning eggs with a spoon as they cook (decidedly dangerous, as splashes of boiling water are inevitable). The best idea involved placing the carton of eggs on its side in the refrigerator the day before the eggs were to be cooked. Evidently, this moves the yolk away from the large end of the egg—which is where the yolk generally settles after packaging—to the center. Now my deviled eggs were truly foolproof.

–Meredith Butcher

Smoothing Things Over

While it's a lot easier to put together a crumb crust (like the one for our Grasshopper Pie, page 7) than to roll out traditional pie dough, that doesn't mean that crumb crusts are problem-free. The crust can be too crumbly and loose, and it often sticks to everything but the pie plate. Here's how Bridget makes even, mess-free crumb crusts every time.

1. Use your hands to distribute the crumbs in an even layer over the bottom and up the sides of the pie plate. Press down lightly.

2. Place a piece of plastic wrap on top of the crust, then run the back of a dinner spoon over the crumbs, smoothing them into the bottom, curves, and sides of the pan.

Rice in a Rush

When making fried rice, cold cooked rice is essential. If you don't have leftover rice on hand (and leaving a fresh batch to cool for several hours isn't practical), Uncle Ben's Ready Rice is your answer. These microwavable pouches of rice are meant to be heated for 90 seconds, but we skipped this step when preparing our **Fried Rice with Ham and Peas** (see recipe card) and simply poured the contents of the package straight into the skillet. While traditional fried rice is usually made with white rice, we preferred the nutty flavor and slightly chewy texture of this brown rice. **–Eva Katz**

Hershey's Kisses Unwrapped

Although the wrapping machines at the Hershey's Company can enrobe up to 1,300 chocolate Kisses a minute, unwrapping them by hand can be considerably more time-consuming. Thanks to recipes like our **Peanut Blossom Cookies** (page 27), Hershey's now produces bags of unwrapped milk chocolate Kisses. Pick up two bags of these ready-to-use Kisses in the candy aisle, so you don't have to unwrap 96 candies for our cookie recipe.

–Cali Rich

Kitchen Know-How
Stuffing a Turkey Breast

To prepare our **Stuffed Turkey Breast** (page 26), you must first butterfly the turkey breast. Sounds hard, but it's actually quite simple, as you can see from the first photo (at right). Once butterflied, the turkey breast is pounded, stuffed, rolled, and tied. The entire process takes less than 10 minutes.

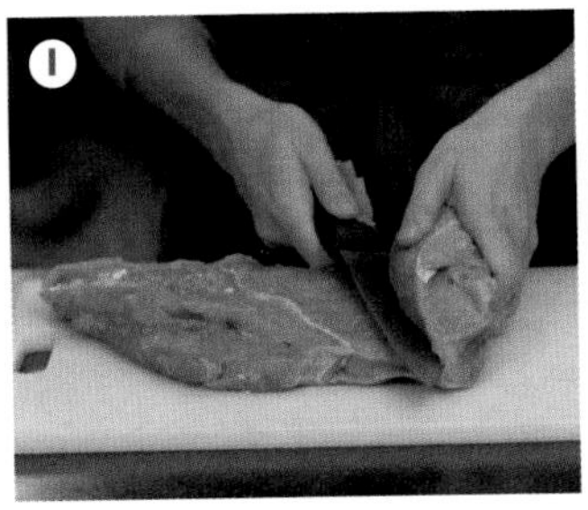

1. With the turkey smooth side down, slice into the thickest part, keeping the knife 1/2 inch above the cutting board and stopping 1/2 inch from the edge of the breast. Open it like a book.

2. Place a sheet of plastic wrap over the turkey and pound lightly with a meat mallet until the turkey breast is an even 1/2 inch thickness throughout.

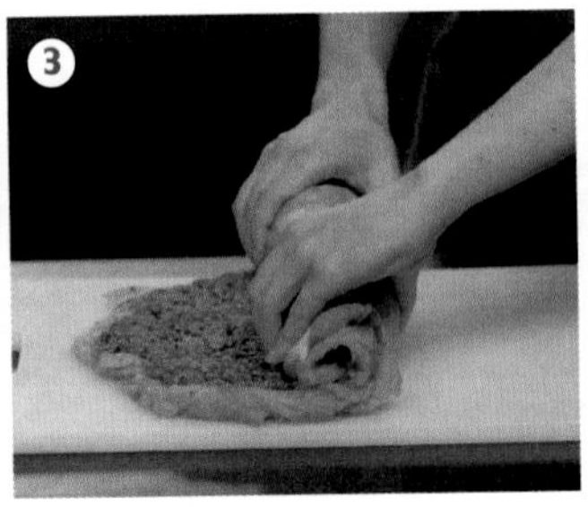

3. Remove the plastic wrap and spread the filling evenly over the turkey, stopping 1/2 inch from sides. Starting with the smaller side nearest you, roll the turkey into a tight cylinder.

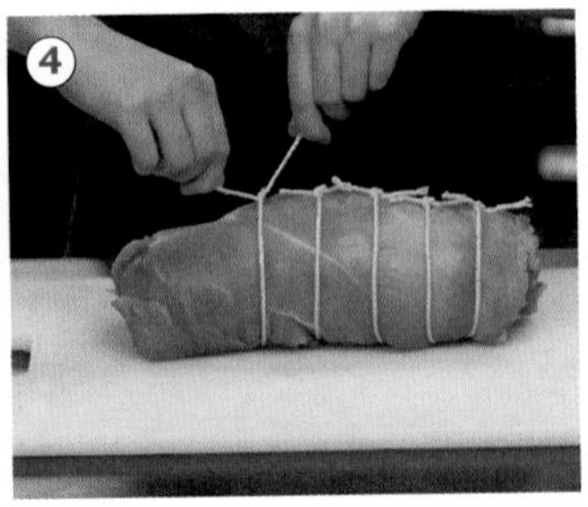

4. Use butcher's twine to tie the turkey breast at 1-inch intervals. Tuck in the ends of the turkey and loop a piece of twine around the ends to keep the stuffing from falling out.

Kitchen Tip: CHOCOLATE CURLS

Although chocolate curls add a professional touch to cakes, cups of cocoa, and our **Grasshopper Pie** (page 7), they are surprisingly easy to make. You'll need block (not bar) chocolate—semisweet, bittersweet, and white chocolate all work well—that's at least 1 inch thick. Allow the block of chocolate to soften up a bit, either by putting it on a plate on a warm windowsill or by microwaving the chocolate on the lowest power setting for 1 minute. It shouldn't melt but just soften a little. Run the blade of a vegetable peeler along the width of the softened chocolate, creating a curl. The longer the block of chocolate, the bigger the curl.

NOT JUST FOR CARROTS
Use a vegetable peeler to shave curls from a slightly softened block of chocolate.

Pickled Banana Peppers

Although authentic recipes do not call for pickled banana peppers, we found that they added a nice kick to our **Cuban Sandwiches** (page 13). Sold in mild or hot (sometimes called "zesty") varieties, sliced banana peppers rings are similar to pepperoncini, but they have a less intense, slightly sweeter flavor. Look for them near the pickles at your supermarket. **–Eva Katz**

How Green Is Your Goddess?

Green Goddess Dressing (page 19) sometimes gets its pastel hue from the addition of avocado, but we thought the dressing tasted better without it. To produce a dressing that's truly green, we prefer to use a blender, which breaks down the herbs, unlocking not only their color but also their full flavor. **–Eva Katz**

MADE BY HAND
As white as tartar sauce.

MADE IN A FOOD PROCESSOR
Nice, light green color.

MADE IN A BLENDER
The richest, brightest color.

Double It

Since **Lemon Pound Cake** (page 17) freezes beautifully, why not make two cakes today and have one in the freezer to serve (up to one month) later? (See "Make Ahead" on page 17 for freezing instructions.) To make two cakes, double all ingredients except the eggs, using 9 eggs (instead of 10). Cream the butter and sugar in step 2 for 6 minutes (rather than 3 minutes) and add the eggs in four additions (rather than three). Divide the batter between two buttered and floured loaf pans and bake as directed, rotating the pans halfway through the baking time.

–Stephanie Alleyne

Madras Curry Powder

Sweeter and hotter than regular curry powder, whose flavor fades and turns bitter after hours of cooking, Madras curry powder can stay the distance in the slow cooker when you're making **Country Captain Chicken** (page 9). But that doesn't mean you have to travel along the old spice route to find it. Madras curry powder is widely available in supermarkets. In the test kitchen, we like Sun Brand Madras Curry Powder, which has a more complex flavor than the other brands we tried. **–Stephanie Alleyne**

The 'On' Ramp

Ramps may be the least known member of the onion family (page 23), unless you're from West Virginia, like I am. Ramps grow in the shady woodlands of the Appalachian Mountains and are a sure sign of spring—the season starts in late March or early April and is over by early May.

The test kitchen loves the distinct flavor of ramps, which is pungent for sure. The greens taste like a cross between a fresh scallion and a yellow onion, with the bite of strong garlic. On the rare occasion that the test kitchen can find ramps, we jump at the chance to sauté them for soups and casseroles or stir-fry them with beef. They're also a great addition to egg and potato dishes. I especially like them in home fries. **–Bridget Lancaster**

Kitchen Know-How
Shake, Rattle, and Peel

Some eggs are easy to peel, while others never seem to let go of their shells. Here's how we handle this pesky task in the test kitchen when preparing **Deviled Eggs** (page 10) and egg salad.

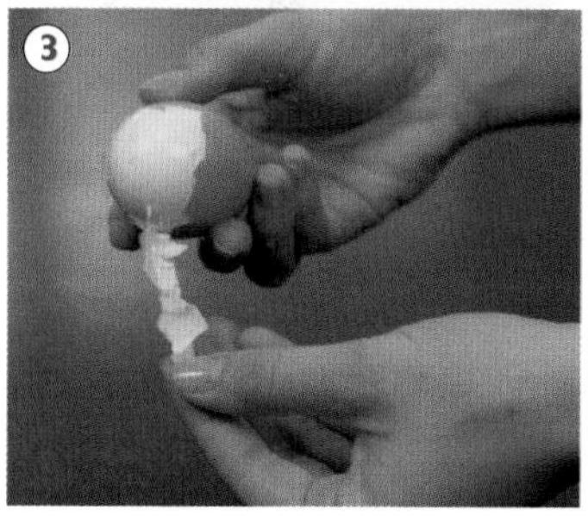

1. Once the eggs have finished cooking, pour out the boiling water and shake the pan back and forth to crack the shells.
2. Transfer the eggs to a bowl of ice water. The cracks will allow more air and water to get in between the white and the shell, making it easier to peel the eggs.
3. Starting at the wider end of each egg, begin to peel away the shell in one strip.

Inside the Test Kitchen Lining Up Cake Layers

It's hard enough to slice a cake into thin, even layers. But if the layers aren't reassembled in their original orientation, the finished cake can look like the Leaning Tower of Pisa. To head off this problem, the test kitchen marks cakes before slicing them. Use this technique if you're making our Ambrosia Cake (see the inside back cover).

1. Using a serrated knife, score the cake in a vertical line, from bottom to top.
2. After slicing the cake into thin layers, reassemble the cake, making sure that the score marks line up.

Food Shopping

FOOD SHOPPING: Milk Chocolates Are Surprisingly Different

Although pastry chefs might debate the merits of various bittersweet chocolates, no one talks about milk chocolate—despite the fact that 65 percent of Americans prefer it to the dark stuff, according to the Chocolate Manufacturers Association. Most of us assume there's no reason to pay "gourmet" prices for a bar of boutique milk chocolate—or is there? To find out, our staff tasted 10 brands of milk chocolate, plain and in chocolate frosting. Tasters were shocked at the wide diversity of flavors and textures among brands.

Milk chocolate must contain at least 10 percent chocolate liquor, which consists of cocoa butter and cocoa solids (the source of chocolate flavor) and 12 percent milk solids; the remainder is sweeteners and flavorings. To figure out exactly what's in each brand, we sent the chocolates out to a food lab, which focused on chocolate solids, fat (the cocoa butter), and sugar.

Most tasters put a premium on flavor. Consequently, the chocolates with the highest percentage of chocolate solids, Scharffen Berger and Dove, were the taste-test winners. Overly sweet chocolates (like Nestlé) or brands with little chocolate flavor (like Cadbury) were downgraded. A second (smaller) group of tasters focused on texture. They placed a premium on creaminess, giving high marks to Lindt, which contained the most fat of the brands tested. Chocolates are listed below in order of preference. **–Keri Fisher**

Top Picks

1

1. **DOVE Milk Chocolate** **80 cents for 1.3-ounce bar**
CHOCOLATE SOLIDS: 7.96% SUGAR: 54% FAT: 32.5%
Though some found the flavor "too sweet," most tasters praised the "great flavor" and agreed that this was a "good all-around piece of milk chocolate."

2

2. **SCHARFFEN BERGER Milk Chocolate** **$4.15 for 3-ounce bar**
CHOCOLATE SOLIDS: 11.18% SUGAR: 40% FAT: 21.4%
Most compared the "dark" flavor favorably to bittersweet chocolate, though a minority called it "burnt." Likeable, but "it doesn't seem like milk chocolate."

3

3. **LINDT Excellence Extra Creamy Milk Chocolate** **$2.50 for 3.5-ounce bar**
CHOCOLATE SOLIDS: 5.22% SUGAR: 50% FAT: 37.5%
Tasters praised the "very creamy" consistency of this top-rated bar that had a "good balance of milk and chocolate." One taster wrote, "What a treat!"

Runners-Up

4

4. **PERUGINA Milk Chocolate** **$2.00 for 3.5-ounce bar**
CHOCOLATE SOLIDS: 6.61% SUGAR: 55% FAT: 30.3%
Some complaints about a "slightly waxy" texture and "not enough" chocolate flavor, but overall very good.

5

5. **NESTLÉ Superior Quality Milk Chocolate** **$2.00 for 5-ounce bar**
CHOCOLATE SOLIDS: 6.46% SUGAR: 60% FAT: 28.6%
Several tasters noted the "chalky, grainy" texture and "fake flavor" that tasted "cheap." Better in our frosting test than when eaten out of hand.

6

6. **HERSHEY'S Milk Chocolate** **$1.59 for 6-ounce bar**
CHOCOLATE SOLIDS: 6.81% SUGAR: 51% FAT: 30.2%
"I bet this is Hershey's," wrote one taster; several others easily recognized the familiar flavor described as "chalky" and "very sweet."

7

7. **GHIRARDELLI Milk Chocolate Baking Bar** **$3.19 for 4-ounce bar**
CHOCOLATE SOLIDS: 5.49% SUGAR: 53% FAT: 32.6%
This "middle-of-the-road" chocolate was praised by fans as "milky sweet" but mostly rejected as "hard and waxy," with an "old musty flavor."

8

8. **NEWMAN'S Own Organics Milk Chocolate** **$1.99 for 2.8-ounce bar**
CHOCOLATE SOLIDS: 7.92% SUGAR: 51% FAT: 32.9%
Tasters complained of the "very mild chocolate flavor" that many felt was dominated by "coffee" overtones.

9

9. **CADBURY Dairy Milk Milk Chocolate** **$1.59 for 4.5-ounce bar**
CHOCOLATE SOLIDS: 3.95% SUGAR: 53% FAT: 30%
Several tasters noted lots of "caramel" undertones "but not much chocolate flavor." As one taster noted, "a little one-dimensional."

10

10. **E. GUITTARD Milk Chocolate** **$2.50 for 2-ounce bar**
CHOCOLATE SOLIDS: 6.05% SUGAR: 46% FAT: 37%
While fans praised this bar as "very milky," most tasters dismissed the "fake chocolate" flavor.

Taste Test Cooking Spray

What started in 1961 as a one-brand, one-can business has evolved into a huge industry, with flavored cooking sprays and specialty sprays for baking and grilling now lining supermarket shelves. You can even make your own cooking spray by buying a hand-pumped aerosol mister and filling it with oil.

But are any of these sprays better than the original PAM (the name stands for Product of Arthur Meyerhoff, who, along with Leon Rubin, brought the product to market in 1961). To find out, we purchased plain, butter-flavored, olive-oil-flavored, baking, and grilling sprays and filled a mister with olive oil, then ran them all through a series of tests: sautéing green beans, baking yellow cakes, toasting croutons, and grilling salmon.

Our results show that you don't need to clutter your cabinet with cans of cooking spray. Only two of these products—plain spray and baking spray (which contains flour)—are useful. Most tasters couldn't detect any butter or olive oil flavor in the flavored sprays, and the grilling spray was a flop—the salmon tore when we tried to flip it. As for the mister, the constant pumping was good exercise, but ultimately tiresome. Sprays are listed below in order of preference. **–K.F.**

Plain Spray

The plain spray performed well in all tests but grilling, in which none of the sprays worked. If you keep only one spray on hand, this is the one.

Baking Spray

Though all the sprays, paired with flour, allowed yellow cakes to release easily from pans, only the baking spray, which has flour mixed in, allowed for easy release with no messy flouring.

Mister

The mister must be pumped manually several times before each use. Though the resulting spray worked just as well as the canned sprays, the extra effort involved just wasn't worth it.

Flavored Sprays

A few tasters noted a "buttery" flavor in the croutons, while others detected an "artificial" flavor in the cake from a pan coated with butter-flavored spray. But most couldn't taste anything in particular in this spray or the olive-oil-flavored spray.

Grilling Spray

We used this spray as directed, applying it to a cold grill grate before heating, but salmon still stuck fast to the grill. To effectively grease a grill, we recommend wiping the hot grate with a wad of lightly oiled paper towels, holding the towels with long-handled tongs.

Equipment Roundup

PARING KNIVES: Can a $5 Knife Outperform a $30 Competitor?

I own more than a dozen different knives (thanks to my wedding registry), but I use only three of them: a chef's knife, bread knife, and paring knife. I use my paring knife not just for "paring" tasks—peeling an apple or turnip, carving the rind off an orange, coring a tomato—but also for jobs suited to a mini chef's knife or a boning knife—dicing a shallot or slipping the blade into the nooks and crannies of a chicken thigh.

To find out which paring knives are the best, I asked six testers of varying hand size and levels of knife skill to peel and core apples, dice shallots, remove the silver skin (a tough, thin membrane) from a pork tenderloin, and core tomatoes. In the test kitchen, we find that 3½-inch blades are the best size for most paring tasks, so I chose knives with blades as close to that size as possible within each brand, with a price limit of $30. Here are some key findings from our tests.

FORGED OR STAMPED: Forged blades are made of molded steel, while stamped blades are simply cut out of a larger piece of metal. Because the forging process can be so time-consuming, forged knives are usually expensive. But we didn't necessarily find them to be any better. The top-rated Forschner features a stamped blade.

THIN AND NARROW: Only a thin blade will slide under an apple peel or a length of silver skin without removing too much of the flesh beneath. The best knives had blades that were no more than a millimeter thick. Thin blades were also more flexible, which was important for peeling round apples and cutting around a tomato core. The Forschner had a very thin and flexible blade, whereas the Farberware and Calphalon had blades that were stiff and thick. In addition, testers rejected wide blades as clumsy, especially on the tomato test, where a narrow blade is key to cutting a tight circle around the core.

SHARP CONTRAST: A knife is only as good as it is sharp. All the knives were sharp right out of the package, but some (such as the Farberware and Chicago Cutlery) dulled so quickly during testing they would require constant sharpening to be of any use.

HANDLING: Despite a wide range of shapes, sizes, and materials, most of the knife handles fit comfortably in the hand. There were, however, some uncomfortable standouts. The rough wooden handle of the Chicago Cutlery knife was dismissed as irritating, while the Messermeister's large molded plastic handle was uncomfortable in all but the largest of hands.

SUMMING UP: The cheapest knife, the lightweight Forschner Fibrox, turned out to be the best, beating models that cost six times as much. For cooks looking for a little more heft, the KitchenAid finished a close second and is a great performer at a good price. Knives are listed in order of preference. **–Keri Fisher**

Highly Recommended

FORSCHNER Fibrox 4-Inch Paring Knife
Price: $4.95
Comments: Testers loved the "great flexibility" of this knife, which slid under silver skin easily and turned the curve of an apple nicely. Though some testers complained that this lightest of all the knives lacked "heft," most agreed that the super-thin, razor-sharp edge more than made up for it.

Recommended

KITCHENAID Cook's Series 3.5-Inch Paring Knife
Price: $9.99
Comments: With the thinnest of all blades and an extremely narrow pointed tip, this knife was a standout in the tenderloin and apple tests. Some testers complained about the heavy handle, but most praised the "smooth" cuts from the "nice sharp blade."

WÜSTHOF Classic 3.5-Inch Paring Knife
Price: $29.95
Comments: Testers praised the "incredibly sharp" blade that made slicing an apple "like cutting butter." Though the "stiff" blade came in handy in the shallot test, most testers agreed that they would prefer a bit more flexibility.

Recommended with Reservations

CALPHALON Contemporary 3.5-Inch Paring Knife
Price: $14.95
Comments: Testers with smaller hands found the molded handle uncomfortable, and all testers found the weight excessive. Though quite sharp, the thick blade was very inflexible.

OXO Good Grips Professional 3.5-Inch Paring Knife
Price: $14.99
Comments: Testers liked the "comfy" no-slip rubber handle but were put off by the thick blade that was "not super-sharp." Though the blade had some bend, most agreed that it "could be more flexible."

MAC Knives 4-Inch Paring Knife
Price: $17.95
Comments: Though the blade was "very sharp and thin," it was also deemed "too long" by most testers, who were uncomfortable with the fact that the cutting edge came so close to the handle.

HENCKELS Classic 4-Inch Paring Knife
Price: $19.95
Comments: The long narrow blade was perfect for removing silver skin but good for little else. Even small-handed testers found the handle too narrow, though the "not-so-flexible" blade was "sharp."

Not Recommended

MESSERMEISTER 4-Inch Four Seasons Paring Knife
Price: $5.95
Comments: The thin, narrow blade won points for flexibility but was "not sharp enough," and its length gave testers little control, making this knife "hard to use." The large plastic handle was too bulky for all but the biggest hands.

CHICAGO Cutlery Walnut Signature 3.5-Inch Paring Knife
Price: $9.95
Comments: Testers universally panned the "boxy" wooden handle that felt "like sandpaper." Though the thin blade was fairly flexible, it was simply "not sharp enough" and failed to perform well on any task.

FARBERWARE Pro 3.75-Inch Paring Knife
Price: $7.99
Comments: With a blade more than twice as thick as those on our top-rated knives, the Farberware lost points across the board. Deemed "so dull" that it smashed rather than sliced shallots and considered "too stiff" for all other tasks.

Gadgets & Gear Magic Knife

The Magic Knife ($14.95) promises "perfect slices every time," thanks to an adjustable spacer attached to a serrated blade. To find out if the Magic Knife delivers on its promise, we tested it in four applications: soft wheat bread, crusty French bread, a large potato, and, as illustrated on the package, a ham. The knife performed well on both types of bread and did an admirable, if not perfect, job slicing a potato into paper-thin rounds. The knife (which adjusts from a few millimeters to 1¼ inches) was inconsistent at the thinnest settings, sometimes producing ragged shavings. The short 6-inch blade didn't stand a chance with the ham (contrary to the package photograph, which likely features a very small ham). Our conclusion: The Magic Knife ensures pretty good (not perfect) slices on small items only.
–K.F.

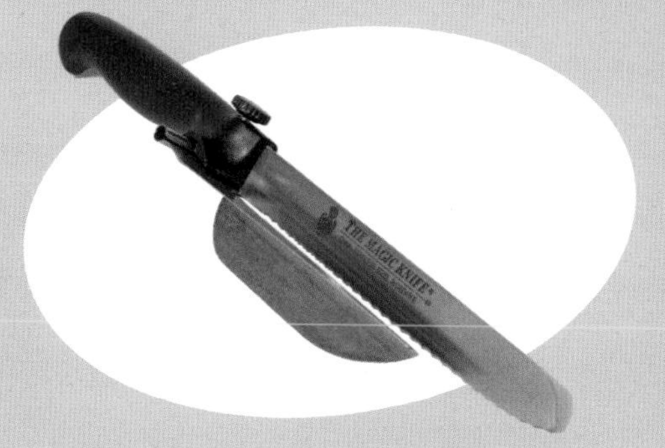

An adjustable spacer ensures pretty good—but not perfect—slices.

When Things Go Wrong in the Kitchen

READERS SHARE FUNNY STORIES ABOUT COOKING MISHAPS

OODLES OF NOODLES

In the first few months of my marriage, I wanted to do everything the way my grandmother did. My husband was just home from Vietnam, and I had recently been discharged from the army as well. One day, I decided that I would make homemade noodles and chicken for supper. I had already prepared the chicken, so I called my grandmother and asked how to make noodles. She told me eggs, flour, and salt. I mixed it all up and decided that it didn't look like enough for one meal, let alone leftovers. So I added more eggs, flour, and salt. By the time I was done, I had added seven eggs and enough flour and salt to match. We ate noodles for more than two weeks and got so sick of them that it was several years before I could even think of making them again. When I told my grandmother what I had done, she laughed so hard she had tears in her eyes.

Colleen Stuckenschneider Sioux Rapids, Iowa

THE YELLOW ALIEN

I come from a family of six, and my parents got into the habit of buying food in bulk. One day my mom and my younger sister were going through the fridge and, to get a better view of what was inside, they removed a huge plastic gallon container of mustard and set it on top of the fridge. Something ended up dislodging the mustard from its perch, the container hit the kitchen floor, and the force of the impact blew off the screw-on lid. It looked as if some alien with thick yellow blood had been cruelly slaughtered in the kitchen.

Peter Isaacson Whittier, Calif.

THE SECRET MARINADE

I grew up in the city, and my dad was certainly not a fisherman. My uncle lived in Montana, and he loved to fish. During one visit, he encouraged my father and me to drive up to Mystic Lake and take his old wooden boat out fishing. Despite our inexperience, we caught some nice-looking lake trout. Most fishermen would have a special cooler for their catch. We simply threw our fish into the bottom of the boat. When evening came, we built a fire to cook them. As we ate, we noticed an unexpected flavor. It wasn't smoke—what was it? Then, suddenly, we knew. The old wooden boat had sprung a few leaks and had been sealed with tar. Our catch had spent the day marinating in tar-flavored water on the bottom of the boat.

Ardy Hagen San Jose, Calif.

LID-LOCKED SALMON

Back in my single days, I would often rush home from work and throw a single serving of salmon in the skillet for a quick meal. I had just bought a new, nonstick skillet and wanted to give it a try. I wanted to cover it, but the skillet didn't come with a lid. No problem, I thought, the lid from my prized copper saucepan looked like a good fit. I dropped the copper lid onto my new nonstick skillet, and it fit, right down inside the pan. But when I tried to pull it back out, it was stuck—I mean really stuck. I called my father, and he recommended a variety of remedies, none of which worked. He promised to take a look at it on his next visit. I guess it didn't register with him that there was a piece of salmon under the lid, and he lived 300 miles away. I kept that silly pan/lid fusion in the freezer for several months before I finally admitted defeat and threw out the skillet, the salmon, and my prized copper lid.

Cindy Matthews Tustin, Calif.

TEXAS TEA

I wanted to surprise my soon-to-be mother-in-law with a chocolate Bundt cake for her birthday and went to work in my fiancé's kitchen. When I added the oil to the batter, my nose wrinkled at the strange aroma wafting from the bottle, but I thought nothing of it and continued to mix my ingredients. When it came time for the finger taste test, I received quite a shock. The batter tasted like motor oil! Thinking that I had measured wrong, I added more cocoa, but the batter still tasted like "Texas tea." Desperate, I added vanilla, thinking it would mask the taste. As I poured the batter into the pan, the strong odor filled the air. Maybe it would bake out, I thought to myself. I clearly needed a miracle, and, as I closed the oven door, I prayed for one. Needless to say, the finished cake tasted like motor oil. I ended up buying a cake. Much later, I confessed to my mother-in-law, and she let me in on a little secret. "Honey," she said, "oil doesn't last forever. It can, and does, go bad. Especially if it's been sitting in my son's kitchen."

Judith Skelton Conroe, Texas

CHERRY BOMB

Although a novice cook, I decided to make cherries jubilee for our new neighbors when we invited them to dinner for the first time. Earlier that summer, I had bought a chafing dish, and this was to be its inaugural use. I researched several versions of the recipe and purchased the right alcohol for the burner. Wanting to be organized, I prepared everything in advance so that all I had to do after dinner was light the burner, add the ingredients to the pan, pour over the kirsch, and set the sauce alight. Unfortunately, I wasn't aware that alcohol disperses in the heat, and I basically created a small vapor bomb around the burner. As my guests sat rapt in expectation of the spectacle, I proceeded to light not only the alcohol but also my sleeve and arm hair! I had wanted to create a lasting impression, and I certainly did. Now when I make cherries jubilee, I call it cherry bomb.

Kathy Rogers Vancouver, B.C., Canada

AN EXPENSIVE, STINKY MISTAKE

Never having used saffron, I didn't understand that the recipe I was following required crushing the saffron threads after measuring, not before. Had I understood this, my soup might not have turned into a crayon-yellow, sickeningly pungent disaster. I was so mad about the expense and time taken to make the ruined chowder that I forced myself to eat it for supper and took a big bowl of it to work for lunch. After stinking up the place, I got offers for lunch from several colleagues the next day. To this day, I still cannot eat anything with saffron in it, and I can smell that stuff coming from a mile away.

Anne Garber Columbus, Ohio

Send us your funniest kitchen disaster stories. Please write to us at Kitchen Disasters, Cook's Country, P.O. Box 470739, Brookline, MA 02447. If you'd like to use e-mail, write to us at kitchendisasters@bcpress.com. If we publish your story, you'll receive a complimentary one-year subscription to *Cook's Country*.

The Great American Cake

Ambrosia Cake

Ambrosia, food of the gods in Greek and Roman mythology, is something a bit more humble in most American households, where it's better known as a chilled fruit salad, often made with mandarin oranges, pineapple, and coconut. The tall and tropical ambrosia cake, made with angel food cake, pineapple curd, and orange and vanilla frostings, has more heavenly aspirations.

To make this cake you'll need:

- 1/4 cup pineapple juice
- 2 large eggs plus 1 egg yolk
- 1/2 cup sugar
- 2 tablespoons unsalted butter
- Pinch salt
- 3 cups vanilla buttercream frosting*
- 1 teaspoon grated zest plus 2 teaspoons juice from 1 orange
- 1 (9-inch) angel food cake*
- 2 (15-ounce) cans mandarin orange slices, drained and cut in half lengthwise
- 2 cups sweetened shredded coconut, toasted
- 1 (20-ounce) can pineapple slices, drained and cut into half moons

For the pineapple curd: Bring pineapple juice to boil in saucepan over medium heat. Whisk eggs, yolk, and sugar in medium bowl. Whisking constantly, slowly pour hot juice into egg mixture, then return mixture to saucepan and cook, stirring constantly, until thick enough to cling to spoon, 2 to 3 minutes. Off heat, stir in butter and salt, then strain into small bowl. Cover surface directly with plastic wrap and refrigerate until thickened, at least 1 hour.

For the orange frosting: Transfer 1 cup vanilla frosting to small bowl. Stir in orange zest and juice.

To assemble: Cut cake horizontally into 4 even layers (see page 29). Place bottom layer on platter. Spread 1/2 cup orange frosting over cake and top with 20 orange slices. Place next layer on top of oranges and spread with pineapple curd. Top with next cake layer and spread with remaining orange frosting and 20 more orange slices. Finish with top cake layer and coat top and sides of cake with vanilla frosting. Press toasted coconut into sides and decorate with orange and pineapple slices.

* Go to www.cookscountry.com for frosting and cake recipes, or use your own.

Recipe Index

(RC) = Recipe Card

Cook's Country

JUNE/JULY 2006

Kansas City Ribs
Sticky, Spicy, and Smoky

Potato Salad
Creamy and Pickle-y!

Better Burgers
Building Flavor Inside Out

ALABAMA CHICKEN
Discovering White BBQ Sauce

TASTING TORTILLA CHIPS
Thin, Crispy, and Salty Win

LEMON MERINGUE PIE
No-Weep Mile-High Topping

GRILLED CHICKEN KEBABS
The Secret? Yogurt Marinade

EASY BERRY SHORTCAKES
No-Roll, No-Cut Biscuits

BLUEBERRY MUFFIN MAKEOVER
50% Less Fat, Brighter Flavor

BEST SLOW-COOKER CHILI
Smoky, Meaty, and Savory

OVEN-FRIED FISH
Crunchy, No-Mess Coating

RATING SPATULAS
Cheapest Model Wins

$1,000 Grand-Prize Winner!

Carrie Vitt of Tucson, Ariz., won first place with a recipe that uses roasted onions, chopped pears, and a sweet citrus dressing to dress up leafy greens. See page 4 for her **Roasted Red Onion and Pear Salad**.

$4.95 U.S./$6.95 CANADA

07>

0 74470 05251 7

Cook's Country

Dear Country Cook,

I often take my 11-year-old, Charlie, up to our lower pond for a 10-minute fishing expedition, the kind that nets one small bass, two hooked fingers, and at least three lures snagged in overhanging branches.

But my most memorable fishing trip was with my then 8-year-old daughter Caroline. We traveled up to New Brunswick in late April with two other father/daughter pairings to fly-fish the Matapedia River for salmon just after the ice had come out. It snowed. It hailed. It rained. And, on the last morning of a freezing three-day expedition, we caught a 6-pounder that was just over the legal limit. I still have the photo of Caroline standing in the canoe, proudly displaying the catch of the day: a fish shining as brightly as her smile.

If you were to ask me about my favorite moment from that trip, I would say it was when Caroline hooked on to a big fish, a good 20 pounds or more. Our guide asked me if I wanted him to help. I said no. She would have to learn for herself. She soon lost that salmon; the big one got away. But the two of us netted something greater, the memory of a chance taken between father and daughter, fishers of life in a small boat on a cold river at the end of the best day of our lives.

Christopher Kimball
Founder and Editor, Cook's Country Magazine

Gone fishing, 1945. Photo by Lambert/Getty Images.

"Home on thRange"

JUNE/JULY 2006

Cook's Country

features

departments

in every issue

Editorial Office: 17 Station Street, Brookline, MA 02445; 617-232-1000; fax 617-232-1572
Subscription inquiries: Cook's Country, P.O. Box 8382, Red Oak, IA 51591-1382
800-526-8447

ON THE COVER: PHOTOGRAPHY: Julie Toy, Jupiter Images/Foodpix. ILLUSTRATION: John Burgoyne.
IN THIS ISSUE: COLOR FOOD PHOTOGRAPHY: Keller + Keller. STYLING: Mary Jane Sawyer, Marie Piraino. ILLUSTRATION: Lisa Perrett.

Cook's Country magazine (ISSN 1552-1990), number 9, is published bimonthly by Boston Common Press Limited Partnership, 17 Station Street, Brookline, MA 02445. Copyright 2006 Boston Common Press Limited Partnership. Application to mail at periodical postage rates pending at Boston, Mass., and additional mailing offices. POSTMASTER: Send address changes to Cook's Country, P.O. Box 8382, Red Oak, IA 51591-1382. For subscription and gift subscription orders, subscription inquiries, or change-of-address notices, call 800-526-8447 in the U.S. or 515-247-7571 from outside the U.S., or write us at Cook's Country, P.O. Box 8382, Red Oak, IA 51591-1382.
PRINTED IN THE USA

Visit us at www.cookscountry.com!
Go online to ask questions, share kitchen tips, and enter recipe contests. You can also take a sneak peek at what we've got cooking for upcoming issues.

Kitchen Shortcuts

READERS SHARE CLEVER TIPS FOR EVERYDAY COOKING CHALLENGES

Popcorn Secret

As a popcorn fanatic, I'm constantly making homemade caramel corn, popcorn balls, and even plain old buttered movie-style popcorn. Over the years, I've developed a method for separating the unpopped kernels from the popped. After popping the corn, I pour all of it onto a cooling rack set inside of a baking sheet. After a quick shake or two, the unpopped kernels fall right through the holes in the rack, leaving nothing but perfect popcorn!

Karen Moss West Point, Utah

Two Platters in One

When grilling, I line my serving platter with plastic wrap and put the raw meat on top. Once I put the meat on the grill, I throw out the plastic wrap and, voilà, I have a clean platter ready for the grilled meat. Keeps my family safe and saves on dishes!

Meredith Eaton
Bloomfield, N.J.

A Pear-fect Tip

I use a melon baller (you can also use a small measuring spoon) to scoop out the stem and blossom end of a fresh pear before peeling it. That gives me a firm finger hold on each end while I peel. Once peeled, the pear can be cut in half and the melon baller used again to scoop out the core. Fast and easy, and no pears slipping out of my hands!

Judy O'Shea
Lethbridge, Alberta, Canada

Cool Idea

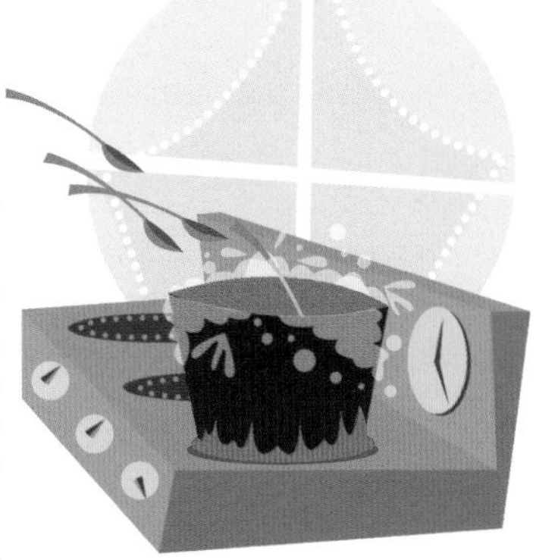

AVOID BOILOVERS

Ever stood there like a deer in the headlights and watched a pot boil over, even after you'd turned off the heat (especially with an electric range)? Throwing a couple ice cubes in the pot would help, but you'd never make it to the freezer in time. Instead, toss in a handful of spoons (the silverware drawer is often right next to the stove). Metal utensils will absorb heat from the water, thereby preventing a boilover. It's much easier to fish a few spoons out of the pot than to clean the entire stovetop.

David Cantu San Antonio, Texas

KEEPING SLEEVES AT BAY

It seems like the dirtier the job, the less my shirt sleeves want to stay rolled up. To keep my long-sleeved shirts in place while I'm breading fried chicken or rolling out pie dough, I roll up my sleeves and place a rubber band on each cuff to keep them in place. Now I can get my hands dirty while keeping my shirt clean.

Amy Flower
Warwick, R.I.

SOFTENING BUTTER—FAST

Ever forget to soften the butter before making a cake? I did, and the only butter I had on hand was frozen. So I put the butter in a large zipper-lock bag (sealed tightly) and slipped the bag into a large bowl of room-temperature water. In about five minutes, the butter was perfectly softened.

Emily Nealy
Pensacola, Fla.

UNSCREWING STUCK JAR LIDS

I pulled the molasses out of my pantry only to find the lid completely stuck on the bottle (I rarely use molasses). I tried to open it using brute force, and then I got smart. I ran the lid under hot water for about 30 seconds, and it came right off. This trick works with honey and maple syrup, too.

Deborah Hoon
Crystal Lake, Ill.

HOT TOWELS FOR A CROWD

Every 4th of July weekend, I host a big barbecue for the whole neighborhood. A few years ago, I got to thinking: Wouldn't a hot, moist towel clean sticky fingers better than paper napkins? I ran out to the hardware store and got a bunch of inexpensive terry-cloth wipes, rolled them up, and poured a cup or two of water over them. I layered the towel rolls in a 6-quart slow cooker set on warm, and they stayed hot and moist for hours!

Roger Berry
Rehoboth Beach, Del.

NO-MESS RICE KRISPIES TREATS

I always had trouble cutting a pan of Rice Krispies Treats into squares with neat edges. The marshmallow eventually makes the knife blade sticky, and dipping the blade into hot water and wiping it clean is another messy proposition. Now I wrap the blade of a bench scraper (the ones with stainless steel blades work best) with Reynolds nonstick foil and cut away without any problem. This tip can be used for cutting brownies and lasagna as well.

Karen Yuen
Los Altos Hills, Calif.

KEEPING THE CHEESE IN THE TACO

It used to drive me crazy when I topped off a taco with shredded cheese only to have the cheese fall right off onto my plate when I tried to take a bite. Now, to make sure the cheese doesn't go anywhere, I put it in the taco shell first, then add the meat and remaining ingredients. Not only does the weight of the meat hold the cheese in place, the heat of the ground beef melts the cheese to gooey greatness!

Kate Nixon
Dover, Mass.

QUICK AND EVEN CUTTING

Here's a quick way to guarantee evenly sized pieces when cutting a head of romaine lettuce for chopped salad, tacos, and the like. Holding the stem end, make the first cut through the length of the head, starting just above the stem. Next, rotate the head 90 degrees and make a second cut in the same manner. Finally, hold the stem while cutting across the head of lettuce (cut very thin strips for shredded lettuce and wider strips for salad-sized pieces). After chopping, just toss the stem end in the trash.

Elena Engelsman
Anaheim, Calif.

If you'd like to submit a tip, please send a letter to Kitchen Shortcuts, Cook's Country, P.O. Box 470739, Brookline, MA 02447. Or e-mail us at shortcuts@bcpress.com. Include your name, address, and phone number. If we publish your tip, you will receive a one-year subscription to *Cook's Country*.

BREAD CRUMBS BY BRUTE FORCE

When making bread crumbs from stale bread, there's no need to break out the food processor. Just put the dried bread in a heavy-duty zipper-lock bag, press out as much air as possible, seal tightly, and then smash with a rolling pin. Once the bread begins to break up, crush the crumbs completely by rolling the pin back and forth over them.

Jane Berger
Washington, D.C.

PUT THE KETTLE TO THE METAL

When I have dinner baking in the oven, I put a pot of water on the stovetop (with the burner turned off). The heat from the oven warms the water so that when my guests are ready for coffee or tea, the water is already warm and comes to a boil quickly.

Dee Dee Miles
Hamilton, N.J.

EASY TRACING TRICK

I am an avid baker but have always found the tracing and cutting of parchment and waxed paper circles to fit the bottom of cake pans to be a pain. Instead, I place the pan on the paper and "trace" around the edge of the pan with a sharp paring knife rather than a pencil. The paring knife perforates the parchment, and all I have to do is lightly tear it out. No scissors necessary.

Kimberly Reuter
Thornton, Colo.

RECYCLE AND GRILL

Before putting anything on the grill, I always wipe down the grates with a few oiled paper towels to prevent sticking. Instead of throwing the paper towels away, I save them and use them to ignite my charcoal chimney starter the next time I grill. I used to use newspaper, but on a still day it takes a while for the smoke to dissipate and my neighborhood smells like burning trash. With the oiled paper towels, I use much less paper and the smell isn't as bad.

Steve Nell
Patterson, La.

SMALLER IS BETTER

My husband and I don't eat much purchased applesauce, but sometimes I need to buy it for recipes. I've found that the snack-sized containers, sold in six-packs, are the perfect size for my purposes. No more half-finished jars sitting around forever in the fridge.

Rachel Billings
Holland, Mich.

PLEASE DON'T EAT THE BRISTLES

I use 1- to 1½-inch-wide natural-bristle brushes to baste meat when I grill. I always have two brushes on hand: one dark-bristled brush for basting light-colored foods and one light-bristled brush for basting dark foods. If a bristle comes loose, it's easy to spot on the contrasting color of the food.

Tony Rotolo
New York, N.Y.

A NEW TAKE ON S'MORES

I bake off a batch of chocolate chip cookies and wrap them in foil the night before we go camping. Once we're at the campsite, I arrange the foil-wrapped cookies on a flat stone near the campfire. By the time we're ready for dessert, the cookies are warm and the chocolate is gooey; all the kids have to do is roast marshmallows and sandwich them between two cookies.

Ramsey Johnson
St. Louis, Mo.

SIMPLE SPOON REST

Instead of using a spoon rest, which creates yet another dirty dish, I use a lid from a jar of one of the ingredients I'm cooking with. The bowl of the spoon fits nicely in the upside-down lid, it has a little lip around the edge to prevent spillage, and when you're done you just throw it away.

Valerie Tate
Cypress, Texas

A 'GRATE' WAY TO THICKEN SOUPS

Here's what I often do to quickly thicken soups, stews, and some sauces. I peel off the skin of a potato (starchy russets work best) and then grate the flesh on a box grater right into what I'm cooking. Because what I'm cooking is already simmering, the potato quickly cooks and dissolves, thickening the mixture.

Tom Gruner
Covington, Wash.

No More Tears

THINK OUTSIDE THE HOUSE

If I happen to be slicing a lot of onions and it's nice outside, I move my cutting board to the table on my screened porch. That way the onion doesn't stink up the kitchen, and the breeze helps to keep the fumes from causing tears.

Patty Logan Leawood, Kan.

Easy Grilled Bacon

When making bacon burgers, I place the bacon in a single layer in a disposable aluminum pan and cook the bacon on the grill while I shape my burger patties. The bacon takes about 10 minutes to become crisp, so by the time I've shaped and cooked the burgers, the bacon's ready to go. After the bacon fat cools, the aluminum tray can be discarded for easy cleanup.

Nancy Britting Havelock, N.C.

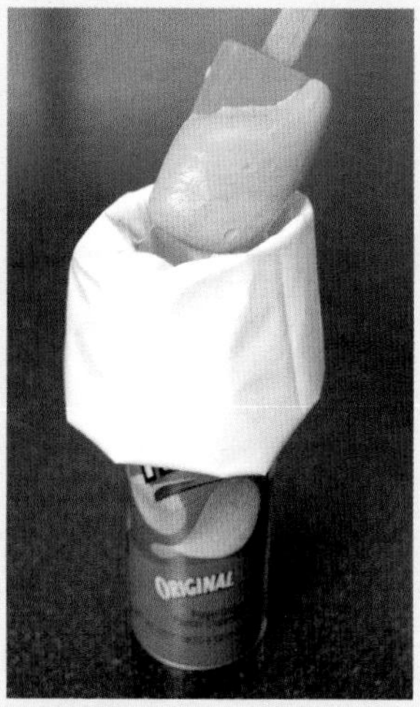

Fuss-Free Pastry Bag

One of the most difficult parts of any icing project is loading the pastry bag without getting the icing all over your hands and the top of the bag. I found that placing the bag inside an empty Pringles can (or, for a larger bag, try an empty Quaker Oats container), with the top of the bag draped over the edges of the can, makes it easy to transfer the icing to the bag.

Jenna Durst Largo, Fla.

Baking Sheet as Organizer

Whenever I'm cooking a big meal, I like to assemble all my ingredients and tools on a rimmed baking sheet before I begin. My setup is sanitary, organized, and easy to move if counter space is needed. It's especially useful when heading out to the grill (I can take everything in one trip), and when I can't find a spot to put down a messy utensil—who cares if it drips on the "tray"?

Dennis Dunn Libertyville, Ill.

Sprinkling a Spoonful of (Powdered) Sugar

For easy and even sprinkling of powdered sugar, I use a hinged tea infuser. Quick to scoop and simple to sprinkle!

Cyndi Leathers
Campbellsville, Ky.

An Elegant Salad Dresses Down the Competition!

Our $1,000 Grand-Prize Winner!

Carrie Vitt Tucson, Ariz.

With roasted onions, fresh pears, goat cheese, almonds, and dried cranberries, this salad tastes as good as it looks.

"The last time I had this salad I was back home in Texas visiting my parents," says contest winner Carrie Vitt. "We all sat out on the porch and ate our dinners under the huge oak trees. As we piled seconds onto our plates, we kept raving about how wonderful the salad was. It was just one of those great summer meals when we were all together, laughing and enjoying a really wonderful meal."

ROASTED RED ONION AND PEAR SALAD SERVES 6

Keep this salad fresh (and the pears from turning brown) by tossing the chopped pears with a couple of teaspoons of lemon juice.

- 2 tablespoons orange juice
- 1 tablespoon lemon juice
- 1 teaspoon Dijon mustard
- 1 teaspoon honey
- 1/4 teaspoon chopped fresh thyme
- 6 tablespoons vegetable or olive oil
- Salt and pepper
- 1 red onion, cut into 1-inch wedges, with root end intact
- 1 head Bibb lettuce, leaves separated but left whole
- 1 (6-ounce) bag baby spinach (about 8 cups)
- 1 ripe pear, cored and cut into 1-inch chunks
- 1/2 cup crumbled goat cheese
- 1/3 cup smokehouse almonds, chopped coarse
- 1/4 cup dried cranberries

1. Adjust oven rack to middle position and heat oven to 400 degrees.

2. Whisk orange and lemon juices, mustard, honey, and thyme together in medium bowl. Gradually whisk in 4 tablespoons oil. Season with salt and pepper.

3. Toss onion wedges with remaining 2 tablespoons oil, 1/4 teaspoon salt, and 1/4 teaspoon pepper. Transfer to baking sheet and roast until brown and soft, 25 minutes, flipping wedges halfway through cooking. Cool 15 minutes.

4. Divide Bibb lettuce leaves among individual salad plates. Toss spinach with 1/4 cup dressing in large bowl. Divide spinach among plates. Arrange roasted onion, pear, goat cheese, almonds, and cranberries on top. Drizzle with remaining dressing and serve.

Raunaq Savur
West Hills, Calif.

STONE FRUIT SALAD WITH CAMEMBERT CROUTONS OVER MIXED GREENS

SERVES 4 TO 6

Raunaq says: "I make this salad at family functions because it highlights ingredients we all love." For a quicker version of this salad, omit the cheese croutons.

- **1/4 cup red wine vinegar**
- **3 tablespoons minced red onion**
- **2 tablespoons chopped chives**
- **1 tablespoon peach or plum preserves**
- **2 teaspoons Dijon mustard**
- **6 tablespoons extra-virgin olive oil**
- **Salt and pepper**
- **1 (8-ounce) wheel Camembert, frozen for 30 minutes**
- **1 large egg, beaten**
- **10 Melba toasts, crushed fine (1/2 cup)**
- **1 small head green leaf lettuce, torn into bite-sized pieces (about 6 cups)**
- **1 small head red leaf lettuce, torn into bite-sized pieces (about 6 cups)**
- **1 plum, pitted and sliced thin**
- **1 peach, pitted and sliced thin**

1. Adjust oven rack to upper-middle position and heat oven to 475 degrees. Line baking sheet with parchment paper.

2. Whisk vinegar, onion, 1 tablespoon chives, preserves, and 1 teaspoon mustard in small bowl. Gradually whisk in oil and season with salt and pepper.

3. Trim rind from cheese; cut into ¾-inch cubes. Set 12 cubes aside; reserve rest of cheese for another use.

4. Mix egg and remaining teaspoon mustard in bowl. Mix Melba crumbs, remaining chives, ¼ teaspoon salt, and ¼ teaspoon pepper in second bowl. Dip cheese cubes in egg mixture, roll in crumbs, and place on baking sheet. Freeze until firm, at least 15 minutes.

5. Bake cheese until light golden brown, 7 to 9 minutes. Cool on baking sheet for 2 minutes. Toss lettuces with dressing and divide among plates. Top each portion with several slices of fruit and 2 or 3 Camembert croutons. Serve.

Kristi Griffith
Jamaica Plain, Mass.

GRILLED VEGETABLE SALAD

SERVES 6

Kristi says: "I always visit my local farmers market to pick up the freshest vegetables to make this great seasonal salad."

Dressing

- **1/4 cup olive oil**
- **3 garlic cloves, minced**
- **2 tablespoons lemon juice**
- **1 tablespoon balsamic vinegar**
- **1 tablespoon Dijon mustard**
- **1/2 teaspoon minced fresh thyme**
- **Salt and pepper**

Salad

- **1 zucchini, sliced into 1/4-inch planks**
- **1 eggplant, sliced into 1-inch rounds**
- **2 red bell peppers, halved, seeded, and pressed flat**
- **1/2 cup olive oil**
- **Salt and pepper**
- **1 red onion, cut into 1/2-inch rounds**
- **1 baguette, sliced into 1-inch rounds**
- **1/3 cup pine nuts, toasted**
- **1 (7-ounce) bag mixed salad greens (about 12 cups)**
- **Shaved Parmesan cheese for garnish**

1. For the dressing: Whisk oil, garlic, lemon juice, vinegar, mustard, thyme, and salt and pepper to taste in bowl.

2. For the salad: Toss zucchini, eggplant, and bell peppers with 3 tablespoons oil in bowl and season with salt and pepper. Brush onion and baguette with remaining 5 tablespoons oil and season with salt and pepper. Grill vegetables and bread until charred on both sides, just 1 or 2 minutes for bread and up to 12 minutes for onions.

3. Chop vegetables roughly and toss with pine nuts and 2 tablespoons dressing in bowl. Toss salad greens with 2 tablespoons dressing in second bowl.

4. Place 3 bread slices on each large plate. Top bread with salad, then vegetables. Drizzle with remaining dressing; garnish with Parmesan. Serve.

Xenia Madill
Columbus, Ohio

FENNEL AND RED GRAPE SALAD WITH CREAMY TARRAGON DRESSING

SERVES 4 TO 6

Xenia says: "I have always loved salads that pair tarragon and grapes, but I recently found that fennel and pecans, especially spiced pecans, go perfectly with this duo. Because I get so many requests for this salad, I have tried to add new twists. For a dramatic presentation, I slice the romaine hearts into quarters lengthwise and stack two on each plate. Then I sprinkle the toppings and dressing over the quarters." Use your favorite store-bought spiced pecans or try our recipe at www.cookscountry.com. For tips on preparing fennel, see page 29.

- **1 tablespoon sour cream**
- **1 tablespoon mayonnaise**
- **1 tablespoon juice plus 1/2 teaspoon grated zest from 1 lemon**
- **5 tablespoons olive oil**
- **1/4 teaspoon sugar**
- **1 tablespoon chopped fresh tarragon**
- **1 tablespoon chopped fresh parsley**
- **Salt and pepper**
- **3 romaine hearts, torn into bite-sized pieces (about 12 cups)**
- **3/4 cup red grapes, halved or quartered, depending on their size**
- **3/4 cup thinly sliced fennel**
- **1/2 cup spiced pecans (see note above)**

1. Whisk sour cream, mayonnaise, lemon juice, olive oil, and sugar together in medium bowl. Whisk in lemon zest, tarragon, and parsley until combined and season with salt and pepper.

2. Arrange romaine hearts in serving bowl and top with grapes, fennel, and pecans. Serve, passing dressing separately at table.

Jason Maresh
Chino Hills, Calif.

BEET, APPLE, AND WALNUT SALAD

SERVES 4 TO 6

Jason says: "I love the classic combination of apple, walnut, and blue cheese with roasted beets. Because this recipe involves more prep than a basic salad, I reserve it for special occasions." To decrease your preparation time, roast and dice the beets the day before and refrigerate them in an airtight container.

- **2 medium beets, trimmed**
- **1 garlic clove, minced**
- **1 tablespoon white wine vinegar**
- **1 teaspoon Dijon mustard**
- **3 tablespoons extra-virgin olive oil**
- **Salt and pepper**
- **1 (5-ounce) bag baby arugula (about 8 cups)**
- **2 tablespoons minced fresh parsley**
- **1 cup walnuts, toasted and chopped**
- **1 Granny Smith apple, cut into 1/4-inch matchsticks**
- **1/2 cup crumbled blue cheese**

1. Adjust oven rack to lower-middle position and heat oven to 400 degrees. Wrap each beet separately in foil and roast until paring knife can be inserted with little resistance, 70 to 80 minutes. Cool until easy to handle, at least 20 minutes. Use paper towels to remove skin and cut beets into ½-inch dice.

2. Whisk garlic, vinegar, mustard, and olive oil together in medium bowl until creamy and fairly smooth. Season with salt and pepper.

3. Toss arugula and parsley with 2 tablespoons dressing and divide among individual salad plates. In separate bowl, toss beets with 1 tablespoon dressing. Top greens with beets, walnuts, apple, and blue cheese. Drizzle with remaining dressing. Serve.

We want your chicken soup recipes for an upcoming contest. Please submit entries by July 31, 2006. Write to us at Recipe Contest, Cook's Country, P.O. Box 470739, Brookline, MA 02447, or send an e-mail to recipecontest@bcpress.com. Include your name, address, and daytime phone number, and tell us what makes your recipe special. The grand-prize winner will receive $1,000. All entries become the property of *Cook's Country*. For more information on this and other contests, go to www.cookscountry.com.

Ask Cook's Country

WE TRY TO ANSWER ANY QUESTION YOU THROW AT US!

HOW TO FREEZE BERRIES

I love to take my 2-year-old son berry-picking, but we can never seem to eat all that we pick. What's the best way to freeze berries?

Jace Martin Asheville, N.C.

Most berries freeze very well—if you follow a few simple steps. We never wash berries before freezing, as berries easily absorb excess water when rinsed; the water expands when frozen, causing the berry skins to rupture. Instead, spread the berries in an even layer on a baking sheet or plate and freeze. After they are frozen solid, transfer the berries to a zipper-lock plastic bag and freeze them for up to two months.

This method ensures that your berries won't freeze in clumps, so you can defrost just as many as you need. A quick rinse helps jump-start the defrosting process. But don't expect frozen berries to have the same texture as fresh. We use frozen berries in recipes that call for cooking the berries or as a topping for hot cereals.

What's the best way to freeze fresh berries?

THE BEST TOMATO PUREE

What, exactly, is tomato puree, and which brand do you like?

Lola Richmond Portland, Ore.

Canned tomatoes are just that—tomatoes that have been peeled and canned. The limited processing makes them ideal for dishes where you want fresh tomato flavor. Tomato puree, on the other hand, is made from tomatoes that have been peeled, seeded, and cooked. The extra processing means you won't get much fresh tomato flavor from puree, but you do get a rich, smooth texture that adds "long cooked" body and depth to whatever you're making.

Because tomato puree is often used in dishes like our chili, which cooks for six to eight hours and is also heavily spiced, we wondered if the brand mattered. To find out, we gathered five popular brands (Progresso, Muir Glen, Hunt's, Redpack, and Contadina), cooked them in our chili, and held a blind tasting. Though some sharp tasters favored the "sweet notes" in the tomato purees made by Muir Glen and Hunt's, most tasters agreed that the differences were "not earthshaking" and that each one was "fine."

WHY OIL AND PIE CRUST DON'T MIX

Is it possible to substitute canola oil for shortening when making a pie crust?

'Kurt' Via e-mail

We prepared our favorite pie crust recipe, which calls for both butter and vegetable shortening, using liquid canola oil in place of the solid shortening. Though the crust made with butter and oil got slightly darker than the crust made according to the recipe, it looked fine. When we broke into the crust, however, all was not fine. Whereas the butter and shortening crust was tender and flaky, the butter and oil crust was crisp and crumbly, not something we look for in a pie crust. Why the discrepancy? Shortening is a solid fat, so it can be worked into small bits that leave behind tiny spaces when they melt in the oven, creating flaky layers. The oil, of course, is already liquid and so leaves no spaces behind as it heats up. The result is a crisp texture, more like that of a cookie.

FREEZING WHIPPED CREAM

I know Cool Whip is stored in the freezer, which got me thinking—can you store tubs of homemade whipped cream in the freezer, too?

Beth Sager Arlington, Mass.

We've had success in the past freezing small dollops of whipped cream for use in hot chocolate or pudding, but we'd never tried freezing whipped cream in bulk. We whipped a cup of cream with some sugar, froze it for the weekend, and then let it thaw at room temperature. While this whipped cream tasted fine, it was much looser than it had been prior to freezing. Because we most often use whipped cream as a final garnish for our homemade desserts, we wouldn't want to cut corners by using a flat, lifeless splotch of whipped cream and therefore don't recommend freezing it in bulk.

SHORTENING IN COOKIES

I see a lot of cookie recipes that call for shortening. Can I substitute butter?

David Milton San Francisco, Calif.

To find out the different effects that shortening and butter can have on cookie dough, we prepared several different kinds of cookies with butter and with shortening. In general, tasters preferred the flavor of the cookies made with butter. For instance, shortening made especially bland chocolate chip cookies. This flavor deficit was less noticeable in snickerdoodles (classic New England cookies). These cookies are so heavily coated with cinnamon-sugar that the differences between the batches made with butter and shortening were harder (although not impossible) to detect.

Why do some cookie recipes call for shortening?

In addition to flavor differences, cookies made with shortening were crispier, and that's largely because shortening adds no water to dough. Unlike butter, which is about 80 percent fat and 20 percent water, shortening is 100 percent fat. Cookies made with butter were softer and cakier.

Our advice? You can use butter in cookie recipes that call for shortening; the cookies may be more flavorful, but they are also likely to be less crisp.

OAT PRIMER

I'm confused about oats. I see recipes that call for rolled oats, quick oats, old-fashioned oats, regular oats, old-fashioned rolled oats . . . and I'm sure there are others. Which of these oats are best for cookies and which are interchangeable?

Nicki Puente Chicago, Ill.

Rolled oats, also known as old-fashioned or regular oats, are whole oats that have been steamed and rolled. If these same oats are also rolled very thinly to make them cook faster, they are called quick oats. Instant oats are cooked and dehydrated; they need no cooking and are easily reconstituted with hot water.

Oats come in four varieties, but only two are suited for baking.

We tried all three types in oatmeal cookies to see which one was best. Both rolled and quick oats produced cookies that tasters described as "chewy" and "oaty." The cookies made with instant oats, however, were deemed "gummy," "raw," and "not acceptable." We've had similar results in other recipes and don't recommend using instant oats in the kitchen. Quick oats and old-fashioned oats can be freely substituted for each other.

One more category of processed oats to consider is steel-cut oats. Sometimes called Scottish or Irish oats, they are neither steamed nor rolled but are simply whole oats that have been cut into smaller pieces. These oats take a long time to cook (about 30 minutes) and are rarely used in baking, although they make a wonderful hot breakfast.

To ask us a cooking question, write to Ask Cook's Country, P. O. Box 470739, Brookline, MA 02447, or send an e-mail to askcookscountry@bcpress.com. See if you can stump us!

Lost Recipes WHOOPIE PIES

YUMMY FLUFF Since 1930, Durkee-Mower Inc. (the makers of Fluff) has been producing a collection of Marshmallow Fluff recipes called *The Yummy Book*. The edition pictured here is from the 1950s and contains recipes for everything from ice cream and fudge to salad dressing and layer cakes.

When it comes to this devilish cream-filled chocolate sandwich cake, everyone wants to take credit for makin' whoopie first.

I've always had a not-so-secret addiction to convenience snack cakes. From Devil Dogs to Oatmeal Cream Pies, if it's packaged in cellophane, I'll eat it. Having been practically raised on the snack combo of a MoonPie and an ice-cold RC Cola, it wasn't a stretch for me to take a shine to whoopie pies on a recent road trip to Maine. Made of two chocolate cookie-like cakes stuffed to the gills with a fluffy marshmallow filling, the whoopie pie is my idea of a good sandwich. It took just one bite for me to wonder: Where did it come from? Why the funny name? And, most important, how could I make this treat at home?

It turns out that Maine and Pennsylvania—the Pennsylvania Dutch of Lancaster County, to be specific—both claim whoopie pies as their own. After weeks of reading through old newspapers and talking to librarians and bakery owners, here's what I learned.

Maine's earliest claim dates back to 1925, when Labadie's Bakery in Lewiston first sold whoopie pies to the public. As I continued my research, I ran across an advertisement for a whoopie pie wrapper contest in the *Portland* (Maine) *Press Herald*. "Collect the most wrappers and a brand new 1950 Plymouth Sedan could be yours!" In small letters under the prize I saw the words "Berwick Cake Co.—Boston." Some research showed that the Berwick Cake Company began manufacturing Whoopie! Pies (the exclamation point was part of the name) in 1927. These sources claim that whoopie pies were named after the musical *Whoopie* (from which came the well-known song "Makin' Whoopie"); *Whoopie* had its debut in Boston 1927. In addition, Marshmallow Fluff, a key ingredient in many whoopie pie recipes, was invented in nearby Lynn seven years earlier.

What about Pennsylvania's claim on whoopie pies? I found an article in a copy of the *Gettysburg Times* from 1982 that spoke of a chocolate cake sandwich with a fluffy cream center. These sandwiches were called gobs and were sold by the Dutch Maid Bakery of Geistown, Pa. While the name was different, the description (and a huge picture) showed that these were no doubt whoopie pies by another name. In 1980, Dutch Maid Bakery purchased the rights to the gob from the Harris and Boyer Baking Company, which had started manufacturing gobs in 1927.

While I wasn't able to resolve the conflicting claims about the origins of the whoopie pie (although I'm pretty confident that they date back to the 1920s), I figured I could bake some up myself. Whoopie pie recipes haven't changed much over the years. Original recipes used a devil's food cake base, with "soda" and "soured milk" to lift the cakes. In today's vernacular, baking soda and buttermilk work well in their place. While the original cakes contained lard, many recipes have switched to shortening or vegetable oil, both of which extend the cakes' shelf life. Although it's considered heresy in the whoopie world, I used butter instead of shortening. Moist and tender, these cakes were snatched up as fast as I could bake them, so I had no concern about shelf life.

Originally, the filling was a whipped frosting made of sugar and lard, but recipes soon switched to marshmallow crème, which was easily purchased under the name of Marshmallow Fluff. Instead of mixing the marshmallow with lard or vegetable shortening, I turned once more to butter. I slathered this fluffy filling between two chocolate cookie-cakes and my whoopie pies were done. And as soon as I put them on a plate, they were history, too. **–Bridget Lancaster**

History never tasted as good as these chocolate cookie-cakes with a fluffy marshmallow filling.

WHOOPIE PIES SERVES 6

Don't be tempted to bake all the cakes on one baking sheet; the batter needs room to spread in the oven.

Cakes

- 2 cups all-purpose flour
- $\frac{1}{2}$ cup Dutch-processed cocoa powder
- 1 teaspoon baking soda
- $\frac{1}{2}$ teaspoon salt
- 1 cup packed light brown sugar
- 8 tablespoons (1 stick) unsalted butter, softened but still cool
- 1 large egg, room temperature
- 1 teaspoon vanilla extract
- 1 cup buttermilk

Filling

- 12 tablespoons ($1\frac{1}{2}$ sticks) unsalted butter, softened but still cool
- $1\frac{1}{4}$ cups confectioners' sugar
- $1\frac{1}{2}$ teaspoons vanilla extract
- $\frac{1}{8}$ teaspoon salt
- $2\frac{1}{2}$ cups Marshmallow Fluff

1. For the cakes: Adjust oven racks to upper-middle and lower-middle positions and heat oven to 350 degrees. Line 2 baking sheets with parchment paper. Whisk flour, cocoa powder, baking soda, and salt in medium bowl.

2. With electric mixer on medium speed, beat sugar and butter in large bowl until fluffy, about 4 minutes. Beat in egg until incorporated, scraping down sides of bowl as necessary, then beat in vanilla. Reduce speed to low and beat in one-third of flour mixture, then half of buttermilk. Repeat with half of remaining flour mixture, then remaining buttermilk, and finally remaining flour mixture. Using rubber spatula, give batter final stir.

3. Using $\frac{1}{3}$-cup measure, scoop 6 mounds of batter onto each baking sheet, spacing mounds about 3 inches apart. Bake until cakes spring back when pressed, 15 to 18 minutes, switching and rotating pans halfway through baking. Cool completely on baking sheets, at least 1 hour.

4. For the filling: With electric mixer on medium speed, beat butter and sugar together until fluffy, about 2 minutes. Beat in vanilla and salt. Beat in Fluff until incorporated, about 2 minutes. Refrigerate filling until slightly firm, about 30 minutes. (Bowl can be wrapped and refrigerated for up to 2 days.)

5. Dollop $\frac{1}{3}$ cup filling on center of flat side of 6 cakes. Top with flat side of remaining 6 cakes and gently press until filling spreads to edge of cake. Serve. (Whoopie pies can be refrigerated in airtight container for up to 3 days.)

Recipe Makeover BLUEBERRY MUFFINS

Lemon syrup and a sprinkle of sugar add a final burst of flavor to our muffins.

Will you still want to wake up for your morning muffin if we take out some of the fat and calories?

Some coffee-shop muffins are so loaded with butter and sugar that they pack 450 calories and 17 grams of fat. While these softball-sized muffins are extreme, even a modest homemade muffin tips the scales at 270 calories and 11 grams of fat—not exactly light fare. While supermarkets and coffee shops sell "reduced-fat" muffins, they are usually so dense, gummy, or artificial tasting that after just one regrettable bite you wish you'd skipped breakfast altogether.

Many new-age muffin recipes suggest replacing the good stuff (butter, sugar, flour, and sour cream) with canola oil, applesauce, wheat germ, whole wheat flour, and soy milk. I was skeptical of these "healthy" ingredients—and, it turns out, with good reason. Muffins made with canola oil were extremely bland ("cardboard tastes better," complained one taster), and applesauce (often used as a butter substitute) made horribly gummy hockey pucks. Healthy flours produced "blueberry bricks," and soy milk imparted a sickly color and an odd saccharine flavor.

After testing (and throwing out) so many truly awful muffins, it was clear to me that omitting the good stuff was not an option. Instead, I started with a classic blueberry muffin recipe as my guide for flavor and texture and then began reducing the amounts of fat- and calorie-heavy ingredients.

The test kitchen's favorite blueberry muffin recipe calls for 1 cup of sugar. Any less got me dry, tough muffins. Switching from the traditional granulated sugar to light brown sugar allowed me to reduce the sugar by ¼ cup and still make a good muffin. That's because brown sugar contains more moisture than granulated sugar.

The test kitchen's favorite muffin recipe calls for 4 tablespoons of butter and 1¼ cups of sour cream. Replacing the sour cream with nonfat buttermilk gave my muffins a nice light texture and good flavor while drastically reducing the fat. Yes, the muffins were less rich, but they were still quite good. Although I had hoped to reduce the butter, anything less than 4 tablespoons made dry and chewy muffins. Fortunately, the reduction in sugar and replacement of sour cream with buttermilk had knocked 80 calories and 6.5 grams of fat from each muffin.

I wanted something extra to distinguish my muffins from the reduced-fat competition. Adding lemon zest and lemon juice to the batter brightened the flavor. Taking this idea a step further, I brushed the warm muffins with a simple lemon syrup (lemon juice and sugar) and sprinkled them with more sugar. You'll need just an extra tablespoon of sugar in total for this topping; that means another 4 calories per muffin, a very small price that is well worth paying.

There's nothing radical about my recipe—no oddball ingredient or technique. And I bet that if you serve my muffins to friends and family, no one will suspect that they are "low fat." But isn't that the idea? **–Meredith Butcher**

LOW-FAT BLUEBERRY MUFFINS MAKES 12

These muffins are best served warm. Store leftovers in an airtight container overnight. Microwave one muffin at a time until warm, about 10 seconds, before serving.

Muffins

- 2 cups plus 1 tablespoon all-purpose flour
- 2 teaspoons baking powder
- ¼ teaspoon baking soda
- ½ teaspoon salt
- 2 large eggs
- ¾ cup packed light brown sugar
- 4 tablespoons unsalted butter, melted and cooled
- ¾ cup nonfat buttermilk
- 1 teaspoon grated zest and 2 teaspoons juice from 1 lemon
- 1 teaspoon vanilla extract
- 1 cup frozen blueberries

Topping

- 1 tablespoon granulated sugar
- 2 teaspoons lemon juice
- 2 teaspoons water

1. For the muffins: Adjust oven rack to middle position and heat oven to 375 degrees. Spray 12-cup muffin tin with nonstick cooking spray. Whisk 2 cups flour, baking powder, baking soda, and salt together in large bowl.

2. Whisk eggs and brown sugar together in medium bowl until thoroughly combined. Gradually whisk in melted butter, then buttermilk, lemon zest, lemon juice, and vanilla until well blended. Fold into dry mixture with rubber spatula (a few streaks of flour should remain). Remove blueberries from freezer and toss with remaining tablespoon flour in small bowl. Gently fold blueberries into batter, being careful not to break berries.

3. Distribute batter in muffin tin and bake until light golden brown and toothpick or skewer inserted into center of muffin comes out clean, 25 to 30 minutes, rotating pan halfway through baking.

4. For the topping: Cool muffins in pan 5 minutes. Meanwhile, heat 2 teaspoons sugar, lemon juice, and water in small saucepan over low heat until sugar has dissolved. Transfer muffins to wire rack, brush tops with lemon syrup, and sprinkle with remaining teaspoon sugar.

And the Numbers . . .

All nutritional information is for a single serving (one muffin).

TRADITIONAL BLUEBERRY MUFFIN
CALORIES: **270**
FAT: **11g**
SATURATED FAT: **7g**

COOK'S COUNTRY LOW-FAT BLUEBERRY MUFFIN
CALORIES: **190**
FAT: **4.5g**
SATURATED FAT: **3g**

Kitchen Know-How
STREAKING AND SINKING

Frozen blueberries actually taste better than most fresh berries (see page 29 for details on our favorite brand), but they need to be handled with care. Keep the blueberries in the freezer until the very last minute. If the berries start to defrost, they will streak the batter blue. And to keep the berries from sinking to the bottom of the batter (in the bowl and in the muffin tin), toss them with 1 tablespoon of flour before gently folding them into the batter.

ONE BAD MUFFIN

We tried many low-fat recipes that were more scary than tasty. This dense, gray muffin was especially bad.

Slow Cooking WEEKNIGHT CHILI

For something so simple, why is ground beef chili made in a slow cooker often greasy, soupy, and downright bland?

The gentle, protected heat of a slow cooker is perfect for the lengthy simmering that turns ground beef, tomatoes, and spices into chili. But this convenience comes at a price. Slow cookers are notorious for dulling even the most assertive flavors. When I dumped the ingredients for my favorite chili recipe into a slow cooker, I found out just how bad this problem can get. After six hours, my "chili" was a greasy, soupy mixture devoid of any spice flavor.

A handful of slow-cooker chili recipes suggested partially cooking ingredients on the stovetop—before adding them to the slow cooker—to develop flavor. Gently sautéing onion and red pepper (preferred over green pepper, celery, and carrot for their mild sweetness) did just that. The potent combination of chili powder, cumin, coriander, oregano, cayenne, and red pepper flakes, chosen for their traditional chili flavors, tasted stale and gritty when added to the slow cooker straight from the jar. I got better results when I added the spices to the onions and peppers as they sautéed, but sometimes the spices scorched. Since spices can go from fragrant to burnt in seconds, I found it easier to toast the spices alone (so I could catch them at the right moment) and then remove them from the pot before cooking the onions and peppers.

Although tasters agreed that chili should be all about the beef, several requested a supplemental smoky flavor. Kielbasa tasted odd in chili, but bacon was a welcome addition. Some tasters were wary of the added grease, but quickly browning the bacon on the stovetop and draining it solved this problem—and increased the meaty flavor of the finished chili.

While slow cookers are great for tenderizing tough cubes of meat, ground beef is another story. Prolonged cooking can make it tough and stringy. I discovered that the degree to which I browned the beef before adding it to the slow cooker made a big difference. When fully browned on the stovetop, the beef emerged tough after six hours in the slow cooker; when left slightly pink, it emerged toothsome and tender.

I had one more issue to resolve: My chili was a bit greasy. I had been using 80 percent lean ground chuck and wondered if a leaner choice would help. Sure enough, the 85 percent lean meat was just as tender and less greasy.

Straining the beef and vegetable mixture before adding it to the slow cooker eliminated any remaining grease.

–Cali Rich

Chili made in a slow cooker never scorches and can cook all day.

SLOW-COOKER WEEKNIGHT CHILI SERVES 10 TO 12

Serve this all-American classic with sour cream and cheese to cool the burn. For less heat, reduce the cayenne pepper to 1/4 teaspoon or omit it altogether. The ground beef will become dry if the chili is cooked for more than 8 hours.

- 1/4 cup chili powder
- 1 tablespoon ground cumin
- 2 teaspoons ground coriander
- 1 teaspoon dried oregano
- 1/2 teaspoon cayenne pepper
- 1/2 teaspoon red pepper flakes
- 8 ounces bacon, chopped fine
- 2 onions, chopped medium
- 1 red bell pepper, chopped medium
- 6 garlic cloves, minced
- 2 pounds 85 percent lean ground chuck
- Salt and pepper
- 1 (28-ounce) can tomato puree
- 1 (28-ounce) can diced tomatoes
- 2 (15.5-ounce) cans dark red kidney beans, drained and rinsed

1. Toast chili powder, cumin, coriander, oregano, cayenne, and pepper flakes in large Dutch oven over medium heat until fragrant, about 2 minutes. Transfer toasted spices to bowl. Add bacon to Dutch oven and cook over medium heat until crisp, 8 to 10 minutes. Transfer bacon to plate lined with paper towels and pour off all but 1 teaspoon fat from pot. Return pot to medium heat, add onions and bell pepper, and cook until softened, about 5 minutes. Stir in garlic and cook until fragrant, about 30 seconds.

2. Add beef, 2 teaspoons salt, and 1 teaspoon pepper. Increase heat to medium-high and cook, using wooden spoon to break up beef into ½-inch pieces, until just slightly pink, about 5 minutes. Drain beef and vegetables in colander.

3. Add tomato puree, diced tomatoes, and toasted spices to empty pot and bring to simmer over medium-high heat, scraping up any browned bits from bottom of pot. Return drained beef and vegetable mixture and bacon to pot, stir to combine, and bring to simmer. Transfer contents to slow-cooker insert.

4. Set slow cooker to low, cover, and cook until tender, 6 to 8 hours, stirring in beans during last hour of cooking. (Alternately, cook on high for 3 to 4 hours.) Adjust seasonings and serve. (Leftovers can be refrigerated for several days or frozen for several months.)

Make Ahead

If you'd prefer to just dump the chili ingredients into the slow cooker before running off to work, you can do all the work the night before. Follow the recipe through step 3, but continue to simmer the assembled chili for 10 minutes. Transfer the chili to an airtight container and refrigerate overnight. In the morning, simmer the chili in a Dutch oven for 10 minutes, then transfer it to your slow cooker and proceed with step 4.

The American Table: A Fair to Remember

Nobody knows exactly when chili con carne was invented, but by the mid-1800s it was a staple in Texas. The rest of the country discovered this iconic dish in 1893 at the Chicago World's Fair. Called the World's Columbian Exposition (in honor of the 400th anniversary of Columbus discovering the New World), the fair drew more than 25 million visitors. The Texas exhibit contained an authentic San Antonio chili stand selling bowls of its signature dish. The chili was a huge hit, and soon enterprising restaurateurs were opening chili joints in every major American city.

Chili wasn't the only culinary icon to get its start at the fair. Juicy Fruit gum, Cracker Jack, Shredded Wheat cereal, and the hamburger were introduced to America at the 1893 fair. And the architecture at the fairgrounds was impressive enough to have served as the inspiration for two of America's better-known fantasy lands: Disneyland (Walt Disney's father was a builder on the project) and Oz, whose creator, L. Frank Baum, visited the fair on several occasions before writing *The Wonderful Wizard of Oz* in 1900. **–Scott Kathan**

All-in-One Burgers

Instead of piling on the toppings, we rethink the seasonings that go inside our burgers.

Key Ingredients

For our burgers, it's not what goes on top that makes them special but what's inside. Here's a peek inside our All-in-One Burgers.

AMERICAN
Cheddar cheese, cooked bacon, yellow mustard, Worcestershire sauce

RANCH
Blue cheese, garlic, ranch dressing mix

TEX-MEX
Taco seasoning, chipotle chiles, cilantro, Monterey Jack cheese

ITALIAN
Sweet Italian sausage, Parmesan cheese, basil

Constantly faced with burger toppings sliding off and landing in my lap rather than my mouth, I was left wondering, could I take the "top" out of the toppings and put those same flavors inside the burger?

I started testing with the 80 percent lean ground beef the test kitchen prefers for grilling. Its relatively high fat content makes for a juicy, flavorful burger; use anything leaner and the burger will be dry.

Flavoring the patties with cheese seemed like a good place to begin, and I chose cheddar (my favorite on burgers), but straight away there were problems. The fat from the cheese created a super-greasy burger, and tasters were put off by the spongy texture.

By switching to leaner ground beef (85 percent lean worked best), I got rid of the greasiness. Adjusting the texture was as simple as cooking the burgers through rather than to the usual medium-rare. Burgers that were cooked through were cohesive and "set" without being dried out.

With the texture under control, I turned to the flavorings. The perfect pairing with cheddar was a mixture of chopped bacon, mustard, and Worcestershire. This burger won over my fellow test cooks, many of whom had been skeptical about the idea of putting toppings on the inside of a burger. They dubbed it the All-American.

Encouraged by their enthusiasm, I moved on to more adventurous burgers and was successful as long as I relied on firm cheeses (soft goat cheese was a disaster) and potent ingredients with minimal moisture (such as garlic, herbs, chiles, and powdered seasoning mixes). My ordinary-looking burgers prove it's what on the inside that really counts.

–Katie Henderson

Build flavor inside burgers with firm cheeses and potent ingredients, such as garlic, chiles, and herbs.

ALL-AMERICAN BURGERS
SERVES 4

- **1 1/2 pounds 85 percent lean ground chuck**
- **1 cup shredded sharp cheddar cheese**
- **8 strips cooked bacon, chopped fine**
- **4 teaspoons yellow mustard**
- **2 teaspoons Worcestershire sauce**
- **1/2 teaspoon salt**
- **1/2 teaspoon pepper**

Break beef into small pieces in medium bowl. Add cheese, bacon, mustard, Worcestershire sauce, salt, and pepper. Using fork, toss until evenly distributed. Divide mixture into 4 equal portions and lightly pack into 1-inch-thick patties. Grill as directed in box on page 11.

RANCH BURGERS **SERVES 4**

- **1 1/2 pounds 85 percent lean ground chuck**
- **2/3 cup crumbled blue cheese**
- **2 garlic cloves, minced**
- **4 teaspoons powdered ranch dressing mix (from packet)**
- **1/2 teaspoon salt**
- **1/2 teaspoon pepper**

Break beef into small pieces in medium bowl. Add cheese, garlic, ranch mix, salt, and pepper. Using fork, toss until evenly distributed. Divide mixture into 4 equal portions and lightly pack into 1-inch-thick patties. Grill as directed in box on page 11.

A Well-Done Burger

Although we usually enjoy our burgers medium-rare, with extra ingredients added, tasters found that the burgers were too soft unless cooked through (basically, well-done).

Burger Grilling Instructions:
When coals are ready and grate is hot, dip wad of paper towels in vegetable oil and use tongs to rub oil over grate. Grill burgers over very hot fire, without pressing down on them, until well seared on both sides and cooked through, 8 to 12 minutes. Transfer to plate, tent with foil, and let rest 5 minutes. Serve.

TEX-MEX BURGERS SERVES 4

- 1½ pounds 85 percent lean ground chuck
- 1 cup shredded Monterey Jack cheese
- ¼ cup minced fresh cilantro
- 4 teaspoons minced canned chipotle chiles in adobo
- 4 teaspoons yellow mustard
- 4 teaspoons taco seasoning (from packet)

Break beef into small pieces in medium bowl. Add cheese, cilantro, chiles, mustard, and taco seasoning. Using fork, toss until evenly distributed. Divide mixture into 4 equal portions and lightly pack into 1-inch-thick patties. Grill as directed in above box.

ITALIAN BURGERS SERVES 4

- ¾ pound 85 percent lean ground chuck
- ¾ pound sweet Italian sausage, casings removed
- ½ cup grated Parmesan cheese
- ¼ cup thinly sliced fresh basil
- 2 garlic cloves, minced
- 4 teaspoons Dijon mustard
- ½ teaspoon salt
- ½ teaspoon pepper

Break beef and sausage into small pieces in medium bowl. Add cheese, basil, garlic, mustard, salt, and pepper. Using fork, toss until evenly distributed. Divide mixture into 4 equal portions and lightly pack into 1-inch-thick patties. Grill as directed in above box.

American Potato Salad

I love American potato salad, but I rarely get it just right—it's either mushy potatoes, bland dressing, or both. Can you come up with a reliable recipe? –Elizabeth Muldoon, Portland, Maine

Yukon Gold potatoes offer the best balance of sturdiness and flavor.

American potato salad contains mayonnaise, mustard, vinegar, pickles, celery, onion, and sometimes hard-cooked eggs. (Personally, I hate eggs in potato salad, but many of my colleagues in the test kitchen think otherwise.) Although this recipe is easy to execute, I have eaten enough sloppy, boring potato salads to agree with you that there's room for improvement.

My first recipe tests focused on the potato variety. I found that firm Red Bliss potatoes made the neatest salad. Unfortunately, my tasters also thought they made the blandest salad. Russet potatoes tasted great but were extremely mushy. Yukon Golds offered the best balance of sturdiness and flavor. While the skins on Red Bliss potatoes are quite palatable, no one liked the papery skins on the Yukon Golds, so I peeled the potatoes before cubing and cooking them.

With the potatoes chosen, it was time to focus on the dressing. Mayonnaise is the base ingredient, but, frankly, it can smother other flavors. I wondered if some other creamy ingredient could perk up my salad. Tasters thought yogurt and buttermilk were too tart but raved when I tried sour cream.

Sweet yellow mustard was my tasters' favorite, beating out Dijon (too spicy) and brown (too ugly). For crunch, I added celery, red onion, and dill pickles. I found a few recipes that supplemented the celery flavor with celery seed, and everyone in the test kitchen approved of this addition.

To further brighten this creamy salad, I tried adding various vinegars and lemon juice, but they tended to overwhelm the other flavors. It wasn't until I added some pickle juice—yes, the liquid in the pickle jar—that my dressing really came together. Why did pickle juice work so well? Dill pickles are packed in a brine made with vinegar that has been diluted with water (so it's not harsh), tempered with sugar, and then flavored with spices and garlic. Pickle juice is also convenient—I already had the jar open.

Although the dressing now had great flavor, it was merely coating the potatoes, not getting inside. Could I get that flavor deep inside the potatoes? The solution was as close as a recipe for French potato salad, in which a simple vinaigrette is drizzled over drained potatoes when they're still hot and is absorbed as they cool. Pouring a mayonnaise-based dressing over hot potatoes would result in a runny mess, but singling out a couple of intensely flavored ingredients—in this case, the mustard and pickle juice—worked perfectly.

–Katie Henderson

Don't Throw Out the Juice

Pickle juice is tossed with just-cooked potatoes to give them a tangy flavor that's not as harsh as straight vinegar and has a gentle sweetness, too.

ALL-AMERICAN POTATO SALAD SERVES 4 TO 6

Make sure not to overcook the potatoes or the salad will be quite sloppy. Keep the water at a gentle simmer and use the tip of a paring knife to judge the doneness of the potatoes. If the knife inserts easily into the potato pieces, they are done.

- 2 pounds Yukon Gold potatoes, peeled and cut into ¾-inch cubes
- 1½ teaspoons salt
- 3 tablespoons dill pickle juice, plus ¼ cup finely chopped dill pickles
- 1 tablespoon yellow mustard
- ¼ teaspoon pepper
- ½ teaspoon celery seed
- ½ cup mayonnaise
- ¼ cup sour cream
- ½ small red onion, chopped fine
- 1 celery rib, chopped fine
- 2 hard-cooked eggs, peeled and cut into ¼-inch dice (optional)

1. Place potatoes in large saucepan with cold water to cover by 1 inch. Bring to boil over high heat, add 1 teaspoon salt, reduce heat to medium-low, and simmer until potatoes are tender, 10 to 15 minutes.

2. Drain potatoes thoroughly, then spread out on rimmed baking sheet. Mix 2 tablespoons pickle juice and mustard together in small bowl, drizzle pickle juice mixture over potatoes, and toss until evenly coated. Refrigerate until cooled, about 30 minutes.

3. Mix remaining tablespoon pickle juice, chopped pickles, remaining ½ teaspoon salt, pepper, celery seed, mayonnaise, sour cream, red onion, and celery in large bowl. Toss in cooled potatoes, cover, and refrigerate until well chilled, about 30 minutes. (Salad can be refrigerated in airtight container for up to 2 days.) Gently stir in eggs, if using, just before serving.

How to MAKE TENDER RIBS

Making tender ribs can be tough work, but we've found a few tips to get that fall-off-the-bone texture every time.

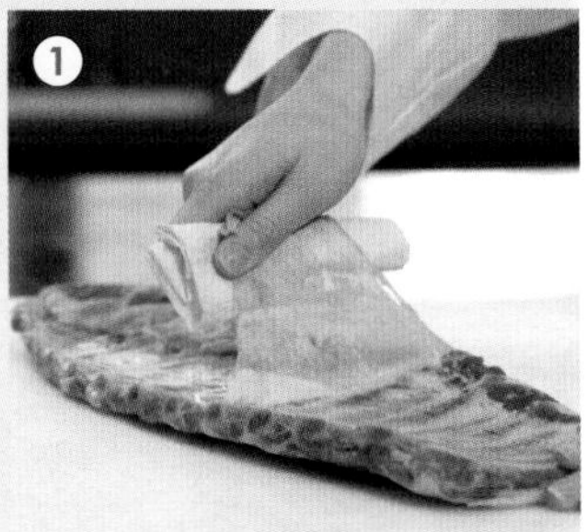

Remove the Membrane
Ribs have a papery membrane on the underside that can make it hard to pull the meat off the bone. Before cooking, loosen this membrane with the tip of a paring knife and, with the aid of a paper towel, pull it off slowly, all in one piece.

Cover with Foil
Barbecuing the ribs for hours on end won't guarantee super-tender meat. Fortunately, you can trap steam and make the ribs tender by covering them with sheets of aluminum foil.

Wrap It Up
During the last hour of barbecuing, wrap the ribs tightly in the foil to keep them from drying out. After removing the ribs from the grill, let them rest for 30 minutes, still wrapped.

Kansas City Sticky Ribs

I was recently in Kansas City and ate the best barbecue ever. (Don't tell my relatives in Texas or I'll get in trouble.) The ribs were so good—sticky, messy, smoky, and sweet—and I want to make them at home. Do you have a recipe that's not too difficult? –Chris Boyce, Longmont, Colo.

One grill produces authentic Kansas City ribs and smoked barbecued beans at the same time.

I love them all: Texas beef ribs, dry-rubbed Memphis ribs, even neon-pink Chinese spareribs. But if I had to pick a favorite, I'm with you—I'd choose Kansas City–style ribs without a second thought. These slow-smoked pork ribs come slathered in a sauce so thick, sweet, and sticky that you need a gross of wet naps to get your hands clean after eating them. But authentic ribs can take all day to prepare. Could I come up with a more reasonable recipe for the home cook?

Aside from the sauce and the smoke, the defining characteristic of KC ribs is their "finger tender" texture: The meat should pull off the bone with very little resistance, and this starts with the right cut. Spareribs are well marbled with fat, which makes them cook up moist and tender. (Baby back ribs are too lean for this recipe.)

Barbecuing is all about utilizing low, indirect heat to turn the ribs smoky and tender. However, keeping a grill at an average temperature of 275 to 300 degrees requires diligence, and adding charcoal every hour (or after every beer, as some recipes suggest) tried my patience (and sobriety). Was there an easier way? Well, yes and no. You can build the charcoal fire hotter at the outset, but you will still need to add charcoal once during the four-hour cooking time. Some things just can't be rushed. (For folks who really don't want to add charcoal, I developed a variation that spends two hours on the grill and then goes into the oven.)

My four-hour ribs were nice and smoky, but they were not as tender as I wanted. They were also too dry. I tried wrapping the ribs with foil (cutting holes in the foil to let smoke in), but this caused them to take on a squishy texture and boiled flavor. What if I just placed the foil on top of the ribs rather than wrapping them? Somewhat to my surprise, this worked nicely. The foil held in some of the steam, helping to make the ribs tender and moist. Because they were still exposed to the fire, they also developed a nice crusty exterior. A simple spice rub helped to further develop the crust.

From here all I had to do was give the ribs a double coating of sauce, once during the last hour on the grill (so that the sauce wouldn't char) and once just before serving. I can make these ribs in much less time than it takes to get to Kansas City—and they taste just as good. –Jeremy Sauer

KANSAS CITY STICKY RIBS SERVES 4 TO 6

Buy St. Louis–style racks (see page 29), which are more manageable than untrimmed pork ribs. We prefer our sauce recipe (see page 14), but store-bought works, too (Texas Best and Bull's-Eye are our favorites).

- **3 tablespoons paprika**
- **2 tablespoons light brown sugar**
- **1 tablespoon black pepper**
- **1 tablespoon salt**
- **1/4 teaspoon cayenne pepper**
- **2 full racks pork spareribs, preferably St. Louis cut, trimmed of any large pieces of excess fat, membrane removed (see photo 1 at left), and patted dry**
- **2 cups wood chips**
- **2 cups barbecue sauce**

1. Combine paprika, sugar, pepper, salt, and cayenne in small bowl. Massage spice rub into both sides of rib racks.

2. Soak wood chips in bowl of water for 15 minutes. Open bottom grill vents completely. Light large chimney starter filled two-thirds with charcoal briquettes (about 60 coals) and burn until covered with fine gray ash. Arrange 13 by 9-inch disposable aluminum pan on one side of grill and pour hot coals into pile on opposite side. Sprinkle 1 cup wood chips over coals, set grill rack in place, and position ribs over pan.

3. Place sheet of aluminum foil directly on top of ribs (see photo 2) and cover grill, positioning lid vents (three-quarters open) directly over ribs.

Barbecue, turning and rotating ribs after 1 hour, until coals are almost spent, about 2 hours.

4. About 20 minutes before coals are spent, light another 60 coals in chimney starter and burn until covered with fine gray ash. Place hot coals from chimney on top of spent coals, and sprinkle remaining cup wood chips over coals. Turn and rotate ribs and barbecue, covered, for 1 hour. Brush ribs liberally on both sides with sauce, wrap tightly with foil (see photo 3 on page 12), and barbecue until very tender, about 1 hour longer.

5. Transfer ribs (still in foil) to cutting board and rest 30 minutes. Unwrap ribs and brush with additional barbecue sauce. Slice ribs between bones and serve with remaining sauce.

KANSAS CITY STICKY RIBS ON A GAS GRILL

Place 2 cups soaked wood chips in small disposable aluminum pan. Place pan directly on primary burner of gas grill, turn all burners to high, and preheat with lid down until chips are smoking heavily, about 15 minutes. Turn primary burner to medium and shut off other burners, adjusting temperature of primary burner as needed to maintain average temperature of 275 degrees. Position ribs over cool part of grill. Barbecue ribs as directed.

EASIEST KANSAS CITY STICKY RIBS

Not keen on tending a grill for 4 hours? Our ribs will taste good even if they spend the last 2 hours of cooking in your oven.

In step 4, instead of adding more charcoal to grill, wrap ribs tightly in foil, place on baking sheet, and bake in 250-degree oven for 1 hour. Remove from oven, brush both sides with barbecue sauce, rewrap with foil, and bake until very tender, about 1 hour longer. Proceed as directed in step 5.

Regional Favorites: Smoky Barbecued Beans

Kansas City might just make the best beans in America.

Whether it's salt pork, bacon, or lard, no recipe for barbecued baked beans is complete without some kind of pork. In Kansas City, many barbecue joints stir "burnt ends"—tough, overcooked bits of smoked brisket (the most common option), ribs, or pulled pork—into their barbecued beans. What likely began as a way to recycle leftovers has become a Kansas City classic, with local restaurants offering burnt-ends sandwiches and burnt-ends platters. I even found several companies that will accept mail-orders for burnt ends.

Beans with smoky bits of barbecued meat sound incredibly appealing, but I wasn't sure how to translate this recipe for the home kitchen. Who has burnt ends in the fridge? I gave up on this idea until a kitchen colleague told me about a recipe from Fiorella's Jack Stack Barbecue, a Kansas City restaurant that suggests cooking the beans on the bottom of the grill—right under the ribs. As the beans simmer in the smoky heat, they catch drippings from the ribs and become unbelievably flavorful—or so my colleague promised. Now this was something I could try at home.

I quickly learned that the beans have to be almost fully cooked when they go into the grill, where they pick up flavor but don't really soften much. Besides, if the beans go into the grill at the outset (when the ribs are rendering most of their fat), they become too greasy. I waited until the ribs had cooked for two hours before adding the pan of beans (I had to open the grill anyway to add more charcoal). This meant I could start the beans on the stovetop at the same time the ribs first went on the grill—and the ribs and beans would be done at the same time.

So how do these beans taste? I live in Boston and like our local baked beans. But, in my opinion, the combination of smoke and pork flavor makes this Kansas City recipe the one to beat. **–Jeremy Sauer**

SMOKY KANSAS CITY BBQ BEANS

SERVES 4 TO 6

This recipe is meant for a charcoal grill. If you're cooking on a gas grill, omit step 3 and finish cooking the beans in a 300-degree oven for 2 to 2 1/2 hours. See the photos on page 28 for tips on making this recipe.

- **4 slices bacon, chopped fine**
- **1 onion, minced**
- **4 garlic cloves, minced**
- **1 pound pinto beans, soaked overnight (see page 28)**
- **6 cups water**
- **1 cup barbecue sauce**
- **1/3 cup packed light brown sugar**
- **2 tablespoons brown mustard**
- **1 teaspoon hot sauce**
- **Salt**

1. Cook bacon in Dutch oven over medium heat until beginning to crisp, about 5 minutes. Stir in onion and cook until softened, about 5 minutes. Add garlic and cook until fragrant, about 30 seconds. Add beans and water and bring to simmer. Reduce heat to medium-low, cover, and cook until beans are just soft, about 1 hour.

2. Stir in 1/2 cup barbecue sauce, brown sugar, mustard, hot sauce, and 2 teaspoons salt and simmer, uncovered, over medium-low heat until beans are tender and sauce is slightly thickened, about 1 hour. (If mixture becomes too thick, add water.) Transfer beans to 13 by 9-inch disposable aluminum pan and wrap tightly with aluminum foil. Using paring knife or skewer, poke holes in foil.

3. In step 4 of Kansas City Sticky Ribs recipe (when new coals are added), nestle pan with beans inside disposable pan already in grill. Replace cooking grate and position ribs directly above beans. Cover grill and cook until beans are smoky and completely tender, about 2 hours. Discard foil, stir in remaining 1/2 cup barbecue sauce, and season with salt. Serve.

Easier Than You Think: Sticky Barbecue Sauce

How do you make the kind of sweet, sticky, smoky sauce that's the hallmark of authentic KC barbecue?

In Kansas City, barbecue is slathered with a thick, sweet, smoky, and sticky tomato-based sauce. This style of sauce is the model for most bottled brands, including KC Masterpiece. Bottled sauces aren't bad, but if you're going to invest a few hours making authentic barbecue, why not make your own sauce?

I started with the usual ingredients—onions, cider vinegar, ketchup, molasses, and mustard—but as my testing continued, I picked up on a few tricks of the trade. Tomato paste and dark corn syrup created the proper "cling" as well as a beautiful sheen. Chicken broth and garlic powder added complexity, and hot sauce kicked in some welcome heat.

Still, I couldn't help feeling like I was missing a secret ingredient. In my research, I ran across several recipes that suggested warm spices like star anise, cloves, and allspice, but they made my sauce taste like pumpkin pie filling. Beer was an interesting addition but not quite what I was after. Then true inspiration struck: What about root beer? After all, root beer's sassafras flavor is indisputably warm, with notes of clove, anise, and vanilla. Sure enough, root beer proved to be the final piece of the puzzle, adding a sweet, slightly spicy flavor that makes my homemade barbecue sauce worth the (minimal) effort.

–Jeremy Sauer

(see recipe on page 14)

Kansas City Barbecue Sauce

continued from page 13

KANSAS CITY BBQ SAUCE MAKES ABOUT 4 CUPS

We like our barbecue sauce extra-thick. If you like a thinner, smoother texture, the sauce can be strained after it has finished cooking.

- 2 teaspoons vegetable oil
- 1 onion, minced
- 4 cups low-sodium chicken broth
- 1 cup root beer
- 1 cup cider vinegar
- 1 cup dark corn syrup
- 1/2 cup molasses
- 1/2 cup tomato paste
- 1/2 cup ketchup
- 2 tablespoons brown mustard
- 1 tablespoon hot sauce
- 1/2 teaspoon garlic powder
- 1/4 teaspoon liquid smoke (optional)

Heat oil in saucepan over medium-high heat until shimmering. Add onion and cook until softened, about 5 minutes. Whisk in remaining ingredients, except for liquid smoke, and bring to boil. Reduce heat to medium and simmer until mixture is thick and has reduced to 4 cups, about 1 hour. Stir in liquid smoke, if using. (Sauce can be refrigerated in airtight container for up to 1 week.)

Good Pop, Bad Pop

Our Kansas City BBQ Sauce is flavored by an unlikely ingredient: root beer. I wondered how other types of soda might fare in my recipe. Birch beer, cream soda, and cola were fine but couldn't top root beer. Other sodas, especially Dr Pepper and Mountain Dew, gave my sauce a medicinal flavor. –J.S.

SECRET INGREDIENT

Spicy Steak Soft Tacos

Whenever we eat Mexican food, I go straight for the steak soft tacos—they're worlds better than the ground-beef kind. Do you have a good recipe? –Amy Gendron, Glens Falls, N.Y.

Frankly, I've never understood the appeal of those ground-beef taco kits, with their stale corn taco shells, boring spice mixes, and watery salsas. I'm with you. I'd much rather have a good steak taco flavored with fresh ingredients. So why does no one make steak tacos at home?

Mexican restaurants sear marinated skirt steak (a flavorful cut from the underside of the steer) in a hot skillet, but skirt steak isn't available in every supermarket. As alternatives, I tested three similar cuts: flank, from the underside of the animal; blade, from the shoulder; and steak tips, from the sirloin. With its slight chew and lean, beefy flavor, flank beat out the competition.

I tried several marinades (most consisted of oil, lime juice, and herbs), but they all gave the steak a spongy texture. And without a powerful, restaurant-caliber burner, the moisture from the marinade caused the steak to steam instead of sear when cooked. The best way to go was a simple dry rub—just a light dusting of chili powder, cumin, and coriander. To give the rub some fresh flavor, I added scallions (common in the tacos sold on the streets of Mexico), jalapeños, and garlic.

What's the best way to cook the steak? Fitting a flank steak large enough to feed a family into a skillet was problematic—the meat curled up the sides of the pan and didn't brown properly. So I flipped the script, first slicing the steak and then searing it. This method might seem odd—I was now essentially stir-frying steak for tacos—but it made the steak easy to manage in the pan (I cooked it in two batches), and the dry rub now covered a larger surface area of the steak, seasoning it more evenly. Still, some of my tasters felt the large slices of meat were a bit unruly once inside the tortillas. Cutting them any smaller led the steak to overcook in the pan before it could brown, so I compromised. After the steak was seared, I chopped it into bite-sized pieces.

I found some Mexican recipes that suggested glazing the browned meat for a final boost of flavor. I tried reducing a bit of tomato sauce and water in the empty skillet and then tossing it with the meat and any juices it had shed. Although this sauce napped the steak nicely, its flavor was one-dimensional. To brighten the sauce, I added a jolt of lime juice and a touch of brown sugar. This intensely flavored sauce made a great glaze. Tucked into a warm flour tortilla with fresh toppings, these meaty tacos leave those tired-tasting kits with ground-beef filling in the dust. –Jeremy Sauer

Soft flour tortillas are the perfect partner for quickly seared steak.

STEAK SOFT TACOS

SERVES 6

To make cutting the steak easier, place the whole flank in the freezer for 20 minutes to firm up. Serve these soft tacos with shredded cheese, lettuce, sour cream, pickled jalapeños, and lots of hot sauce or salsa verde (recipe follows). See page 29 for tips on warming the tortillas.

- **1 flank steak (about 1 1/2 pounds), sliced thin (see photos below)**
- **1 tablespoon chili powder**
- **1 1/2 teaspoons cumin**
- **1 teaspoon coriander**
- **3/4 teaspoon salt**
- **4 garlic cloves, minced**
- **4 scallions, green parts cut into 1-inch lengths, white parts cut in half lengthwise**
- **1–2 jalapeño chiles, minced**
- **4 teaspoons vegetable oil**
- **1/2 cup canned tomato sauce**
- **1/2 cup water**
- **2 teaspoons brown sugar**
- **1 tablespoon lime juice**
- **12 (8-inch) flour tortillas, warmed**

1. Place sliced steak in large bowl and sprinkle evenly with chili powder, cumin, coriander, and salt. Add garlic, scallions, and chiles and toss to combine. (Steak mixture can be refrigerated for up to 2 hours.)

2. Heat 2 teaspoons oil in large skillet over high heat until just smoking. Add half of steak mixture and cook, turning slices once, until just browned, about 1 minute per side. Transfer to bowl. Repeat with remaining oil and steak and transfer to bowl.

3. Off heat, add tomato sauce, water, brown sugar, and lime juice to skillet, scraping up any browned bits with wooden spoon. Meanwhile, use slotted spoon to transfer browned steak mixture to cutting board, leaving accumulated juices in bowl. Chop steak into rough 1-inch pieces.

4. Add reserved juices to skillet and cook until reduced by half, about 6 to 10 minutes over medium heat. Return steak to skillet and cook until meat is glazed and just cooked through, about 2 minutes. Divide among tortillas. Serve.

SALSA VERDE

MAKES ABOUT 1 1/2 CUPS

If using canned tomatillos, skip step 1 and add the drained tomatillos to the food processor in step 2.

- **8 tomatillos, husks removed, or 1 (11-ounce) can tomatillos, drained (see note above)**
- **1/2 onion, chopped rough**
- **1–2 jalapeño chiles, chopped rough**
- **2 garlic cloves**
- **Juice of 1 lime**
- **1/2 cup packed fresh cilantro**
- **1/2 teaspoon salt**

1. Place tomatillos in saucepan, cover with water, and bring to boil over high heat. Once boiling, reduce heat to low and simmer until tomatillos are brownish-green and soft, 5 to 7 minutes. Meanwhile, fill large bowl with ice water. Transfer tomatillos to ice water and cool.

2. Meanwhile, pulse onion, chiles, and garlic in food processor until coarsely ground. Using slotted spoon, transfer tomatillos to food processor along with lime juice, cilantro, and salt. Puree until smooth, scraping down sides as necessary. (Salsa can be refrigerated in airtight container for up to 4 days.)

How to SLICE FLANK STEAK

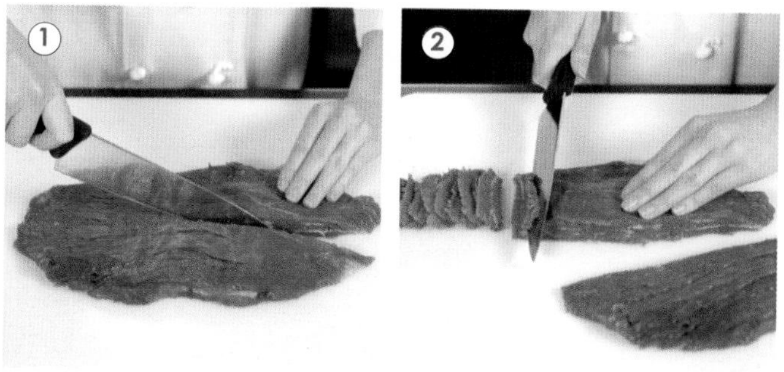

1. Cut the flank steak in half lengthwise. **2.** Working with one half at a time, slice the steak on the bias into 1/4-inch-thick pieces.

Dressing Up: Flavored Lemonade

Mashed strawberries and fresh mint sprigs pump up the flavor in homemade lemonade.

How to Make A MUDDLE

Mashing lemon slices with sugar (a process bartenders call muddling) releases the flavorful oils in the lemon peel, giving our lemonade a deeper, fresher lemon flavor. We found a potato masher works best, but any heavy flat-bottomed object (such as a wine bottle) will work in a pinch.

Nothing says summer better than lemonade. Here's how to make the very best.

Though store-bought lemonade tastes fine, it's never as good as homemade. Yes, freshly squeezed juice makes a big difference. But since I was doing all that squeezing, I thought I'd tap into another source of lemon flavor—the oils in the colored peel—to make truly memorable lemonade.

Strips of zest did little to flavor my test batches, and grated zest made my lemonade gritty. Taking a cue from professional bartenders, who mash mint and sugar together to make mojitos and other tropical cocktails, I sliced lemons and mashed them with the sugar. This lemon syrup was intense—too intense for many tasters—and it was hard work slicing and mashing so many lemons. Luckily, slicing and mashing just one lemon yielded plenty of lemon flavor.

I still had to juice a dozen lemons, but the lemonade I made this way—smooth and without a trace of bitterness—was worth the 10 minutes of squeezing and mixing. And in just five minutes more I could make herbal, fruity, or spicy variations that can't be bought at the supermarket.

–Stephanie Alleyne

BEST LEMONADE

SERVES 6 TO 8

Look for large, slightly soft lemons—they tend to be extra-juicy. Store the lemonade in a covered container in the refrigerator for up to 3 days.

- **1 large lemon, sliced thin, ends discarded**
- **1 1/2 cups sugar**
- **7 cups cold water**
- **2 cups fresh lemon juice (from about 12 lemons)**
- **Ice (for serving)**

Using potato masher, mash lemon slices and sugar in deep bowl until slices release their juice and sugar begins to dissolve. Stir in water and lemon juice until sugar completely dissolves. Strain out lemon slices and chill or pour over ice before serving.

STRAWBERRY LEMONADE

If fresh summer strawberries aren't available, use frozen berries. Just defrost in a microwave set on high for 3 minutes. If you prefer, swap the strawberries for either blueberries or raspberries.

Mash 2 cups fresh strawberries with lemon slices and sugar. Proceed as directed, straining out mashed berries and lemon slices before serving.

MINTY LEMONADE

Mash 1 cup fresh mint leaves with lemon slices and sugar. Proceed as directed, straining out mint leaves and lemon slices before serving.

GINGER LEMONADE

You will need a piece of ginger that's about 3 inches long for this recipe. Use a rasp grater or the small holes on a box grater to grate the ginger.

Mash 4 tablespoons grated fresh ginger with lemon slices and sugar. Proceed as directed, straining out ginger and lemon slices before serving.

I'm Looking for a Recipe

READERS HELP READERS FIND RECIPES

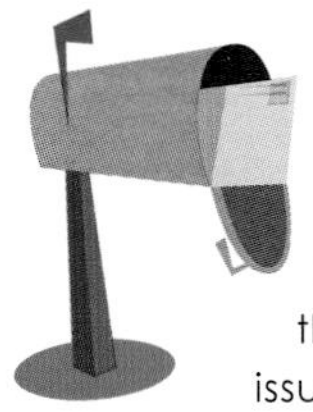

We've Got Mail

Several readers sent us recipes in response to the request for fruit fluff (October/November 2005 issue). We really liked the letter and recipe sent by Annette Baker (right). For the test kitchen's notes on this recipe (and more details on cooking times and procedures), go to **www.cookscountry.com** and click **Looking for a Recipe.** You'll find dozens more recipes submitted by other readers who responded to this page in other issues of *Cook's Country*.

FRUIT FLUFF **Annette Baker** Arlington, Va.

I recognized Karen Morse's request for fruit fluff right away. We call it Grandma's Cheesecake. My husband's grandmother used to make these bar cookies, and now I make them for community potlucks. They are always a hit. This recipe serves 12 and can be refrigerated for a day.

18	**graham crackers, ground fine**
1¼	**cups sugar**
10	**tablespoons butter, melted**
1	**box raspberry Jell-O**
1	**cup hot water**
11	**ounces cream cheese**
1	**(13-ounce) can crushed pineapple, drained**
2	**envelopes Dream Whip**
1	**cup milk**

INSTRUCTIONS: Mix graham cracker crumbs, ¼ cup sugar, and butter and press into 13 by 9-inch Pyrex dish, saving ¼ cup crumb mix for topping. Bake in 350-degree oven until firm, about 12 minutes. Cool. Dissolve Jell-O in hot water. Cool. With electric mixer, whip cream cheese, remaining sugar, and drained pineapple together until smooth, then add Jell-O. Whip Dream Whip with milk until stiff and fold into cream cheese mixture. Pour onto graham cracker crumb base and sprinkle with remaining crumb topping. Refrigerate until set, about 2 hours.

Dixie Stampede Vegetable Soup

Last year, I went to the Dixie Stampede, Dolly Parton's show in Branson, Mo., and I fell in love with the creamy vegetable soup they served. It was smooth and the flavor was perfect. I wrote to them, but they are not willing to share the recipe. This has become an obsession for me. I went back this year and I loved it as much as I did before.

Torie Taibemal
Seward, Neb.

Dairy Queen Frozen Hot Chocolate

I would love to make Dairy Queen–style frozen hot chocolate at home. I have not been able to find a copycat recipe online or in any cookbook.

Amelia Sunderland
Nashville, Tenn.

Coffee-Can Pumpkin Bread

Years ago, a co-worker brought in a loaf of pumpkin bread that she had baked in a coffee can. It was awesomely delicious—rich and spicy. I think it was made with molasses, brown sugar, cinnamon, and ginger. It smelled and tasted like old-fashioned homemade goodness.

Christine Lockett
Amarillo, Texas

Baby-Food Cake

My mother-in-law used to make very moist Bundt cake with jars of fruit baby food. Although she gave me the recipe, it was lost in a move years ago, and I've been unable to find it anywhere. The recipe was at least 30 years old. I hope someone can help since this was my husband's favorite.

Judy Wilde
Albuquerque, N.M.

Sugar Pie

As a child, I remember my grandmother making sugar pie. She would fill an uncooked pie shell with a mound of sugar, then she would fill the "moat" around the sugar with milk or cream, add some cinnamon, and bake it. It was not stirred at all. When finished, the pie looked like a thick white custard with sprinkles of cinnamon. I have tried over and over to make the recipe using books and my memory, but none have turned out right. Many say there is butter or vanilla in the recipe, but I don't recall. I would love to taste this again as it brings back so many wonderful memories.

Sherry Brethorst
Lodi, Wis.

Italian Chocolate Cookies

I'm looking for an Italian cookie that is very dense, even fudge-like, with nuts and raisins and a white glaze. I do have a recipe from my grandmother with cloves, nuts, raisins, coffee, and Dutch cocoa, but it is lighter and more cake-like. The recipe I'm looking for might even contain candied fruit.

Kim Pignone
Via e-mail

No-Bake Fruitcake

Years ago, I had a recipe for no-bake fruitcake. It had dried fruits rather than candied fruits (which I don't like) and lots of nuts. There was some liquor in it, too—perhaps rum? When all the ingredients were combined, you covered it in foil and placed a brick on it for a month until everything melded. It was very tasty and healthy.

Sharon Borovay
Boynton Beach, Fla.

Polish Sour Cream Coconut Cookies

This is a cookie from my childhood. The only place I have ever seen them is in Shamokin, Pa., where my grandmother lived. They sold them at the Acme on certain days, and some of her Polish neighbors made them, too. They are cake-like cookies with white coconut frosting. I am pretty certain there was sour cream in the icing or the cookie or both. My grandmother passed away nearly four years ago, and I would love to have this recipe.

Jennifer Piscitelli
Trumbull, Conn.

Hidden Raspberry Cookies

I'm in search of an Italian cookie recipe that has a hidden raspberry inside. I shop at many Italian bakeries and I've looked in cookbooks and on Web sites, but I've had no luck finding this recipe.

Sheila Briggs
North Andover, Mass.

Brown Sugar Gravy

I'm looking for a recipe that my grandmother called brown sugar gravy. She served it warm over a homemade white cake. I know it was made with flour, not just sugar and butter.

Diane Endres
Via e-mail

Lard Bread

I have been going crazy trying to find a recipe for lard bread. None of the local Italian delis or specialty stores make it, or, if they do, it's not really lard bread.

'Dina'
Via e-mail

Chocolate Mashed Potato Cake

About 50 years ago, I had a friend whose mother used to make a chocolate mashed potato cake, but the recipe was lost when her mother died. It was a heavy, moist cake.

Julie Walter
Worland, Wyo.

German Potatoes and Noodles

My mother was first-generation German-Hungarian. She made a noodle and potato dish that I do not know how to spell, but it sounded like *grenna deah marsh*. When I feel like eating a little of this "soul food," I pop potatoes in the microwave to cook quickly, peel them, and fry them with onions. I then toss egg noodles with the onion and potato mixture and sauté them together until they form a slight crust. It would be nice to say it tastes just like Mom's, but it doesn't.

Judy George
Coral Gables, Fla.

Lebkuchen

Does anyone have a recipe for the German cookies called lebkuchen? My husband's grandmother used to make them, and she forwarded me a recipe that seems to have left out some ingredients. I would love to re-create this recipe for my husband.

Melissa Anthony
Lexington, Ky

Tuna Croquettes with Rice

Back in the late 1960s and early 1970s, my mom used to make tuna croquettes and serve them on white rice with tomato soup poured over the top. It was the best. I know she used to get a lot of her recipes from magazines. I would love to have that recipe.

Alicia C. Cog
Pacifica, Calif.

Are you looking for a special recipe? Let other readers of this magazine help. Just send us your requests, and we will print as many of them as we can. Write to Looking for a Recipe, Cook's Country, P.O. Box 470739, Brookline, MA 02447, or lookingforarecipe@bcpress.com. If you can help with one of the above requests, contact us at the same postal or e-mail address. We will post the responses on www.cookscountry.com.

Find the Rooster!

A tiny version of this rooster has been hidden somewhere in the pages of this issue. If you find it, write to us with its location (plus your name and address), and you will be entered into a random drawing. The first winning entry drawn will receive the Calphalon spatula (our test winner—see page 31), and the next five winners will each receive a free one-year subscription to *Cook's Country*. To enter the contest, write to us at Rooster, Cook's Country, P.O. Box 470739, Brookline, MA 02447, or send us an e-mail at rooster@bcpress.com. Entries are due by July 31, 2006.

Did you find the rooster in the February/March 2006 issue? It was hidden in the potato pancake photo on page 20. Pam Bonner of Marinette, Wis., spotted it and won a Cuisinart skillet.

Quick Cooking

ASIAN CHICKEN LETTUCE WRAPS

Quick Cooking

QUICK TOMATO-BASIL PASTA WITH FRESH MOZZARELLA

Quick Cooking

GRILLED CHICKEN BREASTS WITH GRILLED CORN AND TOMATO SALAD

Quick Cooking

GRILLED PORTOBELLO MUSHROOM BRUSCHETTA

QUICK TOMATO-BASIL PASTA WITH FRESH MOZZARELLA SERVES 4

Look for fresh mini mozzarella balls in the gourmet cheese section of your supermarket.

- 3 tablespoons extra-virgin olive oil
- 4 garlic cloves, minced
- 1/4 teaspoon red pepper flakes
- 1 (28-ounce) can crushed tomatoes
- 1 (14.5-ounce) can diced tomatoes
- 5 tablespoons roughly chopped fresh basil
- 1/4 teaspoon sugar
- Salt
- 1 pound campanelle or fusilli pasta
- 8 ounces fresh mini mozzarella balls, drained and cut in half
- 1/3 cup grated Parmesan cheese

1. Bring 4 quarts water to boil in large pot.

2. Meanwhile, heat 2 tablespoons oil, garlic, and pepper flakes in medium saucepan over medium heat until fragrant but not brown, about 2 minutes. Stir in crushed and diced tomatoes, bring to simmer, and cook until slightly thickened, 15 to 20 minutes. Stir in 3 tablespoons basil, sugar, and 1/2 teaspoon salt.

3. Add 1 tablespoon salt and pasta to boiling water. Cook until al dente. Reserve 1/4 cup cooking water, drain pasta, and transfer back to pot. Stir in sauce and remaining tablespoon oil, and cook over medium heat until heated through (adding reserved water if pasta seems dry), about 1 minute. Stir in mozzarella and season with salt. Serve, sprinkling with remaining 2 tablespoons basil and Parmesan.

ASIAN CHICKEN LETTUCE WRAPS SERVES 4

For best results, use ground chicken made from a mix of light and dark meat.

- 1 head iceberg lettuce
- 3 tablespoons hoisin sauce
- 2 tablespoons soy sauce
- 2 tablespoons water
- 5 garlic cloves, minced
- 2 teaspoons grated fresh ginger
- 2 teaspoons plus 2 tablespoons peanut or vegetable oil
- 1 pound ground chicken
- Salt and pepper
- 1 red bell pepper, diced
- 1 (8-ounce) can water chestnuts, drained and chopped fine
- 5 scallions, chopped

1. Remove 8 large, bowl-shaped leaves from head of lettuce; reserve remaining lettuce for another use. Whisk hoisin sauce, soy sauce, and water together in measuring cup. Combine garlic, ginger, and 2 teaspoons oil in small bowl.

2. Heat 1 tablespoon oil in large nonstick skillet over medium-high heat until just smoking. Cook chicken, stirring to break up clumps, until just cooked through, about 3 minutes. Season with salt and pepper and transfer to bowl.

3. Add remaining tablespoon oil to skillet and heat until just smoking. Add bell pepper, water chestnuts, and scallions and cook until peppers soften, about 3 minutes. Clear center of skillet, add garlic mixture, and cook until fragrant, about 30 seconds. Add chicken and sauce and stir until thickened, about 30 seconds. Spoon mixture into lettuce leaves and serve.

GRILLED PORTOBELLO MUSHROOM BRUSCHETTA

SERVES 4

If you prefer, substitute baby spinach for the arugula.

- 1/3 cup plus 1 tablespoon extra-virgin olive oil
- 3 tablespoons lemon juice
- 7 garlic cloves, 6 minced, 1 whole
- Salt and pepper
- 4 large portobello mushrooms (about 1 1/3 pounds), stemmed
- 4 large slices Italian peasant bread, about 1 inch thick
- 1 (5-ounce) bag baby arugula (about 8 cups)
- 4 ounces goat cheese, crumbled

1. Combine 1/3 cup oil, lemon juice, minced garlic, 1/4 teaspoon salt, and 1/4 teaspoon pepper in large zipper-lock storage bag. Add mushrooms, seal bag, and shake until coated. Let stand at room temperature for about 10 minutes.

2. Meanwhile, cut four 12-inch pieces of foil. Transfer one mushroom, gill side up, to each foil square. Pour remaining marinade over mushrooms and seal foil tightly around mushrooms.

3. Grill foil packets over hot fire, with seam side facing up, until mushrooms are juicy and tender, 7 to 9 minutes. Using tongs, unwrap foil slightly and pour liquid into medium bowl. Unwrap mushrooms and place, gill side up, directly on grill rack. Cook until grill-marked, 30 to 60 seconds, then transfer to plate.

4. While mushrooms are grilling, brush bread with remaining tablespoon oil and toast until grill-marked on both sides, about 1 1/2 minutes per side. Transfer bread to 4 dinner plates and rub each slice with whole garlic clove.

5. Slice mushrooms and toss with arugula and reserved mushroom liquid in large bowl. Season with salt and pepper, then divide mushroom mixture among bread slices. Sprinkle with cheese. Serve.

GRILLED CHICKEN BREASTS WITH GRILLED CORN AND TOMATO SALAD SERVES 4

For this dish, buy chicken breasts that are about 1/2 inch thick.

- 2 ears corn
- 2 teaspoons plus 1/4 cup olive oil
- Salt and pepper
- 2 tablespoons lemon juice
- 2 garlic cloves, minced
- 3 tablespoons chopped fresh basil
- 1 tablespoon Dijon mustard
- 1 tablespoon honey
- 4 boneless, chicken breasts (about 5 ounces each), trimmed
- 1 ripe beefsteak tomato, diced

1. Wrap corn in microwave-safe plastic wrap and microwave on high power until slightly softened, about 3 minutes, turning corn over halfway through cooking. Cool slightly and remove plastic wrap. Brush with 2 teaspoons oil and season with salt and pepper.

2. Whisk lemon juice, garlic, basil, and remaining 1/4 cup oil together in small bowl and season with salt and pepper. Transfer 2 tablespoons dressing to medium bowl and whisk in mustard and honey. Pat chicken dry, season with salt and pepper, and toss in honey-mustard mixture to coat.

3. Grill corn and chicken over hot fire. Grill chicken until cooked through, about 3 minutes per side, transfer to platter, and cover with foil. Grill corn until soft and lightly charred, 5 to 6 minutes. Remove from grill, cool slightly, and cut kernels from cob. Combine corn, tomatoes, and remaining dressing (without honey and mustard) in medium bowl and season with salt and pepper. Serve corn salad with chicken.

Quick Cooking

OVEN-GRILLED REUBEN SANDWICHES

Quick Cooking

QUICK CLAM CHOWDER

Quick Cooking

GRILLED STEAK AND POTATOES WITH GARLIC BUTTER

Quick Cooking

MEDITERRANEAN PORK CHOPS

QUICK CLAM CHOWDER SERVES 6

Serve this summer favorite with saltines or oyster crackers.

4 (6.5-ounce) cans minced clams
3 (8-ounce) bottles clam juice
1½ pounds red potatoes, scrubbed and cut into ½-inch pieces
2 bay leaves
2 teaspoons minced fresh thyme
6 slices bacon, chopped fine
1 onion, minced
2 garlic cloves, minced
¼ cup all-purpose flour
1 cup heavy cream
2 tablespoons chopped fresh parsley
Salt and pepper

1. Drain clams through strainer set over medium bowl. Add bottled clam juice to drained liquid to measure 5 cups (add water if necessary). Bring potatoes, clam juice, bay leaves, and thyme to boil in medium saucepan over high heat. Reduce heat to low to maintain gentle simmer.

2. While potatoes are coming to boil, cook bacon in large Dutch oven over medium heat until just crisp, 5 to 7 minutes. Add onion and cook until softened, about 5 minutes. Add garlic and cook until fragrant, about 30 seconds. Stir in flour and cook for 1 minute.

3. Pour potatoes and cooking liquid into pot with onion mixture, using wooden spoon to scrape bottom of pan. Add clams, cream, and parsley and simmer until potatoes are tender, 5 to 7 minutes. Season with salt and pepper. Serve.

OVEN-GRILLED REUBEN SANDWICHES SERVES 4

Sweet-and-sour cabbage and a zesty mustard-flavored mayonnaise transform this deli classic into something special. "Oven-grilling" allows you to cook the sandwiches all at once (and without turning them) rather than cooking in batches on the stovetop.

⅓ cup cider vinegar
2 tablespoons sugar
1 (16-ounce) bag coleslaw mix
Salt and pepper
¼ cup mayonnaise
¼ cup Dijon mustard
8 slices hearty rye bread
8 slices Swiss cheese (about ½ pound)
1 pound thinly sliced corned beef
2 tablespoons unsalted butter, melted

1. Adjust oven rack to middle position, place baking sheet on rack, and heat oven to 450 degrees. Bring vinegar and sugar to boil in large skillet over medium heat. Stir to dissolve sugar, add coleslaw, cover, and cook, tossing occasionally, until coleslaw is tender, 8 to 10 minutes. Remove lid and simmer until liquid has evaporated, 1 to 2 minutes. Season with salt and pepper.

2. Combine mayonnaise and mustard in small bowl. Spread 1 tablespoon mayonnaise mixture on each bread slice. Layer 1 slice cheese, ½ cup coleslaw, ¼ pound corned beef, and 1 slice cheese on top of bread slice. Top with second slice of bread and compress sandwich with your hands. Repeat to make three more sandwiches. Brush tops and bottoms of sandwiches with melted butter.

3. Transfer sandwiches to preheated baking sheet. Bake until toasted, about 10 minutes. Serve.

MEDITERRANEAN PORK CHOPS SERVES 4

To round out the meal, serve with couscous.

4 boneless rib or center-cut pork chops, about 1 inch thick
Salt and pepper
2 tablespoons olive oil
2 medium zucchini, cut into ¾-inch pieces
3 garlic cloves, minced
¾ cup low-sodium chicken broth
1 tablespoon chopped fresh oregano
2 cups cherry tomatoes, halved
⅓ cup pitted black olives, halved

1. Pat pork chops dry with paper towels and season with salt and pepper. Heat 1 tablespoon oil in large nonstick skillet over medium-high heat until just smoking. Cook chops until well browned on both sides but still pink in center, 3 to 4 minutes per side. Transfer chops to plate and cover with foil.

2. Add remaining tablespoon oil to skillet and heat until just smoking. Add zucchini and salt to taste and cook, stirring, until spotty brown, about 4 minutes. Add garlic and cook until fragrant, about 30 seconds. Add broth and oregano and bring to simmer, using wooden spoon to scrape bottom of pan. Push zucchini to sides of pan, return chops and any accumulated juices to pan, and cook until pork is cooked through and sauce is slightly thickened, about 7 minutes.

3. Transfer chops to serving platter. Add tomatoes and olives to skillet and toss to warm through, about 1 minute. Season with salt and pepper and spoon vegetable mixture over chops. Serve.

GRILLED STEAK AND POTATOES WITH GARLIC BUTTER

SERVES 4

To speed things up, grill the steaks and potatoes at the same time—place the steak on one side of the grill and the potatoes on the other side.

1½ pounds small red potatoes, scrubbed and halved
1 tablespoon olive oil
Salt and pepper
4 tablespoons unsalted butter, softened
2 tablespoons minced fresh parsley
3 garlic cloves, minced
4 boneless strip steaks, about 1 inch thick

1. Toss potatoes and oil in medium microwave-safe bowl and season with salt and pepper. Cover with plastic wrap and microwave on high power until slightly softened, about 4 minutes, tossing potatoes halfway through cooking.

2. Beat butter with fork in medium bowl until light and fluffy. Mix in parsley, garlic, ½ teaspoon salt, and pepper to taste.

3. Sprinkle steaks with salt and pepper. Grill steaks over hot fire until well browned on both sides and internal temperature reaches 125 degrees (medium-rare), 5 to 6 minutes per side. Grill potatoes, starting cut side down and turning several times, until soft and grill-marked, 7 to 8 minutes.

4. Transfer steaks to serving platter and top each steak with 1 tablespoon parsley butter. Cover with foil and let rest 5 minutes. Toss potatoes with remaining tablespoon parsley butter in serving bowl. Serve steaks with potatoes.

Mile-High Lemon Meringue Pie

My husband's all-time favorite dessert is lemon meringue pie, but I need a recipe that's reliable and won't weep. How do I keep the meringue light and fluffy and HIGH? I want the best pie ever. He deserves it!

–Pam Villanova, Ellington, Conn.

A hot sugar syrup "cooks" the egg whites and guarantees a fluffy, no-weep meringue.

Making a modest meringue (beating two or three egg whites with sugar) is tricky enough. Double the amount of topping for a mile-high meringue and you've got double the problems. Weeping (the leaching of liquid from the meringue) was a sad reality in every recipe I tried.

I found that cream of tartar helped make the meringue more stable. But even with cream of tartar in my recipe, the meringue wept. Undercooking is the main problem—the pooling liquid is actually egg white reverting to its liquid form. For regular lemon meringue pies, the test kitchen has solved this problem by spreading the meringue over a piping-hot filling and baking the pie in a hot oven. The hot filling cooks the bottom half of the meringue, while the heat from the oven takes care of the top half.

But when I used this normally reliable method with twice as much meringue, the topping disintegrated into a puddle as I sliced up the first piece of pie. What went wrong? I realized that this method works only with a modest amount of meringue. The center of my super-sized meringue wasn't cooking through. Baking the pie longer was not an option—the top of the meringue burned. I needed to try something different.

Years ago, when I worked as a baker's assistant, I learned about Italian meringue. Boiling-hot sugar syrup is poured into the egg whites as they are whipped. The hot syrup cooks the whites and helps transform them into a soft, smooth meringue that is stable enough to resist weeping. Best of all, this meringue is extra fluffy and billowy. While I needed eight egg whites to achieve mile-high results with a regular meringue, four egg whites yielded plenty of Italian meringue. Doubling the meringue without doubling the whites is a neat trick.

There's only one problem with an Italian meringue. Professional bakers use a candy thermometer to heat the sugar syrup to the correct temperature (between 238 and 245 degrees), but many home cooks don't have this tool. Could I make an Italian meringue without a thermometer? After much trial and error, I found that boiling the sugar syrup for exactly four minutes worked perfectly every time—no matter which stove (or pan) in the test kitchen that I used.

Since I no longer needed a hot filling to cook the meringue, I thought I might be able to let the filling set up in the shell in the fridge. Two hours later (this can even be done the day before), my filling emerged firm yet still silky. Tasters wanted the filling extra lemony and very rich to balance all the meringue. It took a full cup of lemon juice, 2 tablespoons of zest, and 8 yolks—more than I had seen in any other recipe—to please everyone.

With lots of lemon, miles of meringue, and absolutely no weeping, this pie can be counted on to deliver smiles all around the table every time you make it. **–Stephanie Alleyne**

(see recipe on page 18)

Kitchen Know-How
WEEP NO MORE

For our meringue, you don't need a thermometer, but you do need a timer.

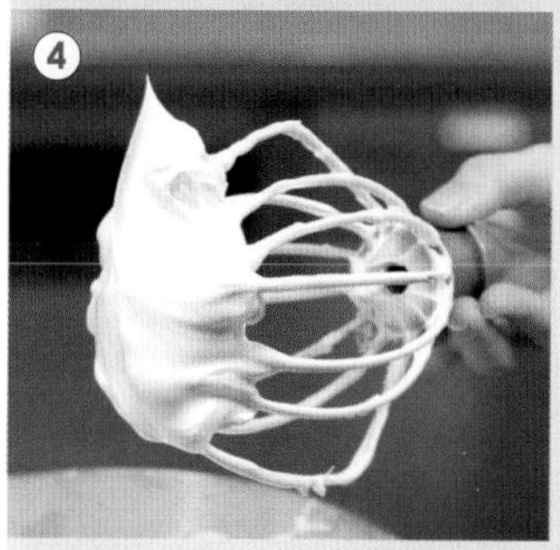

1. After the sugar syrup comes to a full boil, cook it for exactly 4 minutes.
2. Beat the egg whites with the salt and cream of tartar until they hold soft peaks.
3. With the mixer still running, carefully pour the hot sugar syrup directly into the beaten egg whites.
4. Continue beating until the meringue has cooled to room temperature and is thick and fluffy.

Mile-High Lemon Meringue Pie

continued from page 17

MILE-HIGH LEMON MERINGUE PIE SERVES 8 TO 10

If using a hand-held mixer, you will need a very large, deep bowl and should move the beaters vigorously in step 3 to avoid underbeating the egg whites. This pie is best on the day it's made. For the pie shell, go to www.cookscountry.com for our recipe, use your own, or see our recommendation for store-bought crust on page 28.

Lemon Filling

- 1¼ cups sugar
- 1 cup lemon juice (from 6 lemons)
- ½ cup water
- ¼ cup cornstarch
- ¼ teaspoon salt
- 8 large egg yolks (reserve 4 whites for meringue)
- 2 tablespoons grated lemon zest
- 3 tablespoons unsalted butter, cut into pieces and softened
- 1 (9-inch) pie shell, fully baked and cooled

Meringue

- ½ cup water
- 1 cup sugar
- 4 large egg whites (reserved from filling)
- Pinch salt
- ½ teaspoon cream of tartar
- ½ teaspoon vanilla extract

1. For the filling: Whisk sugar, lemon juice, water, cornstarch, and salt together in large nonreactive saucepan until cornstarch is dissolved. Bring to simmer over medium heat, whisking occasionally, until mixture becomes translucent and begins to thicken, about 5 minutes. Whisk in yolks until combined. Stir in zest and butter. Bring to simmer and stir constantly until mixture is thick enough to coat back of spoon, about 2 minutes. Strain through fine-mesh strainer into pie shell and scrape filling off underside of strainer. Place plastic wrap directly on surface of filling and refrigerate until set and well chilled, at least 2 hours and up to 1 day.

2. For the meringue: Adjust oven rack to middle position and heat oven to 400 degrees. Combine water and sugar in small saucepan. Bring to vigorous boil over medium-high heat. Once syrup comes to rolling boil, cook 4 minutes (mixture will become slightly thickened and syrupy). Remove from heat and set aside while beating whites.

3. With electric mixer, beat whites in large bowl at medium-low speed until frothy, about 1 minute. Add salt and cream of tartar and beat, gradually increasing speed to medium-high, until whites hold soft peaks, about 2 minutes. With mixer running, slowly pour hot syrup into whites (avoid pouring syrup onto whisk or it will splash). Add vanilla and beat until meringue has cooled and becomes very thick and shiny, 5 to 9 minutes.

4. Using rubber spatula, mound meringue over filling, making sure meringue touches edges of crust. Use spatula to create peaks all over meringue. Bake until peaks turn golden brown, about 6 minutes. Transfer to wire rack and cool to room temperature. Serve.

Kitchen Wisdom MAKING A MERINGUE MOUNTAIN

These tricks guarantee meringue that looks as good as it tastes.

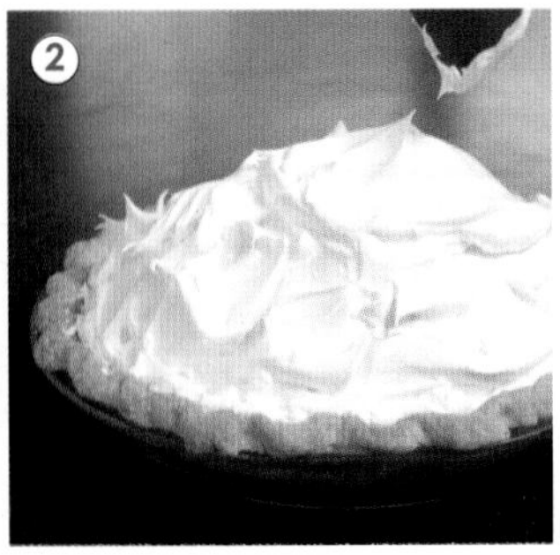

1. Use a rubber spatula to press the meringue onto the edge of the pie crust. This will keep the meringue from shrinking. **2.** Use the spatula to make dramatic peaks and swirls all over the meringue.

Easy Oven-Fried Fish

Is there a way to produce crispy cornmeal batter-fried fish in the oven?

Choose large fillets that are thick enough to allow the coating to crisp in the oven without drying out.

The idea of fried fish fillets coated with cornmeal and cooked to crispy, golden perfection sounds appealing, but we all know what lies in store for the intrepid cook who tries to fry fish: batch upon batch of delicate fish fillets that seem to fall apart no matter how carefully you treat them, a grease-splattered stove, and, of course, the lingering smell of fried fish. This dish is best enjoyed in a restaurant, right? But what about oven-frying? This easier, relatively mess-free technique seemed well worth a try.

Initial tests using cornmeal couldn't have been further off the mark. I might as well have dunked my fish into a sandbox: These fillets cooked up bland, dry, and gritty. Even a generously greased baking sheet failed to help.

I wondered if another corn-based product (one with more fat, perhaps) might give fish the corn crunch I wanted. Taking a "think outside the box" approach, I scoured every section of my supermarket for corn products and came back to the test kitchen with corn flakes, yellow and white tortilla chips, Bugles, Fritos, and cornbread. The corn flakes made a chewy—not crisp—coating on the fish. The coatings made with all varieties of ground corn chips tasted artificial and stale. The cornbread showed the most promise, but it was much too sweet.

Adding some fresh bread crumbs and a savory mix of dry mustard, thyme, garlic powder, cayenne pepper, salt, and black pepper tempered the cornbread's sweetness. Even though the cornbread itself has some fat, the coating was still too crumbly and dry. Mixing the crumbs with melted butter gave the coating a crisp "fried" texture.

Next I had to make sure that the seasoned cornbread would adhere to the fish; simply coating the fillets was not enough. Dredging the fish in flour and then dipping it in buttermilk produced a substantial coating with a tangy flavor.

All I needed to do was fine-tune the cooking method. I was certainly on target but found that the bottoms of the fillets were getting a bit soggy. To solve this problem, I preheated an oiled pan. The fish now hit the pan with a sizzle, just as it would a hot skillet. My oven-fried fish was nicely browned all around and nearly as crispy as pan-fried fish, but it made far less mess and left no lingering fishy odor. –Eva Katz

An Unusual Breading

CORNBREAD

SANDWICH BREAD

Cornmeal, the traditional coating for fried fish, is too dry and sandy to use in the oven. Cornbread adds a similar corn flavor, while fresh bread crumbs temper its sweetness.

OVEN-FRIED FISH SERVES 4

Haddock, cod, or even thicker cuts of catfish work well in this recipe. If you have homemade cornbread on hand, use it.

- 2 **tablespoons vegetable oil**
- 6 **ounces store-bought cornbread (one $3\frac{1}{2}$-inch-square piece)**
- 3 **slices hearty white sandwich bread, quartered**
- 2 **teaspoons dry mustard**
- 1 **teaspoon dried thyme**
- $\frac{1}{4}$ **teaspoon garlic powder**
- $\frac{1}{4}$ **teaspoon cayenne pepper**
- **Salt and black pepper**
- 3 **tablespoons unsalted butter, melted**
- $\frac{1}{2}$ **cup all-purpose flour**
- 1 **cup buttermilk**
- 4 **thick skinless white fish fillets, each $\frac{3}{4}$ to 1 inch thick and 6 to 8 ounces**
- **Lemon wedges**

1. Adjust oven rack to upper-middle position and heat oven to 450 degrees. Pour oil onto rimmed baking sheet and tilt to evenly distribute oil.

2. Pulse cornbread in food processor to coarse crumbs. Transfer crumbs to large bowl. Pulse bread to fine crumbs. Transfer $1\frac{1}{2}$ cups bread crumbs to bowl with cornbread; discard remaining bread crumbs. Toss crumbs with mustard, thyme, garlic powder, cayenne, $\frac{1}{2}$ teaspoon salt, and $\frac{1}{4}$ teaspoon black pepper. Drizzle butter over crumbs and toss until coated.

3. Place flour in shallow baking dish and buttermilk in second shallow baking dish.

4. Place oiled baking sheet in hot oven and heat 10 minutes while preparing fish (don't leave in oven for more than 10 minutes or oil will smoke). Pat fish dry with paper towels and season with salt and pepper. Dip one fillet into flour, shake off excess, coat well with buttermilk, then dredge in crumb mixture, using hands to firmly pack crumbs onto all sides of fish. Transfer breaded fillet to large plate and repeat with remaining fillets.

5. Place breaded fish on preheated baking sheet and bake until coating is crisp and fish is cooked through, 12 to 14 minutes. Serve with lemon wedges.

On the Side: Succotash Salad

Is there a way to rethink succotash to make it lighter and fresher?

Succotash sounds stuffy and old-fashioned— something your grandmother might have prepared. But at its simplest, this summer side dish is nothing more than lima beans and corn cooked with butter and cream. Sounds delicious (and it can be), but even good succotash is awfully rich. Could I rethink this recipe and make it lighter? A room-temperature salad sounded appealing and modern.

Frozen lima beans were completely acceptable. Fresh lima beans were hard to find and not worth the 40 minutes it took to shell and cook them. When it came to the corn, however, fresh was preferable to frozen, which seemed bland by comparison. For more crunch, I added green beans, a common ingredient in succotash recipes. I found it easy to cook all the vegetables in one pot. The green beans needed a head start, but otherwise the timing was simple. Rinsing the cooked vegetables under cool running water set their color and kept them from softening further.

As for the dressing, I chose a simple mixture of olive oil and lemon juice. A little honey brought sweetness to the salad—much as the sweet cream does in the original recipe. For a splash of color and flavor, I finished the salad with minced red onion and chopped fresh basil. This cool, light salad now seems in sync with the warm days ahead. It's perfect with fish (including our Oven-Fried Fish), chicken, or almost anything from the grill. **–Eva Katz**

SUMMER SUCCOTASH SALAD SERVES 4

This salad can be kept covered and refrigerated for up to 1 day. If making the salad in advance, add the basil just before serving.

- 3 **tablespoons olive oil**
- $1\frac{1}{2}$ **tablespoons lemon juice**
- 1 **teaspoon honey**
- $\frac{1}{2}$ **small red onion, minced**
- **Salt and pepper**
- $\frac{3}{4}$ **pound green beans, ends trimmed and cut in half crosswise**
- 2 **ears corn, kernels removed from cobs**
- $\frac{1}{2}$ **pound frozen lima beans**
- 2 **tablespoons chopped fresh basil**

1. Stir oil, lemon juice, honey, red onion, and salt and pepper to taste together in small bowl.

2. Bring $2\frac{1}{2}$ quarts water to boil in large saucepan. Add 1 teaspoon salt and green beans and cook for 1 minute. Add corn and lima beans and cook until tender, about 5 minutes. Drain vegetables into colander and rinse under cold running water until cool. Drain vegetables well and transfer to serving bowl.

3. Toss vegetables with dressing to coat evenly. Stir in basil and season with salt and pepper. Serve.

Reader Mailbag

It's Blueberry Season

Sandy Casella, Shelton, Conn. Robert McCloskey's *Blueberries for Sal* is a favorite book at our house. This photo was taken during our first summer living in the Northeast. We had been looking forward to picking some of those famous blueberries! We went to the Jones Family Farm in Shelton, Conn., on the first day of blueberry season and picked, ate, and then picked some more. Our son Michael, then age 5, showed off some of the berries he used to make blueberry dump cake—his first foray into baking. (He got a little help, of course.)

Thanks for the Memories: ENDLESS SUMMER

Susan Ely, Raleigh, N.C. Childhood memories of summer replay in my mind like old cassette tapes that have lost their covers: Names and dates have been lost or forgotten, but the events are recorded forever in my heart. I can't imagine ever feeling as free and happy as I did during those long, hot Midwestern summers. We decorated our mud pies with orange berries from the mountain ash tree in our neighbor's backyard, sucked on chunks of ice given to us by the milkman, and had endless watermelon seed fights. The highlight of our small-town summers was the Fireman's Festival. The whole town showed up to hear the band, eat hot chicken sandwiches, play bingo, and try to win a teddy bear. Friday-night root beer floats and Saturday-night barbecues sustained us throughout the summers that were as endless as my memories are now.

The Dynamic Duo

Our state fair this year had a recipe contest sponsored by Fleischmann's Yeast called the Dynamic Duo Competition. You had to use any two products that were listed in the rules in your recipe. I decided it would be neat to have my little neighborhood friend Lane (age 6) join in on the fun. We came up with an Italian theme and entered our Sicilian Sausage Bread. To our amazement, we won first place! I think we made a pretty good dynamic duo, even though the competition was about two ingredients, not the people baking them.

Tammy Michalec, Leesville, S.C.

Alabama BBQ Chicken

I was recently at a barbecue place in Alabama and ordered this smoky chicken served with tangy white barbecue sauce. I've never had anything like it. Can you get me the recipe? –John Erwin, San Diego, Calif.

The white—yes, white—barbecue sauce is absorbed almost as quickly as it is brushed onto the smoked chicken.

INSIDE THE TEST KITCHEN:
Chicken Jigsaw Puzzle

To get as much smoke flavor into the chicken as possible, author Meredith Butcher devised this neat arrangement, with the coals on opposite sides of the grill and the chicken halves in the middle, away from direct heat. She found that alternating the direction of the chicken halves allows all four to fit snugly on a standard grill.

While most people think of barbecue sauce as red, sweet, and tomatoey, there are dozens of regional barbecue sauces that don't contain either tomato or a lot of sugar. For example, mustard- and vinegar-based sauces are common in the Carolinas, and the mayonnaise-based sauce you describe is a specialty in northern Alabama. Although I have been fortunate enough to sit down to a plate of this mayonnaise-style BBQ, I have never come across a good recipe for it. Thanks to your letter, I went into the test kitchen and got to work.

While the origins of many recipes can be hazy, it's easy to trace the history of Alabama chicken and white barbecue sauce to just one place: the Big Bob Gibson Bar-B-Q restaurant in Decatur. This barbecue mecca (the *Birmingham News* calls it the best barbecue in the state) has been around since 1925. Bob Gibson started his barbecue career by digging a smoke pit in his backyard. Soon he opened his first restaurant, the descendant of which his grandchildren and great-grandchildren run today. According to grandson Don McLemore, Big Bob (he was 6 feet 4 inches tall and weighed 300 pounds) was best known for his white BBQ sauce. The recipe (a family secret) has not changed in more than 80 years. Although Big Bob used the sauce mostly on hickory-smoked chicken, McLemore says nowadays people put it on everything from pork to potato chips.

Before starting on the white BBQ sauce, I wanted to figure out the best way to smoke the chickens (I wanted to cook two). In the test kitchen, we usually bank the charcoal on either side of the grill and place the bird right in the center, with a drip pan underneath. Hickory is the classic choice at Big Bob's, and I saw no reason to change this part of the recipe. I found that 2 cups of hickory chips placed directly on the coals gave the chickens a nice smoky flavor. Unfortunately, it took nearly two hours to grill two whole chickens, and my fire was beginning to peter out. I didn't want to add more coals, so I looked for ways to reduce the cooking time. Splitting the chickens in half cut the barbecue time to less than an hour and exposed more of the meat to the smoke.

It was time to work on the sauce. I started by ordering a bottle from Big Bob's. The sauce was creamy and tart, with a hint of sweetness and decent heat. Clearly, the sauce started with mayonnaise that was thinned out with vinegar to reach a loose consistency not unlike that of salad dressing. My tasters preferred the sweet-tart flavor of cider vinegar to bland white vinegar, and a little granulated sugar reinforced the subtle sweetness in the sauce. For heat, I relied on black pepper, just like Big Bob. But my tasters wanted more heat, and so did I. A little cayenne and horseradish punched up the sauce without making the heat too overpowering.

According to McLemore, at Big Bob's each smoked chicken is "baptized" by being dunked in a 2-gallon vat of vhite sauce that is continually ·eplenished. I didn't want to nake a vat of sauce. Fortu-nately, I found that brushing he chickens with the sauce wice—once when they came ɔff the grill and again 10 min-ıtes later—was sufficient. I erved extra sauce on the side or dipping the chicken—and naybe some potato chips, too.

–Meredith Butcher

LABAMA BBQ CHICKEN

ERVES 6 WITH LEFTOVERS

f you're going to make the Grilled Chicken Pasta Salad (at ight) using leftover chicken, set ıside 2 cups of shredded chicken ınd make a double batch of the auce, reserving half for the salad.

White BBQ Sauce

- **3/4 cup mayonnaise**
- **2 tablespoons cider vinegar**
- **2 teaspoons sugar**
- **1/2 teaspoon prepared horseradish**
- **1/2 teaspoon salt**
- **1/2 teaspoon black pepper**
- **1/4 teaspoon cayenne pepper**

Chicken

- **1 teaspoon salt**
- **1 teaspoon black pepper**
- **1/2 teaspoon cayenne pepper**
- **2 (3 1/2- to 4-pound) whole chickens, patted dry and split (see page 28)**
- **2 cups hickory wood chips**
- **Vegetable oil for grill grate**

1. For the sauce: Mix all ngredients in blender until mooth, about 1 minute. Refrigerate sauce in airtight container for at least 1 hour or ıp to 2 days.

2. For the chicken: Mix alt, black pepper, and cayenne n small bowl. Rub spice mix-ure all over chicken.

3. Soak wood chips in bowl ɔf water to cover for 15 min-ıtes. Meanwhile, open bottom grill vents completely. Light arge chimney starter filled with charcoal briquettes (about 90 coals) and burn until charcoal is covered with fine gray ash. Place 13 by 9-inch disposable alumi-num roasting pan in center of grill. Pour half of coals into pile ɔn each side of grill, leaving pan n center. Scatter wood chips evenly over coals and set cook-ing grate in place. Cover, with lid vents positioned over center of grill and opened halfway. Let grill heat for 5 minutes.

4. Dip wad of paper towels in oil and oil grate, holding paper towels with long-handled tongs. Place chicken skin side down on center of grill (see photo on page 20). Cover (with half-opened lid vents over chicken).

5. Grill chickens until skin is well browned, 35 to 45 minutes. Flip chickens skin side up and grill, covered, until breast meat registers 165 degrees on instant-read thermometer, 15 to 20 minutes longer.

6. Transfer chickens to cutting board, brush with 2 tablespoons sauce, tent with foil, and let rest 10 minutes. Remove foil and brush chicken with 1 tablespoon sauce. Carve and serve, passing remaining sauce at table.

ALABAMA BBQ CHICKEN ON A GAS GRILL

To hold the wood chips, you will need a small disposable aluminum tray.

Prepare recipe for Alabama BBQ Chicken through step 2. Soak wood chips in bowl of water to cover for 15 minutes, place chips in small aluminum tray, and place tray directly over primary burner. Light grill, turn all burners to high, and close lid, keeping grill covered until wood chips begin to smoke, about 15 minutes. Oil cooking grate. Turn all burners to medium-low. Place chicken skin side down on grill, cover, and proceed with recipe from step 5.

FOOD HISTORY:
Big Bob Gibson Bar-B-Q

Big Bob Gibson's has been serving hickory-smoked barbecue in Decatur, Ala., since 1925. Now run by Big Bob's grandchildren and great-grandchildren, the restaurant has expanded several times. The current pit smoker can cook 175 chickens, 110 slabs of ribs, and 60 whole turkeys at the same time.

What to Do with Leftovers:
Grilled Chicken Pasta Salad

Grilled chicken gets a second chance as the star ingredient in a pasta salad.

No one will guess that this fresh pasta salad starts with leftovers.

Leftover grilled chicken is an asset, but only if you can think of creative ways to use it. Chicken sandwiches are fine but all too predictable. For me, nothing says summer better than pasta salad, so I put away my sandwich bread, shredded my leftover chicken, and made an entirely different meal the next day: grilled chicken pasta salad.

Since my Alabama BBQ Chicken was already hickory-smoked, I decided to create a salad with Southwestern flavors. Sweet corn, black beans, peppers, onions, and cilantro all paired well with the smoke-flavored chicken. I tried both lime vinaigrettes and traditional mayonnaise-based dressings until it dawned on me to use my BBQ sauce (doubling the recipe supplies plenty for both the chicken and the pasta salad). Sure enough, this was a hit with tasters, especially when I added some lime juice. This pasta salad is so fresh and vibrant, no one will guess you started with leftovers.

–Meredith Butcher

GRILLED CHICKEN PASTA SALAD

SERVES 6 TO 8

If you know that you're going to make this chicken salad with leftover Alabama BBQ Chicken, prepare a double batch of the White BBQ Sauce before grilling the chicken and save half for this dish. You'll also need 2 cups of leftover shredded chicken. To make the dish spicier, leave the seeds in the jalapeño.

- **Salt**
- **1 pound corkscrew pasta**
- **1 cup frozen corn**
- **2 cups shredded grilled chicken**
- **1/2 cup canned black beans, drained and rinsed**
- **1 red bell pepper, chopped**
- **1 yellow bell pepper, chopped**
- **1 small red onion, minced**
- **1 jalapeño chile, seeded and minced**
- **1/2 cup chopped fresh cilantro**
- **3 tablespoons lime juice**
- **3/4 cup White BBQ Sauce (at left)**
- **Pepper**

1. Bring 4 quarts water to boil in large pot. Add 1 tablespoon salt and pasta and cook until nearly tender, about 8 minutes. Add corn and cook 1 minute more. Reserve 1/4 cup cooking water, then drain pasta and corn. Transfer pasta and corn to large bowl and refrigerate until completely cooled, at least 30 minutes.

2. Stir in chicken, beans, bell peppers, red onion, jalapeño, cilantro, lime juice, and sauce. Add reserved pasta cooking water, 1 tablespoon at a time, until sauce is loose. Season with salt and pepper to taste. Serve. (Salad can be refrigerated in airtight container for up to 2 days. Check consistency and seasonings before serving.)

FOOD FACT: *Blueberries are one of the few naturally blue foods. In colonial America, blueberries were often boiled in milk and turned into paint. Adding indigo and sage blossoms allowed colonists to create various blues and grays. The paints used in many Shaker homes were often made this way.*

Brown-Sugar Berry Shortcakes

I make a pretty good biscuit for the dinner roll basket, but they turn soggy when I use them to make berry shortcakes. I need something sturdier. Any suggestions? –Caitlyn Linde, Easton, Mass.

Brown sugar flavors the biscuits, berries, and whipped cream topping in this classic American dessert.

How to PREPARE BERRIES

To make sure that they maintain their integrity while they macerate, we mash only one-third of the berries. In addition, we prepare each berry according to its size and structure, as directed below. If you want to use more exotic berries, simply prepare them as recommended for the most similar berry in the list.

Strawberries
- **Hulled, halved, and sliced**

Raspberries
- **Whole**

Blackberries
- **Halved**

Blueberries
- **Whole**

Currants
- **Whole**

By making your own biscuits instead of using those store-bought Twinkie-like sponge cakes, you're already one big step ahead of the crowd. Unfortunately, homemade light and flaky baking-powder biscuits (although perfect for slathering with butter) don't stand a chance against juicy berries. As you've found, traditional biscuits will turn to mush in a matter of seconds. What you need is a bona fide shortcake (basically, a stronger biscuit) with enough structure and flavor to hold its own against the berries and whipped cream topping.

Shortcakes are basically biscuit dough enriched with sugar and fat, usually in the form of eggs or something richer than the usual milk or buttermilk. This fat adds heft and structure, creating a slightly more cakey texture that's perfect for soaking up the juices from the berries.

Starting with a basic baking-powder biscuit recipe, I enriched the dough with an egg and half-and-half (milk was too thin, cream too heavy). This provided the density and crumb that I was after, but the flavor was muted and boring. One test cook suggested I try sour cream in place of the half-and-half, and this gave the shortcakes just the savory, tangy kick I was looking for (similar to buttermilk but richer). Replacing the usual granulated sugar with brown sugar added a caramel note that everyone in the test kitchen enjoyed.

Although these shortcakes now tasted much better, they were squat and gummy on the inside; once I added the sour cream, they lost their tender, pillowy texture. I tried adding more baking powder to improve the rise, but this just gave the shortcakes a chemical flavor. Getting frustrated, I was about to remove the sour cream from the recipe when I realized that I was still treating these shortcakes like biscuits. Up to this point, I had been carefully rolling out the dough and using a biscuit cutter to punch out flat little rounds. But this dough, enriched with egg and sour cream, was more similar to a muffin or cake than a biscuit. What if I streamlined the recipe and skipped the rolling and cutting?

I turned the oven down to a more cake-friendly 375 degrees (biscuits are usually baked at 425 or 450 degrees) and used an ice cream scoop to portion the dough directly from the mixing bowl onto a parchment-lined baking sheet. The large, domed scoops solved my squat shortcake problem, and the oven's moderate heat gave the shortcakes plenty of time to cook through, creating a craggy, rustic exterior and a moist, fluffy interior. For one last touch, I tried brushing the unbaked domes of dough with melted butter and sprinkling them with granulated sugar. The crunchy, crystallized topping added another layer of texture.

As for the berries, I mashed some with brown sugar (preferred over granulated sugar for its more complex flavor) to release their juices but kept most of them whole because I liked their tartness and texture. To tie everything together, I dolloped my berry shortcakes with a tangy whipped topping made from heavy cream, brown sugar (again, everyone liked its caramel flavor), and sour cream. This sweet-tart, old-fashioned dessert is about as far from Twinkies as you can get. **–Jeremy Sauer**

BROWN-SUGAR BERRY SHORTCAKES SERVES 6

Depending on the sweetness of the berries, you may have to use more or less brown sugar. If you don't have a large ice cream scoop, divide the dough into six equal portions and use your hands to form shortcakes in a rough semispherical shape.

Fruit
- **6 cups mixed berries (see How to Prepare Berries at left)**
- **4–6 tablespoons packed light brown sugar**

Shortcakes
- **2 cups all-purpose flour**
- **3 tablespoons packed light brown sugar**
- **1 tablespoon baking powder**
- **1/2 teaspoon salt**
- **8 tablespoons (1 stick) unsalted butter, cut into 1/2-inch pieces and chilled, plus 2 tablespoons unsalted butter, melted (for brushing on shortcakes)**
- **1 large egg**
- **1/2 cup sour cream**
- **2 tablespoons granulated sugar**

Brown-Sugar Cream Topping
- **1 cup heavy cream**
- **1/4 cup sour cream**
- **1/4 cup packed light brown sugar**

1. For the fruit: Crush 2 cups berries and brown sugar in large bowl with potato masher.

Fold in remaining 4 cups berries and let sit at room temperature until sugar has dissolved and berries are juicy, about 30 minutes.

2. For the shortcakes: Adjust oven rack to upper-middle position and heat oven to 375 degrees. Line rimmed baking sheet with parchment paper. Pulse flour, brown sugar, baking powder, and salt in food processor until no lumps of sugar remain. Scatter chilled butter pieces over top and pulse until mixture resembles coarse meal, about 7 pulses. Transfer to large bowl.

3. Whisk egg and sour cream together in small bowl. Stir into flour mixture with rubber spatula until large clumps form. Using hands, knead lightly until dough comes together and no dry flecks of flour remain.

4. Using a large (#10) ice cream scoop, scoop 6 dough rounds onto baking sheet. Brush tops with melted butter and sprinkle with granulated sugar. Bake until golden brown, 25 to 30 minutes, rotating baking sheet halfway through baking time. Cool shortcakes on baking sheet 10 minutes. (Cooled shortcakes can be wrapped tightly in plastic wrap and kept on counter for up to 24 hours.)

5. For the topping: With electric mixer, beat heavy cream, sour cream, and brown sugar to stiff peaks. Split each shortcake in half using serrated knife and place bottoms on individual plates. Spoon portion of fruit over bottoms, top with whipped cream, and cap with shortcake tops. Serve.

SHORTCAKES BY HAND

To make shortcakes without a food processor, freeze the stick of butter until hard and then grate it into the dry ingredients using the large holes of a box grater. Toss gently to distribute the butter evenly and proceed with the recipe.

Getting to Know Berries

We tasted 12 varieties of fresh berries, some familiar and some exotic, to appreciate their unique flavors. Our tasting notes are listed below.

Blackberry
BIG AND JUICY
Also known as brambleberries, these large, purple-black berries grow on tall, thorny bushes, a sign that they belong to the rose family. Blackberries are very juicy and delicate, with a "sweet-sour" flavor similar to that of "fresh cherries."

Blueberry
ALL-AMERICAN
Blueberries exhibit a "pleasant pop" when eaten and have an "acidic, almost lemony" flavor. To distribute blueberries evenly in batters for cakes, muffins, and more, toss them with a little flour before gently folding them in.

Cape Gooseberry
ALL WRAPPED UP
A relative of the tomatillo, this marble-sized berry grows encased in a papery (and poisonous) husk that reveals an edible neon yellow fruit when opened. Cape gooseberries have an "astringent tropical fruit flavor" mixed with a "piney acidity."

Cranberry
SUPER-SOUR
Unlike most fruits, cranberries, which grow in bogs, become more tart ("like underripe grapefruit") as they ripen. Mild-tasting white cranberry juice is made from underripe berries that have not yet turned red. Available fresh only in the fall, these berries freeze well, so buy a few extra bags at Thanksgiving time.

Currant
TART AND TINY
These diminutive berries, which can be red, white, or black, are most commonly associated with the liqueur cassis. Like grapes, currants grow in clusters, but they have large, edible seeds whose sourness and texture make the fruit "reminiscent of pomegranate seeds," with a mild "raspberry flavor."

Fraise des Bois
FRENCH FAVORITE
French for "strawberry of the woods," these tiny wild strawberries are a treasured delicacy in Europe. The seeds give the berries a "grainy texture," but the fruit possesses an aroma "similar to lilacs." Their "intense melon" flavor is best appreciated in dishes where the berries are not heated.

Golden Raspberry
SWEET AS HONEY
These berries are most commonly found in specialty or farmers markets. They are a bit firmer than red raspberries, and their flavor, though not as fruity, is "definitely sweeter," with "highlights of honey."

Gooseberry
VERY BRITISH
These plump berries have a "mouth-puckering tartness" that "recalls slightly underripe grapes." Tart green berries are best cooked with sugar in puddings and jams; sweeter berries (usually yellow or red) are good in salads or as garnishes.

Huckleberry
WILD CHILD
These wild berries are similar to blueberries in appearance but have a deep, wine-colored exterior. They taste "grapey and a little sour," almost like "a cross between a blueberry, a cherry, and a kiwi."

Raspberry
AROMATIC AND COMPLEX
A thorny member of the rose family, this sweet fruit is "aromatic," with a "bright, winey complexity." Be careful when washing raspberries—they become soggy in seconds. Dip them in a bowl of cold water and immediately retrieve. And don't wash until you need them.

Strawberry
FLOWERY AND MEATY
These rotund berries display a "firm, meaty" texture and a "sweet, flowery flavor" balanced with a "surprising amount of acidity." Good strawberries are a brilliant red straight through to the core (a white center is a sign that the berries were picked too early).

Wild Blueberry
SWEET AND PEPPERY
Smaller than their cultivated cousins, wild blueberries have a more "pronounced seediness." Their flavor is more intense, with a "perfumed sweetness" balanced by "peppery acidity." Look for these berries in late summer or buy them frozen (see page 29) any time of year.

Grilled Chicken Kebabs

Every time I make chicken kebabs, they turn out dry and bland. I've tried a bunch of marinades, but nothing seems to help. I also have a tough time getting the meat and vegetables to cook at the same time.

–Sasha Pullman, Long Beach, Calif.

Despite their straightforward appearance, chicken kebabs can be tricky to cook properly. Chicken is very lean, and grilling multiple items on the same skewer usually translates to uneven cooking. My goal was moist, deeply seasoned skewers of skinless, boneless chicken breasts, punctuated by crisp-tender (not singed) vegetables—and I wanted everything to taste of the grill.

To infuse the meat with flavor, I tried several olive oil–based marinades (everything from garlic and lemon to bottled Italian salad dressing). Although the flavor was often quite good, these marinades turned the meat tough and mealy. I switched gears and borrowed a technique commonly used in Greece and the eastern Mediterranean—a marinade made with yogurt, olive oil, garlic, and herbs. Tasters appreciated the mellow tang of the yogurt, but they were even more enthusiastic about the texture of the chicken, which was tender and moist.

Why did marinades with lemon juice and vinegar make the chicken tough and mealy while yogurt made the meat tender? Experts explained that lemon juice and vinegar are much more acidic than yogurt—about 100 times more acidic—and that such strong acids can change the structure of the meat dramatically, in effect, partially cooking it. (Think about raw fish marinated in lemon juice to make ceviche.) In contrast, the milder acidity of the yogurt likely broke down the structure of the meat just enough to help it trap and hold on to moisture, making the cooked kebabs more tender and juicy.

I had the best results when I cut the chicken into 1-inch chunks, which take roughly 12 minutes to cook through—plenty of time for the meat to color nicely and pick up good grilled flavor.

It was now time to choose the vegetables. I tried zucchini and eggplant, but 12 minutes on the grill wasn't enough time for them to achieve that essential grilled flavor and color— these watery vegetables just steamed. I had better results when I tried red onion and sweet bell pepper; their edges charred slightly, but the vegetables remained crisp and juicy at their centers.

At this point, my kebabs were very good, but could I make them better? I remembered my early tests with a lemon-based marinade. Although it did make the meat tough, tasters liked the flavor. Could I make a simple lemon dressing and brush it over the skewers just before serving? A dressing of lemon, garlic, and basil really brightened the flavor of the kebabs, and especially the vegetables, which had not been marinated before cooking.

For a final burst of flavor, I served the kebabs with a cool, tangy yogurt sauce. Although optional, this sauce adds another layer of flavor. Chicken may be quite mild, but I prefer to think of it as a blank canvas, and these highly flavorful kebabs are my small masterpiece.

–Stephanie Alleyne

Threading the chicken and vegetables compactly on skewers prolongs the cooking time and allows everything to develop a nice sear on the grill.

Gadgets & Gear
GRILL BRUSHES

Over the years, we've worn out our fair share of grill brushes. The brass bristles on classic models quickly become clogged with gunk and wear down in a matter of weeks. After testing seven options, we found that the 18-inch Grill Wizard brush ($21.95; www.grillwizard.com) does a much better job than the competition. The unusual design features a replaceable stainless steel "scrubby" pad that cleans even a dirty grill quickly and efficiently. When the pad gets dirty, it can be detached and washed. And when the pad wears down, it can be replaced.

THE BEST BRUSH

Kitchen Know-How
MAKING THE CUT

It's important to cut the onion into bite-sized pieces that will cook at the same rate as the chicken.

Trim the ends and cut the onion into quarters. Peel away the first 3 (outer) layers and discard the inner core. Working with the outer layers only, cut each quarter into 3 even strips. Cut each strip crosswise into 3 pieces.

GRILLED CHICKEN KEBABS
SERVES 4

Don't skimp on the marinating time; any less than 3 hours and the chicken won't be as flavorful or tender. Conversely, marinating for more than 6 hours will make the chicken mushy. Serve with Yogurt-Herb Dipping Sauce.

- 1/2 cup plain yogurt
- 1/2 cup extra-virgin olive oil
- 4 garlic cloves, minced (about 4 teaspoons)
- 2 teaspoons dried thyme
- 2 teaspoons dried oregano
- 1 teaspoon salt
- 1 teaspoon black pepper
- 1/4 teaspoon cayenne pepper
- 4 boneless, skinless chicken breasts (about 1 1/2 pounds), cut into 1-inch cubes
- 2 tablespoons chopped fresh basil
- 3 tablespoons lemon juice
- 2 red bell peppers, cut into 1-inch pieces
- 1 large red onion, prepared according to photo, page 24

1. Whisk yogurt, 1/4 cup oil, 1 tablespoon garlic, thyme, oregano, salt, pepper, and cayenne in large bowl. Stir in chicken. Cover with plastic wrap and refrigerate 3 to 6 hours. Whisk remaining 1/4 cup oil, remaining teaspoon garlic, basil, and lemon juice in small bowl. Cover and refrigerate while chicken is marinating.

2. Remove chicken from yogurt marinade; discard marinade. Thread each skewer with 2 pieces pepper, 1 piece onion, 2 pieces chicken, and 1 piece onion. Repeat twice more, ending with 2 additional pieces of pepper. Grill over high heat until vegetables and chicken are charred around edges on all four sides and chicken is cooked through, about 3 minutes per side. Transfer to serving platter and brush kebabs all over with lemon dressing. Serve.

YOGURT-HERB DIPPING SAUCE
MAKES ABOUT 2 CUPS

Fresh herbs are key in this cool and tangy sauce.

- 1 cup plain yogurt
- 3 tablespoons extra-virgin olive oil
- 2 tablespoons lemon juice
- 1 garlic clove, minced
- 1 tablespoon minced fresh basil
- 1 tablespoon minced fresh mint
- 1/2 teaspoon salt
- 1/4 teaspoon pepper
- 1 cucumber, peeled, halved lengthwise, seeded, and chopped fine

Whisk yogurt, oil, lemon juice, garlic, basil, mint, salt, and pepper in bowl. Stir in cucumber, cover with plastic wrap, and refrigerate until flavors blend, about 30 minutes. (Sauce can be refrigerated for several hours.)

Shopping with the Test Kitchen: Yogurt

When it comes to plain yogurt, you have three choices. Here's what we use (and don't use) in the test kitchen.

WHOLE MILK YOGURT: Made with whole milk, this yogurt is our first choice in sauces and dips, where it's easy to appreciate its rich flavor and creamy texture—it's the best choice in our Yogurt-Herb Dipping Sauce (above). It's also our preference in many quick breads, muffins, and other baked goods.

LOW-FAT YOGURT: Made from 1 or 2 percent milk, this yogurt works well in a range of recipes, including sauces and baked goods. Less rich than its whole milk cousin, but it's hard to taste the difference in most baked goods.

NONFAT YOGURT: Made from skim milk, this lean yogurt often has a hollow flavor and watery texture. Some brands contain stabilizers that can give nonfat yogurt a gelatinous or grainy texture. Not recommended in sauces and will make many baked goods noticeably drier. However, nonfat yogurt does work well in the marinade for our Grilled Chicken Kebabs. Here, the yogurt adds tanginess, not richness or creaminess, so fat content is not an issue.

On the Side: Rice Salad

A foolproof cooking method and lively Mediterranean flavors greatly improve rice salad.

Toasting the rice ensures separate, fluffy grains.

Rice, as one of my cooking teachers was fond of saying, ain't potatoes. Making a salad with rice, therefore, is quite different from making one with potatoes. Rice is not as sturdy as other starches and is easily overcooked and overdressed, resulting in a salad that is mushy, starchy, or gummy.

I cooked long-grain rice (short-grain rice is too sticky for salads) the way I usually do—in a covered pot until all the water was absorbed—and then chilled it. This rice was hard and clumpy. Next I tried treating the rice like pasta, cooking it in a large pot of boiling water. Once it was tender, I drained the rice, rinsed it under cold water to stop the cooking process, and spread the rice on a baking sheet to cool and to keep it from clumping. The rice grains were light and separate (just what I wanted) but a bit waterlogged and frayed.

To solve the waterlogged rice problem, I took a cue from my favorite pilaf recipe, which calls for toasting the rice in oil before cooking it. The rice was now less watery, but it was also heavy and greasy. Dry-toasting the rice, without any oil, was much more successful. This technique not only kept the grains from becoming soggy or frayed when boiled but also coaxed out their nutty flavor.

As for the dressing, I found that less was more. A small amount of oil and vinegar (or lemon juice) did the trick. Warm spices, dried fruits, herbs, and chopped nuts created a nice balance of sweet, bright, and savory flavors that work especially well with grilled meats, including our chicken kebabs.

–Eva Katz

MEDITERRANEAN RICE SALAD
SERVES 6 TO 8

Basmati rice gives this dish a distinct toasty flavor, but any long-grain rice will work.

- 1 cup basmati or other long-grain rice
- Salt
- 2 1/2 tablespoons lemon juice
- 1 teaspoon grated zest plus 2 tablespoons juice from 1 orange
- 1/4 cup extra-virgin olive oil
- 1/2 teaspoon ground cinnamon
- Pepper
- 4 scallions, chopped fine
- 3/4 cup chopped dates, chopped raisins, or currants
- 3/4 cup chopped pistachios or sliced almonds, toasted
- 1/4 cup chopped fresh parsley

1. Bring 4 quarts water to boil in large pot. Meanwhile, toast rice in medium skillet over medium heat, stirring frequently, until faintly fragrant and some grains turn opaque, about 8 minutes.

2. Add 1 1/2 teaspoons salt and toasted rice to boiling water. Return to boil and cook, uncovered, until rice is tender, 8 to 11 minutes. Drain rice, spread on rimmed baking sheet, and cool completely, at least 20 minutes. Transfer cooled rice to serving bowl.

3. Whisk together lemon juice, orange zest and juice, oil, cinnamon, and salt and pepper to taste in bowl. Add scallions, dates, pistachios, parsley, and dressing to bowl with rice and toss to combine. Adjust seasonings and let stand until flavors blend, about 20 minutes. (Salad can be covered and refrigerated for up to 1 day. Bring back to room temperature before serving.)

How to
MAKE BOSTON CREAM CUPCAKES

1. Insert the tip of a small knife at a 45-degree angle about 1/8 inch from the edge of the cupcake and cut all the way around, removing a cone of cake.
2. Cut away all but the top 1/4 inch of the cone, leaving only a small disk of cake.
3. Fill the cupcake with 2 tablespoons pastry cream and top with the disk of cake.
4. Set the filled cupcakes on a wire rack set over parchment paper. Spoon 2 tablespoons of glaze over each cupcake, allowing it to drip down the sides.

Boston Cream Cupcakes

My kids love Hostess cupcakes, but I outgrew their overly sweet, artificial flavor many years ago. I'd love a recipe for cream-filled cupcakes we can all enjoy. –Hannah Scoggins, Columbus, Ohio

I may be biased by living in Boston, but when I think of cream-filled cakes I think of Boston cream pie. Composed of two layers of sponge cake, a custard filling, and a rich chocolate glaze, Boston cream pie (which, of course, is not a pie but a cake) was invented here in 1855 at the Parker House Hotel and is the official dessert of Massachusetts. Why not a Boston cream cupcake?

I found more recipes for the cupcake version of this dessert than you might expect; unfortunately, most of them called for just three ingredients: a box of cake mix, a packet of pudding, and a can of frosting. What I had in mind was something with more homemade flavor, so I turned instead to recipes for the original dessert, which is made with sponge cake. But these recipes weren't quite right either; tasters disliked sponge cupcakes, finding their light, airy texture too insubstantial in small form.

Then I thought of the Hostess cupcakes your kids favor. Soft and moist, those cupcakes have a very fine texture and are incredibly tender. I started with a basic yellow cake, which was a bit too coarse textured. I switched from the traditional creaming method (which calls for beating the butter and sugar first) to the reverse creaming method, which calls for cutting the butter into the dry ingredients, as is done with biscuit dough. These cupcakes were soft, moist, and tender. The reason? The traditional creaming method, which relies on aerating the butter with the sugar, creates large air pockets that result in a coarser crumb. In the reverse creaming method, the butter coats the flour before the batter is aerated, keeping the cake tender and fine crumbed.

A pastry cream filling and rich chocolate glaze take yellow cupcakes to new heights.

Coming up with recipes for the filling and the glaze was easy compared with the work I did on the cupcakes. I wanted a rich, creamy custard that was stiff enough to hold its shape inside the cupcake but still gooey enough to ooze slightly when you bit into it. Heavy cream (rather than milk or half-and-half), three egg yolks, and a good amount of cornstarch gave my pastry cream the perfect consistency. For the glaze, tasters preferred the strong flavor of bittersweet chocolate to semisweet or milk chocolate, and they loved the sheen that corn syrup provided.

Now that I had assembled all of the components, the real challenge began: How was I to get the pastry cream inside the cupcake? Again looking to Hostess for guidance, I found it in the form of a small hole in the bottom of the cupcake, where the filling was piped in. I didn't have a multimillion dollar cream injector, but I did have a pastry bag, so I filled it with pastry cream, stuck the tip into the cupcake, and squeezed. It seemed like I had put a good bit of pastry cream inside, but when tasters took a ɔite they scowled and demanded more filling. It was clear that some of the cake would have to go to make room for more pastry cream.

Though surgery was unavoidable, I was loath to hack up my cupcakes too much. One option was to simply cut off the top, scoop out a bit of the cake, fill the hole, and then replace the top, but the scar was obvious, even when the chocolate glaze was added, and the top tended to slide when tasters took a bite. I had more success by removing a cone-shaped section of cake (see the photos on page 26). Once the glaze was applied, the incision became invisible.

These pretty little cupcakes are not the quickest dessert (nothing beats the convenience of opening a package of Hostess cupcakes), but they taste so good that the adults in your house will be fighting the kids for seconds. **–Keri Fisher**

BOSTON CREAM CUPCAKES MAKES 12

Bake the cupcakes in a greased and floured muffin tin rather than paper cupcake liners so the chocolate glaze can run down the sides of the cooled cakes.

Pastry Cream

- 1 1/3 cups heavy cream
- 3 large egg yolks
- 1/3 cup sugar
- Pinch salt
- 1 tablespoon plus 1 teaspoon cornstarch
- 2 tablespoons cold unsalted butter, cut into 2 pieces
- 1 1/2 teaspoons vanilla extract

Cupcakes

- 1 3/4 cups all-purpose flour, plus additional for dusting muffin tin
- 1 1/2 teaspoons baking powder
- 3/4 teaspoon salt
- 1 cup sugar
- 12 tablespoons (1 1/2 sticks) unsalted butter, softened but still cool, cut into 12 pieces
- 3 large eggs
- 3/4 cup milk
- 1 1/2 teaspoons vanilla extract

Chocolate Glaze

- 3/4 cup heavy cream
- 1/4 cup light corn syrup
- 8 ounces bittersweet chocolate, chopped
- 1/2 teaspoon vanilla extract

1. For the pastry cream: Heat cream in medium saucepan over medium heat until simmering, stirring occasionally. Meanwhile, whisk egg yolks, sugar, and salt together in medium bowl. Add cornstarch and whisk until mixture is pale yellow and thick, about 15 seconds.

2. When cream reaches full simmer, slowly whisk it into yolk mixture. Return mixture to saucepan and cook over medium heat, whisking constantly, until thick and glossy, about 1½ minutes. Off heat, whisk in butter and vanilla. Transfer pastry cream to small bowl, press plastic wrap directly on surface, and refrigerate until cold and set, at least 2 hours or up to 2 days.

3. For the cupcakes: Adjust oven rack to middle position and heat oven to 350 degrees. Spray muffin tin with cooking spray, flour generously, and tap pan to remove excess flour.

4. With electric mixer on low speed, combine flour, baking powder, salt, and sugar in large bowl. Add butter, one piece at a time, and combine until mixture resembles coarse sand. Add eggs, one at a time, and mix until combined. Add milk and vanilla, increase speed to medium, and mix until light and fluffy and no lumps remain, about 3 minutes.

5. Fill muffin cups three-quarters full (do not overfill). Bake until toothpick inserted in center of cupcake comes out clean, 18 to 20 minutes. Cool cupcakes in pan 5 minutes, then transfer them to rack to cool completely.

6. For the glaze: Cook cream, corn syrup, chocolate, and vanilla in small saucepan over medium heat, stirring constantly, until smooth. Set glaze aside to cool and thicken for 30 minutes.

7. Prepare and fill cupcakes as shown in photos 1 through 4 on page 26. Refrigerate until just set, about 10 minutes. (Cupcakes can be refrigerated for up to 2 days; bring to room temperature before serving.)

Bake-Sale Favorites:
Chocolate Oatmeal Cookies

An urban legend spins a new cookie jar favorite.

These cookies offer something for every cookie lover.

There's only one question to ask in the debate over America's favorite cookie: chocolate chip or oatmeal? In this battle, my flag is a windsock, as I can be bribed to switch my allegiance with a warm, just-baked cookie from either side. Luckily for me (and others in the same predicament), the chocolate oatmeal cookie is the perfect compromise.

The most famous version of this cookie is found in a well-traveled chain e-mail titled "The $250 Cookie Recipe." The e-mail tells the tale of a woman who was charged $250 for a cookie recipe at Neiman Marcus—the woman thought she would be charged $2.50. (See page 29 for more information on this tall tale.)

More than just an oatmeal cookie with some chips thrown in, this recipe uses ground oats in place of some of the flour and shaved chocolate in addition to the chips. Although my tasters agreed that this cookie needed more of everything—more oats, more chocolate, more richness—it was a good start.

The ground oats did add great flavor, but they also caused the cookie to lose some of its characteristic oat chew. Stirring some whole oats into the batter solved this problem. To incorporate the caramel-like chew typical of a great chocolate chip cookie, I replaced the granulated sugar with light brown sugar and increased the amount of butter.

As for the chocolate, tasters liked the traditional semisweet chips but weren't wild about the shaved chocolate. After some tinkering, I found that adding melted milk chocolate in its place gave the chocolate its proper due.

Torn between a chocolate chip and an oatmeal cookie? Give this recipe a try (free of charge). **–Bridget Lancaster**

CHOCOLATE OATMEAL COOKIES MAKES 24

This recipe easily doubles. Make sure to cool the baking sheets between batches.

- 1 3/4 cups old-fashioned oats
- 1 cup all-purpose flour
- 3/4 teaspoon baking powder
- 1/2 teaspoon baking soda
- 1/2 teaspoon salt
- 10 tablespoons unsalted butter, softened but still cool
- 1 cup packed light brown sugar
- 1 large egg
- 1 teaspoon vanilla extract
- 3 ounces milk chocolate, melted and cooled
- 1 cup semisweet chocolate chips
- 1 cup pecans or walnuts, chopped

1. Adjust oven racks to upper-middle and lower-middle positions and heat oven to 350 degrees. Line 2 baking sheets with parchment paper. Place 1 cup oats in food processor or blender and process until well ground, about 30 seconds. Transfer to large bowl and stir in flour, baking powder, baking soda, and salt.

2. With electric mixer, beat butter and brown sugar together on medium-high speed until well blended and lumps are gone, about 1 minute. Scrape down sides of bowl. Add egg and vanilla and beat until light and fluffy, about 30 seconds. Add melted chocolate and beat until incorporated, about 20 seconds. Add flour mixture and beat on low speed until just incorporated, about 15 seconds. Add remaining 3/4 cup oats, chocolate chips, and nuts and beat on low speed until evenly distributed, about 10 seconds.

3. Roll 2 tablespoons of dough into balls and space 2 inches apart on baking sheets. Bake, rotating and switching position of pans halfway through baking time, until cookies are cracked and set on top but look moist within cracks, 14 to 18 minutes. Cool cookies on baking sheets on wire racks for 5 minutes, then transfer to wire rack to cool completely. (Cookies can be stored in airtight container for up to 5 days.)

Notes from Our Test Kitchen

TIPS, TECHNIQUES, AND TOOLS FOR BETTER COOKING

Outside the Test Kitchen Beans on the Grill

Our BBQ Beans (page 13) finish cooking on the grill, where they pick up smoke and pork flavors. Here's how to let the flavors in and keep the grease out.

1. When the beans are tender and the sauce is slightly thickened, transfer the beans to a 13 by 9-inch disposable aluminum pan. Wrap tightly in foil and poke several holes in the foil so that the juices from the ribs can flavor the beans.

2. When you're ready to add more coals, nestle the beans in the pan already on the bottom of the grill. Replace the cooking grate, making sure to position the ribs directly above the beans.

Kitchen Creations

Flavored Whipped Cream Toppings

Our tangy Brown-Sugar Cream Topping is the perfect accompaniment to our **Brown-Sugar Berry Shortcakes** (page 22). But brown sugar and sour cream aren't the only ways to jazz up plain old whipped cream. Concentrated flavors from jams, juices, and liqueurs all work well. Here are some test kitchen favorites, perfect with fruit desserts, cakes, or ice cream sundaes. All make about 2$^1/_2$ cups of whipped cream.

TASTE OF THE TROPICS
Beat 1 cup heavy cream and 2 teaspoons light or dark brown sugar to soft peaks. Add 1 tablespoon pineapple juice, $^1/_4$ teaspoon coconut extract, and $^1/_2$ teaspoon vanilla extract and beat to stiff peaks.

FRENCH TOAST
Beat 1 cup heavy cream to soft peaks. Add 1 tablespoon maple syrup and $^1/_2$ teaspoon vanilla extract and beat to stiff peaks.

JUST JAM
Beat 1 cup heavy cream and 1 teaspoon granulated sugar to soft peaks. Add 2 tablespoons of any seedless jam (strawberry, raspberry, apple, plum, or cherry) and beat to stiff peaks.

EGGNOG
Beat 1 cup heavy cream and 1 teaspoon granulated sugar to soft peaks. Add 1 tablespoon bourbon and $^1/_2$ teaspoon vanilla extract and beat to stiff peaks. Sprinkle dollops of whipped cream with grated nutmeg when serving.

PINK LEMONADE STAND
Beat 1 cup heavy cream, 2 teaspoons granulated sugar, and $^1/_2$ teaspoon very finely minced lemon zest to soft peaks. Add 1 tablespoon lemon juice and 1 teaspoon grenadine syrup and beat to stiff peaks. (Omit grenadine for regular lemonade whipped cream.)

Greenskeeper

Our **Creative Salads Contest** recipes (pages 4 and 5) depend on fresh greens. And, as we all know, a perfectly fresh head of lettuce can turn slimy and wilted in no time if not taken care of properly. Instead of letting your greens turn to mush in the depths of your crisper drawer, make good use of your salad spinner. Wash the greens in the water-filled salad spinner bowl (or use your sink for larger batches) and swish the leaves to remove grit. You may need to drain the water and repeat washing if the greens are exceptionally dirty. Once you've spun the clean greens dry, they will last for two days if layered on paper towels in the covered salad spinner or for one week if loosely rolled in several paper towels and sealed in a large plastic bag. **–Cali Rich**

Easy as Pie

A flaky, buttery homemade pie crust is just as important as the filling, but making one is a task that even some of us in the test kitchen find time-consuming, even intimidating. So we wondered: How much would we sacrifice by using a store-bought crust instead? To find out, we tried several types and brands of preformed crusts, either frozen or refrigerated, while developing our **Mile-High Lemon Meringue Pie** (page 18). Frozen crusts, including Mrs. Smith's (also sold as Oronoque Orchards) and Pillsbury Pet-Ritz, are the ultimate timesavers (zero prep needed), but tasters found them pasty and bland, and it was impossible to pry them from the flimsy foil "pie plate" in which they are sold. Pillsbury Just Unroll! Pie Crust ($2.79 for two crusts) was definitely a step above the rest. Though the flavor was a little bland (there's no butter in this pie dough), the crust baked up to an impressive flakiness. Better yet, this fully prepared product comes rolled up and is flexible enough to line one of your own pie plates—with (nearly) no one the wiser. **–Stephanie Alleyne**

PILLSBURY JUST UNROLL!
The hard part is over, and the flavor and texture are fine.

Making Whoopie

We're pretty crazy about our **Whoopie Pies** (page 7), but we know that some of you just want the reward of eating dessert without all the work of making it. So if you don't live in Maine and you're not planning a road trip to Pennsylvania Dutch country, where can you find a good whoopie pie? I mail-ordered some from Isamax Snacks (www.wickedwhoopies.com, 877-447-2629). We liked them! A dozen whoopie pies cost $24, plus shipping. **–Bridget Lancaster**

A Good Soak

Since our **Smoky Kansas City BBQ Beans** (page 13) can take upward of six hours to soften (the characteristically sweet, acidic sauce slows the softening process), we soaked the beans in water overnight before starting them on the stovetop. But what really helped cut time was holding back on the sweet and acidic ingredients (brown sugar, mustard, and hot sauce) for the first hour of cooking. This allowed the beans to soften almost completely before the sweet and sour elements were added. With all the flavors now in the pot, we let the beans simmer for another hour on the stovetop before moving them to the grill.
–Jeremy Saue

Kitchen Know-How

How to Split a Whole Chicken

Our recipe for **Alabama BBQ Chicken** (page 21) calls for whole chickens that you split in half at home. Split chickens cook more quickly than whole birds and are easier to manage on the grill. You'll need kitchen shears (see Gadgets & Gear, page 29) as well as a chef's knife to complete this simple operation.

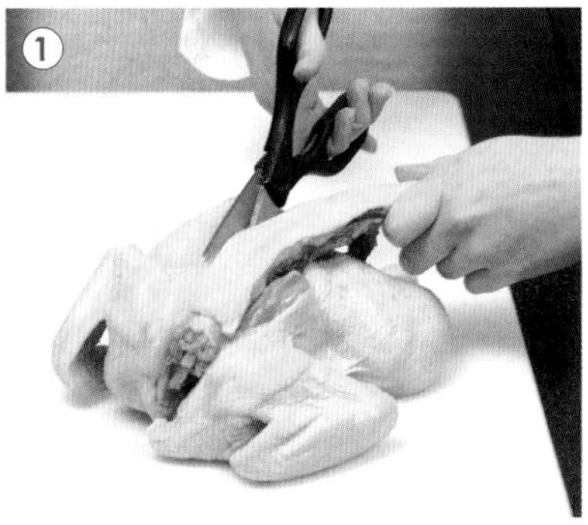

1. Using kitchen shears, cut along both sides of the backbone to remove it.

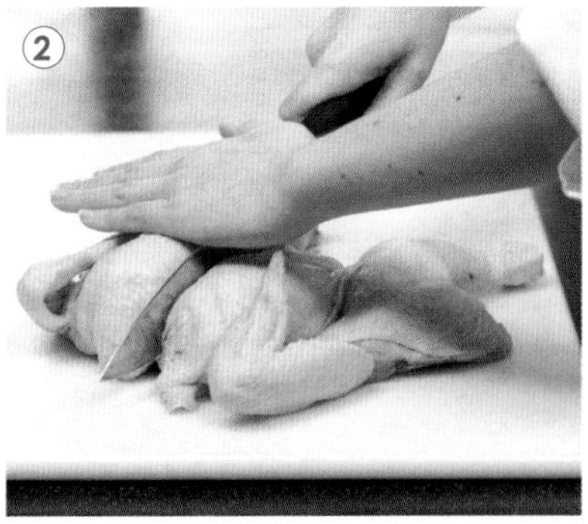

2. Using a chef's knife, split the breastbone to separate the chicken in two.

Gadgets & Gear: KITCHEN SHEARS

When it comes to cutting up poultry, we rely on kitchen shears for the heavy-duty work. A chef's knife is fine for slicing through the thin breastbone, but the blade can chip if you use it to hack through the back or leg bones. We also use kitchen shears to cut lengths of kitchen twine, trim pie dough, and cut out rounds of parchment when lining cake pans.

When shopping for kitchen shears, look for textured handles (so your hands won't slip, even if they become greasy or wet) that feel comfortable in your hand. Also check to see that the blades can open nice and wide. Shears with limited spread won't cut as easily through big bones.

SHEAR MAGIC
We rely on these sturdy Wüsthof Grand Prix Kitchen Shears ($35.95 at www.amazon.com) for cutting up poultry and more.

Butcher Shop: Which Rack Is Right?

When developing our recipe for **Kansas City Sticky Ribs** (page 12), we found that some racks of spareribs were so big they would barely fit on the grill. Because whole spareribs contain the brisket bone and surrounding meat, each rack can weigh upward of 5 pounds. For a more manageable cut, we looked 250 miles east of Kansas City. With "St. Louis" ribs, the brisket bone and surrounding meat are trimmed off to produce a narrower, rectangular rack that usually weighs in at a relatively svelte 3 pounds. In our opinion, St. Louis ribs offer all the taste of whole spareribs without any of the trouble. If you can find only whole spareribs, use the biggest grill possible and be prepared to increase the cooking time significantly. **–Jeremy Sauer**

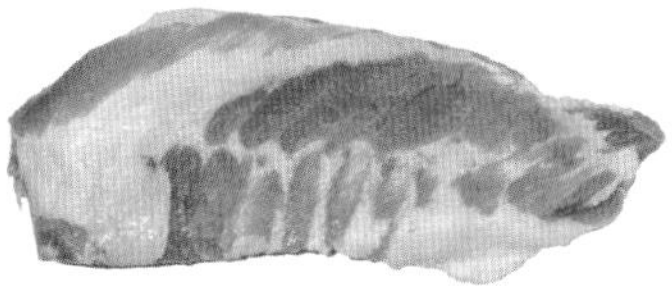

WHOLE SPARERIBS
Bulky and hard to handle on the grill.

ST. LOUIS RIBS
Same great flavor but in a smaller package.

A Cool Rack

A cooling rack is the essential last piece of equipment you need when making many baked goods. Unfortunately, many supermarkets sell traditional row-style racks that can gouge delicate cakes or cupcakes, including our **Boston Cream Cupcakes** (page 27). The problem is the parallel metal bars, which are so thin and flimsy that they can dig into baked goods and leave permanent scars. We prefer grid-style cooling racks with crisscrossing bars. The heavy-gauge bars are tightly woven so they support even the heaviest cake or biggest cookie, and they won't mar their exterior. Grid-style cooling racks are also strong enough to go into the dishwasher and won't rust, as do many flimsy traditional racks. Any serious baker should own at least two of these racks, which are sold in most kitchenware shops. **–Keri Fisher**

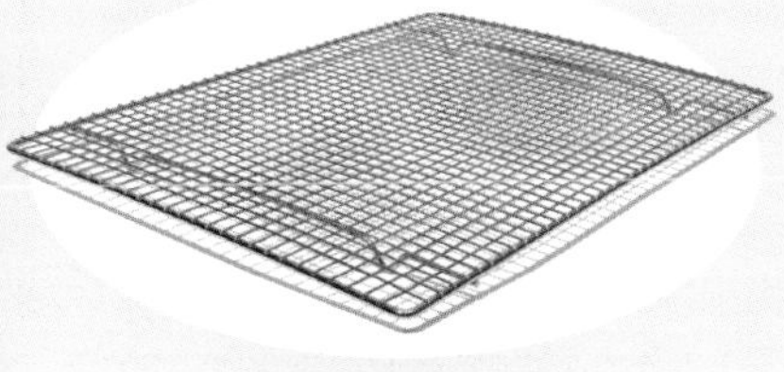

GET ON THE GRID
This heavy-duty, grid-style cooling rack is gentle on baked goods.

Spatula Shopping

Here's where to find the spatulas recommended in our equipment testing on page 31. Cooking.com sells the spatulas made by Calphalon (item #205295, $4.95) and Cuisinart (item #410843, $5.95). Look for the Oxo spatula at Amazon.com (item #77091, $5.99). And if you cook a lot of fish, you may want to check out the Matfer Slotted Pelton Spatula at Cooking.com (item #160964, $6.50).

Hot Tortillas

When developing our recipe for **Steak Soft Tacos** (page 15), we found there was one small but significant detail that our tasters demanded: steaming-hot tortillas. Not only are warm tortillas more pliable and less apt to tear, but they also help to melt cheese and keep fillings hot.

What's the best way to heat tortillas? The microwave worked quickly but left the tortillas soggy and tough. Heating the tortillas over an open flame (such as a gas stovetop) worked great, but each tortilla had to be heated individually. Scattering the tortillas on an oven rack enabled us to heat up to eight at a time, but they had a tendency to dry out. Ultimately, what worked best was to wrap a stack of tortillas in foil before popping them into a 350-degree oven. After about 15 minutes, they were properly heated and ready to go. What's more, when prepared this way, the wrapped tortillas stay hot for 30 minutes. **–Jeremy Sauer**

Buying Blueberries

In the peak of summer, locally grown blueberries are sweet and flavorful, making them the only choice in our test kitchen. But the "fresh" berries sold in our supermarkets most of the year are expensive and either bland or sour. From fall through early summer, we rely on frozen wild blueberries, which, though smaller, have more flavor than their frozen cultivated cousins. We particularly like Wyman's brand from Maine. **–Bridget Lancaster**

FROZEN BERRIES
A good bet any time of year.

Kitchen Know-How
Getting Fennel Fit and Ready

Xenia Madill's prize-winning recipe for **Fennel and Red Grape Salad** (page 5) calls for thinly sliced fennel. Here's how we handle this oddly shaped vegetable in the test kitchen.

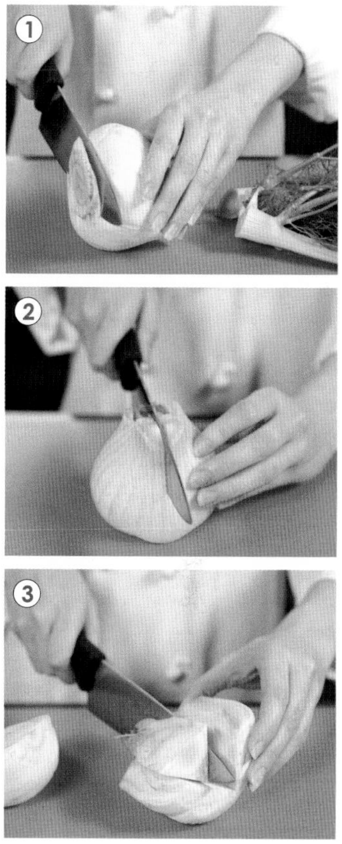

1. Cut off the stem and feathery fronds, then trim a very thin slice from the base of the bulb.
2. Slice the bulb in half lengthwise from top to bottom.
3. Cut out the tough, triangular-shaped piece of the core that rises from the bottom of each half.
The fennel is now ready to be sliced as desired.

The American Table: Famous Food Fables

Everyone on our test kitchen staff has received a well-traveled chain e-mail titled "The $250 Cookie Recipe" (see page 27 for more details)—some of us more than once. Sadly, the legend of the Neiman Marcus cookie is not true. Neiman Marcus not only denies the tale of overcharging a customer (and there's no evidence to show that this ever happened), but the company provides a cookie recipe (chocolate chip, without oats) free for the taking on its Web site.

The $250 Neiman Marcus Cookie isn't the first tale of an outrageously priced recipe. New York's legendary Waldorf-Astoria Hotel had its own story of a customer charged $350 for its Red Velvet Cake recipe. And if $350 sounds like a lot of cash now, keep in mind that this story originated in 1960.

According to Snopes.com, a Web site dedicated to tracking down the truth and fiction behind urban legends, one of the earliest versions of this story can be found in *Massachusetts Cooking Rules, Old and New*. This 1948 cookbook contains a recipe for $25 Fudge Cake, along with a familiar story of a woman overcharged for the recipe. **–Bridget Lancaster**

Food Shopping

TORTILLA CHIPS: Are the Corniest Chips the Best?

My favorite Mexican restaurant serves tortilla chips that are thick, crunchy, and terrifically "corny"; they're as good eaten alone as they are dunked into salsa. It used to be that you had to go out to find chips like this. But now several "upscale" brands sold in supermarkets promise authentic Mexican-style chips. How does this new style of tortilla chip compare with traditional supermarket offerings? To find out, we held a blind tasting of nine brands of tortilla chips.

As a group, the boutique brands lived up to their promise of good flavor: Tasters commented on the "authentic" taste: "Like chips I've had in Mexico," said one. These chips—Green Mountain Gringo, Bearitos, Nana's Cocina, Kettle, and Cape Cod—were consistently rated as having the most corn flavor. Each is made with stone-ground corn, resulting in a coarser-textured chip.

Despite their corny flavor, most of the boutique chips were ultimately rejected by tasters as being "too thick" and "stale." In contrast, the finer-textured chips (several of which are made with corn flour, not stone-ground corn) were described as "thin and crispy" and were perceived as being fresher.

Coarse-textured, super-corny chips might be fine in a Mexican restaurant (where they can be freshly fried), but when bagged for sale at the supermarket this style of chip can come off as stale, especially when compared with thinner chips. Chips are listed in order of preference with tasters' comments. **–Keri Fisher**

Recommended

1. **SANTITAS Authentic Mexican Style White Corn Tortilla Chips**
$1.99 for 18 ounces
Tasters liked the "mild and salty" flavor and "sturdy" texture of these winning chips, whose "great crunch" topped the crispness charts.

2. **TOSTITOS BRAND Tortilla Chips 100% White Corn Restaurant Style**
$3.49 for 13.5 ounces
Though some tasters found these chips "bland, blond, and boring," others praised the "delicately crisp" texture and "fresh" flavor. Most found them "scoop worthy."

3. **GREEN MOUNTAIN GRINGO Tortilla Strips All Natural**
$2.69 for 8 ounces
Tasters liked the "toasted" flavor of these "crunchy," "sturdy" chips, whose long shape made them "good scoopers." Wrote one fan, "Reminds me of chips you get at an authentic Mexican restaurant."

4. **NATURAL TOSTITOS BRAND Yellow Corn Restaurant Style Tortilla Chips**
$2.99 for 9 ounces
Fans praised their "great flavor and texture," though some complained that these large chips "need to be broken prior to dipping."

Recommended with Reservations

5. **SNYDER'S OF HANOVER White Corn Tortilla Chips** **$2.49 for 16 ounces**
"Taste stale and dusty," wrote one taster of these "overly salty and slightly artificial" chips from the famous pretzel maker.

6. **BEARITOS All Natural Organic Tortilla Chips** **$3.69 for 16 ounces**
Despite being "very crisp," with "nice corn flavor," most tasters panned the "gritty," "cardboard" texture that one person likened to "stale Fritos."

7. **NANA'S COCINA Traditional Tortilla Chips** **$3.19 for 16 ounces**
Despite their "very corny," "homemade" flavor, tasters panned the "brittle," "stale" texture of these chips.

Not Recommended

8. **KETTLE Tortilla Chips Little Dippers Organic** **$2.47 for 8 ounces**
"My thumb is bigger than this," wrote one taster of these petite chips. Others liked the "fun shape," but most agreed that these chips tasted "burnt," "stale," and "rancid," though they did have "good crunch."

9. **CAPE COD All Natural White Corn Tortilla Chips** **$2.99 for 8.5 ounces**
Tasters described these chips as "overwhelmingly stale," "tough," and "artificial."

Taste Test Ground Beef

Most recipes simply call for "ground beef," but, as any supermarket shopper knows, the choices are much more varied. The U.S. Department of Agriculture defines "ground beef" as ground fresh and/or frozen beef from primal cuts and trimmings containing no more than 30 percent fat. But that doesn't really help anyone understand the difference between ground round, ground chuck, and ground sirloin. And what about fat content, which can range as low as 7 percent?

To find out if the cut matters, we prepared hamburgers, Bolognese sauce, and meatloaf using each type of ground beef and held a blind tasting, asking tasters to comment on the taste and texture of each sample. The results were clear; differences between the cuts were obvious and noted across the board.

Ground round and ground beef consistently ranked last in our tests, with ground round described as "tough" and "chewy"; less polite tasters deemed the ground beef "livery" and "gross." Tasters preferred ground chuck and sirloin: The ultra-lean sirloin was favored for dishes in which other ingredients added much-needed fat, whereas chuck was preferred in hamburgers. Types of ground beef are listed below in order of preference. **–K.F.**

Ground Chuck
Cut from the shoulder, ground chuck ranges from 15 to 20 percent fat and was favored by our tasters for its "rich" flavor and "tender," "moist" texture. The best choice for burgers.

Ground Sirloin
Tasters praised the ground sirloin as "tender and tasty," especially in the meatloaf and Bolognese sauce, but found it a bit "dry" in hamburgers, though it did have "good beef flavor." Cut from the midsection of the animal near the hip, ground sirloin usually ranges in fat content from 7 to 10 percent.

Ground Round
Lean and tough, ground round comes from the rear upper leg and rump of the cow. Tasters rejected the round as "gristly" and "lacking beef flavor." The fat content ranges from 10 to 20 percent.

Ground Beef
Any cut or combination of cuts can be labeled "ground beef," so consistency is a problem. Because ground beef may have as much as 30 percent fat, greasiness can also be an issue. Our tasters dismissed the ground beef in all applications as "mushy," with an "old boiled beef taste."

Equipment Roundup

PLASTIC NONSTICK SPATULAS: Can a $5 Model Do It All?

Unless you like to eat flaked-off nonstick coating, you need to use a plastic spatula with your nonstick cookware. But with most stores stocking at least five models, how do you know which one is best?

To narrow the field, I decided to focus on one plastic spatula that would fulfill all my cooking needs. A slotted spatula, with slots that allow grease and liquid to drain but that still provide the support of a solid spatula, covers all bases. I gathered 11 brands of plastic nonstick slotted spatulas ranging in price from $4.95 to $14.99 and went to the kitchen to flip pancakes and pan-fry fish fillets and hamburgers. Here are some key findings from my tests.

SIZE MATTERS: After flipping my way through dozens of pancakes, one thing was clear: the larger the blade of the spatula, the better. Small blades caused the pancakes to droop on the sides when I flipped them, dripping batter and sometimes breaking in the process. The size of the slots, on the other hand, did not play a factor in any test; though the slots came in all shapes (circles, rectangles, ovals) and sizes, all the spatulas drained grease from burgers and fish adequately.

THIN IS IN: All of the spatulas featured blades that tapered to a thinner edge, some just at the top and others on all three sides. The best spatulas featured thin blades and even thinner edges. Blades that were too thick were difficult to slide under the pancakes and fish fillets without causing them to bunch up and, in the case of delicate fish fillets, to break. The blade of the top-rated Calphalon spatula was just 2.73 mm, that of the lowest-rated iSi was a whopping 6.5 mm.

PRICE DOESN'T PREDICT STRENGTH: Given the range in price, I thought perhaps the more expensive models might be sturdier than the cheaper ones and better able to support the weight of heavy foods. To test this, I cooked up some hefty 8-ounce hamburgers and flipped them with each spatula. To my surprise, only two spatulas failed this test, bending under the burger's weight, and they were two of the most expensive: the Henckels and the iSi.

HANDLE WITH CARE: While most of the spatulas featured thick plastic handles that were comfortable in the hand, a few had sharp metal edges that made gripping difficult. The Henckels spatula was particularly uncomfortable, with not just one but two sharp edges thanks to the handle's loop design.

SUMMING UP: In the end, the cheapest spatulas were the top performers: The Calphalon and Cuisinart impressed us with their large blades and thin edges. Spatulas are listed in order of preference. **–Keri Fisher**

Recommended

CALPHALON N04 Tools Large Nylon Slotted Spatula
Price: $4.99
Blade area: 16.48 square inches
Blade thickness: 2.73 mm
Comments: The least expensive spatula impressed us with its large blade and very thin edge, which slid under pancakes and fish with ease.

CUISINART Nylon Turner with Soft Grip Handle
Price: $5.95
Blade area: 15.94 square inches
Blade thickness: 2.73 mm
Comments: The large rubber handle was extremely comfortable to hold, and the large blade was tapered on all sides so we could flip from any angle.

OXO Good Grips Nylon Square Turner
Price: $5.99
Blade area: 15.94 square inches
Blade thickness: 3.74 mm
Comments: The long handle was very comfortable, and the thin edge compensated for the fairly thick blade.

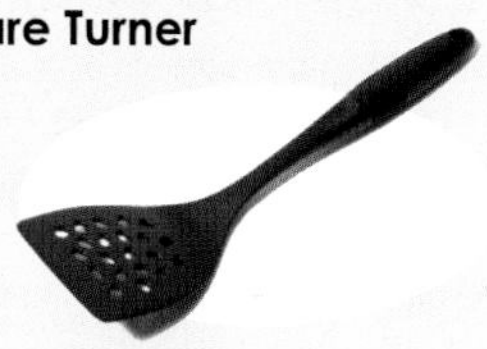

Recommended with Reservations

MESSERMEISTER Pro-Touch Teflon Spatula
Price: $5.95
Blade area: 17 square inches
Blade thickness: 2.6 mm
Comments: This model lost points for the short, thin rubber grip at the end of the handle, which was awkward in all but the smallest hands.

ZYLISS Slotted Turner
Price: $7.49
Blade area: 12.78 square inches
Blade thickness: 3.05 mm
Comments: This spatula shone in all but the pancake test, where the narrow blade resulted in awkward, messy flipping.

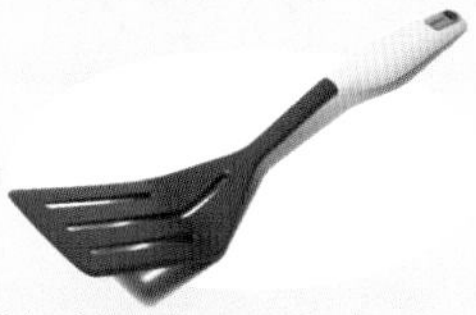

AMCO Nonstick Slotted Spatula
Price: $7.00
Blade area: 12 square inches
Blade thickness: 2.69 mm
Comments: The small blade made flipping large pancakes and fish fillets a messy affair. The thin metal handle also got uncomfortable quickly.

EMERILWARE Nonstick Slotted Turner
Price: $5.99
Blade area: 14.63 square inches
Blade thickness: 4.93 mm
Comments: We liked the large molded handle and tapered edge, but the blade was too thick to slide under foods with ease.

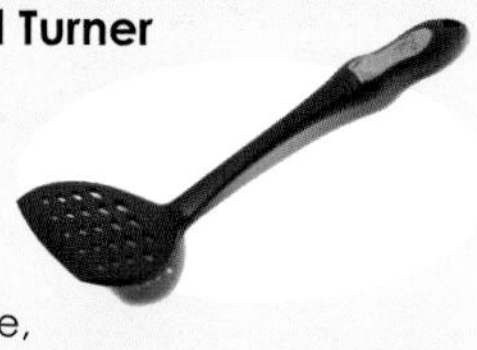

KITCHENAID Silicone Slotted Turner
Price: $9.99
Blade area: 17.81 square inches
Blade thickness: 5.08 mm
Comments: Though it had the largest blade of the lot, it also had one of the thickest, which made flipping greasy foods a slippery task.

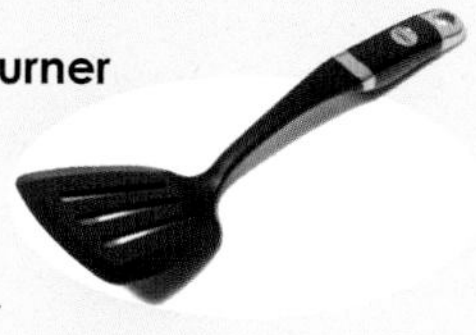

Not Recommended

WMF Profi Plus Nonstick Slotted Spatula
Price: $13.99
Blade area: 9.36 square inches
Blade thickness: 3.7 mm
Comments: The extremely small blade area and very short handle caused this model to flopin all but the hamburger test.

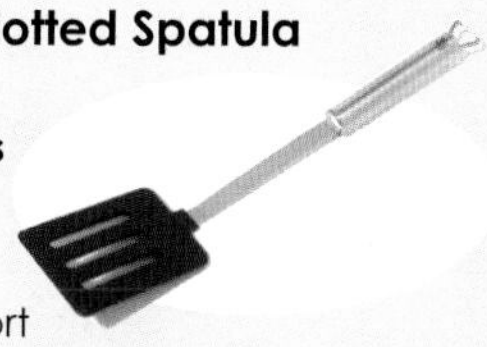

HENCKELS Twin Select Nylon Turner
Price: $14.99
Blade area: 12 square inches
Blade thickness: 3.28 mm
Comments: The most expensive spatula in the group suffered from a small blade and a sharp and extremely uncomfortable metal handle.

iSi K8677 Silicone Meat Turner with Stainless Steel Handle
Price: $12.07
Blade area: 15.13 square inches
Blade thickness: 6.5 mm
Comments: This spatula featured a long, narrow blade that was thick, floppy, and almost jelly-like in texture; sliding it under foods was a daunting task. The thin metal handle was uncomfortable.

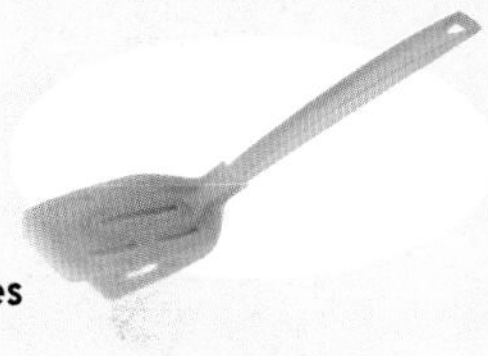

Gadgets & Gear

Plastic Fish Spatulas

Once relegated to restaurant kitchens, fish spatulas are now popular among home cooks as well. The long, narrow, ultra-thin triangular blade is especially designed for sliding under long, narrow, ultra-thin fish fillets. To find out if we really needed one more spatula in the kitchen, we pitted one of our recommended all-around spatulas, the Cuisinart, against a plastic nonstick fish spatula that had performed well in another round of tests, the 12-inch Matfer Slotted Pelton. The Matfer fish spatula sports an ultra-thin blade (just 0.68 mm thick) that did slide under delicate sole fillets more easily than the Cuisinart. But the difference was less dramatic than we expected (the regular plastic spatula worked just fine). What's more, the very small blade of the fish spatula makes it unsuitable for other tasks, such as flipping pancakes and fried eggs. Our conclusion: A good regular plastic spatula is fine for all your flipping needs, even fish. **–K.F.**

The best tool for flipping fish—but is it the only one?

When Things Go Wrong in the Kitchen

READERS SHARE FUNNY STORIES ABOUT COOKING MISHAPS

THE BARKING COFFEE

One day, I decided to make a friend coffee in my one-cup coffeemaker. He complained that it was very weak and funny tasting. To my horror, I realized that I had used a scoop of dog kibbles instead of coffee! I didn't realize that they were in the same kind of container in the cabinet. Needless to say, he has never let me forget about this incident and barks at me whenever I make coffee.

Susan Minkoff Kingston, Pa.

AN ACQUIRED TASTE

Our family usually has corned beef and cabbage on St. Patrick's Day. One year, I attempted to make Irish soda bread myself. As the soda bread was passed around the table, I began to receive quizzical looks. Both of my sons, who are normally not picky eaters, spit the bread out in their napkins, asking what I had done to it. Simultaneously, my father said, "This bread is really good!" We couldn't believe what we were hearing. After the meal, I went back to look at the recipe. Indeed, the recipe called for 2 tablespoons of baking soda, which must have been a misprint. Now, every year, when I begin to discuss what we will be having for St. Patrick's Day, the same chorus is repeated: "Please don't make Irish soda bread again." Then we all chuckle about how Grandpa sat there eating it.

Chris Brandt Winona, Minn.

A PAINFUL MISUNDERSTANDING

I was making a cheesecake for a gathering at my home when I realized I was out of vanilla extract. I ran across the street to a Middle Eastern grocery store. Knowing that the owners spoke very little English, I brought the empty bottle with me so I could show them exactly what I needed. The grocer kindly handed me a tub of what appeared to be snowflakes. The label read "crystallized vanilla" in English, amid some Arabic writing. Another customer in the store, having overheard, told me that crystallized vanilla was just the same as vanilla extract and advised me to use equal amounts in cooking.

Later that night, when I served my laboriously prepared cheesecake, I finally got to try it myself. Swallowing a mouthful of that cheesecake was like ingesting tiny bits of sandpaper mixed with teensy razor blades. I made several more cheesecakes before I had the nerve to serve it to guests again.

Kim Cameron Austin, Texas

STIFF EGGS

At our home, Saturday is Dad's morning to cook. Most Saturdays it is scrambled eggs, sausage, and pancakes or waffles. This one Saturday was no different from any other. I was hustling around the kitchen when I noticed I had forgotten to spray the skillet I was using to cook the eggs. I quickly went to the pantry and got out a can of cooking spray to keep the eggs from sticking. As the eggs continued to cook, I noticed that they didn't look right, but I wasn't paying much attention as I was busy with the waffles and sausage. When we sat down to eat, the first thing out of my wife's mouth was, "What did you do to the eggs?" She said they tasted funny and she was right—they tasted horrible. Evidently, instead of cooking spray, I had used spray starch.

Doug Shutts Grinnell, Iowa

STICKY EVIDENCE

When I was 13 years old and a budding cook, I made many attempts to create fondant, taffy, and divinity candy, all of which failed to set up. My father got tired of all the wasted sugar and told me not to make any more "runny candy." With my parents gone for the afternoon, I decided to attempt saltwater taffy one more time. I decided to give it a little extra cooking to ensure that the candy would set up properly this time. I poured the mixture out onto a buttered cookie sheet and began to pull the taffy. I was shocked to see the candy set up immediately. There was no way to salvage the nearly rock-hard mass, so I decided to destroy the evidence. I went out to the backyard and heaved the candy log as far out into the field as I could.

Later that day, my parents returned home only to be greeted by our German shepherd, Birch, who was whining sadly. Birch had a foreign object lodged in her teeth. As my father pried the sticky mass from the poor dog's teeth, he exclaimed, "Oh, no! Jean's been cooking again!" I was sharply scolded, but I detected a bit of humor in my father's eyes. After that, we finally invested in a candy thermometer.

Jean Becker Fort Wayne, Ind.

A PITFUL CAKE

When I was a newlywed, I wanted to impress my in-laws when they visited our home. My husband grew up in the country and I was a city girl, so I called a friend who also grew up in the country. She offered me some fresh cherries from her tree, and I decided to make one of my favorite cakes. I usually added canned cherries to the batter, but I figured fresh cherries would be even better. I could only imagine how pleased my in-laws would be. Imagine my surprise, when I noticed my mother-in-law graciously removing pits from every bite!

Renee Young New Albany, Ohio

JUMPING CHICKEN

I offended my mother-in-law one evening by making her Hamburger Helper, so she gave me a cookbook for my birthday. Months later, I decided to use the cookbook to make chicken Kiev. The recipe required that I flatten four chicken breasts using a meat mallet. Now, I had no idea what a meat mallet looked like, and I was fairly sure I didn't own one, so I used a can of my husband's beer. With the beer can and half a roll of waxed paper, I was able to brutally smash the chicken. I rolled the chicken around little sticks of butter, but they didn't really stay rolled. Oh, well.

I gently lay the first chicken roll in the pan and—POP! Apparently, when you combine chicken, a stick of butter, and oil that is too hot, the chicken can jump out of the pan and cling to your chest for dear life. I let the oil cool down and tried again. I was a little more successful this time and got the three remaining pieces fried.

My husband was hesitant to try the chicken. After a few bites, he decided it wasn't too bad but didn't want me to attempt it again. He wanted to know why his can of beer looked like it had been abused!

Christine Brungardt Clackamas, Ore.

BAD PIE, GOOD LIMERICK

When I was a 19-year-old college student, I decided to make a blueberry pie for my boyfriend. I didn't have a cookbook at school, so I called home to get a recipe for the pie crust. My 10-year-old sister read me the recipe over the phone. She thought a small "t" meant a tablespoon, so I added a tablespoon of salt. I still can't believe that I didn't question this, but I didn't. My boyfriend, now my husband, took one bite and stopped eating. This inedible pie has been a running joke throughout our marriage. One Valentine's Day I wrote him this limerick:

There was a young lass from St. Kate's
Who decided to bake for a date
The effort was faulty
The pie was so salty
Yet he still made this woman his mate.

Joanne Meierhofer Willmar, Minn.

Send us your funniest kitchen disaster stories. Write to us at Kitchen Disasters, Cook's Country, P.O. Box 470739, Brookline, MA 02447, or to kitchendisasters@bcpress.com. If we publish your story, you'll receive a complimentary one-year subscription to *Cook's Country.*

The Great American Cake

Neapolitan Bundt Cake

This cake originally ran as part of a Betty Crocker cake mix ad campaign in the 1970s, offering the flavors of Neapolitan ice cream: vanilla, chocolate, and strawberry. We tweaked the recipe to accommodate a homemade cake and boosted the chocolate and strawberry flavors as well. Now this is a cake worth revisiting.

To make this cake you'll need:

- 1 **recipe yellow cake batter***
- 1/3 **cup chocolate syrup**
- 2 **tablespoons Dutch-processed cocoa**
- 1/2 **cup seedless strawberry jam**
- 3 **drops red food coloring (optional)**
- 1 **recipe Chocolate Glaze from Boston Cream Cupcakes (page 27)**

For the cake: Divide batter among three bowls. Whisk syrup and cocoa in separate bowl, then gently stir this mixture into one bowl of batter. Stir 1/4 cup jam and food coloring (if using) into second bowl of batter. Grease and flour 12-cup Bundt pan. Pour plain batter into pan. Gently pour in strawberry batter, followed by chocolate batter. Bake on middle rack in 350-degree oven until toothpick inserted in center comes out clean, 60 to 70 minutes. Cool 30 minutes; turn out onto rack to cool completely.

To finish: Melt remaining 1/4 cup jam in small saucepan until pourable. Brush jam all over cake. Using whisk, drizzle Chocolate Glaze over top and sides of cake, allowing glaze to drip down sides. Refrigerate until glaze sets, about 10 minutes. Serve.

*Go to www.cookscountry.com for our yellow cake recipe or use your own recipe (it should yield enough batter for a standard two-layer cake).

Recipe Index

(RC) = Recipe Card

Cook's Country

AUGUST/SEPTEMBER 2006

BBQ Pulled Pork
Authentic Carolina Recipe

Firecracker Fried Chicken
Extra-Spicy, Extra-Light Coating

No-Fear Pie Dough
Flakiest Pat-in-Pan Crust Ever

BEST STEAK FAJITAS
Marinate Twice for Big Flavor

CHOCOLATE CHIP COOKIES
Surprise Ingredient Cuts Fat

GRILLED POTATO SALAD
Smoky Twist on a Classic

RATING THERMOMETERS
Can a Cheap Model Do It All?

GRILLED GLAZED SALMON
Foolproof No-Stick Recipe

CORN OFF THE COB
4 Fresh, Easy Recipes

GARDEN TOMATO SAUCE
Capture Summer in a Skillet

TUNA TASTE TEST
Which Brands Rate Best?

Our $1,000 Contest Winner!
Cindy Rucker of Brooklyn, N.Y., won first place in our salsa contest with a spicy pairing of fruit and chiles. See page 4 for her **Mango-Cucumber Salsa** recipe.

$4.95 U.S./$6.95 CANADA

Cook's Country

Dear Country Cook,

Many years ago, when my wife and I were first invited to our neighbor Jean's farm for dinner, I was struck by the simplicity of the setting: the painted floorboards, the modest Shaker-style table, the bright floral needlepoint placemats (made by her mother, Dorothy), the view across the hay field up toward Walnut Mountain, and, last but not least, the small glass dish of homemade watermelon pickles. Dinner was an excellent stew of woodchuck (I had seconds), a foraged salad including watercress from the brook, and a thick slice of fresh coconut cake. But it was the pickled watermelon rind that still captivates my imagination—a simple thing utterly transformed through necessity.

Our own family still puts up shelves full of jams (blueberry, strawberry, and apricot), and we also harvest honey and boil our own maple syrup. The root cellar is packed with five kinds of potatoes, carrots, beets, and apples for a short while in late fall. Any country cook will tell you that the best recipes are based on need, not excess. Who doesn't love a country ham dinner or a corned beef sandwich served with a thick spear of pickle?

Perhaps the art of home canning is, indeed, headed toward extinction. But home cooking can still save us from the tyranny of convenience. Sure, cooking takes a bit of effort and planning. But who says that a dish of watermelon pickle can't change the world? At the very least, a plate of home cooking can make your day. And, as Jean is apt to say, one good day might just lead to another.

Christopher Kimball
Founder and Editor, *Cook's Country Magazine*

Canning Demonstration Ilene Holder, a Four-H Club member, gives a demonstration in canning. Holmes County, Mississippi. August 1935. (Photo by George W. Ackerman/© CORBIS)

"Home on the Range"

AUGUST/SEPTEMBER 2006

Cook's Country

departments

features

in every issue

Editorial Office: 17 Station Street, Brookline, MA 02445; 617-232-1000; fax 617-232-1572
Subscription Inquiries: Cook's Country, P.O. Box 8382, Red Oak, IA 51591-1382
800-526-8447

ON THE COVER: PHOTOGRAPHY: James Carrier Photography/Stockfood America. ILLUSTRATION: John Burgoyne.
IN THIS ISSUE: COLOR FOOD PHOTOGRAPHY: Keller + Keller. STYLING: Mary Jane Sawyer, Marie Piraino. ILLUSTRATION: Lisa Perrett.

Cook's Country magazine (ISSN 1552-1990), number 10, is published bimonthly by Boston Common Press Limited Partnership, 17 Station Street, Brookline, MA 02445. Copyright 2006 Boston Common Press Limited Partnership. Application to mail at periodical postage rates pending at Boston, Mass., and additional mailing offices. POSTMASTER: Send address changes to Cook's Country, P.O. Box 8382, Red Oak, IA 51591-1382. For subscription and gift subscription orders, subscription inquiries, or change-of-address notices, call 800-526-8447 in the U.S. or 515-247-7571 from outside the U.S., or write us at Cook's Country, P.O. Box 8382, Red Oak, IA 51591-1382.
PRINTED IN THE USA

Visit us at www.cookscountry.com!
Go online to ask questions, share kitchen tips, and enter recipe contests. You can also take a sneak peek at what we've got cooking for upcoming issues.

Kitchen Shortcuts

READERS SHARE CLEVER TIPS FOR EVERYDAY COOKING CHALLENGES

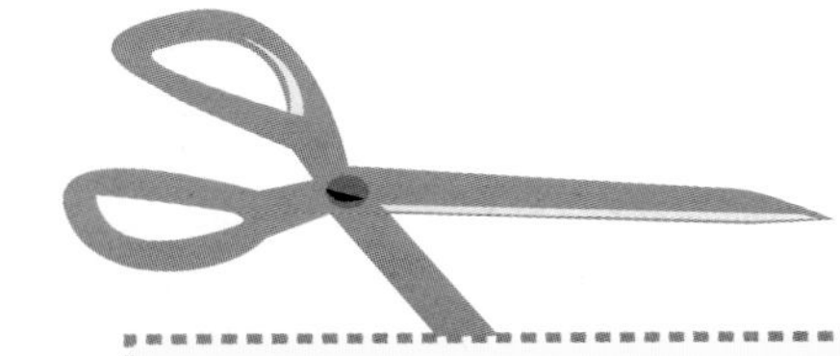

One-Stop Chopping

I discovered an advantage of storing chocolate in the freezer: When it's frozen, there's no need to chop it into pieces with a knife; it will shatter if you give it just one hard smack on the countertop. (And because it's still in its wrapper, the pieces don't shoot all over the counter.) All you need to do is pour the "chopped" chocolate into a double boiler for melting.

Timothy Jack Ward Chappaqua, N.Y.

DOUBLE DUTY

Flower Power

To avoid getting stuck by trussing pins, skewers, meat thermometers, and other sharp items stored in kitchen drawers, I turn to my florist. Every time I buy fresh flowers, I save the small green plastic water-holding tubes attached to the stems. After washing the tubes and letting them dry, I slip the pointy end of an item inside the tube. No more pricked fingers.

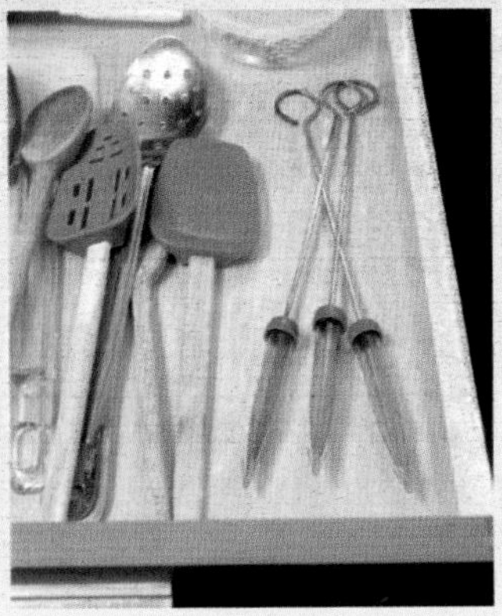

Ann Chin
Paramus, N.J.

Hang Time

Handy Hanger

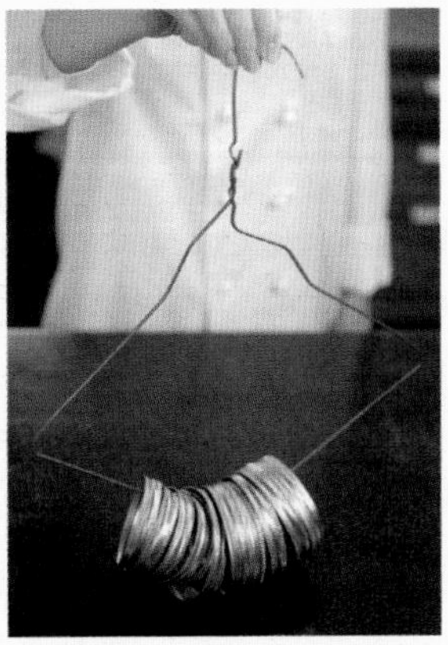

In the summer, I do a lot of canning, so it's always a struggle keeping my jar rings in order. My solution is to take a wire coat hanger, stretch it into a diamond shape, and unloop the secured end. I slip the rings on the hanger and then re-secure the open end. When I'm canning, I keep the hanger handy by hanging it on a cupboard knob. Now I'm never at a loss for a ring when I need one.

Bonnie Farley Henry, S.D.

Teaching Tomorrow's Bakers

NO-MESS PASTRY BAG

My sons are learning how to use a pastry bag to decorate cookies. One of their biggest frustrations is having the frosting pop out of the top of the bag when they squeeze it. My solution: I fill the pastry bag, twist the top shut, then use a twist tie to secure it. A rubber band also works well, but the twist tie makes it easier to open the bag when adding more icing.

Tracy Schuhmacher Penfield, N.Y.

KEEPING FRESH FRUIT FRESHER

During the summer months, I like to keep a large bowl of cut-up fruit in the refrigerator for snacking. Unfortunately, after a few hours of sitting in its own juices, the fruit does not look very appetizing. My solution is to place an inverted saucer or pie plate in the bottom of the bowl before adding the fruit. This way, the fruit sits on top of the inverted dish and the juice collects underneath it. No more soggy fruit.

Mary Lou Laskus
Allendale, Mich.

WHY SCREAM FOR ICE CREAM?

My family loves homemade ice cream, but we hate the racket the ice cream maker makes in the kitchen as it churns. Then I discovered that I could fit the machine inside my refrigerator (snaking the cord out the bottom of the door). Voilà—a quiet kitchen once again. By all means check on it regularly, but this makes for a much more peaceful kitchen.

Scott Smith
Cumberland, R.I.

COFFEE FILTER AS LID

While microwaving a cup of soup at the office, I realized I'd left the vented lid of my soup mug at my desk. Not wanting a splattered mess, I grabbed a round coffee filter and placed it upside down over the mug. The wavy edges of the filter fit perfectly over the cup, making a loose cover that's perfect for microwaving—and it's handy, cheap, and disposable.

Jennifer Judson
Tulsa, Okla.

CUTTING-BOARD CUSHION

Even in a good-sized kitchen it can be hard to figure out where to store a large cutting board. I never knew where to store mine until I started thinking outside the kitchen—and in the living room. Now I store my largest cutting board under a cushion on the sofa frame (a chair will work just as well). This has not only saved me precious space in the kitchen but has done wonders for my sore back! (And my cutting board is only ½ inch thick.) I just make sure to wash the board before I use it in the kitchen.

Krandall Kraus
San Francisco, Calif.

A CAN-DO ATTITUDE

Tired of using a spoon or spatula to dig out the contents of an opened can, I was happy to discover an easier way: Simply turn the can over and pierce the bottom with a can opener, then give the can a couple of quick shakes or a few raps on the countertop and the contents will plop out easily. (Just make sure you place a bowl underneath the can before you get started.)

Lynni Boulton
Moscow, Idaho

SPOUTING OFF

How many times have you opened a bottle of salad dressing and poured half the bottle on your salad because the bottle was lacking a plastic spout? I solved this problem by saving the spouts from spent bottles. I've found that most spouts fit just about any bottle. This has saved me a lot of wasted salad dressing.

Ann Mantooth
Knoxville, Tenn.

STORE CANS UPSIDE DOWN

I've found that storing canned goods upside down has two benefits. First, the tops stay cleaner (so dust and so forth won't get into the food when you open the can—a problem, especially if you store things in a basement). Second, the cans empty more easily (especially when it comes to foods like beans) because the contents are already pressed against the top.

Dianne Sedlar
St. Louis, Mo.

If you'd like to submit a tip, please send a letter to Kitchen Shortcuts, Cook's Country, P.O. Box 470739, Brookline, MA 02447. Or e-mail us at **shortcuts@bcpress.com.** Include your name, address, and phone number. If we publish your tip, you will receive a one-year subscription to *Cook's Country*.

EASY CHOCOLATE PIPING

When I want to melt chocolate for decorative piping, instead of messing with a double boiler or dirtying more dishes, I kill two birds with one stone. I pour chocolate chips into a large zipper-lock freezer bag and microwave the bag at 20-second intervals until the chips are just melted. Then I cut a tiny strip from a bottom corner of the bag and use it just like a piping bag. There's no mess at all, and cleanup is as simple as tossing the bag in the trash.

Catherine Phillips
Vanceboro, N.C.

THE DAILY TRASH BAG

Since I'm usually cooking breakfast when the newspaper arrives, I decided to make use of the plastic bag the paper comes in. I place the bag next to my cutting board and fill it with vegetable peelings, eggshells, butter wrappers, coffee grounds—whatever scraps are left from making breakfast. Once I'm finished, I just tie the end in a knot and throw it away. No mess, no hassle.

Susan Trantham
Lufkin, Texas

TASTIER SWEET TEA

Try a teaspoon or two of a powdered drink mix (lemonade, Hi-C, even Tang!) instead of sugar to sweeten a glass of iced tea. It adds a flavor boost and sweetens at the same time.

Charlotte Bryant
Greensburg, Ky.

FLOUR SPRINKLER

I make bread quite often and needed a quick, clean, and convenient way to sprinkle flour onto my countertop. I found my solution in an old spice jar. With its plastic shaker top, it is the perfect dispenser for flour, and the screw-on metal lid keeps the flour dry during storage. It's also easy to refill.

Carrie Icard
Price, Utah

FIX FOR BURNING SUGAR SYRUP

Whenever I'm working with boiling sugar—whether I'm making caramel, candy, or just boiling sugar syrup for sorbet—I always set up a bowl of ice water right next to my cutting board. Even a tiny spatter of the molten sugar will cause a nasty burn if it sticks to your skin. When this occurs I simply plunge my hand into the ice water to quickly ease the burn.

Christina Hurn
Santa Fe Springs, Calif.

NEW USE FOR MAGNETS

The interior walls and ceiling of most refrigerators are made of metal, and I realized I could use this to my advantage. How? I use magnetic clips to fix small bags of leftovers or other food items to the ceiling and sides of the fridge. The bags are easy to spot, and they make good use of otherwise unused space.

Marina Windsor
Baltimore, Md.

'GRAB BAG' BREAD

To save money I like to buy in bulk, and to save time I like to cook in bulk. Every so often, I line up several zipper-lock plastic freezer bags and measure out the dry ingredients for my favorite bread: flour, yeast, salt, sugar, seasonings, and so on. When I want to make bread, all I need to do is grab a bag from the freezer, dump the contents into my bread machine, and add the wet ingredients. Bread making couldn't be quicker or easier.

Amy Siegel
Clifton, N.J.

THE END OF THE PAPER CHASE

My family tapes clear plastic page protectors to the inside of kitchen cabinet doors. The plastic sheaths are perfect for storing instruction manuals for kitchen appliances, ingredient conversion guides, and even clippings of recipes that we plan on making soon.

Nancy Johnson
Troy, Mich.

POP SECRET

To remove unpopped kernels from a bag of microwave popcorn, open the bag just enough for the small kernels to fall out, then turn the bag upside down and shake. The hard kernels will spill out, leaving the larger popped kernels behind.

Abigail Wilding
Bedford, N.H.

Hot Idea

Warming Taco Shells

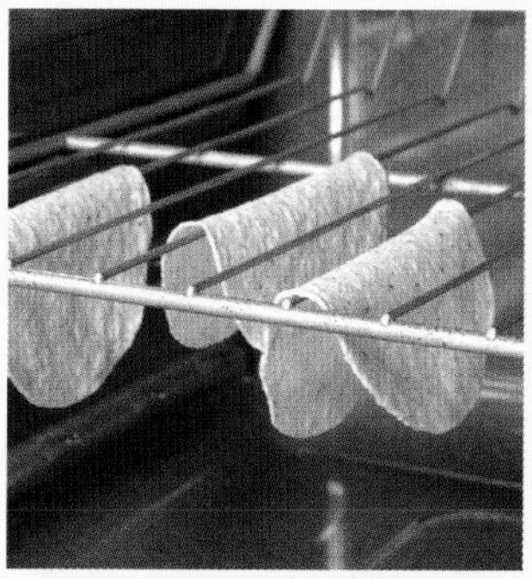

A quick and easy way to heat store-bought taco shells is to hang them upside down from the bars of your oven rack. The shells warm evenly and are very easy to remove.

Eileen J. Marsh
Pittsford, N.Y.

Shear Genius!

Last Thanksgiving we had eight children—seven of them 5 years old or younger—stay with us for the long weekend.

My son's wife was preparing a bowl of spaghetti for her two small ones and asked for the kitchen shears. She then cut the cooked pasta into small pieces quickly and evenly. The shears were much more effective than a knife and fork. What a good idea.

Terri Hathaway
Dorset, Vt.

Pulling Hot Pork

I regularly smoke and pull about a hundred pounds of pork each summer for school fundraisers and other events, and pulling that much steaming-hot pork wreaks havoc on my hands. I've tried using two forks to shred the meat, but it takes too long. Now whenever I'm pulling pork (or handling any hot food), I wear a pair of thin cotton gloves underneath a pair of foodsafe latex or vinyl gloves. Now I can handle the heat no matter how much pork I'm pulling!

Karen Barshinger
Cedar Rapids, Iowa

Pie-Crust Protector

Whenever I make a pie, the edges of the crust always brown too quickly. I used to make a ring out of foil to protect the edges, but it often fell off. Now I use the removable bottom ring from my tart pan. I turn it upside down, and it covers the edges of the crust perfectly.

Michele Quinn
Holly Hill, Fla.

Keeping Critters at Bay

FROZEN TRASH

This tip may seem obvious, but it has saved me a lot of trouble. Our garbage is picked up once a week, and there are lots of wild animals where we live (raccoons are a real problem), so we can't compost. Rather than stinking up the kitchen with a trash can full of garbage, I keep a plastic grocery bag in the freezer and store food scraps there. On garbage-collection day, the bag goes into the trash a frozen mass. No smell, no mess, and not very appealing to raccoons. Very helpful during the warm summer months.

Ross Bishop Palmyra, Va.

A Spicy, Fruity Salsa Heats Up the Competition

Our $1,000 Grand-Prize Winner

Cindy Rucker
Brooklyn, N.Y.

This spicy tropical salsa is perfect with grilled fish.

Cindy, who grew up in Oklahoma, says Mexican fare is her favorite comfort food. "Growing up close to the border, I was always around the aromas and spices of Mexican cuisine, and as an adult it is the food that still fills my table." In her kitchen, Cindy has experimented by pairing fruits with chiles to make salsas, and mango and super-hot habaneros are a favorite. "I love that mango is light and refreshing, yet it can hold its own against the sharp but slightly fruity habanero. This salsa is perfect with any grilled fish, including tilapia tacos, my favorite." Cindy tells us that this tasty salsa helped her win her husband's heart while they were dating. See page 31 for tips on seeding a cucumber.

MANGO-CUCUMBER SALSA

MAKES ABOUT 4 CUPS

Make sure that the mango is not overly ripe to ensure easy cutting and scooping.

- **1 tablespoon extra-virgin olive oil**
- **1 tablespoon lime juice**
- **1 teaspoon sugar**
- **1 large mango, peeled, pitted, and cut into 1/4-inch pieces**
- **1/2 large cucumber, peeled, seeded, and cut into 1/4-inch pieces**
- **6 radishes, cut into 1/4-inch pieces**
- **1 garlic clove, minced**
- **1/2 habanero chile, seeded and minced**
- **1/2 small red onion, minced**
- **2 tablespoons chopped fresh basil**
- **Salt and pepper**

1. Stir oil, lime juice, and sugar together in small bowl until sugar is dissolved.

2. Toss mango, cucumber, radishes, garlic, habanero, onion, and basil in large bowl. Stir in lime juice mixture until combined. Season with salt and pepper to taste. Serve. (This salsa is best served within 1 hour. To make ahead, mix all ingredients except mango together and refrigerate up to 1 day. When ready to serve, add mango and toss gently.)

David Hooper
Aurora, Colo.

Roxanne Chan
Albany, Calif.

Kim Forton
Lee's Summit, Mo.

Tom Stupek
Rio Verde, Ariz.

GRILLED SALSA VERDAVID

MAKES 3 1/2 CUPS

David writes: "I love this salsa on everything from tortilla chips to eggs!" If you can't find fresh tomatillos for David's version of salsa verde, substitute one 11-ounce can of tomatillos, drained, and add it directly to the food processor in step 2.

- **8 medium tomatillos, husks removed**
- **2 Anaheim chiles**
- **3 jalapeño chiles**
- **1/2 medium onion, quartered through root end**
- **1/2 small zucchini, quartered lengthwise**
- **5 garlic cloves, peeled and left whole**
- **3 tablespoons extra-virgin olive oil**
- **2 tablespoons lime juice**
- **1 tablespoon orange juice**
- **1 tablespoon honey**
- **1 1/2 teaspoons ground cumin**
- **Salt and pepper**

1. Light grill. Toss tomatillos, chiles, onion, zucchini, garlic, and 2 tablespoons oil in medium bowl. Thread garlic on metal skewer. Grill vegetables over hot fire until charred on all sides, about 3 minutes for garlic, 6 minutes for jalapeños and zucchini, and 9 minutes for tomatillos, Anaheim chiles, and onion. While still hot, steam chiles in a closed paper bag, about 10 minutes. When cool enough to handle, skin and seed chiles and core tomatillos.

2. Whisk lime juice, orange juice, honey, cumin, and remaining tablespoon oil in small bowl. Pulse mixture with grilled vegetables in food processor until smooth. Season with salt and pepper to taste, cover with plastic wrap, and refrigerate until flavors meld, at least 1 hour or up to 2 days.

SPANISH SUNSHINE SALSA

MAKES 3 CUPS

Roxanne writes: "I grow a variety of produce, including tomatoes and oranges, and get constant inspiration for recipes from whatever is popping up. This recipe was created to please my teenage son, who is crazy about olives. Use it as an accompaniment to grilled meat or fish."

- **4 medium tomatoes, seeded and cut into 1/4-inch pieces**
- **Salt**
- **1 seedless orange, peeled, sectioned, and cut into 1/4-inch pieces**
- **1/2 cup Spanish green olives, pitted and quartered**
- **3 scallions, chopped fine**
- **1/4 cup chopped fresh parsley**
- **1 garlic clove, minced**
- **2 tablespoons lemon juice**
- **1 tablespoon extra-virgin olive oil**
- **1/4 teaspoon sugar**
- **Pepper**

1. Toss tomatoes and 1/4 teaspoon salt in medium bowl. Transfer to colander set over large bowl to drain excess moisture, about 30 minutes.

2. Return tomatoes to bowl and toss with remaining ingredients, including salt and pepper to taste. Cover with plastic wrap and refrigerate until flavors meld, at least 1 hour or up to 2 days.

NOTE: For most recipes that use fresh orange segments, it's important to remove the bitter pith and membranes. In the test kitchen, we use a paring knife to cut away the peel and white pith. Then we remove just the fruit flesh by cutting to the center inside the two membranes of each section.

TOASTED CORN AND BLACK BEAN SALSA

MAKES ABOUT 5 CUPS

Kim writes: "This is one of our favorite snacks to enjoy on its own or with tortilla chips. It's great for parties because everyone loves it and it's amazingly healthy." If you can't find queso fresco (a Mexican cheese), use farmers cheese or omit the cheese altogether.

- **3 tablespoons extra-virgin olive oil**
- **1 large ear corn, kernels removed (about 1 cup)**
- **1/2 teaspoon ground cumin**
- **1/8 teaspoon cayenne pepper**
- **3 tablespoons lime juice**
- **Salt and pepper**
- **2 medium tomatoes, seeded and cut into 1/4-inch pieces**
- **1 (15.5-ounce) can black beans, drained and rinsed**
- **1/2 red bell pepper, seeded and chopped fine**
- **1 serrano chile, seeded and minced**
- **2 scallions, chopped fine**
- **1/2 cup crumbled queso fresco**

1. Heat 1 tablespoon oil in medium skillet over medium-high heat until shimmering. Add corn and cook until deep golden brown, about 4 minutes. Add cumin and cayenne and cook until fragrant, about 30 seconds. Transfer to large bowl.

2. Whisk remaining 2 tablespoons oil, lime juice, 1/4 teaspoon salt, and 1/4 teaspoon pepper in small bowl. Add to corn mixture along with tomatoes, beans, bell pepper, chile, scallions, and cheese. Toss well and check seasoning. Cover with plastic wrap and refrigerate until flavors meld, at least 1 hour or up to 1 day.

PINEAPPLE-AVOCADO SALSA

MAKES ABOUT 2 CUPS

Tom writes: "I was serving fish to my entire in-law clan one Sunday afternoon and decided to try something different to accompany it. I came up with this fresh and quick salsa, and everyone was more than pleased."

- **1/2 small ripe pineapple, peeled, cored, and cut into 1/2-inch pieces**
- **1/2 red bell pepper, seeded and chopped fine**
- **1 ripe avocado, pit and skin removed, and diced**
- **2 tablespoons chopped fresh cilantro**
- **1 small jalapeño chile, seeded and minced**
- **2 teaspoons dark brown sugar**
- **3 tablespoons lime juice**
- **Salt and pepper**

Gently toss pineapple, bell pepper, avocado, cilantro, and chile in medium bowl. Stir brown sugar and lime juice together in small bowl until sugar is dissolved, then stir into pineapple mixture until combined. Season with salt and pepper to taste. Serve. (This salsa is best served within 1 hour. To make ahead, mix all ingredients except avocado together and refrigerate up to 1 day. When ready to serve, add avocado and toss gently.)

We want your bar-cookie recipes for an upcoming contest. Please submit entries by September 30, 2006. Write to us at Recipe Contest, Cook's Country, P.O. Box 470739, Brookline, MA 02447, or e-mail us at recipecontest@bcpress.com. Include your name, address, and daytime phone number, and tell us what makes your recipe special. The grand-prize winner will receive $1,000. All entries become the property of *Cook's Country*. For more information on this and other contests, visit our Web site at **www.cookscountry.com.**

Ask Cook's Country

WE'LL ANSWER ANY QUESTION YOU THROW AT US!

BAY WATCH

I use bay leaves in cooking, but I don't really know anything about them. How do they affect the flavor of a dish? Can you use too many? What's the best way to store them?

Michael Cox San Diego, Calif.

Dried bay leaves are extremely potent. Most recipes (including ours) call for just one or two leaves for a large pot of food. How does that potency translate to the flavor of the finished dish? To find out, we prepared three batches of a simple chicken broth, one using two bay leaves (as the recipe indicated), one using no bay leaves, and one using four bay leaves. (There are two kinds of bay leaves: Turkish and Californian. We prefer the milder flavor of the more common Turkish bay leaves and used them in our tests.) The broth made without bay leaves was panned as "bland" and "watery," with "no flavor." Too many bay leaves, however, left the broth "bitter," "piney," and "sour." Just the right amount—in this case, two bay leaves—produced a broth that was "balanced," "nicely seasoned," and "herby."

Next we ran some tests to see what kind of storage would best help this intensely flavored herb retain its potency, using bay leaves from a freshly opened jar; from a jar that had been opened three months before, the lid replaced, and the jar stored at room temperature; and from a zipper-lock freezer bag that had been stored in the freezer for three months. We were amazed at the degree of flavor loss in the leaves stored in the jar; the fresh bay leaves tasted nearly twice as flavorful. The leaves stored in the freezer were nearly as good as those from the freshly opened jar.

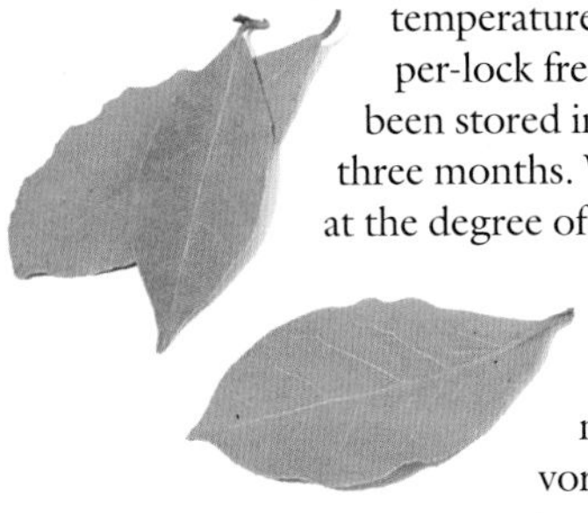

Dried bay leaves are intensely flavored, but they can lose their potency if not stored in an airtight container in the freezer.

ADJUSTABLE CUP

I know you use one kind of measuring cup for dry ingredients and another kind for liquids, but what do you use for ingredients like yogurt and mayonnaise?

Judie Morton Duncanville, Texas

It's important to use the proper measuring cup to ensure accurate measurement. Liquids spill easily when measured in cups meant for dry ingredients, and it's nearly impossible to get an accurate measure of a dry ingredient in a cup meant for liquids (you can't neatly level off a liquid measure). For semisolids like yogurt, mayonnaise, and peanut butter, we turn to adjustable cups, marketed under the brand names Wonder Cup and Adjust-A-Cup (we prefer the latter, whose measurement markings won't fade even after repeated dishwashing). These cups consist of a clear acrylic tube marked with measurement increments and a plunger-type insert. To use one, you just pull the plunger down to the desired measurement, fill the container, then turn the cup upside down over a bowl and push out the ingredients. If you don't have an adjustable measuring cup, we recommend using dry measuring cups for semisolids so you can scrape the item level with the cup; just be sure to scrape out the cup with a flexible rubber spatula.

For easy measurement of semisolids, we prefer the fade-resistant Adjust-A-Cup.

PICKIN' CHICKEN

Do you have a rule of thumb for how much cooked meat to expect from a roasted chicken? I'm thinking in terms of using the meat for recipes that call for cooked/leftover meat, not figuring portions.

Dana Thompson Gresham, Ore.

We roasted 3-, 4-, and 5-pound chickens and then picked them clean to find out how much meat we could get per pound. The birds averaged about 1 cup of cooked picked chicken per pound of raw chicken (the 3-pound raw chicken yielded about 3 cups cooked chicken), and the proportion of white meat to dark was about 2 to 1. If you're purchasing a cooked chicken from the market, remember that chickens lose about 25 percent of their weight when cooked, so plan on a 2½-pound cooked chicken for 3 cups picked meat.

MICROWAVED CORN?

Do you have a good way to microwave corn on the cob? I hate having to heat up my kitchen with a big pot of boiling water in the middle of August.

Lynn Anderson Hayden Lake, Idaho

We tried several methods for microwaving corn and came up with one that worked, producing sweet, firm kernels rather than mealy, starchy ones. Here's how to do it: Remove the husk and silk from four ears of corn. In a shallow-sided microwavable dish, melt two to three tablespoons of butter. Add the corn and toss to coat. Cover the dish with plastic wrap and cook at high power for six to eight minutes, depending on the size of the ears (the corn is done when the kernels yield gently to pressure). The fat protects the kernels, keeping moisture inside. If your microwave is big enough, this method can be adapted for more ears of corn. Simply add one to two minutes per additional ear (or subtract if you wish to cook fewer ears).

FREEZING ONIONS

I tried Vidalia onions for the first time, and I have to say WOW! *They taste great, but they are a little pricey, and they're so big. Can they be frozen? I hate to let them go to waste.*

"Dagger" via e-mail

We froze several Vidalia onions over the weekend and then thawed them out, with the goal of comparing them with fresh Vidalia onions in a raw and cooked blind tasting. Unfortunately, we never got that far. Once thawed, the previously frozen onions were little more than sodden sponges: mushy, waterlogged, and clearly of no culinary use. Why the total destruction? Onions have an extremely high water content—as much as 90 percent. When the onions freeze, the water expands, destroying the cell walls and thus making the onion soft and unpalatable once thawed. Skip the freezing and buy Vidalias only when you know you are going to use them. And store them in a cool, dry place.

MILK VERSUS HALF-AND-HALF

What, exactly, is half-and-half, and how does its fat content compare with that of milk? How do they compare when used in recipes?

Tony Discoe Newport Beach, Calif.

According to the U.S. Department of Agriculture, half-and-half must contain 10.5 to 18 percent fat, while whole milk must contain at least 3.5 percent fat. To find out how milk and half-and-half compared in recipes, we chose three test kitchen favorites that call for the latter—vanilla pudding, mashed potatoes, and shortcakes (minus the strawberries)—and prepared one batch of each with half-and-half and another with whole milk. Differences were most obvious in the potatoes, where the batch made with half-and-half was described as "much creamier," with a "smoother texture" and "more buttery flavor" than the batch made with milk. Though the vanilla pudding made with milk was looser than that made with half-and-half, flavor differences were slight. Most tasters said, "I'd be happy with either." Differences were least noted in the shortcakes, where tasters commented that the "flavors aren't that different." In baked goods that call for half-and-half you can probably get away with using whole milk, but in dishes where you're looking for creaminess (not just fat and flavor), the differences will be notable although generally not unacceptable.

Half-and-half has roughly three times the fat of whole milk.

To ask us a cooking question, write to Ask Cook's Country, P. O. Box 470739, Brookline, MA 02447. If you prefer e-mail, write to askcookscountry@bcpress.com. See if you can stump us!

Recipe Makeover CHOCOLATE CHIP COOKIES

A "mystery ingredient" makes these cookies so good, no one will guess they're low fat.

For maximum chocolate flavor, we sprinkle some of the chips over the dough balls just before they go into the oven.

It's no wonder that big and chewy bakery chocolate chip cookies taste so good. With huge amounts of chocolate chips, butter, and sugar, they easily tip the scale at more than 200 calories and 8 grams of fat per cookie. When you consider that most "healthy" recipes use ingredients like applesauce, banana puree, molasses, and carob chips, it's pretty easy to understand why the bakeries are still in business. I made five different recipes for low-fat cookies, and the best of the lot were merely tasteless; the worst ones had unpleasant flavors, were tiny, or both. Could I make a low-fat chocolate chip cookie that didn't look or taste like a diet cookie?

Using the test kitchen's thick and chewy chocolate chip cookie recipe as a model, my first inclination was to reduce the amount of high-fat ingredients. After many tests in which I reduced butter, sugar, and eggs by varying amounts, I succeeded in creating a great-tasting low-fat chocolate chip cookie. But there was a problem: Since most of the butter had been taken out, within an hour of coming out of the oven, my tender and chewy cookies had turned into rocks.

I searched for a low-fat ingredient that could replicate butter's tenderizing power without changing the flavor profile of the cookie. Applesauce, a common ingredient in "healthy" baked goods, seemed like a good place to start. Unfortunately, my tasters complained not only of a strange aftertaste but also that the cookies looked more like corrugated cardboard than dessert. Molasses kept the cookies moist and tender, but the cookies were a strange brown color and had a strong molasses flavor. The only thing that raised my spirits was watching my colleagues cringe when they bit into the banana-puree cookies, which one taster described as "insulting to cookies everywhere."

With my frustration mounting, I tried one last "healthy" ingredient to make sure I had exhausted my options before moving on—homemade date puree, made from cooking and mashing dried dates. I replaced three-quarters of the butter in my favorite full-fat recipe with date puree and held my breath as tasters sampled this batch. I was pleasantly surprised when tasters said these cookies had a rich, sweet flavor, with only a slight, almost unidentifiable hint of "fruitiness." Now, thanks to my new "butter substitute," I had flavorful and tender cookies that stayed moist for days, not hours.

While the slight hint of fruitiness from the dates wasn't unpleasant, I didn't want even a trace of "unusual" flavor in these cookies. Unfortunately, as soon as I reduced the amount of fruit puree, the cookies turned back into rocks. Pressing the cooked dates through a sieve helped eliminate any date chunks in the cookies, but the fruit flavor was still present. Rather than taming the fruit flavor, one of my colleagues suggested trying to pump up the butter flavor by melting and browning it. Sure enough, the nutty, concentrated flavor of the browned butter boosted the buttery flavor of the cookies, adding just enough richness to mask any remaining hints of date. And since this batter was so flavorful, I could now cut the full cup of chocolate chips (many recipes call for even more) back to just half a cup—and my cookies still tasted chocolaty.

Although I was originally pessimistic about using a "healthy" fat substitute in my low-fat chocolate chip cookies, I was

(continued on page 8)

Secret Ingredients: THE DATING GAME

Could we really cut the fat and calories of a typical chocolate chip cookie without sacrificing flavor and chew? Yes, thanks to the addition of pureed dates and a mere 3 tablespoons of browned butter.

DATES

Cooked, pureed dates add moisture and chew to our cookies.

BROWNED BUTTER

Browning the butter intensifies its flavor, so just a little butter can taste like a lot.

And the Numbers . . .

All nutritional information is for one serving (one cookie).

TRADITIONAL CHOCOLATE CHIP COOKIES
CALORIES: **220**
FAT: **8g**
SATURATED FAT: **5g**

COOK'S COUNTRY LOW-FAT CHOCOLATE CHIP COOKIES
CALORIES: **120**
FAT: **3g**
SATURATED FAT: **2g**

THE JAGGED EDGE

While browned butter and date puree gave us cookies that tasted every bit as good as regular chocolate chip cookies, they did have one effect we weren't crazy about—strange, shiny, smooth tops instead of the craggy tops we expect in chocolate chip cookies. To make sure that our low-fat cookies look appealing, we found it necessary to perform a little assembly magic.

1. Roll 2 tablespoons of dough into a ball. Hold the dough ball with the fingertips of both hands and pull it into two equal halves, creating jagged edges.
2. Rotate the cookie halves so that the jagged surfaces are facing up. Press the two halves together at their base so that they form a single ball.
3. Space the balls of dough, jagged side up, 2 inches apart on the prepared baking sheets.

Low-Fat Choclate Chip Cookies

continued from page 7

happy to be proven wrong. The combination of date puree and browned butter makes a tender cookie that can stand up to any bakery cookie in flavor, size, and staying power. And with only 120 calories and 3 grams of fat, you can even have two. **–Meredith Butcher**

BIG AND CHEWY LOW-FAT CHOCOLATE CHIP COOKIES

MAKES 18 COOKIES

Dried dates can be found in the nut and dried fruit section of the supermarket. Be sure to buy dates that are still supple. See page 31 for tips on browning butter.

- **1 cup water**
- **4 tablespoons finely chopped dates**
- **3 tablespoons unsalted butter**
- **2 cups all-purpose flour**
- **1/2 teaspoon baking soda**
- **1/2 teaspoon salt**
- **1 1/4 cups packed light brown sugar**
- **1 large egg**
- **2 teaspoons vanilla extract**
- **1/2 cup semisweet chocolate chips**

1. Adjust oven rack to middle position and heat oven to 325 degrees. Line 2 baking sheets with parchment paper.

2. Bring water to boil in small saucepan over medium-high heat. Add dates and simmer until tender and most of water has evaporated, about 20 minutes.Using rubber spatula, press dates through fine-mesh strainer into medium bowl. Scrape dates remaining in strainer into bowl (you should have 1/4 cup puree).Cook butter in small saucepan over medium heat until nutty brown, about 4 minutes. Let cool.

3. Whisk flour, baking soda, and salt in medium bowl. With electric mixer on medium speed, beat melted butter, brown sugar, and date puree in large bowl until blended. Beat in egg and vanilla until combined. Add flour mixture and mix on low until just combined. Reserve 2 tablespoons chips, and stir remaining chips into batter by hand.

4. Following photos on page 7, form dough into 18 cookies and space them 2 inches apart on prepared baking sheets. Press remaining 2 tablespoons chips evenly over cookies.

5. Bake until edges are light golden brown and centers are soft and puffy, 15 to 18 minutes, rotating baking sheet front to back halfway through baking. Cool cookies completely on baking sheets. Serve. (Cookies will keep in airtight container at room temperature for up to 3 days.)

Lost Recipes BLUEBERRY BOY BAIT

Forget the funny name—after one bite of this moist and simple blueberry coffee cake, you'll be hooked, too.

A summer without fresh baked blueberry desserts is like a trip to the beach without a sunburn—it just ain't gonna happen. But when a friend had me over for a cup of coffee, she brought something new to the table. Much more than a moist yellow sheet cake topped with a layer of blueberries and crisp cinnamon sugar, it was possibly the best coffee cake I'd ever eaten. I asked what it was. "Blueberry Boy Bait," she replied. I asked for the recipe. "Family secret," she answered. Some friend.

I just had to find this recipe. A 1964 edition of the *Appleton* (Wisconsin) *Daily Herald* as well as two Chicago papers—a 1971 *Suburban Economist* and a 1956 *Daily Herald*—featured nearly identical recipes for Blueberry Boy Bait. But none of the recipes explained the name, and none of them were good—they all produced a dry, cottony cake with hard nuggets of streusel.

In a 1954 edition of the *Chicago Tribune*, I finally found the person who started it all. A 15-year-old girl named Adrienne (aka Renny) Powell of Chicago entered her dessert—Blueberry Boy Bait—in the junior division of the 1954 Pillsbury Grand National Baking Contest. She won second place, which included a $2,000 cash prize plus a promise to print her recipe in *Pillsbury's 5th Grand National Recipes Cookbook*. Renny named the cake (a family recipe) for the effect it had on teenage boys—one bite and they were hooked. This left me with one question: Where was this recipe when I was a teenager?

I was happy to finally find Ms. Powell, but her original recipe was tricky. I found a simpler version in the 1969 *Pillsbury's Bake Off Dessert Cookbook*. This cake was moist and tender, and I especially liked that blueberries were stirred into the cake batter as well as on top, making every bite berry-packed. But the best part was the topping. No more dry, crumbly streusel—just a sprinkling of sugar and cinnamon, which baked up into sweet, crispy flakes, just like my friend's cake.

My adjustments were minor. For deeper flavor, I exchanged the shortening for butter and half of the granulated sugar for brown sugar. For more structure, I added an extra egg. And since this cake has "blueberry" in its name, I doubled the amount.

Finally, I invited my friend over for coffee and watched as she silently ate a piece of my Blueberry Boy Bait. "Tastes just like humble pie," she said, grinning. "Where'd you get the recipe?" "Family secret," I said.

–Bridget Lancaster

This coffee cake has a crunchy cinnamon-sugar topping and is chock-full of sweet blueberries.

BLUEBERRY BOY BAIT

SERVES 12

If using frozen blueberries, do not let them thaw, as they will turn the batter a blue-green color.

Cake

- **2 cups plus 1 teaspoon all-purpose flour**
- **1 tablespoon baking powder**
- **1 teaspoon salt**
- **16 tablespoons (2 sticks) unsalted butter, softened**
- **3/4 cup packed light brown sugar**
- **1/2 cup granulated sugar**
- **3 large eggs**
- **1 cup whole milk**
- **1/2 cup blueberries, fresh or frozen (see note above)**

Topping

- **1/2 cup blueberries, fresh or frozen (see note above)**
- **1/4 cup granulated sugar**
- **1/2 teaspoon ground cinnamon**

1. For the cake: Adjust oven rack to middle position and heat oven to 350 degrees. Grease and flour 13 by 9-inch baking pan.

2. Whisk 2 cups flour, baking powder, and salt together in medium bowl. With electric mixer, beat butter and sugars on medium-high speed until fluffy, about 2 minutes. Add eggs, one at a time, beating until just incorporated. Reduce speed to medium and beat in one-third of flour mixture until incorporated; beat in half of milk. Beat in half of remaining flour mixture, then remaining milk, and finally remaining flour mixture. Toss blueberries with remaining 1 teaspoon flour. Using rubber spatula, gently fold in blueberries. Spread batter into prepared pan.

3. For the topping: Scatter blueberries over top of batter. Stir sugar and cinnamon together in small bowl and sprinkle over batter. Bake until toothpick inserted in center of cake comes out clean, 45 to 50 minutes. Cool in pan 20 minutes, then turn out and place on serving platter (topping side up). Serve warm or at room temperature. (Cake can be stored in airtight container at room temperature up to 3 days.)

Slow Cooking SMOTHERED PORK CHOPS

Smothered pork chops are great in the skillet, but will they work in a slow cooker?

The best smothered pork chops are fall-off-the-bone tender, covered with caramelized onions, and enriched with a deeply flavored onion gravy. I wondered if I could slow this recipe down to an eight-hour braise in my slow cooker, starting it in the morning and having it ready by the time I got home from work. More important, would it still be as good as the original?

The test kitchen's favorite skillet recipe uses relatively thin ¾-inch rib chops, so that's where I started. It took exactly eight hours to disprove the notion that you can't overcook anything in a slow cooker. The chops were dry and stringy, while the onions were surprisingly undercooked and swollen. To round out the failure, the sauce was watery and bland. Center-cut loin chops of similar size fared no better. It seemed that thin was not in, and I had to move to thicker chops. I was certain that huge 2-inch-thick chops, special-ordered from my butcher, were going to be the answer. I just had to determine which was better, rib or center-cut chops. To my dismay, both of these cuts also overcooked in eight hours, even on the low setting.

I wasn't willing to cut back on my cooking time, so I had to find another solution to overcooked chops. A test kitchen colleague suggested blade chops, which are cut from the shoulder end of the loin and contain a lot of fat and connective tissue. The fat melted into the meat, keeping it moist and tender, and the connective tissue all but disappeared over the course of eight hours. Best of all, there was no need to special-order extra-thick chops, since readily available ¾-inch blade chops worked perfectly.

Unfortunately, the same couldn't be said for the gravy and onions. It was becoming clear that the "dump and cook" method of loading the slow cooker with raw ingredients wasn't going to produce enough flavor. By first browning the chops on the stovetop in bacon fat, I not only added color and richness to the chops but also created a savory foundation for my sauce. When the chops were nicely seared, I removed them and cooked the onions—with garlic, thyme, and a bay leaf—in the empty pan. Tasters wanted more sweetness, and a little brown sugar added to the mix gave them just that (and helped to speed up the browning of the onions).

With the chops and the flavor of the onions and gravy set, my last challenge was to get the texture of the onions and gravy right—the sauce was still too watery. More onions thickened it, but they also threw off the flavor. Fortunately, my solution was sitting on the counter right next to the slow cooker: the blender. I removed the cooked onions from the sauce and pureed them with a cup of cooking liquid, then reduced that sauce in a saucepan (adding cornstarch to help it thicken) before pouring it back over the chops. I now had a thick, rich, emulsified gravy that truly smothered each chop.

I finished the sauce with a splash of cider vinegar to brighten things up, then garnished the chops with the bacon I'd cooked earlier as well as some chopped parsley. Now I had a recipe that was even better than the original—and it practically cooked itself while I was at work all day. **–Meredith Butcher**

Chop Shop

The secret to great slow-cooked smothered pork chops is choosing the right chop. The excess fat on a blade chop melts away after eight hours in the slow cooker.

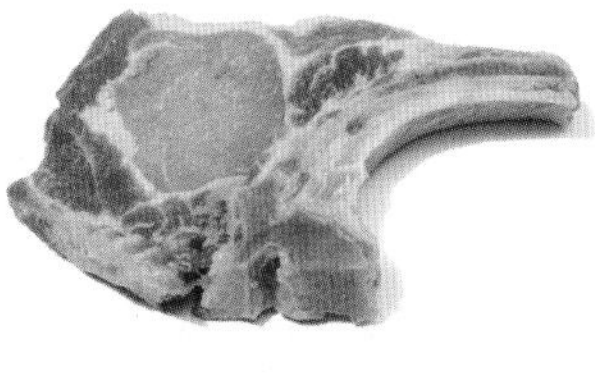

BLADE
The fat in these inexpensive chops keeps them from drying out in a slow cooker.

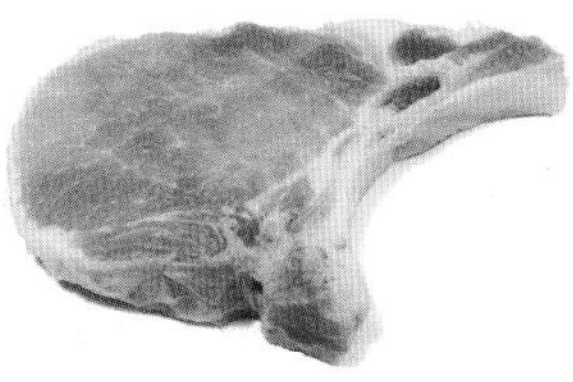

RIB
Our favorite for grilling and sautéing, but too lean for all-day cooking.

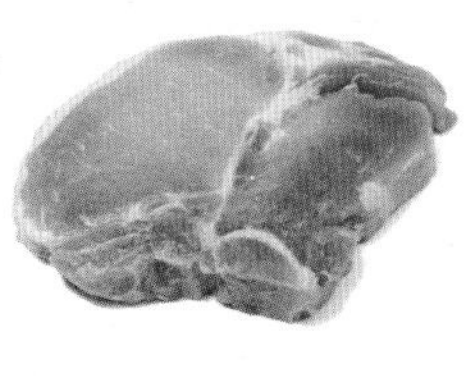

CENTER CUT
Our second choice for grilling and sautéing, but, again, too lean for the slow cooker.

Our smothered chops are fall-off-the-bone tender.

SLOW-COOKED SMOTHERED PORK CHOPS SERVES 6

These pork chops are so tender that you'll need to remove them from the slow cooker with a spoon.

- 4 slices bacon, chopped fine
- Vegetable oil (if necessary)
- 6 bone-in blade-cut pork chops, about ¾ inch thick
- Salt and pepper
- 3 yellow onions, halved and sliced into ½-inch half-moons
- 1 teaspoon plus 1 tablespoon light brown sugar
- ¼ cup plus 2 tablespoons water
- 3 garlic cloves, minced
- 2 teaspoons minced fresh thyme
- 3 cups low-sodium chicken broth
- 1 tablespoon soy sauce
- 2 bay leaves
- 1 tablespoon cornstarch
- 1 tablespoon cider vinegar
- 1 tablespoon minced fresh parsley

1. Fry bacon in large skillet over medium heat until lightly browned, about 8 minutes. Using slotted spoon, transfer bacon to paper towels, leaving fat in pan (you should have 2 tablespoons fat; if not, supplement with oil). Refrigerate bacon.

2. Heat fat over high heat until smoking. Meanwhile, pat pork chops dry with paper towels and sprinkle with salt and pepper. Cook 3 chops until golden brown on both sides, about 3 minutes per side. Transfer chops to slow-cooker insert. Repeat with remaining chops and transfer to slow-cooker insert.

3. Pour off all but 1 teaspoon fat from skillet; add onions, 1 teaspoon brown sugar, ¼ teaspoon salt, and ¼ cup water to now-empty skillet. Using wooden spoon, scrape browned bits from pan bottom and cook over medium-high heat until onions are soft, about 6 minutes. Stir in garlic and thyme and cook until fragrant, about 30 seconds longer. Pour onion mixture over chops in slow-cooker insert. Add broth, soy sauce, and remaining 1 tablespoon brown sugar to skillet, bring to boil, and add bay leaves. Pour mixture over onions in slow cooker.

4. Cover slow cooker and cook on low until pork is very tender, about 8 hours (or cook on high for 4 hours).

5. When ready to serve, reheat bacon in large saucepan until crisp and transfer to small bowl. Carefully transfer chops to serving platter with large spoon and tent with foil. Discard bay leaves and pour liquid through mesh strainer into now-empty saucepan. Transfer solids to blender with 1 cup liquid and blend until smooth. Stir back into remaining liquid in saucepan. Mix cornstarch and remaining 2 tablespoons water together in small bowl and stir into sauce. Cook over medium heat until thickened, about 8 minutes. Add vinegar, season with salt and pepper, pour over chops, and sprinkle with bacon and parsley. Serve.

Make Ahead

The recipe can be prepared through step 3 a day in advance. Refrigerate the chops separately and the onion and broth mixtures together. In the morning, place the chops in the slow-cooker insert; bring the broth and onion mixture to a boil in a skillet, and pour it over the chops. Proceed as directed.

Lexington-Style Barbecued Pulled Pork

Break out the white bread and pile on the pickle chips for a true taste of North Carolina barbecue.

Being born and raised in North Carolina, I consider myself a pulled pork fanatic—so long as it's Lexington-style barbecue. I just love the sweet, vinegary sauce and the smoky meat, but I'm pretty intimidated by the hours and hours of grilling. Can this recipe be simplified without sacrificing flavor? –Barbara J. Bradley, Glen Ellyn, Ill.

How to SET UP THE GRILL

Indirect heat is the key to low and slow BBQ. Place the roast on the side of the grill opposite the lit coals.

Back in my restaurant days, I lived in the Carolinas for a spell. To be honest, I don't remember too much about it except for the Lexington-style barbecue (named after Lexington, N.C., the self-proclaimed "barbecue capital of the world"). The slow-cooked pork shoulder was so tender, so sweet, and so smoky that it seemed almost unnatural. But what really hooked me was that sauce—thin and pungent, tart with vinegar and spicy with pepper, its acidity expertly balanced by just a hint of sugar and ketchup. When combined with the succulent, meaty pork shoulder, it added just enough bite to tighten my jaw and whet my appetite.

But making Lexington-style pulled pork at home can be trying, because it calls for hours and hours of diligent grill tending. To see if there was a less labor-intensive way to produce authentic-tasting Lexington barbecued pork, I hit the books. To reduce the cooking time while still maintaining barbecue flavor, some recipes rely on indoor smokers or even braise the pork shoulder with liquid smoke, but these methods seemed disingenuous. In the test kitchen, we often start large pieces of meat on the grill before finishing them in the oven. Theoretically, this allows the meat to take on a smoky, barbecued flavor without having it sit over a live fire all day.

My first tests using this technique resulted in fork-tender meat in just four to five hours (two on the grill, the rest in the oven), but the smoke flavor that the grill provided dissipated during its time in the oven, leaving the pork tasting like it had been simply roasted. To bump up the flavor, I coated the pork with a basic barbecue rub (many recipes use just salt and pepper) before placing it on the grill. To make sure the smoke got down into the meat, I doubled the amount of wood chips called for in most recipes, burning through 4 cups of chips in just two hours of grilling. With this treatment, the pork developed a deep red crust (called bark in barbecue circles) and a rich, thick smoke ring that stayed with the pork even after a couple hours in the oven.

Covering the pork and finishing it in a 325-degree oven created moist heat that melted the collagen, turning the tough pork shoulder into a savory, fork-tender piece of meat. It had just the right amount of smoke and seasoning, but now it needed its complement, a splash of that characteristic sweet and sour Lexington-style barbecue sauce.

The beauty of this sauce is its simplicity—after all, it's nothing more than vinegar, sugar, pepper, and ketchup. But even with so few ingredients, it still took some testing to get the balance of flavors just right. As a base, cider vinegar was the clear favorite for its fruity taste. But it did have an edge, which was easily curbed by adding an equal amount of water. For a touch of sweetness, I added granulated sugar and just enough ketchup to give the sauce body and a rosy color. As for the heat, although hot sauce was a common theme in my research, I found the flavor to be distracting. Black pepper added a nice earthy bite, and a pinch of red pepper flakes gave the sauce a kick that matched the pungency of the vinegar. Finally, I was ready to put it all together.

After I pulled the pork into shreds, I gave it a little splash of sauce, piled it high on my plate, then served myself some coleslaw and pickle chips. Every forkful of that smoky meat brought me back to North Carolina. **–Jeremy Sauer**

LEXINGTON-STYLE PULLED PORK

SERVES 8 TO 10

Pork butt (often labeled Boston butt) is usually sold boneless and wrapped in netting but is sometimes available on the bone. If barbecuing a bone-in roast, or if your pork butt weighs more than 5 pounds, plan on an extra 30 to 60 minutes of oven cooking time.

Spice Rub and Pork

- **2 tablespoons paprika**
- **2 tablespoons pepper**
- **2 tablespoons brown sugar**
- **1 tablespoon salt**
- **1 (4- to 5-pound) boneless pork shoulder roast**
- **4 cups wood chips**

Lexington BBQ Sauce

- **1 cup water**
- **1 cup cider vinegar**
- **1/2 cup ketchup**
- **1 tablespoon sugar**
- **3/4 teaspoon salt**
- **1/2 teaspoon pepper**
- **1/2 teaspoon red pepper flakes**

1. For the spice rub and pork: Combine spices, sugar, and salt in small bowl, breaking up any lumps as necessary. Massage entire pork roast with spice mixture. (Roast may be wrapped tightly and refrigerated for up to 1 day.)

2. Soak wood chips in bowl of water to cover for 15 minutes. Open bottom grill vents. Light large chimney starter filled halfway with charcoal briquettes (about 50 coals) and burn until charcoal is covered with fine gray ash. Pour coals into pile on one side of grill and scatter wood chips over coals. Set cooking grate in place, cover, and let grill heat up 5 minutes. Scrape grate clean.

3. Position pork on cooler side of grill. Cover, positioning half-open lid vents directly over meat, and cook until meat has dark, rosy crust and charcoal is spent, about 2 hours.

4. Meanwhile, adjust oven rack to lower-middle position and heat oven to 325 degrees. Transfer pork to large roasting pan, wrap pan and pork tightly in foil, and roast in oven until fork inserted into pork can be removed with no resistance (see page 30), 2 to 3 hours. Remove from oven and rest, still wrapped in foil, for 30 minutes.

5. For the sauce: Whisk together all ingredients until sugar and salt are dissolved. Using hands, pull pork into thin shreds, discarding fat if desired. Toss pork with ½ cup vinegar sauce, serving remaining sauce at table.

LEXINGTON-STYLE PULLED PORK FOR GAS GRILL

Seal 4 cups soaked wood chips in foil packet (see page 31). Place packet on primary burner of gas grill, turn all burners to high, and preheat with lid down until chips are smoking heavily, about 15 minutes. Turn primary burner to medium and shut off other burners, adjusting temperature of primary burner as needed to maintain average temperature of 275 degrees. Position pork over cool part of grill. Barbecue as directed.

The American Table: North Carolina Barbecue Battle

Although North Carolinians agree that pork is the barbecue meat of choice, they're divided when it comes to exactly what cut of pork and what type of sauce should be used. In the eastern part of the state, it's just not barbecue unless it's a whole hog. Known in the Carolinas as a pig pickin', this type of barbecue starts with a split hog and ends with succulent meat and crackling-crisp skin. The meat is then literally picked from the bones and lightly seasoned with a thin vinegar and pepper sauce. Western Carolinians eschew the whole hog and go straight for the shoulder—the most marbled and meatiest chunk of the animal. The pork shoulder is cooked just like the whole hog (slow and low over a wood or charcoal fire), but the sauce further stokes the debate. Although still vinegar-based, the barbecue sauce in the western areas is enriched with just enough ketchup and sugar to take the edge off the acidity.

How to FINISH THE PORK

1. After taking the pork off the grill, transfer it to a roasting pan, cover the pan with foil, and finish in a 325-degree oven.

2. Wearing kitchen gloves to protect your hands from the heat, shred (or "pull") the pork into thin strands, adding sauce as you go.

On the Side: Creamy Buttermilk Coleslaw

We love the tang of a buttermilk dressing, but not when it makes the slaw watery. Could we keep the tang and improve the consistency?

Whether served on the side or piled high right on top, it's hard for me to imagine eating barbecue without cool, creamy coleslaw. A tangy buttermilk coleslaw is my favorite, but not when the slaw makes a watery pool on my plate. Part of the problem is the buttermilk, which tastes great but makes a thin dressing. The other part of the problem is the cabbage, which sheds liquid as the slaw sits and turns the already-thin dressing downright watery. Many recipes tackle this problem by salting the shredded cabbage to remove excess water before dressing it. The salting worked like a charm, as the salted cabbage shed nearly 1/3 cup of liquid after just one hour.

But this method doesn't address the bigger problem: the thin buttermilk. To thicken the dressing, I wanted to add a creamier ingredient. Mayonnaise had the right body, but it dulled the buttermilk flavor. Sour cream had great tang, but it left the dressing thin. The solution was to use both mayonnaise (to thicken the dressing) and sour cream (to restore some tang). **–Eva Katz**

CREAMY BUTTERMILK COLESLAW

SERVES 8 TO 10

Make this slaw up to 1 hour before serving.

- **1 medium head green cabbage, cored and chopped fine**
- **2 large carrots, peeled and shredded on box grater**
- **Salt**
- **2/3 cup buttermilk**
- **1/2 cup mayonnaise**
- **1/4 cup sour cream**
- **8 scallions, chopped fine**
- **2 tablespoons sugar**
- **1 teaspoon Dijon mustard**
- **1/4 teaspoon pepper**

1. Toss shredded cabbage and carrots with 1 teaspoon salt in colander set over medium bowl. Let stand until wilted, about 1 hour. Rinse cabbage and carrots under cold water, drain, dry well with paper towels, and transfer to large bowl.

2. Stir in remaining ingredients plus salt to taste. Refrigerate until chilled, about 15 minutes. Adjust seasonings and serve.

Extra-Light, Extra-Crispy Waffles

Frozen Eggo waffles are the breakfast standard in my house, but when supplies ran low last weekend I broke down and made the real deal. What a mistake—they were as soggy as wet cardboard. How do you get toaster-crisp texture straight from a waffle iron? –Edie Shannon, Charlotte, N.C.

Gadgets & Gear:
WAFFLE IRON 101

Forget the bells, whistles, and colored lights on fancy new waffle irons. Many new waffle irons have signals that are intended to alert you when the waffle is ready, but they are often off the mark. Watch the clock when cooking your first waffle and take a peek under the lid. Note the time it takes to produce a golden brown, crispy waffle and use that as a guide for future batches.

Although frozen waffles are little more than vehicles for syrup and butter, they are convenient and they are consistently crisp, unlike some "from scratch" waffles I've had. Waffles should be exceptionally crisp on the outside and light on the inside. And if I'm going to make them myself, they'd better taste good.

I gathered a slew of recipes, summoned my tasters, and fired up the irons. These recipes all included a basic combination of flour, sugar, leavener (baking powder or soda), eggs, fat (butter or oil), and milk or buttermilk. Some recipes incorporated interesting ingredients like club soda (for light texture) or cooked grits (for toothy bite), but tasters were not impressed. These waffles definitely had more flavor than frozen, but their texture was problematic. A few of the waffles were nice and crisp hot off the iron but then became soggy on the plate.

I noticed that two of the most promising recipes had a common ingredient: beaten egg whites. Although most waffle recipes don't call for separating the eggs, beaten egg whites add lightness to everything from cakes to soufflés, and they worked wonders on waffles, too.

Now my waffles were lighter and fluffier, but they were not nearly crisp enough. I realized that while the design of a toaster allows excess moisture to escape, a waffle iron traps steam from the batter and increases the likelihood of a soggy outcome. When I want crispness in other recipes, I usually rely on oil (which is 100 percent fat) rather than butter (which is 80 percent fat and 20 percent water). Would the same trick work with waffles? Though several tasters, including me, were partial to the nutty flavor of waffles made with butter, the waffles made with oil were crispier.

Butter was out and oil was in, but my waffles were still a bit soggy. I couldn't get rid of all the moisture—a waffle without milk just isn't possible. Cornstarch is commonly used to combat excess moisture in all kinds of recipes, and I wondered how it would affect my waffles. I replaced some of the flour with cornstarch, working my way up from a scant 2 teaspoons (which made little difference) to a hefty ¾ cup. My waffles were finally both light and crispy, but could I make them extra-light and extra-crispy?

While discussing my recipe with a colleague, I noticed that another cook had prepared a batch of Rice Krispies Treats. I tried one, and the crackling crunch and mild malt flavor brought my waffles to mind. I joked that I should toss some of the cereal into my batter. With nothing to lose, I did just that and couldn't believe the results. The Rice Krispies added a malty, slightly sweet flavor that tasters loved, and each puffed grain of rice produced a tiny pocket of air in the waffles. My waffles were seriously crisp, and the Rice Krispies seemed to disappear as the batter cooked, leaving behind only their crunch and lightness.

Best of all, my waffles retained their crispy structure, even with a generous topping of butter and syrup. I think it's time to "leggo" of your Eggo waffles for something a lot tastier. **–Cali Rich**

To ensure crisp, light waffles, our novel recipe relies on beaten egg whites, cornstarch, and a breakfast cereal.

Ready When You Are

KEEPING THEM WARM: Our waffles are best served right off the waffle iron, but they can be reheated so everyone can eat at once. Transfer the cooked waffles to a wire rack set on top of a baking sheet in a 400-degree oven and bake until crisp and hot, 3 to 5 minutes.

KEEPING THEM FROZEN: Like the convenience of frozen waffles but don't like their stale flavor? Our waffles freeze beautifully. After cooling the waffles, wrap each in plastic, then freeze in a zipper-lock bag for up to one month. To serve, place the waffles on a wire rack set on a baking sheet and bake in a 400-degree oven until crisp and hot, about 5 minutes.

PUFF DADDY This puffed rice cereal makes a "treat" of our crispy waffles.

LIGHT AND CRISPY WAFFLES MAKES EIGHT 7-INCH ROUND WAFFLES

All waffle irons are not created equal. If your first waffle comes off the iron too pale or too dark, adjust the heat as necessary. Make sure to fill the waffle iron as directed; if you don't use enough batter, the Rice Krispies can scorch. Serve with syrup (see recipes on page 30).

- **1 1/4 cups all-purpose flour**
- **1 cup Rice Krispies**
- **3/4 cup cornstarch**
- **1/4 cup sugar**
- **1 teaspoon baking powder**
- **1/2 teaspoon baking soda**
- **3/4 teaspoon salt**
- **2 large eggs, separated**
- **1 1/2 cups milk**
- **1 teaspoon vanilla extract**
- **1/2 cup vegetable oil**

1. Preheat traditional waffle iron to medium. Meanwhile, stir flour, Rice Krispies, cornstarch, sugar, baking powder, baking soda, and salt together in large bowl. Whisk egg yolks, milk, vanilla, and oil together in medium bowl.

2. With electric mixer or balloon whisk, beat egg whites in bowl to soft peaks. Pour milk mixture over dry ingredients and whisk until combined. Whisk in beaten whites until just combined. Do not overmix; a few streaks of whites should be visible.

3. Pour 2/3 cup batter into center of preheated waffle iron and use back of dinner spoon to spread batter toward outer edges (batter should reach about 1/2 inch from edges of iron before closing lid). Close lid and cook until deep golden brown, 3 to 4 minutes. Serve immediately.

LIGHT AND CRISPY BELGIAN WAFFLES

Some Belgian waffle makers make one waffle at a time, while others make two. For single waffle makers, use 2/3 cup batter per waffle. For double waffle makers, use 1 1/3 cups batter in total.

Bake-Sale Favorites: Peach Squares

I haven't had much luck baking peach squares. They always come out too wet and crumbly, and they aren't loaded with the intense flavor of peaches that I want. Can you help? –Pamela Hopkins, Henrietta, Ga.

A peach square should be packed with peach flavor and be sturdy enough so that it can be eaten out of hand—just like the perfect summer peach. But judging from the half-dozen recipes I made at the outset of my research, both of those qualities are pretty rare in most peach squares.

The biggest discovery I made in my testing was frozen peaches. Not only were they more convenient than fresh (no peeling, pitting, and chopping), but their quality was more consistent. Chopping the peaches in the food processor before cooking them down in a skillet with peach preserves gave me a rich, deeply flavored filling, and because excess liquid evaporated during cooking, the filling also had just the right texture: not wet but jammy, with bits of peach to bite into.

I developed a simple streusel that works as both crust and topping, so these peach squares are as easy to make as they are to eat. **–Katie Henderson**

How to MAKE PEACH SQUARES

One mixture is used for both the crust and the topping.

1. Sprinkle the flour, sugar, and nut mixture over the pan and press down firmly, using the flat bottom of a measuring cup to form an even layer.
2. After the crust has been baked, layer the hot peach filling into the pan, then pinch the remaining streusel (the crust mixture with more brown sugar added) into dime-sized pieces and sprinkle it over the peach filling.

Peachy Keen

For intense fruit flavor, our recipe bypasses fresh fruit for these two year-round staples.

FROZEN FRUIT
More reliable than fresh and always available.

PEACH PRESERVES
Adds intensity as well as bits of fruit.

PEACH SQUARES MAKES 24

Although any brand of frozen peaches or peach preserves will work, the test kitchen prefers Whole Foods 365 frozen peaches and Smucker's preserves.

- **1 1/2 cups all-purpose flour**
- **1 3/4 cups sliced almonds**
- **1/3 cup granulated sugar**
- **1/3 cup plus 1 tablespoon packed light brown sugar**
- **Salt**
- **12 tablespoons (1 1/2 sticks) cold unsalted butter, cut into 1/2-inch pieces**
- **1 1/2 pounds frozen peaches, partially thawed**
- **1/2 cup peach preserves**
- **1/2 teaspoon grated lemon zest and 1 teaspoon lemon juice**

1. Adjust oven rack to middle position and heat oven to 375 degrees. Line 13 by 9-inch baking pan with aluminum foil, allowing excess to overhang pan edges. Spray pan with cooking spray. Process flour, 1 1/4 cups almonds, granulated sugar, 1/3 cup brown sugar, and 1/2 teaspoon salt in food processor until combined, about 5 seconds. Add butter and pulse mixture until it resembles coarse meal (some pea-sized pieces of butter will remain), about twenty 1-second pulses.

2. Transfer 1/2 cup flour mixture to small bowl and set aside. Press remaining flour mixture firmly and evenly into bottom of prepared baking pan (see photo 1). Bake until golden brown, about 15 minutes. Meanwhile, toss remaining 1 tablespoon brown sugar with reserved flour mixture. Set aside.

3. While crust is baking, remove blade from food processor and wipe out workbowl. Pulse peaches and preserves in food processor until mixture has 1/4-inch chunks, about five 1-second pulses (if larger chunks remain, scrape down sides and pulse 2 more times). Cook peach mixture in large nonstick skillet over high heat until thickened and jam-like, about 10 minutes. Off heat, add pinch salt, lemon zest, and lemon juice. Pour mixture over hot crust.

4. Using fingers, pinch reserved flour mixture to create dime-sized clumps (see photo 2) and sprinkle over peaches. Sprinkle remaining 1/2 cup almonds over top and bake until almonds are golden brown, about 20 minutes. Cool to room temperature, at least 2 hours. Using foil overhang, lift from pan and cut into 24 squares. Squares are best served on day they are baked. (See page 30 for reheating instructions.)

No-Fuss Grill-Roasted Turkey Breast

My husband, Andy, loves to roast a whole turkey on the grill. But it's always a big production and an all-day affair. Is grilling a whole turkey breast a simpler option? –Sallie Barrett, Chapel Hill, N.C.

Our recipe delivers moist, juicy meat with just the right balance of sweet and smoky flavors.

A bone-in, skin-on whole turkey breast cooks relatively quickly on the grill, but that doesn't mean that grilling a turkey breast is without its challenges. Our early tests yielded plenty of dry, bland turkey breasts with soggy skin.

When you're cooking a whole turkey, brining (that is, soaking the turkey in salt water before cooking) will keep delicate white meat from drying out as you wait for the dark meat to finish cooking. With an all-white-meat turkey breast, however, brining is unnecessary. As long as we took the turkey breast off the grill when the internal temperature reached 160 degrees (use an instant-read thermometer—see page 29), the meat didn't overcook. But it was still very bland.

We've had good luck in the test kitchen using salt rubs to season meat. We tried rubbing a combination of salt and dark brown sugar under and over the skin just before grilling; this gave us a tasty crust, but the seasoning didn't penetrate into the meat. When we left the rub on overnight (covered in plastic wrap in the refrigerator), however, the resulting turkey breast was juicy and deeply seasoned. Why does this work? Initially, the salt will draw moisture out of the bird. But given enough time, the salt and water flow back into the bird, actually seasoning it throughout.

We now had well-seasoned, moist white meat, but the skin was still rubbery. Since our rubbed turkey breast was covered in plastic overnight, some condensation formed on the outside of the skin. We needed to wipe the skin dry in order to give it the best chance to crisp up. By applying a second rub of dark brown sugar and black pepper under and over the skin right before we put the breast on the grill, we were able to replace some of the seasoning we had just wiped away. This second rub also gave the roast a spicy kick (from the pepper) and a more crisp, coffee-colored skin (from the brown sugar). The skin was now much better, and it was further improved when pierced before grilling, which allowed some of the fat to drain away.

Up until this point, we had been roasting our turkey breast over the cool side of a single-banked fire—that is, we pushed all the coals over to one side of the grill, put the turkey over the bare side, and cooked it with the grill lid on. Halfway through roasting, we rotated the meat to ensure even cooking, but this meant we had to open the lid, costing us precious heat and cooking time. By rearranging the coals in a double-banked formation, with two piles of coal on opposite sides of the grill floor, and putting the turkey breast in the middle, we were able to generate indirect but even heat from both sides. We now had no need to turn the turkey or open the lid, so we could walk away from the bird while it roasted.

To add more smoke flavor to the turkey, most recipes add hickory chips to the charcoal, with some calling for as much as 3 cups. But we found that such a large amount of chips left the turkey tasting like the inside of the grill lid. Tasters

Three Steps to CRISPIER SKIN

Don't be tempted to rub the turkey breast with both salt and pepper at the outset. The salt rub is left on overnight to fully season the turkey, but it dissolves and causes moisture to bead up on the skin that will inhibit crisping. Wiping away the moisture avoids this problem, but you wouldn't want to wipe away the pepper. Wait to pepper the turkey until it has been patted dry and is ready for the grill.

1. Lift Once Using your hands, carefully loosen the skin from the meat.
2. Season Twice Massage the brown sugar and salt on and under the skin. After refrigerating the bird overnight, wipe away excess moisture on the skin, then season again with brown sugar and pepper.
3. Skewer All Over Use a skewer to poke numerous holes in the skin so the fat can render easily.

felt that ½ cup of chips added just enough smokiness without overwhelming the mild flavor of the breast meat. Now we had smoky, well-seasoned, and juicy meat that our tasters were fighting over—and our turkey didn't require any babysitting on the grill. **–Meredith Butcher and Cali Rich**

GRILL-ROASTED TURKEY BREAST SERVES 6 TO 8

During cooking, resist the urge to peek under the lid, as heat will escape and prolong the cooking time.

- **1 whole, bone-in, skin-on turkey breast (about 5 pounds)**
- **3 tablespoons dark brown sugar**
- **1 tablespoon salt**
- **2 teaspoons pepper**
- **½ cup wood chips, preferably hickory**

1. Rinse turkey and pat dry with paper towels. Mix 2 tablespoons brown sugar and salt in bowl. Loosen skin from turkey and rub with sugar and salt mixture, following photos 1 and 2 on page 14. Tightly wrap turkey with plastic wrap, place on plate, and refrigerate for at least 8 hours or overnight.

2. Unwrap turkey and pat dry with paper towels. Mix remaining tablespoon brown sugar and pepper in bowl. Rub mixture under and over turkey breast skin. Using skewer, pierce turkey skin all over, following photo 3.

3. Soak wood chips in bowl of water to cover for 15 minutes. Open bottom vent on grill. Light large chimney starter filled with charcoal briquettes (about 100 coals) and burn until charcoal is covered with fine gray ash. Place 13 by 9-inch disposable aluminum roasting pan in center of grill. Pour half of coals into pile on one side of grill and remaining coals on other side, leaving pan in center. Scatter wood chips evenly over coals, set cooking grate in place, cover (open lid vent completely), and let grill heat for 5 minutes. Scrape cooking grate clean.

4. Place turkey, skin side up, on center of grate (grill temperature should register about 400 degrees). Cover and grill until skin is well browned and crisp and thickest part of meat registers 160 degrees on instant-read thermometer, about 1½ hours (grill temperature will cool down to about 325 degrees). Wearing oven mitts or using wad of paper towels, transfer breast to cutting board, cover loosely with foil, and let rest for 20 minutes. Carve and serve.

GRILL-ROASTED TURKEY BREAST FOR GAS GRILL

Prepare recipe for Grill-Roasted Turkey Breast through step 2. Soak wood chips in bowl of water to cover for 15 minutes, seal in foil packet (see page 31), and place over primary burner. Turn all burners to high and close lid, keeping grill covered until wood chips begin to smoke, about 15 minutes. Scrape cooking grate clean. Leave primary burner on high and turn off all other burners. Place turkey breast on cool part of grill and proceed with recipe from step 4, rotating breast, still skin side up, halfway through cooking. Adjust primary burner as necessary to maintain temperature of 350 to 375 degrees.

Good Wood

You can use any hardwood as fuel for grilling or smoking (soft woods like pine contain too much resin and give foods an unpleasant flavor), but most stores carry only hickory and mesquite. In the test kitchen, we've found that mesquite is too assertively flavored for smoking applications, but it can give good, musky flavor to meats that don't spend too much time on the grill. Our favorite all-purpose wood for grilling and smoking is hickory, which gives food a subtle, slightly sweet flavor.

On the Side: Barbecued Macaroni Salad

Pasta salad takes a road trip to the barbecue belt to create this smoky, spicy side dish.

As an accompaniment to a char-grilled burger or smoke-ringed rack of ribs, plain old macaroni salad can seem awfully boring. Mayonnaise and pasta aren't exactly the most exciting (or flavorful) ingredients. When a colleague told me about macaroni salad with barbecue flavors, I thought I had the perfect way to shake up this often-dull recipe.

Unfortunately, most of the recipes I found simply drowned the pasta in ketchupy barbecue sauce and were much too sweet and sticky. In the end, I found that a combination of barbecue sauce and mayonnaise proved more effective; the assertive tang of the barbecue sauce was nicely balanced by the neutral creaminess of the mayonnaise.

To punch up the barbecue flavor, I added chili powder, garlic powder, cider vinegar, and hot sauce. For freshness and texture, bell pepper, celery, and scallions introduced just the right vegetal bite. This spicy summertime side dish definitely won't hide in the background—in fact, it might just steal the show.

–Jeremy Sauer

BBQ MACARONI SALAD
SERVES 8 TO 10

We like the sweet, smoky flavor of Texas Best or Bull's-Eye barbecue sauce here, but feel free to substitute your favorite. As the salad sits, it can become dry; just before serving, stir in a few tablespoons of warm water to bring back its creamy texture.

- **Salt**
- **1 pound elbow macaroni**
- **1 red bell pepper, seeded and chopped fine**
- **1 rib celery, chopped fine**
- **4 scallions, sliced thin**
- **2 tablespoons cider vinegar**
- **1 teaspoon hot sauce**
- **1 teaspoon chili powder**
- **⅛ teaspoon garlic powder**
- **Pinch cayenne pepper**
- **1 cup mayonnaise**
- **½ cup barbecue sauce (see note above)**
- **Pepper**

1. Bring 4 quarts water to boil in large pot. Add 1 tablespoon salt and macaroni and cook until nearly tender, about 5 minutes. Drain in colander and rinse with cold water until cool, then drain once more, briefly, so that pasta is still moist; transfer to large bowl.

2. Stir in bell pepper, celery, scallions, vinegar, hot sauce, chili powder, garlic powder, and cayenne pepper, and let sit until flavors are absorbed, about 2 minutes. Stir in mayonnaise and barbecue sauce and let sit until salad is no longer watery, about 5 minutes. Season with salt and pepper and serve. (The salad can be covered and refrigerated for up to 2 days. Check seasonings before serving.)

MEATY BBQ MACARONI SALAD

Our BBQ Macaroni Salad tastes great alongside any grilled fare, but for a heartier salad you can add browned sausage, kielbasa, or deli ham.

Heat 1 teaspoon vegetable oil in nonstick skillet over medium-high heat until shimmering. Add 8 ounces smoked sausage, kielbasa, or deli ham, cut into ½-inch chunks, and cook until browned, about 5 minutes. Transfer meat to paper-towel-lined plate and proceed with recipe, adding browned meat with vegetables in step 2.

I'm Looking for a Recipe

READERS HELP READERS FIND RECIPES

We've Got Mail

Several readers sent us recipes in response to the request for Prune Cake (October/November 2005 issue). We really liked the recipe sent by Heather Ghanem (at right). For the test kitchen's notes on this recipe (with more details on cooking times and procedures), go to **www.cookscountry.com** and click **Looking for a Recipe**. You'll find dozens more recipes submitted by other readers who responded to this page in other issues of *Cook's Country*.

PRUNE CAKE **Heather Ghanem** Via e-mail

This is my grandmother's recipe. Serve slices with a dusting of confectioners' sugar.

1	cup sugar
1½	sticks butter
3	eggs
3	tablespoons sour cream
2	cups flour
1	teaspoon cinnamon
1	teaspoon baking soda
1	teaspoon allspice
1	cup prunes, cooked
1	cup chopped walnuts

INSTRUCTIONS:

Cream sugar and butter. Add eggs and beat thoroughly. Add sour cream alternately with sifted dry ingredients. Add prunes and walnuts. Pour into angel food pan. Bake at 325 degrees for 44 to 48 minutes, or until inserted toothpick comes out clean.

Grape Juice Pie

My grandmother used to make a grape juice pie, which was my favorite as a child. It was made from Welch's grape juice, but that's about all I can remember. I've tried to reproduce it, but I have had no luck.

Sharon Lockett
Aiken, S.C.

Dressel's Chocolate Cake

My mom will be celebrating her 100th birthday this year. For as long as I can remember, we had birthday cakes made by Dressel's Bakery, located in the Chicago area. My parents, my husband, my children, and my grandchildren enjoyed a Dressel's chocolate cake on each and every birthday. They closed some years ago, and I would like to surprise my mom with a chocolate fudge whipped cream cake for her 100th birthday. The cake had two layers of dark chocolate cake with about an inch of whipped cream in between the layers. The outside was frosted with whipped cream, and the sides were then covered with very finely chopped nuts. This recipe would bring back many memories for my mom and our whole family.

Pat McCoy
Johnsburg, Ill.

Whole Wheat Chocolate Chip Cookies

Several years ago, while in Charlotte, N.C., I purchased a 4-ounce chocolate chip cookie at a mall. The following ingredients were listed on the package: whole wheat flour, oatmeal, brown sugar, butter, eggs, water, salt, baking powder, molasses, chocolate chips, and walnuts. I have hunted all over for such a recipe and I cannot find one. I am going to experiment with the ingredients in different amounts and see what happens, but I thought perhaps someone might have the recipe.

Jane Carmean
Mansfield, Ohio

Mamie Eisenhower Fudge

My husband says his mother used to make something she called Mamie Eisenhower Fudge. The recipe used at least six different kinds of chocolate, and, apparently, it was wonderful. I have not been able to find a recipe that calls for more than two kinds of chocolate. Can anyone help?

Jeanette Rector
Owasso, Okla.

Mrs. Muskie's Birthday Cake

Around 1970, when Edmund Muskie from Maine was running for president, there was a recipe published in our local paper called Mrs. Muskie's Birthday Cake. It was a rich, three-layer white cake made with butter and sour cream. Between the layers there was a strawberry filling, and the whole thing was frosted in whipped cream. It was to die for. I made the cake many times for special events, birthdays, garden weddings, etc. Somewhere along the way I lost the recipe and I would love to have it again.

Martha Harausz
Albany, N.Y.

Antonia's Goat Cheese Soufflé

About four years ago, I was in Key West, Fla., and I had the best twice-baked goat cheese soufflé at Antonia's restaurant. I have been back since then, but the restaurant has changed owners. They still have a soufflé, but nothing like the one I had the first time I went there. Does anyone have this recipe?

Libby Frazier
Boca Grande, Fla.

The Blue Ridge Pig Potato Salad

I used to travel to Virginia for work and would always stop near the small village of Nellysford for lunch. The Blue Ridge Pig was in a converted gas station and extremely rough, but it had the most unusual potato salad I have ever eaten. The potatoes were partially mashed with what I think was oil, green onions, dill, lots of celery, and maybe dill pickles and pickle juice. I have never forgotten it and have never found a recipe even close to that delectable version.

Edye Haynes
Mayfield, Ky.

Cherry Blossom Rolls

I am desperate to find a recipe I had back in the 1970s. It was a sweet yeast dough with a filling of flaked coconut, chopped maraschino cherries, and almond flavoring. It may have contained chopped dried apricots as well, but I am not sure. The dough was rolled into pinwheels, and I believe they were put into muffin tins to rise, hence the name cherry blossom rolls. I used to make this recipe every year for almost 20 years. I lost the recipe about nine years ago. It may have come from the Robin Hood flour company in Canada.

Patricia Julian
Via e-mail

Maas Brothers Spinach Florentine

When I was a little girl and living in Clearwater, Fla., we used to shop at Maas Brothers. After we shopped, we would go into the restaurant and we would always order a cold salad called spinach Florentine. I remember that it had spinach and maybe cottage cheese as two of the major ingredients.

Susan Pedrosa
Woodstock, Ontario
Canada

Shrewsbury Biscuits

Recently, I was in Pune, India, and I ate the most amazing cookie, called a Shrewsbury biscuit. It was like the best shortbread I have ever tasted; it was crisp, not soft, mealy, dry, or crumbly, the way some shortbread can be. I am told that it is an artifact from when the British ruled in India. The British eventually left, but India kept the cookie. I would love to get this recipe!

Gloria Tsoi
Somerville, Mass.

Grape-Nuts Custard Pudding

I think I could create a recipe for Grape-Nuts custard pudding, but I would prefer a recipe. It's easy to overdo the Grape-Nuts and end up with an overly thick crust. My grandmother's version had a light and flavorful crust, just enough Grape-Nuts to make a sweet and nutty layer on top, and loads of creamy custard underneath. I'm not sure if she used lemon zest and juice or just vanilla and nutmeg. I haven't made it since my boys were younger. My husband has asked for it several times.

Carolyn Barker
Naples, Maine

Are you looking for a special recipe?
Let other readers of this magazine help. Just send us your requests, and we will print as many of them as we can. Write to Looking for a Recipe, Cook's Country, P.O. Box 470739, Brookline, MA 02447, or send an e-mail to lookingforarecipe@bcpress.com. If you can help with one of the above requests, contact us at the same postal or e-mail address. We will post responses to recipe requests on **www.cookscountry.com.**

Find the Rooster!

A tiny version of this rooster has been hidden somewhere in the pages of this issue. If you find it, write to us with its location (plus your name and address), and you will be entered into a random drawing. The first winning entry drawn will receive the Thermapen thermometer (our test winner—see page 29), and the next five winners will each receive a free one-year subscription to *Cook's Country*. To enter the contest, write to us at Rooster, Cook's Country, P.O. Box 470739, Brookline, MA 02447, or e-mail us at **rooster@bcpress.com.** Entries are due September 30, 2006.

Did you find the rooster in the April/May 2006 issue? It was hidden in the test kitchen photo on page 13. Matthew Davis of Stevens Point, Wis., spotted it and won a Calphalon spatula.

30-Minute Supper

GRILLED BEEF KEBABS WITH GREEK SALAD

30-Minute Supper

PAN-SEARED PORK CHOPS WITH PARSLEY-OLIVE SALSA

30-Minute Supper

SIZZLING GARLIC SHRIMP

30-Minute Supper

GRILLED CHICKEN WITH SESAME NOODLES

PAN-SEARED PORK CHOPS WITH PARSLEY-OLIVE SALSA

SERVES 4 TO 6

For this recipe, we like bone-in rib or center-cut chops between 1/4 and 1/2 inch thick. Toast the pine nuts in a small skillet over medium heat until golden in color.

- **1/3 cup chopped fresh parsley**
- **1/3 cup green olives with pimentos, chopped fine**
- **1/3 cup pine nuts, toasted (see note above) and chopped**
- **3 tablespoons capers, rinsed and chopped**
- **1 garlic clove, minced**
- **1 tablespoon lemon juice**
- **3 tablespoons olive oil**
- **Salt and pepper**
- **1/4 cup all-purpose flour**
- **6 thin pork chops (about 1 1/2 pounds), trimmed**
- **1 tablespoon unsalted butter**

1. Combine parsley, olives, pine nuts, capers, garlic, lemon juice, 1 tablespoon oil, and salt and pepper to taste in small bowl.

2. Place flour in shallow dish. Pat pork chops dry with paper towels, season with salt and pepper, dredge in flour, and shake to remove excess flour. Heat remaining 2 tablespoons oil and butter in large skillet over high heat until foaming subsides. Cook 3 chops until well browned on both sides, 1 1/2 to 2 minutes per side. Transfer chops to serving platter, cover with foil, and repeat with remaining chops. Serve with parsley-olive salsa.

GRILLED BEEF KEBABS WITH GREEK SALAD

SERVES 4

During the summer months, stew meat is often labeled as kebab meat. Grilled pita is a great accompaniment to this dish.

- **2/3 cup extra-virgin olive oil**
- **2 teaspoons minced fresh oregano**
- **2 garlic cloves, minced**
- **1 1/2 pounds beef stew or kebab meat, preferably chuck (see note above)**
- **Salt and pepper**
- **4 tablespoons red wine vinegar**
- **1 (10-ounce) package chopped romaine lettuce**
- **2 large ripe tomatoes, cored and cut into 10 wedges each**
- **1 cucumber, peeled, halved lengthwise, seeded, and cut into 1/2-inch-thick slices**
- **1/3 cup loosely packed torn fresh mint**
- **1/2 cup large kalamata olives, pitted and chopped coarse**
- **1 cup crumbled feta cheese**

1. Combine oil, oregano, and garlic in small bowl. Toss 3 tablespoons oil mixture with beef cubes in bowl and season with salt and pepper. Whisk vinegar into remaining oil mixture to make dressing.

2. Toss lettuce, tomatoes, cucumber, mint, olives, and feta in large serving bowl.

3. Thread four 12-inch metal skewers with beef; discard any leftover marinade. Grill over high heat, turning often, until charred and cooked through, 6 to 8 minutes. Transfer to serving platter and drizzle with 3 tablespoons dressing.

4. Just before serving, toss salad with remaining dressing. Adjust seasonings. Serve with kebabs.

GRILLED CHICKEN WITH SESAME NOODLES

SERVES 4 TO 6

If you prefer, you can substitute 12 ounces dried spaghetti for the Asian noodles.

- **3 garlic cloves, minced**
- **2 tablespoons minced fresh ginger**
- **1/2 cup soy sauce**
- **3 tablespoons rice vinegar**
- **2 teaspoons hot sauce**
- **3 tablespoons light brown sugar**
- **2 tablespoons toasted sesame oil**
- **4 boneless, skinless chicken breasts (about 1 1/2 pounds)**
- **1/4 cup peanut butter**
- **Salt**
- **1 pound fresh Asian noodles**
- **6 scallions, sliced thin**

1. Bring 4 quarts water to boil over high heat. Meanwhile, whisk garlic, ginger, soy sauce, vinegar, hot sauce, brown sugar, and oil in small bowl. Toss chicken with 3 tablespoons garlic mixture in bowl. Puree remaining garlic mixture and peanut butter in blender until smooth.

2. Add 1 tablespoon salt and noodles to boiling water and cook until al dente. Drain well, rinse under cold running water until cool, and drain again. Toss noodles, peanut sauce, and scallions in large bowl. Adjust seasonings.

3. Grill chicken breasts over high heat until cooked through, 2 to 3 minutes per side. Slice chicken and serve with noodles.

SIZZLING GARLIC SHRIMP

SERVES 4

Serve this dish with crusty bread and a salad.

- **1 1/2 pounds large shrimp, peeled and deveined**
- **Salt and pepper**
- **1/4 cup extra-virgin olive oil**
- **6 garlic cloves, sliced thin lengthwise, plus 1 clove minced**
- **1 red bell pepper, seeded and diced**
- **1/4 teaspoon red pepper flakes**
- **1/4 cup dry sherry**
- **2 tablespoons chopped fresh parsley**
- **2 tablespoons unsalted butter, softened**
- **1 tablespoon lemon juice, plus lemon wedges for serving**

1. Pat shrimp dry and toss with 1/4 teaspoon salt and 1/4 teaspoon pepper in medium bowl.

2. Cook oil and sliced garlic in large skillet over medium heat, stirring often, until garlic is golden and crisp, 3 to 4 minutes. Using slotted spoon, transfer garlic to small bowl. Add bell pepper and pepper flakes to skillet and cook until bell pepper is soft, about 3 minutes. Increase heat to high, add shrimp, and cook until edges turn pink, about 1 minute. Flip shrimp, add sherry, and simmer until shrimp are just cooked through, about 1 minute. Using slotted spoon, transfer shrimp to serving platter.

3. Add minced garlic, parsley, butter, and lemon juice to skillet and simmer until thickened, about 1 minute. Adjust seasonings, pour sauce over shrimp, and scatter browned garlic chips on top. Serve with lemon wedges.

30-Minute Supper

CALIFORNIA CHICKEN BURRITOS

30-Minute Supper

GRILLED SAGE PORK TENDERLOIN WITH CRANBERRY-APPLE RELISH

30-Minute Supper

PASTA WITH CHICKEN CACCIATORE SAUCE

30-Minute Supper

SAUTÉED FISH FILLETS WITH FRESH ITALIAN BREAD CRUMBS

GRILLED SAGE PORK TENDERLOIN WITH CRANBERRY-APPLE RELISH SERVES 4

Remove the thinner tail-end tenderloin pieces from the grill earlier to keep them from overcooking.

- **3 tablespoons plus 1/4 cup apple jelly**
- **2 tablespoons plus 1 teaspoon coarse grainy mustard**
- **2 tablespoons chopped fresh sage**
- **Cayenne pepper**
- **2 pork tenderloins (1 1/2 to 2 pounds total), cut crosswise into 1 1/2-inch pieces**
- **Salt and pepper**
- **1/2 cup dried cranberries**
- **1/2 teaspoon cider vinegar**
- **1 large Granny Smith apple, cored and diced**

1. Combine 3 tablespoons jelly, 2 tablespoons mustard, sage, and 1/4 teaspoon cayenne in medium bowl. Season pork with salt and pepper and toss in bowl with jelly-mustard mixture.

2. Combine cranberries, remaining 1/4 cup jelly, and vinegar in medium microwave-safe bowl. Cover with plastic, poke holes in plastic, and microwave on high power until cranberries are plump, about 1 minute. Stir in apple, remaining 1 teaspoon mustard, and 1/8 teaspoon cayenne and season with salt.

3. Grill pork over high heat until golden brown on exterior and slightly pink in center, about 3 1/2 minutes per side. Transfer pork to serving platter. Serve with cranberry-apple relish.

CALIFORNIA CHICKEN BURRITOS

SERVES 4

Garnish with sliced avocado, chopped romaine lettuce, and sour cream. If you don't have cooked rice on hand, you can use Uncle Ben's Ready Rice.

- **2 tablespoons vegetable oil**
- **1 (15.5-ounce) can black beans, drained**
- **1/2 cup water**
- **1 cup prepared chunky salsa, drained and juices reserved**
- **1 small canned chipotle chile, minced, plus 1 teaspoon adobo sauce**
- **3 garlic cloves, minced**
- **Salt and pepper**
- **2 cups cooked rice (see note above)**
- **1 1/2 cups shredded rotisserie chicken**
- **3 cups shredded cheddar cheese**
- **4 (10-inch) flour tortillas**

1. Adjust oven rack to middle position and heat oven to 450 degrees. Heat oil in large nonstick skillet over medium-high heat until just beginning to smoke. Add black beans, water, reserved salsa juices, chile, and adobo sauce and cook until liquid has evaporated and beans are soft, about 5 minutes. Add garlic and cook until fragrant, about 30 seconds. Using potato masher, mash beans lightly. Season with salt and pepper.

2. Place rice in medium microwave-safe bowl, cover with plastic wrap, poke holes in plastic, and microwave on high power until hot, about 90 seconds. Stir in salsa, chicken, and 1 1/2 cups cheddar. Spread one-quarter of black bean mixture down center of each tortilla, leaving 2-inch border at ends. Mound rice mixture on beans and fold tortillas to form burritos. Transfer to baking sheet, sprinkle with remaining 1 1/2 cups cheddar, and bake until cheese is bubbly, about 10 minutes. Serve.

SAUTÉED FISH FILLETS WITH FRESH ITALIAN BREAD CRUMBS SERVES 4

Use 3/4- to 1-inch-thick pieces of fish, each weighing about 6 ounces. This will allow you to cook all four pieces in one batch.

- **1/4 cup packed fresh parsley**
- **2 garlic cloves, minced**
- **1 slice hearty white sandwich bread, torn into 1-inch pieces**
- **4 tablespoons olive oil**
- **1 teaspoon grated zest and 3 tablespoons juice from 2 lemons**
- **Salt and pepper**
- **1/2 cup all-purpose flour**
- **4 boneless, skinless thick white fish fillets (see note above)**
- **1/4 cup water**
- **3 tablespoons unsalted butter**

1. Process parsley and garlic in food processor until minced. Add bread and pulse into fine crumbs. Cook crumbs with 1 tablespoon oil in large nonstick skillet over medium-high heat until browned, about 5 minutes. Stir in zest and season with salt and pepper. Transfer mixture to small bowl and wipe out skillet.

2. Place flour in shallow dish. Pat fish dry with paper towels, season with salt and pepper, dredge in flour, and shake to remove excess flour. Heat remaining 3 tablespoons oil in skillet over medium-high heat until shimmering. Cook fish, without moving, until golden brown, 3 to 4 minutes. Flip and cook until thickest part of fillets flakes easily, 2 to 3 minutes.

3. Transfer fillets to serving plate and tent with foil. Reduce heat to medium, add lemon juice and water, and use wooden spoon to scrape browned bits from bottom of pan. Simmer until thick and syrupy, about 4 minutes. Pour in accumulated juices from fish, whisk in butter, and adjust seasonings. Pour sauce over fish and sprinkle tops with seasoned crumbs. Serve.

PASTA WITH CHICKEN CACCIATORE SAUCE

SERVES 4 TO 6

To save time, chop the parsley and grate the cheese while the sauce is simmering.

- **4 tablespoons olive oil**
- **1 pound boneless, skinless chicken breasts, cut into 1/4-inch-thick strips**
- **Salt and pepper**
- **1 small onion, minced**
- **10 ounces white mushrooms, quartered**
- **4 garlic cloves, minced**
- **1/2 cup dry red wine**
- **1 (28-ounce) can diced tomatoes**
- **2 teaspoons minced fresh thyme**
- **1 pound penne pasta**
- **1/4 cup chopped fresh parsley**
- **1 cup grated Parmesan cheese**

1. Bring 4 quarts water to boil in large pot over high heat. Heat 2 tablespoons oil in large nonstick skillet over high heat until just beginning to smoke. Season chicken with salt and pepper and cook until no longer pink, about 3 minutes. Transfer chicken to plate.

2. Add remaining 2 tablespoons oil, onion, mushrooms, and 1/2 teaspoon salt to skillet and cook over medium-high heat until browned, 6 to 8 minutes. Add garlic and cook until fragrant, about 1 minute. Add wine, tomatoes, and thyme; increase heat to high and simmer until sauce thickens, about 7 minutes. Return chicken to sauce.

3. Meanwhile, add 1 tablespoon salt and pasta to boiling water and cook until al dente. Reserve 1/2 cup pasta cooking water, then drain pasta and return to pot. Add sauce and simmer over medium heat until hot, about 1 minute, adding reserved pasta water as needed. Off heat, stir in parsley and Parmesan. Adjust seasonings and serve.

Fresh Corn Side Dishes

A quick sauté transforms this summer staple into a standout.

I wasn't a fan of corn as a child, probably because the mushy, bland stuff my mom served was either drowning in cream or swimming in a pool of butter, tasting like anything but fresh corn. As an adult, I grew to love fresh corn on the cob, quickly boiled and lightly buttered, but it can get boring. I wanted to serve corn off the cob in dishes that were a bit more lively.

Removing corn from the cob isn't a difficult task, but many home cooks do a poor job of it. While a perfect "de-cobbing" would cleanly cleave every kernel from the cob, in the real world the knife usually cuts open the kernels, releasing (and wasting) the sweet "milk" inside and leaving part of the kernel behind. To capture every bit of sweetness from the cobs, I "milked" them after removing the kernels by scraping the back of the knife up and down each side of the cob. I then added the resulting milk to the kernels (getting anywhere from 1 to 2 tablespoons per cob).

Good summer corn is very sweet on its own, and I found many recipes for corn side dishes that simply called for raw corn cut fresh from the cob. But when I offered the raw corn to my tasters they rejected it as tough and starchy. I didn't want to cook the corn too much (and thus lose its fresh flavor), however, so I tried two quick-cooking options: blanching and sautéing. Tasters preferred the flavor of the sautéed corn, and the method allowed me to incorporate other flavors easily. With herbs, bacon, chiles, and citrus juice, these side dishes taste like fresh corn on the cob—only better.

–Keri Fisher

How Sweet It Is(n't)

While many varieties of fresh corn have been bred for maximum sweetness, you never know exactly how sweet corn is until you get it home. If your corn isn't as sweet as you like, add 1 to 2 teaspoons of sugar to the skillet with the corn.

GARDEN FRESH CORN

SERVES 4

Fresh garden herbs and zucchini make this a perfect end-of-summer dish. A variety of soft herbs is especially nice, but the recipe also works well with just one or two herbs. Mint would be a good addition.

- 1 tablespoon vegetable oil
- 2 small zucchini, diced
- 5 medium ears corn, prepared according to photos (about 3 cups kernels)
- 3 garlic cloves, minced
- 2 tablespoons minced fresh basil
- 1 tablespoon minced fresh chives
- 1 tablespoon minced fresh parsley
- 1 1/2 teaspoons lemon juice
- Salt and pepper

Heat oil in large skillet over medium-high heat until hot but not smoking. Add zucchini and cook until softened and browned at edges, about 3 minutes. Add corn and cook until deep yellow and softened, about 2 minutes. Add garlic and cook until fragrant, about 30 seconds. Off heat, stir in herbs, lemon juice, and salt and pepper to taste. Serve.

SMOKY SOUTHWESTERN CORN

SERVES 4

This spicy corn side dish goes perfectly with our Skirt Steak Fajitas (page 18).

- 1 tablespoon vegetable oil
- 1 small red onion, diced
- 1 medium red bell pepper, seeded and diced
- 5 medium ears corn, prepared according to photos (about 3 cups kernels)
- 1 teaspoon chopped canned chipotle chile in adobo sauce
- 3 tablespoons minced fresh cilantro
- 2 teaspoons lime juice
- Salt and pepper

Heat oil in large skillet over medium-high heat until hot but not smoking. Add onion and cook until softened and browned around edges, about 3 minutes. Add red pepper and cook until softened, about 1 minute. Add corn and cook until deep yellow and softened, about 2 minutes. Off heat, stir in chipotle, cilantro, lime juice, and salt and pepper to taste. Serve.

SPICY CREAMED CORN WITH BACON AND SCALLIONS

SERVES 4

If you don't have shallots, use one small red onion instead.

- 6 slices bacon, chopped
- 3 medium shallots, minced
- 5 medium ears corn, prepared according to photos (about 3 cups kernels)
- 2/3 cup heavy cream
- Pinch cayenne pepper
- 2 medium scallions, sliced thin
- Salt and pepper

Cook bacon in large skillet over medium-high heat until crisp, 8 to 10 minutes. Transfer bacon to plate lined with paper towel and pour off all but 1 tablespoon fat from skillet. Add shallots and cook until soft, about 2 minutes. Add corn and cook until deep yellow and softened, about 2 minutes. Add cream and cayenne pepper and cook until reduced and thickened, about 2 minutes. Toss in scallions and bacon and season with salt and pepper to taste. Serve.

FRESH CORN WITH SAUSAGE AND SAGE

SERVES 4

For more maple flavor, try using maple breakfast sausage. Even if your corn isn't super-sweet, you probably won't need to add sugar to this recipe; the maple syrup will compensate.

- 1 tablespoon vegetable oil
- 5 ounces crumbled breakfast sausage (about 3/4 cup)
- 1 medium red bell pepper, seeded and diced
- 5 medium ears corn, prepared according to photos (about 3 cups kernels)
- 1 teaspoon chopped fresh sage
- 1 tablespoon chopped fresh thyme
- 2 tablespoons maple syrup
- Salt and pepper

Heat oil in large skillet over medium-high heat until hot but not smoking. Cook sausage until lightly browned with some pink spots remaining, about 2 minutes. Add red pepper and cook until softened, about 1 minute. Add corn and cook until deep yellow and softened, about 2 minutes. Off heat, stir in sage, thyme, maple syrup, and salt and pepper to taste. Serve.

Kitchen Wisdom

LEND ME YOUR EARS

To get every bit of sweet summer goodness from fresh corn, we cut the kernels from the cobs, then use the back of a knife to scrape all the milk from the cobs.

1. Cut the kernels from the ears.
2. Run the back of the knife down each corn cob to scrape away the "milk."

Light cooking keeps summer corn super-sweet and fresh.

The Best Steak Fajitas

My husband and I love the skirt steak fajitas at our local Mexican restaurant. We have tried to make them at home, but they never taste right, and the steak is tough and chewy. Can you help us? –Renee Hinz, Altamont, Ill.

The success of restaurant fajitas is partly due to the rich beefy flavor of skirt steak, a cut located between the abdomen and chest cavity of the steer. But skirt steak can be tough if not handled properly. Many recipes "skirt" this problem by calling for flank steak. Although more tender, flank steak can't match the meaty flavor of a well-marbled skirt steak. Could I make skirt steak as tender as flank steak? Along the way I wanted to develop a superior marinade, too.

Lime juice is the key flavor in any fajita marinade. However, despite what many "experts" claim, I found that lime juice doesn't tenderize meat. Yes, it adds flavor, but its acidity can actually make the outside of the meat mushy. As for other marinade flavors, tasters particularly liked Worcestershire sauce (which enhanced the meatiness of the steak), cumin (for its earthy flavor), a fresh chile, and brown sugar.

But I wasn't having much luck on the tenderness front until I added soy sauce to my marinade. Not only did the soy sauce add great flavor, but it also seemed to make the meat slightly more tender and especially juicy.

Why was the soy sauce so successful? After doing some research, I realized that it was acting like a brine—a salt-water solution that helps meat hold on to its natural moisture and makes it more tender. Now my marinade tasted great and the meat was slightly more tender, but could I do even better?

I tried pounding the steaks with a mallet to help break down tough fibers, but pounding made the steaks too thin for fajitas. Pricking the steaks with a fork (to break down the muscle fibers) proved to be a better route to tenderness. And, as a bonus, it also helped the marinade penetrate and flavor the meat in only 30 minutes.

I think the best fajitas are grilled, and peppers and onions are a must as accompaniments. Grilling both meat and vegetables was easy enough: First, I built a hot fire in one half of the grill and grilled the onions and peppers. Once the vegetables were cooked, I slid them to the cool part of the grill and seared the steaks over the hot coals. To make sure the steaks retained as much moisture as possible, I found it necessary to let the grilled meat rest for five minutes. While the meat rested, I toasted the tortillas over the dying coals.

My fajita recipe seemed perfect, except for one small thing: The smoke from the grill was drowning out the lime flavor. Adding more lime juice to my marinade didn't help. But what if I marinated the steaks a second time—after grilling, as they rested? Sure enough, drizzling the steaks with some fresh marinade did the trick. My fajitas are as tender and as flavorful as any I've ever eaten in a restaurant. I hope you agree.

–Katie Henderson

High-heat grilling and a double marinade for the steak are what give our fajitas their bright, bold flavor.

SKIRT STEAK FAJITAS

SERVES 4

Toast the cumin in a dry skillet over medium heat until fragrant (about 1 minute), then remove the pan from the heat so the cumin won't scorch. Serve the fajitas as is or with salsa, shredded cheese, and/or sour cream. To use flank steak instead of skirt steak, see page 31.

- **1/2 cup lime juice**
- **1/4 cup vegetable oil**
- **3 garlic cloves, minced**
- **2 tablespoons soy sauce**
- **2 teaspoons ground cumin, toasted (see above note)**
- **2 teaspoons light brown sugar**
- **1 jalapeño chile, seeded and chopped fine**
- **1 tablespoon minced fresh cilantro**
- **2 skirt steaks, each about 3/4 pound**
- **2 large onions, cut into 1/2-inch slices**
- **3 large bell peppers (1 red and 2 green), tops and bottoms removed, then cut in half lengthwise and seeded**
- **12 (6-inch) flour tortillas**

1. Whisk lime juice, 2 tablespoons oil, garlic, soy sauce, cumin, brown sugar, and chile in bowl. Transfer 1/4 cup marinade to bowl, add cilantro, and set aside. Prick steaks with fork about 50 times on each side, then cut each steak in half crosswise. Place steaks in large zipper-lock plastic bag, pour in marinade without cilantro, seal bag, and refrigerate at least 30 minutes or up to 2 hours. Remove steaks from bag, pat dry with paper towels, and discard marinade in bag.

2. Light large chimney starter filled with charcoal briquettes (about 100 coals) and burn until coals are covered with fine gray ash. Pour coals into pile on one side of grill. Set cooking grate in place, cover, and let grill heat up 5 minutes. Scrape cooking grate clean.

3. Meanwhile, brush onions and peppers with remaining 2 tablespoons oil. Grill onions and peppers, turning occasionally, until charred and softened, 8 to 12 minutes (peppers will cook more quickly). Move vegetables to cool side of grill. Grill steak directly over coals until seared on both sides but still pink in center, 4 to 6 minutes per side. Transfer steak and vegetables to serving platter, pour cilantro marinade over, cover with foil, and let rest 5 minutes.

4. Meanwhile, toast tortillas over hot fire, about 10 seconds per side. Wrap in aluminum foil to keep warm. Slice steak as shown in photo below and cut vegetables into finger-length pieces. Serve immediately with warm tortillas.

SKIRT STEAK FAJITAS ON A GAS GRILL

Follow recipe for Skirt Steak Fajitas through step 1. Heat all burners on high for 15 minutes. Scrape cooking grate clean. Grill vegetables, with lid down, as directed in step 3. Turn off one burner, then move vegetables to cool side of grill. Proceed as directed, grilling steak on hot side of grill.

Kitchen Wisdom

THE RIGHT SLICE

Once the steak has rested, slice the meat across the grain into thin pieces.

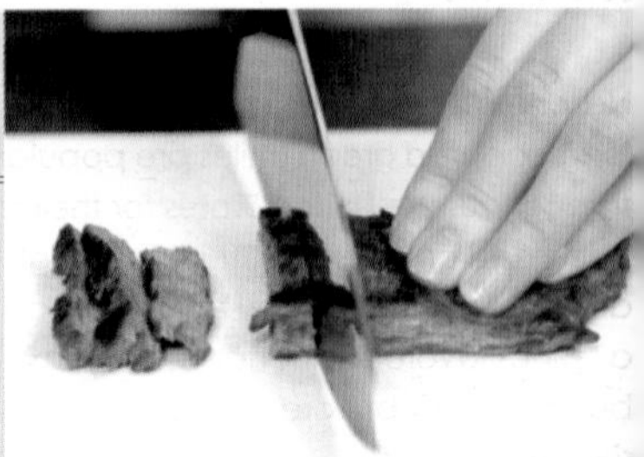

Getting to Know Fresh Chiles

Fresh chiles not only have varying heat levels, but they also have different flavor profiles. We picked up 12 varieties and tasted them in tomato salsa. Listed below are tasting notes in addition to a heat rating of 1 to 5 peppers for each chile (zero is equivalent to a green bell pepper, and 5 is the hottest).

Jalapeño

OLD RELIABLE

The jalapeño, perhaps the best-known chile, is named after Xalapa (or Jalapa), the capital city of the state of Veracruz, Mexico. These emerald green chiles have a moderate heat and a "light, grassy" flavor, with a "bitter" quality "similar to green bell pepper."

Red Fresno

JALAPEÑO LOOK-ALIKE

These bright, cone-shaped chiles are often mistaken for red jalapeños. Their flavor is "sweet-sour," with a "sneaky heat" and a "smoky, musky aftertaste." Their thin walls and tender skin make them nice in raw preparations, such as salsas and salads.

Poblano

PERFECT FOR STUFFING

These large, blackish green chiles are most often associated with *chiles rellenos*, the Mexican version of stuffed peppers. Their heat is "tame, but noticeable," like "a bell pepper on steroids." Served raw, their flavor is "vegetal and earthy," but it sweetens with cooking.

Long Green

JOLLY GREEN GIANT

Long and wrinkled, these supermarket staples are sometimes mislabeled "pepperoncini" or "Anaheim" but are most closely related to the New Mexico green chile. Their flavor is "herby, with a sharp bite" and a "mild, building heat." Perfect for a chunky tomato salsa or salsa verde.

Habanero

THE KING OF CHILES

Considered the hottest of the hot, these lantern-shaped chiles have just as much flavor as they do heat. They possess a "pungent floral aroma," a "pear-like" taste, and an "intense, throat-tingling heat." Use sparingly in cooked dishes or add to marinades and salsas.

Scotch Bonnet

TUTTI-FRUTTI

Named for its resemblance to a Scottish toque, this relative of the habanero is native to the Caribbean. The base for the hottest of hot sauces, these chiles are "incredibly aromatic and fruity," garnering comparisons to "peaches," "melons," and "papayas." Use sparingly in cooked dishes or add to marinades and salsas.

Thai

BIRD'S BEAK

These tiny, multicolored chiles may look ornamental, but they mean business. Sometimes labeled bird or Thai bird chiles because of their resemblance to a bird's beak, these chiles have a flavor similar to that of "black peppercorns" and a heat that "hits quick and lasts long." Use sparingly in cooked dishes.

Cherry Pepper

ANTIPASTO PEPPER

These small, Ferrari-red, spherical chiles are also known as Hungarian cherry peppers. A common addition to antipasto platters, these chiles can be either hot or sweet and are often found pickled and stuffed. Their flavor is "definitely fruity," with a "lemon-lime aftertaste" and a "nice, round heat."

Anaheim

SO-CAL FAVORITE

Named after the California city, these long, tapered green chiles are popular throughout the United States for their mild spice and crisp texture. They are "high in acidity," with a "lemony bitterness" and a "pine-flavored" aftertaste. They can be eaten raw but are often stuffed and roasted or fried.

Serrano

FRESH AND CLEAN

Often mistaken for jalapeños, these chiles can be distinguished by their slender shape and brazen heat. They have a "very fresh, clean flavor," with hints of "grapefruit" and "tomato." Serrano chiles pack quite a punch, but the heat comes and goes quickly. Use raw in salsa or cooked in chilis and curries.

Banana

LONG AND LEAN

These yellowish green chiles, referred to as banana peppers because of their shape and length, may also be called Hungarian wax peppers. Their heat is "high and nasal," like "white peppercorns or cinnamon," and their flavor is "waxy, like a cucumber," with a "bitter, immature finish." Use raw in salsa or stuff and roast.

Dutch

MILD AND MELONY

Also known as Holland chiles, these long red chiles are thin fleshed, with a nice fresh crunch. Their flavor is "mild and sweet" and "melon-like," with a "vinegary bite." Use them raw, or roast for a sweeter flavor.

Firecracker Chicken

My uncle was famous for his firecracker chicken. He'd marinate boneless chicken breasts in a mash of chile peppers from his garden and then fry them up until they were golden and crunchy. He's not with us anymore, and he didn't leave us a recipe. Have you ever heard of anything like this? –Harry Martins, Springfield, Mo.

Our spicy firecracker sauce pulls triple duty as a marinade, as part of the batter, and as a finishing sauce for these crunchy strips of fried chicken.

All recipes for firecracker chicken have one thing in common—tongue-tingling heat capable of satisfying any chilehead's cravings for fire. Like your uncle's version, most recipes marinate boneless chicken breasts in hot sauce; the chicken is then breaded, pan-fried, and served with more hot sauce.

My first question was simple: Did I have to make my own hot sauce, or could I just use bottled sauce? Commercial hot sauce wasn't bad, but my tasters wanted something more fresh and interesting, like what your uncle made.

The recipes I tested agreed on the chiles, but there was little consensus on the other base ingredients for the spicy marinade/finishing sauce. After testing numerous condiments in my fridge, I settled on an unlikely foundation for my sauce. Yellow (aka "hot dog") mustard had a bright flavor and color, a welcome pungency, and a consistency that helped it cling nicely to the fried chicken. As for the spice, tasters liked habanero chiles for their unapologetic burn, but they wanted a more complex heat. I added pickled banana peppers (plus some of their pickling juices) for a nice acidic tang and dry mustard for its sinus-clearing heat.

It was time to move on to the chicken. In classic fried chicken, the coating adheres to the cut-up chicken parts because the skin is very tacky. But I was using strips of boneless, skinless breasts and encountered problems from the start. To fortify the coating, I used a method the test kitchen developed for our buttermilk fried chicken recipe and incorporated some of the liquid (in this case, the mustard sauce) into the flour. The sauce gave the flour the texture of wet sand, so it stuck to the chicken in irregular clumps. When fried, this lumpy texture created thick, crispy pockets of coating that my tasters loved. Unfortunately, the coating still wasn't sticking to the chicken.

I eventually figured out the problem. The chicken had soaked up enough of the firecracker marinade to cause it to steam when it hit the hot oil; the extra liquid steamed the coating right off. Two things helped—letting the coated chicken dry out in the refrigerator for 15 minutes and adding baking powder and cornstarch to the coating (to absorb moisture and encourage browning). The coating was now more clingy but still not quite clingy enough.

The proteins in eggs can "glue" coatings onto countless foods, so I dried the marinated chicken with paper towels, dipped it in beaten eggs, and then rolled it in the moistened flour coating. Sure enough, this chicken fried up beautifully, with a crispy, crunchy coating that adhered to the chicken. But now my tasters didn't like the "eggy flavor" this method added!

Using just the egg whites reduced the egg flavor, but the whites were so thin that they didn't hold the coating. I mulled over different ways to thicken the egg whites before it hit me—why not just beat the egg whites? The foamy egg whites held on to a ton of coating. My firecracker chicken finally packed a crunch—and a kick—that was worthy of its name. **–Jeremy Sauer**

How to Make CRUNCHY CHICKEN

1. Dip the chicken in the foamy egg whites to anchor the coating.
2. Pat the moistened coating mixture onto the chicken to ensure adhesion.
3. Let the breaded chicken strips rest in the refrigerator for 15 minutes and then pan-fry them in oil until very crisp.

SOME LIKE IT HOT We use four elements of heat—dry mustard, bottled mustard, pickled peppers, and fresh chiles—to give our Firecracker Sauce its spicy kick.

FIRECRACKER CHICKEN

SERVES 6

If you really like spicy foods, try adding another habanero or two; if you are spice-averse, substitute jalapeños. We like to drizzle the sauce over the chicken strips just before serving, but the sauce is just as good served on the side for dipping.

Firecracker Sauce

- 1/2 cup sliced pickled banana peppers, chopped fine, plus 1/4 cup pickling liquid
- 1/4 cup lemon juice
- 1/4 cup vegetable oil
- 1/4 cup yellow mustard
- 3 tablespoons dry mustard
- 2 tablespoons chili sauce
- 2 tablespoons brown sugar
- 3 garlic cloves, minced
- 1 habanero chile, minced
- 4 scallions, sliced thin

Chicken

- 6 boneless, skinless chicken breasts (about 2 1/2 pounds), trimmed
- 2 cups all-purpose flour
- 1/2 cup cornstarch
- 1 tablespoon salt
- 1 teaspoon baking powder
- 4 large egg whites
- 1 cup vegetable oil

1. For the sauce: Whisk ingredients together in large bowl.

2. For the chicken: Cover chicken breasts with plastic wrap and pound lightly with meat mallet until about ½ inch thick. Slice breasts in half lengthwise and transfer to large zipper-lock storage bag. Add ¼ cup Firecracker Sauce to bag, seal, and gently squeeze bag to coat chicken with sauce. Refrigerate for 30 minutes (or up to 2 hours).

3. Meanwhile, in large bowl, combine flour, cornstarch, salt, and baking powder. Add 6 tablespoons Firecracker Sauce and, using hands, combine until mixture resembles coarse, wet sand.

4. In another large bowl, whisk egg whites until foamy. Remove chicken from marinade and pat dry with paper towels. Working with one strip at a time, dip chicken in egg whites and transfer to flour mixture, pressing lightly to adhere. Place chicken pieces on wire rack set on rimmed baking sheet and refrigerate 15 minutes (or up to 4 hours).

5. Adjust oven rack to middle position and heat oven to 200 degrees. Heat oil in large skillet over medium-high heat until shimmering. Carefully place half of chicken strips in oil and fry until golden brown and cooked through, 2 to 4 minutes per side. Transfer to baking sheet lined with paper towels and place in warm oven. Repeat with remaining chicken strips. Transfer chicken to platter, drizzle with remaining sauce, and serve.

The American Table: Southern Fried Chicken

Few foods are more closely associated with American cooking, especially Southern cooking, than fried chicken. Almost every cuisine around the world has some version of this dish, but what makes Southern fried chicken unique is the combination of herbs and spices and the thick, crunchy coating.

Some sources suggest that Scottish immigrants to the South brought with them the tradition of frying chicken. As the dish grew in popularity, so did arguments about its proper preparation. Should shortening, bacon drippings, lard, or oil be used as the frying medium? Should a batter or seasoned flour be used to coat the chicken? Should the chicken be deep-fried (that is, submerged in fat as it cooks) or pan-fried (with the fat coming halfway up the sides of each piece)?

The basic fried chicken recipe has spawned countless variations, everything from firecracker (with its spicy sauce) to Maryland fried chicken, which is served with a brown pan gravy.

Perhaps America's most famous fried chicken recipe is Kentucky fried chicken. Harland Sanders created his famous recipe in the 1930s. It relies on a secret blend of 11 herbs and spices and became so popular at his restaurant in Corbin, Ky., that the governor awarded Sanders the honorary title of Colonel.

The Colonel's big innovation was the use of a pressure cooker, which cut cooking time from half an hour to just minutes. When his restaurant was forced to close 1952, the Colonel (already in his 60s) hit the road and began selling his recipe to other restaurants. In 1964, the Colonel had more than 600 franchised outlets and sold his interest for $2 million, not only earning him fame and fortune but guaranteeing that fried chicken would become the most famous recipe from the American South.

What to Do with Leftovers: Firecracker Chicken Salad

The Asian flavors and subtle heat of this salad will wake up your taste buds.

With upward of 15 test cooks lined up for a taste of our Firecracker Chicken, it wasn't often that we had leftovers. But when you're not cooking for an entire test kitchen, what's the best way to use up yesterday's fried chicken? Our favorite preparation morphs our super-spicy Firecracker Chicken into a restaurant favorite—Chinese-inspired chicken salad.

To transform our searing Firecracker Sauce into salad dressing, we added sour cream, which gave it body and tamed the heat. This thick dressing needs sturdy lettuce—we like crisp, cool romaine best. To balance the heat, we added sweet-tangy mandarin orange segments. Fresh bell pepper and crispy chow mein noodles offered a welcome crunch. As for the chicken, we found it best to reheat the leftovers in a 350-degree oven just to recrisp the coating. From there, we chopped the chicken (to stretch a small amount of leftover chicken) and tossed it with lettuce for a substantial (and spicy) suppertime salad. **–Jeremy Sauer**

FIRECRACKER CHICKEN SALAD SERVES 4

If you like really spicy foods, add some minced fresh chile to this quick salad.

- 4 strips Firecracker Chicken
- 1/4 cup Firecracker Sauce
- 2 tablespoons sour cream
- 1 head romaine lettuce, torn into 1/2-inch pieces
- 1 red bell pepper, seeded and chopped fine
- 1 (15-ounce) can mandarin orange segments, drained
- 1 cup chow mein noodles
- 4 scallions, sliced thin

1. Adjust oven rack to middle position and heat oven to 350 degrees. Place chicken strips on wire rack set on rimmed baking sheet and bake for 10 to 15 minutes.

2. Meanwhile, whisk together Firecracker Sauce and sour cream.

3. Combine lettuce, bell pepper, oranges, chow mein noodles, and scallions in large bowl. Add sauce mixture and toss to combine. Remove chicken strips from oven and chop into 1-inch pieces. Divide salad among plates and top with crispy chicken pieces. Serve.

Easy Pat-in-the-Pan Pie Dough

Lose your rolling pin, your pie weights, and your fear—forever.

At a Glance

NO-FEAR PIE CRUST

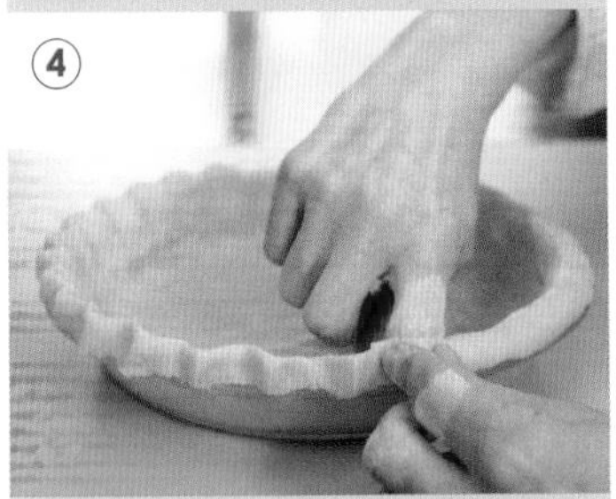

1. Hold the pie plate up to the light to check the thickness of the dough; it should be translucent, not opaque. Pay attention to the curved edges. **2.** Roll the reserved dough into three 8-inch ropes. Arrange the ropes around the perimeter of the pie plate, leaving small (about 1-inch) gaps between them. **3.** Squeeze the ropes together. **4.** Create a fluted edge, dipping your fingers in flour if the dough is sticky.

When it comes to frustration, few tasks can rival that of making pie dough. The rules are both precise (for optimal flakiness the fat must be very cold and cut into the flour just so) and maddeningly vague (recipes typically call for 4 to 6 tablespoons of ice water, or more as needed—whatever that means). I can barely draw a circle, much less roll one from raw, cold pie dough. And moving a floppy disk of pastry off the counter and into a waiting pie plate is easier said than done. A pie shell that shrinks in the oven (despite being covered with weights) is the final indignity. There are so many places that pie dough can go wrong, no wonder most cooks throw in the pastry cloth and buy a prebaked pie shell.

The problem with this solution is flavor. Most store-bought crusts are made with shortening, not butter, and offer nothing other than flaky texture. I wanted a totally reliable recipe for a pie shell that baked up flaky and full of buttery flavor.

Of course, I'm not the first baker in search of pie-pastry nirvana. Many recipes call for a pat-in-the-pan crust (the dough is shaped right in the pan, like a graham cracker crust), and I decided to give it a try.

After making more than 20 pat-in-the-pan crusts, I was discouraged. Without exception, my tests yielded dough that was either too sticky or too stiff to press into a pie plate thinly and evenly, and none baked up flaky enough to replace the store-bought standby. You can imagine my surprise when my 23rd test—a crust with cream cheese—fooled several pie snobs in the kitchen. They had assumed this good-looking, flaky crust was made with a rolling pin, not my humble fingers.

With the heel of your hand, press our easy-to-handle dough into a pie plate. Use a glass pie plate so you can easily judge the thickness of the dough.

Why was cream cheese so successful? It turns out that acidity promotes tenderness. But not any old acidic ingredient will work. Vinegar made a sour crust, and sour cream and buttermilk made the dough too sticky. Dense cream cheese made the dough easier to manipulate. I found this dough could handle a whopping 12 tablespoons of fat, almost twice as much as a standard pie dough, and it didn't require ice water. It was easy, it was flaky, and it tasted great.

This dough also relies on an unusual mixing method. Softened butter and cream cheese are beaten together and then mixed with flour, sugar, and salt. The fat in the cream cheese coats the particles of flour and prevents toughness, a problem in many crusts. This recipe has one more unexpected benefit: There's no need to hold the crust in place with foil and pie weights. As long as the dough is chilled when it goes into the oven, it won't shrink.

–Stephanie Alleyne

NO-FEAR PIE CRUST

MAKES ONE 9-INCH PIE SHELL

The pastry can be pressed into the pie plate and refrigerated for up to 2 days or double-wrapped in plastic and frozen for up to 1 month. Once baked and cooled, the shell can be wrapped tightly in plastic and stored at room temperature for up to 1 day.

- **1¼ cups all-purpose flour**
- **2 tablespoons sugar**
- **¼ teaspoon salt**
- **8 tablespoons (1 stick) unsalted butter, softened but still cool**
- **2 ounces cream cheese, softened but still cool**

1. Lightly coat 9-inch Pyrex pie plate with cooking spray. Whisk flour, sugar, and salt together in bowl.

2. With electric mixer at medium-high speed, beat butter and cream cheese in large bowl, stopping once or twice to scrape down beater and sides of bowl, until completely homogenous, about 2 minutes. Add flour mixture and combine on medium-low until mixture resembles coarse cornmeal, about 20 seconds. Scrape down sides of bowl. Increase mixer speed to medium-high and beat until dough begins to form large clumps, about 30 seconds. Reserve 3 tablespoons of dough. Turn remaining dough onto lightly floured surface, gather into ball, and flatten into 6-inch disk. Transfer disk to greased pie plate.

3. Press dough evenly over bottom of pie plate toward sides, using heel of your hand. Hold plate up to light to ensure that dough is evenly distributed (see photo 1 at left). With your fingertips, continue to work dough over bottom of plate and up sides until evenly distributed.

4. On floured surface, roll reserved dough into 12-inch rope. Divide into three pieces, roll each piece into 8-inch rope, and form fluted edge (photos 2 through 4). Wrap in plastic and refrigerate at least 1 hour.

5. Adjust oven rack to middle position and heat oven to 325 degrees. Lightly prick bottom of crust with fork. Bake until golden brown, 35 to 40 minutes. Cool on wire rack. (If large bubbles form, wait until crust is fully baked, then gently press on bubbles with kitchen towel. Bubbles will settle as crust cools.)

Raspberry Chiffon Pie

I like the ease of a no-bake raspberry chiffon pie, and the creamy pink filling looks great, but the recipes I've tried never taste like fresh berries. Any ideas? –Rachel Sullivan, Meredith, N.H.

At its best, raspberry chiffon is light, billowy, and creamy. Rarely, however, is it intensely flavored. That's because the filling doesn't contain much fruit—it's mostly whipped egg whites and/or heavy cream, sugar, and gelatin (which allows the filling to set, without baking, in the refrigerator). Chiffon pies that rely on potent ingredients, such as lemon or coconut, can be flavorful, but after eating a half-dozen of my raspberry chiffon pies my tasters were not very excited. The pink pies were pretty, but they tasted more like sweet foam than fruit.

My first thought was to add more raspberries. From these tests, I learned that the best recipes cooked the berries and sugar into a puree, which was strained to remove the seeds. Why not just add more of this puree? The solution was not so simple. Tasters preferred fillings made with gelatin-stabilized whipped cream to those made with gelatin-stabilized egg whites (the latter were billowy but not really creamy and smooth). Unfortunately, the cream filling could only "hold" so much fruit puree before it would collapse and refuse to set.

How could I help stiffen the chiffon filling? More gelatin helped (3 tablespoons was ideal), but there was a limit—I didn't want a bouncy Jell-O pie. A little cream cheese thickened the whipped cream and added more richness. In the end, these measures allowed me to add 1/3 cup of raspberry puree to the filling. A good start, but my tasters wanted more fruit flavor.

Replacing the usual plain gelatin with raspberry-flavored gelatin bumped up the fruit flavor and gave the filling a vibrant color, but I was now officially out of ideas. My filling had better flavor than most recipes, but it wasn't what I would call intense. Then inspiration struck.

Many diners serve no-bake berry pies. The filling is basically sweetened fruit thickened with pectin (the stuff used to turn fruit into jam). Frankly, I think these pies are too jammy and sweet, especially when you get a fat slice, but what if I used this kind of filling in a thin base layer for my chiffon pie?

This idea worked perfectly. I cooked frozen berries (one-quarter the price of fresh berries) until they started to break down and then added the pectin, followed by the sugar. The mixture thickened beautifully and the flavor was intense. I set aside some of this smooth puree to flavor the chiffon filling and poured the rest (with fresh fruit added for texture and flavor) into a prebaked pie shell. After about 10 minutes on the counter, this jam-like mixture set into a thin, dark red layer of pure raspberry flavor.

Next I prepared the chiffon filling (with the reserved berry mixture), spooned it over the fruit layer, and let the gelatin work its magic in the refrigerator. Three hours later, I had a perfectly set, sliceable pie with great color and intense raspberry flavor. With a crown of lightly sweetened whipped cream, my pie finally tasted as good as it looked.

–Stephanie Alleyne

RASPBERRY CHIFFON PIE

SERVES 8 TO 10

The heavy cream must be ice cold; if not, it won't hold stiff peaks, no matter how long or hard you beat it. Soften the cream cheese at room temperature; the microwave will cause the cheese to separate.

Fruit Layer

- 1 (12-ounce) bag frozen raspberries (2 cups)
- 3 tablespoons pectin (Sure-Jell)
- 1 1/2 cups sugar
- Pinch salt
- 1 cup fresh raspberries
- 1 (9-inch) pie shell, baked and cooled (see page 22)

Chiffon Layer

- 3 tablespoons raspberry-flavored gelatin
- 3 tablespoons boiling water
- 3 ounces cream cheese, softened
- 1 cup heavy cream, chilled

Whipped Cream Topping

- 1 1/4 cups heavy cream, chilled
- 2 tablespoons sugar

1. For the fruit layer: Cook frozen berries in medium saucepan over medium-high heat, stirring occasionally, until berries begin to give up their juice, about 3 minutes. Stir in pectin and bring to full boil, stirring constantly. Stir in sugar and salt and return to full boil. Cook, stirring constantly, until slightly thickened, about 2 minutes. Pour through fine-mesh strainer into medium bowl, pressing on solids to extract as much puree as possible. Scrape puree off underside of strainer into bowl.

2. Transfer 1/3 cup raspberry puree to small bowl and cool to room temperature. Gently fold fresh raspberries into remaining puree. Spread fruit mixture evenly over bottom of pie shell and set aside.

3. For the chiffon layer: Dissolve gelatin in boiling water in large bowl. Add cream cheese and reserved 1/3 cup raspberry puree and beat with electric mixer on high speed, scraping down sides of bowl once or twice, until smooth, about 2 minutes. Add 1 cup cream and beat on medium-low until incorporated, about 30 seconds. Scrape down bowl. Beat on high speed until cream holds stiff peaks, 1 to 2 minutes. Spread evenly over fruit in pie shell. Cover pie with plastic wrap. Refrigerate until set, at least 3 hours or up to 2 days.

4. For the whipped cream topping: When ready to serve, beat 1 1/4 cups cream and sugar to stiff peaks. Spread or pipe over chilled filling. Serve.

Two Layers, Two Thickeners

FOR THE FRUIT LAYER

For the bottom layer, we used Sure-Jell (pectin) to achieve a concentrated raspberry flavor and texture. There are two formulations of Sure-Jell. We found that the original formula (sold in the bright yellow box) made the smoothest, thickest bottom layer of fruit.

FOR THE CHIFFON LAYER

A few tablespoons of raspberry gelatin made for great stability and color in the creamy chiffon layer and reinforced the berry flavor.

This raspberry pie is creamy, light, and packed with fruit flavor.

Kitchen Know-How
A BETTER WAY TO STUFF PEPPERS

1. Cut each pepper in half through the stem end to create two shallow boats. Discard the core and seeds.
2. When ready to bake, unwrap the stuffed pepper halves, cover the filling with foil, and poke several holes in the foil to allow excess liquid to evaporate.
3. Place the pepper halves foil side down over the vents on the slotted top of a broiler pan.

Stuffed Peppers from the Freezer

Stuffed peppers are often soggy and tasteless, and freezing them only makes matters worse. We wanted our stuffed peppers to freeze well and to taste even better.

Stuffed peppers don't freeze well. Freezing dulls the flavor of the filling and makes the peppers mushy (the water in the peppers expands as it freezes, causing the cell walls, which give the pepper structure, to rupture). I solved the flavor problem by adding potent ingredients like sausage, Parmesan cheese, and fresh herbs to the filling. To repair the peppers' mushy consistency, I thought I might be able to make the freezer's softening power work for me and eliminate the usual step of blanching the peppers before stuffing them. After conducting side-by-side tests, I concluded that you can either blanch the peppers or you can freeze them, but you can't do both. For my freezer recipe, blanching was out.

Excessive oven time and moisture were my next big challenges. I found that baking the frozen peppers straight from the freezer was the best way to preserve their flavor and texture, but the filling was taking two hours to reach a safe temperature, by which time the peppers were swimming in a sea of their own juices. Splitting the peppers through the stem (instead of lopping off the top) halved the cooking time and made them more stable, but they still needed to be elevated above their cooking juices. Baking my shallow stuffed-pepper "boats" on a broiler pan let most of the pepper juice drain away, but some remained trapped in the filling. I found that piercing each pepper several times with a fork allowed this last bit of excess moisture to drain.

My peppers were better, but now tasters complained (rightfully so) about the tough pepper skin. Trying to mimic the soft, toasty sweetness of roasted red peppers, I made a new batch in which I brushed the pepper skins with oil, covered the filling side with foil to hold in the filling, and roasted the peppers, skin side up, in a 450-degree oven. In only 30 minutes, the skin and flesh of the peppers were browned and tender. Since I was now baking the stuffed peppers upside down, I found that it was most effective to poke the drainage holes in the foil covers rather than the peppers themselves.

I had won over all the test kitchen skeptics who doubted that stuffed peppers could be this good, and a final layer of gooey melted cheese was just the right finishing touch for this resuscitated classic.

–Cali Rich

A rich filling with ground beef, Italian sausage, and two kinds of cheese enlivens this summer classic.

FROM-THE-FREEZER STUFFED PEPPERS

SERVES 4 TO 6

If you don't have leftover rice on hand, we recommend Uncle Ben's Ready Rice. We prefer sweet red peppers in this recipe; green peppers, while traditional, were too bitter. Ground turkey can be substituted for the beef.

Peppers and Stuffing

- 1 tablespoon olive oil
- 1 medium onion, chopped fine
- 8 ounces ground beef, preferably 85 percent lean
- 4 ounces hot or sweet Italian sausage, casings removed
- Salt and pepper
- 4 garlic cloves, minced
- 2 cups leftover cooked rice
- 1 (14.5-ounce) can diced tomatoes, drained
- 1 cup shredded mozzarella cheese
- 1/2 cup grated Parmesan cheese
- 3 tablespoons chopped fresh parsley
- 4 medium red bell peppers, cut in half through stem end (stem left intact), cored, and seeded

For Serving

- 2 tablespoons olive oil
- Salt and pepper
- 1 cup shredded mozzarella cheese

1. For the peppers: Heat oil in large skillet over medium heat until shimmering. Cook onion until softened and beginning to brown, about 5 minutes. Increase heat to medium-high and add beef, sausage, ½ teaspoon salt, and ¼ teaspoon pepper; cook, breaking meat into small pieces with wooden spoon, until meat begins to brown, 6 to 8 minutes. Add garlic and cook until fragrant, about 30 seconds. Drain mixture in colander for 1 minute.

2. Transfer meat mixture to large bowl and mix with rice, tomatoes, mozzarella, Parmesan, parsley, ½ teaspoon salt, and ¼ teaspoon pepper. Refrigerate until well chilled, at least 20 minutes.

3. Spoon filling evenly into bell peppers. Wrap each pepper with 2 layers of plastic wrap and 1 layer of foil. Place in baking dish and freeze until firm. Transfer to zipper-lock plastic bag and freeze up to 2 months.

4. When ready to serve: Adjust oven rack to middle position and heat oven to 450 degrees. Cut 8 pieces foil large enough to just cover stuffing in peppers, and spray with cooking spray. Unwrap peppers and cover filling sides with new foil squares. Using skewer, poke several holes through foil. Place peppers, foil side down, over vents of slotted broiler-pan top set over broiler-pan bottom. Brush peppers with oil and season with salt and pepper to taste. Bake until peppers are spotty brown, 30 to 35 minutes. Flip peppers filling side up, remove foil, and sprinkle with mozzarella. Bake until cheese is melted, about 5 minutes. Let rest 5 minutes before serving.

FROM-THE-FREEZER STUFFED PEPPERS WITH WHITE BEANS

SERVES 4 TO 6

In step 1, omit beef and sausage. Cook onion, salt, and pepper until onion is golden brown, about 7 minutes. Add garlic and cook until fragrant. Do not drain. Stir in one 15-ounce can drained and rinsed cannellini beans. Stir into rice mixture.

Grilled Potato Salad

Grilled potato salad that's worth the effort.

Dress this salad twice—once when the vegetables come off the grill (and can soak up flavors) and again right before serving.

Smoky grilled potatoes dressed in a highly seasoned vinaigrette are a relative newcomer to America's grilling repertoire, but they are a worthy addition. Unfortunately, it takes a lot of precision tong or spatula work to check and flip all those potatoes. Working with skewers isn't any easier, as the potato slices spin around or break off the skewers entirely. Could I find an easier approach that would convince me to fire up the grill for a potato salad? It was worth a try.

Waxy Red Bliss potatoes are the best choice for the grill because they hold their shape better than any other type. In my testing, I found that grilling raw potatoes without precooking them was not an option; the outsides burned by the time the insides were tender. Simmering the potatoes in water on the stovetop was a better solution—the potatoes grilled up nicely charred on the outside and creamy on the inside.

I had started my testing using the smallest red potatoes (about 1½ inches in diameter). I cut them in half, partially cooked them in water, laid them on the grill cut side down, then flipped them once during cooking. While this seemed like the simplest way to go, I was contending with 40 or so potato pieces to be flipped on the grill, which was too much work in my book—especially for a side dish.

I moved on to the larger potatoes. Instead of cutting them into chunks, I cut them into thick planks (about four to five per potato) before precooking. Now I was grilling about 25 pieces of potato instead of 40 or more. (The planks were not only easier to grill, but they also absorbed a lot of dressing, helping to season the salad throughout.) Noticing that I had some spare room on the grill, I threw on an onion and a bell pepper, which added more smoky flavor and color to the salad.

I knew I wanted to dress the grilled potatoes and veggies with a vinaigrette, but what kind? White wine vinegar added a sharp, tangy bite, and extra-virgin olive oil contributed good flavor and creaminess. Adding the strong flavors of garlic, capers, and parsley to the dressing provided the necessary bold counterpoints, and the dish was a hit. Now I had a potato salad worthy of firing up the grill. **–Eva Katz**

GRILLED POTATO SALAD SERVES 6

This salad is best served at room temperature; this gives the potatoes time to soak up the flavors of the dressing. If you choose to serve it warm, let the salad rest for 15 minutes before serving to allow the flavors to meld. Look for potatoes that are 3 to 4 inches around; you will need about six for this recipe.

- **3 tablespoons white wine vinegar**
- **2 garlic cloves, minced**
- **Pepper**
- **9 tablespoons extra-virgin olive oil**
- **2 pounds medium red potatoes, scrubbed (see note above)**
- **1 large red onion**
- **1 large red bell pepper**
- **Salt**
- **3 tablespoons capers, drained and rinsed**
- **3 tablespoons chopped fresh parsley**

1. Whisk vinegar, garlic, ¼ teaspoon pepper, and 6 tablespoons oil in large bowl. Reserve ¼ cup dressing and set aside for finishing salad.

2. Slice potatoes into ¾-inch planks, unpeeled onion into ½-inch rounds, and bell pepper according to photos below. Bring potatoes, 1 teaspoon salt, and enough water to cover potatoes by 1 inch to boil in large saucepan over high heat. Reduce heat to medium and simmer until edges of potatoes begin to soften but centers are still firm, about 10 minutes. Drain potatoes thoroughly in colander, transfer to medium bowl, and toss with 2 more tablespoons oil. Toss onion and pepper with remaining tablespoon oil in separate bowl. Season vegetables with salt and pepper to taste.

3. Grill vegetables, uncovered, over moderate fire until well charred on both sides, 5 to 10 minutes per side (onions and peppers will take less time than potatoes). Remove vegetables from grill. Using tongs, remove skin from onions. Cut onions and peppers into ¾-inch pieces and potatoes into quarters.

4. Toss grilled vegetables with dressing (not ¼ cup reserved dressing). Toss in capers and cool salad to room temperature, about 15 minutes. Just before serving, toss with remaining ¼ cup dressing and parsley. Adjust seasonings and serve.

How to PREPARE PEPPERS FOR THE GRILL

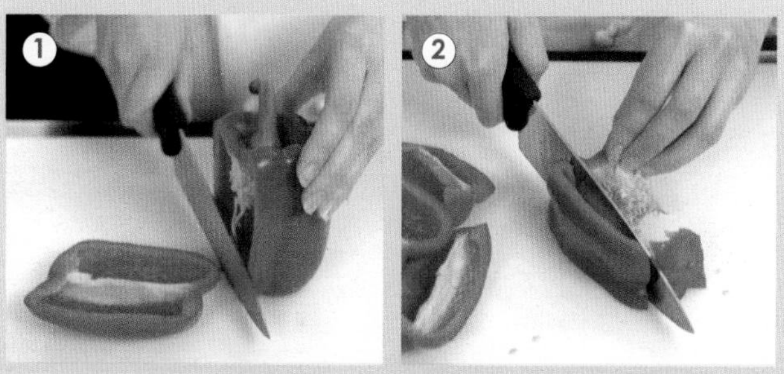

1. Holding the pepper upright, slice off a large fleshy piece from either side of the stem. **2.** Slice off the remaining smaller pieces.

Summer Coooking 101:
How to Grill Vegetables

Grilling is the best way to cook many summer vegetables. Here's a list of vegetables we like to grill, with preparation information and timing. Before grilling, toss all of these vegetables (except for corn on the cob) with olive oil and season with salt and pepper. Use a moderate fire (a roaring fire will torch delicate vegetables). Serve grilled vegetables hot or at room temperature.

Asparagus
TO PREPARE: Snap off tough ends.
GRILL FOR: 5 to 7 minutes, turning once.

Bell Peppers
TO PREPARE: Stem, seed, and cut into large pieces.
GRILL FOR: 10 to 12 minutes, turning once.

Corn on the Cob
TO PREPARE: Remove all but inner layer of husk and snip off silk.
GRILL FOR: 8 to 10 minutes, turning every 2 minutes or so.

Eggplant
TO PREPARE: Trim ends and cut crosswise into ¾-inch-thick rounds.
GRILL FOR: 8 to 10 minutes, turning once.

Fennel
TO PREPARE: Remove feathery fronds and stalks. Trim base of bulb and slice vertically into ½-inch-thick planks.
GRILL FOR: 8 to 10 minutes, turning once.

Portobello Mushrooms
TO PREPARE: Discard stems and wipe caps clean.
GRILL FOR: 8 to 12 minutes, turning once.

White or Cremini Mushrooms
TO PREPARE: Wipe clean and skewer.
GRILL FOR: 8 to 12 minutes, turning every 3 minutes.

Onions
TO PREPARE: Peel, cut crosswise into ½-inch-thick rounds, and skewer. Or, leave skin on, don't skewer, and peel before serving.
GRILL FOR: 10 to 12 minutes, turning once.

Zucchini or Summer Squash
TO PREPARE: Trim ends and slice lengthwise into ½-inch-thick planks.
GRILL FOR: 8 to 10 minutes, turning once.

Sweet and Saucy Grilled Salmon

Glazed salmon gives me fits because it sticks to the grill. I've had the best luck grilling it skin side down and not turning it at all. The salmon doesn't stick, but the fish isn't really grilled. There's got to be a better way.

–Stephen Green, Nepean, Ontario, Canada

Our "secret" technique will forever change the way you grill salmon.

Salmon is perfect for glazing and for grilling, but try to do both things at once and the fish desperately wants to stick to the grate. The sweet, smoky flavor of glazed grilled salmon makes this recipe very appealing, as does the fact that the mess and dreaded fishy odors stay outside. But how could I make this recipe less frustrating?

Salmon sticks to the grill all by itself. A glaze just compounds the problem, so the glaze had better be good. I tried recipes with maple syrup, honey, brown sugar, jellies, or jams as the base ingredient. My tasters preferred the concentrated sweetness of the jelly-based glazes, which also had just the right consistency to coat and cling to the salmon.

But no matter how much I scrubbed the grill grate or how well I oiled it, time after time the sticky, sweet glaze adhered to the grill and wouldn't let go, causing the salmon to tear when I tried to get a spatula under it. My recipe was literally going up in smoke. I tried cooking the salmon skin side down and not flipping it, sacrificing the skin to the grill when I removed the flesh above it. This worked, but my tasters rightfully complained that this salmon didn't have grill marks—or much grill flavor. I needed a better solution.

At home, I regard my grill as an outdoor stove, often putting saucepans right on the grate next to whatever I'm grilling. I wondered if I could use a disposable aluminum pie plate as a mini-skillet, so I threw one on the hot grill and tossed a piece of salmon in it. I got some encouraging results: partial browning, some smoke flavor, and no sticking when I flipped the salmon. To get more browning and grill flavor, I downgraded from a thick pie plate to individual pieces of aluminum foil, and this worked like a charm. Now I was getting great grill marks, full smoke flavor, no sticking, and, if I removed the skin (which most people discard anyway), I could glaze both sides of the salmon. The extra glaze even caramelized in the foil "boat," adding another great dimension of flavor. **–Katie Henderson**

SWEET AND SAUCY GRILLED SALMON

SERVES 4

Use any brand of heavy-duty aluminum foil to make the grill trays, but be sure to spray the foil with nonstick cooking spray. Alternatively, you can use Reynolds Release Nonstick Aluminum Foil and skip the cooking spray.

- **1 teaspoon grated zest and 2 tablespoons juice from 1 large lime**
- **2 garlic cloves, minced**
- **2 scallions, chopped rough**
- **1/2 cup packed fresh cilantro leaves and stems**
- **1/2 cup jalapeño jelly**
- **2 tablespoons unsalted butter**
- **4 salmon fillets (each 6 to 8 ounces and 1 1/4 inches thick), skin removed (see page 30)**
- **Salt and pepper**

1. Process lime zest, lime juice, garlic, scallions, cilantro, and jelly in food processor or blender until smooth. Heat glaze in small saucepan over medium heat until just bubbling, 2 to 3 minutes. Remove from heat and transfer 1/4 cup glaze to small bowl to cool slightly. Stir butter into glaze remaining in saucepan, cover, and set aside.

2. Light large chimney starter filled with charcoal briquettes (about 100 coals); burn until coals are covered with fine gray ash. Pour coals over three-quarters of grill; set cooking grate in place, cover, and let grill heat up for 5 minutes.

3. Following photos, use heavy-duty foil to make four 7 by 5-inch trays. Coat trays with cooking spray. Season salmon with salt and pepper, brush each side of each fillet with 1/2 tablespoon reserved glaze (without butter), and place skinned side up on trays.

4. Place trays with salmon over hot fire and grill until glaze forms golden brown crust, 6 to 8 minutes. (Move fillets to cooler part of the grill if they darken too soon.) Using tongs, flip salmon and cook 1 minute. Spoon half of buttered glaze on salmon and cook until center of each fillet is still just translucent, about 1 minute. Transfer salmon to platter and spoon remaining buttered glaze over it. Serve.

ORANGE-SESAME GLAZE

Replace lime zest and juice with lemon zest and juice, and replace jalapeño jelly with orange marmalade. Puree 2 tablespoons oyster-flavored sauce and 1 teaspoon toasted sesame oil with other glaze ingredients. Add 1 teaspoon toasted sesame seeds along with butter.

SPICY APPLE GLAZE

Replace lime zest and juice with 2 tablespoons cider vinegar and replace jalapeño jelly with apple jelly. Puree 1/2 teaspoon red pepper flakes with other glaze ingredients.

Test Kitchen Secrets
NO MORE STICKING

Few culinary pitfalls are as irksome as fish stuck to the grill. Fish baskets leave no attractive grill marks, and the fish often sticks to the basket. We had better luck with homemade foil trays coated with cooking spray.

1. Cut out four rectangles of heavy-duty aluminum foil and crimp the edges until each tray measures 7 by 5 inches.
2. Place one seasoned and glazed salmon fillet, skinned side up, on each foil tray.
3. After the glaze forms a golden brown crust around the edges of the fish, use tongs to flip each fillet.
4. Spoon half the buttered glaze over the salmon while it's on the grill so the glaze can thicken slightly.

On the Side: Cucumber Salad

What's the secret to a crisp salad with big flavors and a dressing that's not watery?

A cool salad made with crisp cucumbers is a quick, refreshing companion to any grilled dish. The cucumbers' high water content is part of what makes them so refreshing, but once sliced they shed some of this water, which dilutes any dressing. One solution to this problem is to salt the cucumbers before dressing them, which rids them of excess water. But this takes at least an hour. For a weeknight dinner, I wanted something faster.

Instead of trying to fight the problem of the diluted dressing, I thought I might be able to work with it. I simmered rice vinegar and sugar (a classic Asian flavor combination) in a small saucepan until the mixture was reduced by half; this took just five minutes and gave my dressing a very concentrated flavor base. I then added the other ingredients—lime juice, ginger, fresh chile, and toasted sesame oil—to the dressing and tossed it with the cucumbers. The water from the cucumbers diluted my double-strength dressing to just the right potency. Sometimes it's best not to fight Mother Nature. **–Eva Katz**

SPICY ASIAN CUCUMBER SALAD SERVES 4

You can substitute 1/4 teaspoon red pepper flakes for the fresh red chiles. Add them to the saucepan with the vinegar and sugar.

- 1/2 **cup rice vinegar**
- 2 **tablespoons sugar**
- 2 **tablespoons lime juice**
- 2 **tablespoons minced fresh ginger**
- 1 1/2 **tablespoons minced red chile (about 1 large chile)**
- 1 **tablespoon toasted sesame oil**
- 3 **cucumbers, peeled, seeded (see page 31), and cut crosswise into 1/4-inch slices**
- 4 **scallions, white and light green parts, sliced thin**
- 1/4 **cup loosely packed fresh basil, chopped**
- **Salt and pepper**

1. Bring vinegar and sugar to boil in saucepan over medium-high heat. Reduce heat to medium-low and simmer until mixture reduces by half, 5 to 6 minutes. Transfer to medium bowl and cool to room temperature.

2. Whisk in lime juice, ginger, chile, and sesame oil. Toss in cucumbers, scallions, and basil; season with salt and pepper, and let sit for 10 minutes or up to 1 hour. Serve.

From Your Garden: Fresh Tomato Sauce

For a sauce that really tastes like tomatoes, keep the recipe simple.

Summer tomatoes require almost nothing—other than a little salt—to make them taste good. A fresh tomato sauce for pasta should follow this same philosophy. The best recipes are nothing more than garlic, olive oil, tomatoes, herbs, and salt. But the way you treat these ingredients makes a big difference in the quality of your sauce.

Most recipes add garlic to hot oil, which I've found is a big mistake. The garlic goes from raw and biting to burned and acrid in seconds. Starting the garlic and oil together in a cold pan is a much safer method that gives the finished sauce a subtle, not bitter or overpowering, garlic flavor.

As for the tomatoes, no one in the test kitchen liked the leathery curls of skin that the tomatoes shed as they cooked. Peeling the tomatoes is a must. At first, I thought that seeding the tomatoes would be necessary, too. But without the moisture that surrounds the seeds, the sauce was dry and began to scorch before the tomatoes softened properly. Having the liquid from the seeds in the pan gave the meaty tomatoes sufficient time (about 20 minutes) to break down and form a chunky but cohesive sauce. And no one minded the seeds themselves, which disappeared into the sauce by the end of cooking.

In a tasting of sauces made with extra-virgin and regular olive oil, tasters preferred the rich, fruity flavor of extra-virgin oil. And when it came to herbs, less was more. I tried a whole garden's worth of fresh herbs, singly and in different combinations; tasters preferred the simplicity of a little chopped fresh basil and nothing else. While this sauce can go from garden to table in about half an hour, it's also sturdy enough to freeze and enjoy months later as a sweet reminder of summer.

–Stephanie Alleyne

FRESH TOMATO SAUCE MAKES ABOUT 2 CUPS, ENOUGH FOR 1 POUND OF PASTA

To keep the garlic from burning, start the olive oil and garlic in a cold pan. Add a pinch of sugar to the cooked sauce if your tomatoes aren't as sweet as you'd like. If the sauce seems too thick, toss the sauce and pasta with a little reserved pasta cooking water to help spread the sauce evenly.

- 3 **tablespoons extra-virgin olive oil**
- 4 **garlic cloves, minced**
- 2 **pounds beefsteak tomatoes (about 4 large), cored, peeled (see photos, page 31), and cut into 3/4-inch chunks**
- **Salt**
- 1/4 **cup chopped fresh basil**
- **Pepper**

Stir oil and garlic together in large skillet. Turn heat to medium and cook until garlic is sizzling and fragrant, about 2 minutes. Stir in tomatoes and 1/2 teaspoon salt. Bring to rapid simmer and cook, stirring occasionally, reducing heat if sauce begins to stick to bottom of pan, until thickened and chunky, 15 to 20 minutes. Remove from heat. Stir in basil and season with salt and pepper to taste.

Tomato Sauce for the Freezer

MAKE MINE A DOUBLE For a taste of summer in the dead of winter, make a double batch of sauce and freeze half (or all) of it. Double the ingredients, increasing the cooking time to about 30 minutes. Cool the sauce completely. Transfer to a 2-cup freezersafe container. Press a layer of plastic wrap directly on the surface of the sauce, cover, and freeze for up to 3 months. Defrost in the microwave or in the refrigerator overnight.

Food Shopping

TUNA: Are the New Pouches Better than Traditional Cans?

In recent years, pouched tuna has appeared in supermarkets, promising a fresher, less processed, better-tasting alternative to canned tuna. But is pouched tuna really better than its canned cousin?

A preliminary tasting showed that tasters had a strong preference for solid white albacore tuna packed in water, which is the mildest variety of processed tuna; chunk light tuna had unappealing strong flavors, and albacore packed in oil was too mushy. We rounded up the top five national brands of canned albacore tuna in water and tasted them blind against three pouched water-packed albacore products.

The results were, in a word (no, not fishy), startling. Out of the eight tunas sampled, tasters chose two canned products—Chicken of the Sea and StarKist—as their overall favorites; in fact, canned tunas took four of the top five spots.

Why didn't the pouched products, which require less processing and therefore should have fresher flavor, swim away with the lead? When it comes to tuna, more flavor is not necessarily a good thing. Our tasters preferred the milder brands (whether pouched or canned) and downgraded Bumble Bee (the big loser in this tasting) for tasting too fishy. And given the minimal flavor differences in the mild tunas, our tasters focused on texture—and here's where the canned tunas won the race.

Because the cans are about three times as thick as the pouches (1½ inches versus about half an inch), the tuna must be broken down to get it into the pouch; the cans hold larger pieces of fish. Larger pieces mean that canned tuna has larger flakes than pouched tuna. In the end, we found texture to be more variable than flavor, and meaty canned tuna was preferred to mushier pouched tuna. The tunas are listed below in order of preference. **–Scott Kathan**

Top Picks

1. **CHICKEN OF THE SEA Solid White Albacore Tuna in Water**
$1.39 for 6-ounce can
Tasters liked its "good, mild flavor," "moist texture," "chunky appearance," "large, beautiful flakes," and "taste of the ocean."

2. **STARKIST Solid White Albacore Tuna in Water**
$1.39 for 6-ounce can
Texture ruled with this "firm," "flaky," and "moist" tuna that was praised for its "fresh taste," "perfect salt level," and "mellow flavor."

Runners-Up

3. **STARKIST Premium Chunk White Albacore Tuna in Water**
$3.69 for 7.06-ounce pouch
Seasoning seemed to be the key in this "tangy," "tart," "salty and briny" tuna. Tasters especially appreciated its "clean" and "bright" flavor.

4. **GEISHA Albacore Solid White Tuna in Water**
$1.29 for 6-ounce can
Fans appreciated this tuna's "dense," "meaty," and "chunky" texture, saying that it "looks like real fish." The flavor was deemed "very mild."

5. **3 DIAMONDS Fancy Albacore Solid White Tuna in Water**
$1.29 for 6-ounce can
While tasters liked its "juicy and moist" texture, some were put off by this tuna's "strong fish taste." As one taster wrote, "This is why people don't like seafood."

6. **CHICKEN OF THE SEA Premium Albacore Tuna in Water**
$3.67 for 7.1-ounce pouch
This tuna elicited mixed comments, ranging from "clean flavor" to "stinky." A few tasters thought this tuna was "meaty," but there were many complaints about "pre-chewed" texture.

Don't Bother

7. **BUMBLE BEE Solid White Albacore Tuna in Water**
$1.29 for 6-ounce can
Tasters compared this "harsh," "sour" tuna to anchovies, sardines, and even "old salmon." The "bloody" appearance and "dry" texture didn't help.

8. **BUMBLE BEE Premium Albacore Tuna in Water**
$3.39 for 7.06-ounce pouch
Several tasters likened this sample to cat food, describing the texture as "previously chewed," "ultra-chopped," and "mealy." Its "strong fishiness" sunk this tuna to the bottom of our list.

Taste Test Pickles

Pickles are available in two basic varieties: processed and fresh. The shelf-stable pickles you find on supermarket shelves, with brand names like Cain's, Gedney, Heinz, and Vlassic, are processed. The pickles you find in the refrigerator section, which include many small regional producers as well as the national brand Claussen, are fresh.

Processed pickles are either heavily salted or packed in salt water and are then left to ferment for a period of weeks or months. The salt retards spoilage and draws out moisture, while naturally occurring bacteria convert the natural sugars in the cucumbers into lactic acid, which also acts as a preservative and lends a distinctive flavor. Processed pickles are then packed in a vinegar solution. Fresh pickles are not fermented but are quickly cured with a seasoned vinegar solution that contains salt. They are typically crispier and more vibrantly colored than processed pickles.

We tasted five styles of pickles (listed below), both processed and fresh. Our tasters preferred the crunch, brighter color, and fresher flavor of the fresh pickles. Many of the processed pickles were described as "musty tasting," and tasters complained about their "unnatural hue" and "overpowering salt and vinegar rush." **–S.K.**

Dill/Kosher Dill
The most basic cucumber pickle, flavored with salt, vinegar, and dill; "kosher" does not refer to Jewish dietary laws but signifies the addition of garlic (although most "regular" dills also contain garlic). Tasters found these pickles "pleasant and refreshing," with "grassy," "dilly" flavor.

Polish/Hearty Garlic Dill
This spicier version of dill pickles has a "good spicy bite," according to our tasters. Comments ranged from "lots of garlic" to "peppery but not hot."

Half-Sour
Very fresh and crisp. Tasters called these "super-crunchy" and "close to perfect."

Bread and Butter
These sweet/tart pickles are seasoned with mustard, sugar, and sometimes onions and bell peppers and are often sold in waffle-cut disks. Tasters noted the "nice balance of sweet and tart" and "mustardy and fruity" flavors. Overall, "crisp and tart."

Sweet Gherkin
These small, sweet pickles are made with immature cucumbers and often flavored with cinnamon, ginger, and nutmeg. Tasters' opinions ranged from "nice cinnamon flavor" to "tastes like Big Red gum" and "too sweet."

Equipment Roundup

INSTANT-READ THERMOMETERS: Are Inexpensive Brands Any Good?

In the test kitchen we use an instant-read thermometer to determine when meat, poultry, and even bread are optimally cooked. We also use it to check the temperature of sugar syrup when making meringues, caramel sauce, and candy and to test oil temperature when frying.

Our favorite instant-read thermometer is the ThermoWorks Super-Fast Thermapen, a test kitchen workhorse that quickly provides accurate readings across a broad range of temperatures. But at $85, the Thermapen isn't cheap.

In the past, the only inexpensive instant-read thermometers available were mediocre dial-face models. Dial-face thermometers are hard to read, and their sensors are in the wrong place—more than an inch up the stem. In contrast, digital instant-read thermometers have their sensors on the very tip of their probe, making them easy to use in both shallow liquids and deep roasts.

In recent years, cheaper digital instant-read thermometers have become available. Could any of them approach the performance of our trusty Thermapen? We purchased eight digital instant-read thermometers, all priced under $25, and put them through their paces in the kitchen. Thermometers are listed in order of preference at right.

ON THE MONEY: A thermometer must be accurate; otherwise, what's the point? Three of the models we tested (Cooper-Atkins, CDN Candy, and Polder 363-90) weren't perfectly accurate in boiling water and/or ice water. What's more, none of the offenders featured a calibrating function.

SPEED MATTERS: When you're taking the temperature of hot oil, you want a reading as soon as possible. When using the thermometers in hot oil, testers' hands became uncomfortably hot with the slower models. Fast response time proved to be an especially important factor in our ratings.

IS BIGGER BETTER? Bigger is better, but only to a point. With its mammoth 8$\frac{1}{4}$-inch probe, the CDN Candy thermometer had no trouble finding the center of our biggest roast, but it was cumbersome with smaller items. At the other end of the spectrum, the probes on the CDN Q2-450, Cooper-Atkins, and Polder 371 were too short (just 2$\frac{3}{4}$ inches) to reach the center of a big roast. The ideal probe length is 4 to 5 inches.

DESIGN DETAILS: Most of the "extra" features—including auto shut-off and minimum/maximum temperature memory—were deemed nonessential, but testers did value thermometers that could be calibrated. They also liked thermometers that registered a wide range of temperatures, from below zero (for frozen items) to 400 degrees.

SUMMING UP: None of our cheap contenders could match the speed, temperature range, or accuracy of the Thermapen, but a few—notably the CDN DTQ450 and the Maverick—came pretty close, and for a fraction of the price.

–Scott Kathan

Highly Recommended

THERMOWORKS Super-Fast Thermapen 211-476
Price: $85.00
Average Response Time: 5 seconds
Comments: Simply the best: fast, accurate, and easy to use. The Thermapen also has the widest temperature range (–58 to 572 degrees).

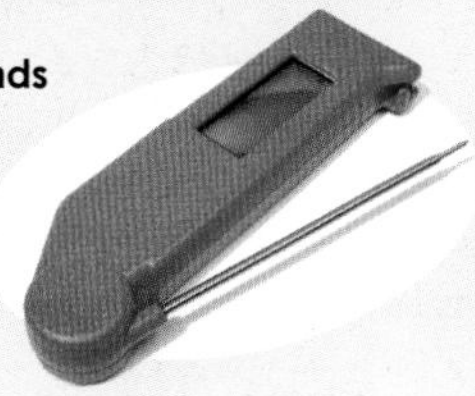

CDN ProAccurate Quick Tip Digital Cooking Thermometer DTQ450
Price: $17.95
Average Response Time: 9 seconds
Comments: The CDN Quick Tip was fast and accurate and had every feature we deemed necessary, including a calibration button. Not quite as fast as the mighty Thermapen, but fast enough.

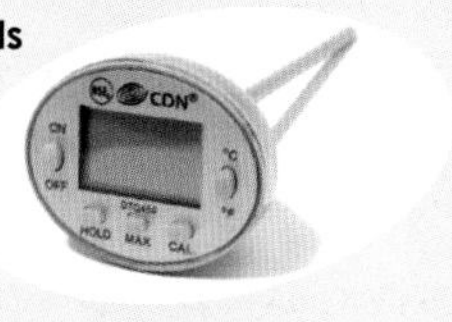

Recommended

MAVERICK Redi-Chek Professional Chef's Digital Thermometer DT-01
Price: $12.95
Average Response Time: 14 seconds
Comments: While this no-frills model is rated to only 302 degrees, it accurately registered the temperature in 350-degree frying oil. While every reading was accurate, the lack of a calibration function might spell trouble down the road.

CDN ProAccurate Quick Tip Digital Cooking Thermometer on a Rope Q2-450
Price: $16.95
Average Response Time: 11 seconds
Comments: The short (2$\frac{3}{4}$-inch) stem is a problem with big roasts and large loaves of bread. Otherwise, a top-notch thermometer, with a wide temperature range (–40 to 450 degrees) and a calibration function.

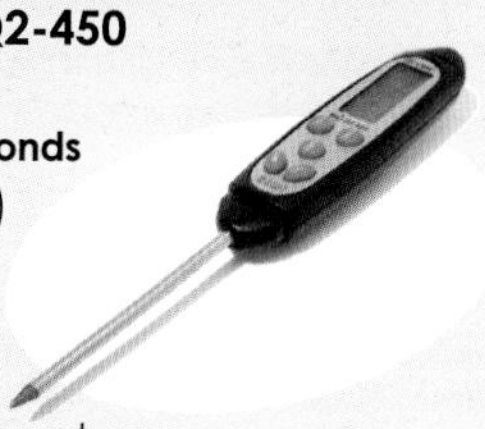

POLDER Instant-Read Thermometer 371
Price: $19.99
Average Response Time: 15 seconds
Comments: This looks exactly like the CDN Q2-450 (complete with short probe), but its response time was four seconds slower. Otherwise, very serviceable.

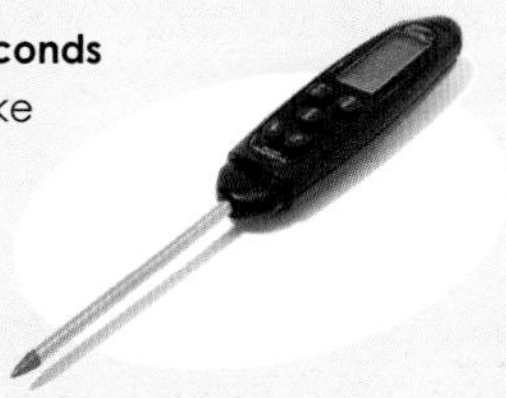

CDN ProAccurate Candy & All-Purpose Thermometer DTC375
Price: $24.99
Average Response Time: 18 seconds
Comments: The oversized probe (8$\frac{1}{4}$ inches long) was handy with a big roast and in hot oil, but it left a large exit wound in a steak. Programmed candy alarms and clip are handy.

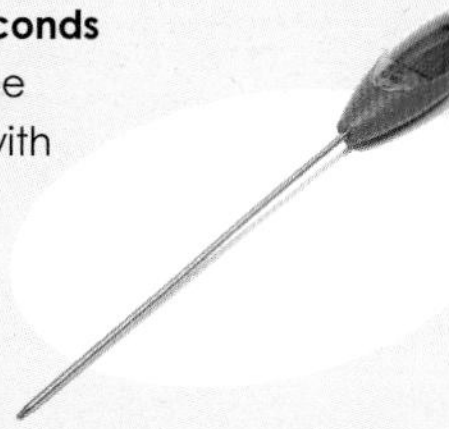

Recommended with Reservations

POLDER Digital Instant Read Thermometer 363-90
Price: $19.99
Average Response Time: 20 seconds
Comments: A relatively slow average response time and lack of calibration function are flaws. The side-oriented display is no better (or worse) than the classic top-oriented design.

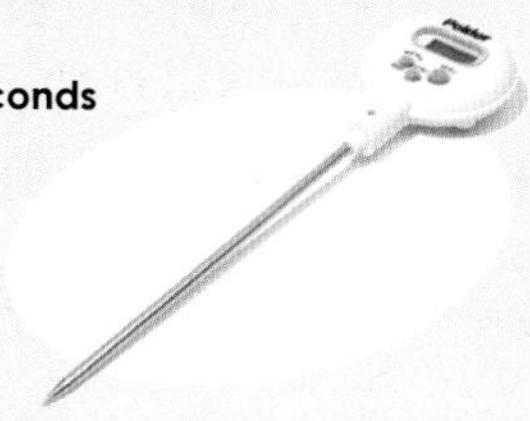

TAYLOR Classic Instant Read Thermometer 9840
Price: $16.99
Average Response Time: 21 seconds
Comments: Slow response time is the biggest concern with this thermometer. No calibration function.

COOPER-ATKINS Waterproof Digital Thermometer DPP400W
Price: $24.00
Average Response Time: 28 seconds
Comments: Its relatively poor showing in accuracy tests is a minor practical flaw; a calibration function would help. The short (2$\frac{3}{4}$-inch) stem is a more serious drawback, as is the slow response time. The tiny buttons can be hard to manipulate.

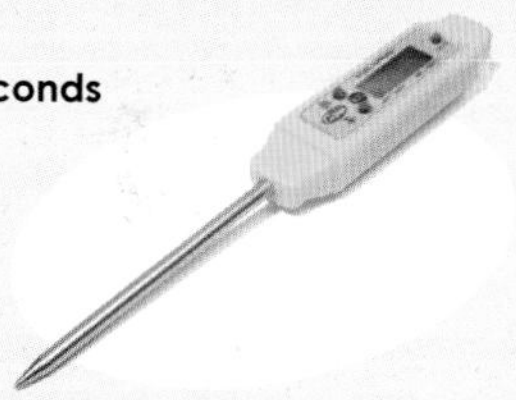

Calibrating Instant-Read Thermometers

Even the best instant-read thermometers eventually need to be recalibrated. Many instant-read thermometers, both dial-face and digital, can be calibrated at home. We think this feature is essential. Here's how to recalibrate a thermometer with this function.

Make a slurry of ice and cold tap water in a glass or bowl; allow to sit for two minutes to let the temperature stabilize. Put the probe in the slurry, being careful not to touch the sides or bottom of the glass or bowl. On a digital thermometer, press the "calibrate" button to 32 degrees; on a dial-face thermometer, turn the dial to 32 degrees (the method differs from model to model, but many require pliers to turn a small knob on the back).

–S.K.

To calibrate a thermometer, immerse the probe in ice water and adjust the temperature to 32 degrees.

Notes from Our Test Kitchen

TIPS, TECHNIQUES, AND TOOLS FOR BETTER COOKING

Kitchen Creations
Flavored Syrups

It's hard to improve on maple syrup and a pat of butter atop steaming waffles or pancakes, but if you're looking to spice up your short stack, these variations are sure to please.

BUTTER PECAN SYRUP
MAKES ABOUT 2 CUPS

- **1 1/2 cups maple syrup**
- **2 tablespoons unsalted butter**
- **1/2 cup pecans, toasted and chopped**
- **1/4 teaspoon vanilla extract**
- **Pinch salt**

Simmer all ingredients in small saucepan over medium-low heat until slightly thickened, about 5 minutes.

BLUEBERRY HILL SYRUP
MAKES ABOUT 1 3/4 CUPS

- **1/2 cup frozen blueberries**
- **1 1/2 cups maple syrup**
- **1/4 teaspoon grated lemon zest**
- **Pinch salt**

Mash blueberries in small saucepan over medium heat until moisture has evaporated, about 5 minutes. Whisk in remaining ingredients and cook over medium-low until slightly thickened, 5 to 7 minutes.

APPLE-CINNAMON SYRUP
MAKES ABOUT 1 3/4 CUPS

- **1 1/2 cups maple syrup**
- **1/3 cup apple jelly**
- **1/4 teaspoon cinnamon**
- **Pinch salt**

Simmer all ingredients in small saucepan over medium-low heat until slightly thickened, 5 to 7 minutes.

Peach Square Revival

Our **Peach Squares** (page 13) are best served on the day they are made because the crust can become soggy with time. However, it is possible to revive the squares. Simply place leftover squares side by side (with no spaces in between the squares) on a baking sheet and heat in a 350-degree oven until the bottoms are crisp, 10 to 12 minutes. Allow to cool back to room temperature before eating.

Taming the Heat

Most of the heat in a chile pepper resides in the ribs and seeds. To temper that heat, just cut it open, pull out and discard the core and seeds, and cut away and discard the ribs. For maximum burn, leave the seeds and ribs intact. When working with hot peppers, it's a good idea to wear rubber gloves and to wash your knife and cutting board as soon as you're done. Also remember that smaller chiles are usually much hotter than larger chiles.

Cut off the top of the chile, discard the core and seeds, and cut a slit down the side. Open the chile and press it flat on a cutting board. Keeping the knife parallel to the cutting surface, gently trim off the white ribs.

INSIDE THE TEST KITCHEN
Not Fork-Tender

You may have noticed that many barbecue recipes (ours included) throw around the term "fork-tender" pretty freely. But what exactly does it mean? In the case of our **Lexington-Style Pulled Pork** (page 11), it's the point where the pork has reached the ideal tenderness—a state in which the meat can be shredded using nothing more than two forks (or two hands for that matter). But aside from removing the roast from the oven and tearing it apart, how can you tell if it's done? We like to stick a fork straight into the top of the roast and lift. If the fork comes out with little or no resistance, it's fork-tender. If the fork is difficult to remove from the roast, as associate editor Jeremy Sauer is finding in this case, it's not quite fork-tender and should be cooked longer.

Whisk Assessment

When you're getting ready to beat some eggs or whip some cream by hand, there's no better tool than an old-fashioned wire whisk. But which one is best? The long, lean "sauce" whisk or the Rubenesque "balloon" whisk? As it turns out, they serve very different purposes. A sauce whisk has a slender, tapered shape that can reach into the corners of pots and pans, making it ideal for whisking butter into a pan sauce or making a stovetop custard. On the other hand, the balloon whisk is best used away from the stove, where its wide girth helps incorporate air into liquid ingredients, making it a better choice when whipping cream or egg whites.

When used head to head with the sauce whisk to whip egg whites, the balloon whisk made quick work of the job; the sauce whisk required much more effort. That being said, since they serve fairly different purposes (and are both relatively inexpensive), we recommend keeping both types of whisk in your equipment drawer.

–Jeremy Saue

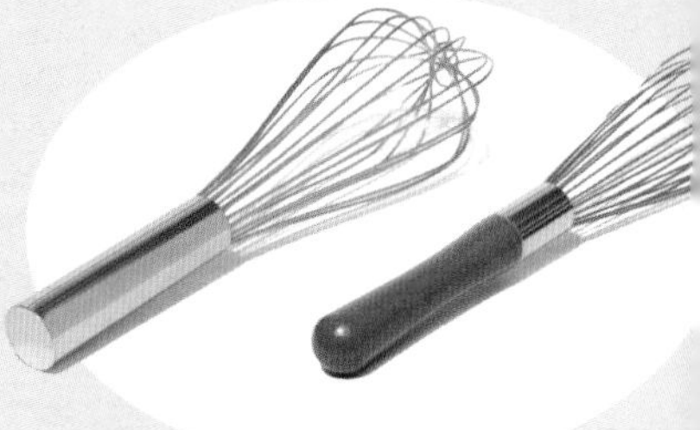

DIFFERENT WHISKS FOR DIFFERENT JOBS

A hefty balloon whisk (left) is best suited to heavy-duty tasks away from the stove. A sauce whisk (right) is used for more delicate tasks.

Kitchen Know-How
The Skinny on Salmon

Many grilled salmon recipes use skin-on fillets, but we prefer to trim off the skin for our **Sweet and Saucy Grilled Salmon** (page 26), making a flavorful, glazed crust possible on both sides of the fish. A good fishmonger should be able to remove the skin for you. If that's not possible, you'll need to do the work yourself. Armed with a sharp knife and a little know-how, skinning salmon is a breeze. (A flexible boning knife works best, but if you don't have one a chef's knife works as well.)

1. Using a sharp boning knife, insert the blade just above the skin about 1 inch from one end of the fillet. Cut through the nearest end, keeping the blade just above the skin.

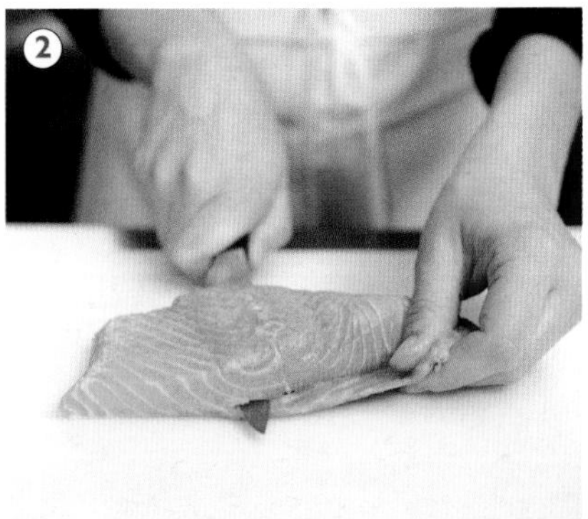

2. Roate the fish and grab the loose piece of skin. Run the knife between the flesh and the skin, making sure the knife is just above the skin, until the skin is completely removed.

Shopping with the Test Kitchen: Two Steaks for Fajitas

Although we prefer the beefier flavor of skirt steak, it's not as widely available as flank steak, which will also work well in our **Skirt Steak Fajitas** (page 18). Both steaks share similar characteristics (long and thin and very flavorful), so how do you tell them apart? Skirt steak is narrower, and the grain runs crosswise. Flank steak is wider, and the grain runs lengthwise. When shopping for skirt steak, choose fattier cuts, which will add a lot of flavor to the fajitas. If using flank steak, cut the meat into thirds lengthwise rather than in half crosswise.

SKIRT STEAK
The grain runs crosswise.

FLANK STEAK
The grain runs lengthwise.

Browned Butter

In our **Big and Chewy Low-Fat Chocolate Chip Cookies** (page 8), the nutty flavor of browned butter helps to mask the taste of pureed dates (which normally is not unpleasant but is odd in a chocolate chip cookie). Browned butter is made by slowly melting and cooking butter over moderate heat; as the water in the butter evaporates, the milk solids caramelize. But making browned butter can be tricky, as it can quickly turn to burned butter if not watched closely. In the test kitchen, we prefer a stainless steel pan for browning butter, as the shiny surface makes it easy to gauge the true color of the butter. The dark finish on nonstick pans makes this difficult.

–Meredith Butcher

JUST MELTED
Not browned butter.

PERFECTLY BROWNED BUTTER
Golden and nutty flavored.

WENT TOO FAR
This butter is burnt.

A Smokin' Gas Grill

Our recipes for **Lexington-Style Pulled Pork** (page 11) and **Grill-Roasted Turkey Breast** (page 15) were developed using a charcoal grill, which is the traditional choice when you want to use wood chips to produce flavorful smoke. It takes some ingenuity to use wood chips on a gas grill (tossing them onto the burners results in immediate combustion and little smoke), but we've developed a method that produces good results.

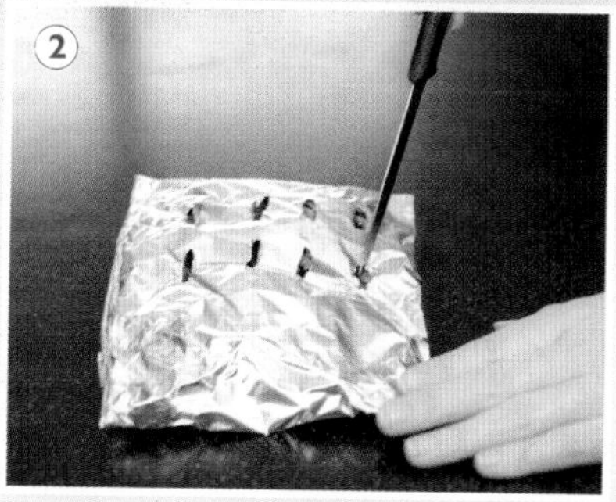

1. Place the soaked and drained chips in the center of an 8-inch square piece of heavy-duty aluminum foil. Fold the foil over the chips and crimp all sides to seal well.
2. Using a paring knife, cut slits in top of the foil packet and place it directly on the primary burner (the burner that will remain on during the entire cooking time). When protected in this way, the chips should smoke for 30 to 40 minutes.

A Seedy Situation

In addition to the common Kirby cucumber, many supermarkets sell English (or hothouse) cucumbers. English cukes are longer and more slender than their American cousins, and here in the test kitchen we prefer them because their thin skin is perfectly edible, their flesh is slightly firmer, and they have fewer (and smaller) seeds than Kirby cucumbers.

Because some markets don't always carry English cucumbers, our recipe for **Spicy Asian Cucumber Salad** (page 27) was developed with Kirbys, which need to be peeled and seeded. Here's a quick way to seed a cucumber.

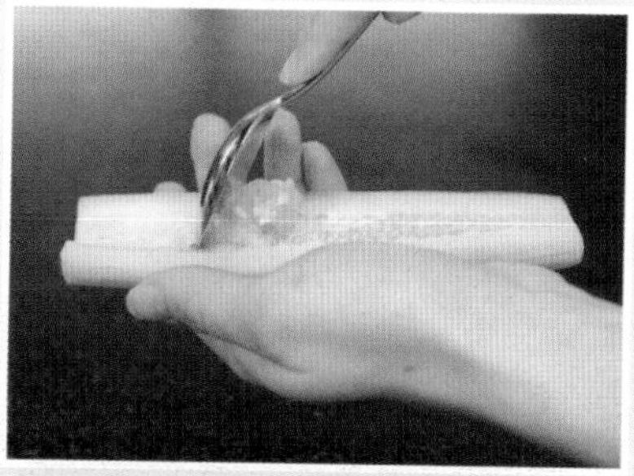

Peel and halve the cucumber lengthwise. With a spoon, use just enough pressure to scoop away the seeds and the surrounding liquid.

Thermometer Shopping

Here's where to find the winning digital instant-read thermometers rated on page 29. Thermoworks.com sells many types of Thermapens, including our favorite, the Super-Fast Thermapen ($85). The CDN (model DTQ450, $17.95) can be purchased at cdn-timeandtemp.com.

Equipment Update

In our February/March 2006 equipment roundup, we tested inexpensive (under $50) nonstick skillets and recommended the Wearever Collections Premium Nonstick Aluminum Skillet as a "Best Buy." It has come to our attention that this skillet is no longer available. To find a comparable replacement, we tested three similar inexpensive 12-inch, nonstick skillets from the same manufacturer: the Wearever Balance, the Wearever Hard-Anodized, and the Wearever Excellence. We put each pan through the original battery of tests—flipping omelets, sautéing onions, and pan-searing salmon—to determine evenness of heating, the presence of hot spots, the pace of sautéing, and performance at high temperatures.

Though all three skillets performed adequately and released food effortlessly, one stood out for its superior design and performance. The Hard-Anodized model ($29.99 at Amazon.com) is lighter than the others, has an elongated stainless-steel handle, and feels comfortable in your hands—even when maneuvering the skillet to swirl oil or flip eggs.

A NEW NONSTICK SKILLET
This Wearever nonstick pan offers good performance at a reasonable price.

Kitchen Know-How
Peeling Tomatoes

Just a few seconds in boiling water is all it takes to loosen the skins from delicate summer tomatoes without cooking the flesh. Save yourself a step by using the same pot of water to cook the pasta.

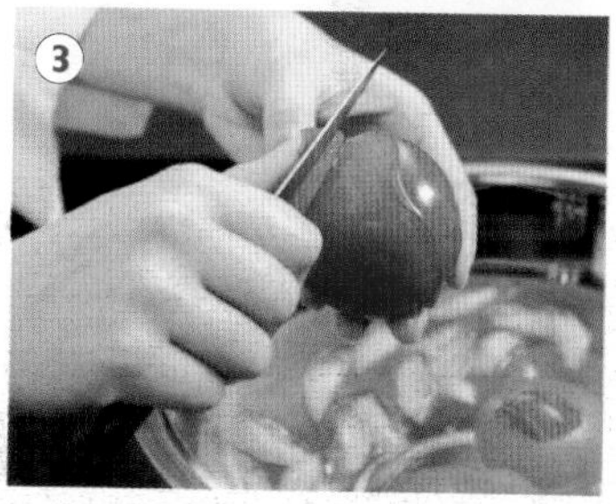

1. Peeled tomatoes are slippery, so core them before blanching. **2.** Place the tomatoes (no more than four at a time) in boiling water. Blanch until the skins just begin to split around the cored area, about 15 seconds. Use a slotted spoon to transfer the tomatoes to a bowl of ice water. **3.** Once the tomatoes are cool, the skins slip right off with a little help from a paring knife.

When Things Go Wrong in the Kitchen

READERS SHARE FUNNY STORIES ABOUT COOKING MISHAPS

TWO WINNERS

A few months ago my children baked cakes to enter into a cooking contest. My daughter, who is 11 years old, made a lemon pound cake. She worked arduously, scraping rinds and squeezing lemons, and it was a long and messy process, but it turned out beautifully. My son, on the other hand, a typical 9-year-old boy, made a crazy chocolate cake concoction using a boxed mix as the starting base. My daughter was sure that she would win because her cake was made from scratch. As the cakes cooled on the counter, we left the house to do a quick errand. We returned home 30 minutes later to find the lemon pound cake half eaten. Apparently, we had left a chair pushed up against the counter, making it easy for our dog, Scrappy, to reach the cakes. There was an eruption of tears and doggie threats. Then my daughter started laughing and blurted to her brother, "I would have won first prize. Even the dog chose my cake over yours!" Being a good sport, my son put both their names on the chocolate cake and they wound up with the third-place prize!

Karina Schumacher Elburn, Ill.

NOT SO TASTY TREATS

When our children were younger, my husband and I went to visit my sister over the Christmas holidays. She had put out several containers of holiday goodies for us on her kitchen bar. Because the children were coming, she had taken the bowl of cat food off the floor and placed it on the counter. As my husband was sampling some of the prepared snacks, he picked up a handful of dry cat food and tossed it in his mouth, just as he would with a handful of peanuts. We all watched in horror. My husband has never lived that episode down. Even now, 25 years later, when we go to visit my sister, she always offers him some cat food.

Catherine Phillips Vanceboro, N.C.

MIXER MADNESS

While cleaning up the kitchen counter one day, I saw some food particles on the KitchenAid mixer. I was in the midst of wiping them off when I accidentally moved the power switch from "off" to "high." The paddle blade was still in the mixer and it quickly whisked my cleaning rag out of my hand, twirling it violently. The mixer gyrated toward the kitchen window, and my cleaning rag caught the kitchen curtains and pulled them down, curtain rod and all, and everything was twirling around so violently I could not reach the switch to turn it off! I quickly ran to our electric box and turned the breaker for the kitchen circuit off to stop the machine. The curtains were torn to shreds and the curtain rod was wound around the paddle of the mixer. Since then, I have been very careful to keep the mixer disconnected when cleaning it!

Bruce Clark Interlaken, N.Y.

SECRET INGREDIENT

When my husband and I were first married, he was always trying to impress me with his cooking prowess. One of his more beloved wedding gifts was a new gas grill. Needless to say, we ate a lot of bratwurst and hamburger that summer. I came home from shopping one Saturday afternoon and he had made a meal of grilled hamburgers, rice, and green beans. I took one bite of the hamburger. "What do you think?" he asked. "I used a secret ingredient." I responded that it was interesting and tried to take another bite. As I choked down the second bite, I asked what his secret ingredient was. "Vanilla," he responded. After I finished the rice and green beans, we had a little discussion about vanilla extract and when not to use it.

Emily Speight Waukegan, Ill.

KILLER MEAT LOAF

Years ago, when I first learned to cook, my neighbor gave me her favorite sweet-and-sour meat-loaf recipe, which she swore by. The recipe called for 4 ounces of bread crumbs, and when I weighed them, the yield was 3 cups. I poured the bread crumbs into the bowl, and the resulting mixture was the oddest beige color, but I baked it anyway. When I took the meat loaf out and glazed it with the sweet-and-sour sauce, it looked like a glazed adobe brick and was just as hard. It was impossible to cut, so I threw the meat loaf in the trash.

A few evenings later, my neighbor, who was a tall, proper Southern lady with big blonde hair and a Louisiana accent, was at my front door waving the meat loaf in my face, uttering barnyard expressions and telling me how she almost killed herself on my meat loaf. As it turned out, her dog had gotten into my trash, and after attempting to eat the meat loaf, he had dropped it on her back porch. She later tripped over the meat loaf in the dark and assumed that I had left it there because I didn't like her recipe. We have been laughing about the night of the killer meat loaf for over 40 years now!

Cynthia Williams Phoenix, Ariz.

DON'T LOOK IN THE GARAGE

When my cousin Emily was visiting, we baked dozens and dozens of cookies. When we finished our "World's Best Cookie" recipe, which required a ton of ingredients, including pricey hazelnuts, we noticed that the dough had a strange bitter taste. As we looked over the list of ingredients, we tried to figure out what could have gone wrong. It was then that I noticed a bulk-sized bottle of cooking oil on the counter. I winced as I asked Emily what oil she had used in the recipe. She replied, "There was no oil left in the pantry, but I found some more in your garage." She had used rancid frying oil and bacon fat from an old container that we kept in our garage!

Mary P. Morgan Cumberland, R.I.

LOUDER THAN BOMBS

During World War II, my parents and other relatives lived together in a big house in Washington, D.C. My grandmother decided that she was going to contribute to the war effort and can some tomatoes. Grandma was not a particularly experienced cook and had probably never canned tomatoes in her life. Nonetheless, she persevered with her project, and, by the end of the day, all the tomatoes were sealed in their jars and lined up neatly on shelves in the basement.

Some time later, the entire household was awakened in the middle of the night by the sound of explosions. Being only two short blocks from Walter Reed Hospital, they all feared that the Germans were bombing. Everyone was scurrying around the house trying to ascertain what was happening, when they realized that the explosions were taking place in their own house; in fact, in their very own basement! They timidly opened the basement door and found tomatoes on the ceiling, on the walls, on the floor, and all over everything else. Grandma had failed in some step of the canning process, and the tomatoes had spoiled in their jars. **Stanley E. Rose** Silver Spring, Md.

Send us your funniest kitchen disaster stories. Please write to us at Kitchen Disasters, Cook's Country, P.O. Box 470739, Brookline, MA 02447. Or send an e-mail to **kitchendisasters@bcpress.com.** If we publish your story, you'll receive a complimentary one-year subscription to *Cook's Country*.

The Great American Cake

Baked Alaska

At first glance, this cake may look like a giant snowball, but tap under that thick layer of toasted meringue and you've struck gold—ice cream encased in tender pound cake. Although ice cream baked in pastry was a favorite dessert served by Thomas Jefferson, the meringue-crusted version we know today was named in 1869 at New York's famed Delmonico's restaurant to celebrate the purchase of Alaska.

To make this cake you'll need:

- **1 (16-ounce) frozen pound cake, thawed and cut into 1/4-inch-thick slices, with edges trimmed**
- **2 tablespoons plus 1 cup sugar**
- **3/4 cup water**
- **2 pints ice cream or sherbet, softened**
- **4 large egg whites**
- **1/4 teaspoon cream of tartar**
- **Pinch salt**
- **1/2 teaspoon vanilla extract**

For the cake: Line 1 1/2-quart bowl with plastic wrap, letting ends of wrap overhang bowl. Line bowl with even layer of cake slices, positioning slices with no spaces in between. Stir 2 tablespoons sugar and 1/4 cup water until sugar dissolves, and brush mixture over cake slices. Fill bowl with ice cream and smooth surface. Top with remaining cake slices. Cover with overhanging wrap, weigh down top with plate, and freeze until firm, at least 6 hours or up to 1 week.

To serve: Adjust oven rack to middle position and heat oven to 425 degrees. Boil 1 cup sugar with remaining 1/2 cup water until syrupy, about 4 minutes. With electric mixer, beat egg whites on medium-high speed until foamy. Add cream of tartar and salt and beat to soft peaks. Slowly add sugar syrup and vanilla and beat until thick and cooled, about 6 minutes. Remove plastic and invert cake onto ovensafe platter. Cover cake with meringue and bake until golden brown, about 5 minutes. Serve immediately.

Recipe Index

RC = Recipe Card

Cook's Country

OCTOBER/NOVEMBER 2006

Best Mashed Potatoes
Super-Creamy, Super-Easy

Blackout Cake
For Chocolate Lovers Only!

Foolproof Stuffed Turkey
No More Dry White Meat

PECAN CHICKEN CUTLETS
Crunchiest-Ever Crust

SLOW-COOKER BRISKET
Tender Beef, Rich Sauce

HOW TO BUY KNIVES
Best Collection under $100

MINI MEAT LOAVES
Ready in Just 30 Minutes

LOW-FAT ALFREDO SAUCE
No Cream, No Problem

CIDER-GLAZED PORK LOIN
Building Big Apple Flavor

PUMPKIN-PRALINE PIE
Perfecting a New Classic

PHILLY CHEESESTEAK
In Search of the Real Deal

ROASTED FALL VEGETABLES
A Fresh Look at Root Veggies

Our $1,000 Contest Winner!
Lisa Ashton of Aston, Pa., won first place in our holiday side-dish contest with a recipe that uses bacon, cheddar cheese, and sour cream to dress up cauliflower. See page 4 for her **Creamy Cauliflower Casserole.**

$4.95 U.S./$6.95 CANADA

Cook's Country

Dear Country Cook,

Pie! No three-letter word ever meant more to me growing up on a mountain farm in Vermont. That's because the town baker, Marie Briggs, made it look so easy, yet I knew from personal experience that pie making was enshrouded in mystery. Rolling out dough that didn't fall apart, that easily transferred to the pie dish, and that tasted light and flaky when baked—that was kitchen alchemy.

Country life is filled with secrets. A neighbor recently joined the local grange and discovered meetings full of ritual, secret passwords, and, of course, cooking contests. (She won second place in the statewide championship for her Hot Milk Cake.) And when I recently came across a perfect 50-foot hand-dug well on my family's property, it was a puzzle, an amazing feat of ancient engineering.

But for pie lovers, there is no mystery in the annual firehouse chicken and biscuit dinner. It is the Olympics for pie makers. There is strict ritual to the event. There are a dozen long tables, and the feed doesn't begin until exactly 5 p.m. At that time, those at the first table get up, follow the leader, march around the inside of the firehouse, then get into line for dinner, which is served with sides of mashed potatoes, beets, and corn pudding. The best part is the dessert table. This year, I chose the coconut cream pie and wasn't disappointed. I must have looked just like the kid in the photo because I was grinning so much.

Pie. Just one more reason why the country life is worth living.

Christopher Kimball
Founder and Editor, Cook's Country Magazine

Boy Eating a Piece of Pumpkin Pie, November 1957. A young boy enjoys a slice of pumpkin pie at a Thanksgiving bazaar at Calvary Methodist Church in Washington, D.C. © Wally McNamee/CORBIS.

OCTOBER/NOVEMBER 2006

Cook's Country

4

7

10

features

departments

in every issue

Visit us at cookscountry.com!
Go online for hundreds of recipes, food tastings, and up-to-date equipment reviews. You can get a behind-the-scenes look at our test kitchen, talk to our cooks and editors, enter recipe contests, and share recipes and cooking tips with the *Cook's Country* community.

Editorial Office: 17 Station Street, Brookline, MA 02445; 617-232-1000; fax 617-232-1572
Subscription Inquiries: Cook's Country, P.O. Box 8382, Red Oak, IA 51591-1382
800-526-8447

ON THE COVER: PHOTOGRAPHY: StockFood/Hunter. ILLUSTRATION: John Burgoyne.
IN THIS ISSUE: COLOR FOOD PHOTOGRAPHY: Keller + Keller. STYLING: Mary Jane Sawyer, Marie Piraino. ILLUSTRATION: Lisa Perrett.

Cook's Country magazine (ISSN 1552-1990), number 11, is published bimonthly by Boston Common Press Limited Partnership, 17 Station Street, Brookline, MA 02445. Copyright 2006 Boston Common Press Limited Partnership. Periodicals postage paid at Boston, Mass., and at additional mailing offices, USPS #023453. POSTMASTER: Send address changes to Cook's Country, P.O. Box 8382, Red Oak, IA 51591-1382. For subscription and gift subscription orders, subscription inquiries, or change-of-address notices, call 800-526-8447 in the U.S. or 515-247-7571 from outside the U.S., or write us at Cook's Country, P.O. Box 8382, Red Oak, IA 51591-1382.
PRINTED IN THE USA

Kitchen Shortcuts

READERS SHARE CLEVER TIPS FOR EVERYDAY COOKING CHALLENGES

Recipe Rolodex

KEEP IT CLEAN

I save all my recipes in one of those small photo albums with the plastic inserts, which keeps them nice and neat. I also label the albums, so that whenever I need a recipe I always know where to look.

Anna Couperthwait
Dunwoody, Ga.

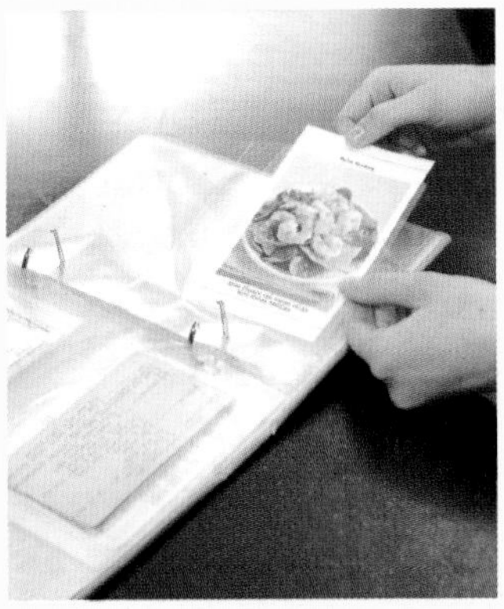

Measuring Scoops

I use spring-loaded ice cream scoops to measure my shortening and peanut butter. They come in different sizes that will hold 1/4, 1/3, and 1/2 cups. With these, I can measure any amount I need. They are a lot less messy than trying to fill a regular measuring cup.

Marcia Blosser
Yates Center, Kan.

Press-in Pie Crust

When making a graham cracker pie crust, the most difficult part of the job is pressing the crumbs into the pie plate. To save time and trouble when making a 9-inch pie, I use my 8-inch pie plate to press and smooth the crumbs into the larger pie plate. Give it a try!

John P. Jones
Sarasota, Fla.

Neat Trick!

RECIPE HANGER

To keep recipes from magazines (and elsewhere) at hand without risk of getting them dirty, I use a clothes hanger with clips. I hang the hanger from the cupboard door and use the clips to secure the magazine. It keeps my recipe at eye level, and it keeps my magazines—including this one—nice and clean!

Jody A. Leathers Winslow, Maine

IMPROVISED COOLING RACK

Around the holidays, I bake tons of cookies and cakes to give to friends and family, so I'm always short on cooling racks. Fortunately, I've learned to improvise. Now I use my muffin tins as a cooling rack—I just turn them upside down and place the hot pans right on top.

Erin Conlan
Essex, Conn.

FROZEN SOAP PADS

I like using soap pads, but I don't enjoy seeing them turn my sink into a rusty mess before they're all used up. Now once I use a pad I store it in a plastic bag in the freezer. Just a quick rinse under the tap and it's ready to use again. This way the pad wears out before it rusts.

Joyce Uglow
Watertown, Wis.

SMOOTH OPERATOR

For heavy appliances that are kept on the counter (food processor, bread machine, rice cooker, etc.), cut a piece of clean cardboard that will fit underneath the appliance without showing. The cardboard makes it easy to slide the appliance across the countertop. When you're done using the appliance, it slides just as easily back to the storage space—no heavy lifting necessary.

Martha Tabacco
Farmington Hills, Mich.

THINK AHEAD

When I make icebox cookie dough (or any make-ahead freezer recipe), I write the baking directions (oven temperature, position of oven racks, cooking time, etc.) right on the zipper-lock freezer bag with a permanent marker. Then I don't have to search for the recipe card when it's time to bake.

Barbara K. Filippelli
Pawling, N.Y.

MAKING SPACE

I've got a pretty small kitchen, so I came up with this shortcut for making more counter space. I open a drawer and cover it with a cookie sheet (a cutting board works great, too). The cookie sheet makes for instant "counter" space, where I can stack extra dishes or serving platters.

Kathryn Jandeska
River Forest, Ill.

AN EGG-CELLENT TIP

After I hard-cook and cool my eggs, I always write the date on the shells with a Magic Marker. That way I know which eggs in the fridge are hard-cooked and how old they are.

Pat Rininger
Massillon, Ohio

EASIEST EGG SALAD

When I make egg salad for sandwiches, I have to cut up the egg, then smash and season it before adding the mayo. This process leaves a mess on the counter, the bowl, and my hands. I discovered that I can do it with no mess at all by smashing the eggs inside a zipper-lock bag with the mayonnaise and seasonings. Voilà! It's ready for sandwiches.

Lisa Brown
Port Angeles, Wash.

NONSTICK CHEESE SLICING

When cutting semisoft cheeses like cheddar and Monterey Jack, wrap your knife blade with a sheet of parchment paper (freezer wrap and waxed paper work, too). The cheese won't stick to the paper or the blade!

Kathy Luckenbach
Astoria, Ore.

BOUQUET OF HERBS

To keep parsley and other leafy herbs fresh, snip the stem ends and stand the herbs in a small vase with a few inches of water. Set it on the counter as you would cut flowers—they'll stay fresh and look great!

Becky Bruce
Cedar Falls, Iowa

If you'd like to submit a tip, please send a letter to Kitchen Shortcuts, Cook's Country, P.O. Box 470739, Brookline, MA 02447. Or to send your tip by e-mail, visit **cookscountry.com/emailus.** Include your name, address, and phone number. If we publish your tip, you will receive a free one-year subscription to *Cook's Country.*

SQUEEGEE-CLEAN

Anytime I bake, I end up with flour, sugar, and everything else all over the kitchen counter. To simplify cleanup, I like to use an inexpensive squeegee to scrape the mess off the counter. It makes cleanup very quick and saves a lot of paper towels.

Catherine McKinley
Akron, Ohio

SIMMER WHILE YOU SLEEP

The night before preparing my Thanksgiving turkey, I remove the giblets and neck from the cavity of the turkey and place them in the slow cooker (set on low) with water, celery, onion, and a bay leaf. When I wake up in the morning, the giblets are soft and ready to chop for the stuffing or gravy, and I have turkey broth to use in both, too.

Peggy Weed
Yakima, Wash.

BEST WAY TO CUT CHEESECAKE

The easiest way to cut sweets like cheesecake and cookie dough is not with dental floss but with a nylon classical guitar string. One end can be looped around a wooden dowel or spoon handle, and the string can be washed and reused. It even makes a wonderful sound if you stretch it tight enough (just kidding).

Howard Raber
Galena, Ill.

READ IT AND SWEEP

It seems like I can never find my dustpan when I need it. As a quick and easy substitute, I use my grandmother's old trick. I wet the edge of a sheet of newspaper with water and place it on the floor. The wet edge of the paper sticks fast to the floor, so I can sweep dust and dirt right over it and onto the rest of the paper. From there I just gather up the paper to contain the dirt and throw it all away!

Virginia Ruan
Gaithersburg, Md.

UNDERCOVER TURKEY

Low-fat ground turkey breast is appealing more and more to health-conscious families. But introducing it to kids (or even your spouse) can be tricky if they turn up their noses at the "white stuff" in their tacos or spaghetti sauce. When browning ground turkey meat, try adding a touch of Kitchen Bouquet or soy sauce to the pan; it immediately turns the white turkey meat brown, and it adds a bit of flavor.

Mary Caywood
Memphis, Tenn.

COUPON HOLDER

I frequently forget to give my coupons to the cashier at the supermarket checkout. I solved the problem by making out my grocery lists on inexpensive white envelopes. Once the grocery list is complete, I tuck the coupons I want to use inside the envelope.

Leah Anderson
San Jose, Calif.

NEAT KNEADING

I enjoy meat loaf, but it can be messy to prepare. To eliminate the need to clean the mixing bowl and wash my hands repeatedly, I put all of the ingredients in a large zipper-lock bag. (A 1-gallon bag comfortably holds 2 pounds of ground meat, plus any number of other ingredients.) I then remove as much air as possible, seal the bag, and proceed to "knead" the mixture until the ingredients are thoroughly combined.

Robyn Johnson
La Quinta, Calif.

TACOS FOR ONE

I love beef tacos, but I live alone and I don't want to purchase ground beef by the pound (it always ends up going to waste). As a solution, I keep hamburger patties in my freezer. Whenever I want a quick taco or two, I just toss a burger in a nonstick skillet over medium heat. As the meat thaws, I mash it up with a wooden spoon and add my special mix of herbs and spices. In no time at all, it's browned and ready to go.

Donald Zwier
Grayslake, Ill.

Hot Tip!

RON IT OUT

have a tiny kitchen with very little counter space, o whenever I bake cookies, I always run out of oom after the first tray. To make some extra space, pull out the ironing board and set it up to hold the rays of cookies while they cool.

Sarah Bullard Brighton, Mass.

Foil Cookie Sheet

If I want to make a bunch of cookies in a hurry, I create the largest cookie sheet that will fit in my oven. I use a few sheets of aluminum foil to cover one of the oven racks and put the cookie dough right on the foil. The cookies bake evenly, and, as an added bonus, I don't have to wash any cookie sheets.

Karine Karpati
Cupertino, Calif.

Fill 'er Up

I used to have such trouble getting rid of the oil after frying french fries. Now I let the oil cool and pour it through a funnel into an empty screw-top orange juice container. I just screw on the top, and the carton is ready for the garbage!

Tobin Cataldo
Birmingham, Ala.

DOUBLE DUTY

Preheated Plates

If I'm making a recipe that needs to be cooled for a period of time before being served (lasagna, for example), I cool the hot pan on top of my dinner plates (ovensafe plates, not the fine china!) instead of on a cooling rack or trivet. This way I can serve the food on warm plates.

Jane M. Ashworth Beavercreek, Ohio

Dip and Sift

Whenever I need to lightly flour a surface to roll out pastry crust or knead bread, I use my large perforated spoon. It makes short order of dipping and sifting, and it's easy to return any unused flour to the bin.

Deb Zihlman
Fort Worth, Texas

A Creamy Casserole Rejuvenates Ho-Hum Cauliflower

Cream cheese helps thicken and stabilize a super-easy, extra-creamy sauce for this cauliflower casserole.

Our $1,000 Grand-Prize Winner!

Lisa Ashton
Aston, Pa.

Lisa says: "My kids enjoy most vegetables and like to try new things, but cauliflower never grabbed them. Then I tweaked my mother's recipe a few times to make it more kid-friendly—all kids love cheese and bacon. I make this dish a lot for parties, and in my Italian family there's no shortage of parties."

CREAMY CAULIFLOWER CASSEROLE WITH BACON AND CHEDDAR

SERVES 6 TO 8

Roughly chopped cauliflower acts as a casserole "filler," much like rice or pasta, while the large florets add texture.

- 8 slices bacon, chopped, cooked until crisp, and cooled
- 3 cups shredded cheddar cheese
- 1 tablespoon chopped fresh parsley
- Salt
- 2 large cauliflower heads, trimmed and cut into 1-inch florets (about 8 cups)
- 4 ounces cream cheese
- 1/4 cup heavy cream
- 1/4 cup sour cream
- 1/2 teaspoon pepper

1. Mix bacon, ½ cup cheese, and parsley in small bowl. Set aside for topping.

2. Adjust oven rack to middle position and heat oven to 350 degrees. Bring 4 quarts water to boil in large pot. Add 1 tablespoon salt and cauliflower and cook until tender, about 7 minutes. Drain and rinse cauliflower with cold water. Transfer half of cauliflower to cutting board and roughly chop. (Topping and cauliflower may be refrigerated separately for up to 1 day.)

3. Melt cream cheese in now-empty pot over low heat. Stir in heavy cream and remaining 2½ cups cheese and cook until cheese starts to melt, about 3 minutes. Off heat, stir in sour cream, cauliflower, ½ teaspoon salt, and pepper. Transfer mixture to 2-quart baking dish, sprinkle with topping, and bake until browned and bubbly, about 15 minutes. Serve.

Our Runners-Up

Lisa Renshaw
Kansas City, Mo.

WHIPPED EGGNOG SWEET POTATOES

SERVES 6 TO 8

Lisa says: "I created this recipe with my son in mind, since he enjoys both sweet potatoes and eggnog. And after serving it year after year, I found it's the only side dish that never has any leftovers." The praline-like topping is optional, but it's definitely worth making.

- **1 large egg white, beaten**
- **1/2 cup cashews, toasted, cooled, and chopped fine**
- **4 tablespoons brown sugar**
- **1 teaspoon cinnamon**
- **2 pounds sweet potatoes, peeled and cut into 1-inch cubes**
- **1/3 cup heavy cream**
- **4 tablespoons butter, softened**
- **1/2 cup eggnog**
- **1 teaspoon grated zest plus 2 tablespoons juice from 1 orange**
- **1/4 teaspoon nutmeg**
- **1 teaspoon salt**

1. Adjust oven rack to middle position and heat oven to 300 degrees. Line baking sheet with parchment paper.

2. Toss egg white with nuts in large bowl. Mix 2 tablespoons brown sugar with cinnamon in medium bowl. Stir in nuts, spread on prepared baking sheet, and bake until hardened and candy-like, about 30 minutes. Let mixture cool completely, then crumble into small pieces. (Topping can be stored in airtight container for up to 5 days.)

3. Steam sweet potatoes in steamer basket set in large covered saucepan with 1 inch of boiling water until tender, about 20 minutes. Drain.

4. With electric mixer on medium speed, beat heavy cream in large bowl until stiff peaks form. Transfer to medium bowl. Beat sweet potatoes in now-empty bowl at medium-high speed until smooth, about 5 minutes. Beat in butter, remaining 2 tablespoons brown sugar, eggnog, orange zest and juice, nutmeg, and salt. Fold whipped cream into sweet potatoes, transfer to serving bowl, and sprinkle with nut mixture. Serve.

Peg Nelson
Milton, Mass.

CHERRY-APPLE DRESSING

SERVES 8 TO 10

Peg says: "A few years ago I decided to spice things up by adding cherries and apples to my cornbread stuffing recipe." If using homemade cornbread, you'll need an 11 by 8-inch pan of cornbread.

- **2 (18-ounce) packages store-bought cornbread, cut into 3/4-inch cubes (about 12 cups, including crumbs)**
- **2 cups dried cherries**
- **4 cups low-sodium chicken broth**
- **12 ounces bulk breakfast sausage**
- **2 small onions, chopped fine**
- **3 celery ribs, chopped fine**
- **1 garlic clove, minced**
- **1 tablespoon minced fresh sage**
- **1 teaspoon minced fresh thyme**
- **1 teaspoon salt**
- **1 teaspoon pepper**
- **2 tablespoons unsalted butter**
- **2 Granny Smith apples, peeled and grated**
- **1 large egg, beaten**

1. Adjust oven racks to upper-middle and lower-middle positions and heat oven to 250 degrees. Bake cornbread on 2 baking sheets until dried and crisp, 50 to 60 minutes. Cool completely, then transfer to large bowl.

2. Increase oven temperature to 400 degrees. Mix cherries and ½ cup broth in small bowl. Set aside.

3. Brown sausage in Dutch oven over medium-high heat, breaking up clumps, 5 to 7 minutes. Using slotted spoon, transfer sausage to plate. Add onions and celery to pot and cook until softened, 6 to 8 minutes. Stir in garlic, sage, thyme, salt, and pepper and cook until fragrant, about 1 minute. Transfer to bowl with cornbread. Melt butter in now-empty pot. Add apples and cook until just tender, about 6 minutes. Transfer to bowl with cornbread. Add cherry mixture to cornbread along with remaining 3½ cups broth, egg, and cooked sausage.

4. Transfer mixture to 3-quart baking dish and bake until top is golden brown and crisp, about 25 minutes. Serve.

Cheryl Ewing
Ellwood City, Pa.

ITALIAN-STYLE GREEN BEANS

SERVES 6 TO 8

Cheryl says: "My family grew tired of the good ol' green bean casserole that I loved to serve year after year on the holidays. So one year I decided to shake things up and created this recipe from ingredients I already had in my refrigerator and pantry. My family loved it—and they still love it, almost 20 years later." If you want to get a head start on this recipe, you can prepare the beans as directed in step 1 and store them in the refrigerator for up to 2 days.

- **Salt**
- **2 pounds green beans, ends trimmed**
- **2 tablespoons extra-virgin olive oil**
- **1 medium onion, chopped fine**
- **2 portobello mushroom caps, sliced thin**
- **2 red bell peppers, seeded and chopped fine**
- **1 garlic clove, minced**
- **1 (14.5-ounce) can diced tomatoes, drained**
- **1 tablespoon red wine vinegar**
- **1/4 teaspoon dried oregano**
- **Pepper**
- **3/4 cup shredded mozzarella cheese**
- **1/4 cup grated Parmesan cheese**

1. Adjust oven rack to middle position and heat oven to 450 degrees. Bring 4 quarts water to boil in Dutch oven. Add 1 tablespoon salt and beans and cook until tender, about 6 minutes. Drain and set aside. (The beans can be refrigerated for up to 2 days.)

2. Heat oil in now-empty Dutch oven over medium-high heat until shimmering. Add onion and mushrooms and cook until soft and liquid has evaporated, about 8 minutes. Add peppers and cook until soft, about 8 minutes. Add garlic and cook until fragrant, about 30 seconds. Stir in tomatoes, vinegar, oregano, and green beans. Season with salt and pepper.

3. Transfer mixture to 2-quart baking dish. Sprinkle with cheeses and bake until cheese is melted and bubbly, about 7 minutes. Serve.

Susan Asanovic
Wilton, Conn.

CHRISTMAS TREE CHARD

SERVES 6 TO 8

Susan says: "I love this colorful dish around the holidays. Just looking at it makes everyone feel cheerful. It's also a great way to serve dark greens to kids since they love the colors and the fruit."

- **3 tablespoons extra-virgin olive oil**
- **5 garlic cloves, minced**
- **2 bunches red chard, stemmed, cut into thin strips, and chopped (about 6 cups)**
- **2 bunches green chard, stemmed, cut into thin strips, and chopped (about 6 cups)**
- **Salt and pepper**
- **1 medium red onion, chopped fine**
- **1 teaspoon minced fresh rosemary**
- **3/4 cup cranberry juice**
- **2 teaspoons light brown sugar**
- **1/2 cup pine nuts, toasted**
- **1/4 cup dried cranberries**

1. Cook 2 tablespoons oil and half of garlic in Dutch oven over medium heat until garlic is just golden, about 3 minutes. Add chard, season with salt and pepper, cover, and cook, stirring occasionally, until chard is wilted, about 5 minutes. Transfer chard to large bowl.

2. Heat remaining 1 tablespoon oil in now-empty pot over medium heat until shimmering. Cook onion until softened, about 5 minutes. Add remaining garlic and rosemary and cook until fragrant, about 1 minute. Add cranberry juice and brown sugar and reduce until syrupy, about 2 minutes. Return chard to pot and toss with pine nuts and dried cranberries. Adjust seasonings. Serve.

We want your summer pasta sauce recipes for an upcoming contest. Please submit entries by November 30, 2006. Write to us at Recipe Contest, Cook's Country, P.O. Box 470739, Brookline, MA 02447. Or to contact us by e-mail, visit **cookscountry.com/emailus.** Include your name, address, and daytime phone number, and tell us what makes your recipe special. The grand-prize winner will receive $1,000. All entries become the property of *Cook's Country*. For more information on this and other contests, go to **cookscountry.com.**

Ask Cook's Country

WE'LL ANSWER ANY QUESTION YOU THROW AT US!

KEEPING KETCHUP

Should ketchup be stored in the refrigerator once opened? I recently noticed that there is nothing on the bottle that says "Refrigerate after opening." I really don't like cold ketchup, but does it go bad?

Greg Allen Port Townsend, Wash.

Although Heinz (America's top-selling brand) does not specify storage instructions on the bottle, the company does recommend refrigerating opened bottles of ketchup. High levels of acidity (from both the tomatoes and the vinegar) prevent ketchup from spoiling quickly at room temperature, but we wondered how long it would take for the flavor to be affected. To find out, we pitted refrigerated ketchup bottles against bottles left on the counter for specific amounts of time. The opened ketchup left on the counter for one week tasted fine, but samples left out for two weeks, one month, and two months tasted progressively "washed out" and "stale" compared with the more "robust," "brighter" flavor of the refrigerated ketchup. Our advice is to keep ketchup in the refrigerator and warm small amounts as needed in the microwave to take the chill off.

CONVENIENCE GARLIC

Whenever I go shopping, I see little bottles of peeled or chopped garlic. I wonder about the quality of these products. Are they as good as heads of fresh, unpeeled garlic?

Philip Boccia New Hyde Park, N.Y.

We go through a lot of garlic in the test kitchen, so we know firsthand that peeling and mincing many cloves can be tedious. Wondering if all this work was necessary for fresh garlic flavor, we bought two convenience garlic products—peeled whole cloves and minced jarred bits—and tested them against fresh garlic in two recipes: aioli (garlic mayonnaise) and spaghetti with garlic and oil. The minced product, which preserves the garlic in a solution of water and phosphoric acid, ruined both recipes with musty, bitter flavors, but the peeled cloves were pretty good, running a close second to the fresh garlic in both recipes.

MINCED GARLIC
Don't bother.

PEELED CLOVES
Almost as good as fresh.

Produce departments in some supermarkets carry small containers of cloves peeled in-house, which are significantly fresher than those bottled by a manufacturer; either way, look for cloves that are unblemished, creamy white in color, and firm. While heads of fresh garlic will keep for weeks (if not longer) in a cool, dry place with plenty of air circulation, peeled cloves are best stored in their container in the refrigerator and used within a few weeks.

STORING TOASTED NUTS

I always toast the nuts I use for baking. If I do this ahead of time, will the nuts keep their toasted flavor and texture for a few days?

Gail Coppola Waltham, Mass.

Keeping toasted nuts on hand seemed like a great idea, so we skillet-toasted four kinds (walnuts, pecans, blanched slivered almonds, and pine nuts), stored one batch at room temperature and another in the fridge, and tasted them against freshly toasted samples at four time intervals: 24 hours, 48 hours, one week, and one month.

While all of the nuts tasted best when toasted fresh, both the refrigerated and room-temperature stored toasted almonds fooled many tasters, who found little difference even between the day-old and month-old toasted nuts. Walnuts and pecans, while not unpleasant, staled slightly after 48 hours and lost some of their toasty flavors. Pine nuts fared worst in both lineups; the day-old samples tasted noticeably duller, and the month-old nuts garnered comments such as "funky" and "rancid."

Why did pine nuts fare so poorly in this test while almonds did so well? Pine nuts contain a lot of unsaturated fat, which is highly susceptible to rancidity when exposed to oxygen and heat (one reason why pine nuts should always be refrigerated). Almonds contain less fat than walnuts and pecans, but, more important, the flash-boiling process used to blanch almonds also cooks them slightly, making them less susceptible to spoilage.

FREEZING LEMONS

Can you freeze lemons and then thaw them for juicing?

'Trinketbuyer' Via e-mail

We don't recommend freezing lemons at home. After sampling lemonade and glazed lemon cookies made with both fresh and frozen-then-thawed lemons, tasters had no trouble figuring out which batch was made with the latter, identifying "insipid," "dull," and "bitter" flavors. Some research explained our findings. When lemons (and other citrus fruits) are frozen slowly—as happens in most home freezers—the water in the fruit expands as it freezes, forming large ice crystals that tear through cell walls. This causes the release of enzymes that give the fruit off-flavors when it thaws. If you find yourself with an overabundance of lemons, juice them and freeze the juice in an ice-cube tray, then transfer the cubes to a freezer zipper-lock bag for up to two months. Tasters noticed only minor flavor differences between frozen and fresh juice.

When life gives you lemons, squeeze them and freeze the juice.

BEST WAY TO WASH A KNIFE

I've always heard that it's important to wash knives by hand rather than in the dishwasher. But a friend (and accomplished cook) recently told me that he thought that was to protect the wooden handles rather than the blades. Is this true?

'Mtamy' Via e-mail

There are many reasons to hand-wash your knives, no matter what the handle material (although prolonged submersion in water can damage handles made of natural materials like wood, bone, and horn). The excessive motion inside the dishwasher can cause the knife blade to bump up against other surfaces, damaging the blade. The extreme changes in temperature can cause the metal rivets and joints in the handle to expand and contract and eventually loosen. Finally, dishwashing detergents are harsh and can eat away at the blade. We recommend hand-washing knives in mild soapy water and drying them thoroughly and immediately after each use.

PARCHMENT VERSUS WAXED PAPER

What's the difference between parchment paper and waxed paper? Can I use them interchangeably in the kitchen?

Marcus Willingham San Francisco, Calif.

Similar as they may appear, parchment and waxed papers are not contenders for all kitchen tasks. Parchment paper is treated with sulfuric acid and then coated with a sheer layer of silicone; combined, these treatments create parchment paper's hard, heat- and moisture-resistant nonstick surface. Waxed paper is made from very thin, porous, gauze-like paper that is triple-coated with a food-grade paraffin wax. The wax provides strength and moisture resistance, but it is heat-sensitive and chars at low temperatures. That said, waxed paper is ovensafe for lining cake pans, where the batter protects it from direct heat, but stick with parchment paper when lining cookie sheets.

To ask us a cooking question, write to Ask Cook's Country, P.O. Box 470739, Brookline, MA 02447. Or to contact us by e-mail, visit **cookscountry.com/emailus.** See if you can stump us!

Lost Recipes CHOCOLATE BLACKOUT CAKE

Brooklyn still mourns the loss of the Dodgers and Ebinger's Baking Company, but at least New Yorkers (and anyone else who likes a good chocolate cake) can re-create this well-loved recipe at home.

LOST ICON
Ebinger's Baking Company opened in 1898 on Flatbush Avenue in Brooklyn and grew into a chain of more than 60 stores before going bankrupt in 1972. Started by Arthur Ebinger, a baker who emigrated from Germany with a vast collection of recipes, the business grew to include his wife and their three sons. During its heyday, Ebinger's was a point of bragging rights for Brooklynites, as celebrities and the well-to-do from Manhattan never went to Brooklyn without taking home a cake or one of Ebinger's other specialties, which included challah, rye bread, pumpkin pie, Othellos (filled mini-sponge cakes covered in chocolate), and crumb buns.

The craggy, textured exterior of Chocolate Blackout Cake gives this classic dessert its signature look.

Mention Ebinger's to most Brooklynites over the age of 40 and you'll see a sparkle of nostalgia in their eyes. Bring up Chocolate Blackout Cake and you might actually see a tear or two. When the Brooklyn-based chain of bakeries closed its doors, the borough went into mourning. On that fateful day, August 27, 1972, the *New York Times* ran a story titled, "Tears Replace the Coffee Cakes." Of all the lost Ebinger's recipes, none have received more attention in the past 35 years than its Chocolate Blackout Cake.

A forerunner of "death by chocolate" confections, Chocolate Blackout Cake is decidedly decadent, marrying fudgy, dark chocolate layers with a rich, creamy chocolate pudding that acts as both filling and frosting. But what really sets this cake apart is yet another dimension of chocolate flavor—its signature shaggy coating of chocolate cake crumbs.

Blackout Cake got its name from the blackout drills performed by the Civilian Defense Corps during World War II. When the navy sent its ships to sea from the Brooklyn Navy Yard, the streets of the borough were "blacked out" to avoid silhouetting the battleships against the cityscapes of Brooklyn and Manhattan. The cake was so named because of its darkly chocolate—practically "black"—appearance. According to some, the crumbled cake crumbs on top are reminiscent of a city skyline.

Ebinger's original recipe was never published, leaving cookbook authors and Brooklyn grandmothers to rely on their taste buds to reproduce "authentic" versions. I compiled a folder of promising recipes, but the only things they had in common were long ingredient lists and complicated cooking techniques. I wanted a great-tasting cake, but it also had to be simple and easy.

I started with the cake layers. For big chocolate flavor, most recipes rely on regular cocoa powder, but I found it too astringent. The less acidic Dutch-processed cocoa was better, but I wanted even more chocolate flavor. I tried adding melted chocolate, but the cake became dense and gummy.

I had better luck when I used a few test kitchen tricks to bring out the subtleties of the cocoa. The tang of buttermilk carried the chocolate flavor; other dairy products seemed to mute it. Adding brewed coffee to the batter enhanced the nuances of the cocoa, as did a combination of brown and white sugar. But still I pined for more depth. Borrowing a spice-blooming technique from the savory kitchen, I added the cocoa powder to the butter that I was already melting for the cake. As the pungent aroma of cocoa filled the kitchen, I knew that I would be rewarded for my gamble. The cake made with toasted cocoa was dark and rich, with a distinct chocolate flavor.

To keep things simple, I decided to mix the cake batter right in the saucepan with the butter and cocoa. Although unconventional, this streamlined method yielded a perfect cake and saved me a load of time (and a load of dishes).

The traditional pudding component of the cake should be velvety, with a dark chocolate tang, yet viscous enough to cling to the sides of the cake like a frosting. Some recipes achieve this with a bitter mixture of cocoa, chocolate, cornstarch, and water. Given the already-pronounced chocolate flavor in the cake, my tasters preferred a sweeter, more dairy-rich chocolate flavor in the pudding. A combination of half-and-half and milk gave the pudding a satiny quality, while unsweetened chocolate produced the most depth of flavor.

Once the two cake layers and the pudding had cooled, it was time to assemble this skyscraper. I divided the cakes along their equators, planning to use three of the four resulting rounds as layers and the fourth for the crumbled cake topping. I spread a generous amount of pudding between the layers and coated the exterior of the cake with the rest. To finish it off, I crumbled the reserved layer and sprinkled it over the top of the cake and pressed the crumbs into the sides. After just one bite, I realized why Brooklynites still talk about this cake 35 years after the closing of Ebinger's. **–Jeremy Sauer**

CHOCOLATE BLACKOUT CAKE

SERVES 10 TO 12

Be sure to give the pudding and the cake enough time to cool or you'll end up with runny pudding and gummy cake.

Pudding

- **1 1/4 cups granulated sugar**
- **1/4 cup cornstarch**
- **1/2 teaspoon salt**
- **2 cups half-and-half**
- **1 cup whole milk**
- **6 ounces unsweetened chocolate, chopped**
- **2 teaspoons vanilla extract**

(recipe continued on page 8)

How to ASSEMBLE BLACKOUT CAKE

1. Using your hands, crumble one cake layer into medium-sized crumbs.

2. Spread the pudding all over the top and sides of the cake.

3. Sprinkle the reserved cake crumbs all over the top and sides of the cake, then use your hands to gently press the crumbs into the pudding.

Chocolate Blackout Cake

continued from page 7

Cake Layers

- 8 tablespoons (1 stick) unsalted butter, plus extra for greasing pans
- $1\frac{1}{2}$ cups all-purpose flour, plus extra for dusting pans
- 2 teaspoons baking powder
- $\frac{1}{2}$ teaspoon baking soda
- $\frac{1}{2}$ teaspoon salt
- $\frac{3}{4}$ cup Dutch-processed cocoa
- 1 cup brewed coffee
- 1 cup buttermilk
- 1 cup packed light brown sugar
- 1 cup granulated sugar
- 2 large eggs
- 1 teaspoon vanilla extract

1. For the pudding: Whisk sugar, cornstarch, salt, half-and-half, and milk in large saucepan. Set pan over medium heat. Add chocolate and whisk constantly until chocolate melts and mixture begins to bubble, 2 to 4 minutes. Stir in vanilla and transfer pudding to large bowl. Place plastic wrap directly on surface of pudding and refrigerate until cold, at least 4 hours or up to 1 day.

2. For the cake layers: Adjust oven rack to middle position and heat oven to 325 degrees. Butter and flour two 8-inch cake pans. Whisk flour, baking powder, baking soda, and salt in bowl.

3. Melt butter in large saucepan over medium heat. Stir in cocoa and cook until fragrant, about 1 minute. Off heat, whisk in coffee, buttermilk, and sugars until dissolved. Whisk in eggs and vanilla, then slowly whisk in flour mixture.

4. Divide batter evenly between prepared pans and bake until toothpick inserted in center comes out clean, 30 to 35 minutes. Cool layers in pans 15 minutes, then invert onto wire rack. Cool to room temperature, at least 1 hour.

5. To assemble the cake: Cut each cake in half horizontally. Crumble one cake layer into medium crumbs and set aside. Place one cake layer on serving platter or cardboard round. Spread 1 cup pudding over cake layer and top with another layer. Repeat with 1 cup pudding and last cake layer. Spread remaining pudding evenly over top and sides of cake. Sprinkle cake crumbs evenly over top and sides of cake, pressing lightly to adhere crumbs. Serve. (Cake can be refrigerated for up to 2 days.)

Recipe Makeover FETTUCCINE ALFREDO

Can you eliminate all of the cream and most of the butter and still have a pasta dish worth eating?

Ready in just 20 minutes, fettuccine Alfredo is perfect for weeknight cooking. But once most home cooks see that standard recipes contain $1\frac{1}{2}$ cups of heavy cream, a stick of butter, and 2 cups of cheese, they consign this dish to the occasional restaurant indulgence. That's a shame, because fettuccine Alfredo is actually better suited to home preparation; the creamy sauce turns cold and stiff if it sits for even a few minutes, as invariably happens in restaurants. Could I develop a recipe that would lose much of the fat while retaining the rich flavor of traditional Alfredo?

Many low-fat Alfredo recipes cut calories simply by switching out the cream for lower-fat dairy products such as half-and-half, whole milk, or evaporated milk.

I tried adding a cornstarch slurry (cornstarch dissolved in liquid) to each of these dairy products to replicate the thickening effect of heavy cream. Tasters preferred the product with the most fat, the half-and-half, praising its rich flavor. But they also commented that the half-and-half/cornstarch combination wasn't producing a properly thickened sauce.

I had better luck using a roux (a cooked mixture of butter and flour) to thicken my sauce. With very little roux (just 1 tablespoon of butter and 2 teaspoons of flour), I was able to thicken the sauce nicely.

With an effective thickener in place, I had hoped to use something less fattening than half-and-half. After several tests, tasters settled on $\frac{3}{4}$ cup whole milk and just $\frac{1}{4}$ cup half-and-half for a happy medium of creamy texture, rich taste, and reduced fat. As for the cheese, my tasters demanded a full cup of Parmesan, which contributed just 4 grams of fat per serving but added nutty, complex flavor.

My sauce was now pretty good, but a few tasters rightfully complained that it seemed "too sweet" and "too milky." A pinch of nutmeg and plenty of black pepper added some savory notes, but simmering a crushed garlic clove in the sauce was a key discovery. The sharpness of the garlic worked perfectly to cut any hint of sweetness and added another dimension of flavor to the sauce as well.

I had made tremendous progress (cutting nearly three-quarters of the fat from the original recipe), but even my silky, rich sauce clumped and clotted if not served right away. I found that tossing the pasta and sauce with $\frac{1}{3}$ cup of the pasta cooking water thinned the sauce enough to stave off the inevitable thickening that occurred as it cooled. And by heating my serving bowls with hot water before filling them with pasta, I was able to keep my rich Alfredo hot and at the proper consistency for a longer period of time.

–Cali Rich

Our low-fat Alfredo is quick and easy, and big on creamy, rich flavor and texture.

And the Numbers...

All nutritional information is for a single serving.

TRADITIONAL FETTUCCINE ALFREDO
CALORIES: **580**
FAT: **43g**
SATURATED FAT: **27g**

COOK'S COUNTRY LOW-FAT FETTUCCINE ALFREDO
CALORIES: **320**
FAT: **12g**
SATURATED FAT: **6g**

LOW-FAT FETTUCCINE ALFREDO

SERVES 4 AS A FIRST COURSE

Make the sauce while the pasta water is heating up. Once the sauce is done, you should be ready to cook the pasta. Fresh pasta is more porous than dried, and we recommend it here because it will better absorb the sauce.

- 1 tablespoon unsalted butter
- 2 teaspoons all-purpose flour
- $\frac{3}{4}$ cup whole milk
- $\frac{1}{4}$ cup half-and-half
- 1 garlic clove, peeled and lightly crushed
- Salt and pepper
- Pinch nutmeg
- 1 cup grated Parmesan cheese
- 1 (9-ounce) package fresh fettuccine

1. Bring 4 quarts water to boil in large pot over high heat. Using ladle, fill each of 4 individual serving bowls with about $\frac{1}{2}$ cup boiling water. Set aside.

2. Heat butter over medium heat in large saucepan until foaming. Whisk in flour until mixture is smooth and golden, 1 to 2 minutes. Whisk in milk, half-and-half, garlic, $\frac{1}{2}$ teaspoon salt, $\frac{1}{2}$ teaspoon pepper, and nutmeg and bring to simmer. Reduce heat to medium-low and simmer until sauce is slightly thickened, 1 to 2 minutes. Discard garlic, stir in Parmesan, and remove from heat.

3. Stir 1 tablespoon salt and pasta into boiling water and cook, stirring constantly, until al dente, 2 to 3 minutes. Reserve 1 cup pasta cooking water, then drain pasta.

4. Return sauce to low heat, add $\frac{1}{3}$ cup pasta water and cooked pasta; toss until evenly coated. Cook until sauce has thickened slightly, about 1 minute. Add more cooking water as needed to thin sauce to proper consistency and adjust seasonings. Working quickly, empty water from warmed bowls and fill with pasta. Serve immediately.

Slow Cooking BEEF BRISKET

A big, tough piece of brisket is perfect for the slow cooker, but not if the meat ends up swimming in a watery sauce.

Everyone knows brisket is tough and needs prolonged cooking to make it tender, which, of course, is just what the slow cooker does best. Or so I thought. I wanted to adapt a traditional braised brisket recipe with a potent onion and red wine sauce for my slow cooker. I browned the brisket, cooked the onions, and then added both to the slow cooker along with broth, red wine, tomato paste, and herbs. Nine hours later, I had a shrunken (but tender) brisket swimming in a vast sea of watery, greasy sauce.

What I came to realize is that brisket (unlike most cuts of meat) releases a lot of liquid as it cooks—up to 4 cups by my measurements. Given the copious brisket juices, it was a mistake to add much more liquid to the slow cooker. In an effort to trim the liquid, I replaced 1 cup of red wine with 2 tablespoons of red wine vinegar, a concentrated ingredient that added depth with a touch of acidity. Then I cut the amount of broth in half and used flour to thicken the sauce. But because each brisket I cooked lost varying amounts of liquid, the resulting sauces were either too thick or thin. In the end, I found the only way to achieve a consistent result was to reduce the sauce on the stovetop at the end of cooking. Finishing the sauce on the stovetop also allowed me to skim off excess fat.

With my sauce taken care of, I revisited the meat. Although many slow-cooker recipes advocate a dump-and-cook approach, in the test kitchen we've found that browning meat before it goes into the slow cooker is a crucial step. But given how much my brisket was shrinking, I had to start with a really big piece. Unfortunately, a 5-pound brisket doesn't fit neatly in any skillet I own. Could I flavor the meat another way?

I thought of my other favorite brisket recipe—barbecued brisket. Rubbing the meat with spices and letting it "cure" in the refrigerator overnight is a key step in that recipe. Could I replace the barbecue spices with onion powder, garlic powder, paprika, cayenne pepper, and salt? Sure enough, this simple spice rub added a lot of flavor. Pricking the meat with a fork before applying the spices helped them to penetrate even more. In side-by-side tests, my tasters said the spice rub added even more flavor than browning—and it was a whole lot easier.

Now that I wasn't browning the brisket, I wondered if I could lose this step for the onions. No matter what I tried, the sauce tasted weak and watery unless I took 20 minutes to brown the onions and build a sauce. Logistically, it was easy to season the brisket and make the onion gravy the night before. With the two main components in the fridge, in the morning I could get everything (including some fresh herbs) into the slow cooker in the time it took to make two slices of toast. **–Katie Henderson**

SLOW-COOKER BRISKET AND ONIONS

SERVES 8

The leaner flat-cut brisket is the better choice for this recipe. The thicker point cut is much fattier—a good thing on the grill, where the excess fat can drip away, but a disadvantage in a slow cooker, where the fat can make the sauce greasy. If you end up with an especially thick piece of brisket, extend the cooking time to 11 hours.

- **1 tablespoon vegetable oil**
- **3 large onions (about 2 pounds), halved and sliced 1/2 inch thick**
- **1 tablespoon light brown sugar**
- **Salt**
- **1 tablespoon tomato paste**
- **2 tablespoons all-purpose flour**
- **3 garlic cloves, minced**
- **1 3/4 cups low-sodium chicken broth**
- **2 tablespoons plus 1 teaspoon red wine vinegar**
- **1 tablespoon paprika**
- **2 teaspoons onion powder**
- **1 teaspoon garlic powder**
- **1/8 teaspoon cayenne pepper**
- **1 (5-pound) flat-cut beef brisket, trimmed of excess fat**
- **3 sprigs fresh thyme**
- **3 bay leaves**

1. Heat oil in large skillet over medium-high heat until shimmering. Cook onions, brown sugar, and 1/4 teaspoon salt until onions are golden, 10 to 12 minutes. Stir in tomato paste and flour and cook until darkened, about 2 minutes. Add garlic and cook until fragrant, about 30 seconds. Stir in broth and cook until sauce thickens, about 4 minutes. Off heat, stir in 2 tablespoons vinegar and transfer mixture to bowl.

2. Combine 1 teaspoon salt, paprika, onion powder, garlic powder, and cayenne in bowl. Using fork, prick brisket all over. Rub spice mixture over brisket and wrap tightly in plastic. Cover bowl with onion mixture with plastic wrap. Refrigerate brisket and bowl with onion mixture overnight.

3. The next morning, add half of onion mixture to slow-cooker insert. Add thyme and bay leaves and place brisket, fat side up, on top. Spread remaining onion mixture over brisket. Set slow cooker to low, cover, and cook until brisket is fork-tender, 9 to 10 hours (or cook on high for 5 to 6 hours). Turn cooker off and allow brisket to rest for 30 minutes.

4. Transfer brisket to cutting board, cut across grain into 1/2-inch slices, and transfer to serving platter. Tent with foil. Pour sauce into large skillet, discard herbs, and simmer over high heat until slightly thickened, 8 to 10 minutes. Skim fat, add remaining vinegar, then pour half of sauce over brisket. Serve with remaining sauce on side.

To make the meat especially juicy and easy to slice, turn off the slow cooker and let the fully cooked brisket rest in the sauce for half an hour before carving it.

Kitchen Know-How
THE INCREDIBLE SHRINKING BRISKET

Don't be alarmed if the edges of the brisket sit above the liquid in the slow-cooker insert. As the brisket cooks, it will shrink and the edges will become submerged in the liquid.

Pecan-Crusted Chicken

I like the idea of coating chicken cutlets with ground pecans. But the nuts either fall off or burn. What am I doing wrong? –Jenna Campbell, Ann Arbor, Mich.

Test Kitchen Tip
PRODUCING PERFECT CUTLETS

Chicken breasts are too thick to use in this recipe (the outside will burn long before the meat cooks through), and packaged cutlets are often too thin (the meat overcooks before the coating browns). For crisp, browned cutlets that are perfectly cooked through, it's best to buy chicken breasts and cut them in half yourself. Each breast should yield two pieces that are about 1/2 inch thick.

Adding a pecan crust is a great way to dress up boring chicken cutlets. Too bad this easy-sounding recipe is so problematic. Ground nuts don't readily adhere to the chicken, and, when they do, they usually burn long before the chicken is cooked through.

After testing several recipes, it was easy to see why everything goes so wrong. Most recipes use only beaten eggs to adhere the nuts to the chicken. I found that eggs alone aren't tacky enough to secure the heavy coating, so the nuts fall off in the pan. I tried the classic breading procedure for cutlets—coating them first in flour, then eggs, and finally the nuts. This method kept the crust in place during frying, but as soon as my tasters put fork to chicken, the crust fell away in sheets.

I decided to focus on making the eggs "stickier." After several false starts, I hit upon the solution—Dijon mustard, which turned the eggs thick and gluey. It occurred to me that my egg-mustard mixture was on its way to being a marinade, so I kept going, stirring in minced garlic, salt, pepper, and a little tarragon (to complement the sweetness of the pecans). Not only did the pecan crust stay put in the pan and on the plate, but just 10 minutes in the marinade made the chicken taste much better.

I still had one big problem, though: The nuts were burning. Unlike bread-crumb crusts, which need a fair amount of time in a hot skillet to crisp up, nut crusts brown quickly because of their high oil content. Some recipes solve this burning issue by baking the coated chicken cutlets, but no one in the test kitchen liked the pallid, soggy results. For a really crisp coating, pan-frying seemed to be my only option.

To keep the nuts from burning, I tried mixing them with some fresh bread crumbs. Their flavor was neutral (other options, such as crushed crackers and cereal, were too distracting), and the crumbs did indeed help to keep the nuts from burning. A few teaspoons of moisture-absorbing cornstarch ensured an ultra-crisp crust, and a pinch each of cinnamon and brown sugar highlighted the subtle sweetness of the pecans. **–Stephanie Alleyne**

To build flavor, we soak the chicken in a highly seasoned mixture of egg, garlic, and herbs before adding the pecan crust.

PECAN-CRUSTED CHICKEN CUTLETS

SERVES 4

Do not process the pecans too finely or their natural oils will be released and you'll end up with pecan paste.

- **2 large eggs**
- **4 teaspoons Dijon mustard**
- **3 garlic cloves, minced**
- **2 teaspoons dried tarragon**
- **Salt and pepper**
- **4 boneless, skinless chicken breasts (about 1 1/2 pounds), halved horizontally**
- **2 cups pecans**
- **2 slices hearty white sandwich bread, torn in half**
- **4 teaspoons cornstarch**
- **1 tablespoon dark brown sugar**
- **1/8 teaspoon cinnamon**
- **1 cup vegetable oil**

1. Adjust oven rack to middle position and heat oven to 250 degrees. Line rimmed baking sheet with wire rack. Whisk eggs, mustard, garlic, tarragon, ½ teaspoon salt, and ½ teaspoon pepper in large bowl. Add chicken, coat well, cover with plastic wrap, and refrigerate while preparing nut mixture.

2. Pulse pecans in food processor until finely chopped, with some pebble-sized pieces. Transfer to pie plate or shallow rimmed dish. Pulse bread in food processor until finely ground. Add bread crumbs to nuts and stir in cornstarch, brown sugar, ½ teaspoon pepper, ¼ teaspoon salt, and cinnamon.

3. Working one at a time, remove cutlets from egg mixture, letting excess drip back into bowl. Thoroughly coat chicken with nut mixture, pressing on coating to help it adhere, and transfer to large plate.

4. Heat ½ cup oil in large nonstick skillet over medium-high heat until shimmering. Place 4 cutlets in skillet and cook until golden brown on both sides, 3 to 4 minutes per side (lower heat if crust is browning too quickly). Transfer chicken to rack on baking sheet and keep warm in oven. Discard oil and solids from skillet and repeat with remaining oil and cutlets. Season cutlets with salt and pepper and serve immediately.

On the Side: Orange-Cranberry Rice Pilaf

A few seasonal ingredients make ordinary pilaf a standout side dish.

At its most basic, rice pilaf is long-grain rice first toasted in butter or oil, until the grains are fragrant and nutty, and then simmered in water. Onions, dried fruits, herbs, and spices are often added for depth of flavor and texture. With oranges and cranberries in season at this time of year, I thought their flavors might add an interesting twist to regular pilaf.

Using the test kitchen's recipe for basic rice pilaf, I cooked onion in butter until soft and then stirred in 1 1/2 cups of long-grain rice. To infuse the rice with orange flavor, I tried replacing 1 cup of the water (our recipe calls for 2 1/4 cups) with fresh squeezed orange juice. My instincts were right on, but the proportion was way off. Just 1/2 cup of juice proved potent enough to flavor the rice. Swapping the remaining water for chicken broth gave my pilaf richness and tempered the sweetness of the juice. A few strips of zest added more orange flavor without adding sweetness.

As for the cranberries, I used dried and found they were best sprinkled on top of the rice while it rested off heat for 10 minutes (if added earlier, the fruit became bloated and discolored the rice). Whole dried cranberries proved too leathery; chopping them was a simple solution. **–Stephanie Alleyne**

ORANGE-CRANBERRY RICE PILAF

SERVES 4 TO 6

Use a vegetable peeler to obtain the wide strips of orange zest. Although you may be inclined to substitute basmati for the long-grain rice, we advise against it; basmati did not work as well. See page 30 for details.

- **3 tablespoons unsalted butter**
- **1 small onion, chopped fine**
- **Salt**
- **1 1/2 cups long-grain rice**
- **1 3/4 cups low-sodium chicken broth**
- **3 strips zest plus 1/2 cup juice from 1 to 2 oranges**
- **1 bay leaf**
- **1/2 cup dried cranberries, chopped fine**
- **6 scallions, chopped fine**
- **Pepper**

1. Melt butter in large saucepan over medium heat. Add onion and 1/2 teaspoon salt and cook until softened, about 3 minutes. Stir in rice and cook, stirring occasionally, until fragrant and edges begin to turn translucent, about 3 minutes.

2. Stir in broth, orange zest and juice, and bay leaf and bring to boil over medium-high heat. Cover, reduce heat to low, and cook until liquid is absorbed and rice is tender, about 20 minutes. Quickly sprinkle cranberries and scallions over rice (do not stir), replace lid, and let rice stand off heat 10 minutes. Discard bay leaf and zest and fluff rice with fork. Season with salt and pepper to taste. Serve.

On the Side: Double-Corn Cornbread

Can North and South unite over cornbread?

It's funny that something as humble as cornbread can be so polarizing. In the North, cornbread is cakey and sweet, while Southerners demand theirs thin, crusty, and utterly savory. For me, cornbread should offer the best of both worlds—neither too muffin-like nor too austere. Ideally, my cornbread would fall politely between the extremes: tender and slightly sweet, yet dark and crunchy. I also wanted it bursting with bold corn flavor. The question, then, was how best to marry the two regional styles without inciting civil war in the test kitchen.

I started with the cornmeal. Most self-respecting Southerners insist on white cornmeal, while Northerners prefer yellow. But in tests pitting white against yellow, my blindfolded tasters (from both sides of the Mason-Dixon line) were hard-pressed to detect significant differences. In short: Either one works fine. Now the question was, how much? Southern recipes call for more cornmeal than flour (typically 1 1/2 cups cornmeal to a mere 1/2 cup flour), while Northern cornbread usually reverses the ratio. For cornbread that was neither too crumbly nor too cake-like, I had the best luck using equal amounts of each.

In search of more corn flavor, I found several recipes that swapped the buttermilk I had been using for a combination of sour cream (for tang) and a can of creamed corn. My tasters loved the added richness imparted by the sour cream but found the canned corn tinny. Not wanting to give up on creamed corn just yet, I made a quick homemade version by pureeing defrosted frozen kernels with the sour cream. This mixture, along with two eggs for moisture and structure and a shot of hot sauce for kick, gave my cornbread great flavor.

Some recipes use bacon fat to enrich the cornbread, while others rely on melted butter. The bacon fat imparted good flavor, but having to cook bacon was an extra step I wanted to avoid. Melted butter was the easier choice, and it created a nice, golden brown crust.

The most controversial ingredient was the sugar. It is taboo in Southern recipes, while Northern recipes often call for as much as 1/2 cup. To enhance the natural sweetness of the corn without making sweet corn muffins, I settled on 2 tablespoons.

Regardless of region, cornbread fares best in a super-hot oven, and 450 degrees proved the best temperature to form a craggy crust. This blast of heat also got the most from the leaveners. For the crunchiest, brownest bottom crust, a preheated pan (preferably cast iron, the traditional Southern choice) is a must. The key is to preheat the pan until it's ripping hot. The batter should sizzle as it hits the pan. **–Stephanie Alleyne**

DOUBLE-CORN CORNBREAD

SERVES 8 TO 10

A cast-iron skillet (or any ovensafe pan) is our first choice for this recipe, but a 9-inch cake pan will also work. Instead of heating it on the stovetop, place the cake pan with the oil in the preheated oven for 5 minutes before adding the batter.

- **1 cup cornmeal (yellow or white)**
- **1 cup all-purpose flour**
- **2 tablespoons sugar**
- **2 teaspoons baking powder**
- **1/4 teaspoon baking soda**
- **3/4 teaspoon salt**
- **1 cup frozen corn, thawed**
- **1 cup sour cream**
- **2 large eggs**
- **1/2 teaspoon hot sauce**
- **4 tablespoons unsalted butter, melted**
- **2 teaspoons vegetable oil**

1. Adjust oven rack to middle position and heat oven to 450 degrees. Whisk cornmeal, flour, sugar, baking powder, baking soda, and salt in large bowl. Pulse corn, sour cream, eggs, and hot sauce in food processor until corn is coarsely chopped and mixture is combined. Fold corn mixture into cornmeal mixture, then stir in melted butter.

2. Heat oil in 10-inch skillet over medium-high heat until just beginning to smoke. Take skillet off heat; quickly add batter and place skillet in oven. Bake until toothpick inserted in center comes out clean, about 25 minutes. Cool cornbread in skillet on wire rack for 20 minutes (handle will be hot). Serve warm.

Meaty Freezer Lasagna

LASAGNA FOOD FACT:

According to food historians, lasagna originally consisted of thin layers of sun-dried dough that was more like flat bread than what we think of as lasagna. In medieval times the dough was often layered with a sweet, creamy filling. It wasn't until the widespread cultivation of the tomato plant in the 1700s that lasagna began to take on its familiar, modern form as a baked noodle casserole.

No Boil, No Fuss

No-boil noodles, which are precooked and dehydrated before packaging, freeze beautifully and bake up tender but not mushy—if handled correctly.

TIME SAVER

How do you get the convenience of Stouffer's but the taste of homemade?

When Vernon Stouffer began freezing and selling the most popular dishes on the menu of his family restaurant in post–World War II Cleveland, he helped create American convenience cooking. Lasagna has long been one of the company's frozen offerings, and it's not hard to understand why. Lasagna is so time-consuming to assemble that many people don't mind the tired flavor and softened texture that characterize even homemade frozen lasagnas. Still, wouldn't it be nice to pull a really good lasagna out of the freezer?

Turning to one of the test kitchen's favorite recipes, I assembled the requisite components: a batch of hearty tomato meat sauce, a rich mixture of egg and Parmesan and ricotta cheeses, a generous bowl of shredded mozzarella, and a pile of no-boil noodles (boiling and draining conventional noodles was too much work for a "convenience" recipe). I froze the layered casserole for several days, thawed it overnight in the refrigerator, and baked it. Unfortunately, the freezer had a punishing effect on this otherwise reliable recipe. The flavors were dull, and the noodles were so flimsy that they nearly disintegrated between the substantial layers of sauce and cheese. Stouffer's was looking pretty good.

The flavor issues were pretty easy to fix. I replaced some of the ground beef with ground pork and increased the amounts of red pepper flakes and fresh basil. But what could I do about the texture of the noodles? Stacking double layers of no-boil noodles seemed like a good idea, but this distorted the ratio of pasta to sauce and cheese.

I was close to accepting the flimsy noodles when it occurred to me that the problem with freezing no-boil noodles might be in the thawing. Instead of defrosting the lasagna overnight in the refrigerator (as directed in many recipes), I followed Stouffer's lead and popped the frozen lasagna into a 375-degree oven. Sure enough, the frozen block emerged perfectly cooked. One hour and 15 minutes of covered cooking allowed steam to permeate the entire casserole, softening the no-boil noodles to the perfect texture. I then removed the foil and continued baking the lasagna for another 30 minutes to evaporate excess moisture and to crisp the cheesy crust.

This straight-from-the-freezer method not only ensures toothsome noodles but eliminates the time-intensive step of defrosting. Vernon Stouffer had a good idea—I just made it better.

–Cali Rich

No need to defrost—our rich, meaty lasagna goes straight from the freezer to the oven.

FROM-THE-FREEZER MEATY LASAGNA

SERVES 6 TO 8

This lasagna can be assembled and frozen for up to 2 months before being baked.

Tomato Meat Sauce

- 1 1/2 tablespoons olive oil
- 1 onion, chopped fine
- 6 garlic cloves, minced
- 1/4 teaspoon red pepper flakes
- 1/2 pound 85 percent lean ground chuck
- 1/2 pound ground pork
- 1 teaspoon salt
- 1/2 teaspoon pepper
- 1/4 cup heavy cream
- 1 (28-ounce) can tomato puree
- 1 (28-ounce) can diced tomatoes, drained
- 1/4 cup chopped fresh basil

Ricotta, Mozzarella, and Pasta Layers

- 1 3/4 cups whole milk ricotta cheese
- 1 1/4 cups grated Parmesan cheese
- 1/4 cup chopped fresh basil
- 2 large eggs, lightly beaten
- 1/4 teaspoon salt
- 1/4 teaspoon pepper
- 12 no-boil lasagna noodles from one 8- or 9-ounce package
- 5 cups shredded whole milk mozzarella cheese

1. For the sauce: Heat oil in large Dutch oven over medium heat until shimmering, about 2 minutes. Add onion and cook until softened, about 2 minutes. Add garlic and pepper flakes and cook until fragrant, about 30 seconds. Increase heat to medium-high, add ground meats, salt, and pepper, and cook, breaking meat into small pieces, until meat is no longer pink but not browned, about 4 minutes. Add cream and simmer until liquid evaporates and only fat remains, about 4 minutes. Stir in tomato puree, diced tomatoes, and basil and bring to simmer. Reduce heat to low and simmer until flavors blend, about 3 minutes. Remove pot from heat, cool sauce for 20 minutes, then refrigerate until cool, at least 20 minutes.

2. For the pasta layers: Mix ricotta, 1 cup Parmesan, basil, eggs, salt, and pepper in bowl. Spread ¼ cup meat sauce over bottom of 13 by 9-inch baking dish. Place 3 noodles crosswise on top of sauce, evenly space 9 tablespoons ricotta mixture over noodles, and sprinkle evenly with 1¼ cups mozzarella; spoon 1½ cups sauce over cheese. Repeat layering of noodles, ricotta mixture, mozzarella, and sauce two more times. Place 3 remaining noodles on top and spread with remaining sauce. Cover with remaining 1¼ cups mozzarella and remaining ¼ cup Parmesan.

3. Spray large sheet of aluminum foil with nonstick cooking spray and tightly cover lasagna. Wrap with plastic wrap several times and cover with another layer of foil. Freeze.

4. When ready to serve: Adjust oven rack to middle position and heat oven to 375 degrees. Remove all wrapping except foil layer that is flush against lasagna. Bake 1 hour and 15 minutes, then remove foil. Continue baking until cheese is spotty brown and sauce is bubbling, about 30 minutes. Let lasagna cool for 15 minutes. Serve.

Cheesy Garlic Bread

I've tried to make cheesy garlic bread on several occasions, but I find it difficult to get the flavors into the bread. Any suggestions? –Karen Brown, Franklin, Tenn.

A few simple steps are all it takes to tame garlic's sharp bite and bring out its sweet side.

Based on my experience, garlic bread—with cheese or not—often consists of greasy, soggy bread with a layer of bitter garlic flavor on top and no flavor at all in the middle. Great garlic bread should be light and fluffy on the inside and crunchy on the outside, with the deep perfume of nutty garlic and rich butter throughout. My first step was to develop a foolproof garlic bread recipe. I could tackle the cheese component later.

I tried raw, roasted, and toasted garlic in combination with butter and olive oil to see which, if any, would yield the right balance of garlic flavor. I tried mashed garlic, sliced garlic, and chopped garlic. In most cases, the flavors were so bitter and pungent my eyes watered. Starting with minced garlic and cold butter in a pan over low heat brought out the nuttiest flavors, but tasters complained about biting into chunks of sharp garlic. Grating the cloves eliminated any larger bits, and when cooked over low heat the garlic turned into a sticky, golden paste that was perfect for slathering on bread.

Selecting the bread was easy. Italian supermarket bread was immediately eliminated because of its thin crust and soft, spongy interior. With its crisp crust and chewy interior, a supermarket baguette was a far better choice.

Up to this point, I had been slicing the loaf horizontally and baking the halves open-faced until warm and toasty. The garlic-butter mixture was flavoring the top of the bread, but the rest of the loaf was bland. I solved the problem by wrapping the slathered bread in foil and letting the garlic butter steam for 15 minutes. Unwrapping the bread and opening up the layers for another short stint in the oven made my garlic bread crisp.

As for the cheesy crust, some tasters preferred Parmesan for its potent flavor, while others favored gooey cheeses like mozzarella. Rather than taking the time to grate and shred several cheeses, I picked up a packaged blend of shredded Italian cheeses that satisfied everyone. A quick blast of heat from the broiler melted the cheese and helped crisp the bread even further.

–Meredith Butcher

Kitchen Know-How
SLOW AND LOW FOR GOOD GARLIC FLAVOR

If you cook garlic too quickly, it will burn and turn bitter. To bring out its sweet, nutty flavor, grate the garlic (there should be no large bits), cook it over low heat with some butter, and add a little water (to further reduce the risk of scorching).

CHEESY GARLIC BREAD
SERVES 6 TO 8

The serrated edges on a bread knife can pull off the cheesy crust. To prevent this, place the finished garlic bread cheese side down on a cutting board. Slicing through the crust (rather than the cheese) first will keep the cheese in place.

- **5 garlic cloves, grated**
- **8 tablespoons (1 stick) unsalted butter, softened**
- **1/2 teaspoon water**
- **1/4 teaspoon salt**
- **1/4 teaspoon pepper**
- **1 (18- to 20-inch) baguette, sliced in half horizontally**
- **1 1/2 cups shredded Italian cheese blend**

1. Adjust oven rack to lower-middle position and heat oven to 400 degrees. Cook garlic, 1 tablespoon butter, and water in small nonstick skillet over low heat, stirring occasionally, until straw colored, 7 to 10 minutes.

2. Mix hot garlic, remaining butter, salt, and pepper in bowl and spread on cut sides of bread. Sandwich bread back together and wrap loaf in foil. Place on baking sheet and bake for 15 minutes.

3. Carefully unwrap bread and place halves, buttered sides up, on baking sheet. Bake until just beginning to color, about 10 minutes. Remove from oven and set oven to broil.

4. Sprinkle bread with cheese. Broil until cheese has melted and bread is crisp, 1 to 2 minutes. Transfer bread to cutting board with cheese side facing down. Cut into pieces. Serve.

Parmesan 101

We use a lot of Parmesan cheese in the test kitchen, but not all of it is the genuine article, true Parmigiano-Reggiano, which has been made for more than 800 years in northern Italy. Here are some tips for buying, storing, and grating this versatile cheese.

Buying

Nothing beats the spicy, nutty flavor of authentic Parmigiano-Reggiano. Always buy a wedge with a piece of the rind attached; this way, you can see the signature imprint stamped on the rind and know that you are getting what you're paying for.

American-made DiGiorno Parmesan costs about half as much as Parmigiano-Reggiano, and in a test kitchen taste test, it beat all other substitutes for the real deal. We don't recommend using the boxed powdered stuff under any circumstances; it is made from inferior cheese and usually contains additives.

Storing

Keep your Parmesan tightly wrapped in butcher's paper, waxed paper, or plastic wrap and store it in a drawer in the refrigerator. If eating as a table cheese, allow Parmesan to come to room temperature before serving. If you want grated Parmesan, buy a whole piece, grate it yourself, and store it in the freezer or refrigerator, in an airtight container, for about 3 weeks; our taste tests concluded that for cooking applications, there is little difference between freshly grated and pregrated Parmesan that has been handled well (after 3 weeks, the pregrated cheese begins to suffer in flavor and texture). And don't throw away the rinds—they add body and flavor to soups and stews.

Grating

A simple vegetable peeler is good for shaving curls of Parmesan into salads and vegetables and even on steaks. For fine grating—which most recipes call for—the small holes of a box grater work well enough, but the test kitchen prefers a rasp-style grater, which produces light, feathery strands of cheese with very little work. Our favorite is the Microplane Zester/Grater (model 40020, pictured at left grating garlic; $12.95 at microplane.com).

Roasted Fall Vegetables

Creative glazes and a novel cooking method transform humble root vegetables into exciting side dishes.

It is fair to say that root vegetables have an image problem. It's easy to understand why, since they are often prepared in pretty unappealing ways. Carrots are naturally sweet, but turnips, parsnips, and celery root are more assertive. These vegetables need to be cooked properly and paired with the right flavors to bring out their sweet earthiness.

Cooking vegetables in the oven allowed me to work with a large volume, and it minimized hands-on fussing. But root vegetables have a tough, fibrous texture, and roasting them on a sheet pan made them leathery and dry. To transform fibrous vegetables into silky, tender morsels, I found that cooking them with some liquid was key (think braises and stews). I found I could achieve a similar effect in the oven by adding a small amount of liquid to the baking dish with the vegetables and then covering the dish with foil. About halfway through the cooking time, I removed the foil, allowing the liquid to evaporate and the flavors to concentrate. The vegetables even caramelized in spots.

As an added benefit, I found that root vegetables do an amazing job of absorbing the flavors they are cooked with and that my cooking method was ideally suited to transforming their stodgy personality. Water (rather than overpowering chicken broth) mixed with flavorful ingredients (such as onions, herbs, chiles, vinegar, and ginger) infused the vegetables with just enough flavor without masking their unique character.

All the recipes I developed call for a thick sweetener (jelly, jam, or syrup) to help bring out the natural sweetness of the vegetables and tame any inherent bitterness. These sweeteners also promote a glossy, glaze-like appearance, as does a little butter stirred in just before serving. My oven-glazing method is easy and will elevate even the most humble root vegetable to superstar status. **–Eva Katz**

ROASTED GLAZED TURNIPS WITH BACON AND BALSAMIC VINEGAR SERVES 6

Use only purple-top turnips for this recipe; yellow turnips (rutabagas) take longer to cook.

- **2 pounds purple-top turnips, peeled and cut into 3/4-inch cubes**
- **4 shallots, peeled and sliced thin**
- **2 tablespoons maple syrup**
- **2 tablespoons balsamic vinegar**
- **1 tablespoon chopped fresh rosemary**
- **Salt and pepper**
- **3 tablespoons unsalted butter (1 tablespoon melted and 2 tablespoons cubed)**
- **1/2 cup water**
- **6 slices bacon, cut into 1/4-inch strips and cooked until crisp**

1. Adjust oven rack to middle position and heat oven to 450 degrees. Toss turnips, shallots, syrup, vinegar, rosemary, ½ teaspoon salt, ⅛ teaspoon pepper, and melted butter in 13 by 9-inch Pyrex baking dish. Pour water over vegetables, cover with foil, and roast until turnips begin to soften, about 25 minutes.

2. Remove foil and continue to roast, tossing occasionally, until turnips are tender and spotty brown and liquid is reduced to thick glaze, 25 to 30 minutes. Add bacon and cubed butter and toss. Adjust seasonings and serve.

ROASTED GLAZED PARSNIPS AND CARROTS WITH ORANGE AND THYME SERVES 6

This recipe can be made with 2 pounds of carrots and no parsnips.

- **1 pound carrots, peeled and cut into 2 by 1/2-inch sticks**
- **1 pound parsnips, peeled and cut into 2 by 1/2-inch sticks**
- **2 teaspoons minced fresh thyme**
- **1 tablespoon cider vinegar**
- **3 tablespoons orange marmalade**
- **1 teaspoon grated fresh ginger**
- **Salt and pepper**
- **3 tablespoons unsalted butter (1 tablespoon melted and 2 tablespoons cubed)**
- **1/2 cup water**

1. Adjust oven rack to middle position and heat oven to 450 degrees. Toss carrots, parsnips, 1 teaspoon thyme, vinegar, marmalade, ginger, ½ teaspoon salt, ⅛ teaspoon pepper, and melted butter in 13 by 9-inch Pyrex baking dish. Pour water over vegetables, cover with foil, and roast until vegetables just begin to soften, about 20 minutes.

2. Remove foil and continue to roast, tossing occasionally, until vegetables are tender and browned and liquid is reduced to thick glaze, 20 to 25 minutes. Add remaining teaspoon thyme and cubed butter and toss. Adjust seasonings and serve.

ROASTED GLAZED CELERY ROOT WITH LEEKS AND GRAPES SERVES 6

Be sure to rinse the leeks well to remove any dirt.

- **2 pounds celery root, peeled and cut into 3/4-inch pieces (see page 30)**
- **2 large leeks, white and light green parts only, cut in half lengthwise, then sliced thin**
- **3 tablespoons grape jelly**
- **Salt and pepper**
- **3 tablespoons unsalted butter (1 tablespoon melted and 2 tablespoons cubed)**
- **1/4 cup water**
- **1 cup seedless red grapes, halved**
- **2 teaspoons chopped fresh tarragon**

1. Adjust oven rack to middle position and heat oven to 450 degrees. Toss celery root, leeks, jelly, ½ teaspoon salt, ⅛ teaspoon pepper, and melted butter in 13 by 9-inch Pyrex baking dish. Pour water over vegetables, cover with foil, and roast until celery root softens, about 20 minutes.

2. Remove foil, toss in grapes, and continue to roast, tossing occasionally, until vegetables are tender and liquid is reduced to thick glaze, 20 to 25 minutes. Add tarragon and cubed butter and toss. Adjust seasonings and serve.

Our oven-glazing technique makes root vegetables (in this case, turnips) look good—and taste even better.

Visit us at cookscountry.com!
For a variation on this recipe, visit **cookscountry.com** and look for the Cook's Country Extra box. Type in SQUASH for access to a recipe for **Roasted Carrots with Chili and Lime.** This recipe will be available free through December 31, 2006.

Cider-Glazed Pork

I recently tried a recipe for cider-glazed pork loin. It seemed like the perfect fall dinner, but I was disappointed when the glaze came out soupy, with very little apple flavor. I was expecting the cider to cook down and coat the roast. Where did I go wrong?

–Marjorie McClendon, St. Paul, Minn.

Kitchen Know-How

TAKE THE TIME TO TIE

A pork loin is often narrow at one end and thick at the other, and its overall shape is pretty flat. Tying the roast at $1\frac{1}{2}$-inch intervals with butcher's twine produces a rounder roast that cooks more evenly and carves into more attractive slices.

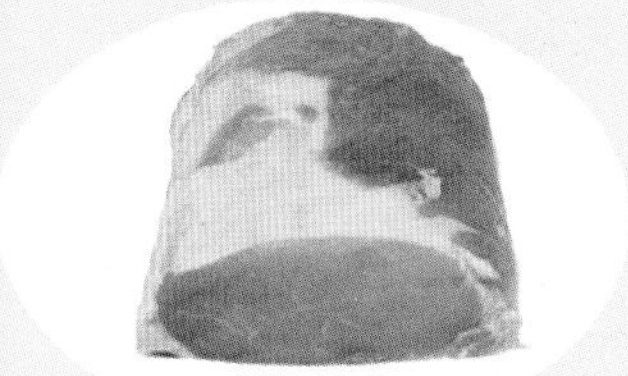

BEFORE

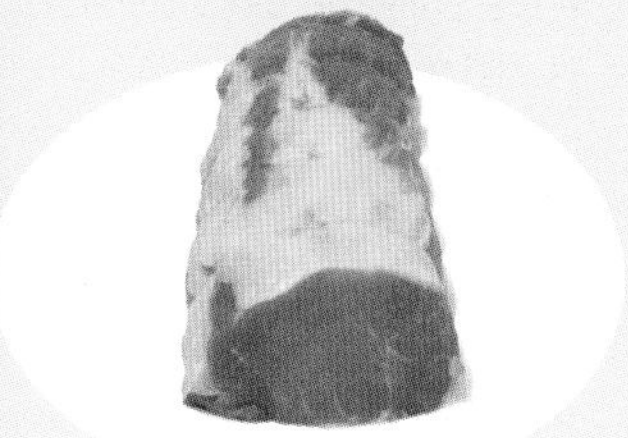

AFTER

Big Apple Flavor

Cider alone couldn't produce the big apple flavor we wanted in the glaze for our pork loin. Apple butter (super-concentrated applesauce) pumped up the flavor of the glaze and helped it cling to the roast.

APPLE BUTTER   APPLE CIDER

American pigs have had most of the fat bred out of them over the last half-century, and, as a result, pork loin—a lean cut to begin with—can be pretty dry and bland. A sticky-sweet cider glaze can hide these flaws, but just pouring cider over a roast and shoving it into the oven doesn't work. When I tried this most obvious method, I was shocked to find that the cider made the meat worse: The roast refused to brown as it sat in a watery pool of cider. Glazing a pork roast requires a bit more finesse.

My first goal was to develop a reliable roasting method without a glaze. To improve browning (and thus add flavor), I tried roasting the meat in a very hot oven. While most recipes call for 375 or 400 degrees, I discovered that the oven has to be cranked up to at least 450 degrees to brown the exterior. Unfortunately, the meat (especially the outer portion) was chalky and dry by the time the center was done. In the end, I found that browning the pork loin in a skillet and then transferring it to a moderate oven (375 degrees) produced a more evenly cooked, juicier roast.

With my roasting technique under control, it was time to focus on the glaze. To help the glaze cling to the meat, I thought I'd trying simmering the cider in the (now-empty) pan I had used to brown the pork. Simmering thickened the cider and punched up the apple flavor, but the glaze still wasn't sticky enough. To make it more syrupy, I tried adding maple syrup, honey, and brown sugar. The maple and honey competed with the apple flavor, and the brown sugar was so sweet it caused my glaze to scorch. Next I tried adding applesauce, apple jelly, and apple butter. The applesauce was too grainy and the jelly too sweet, but the apple butter was just right, contributing substance as well as apple flavor. Shallots and herbs rounded out the flavors of the glaze.

I tested adding the glaze at different stages throughout the cooking process and finally settled on the halfway point. Added earlier, the glaze burned; added later, it didn't reduce enough. I also found it imperative to use a fairly small baking dish. In a shallow broiler pan, the glaze evaporated too quickly. The pork loin fit snuggly in a 13 by 9-inch baking dish, where it sat in a deeper pool of glaze.

While my nicely glazed roast pork loin was resting, I noticed that it was "leaking" juices onto the cutting board. Adding those juices to the glaze remaining in the baking dish produced an intensely flavored sauce I could serve with the sliced pork. With a glaze that does double duty as a sauce, my recipe gives pork loin the powerful flavor boost it needs. **–Katie Henderson**

Stovetop searing followed by roasting with an apple glaze combine to give our pork roast a deep, rich flavor.

CIDER-GLAZED ROAST PORK LOIN SERVES 6

Make sure to tie the roast (see photo at left) if your butcher hasn't already done so.

- **1 (3-pound) boneless center-cut pork loin, tied**
- **Salt and pepper**
- **2 tablespoons vegetable oil**
- **6 small shallots, peeled (and halved if large)**
- **2 cups apple cider**
- **1/2 cup apple butter**
- **1 bay leaf**
- **1 sprig fresh thyme**
- **1 teaspoon cider vinegar**

1. Adjust oven rack to middle position and heat oven to 375 degrees. Pat pork loin dry with paper towels and season with salt and pepper.

2. Heat 1 tablespoon oil in large skillet over medium-high heat until just smoking. Place pork loin, fat side down, in skillet and cook, turning it several times, until browned on all sides, 8 to 10 minutes. Transfer pork, fat side down, to 13 by 9-inch baking dish and roast until thermometer inserted in thickest part registers 85 degrees, about 25 minutes.

3. While pork roasts, cook remaining tablespoon oil and shallots in empty skillet over medium heat until golden brown, 3 to 5 minutes. Increase heat to high, add cider, apple butter, bay leaf, and thyme and bring to boil. Cook until thickened, about 8 minutes.

4. After pork has roasted for 25 minutes, pour glaze over pork and, using tongs, roll pork to coat with glaze. Cook until internal temperature registers 145 degrees, 20 to 30 minutes more, turning once halfway through to recoat with glaze. Transfer pork to cutting board, tent with foil, and let rest 20 minutes. Transfer glaze to small saucepan and whisk in vinegar.

5. Before slicing pork, pour accumulated juices from roast into glaze and warm glaze over low heat. Cut roast into 1/4-inch slices, transfer to platter, and spoon 1/2 cup glaze over top. Serve, passing remaining glaze at table.

I'm Looking for a Recipe

READERS HELP READERS FIND RECIPES

We've Got Mail

Several readers sent us recipes in response to the request for a zucchini crisp recipe (June/July 2005). We really liked the recipe sent by Amy Grice (right). Go to **cookscountry.com** and click **Looking for a Recipe** to find dozens more recipes submitted by readers who responded to other recipe requests in previous issues of *Cook's Country*.

ZUCCHINI CRISP **Amy Grice,** Schenectady, N.Y.

Amy found this unusual recipe online, and our test kitchen made a few modifications to streamline this sweet way to use up a bumper crop of zucchini. Serve with vanilla ice cream.

7	**medium zucchini, peeled, seeded, and chopped into 1/2-inch pieces (7 cups)**
1/2	**cup lemon juice**
1 1/2	**cups sugar**
2	**teaspoons cinnamon**
1/2	**teaspoon nutmeg**
4	**cups all-purpose flour**
	Salt
12	**tablespoons (1 1/2 sticks) unsalted butter, chilled and cut into 1-inch pieces**

INSTRUCTIONS: Preheat oven to 375 degrees. Coat a 13 by 9-inch baking dish with cooking spray. Place zucchini and lemon juice in medium saucepan. Cook, covered, over medium-low heat, stirring occasionally, until tender, about 15 minutes. Stir in 3/4 cup sugar, 1 teaspoon cinnamon, and nutmeg. Simmer 1 minute longer and remove from heat. Pulse flour, remaining 3/4 cup sugar, and 1/4 teaspoon salt in food processor. Pulse in butter until the mixture resembles coarse crumbs. Stir 1/2 cup crumb mixture into zucchini mixture. Press half of remaining crumb mixture into the prepared pan. Spread zucchini mixture evenly over crust. Crumble remaining crumb mixture over zucchini and sprinkle with 1 teaspoon cinnamon. Bake for about 35 minutes or until golden brown.

Dublin Pie

When I was in Dublin, Ireland, I had this magnificent pie made with a chocolate crust, a chocolate mousse bottom, a creamy white chocolate filling, and a Dime Bar (Heath Bar) topping. From what I have heard, it's made with a type of sugar that you cannot find in the United States. Does anyone have a recipe for this pie?

Lisa Poggas
Castle Rock, Colo.

Scottish Oat Cakes

I am searching for a loved but lost recipe called Scottish oat cakes. Many years ago, when I was a teenager, we had an intern named Sally from the Princeton seminary at our small country church. One day, she offered me the most wonderful oatmeal cookie cake, called a Scottish oat cake, made from a recipe that had been in her family for many generations. The recipe had almost equal amounts of old-fashioned rolled oats and flour. It also had shortening, salt, baking powder, and milk. The dough was mixed by hand, and the cakes were baked on cookie sheets until lightly golden brown on the bottoms and dense and chewy inside. I held on to this recipe for many years as I moved from place to place, but it is now gone. I hope someone can help.

Linda Hutchinson
Blacksburg, S.C.

Friendship Cake

A friend of mine is looking for a recipe for friendship cake. It begins with a starter (similar to sourdough) that takes about 30 days to mature and requires feeding during that time. Before baking the cake, the starter is divided and given to seven friends, hence the name, friendship cake.

Mary Weinstein
Alpine, Calif.

Taraleekoos

I have misplaced my recipe for an Italian wedding cookie. It is finger shaped and hard, like biscotti, and is topped with sesame seeds. My recipe made seven or eight dozen cookies, and although I have made several variations of this recipe, none have lived up to the original. For some unknown reason the cookies were given the name Taraleekoos.

Dharma Muscarella
South Wales, N.Y.

Aebleskive

I have a pan that has been hanging on my kitchen wall as a decoration, and I recently discovered that it is what is known as an aebleskive pan. Now that I know what kind of pan it is, I want to make the sweet dumpling-type pastry that the pan produces. Can anyone supply a good recipe?

Ernie Mainland
Petoskey, Mich.

Goody Goody Butterscotch Pie

In the 1950s there was a drive-in restaurant in West Los Angeles called The Goody Goody. They made a butterscotch pie that was to die for. I don't think the filling had any milk or cream in it, but it was caramelized and gooey, just like melted butterscotch. It also had a meringue topping. I have been looking for a recipe for this heavenly pie for 50 years.

Vicki Olsen
Via e-mail

Eugene's Plantation Dressing

Back in the 1960s there was a restaurant in Milwaukee, Wis., called Eugene's. They served a Thousand Island–type salad dressing with cheese curds in it. It was called Plantation Dressing and was my favorite as a kid. I would love to find this recipe.

Mike Levand
Lenexa, Kan.

Zucchini Chocolate Cake

Years ago, I clipped a recipe out of the newspaper for zucchini chocolate cake. A local housewife sent the recipe in to the newspaper, and she had won an award for it. I made this cake all the time, but when I moved I lost the recipe. I've tried many cookbook recipes, but they are not the same—too dry and dull. Does anyone have a recipe for a truly delicious zucchini chocolate cake?

Don Durkee
Via e-mail

Treacle Pudding

When I was a young girl, my family moved to England. We were the only Americans around, and we assimilated ourselves completely into the British culture. One thing I remember fondly was something we used to eat called treacle pudding. It was an upside-down cake baked with syrup in the bottom of the pan—the syrup ended up on top when the cake was released. Since I've moved back to the States, I have yet to find the same thing here. Does anyone have a recipe?

Kirstin Fitrell
Via e-mail

Havana Cake

My sister and I would love to find a recipe for Havana Cake, a layer cake that Ackerman's Bakery in Chicago used to make about 30 years ago. It was a yellow layer cake with about an inch of filling between the layers. The chocolate-nut filling was somewhere between the consistency of mousse and pudding. The sides of the cake were covered with chocolate curls.

Gail Pravatiner
Brooklyn Park, Minn.

Peanut Butter Crunch Bars

I went to school in Bolingbrook, Ill., and peanut butter crunch bars were my favorite dessert on the lunch menu. They were wonderfully creamy peanut butter bars with a slight rice cereal crunch, and they were topped with a thin, brittle chocolate coating. They were always served slightly cooled. I've tried different recipes, but they are always too sweet, too dry, or too cakey. I would love to make this treat for my own children.

Kim Shields
Keller, Texas

Whole Cake

My mother, who was born in southern Indiana in 1907, used to make a quick bread in a cast-iron skillet. She called it whole cake, but it was not sweet. She mixed up a batter, poured it into a skillet with some melted lard, and baked it. It would rise to about two inches, and it was crispy on the bottom. Unfortunately, none of her recipes were written down, and when she died in 1978 her recipes went with her. Does anyone have a recipe for whole cake?

Pat Neely
Indianapolis, Ind..

Are you looking for a special recipe? Let other readers of this magazine help. Just send us your requests, and we will print as many of them as we can. Write to Looking for a Recipe, Cook's Country, P.O. Box 470739, Brookline, MA 02447, or visit **cookscountry.com/emailus.** If you can help with one of the above requests, contact us at the same postal or e-mail address. We will post the responses on **cookscountry.com.**

Find the Rooster!

A tiny version of this rooster has been hidden somewhere in the pages of this issue. If you find it, write to us with its location (plus your name and address), and you will be entered into a random drawing. The first winning entry will receive the four individual Forschner knives pictured on page 29; the next five winners will each receive a complimentary one-year subscription to *Cook's Country*. To enter the contest, write to Rooster, Cook's Country, P.O. Box 470739, Brookline, MA 02447. Or to send your entry by e-mail, visit **cookscountry.com/emailus.** Entries are due by November 30, 2006.

Did you find the rooster in the June/July 2006 issue? It was hidden on page 21 in the Grilled Chicken Pasta Salad photo. Johnny Sue Frazee of Frankton, Ind., spotted it and won a Calphalon spatula and a one-year subscription to *Cook's Country*.

30-Minute Supper

GARLICKY PORK CUTLETS WITH PROSCIUTTO, LEMON, AND SAGE

30-Minute Supper

PEPPER-CRUSTED STEAK WITH WORCESTERSHIRE-BUTTER SAUCE

30-Minute Supper

EASY MINESTRONE

30-Minute Supper

HONEY-SESAME PORK TENDERLOIN WITH SPICY SCALLION SALAD

PEPPER-CRUSTED STEAK WITH WORCESTERSHIRE-BUTTER SAUCE SERVES 4

You will need a 12-inch skillet for this recipe. To ensure even browning, look for steaks no wider than 3 inches.

4 strip steaks (8 to 10 ounces each), about 1 inch thick
Salt
1 tablespoon coarsely ground pepper
1 tablespoon vegetable oil
1 shallot, minced
1/2 cup red wine
1/2 cup low-sodium chicken broth
1/4 cup Worcestershire sauce
1 teaspoon minced fresh thyme
2 tablespoons unsalted butter

1. Pat steaks dry with paper towels and season with salt. Rub one side of each steak with pepper. Heat oil in large skillet over medium-high heat until just smoking. Place steaks with peppered side down in skillet and cook until well browned on both sides, 3 to 5 minutes per side. Transfer to plate and tent with foil.

2. Add shallot to empty skillet and cook until softened, about 1 minute. Add wine, broth, Worcestershire, and thyme and simmer, scraping up browned bits with wooden spoon, until reduced by half, about 5 minutes. Add accumulated steak juices back to pan, whisk in butter, and season with salt. Pour sauce over steaks. Serve.

GARLICKY PORK CUTLETS WITH PROSCIUTTO, LEMON, AND SAGE SERVES 4

If you can't find prosciutto, substitute 6 thin slices of deli ham.

8 boneless pork chops (3 to 4 ounces each), about 1/4 inch thick
8 slices prosciutto (see note above)
1/2 cup all-purpose flour
4 tablespoons vegetable oil
6 garlic cloves, sliced thin
1 cup low-sodium chicken broth
1 tablespoon lemon juice
1 teaspoon minced fresh sage
2 tablespoons unsalted butter
Salt and pepper

1. Pat pork chops dry with paper towels. Lay 1 slice prosciutto on each chop. Cover chops with plastic wrap and, using meat pounder, pound each until 1/8 inch thick. Dredge cutlets in flour, shaking to remove excess flour.

2. Heat 2 tablespoons oil in large skillet over medium-high heat until just smoking. Add half of cutlets, prosciutto side down, and cook until light golden brown on first side, about 3 minutes. Flip cutlets and cook until just cooked through, about 1 minute. Transfer to plate, tent with foil, and repeat with remaining oil and cutlets.

3. Add garlic to empty skillet and cook until fragrant, about 30 seconds. Add broth and simmer, scraping up browned bits with wooden spoon, until reduced by half, about 5 minutes. Add accumulated pork juices back to pan and whisk in lemon juice, sage, and butter. Season with salt and pepper and pour sauce over cutlets. Serve.

HONEY-SESAME PORK TENDERLOIN WITH SPICY SCALLION SALAD SERVES 4 TO 6

To ensure even cooking, use tenderloins that weigh between 12 and 16 ounces each. For an extra kick, don't seed the chile.

2 tablespoons sesame seeds
3 tablespoons vegetable oil
2 pork tenderloins (1 1/2 to 2 pounds total)
Salt and pepper
1/2 cup honey
1/2 cup plus 2 tablespoons cider vinegar
1 cucumber, peeled, halved lengthwise, seeded, and sliced thin
1 jalapeño chile, seeded and sliced thin
8 scallions, sliced thin on bias

1. Toast sesame seeds in large nonstick skillet over medium-high heat until golden, about 3 minutes. Transfer sesame seeds to small bowl.

2. Heat 1 tablespoon oil in empty skillet over medium-high heat until just smoking. Pat pork dry with paper towels and season with salt and pepper. Cook tenderloins until browned on all sides, 5 to 8 minutes. Reduce heat to medium, add honey and 1/2 cup vinegar, and cook, turning tenderloins to coat, until mixture is syrupy and instant-read thermometer inserted in center of tenderloin registers 145 degrees, about 10 minutes. Transfer pork to cutting board, tent with foil, and let rest 5 minutes. Set skillet with honey mixture aside.

3. Combine cucumber, jalapeño, scallions, remaining 2 tablespoons oil, remaining 2 tablespoons vinegar, and 2 teaspoons sesame seeds in bowl. Adjust seasoning with salt and pepper.

4. Cut pork into 1/2-inch-thick slices, transfer to platter, drizzle with reserved honey mixture, and sprinkle with remaining sesame seeds. Serve with scallion salad.

EASY MINESTRONE SERVES 4 TO 6

Use small pasta shapes such as orzo and ditalini in this rustic soup. A combination of frozen zucchini, carrots, broccoli, and beans (sometimes labeled "Italian Blend") works well here.

6 cups low-sodium chicken broth
1 (15.5-ounce) can cannellini beans, drained and rinsed
1 (28-ounce) can diced tomatoes
2 tablespoons extra-virgin olive oil, plus extra for serving
2 onions, chopped fine
4 garlic cloves, minced
1/2 cup dry pasta (see note above)
1 (16-ounce) bag frozen mixed vegetables (see note above)
1/4 cup minced fresh basil
Salt and pepper

1. Bring broth, beans, and tomatoes to boil in large saucepan.

2. Meanwhile, heat oil in Dutch oven over medium-high heat until shimmering. Add onions and cook until softened, about 5 minutes. Add garlic and cook until fragrant, about 30 seconds. Stir in broth mixture and pasta and simmer until pasta is tender, about 10 minutes.

3. Stir in vegetables and basil and cook until heated through, about 2 minutes. Season with salt and pepper. Serve with additional olive oil for drizzling.

30-Minute Supper

BAKED CHICKEN BREASTS WITH PARMESAN-GARLIC CRUST

30-Minute Supper

SHRIMP AND SCALLOP SKEWERS WITH HOISIN-GINGER SAUCE

30-Minute Supper

SPAGHETTI WITH GARLIC, OLIVE OIL, AND SPICY BREAD CRUMBS

30-Minute Supper

HEARTY SCRAMBLED EGGS WITH TEXAS TOAST

SHRIMP AND SCALLOP SKEWERS WITH HOISIN-GINGER SAUCE SERVES 4

You will need four to six 10-inch bamboo skewers for this recipe. Feel free to use all shrimp or all scallops, if desired. Sea scallops often come with a tendon that should be removed before cooking; see page 31 for more information.

- **1/2 cup hoisin sauce**
- **1/2 cup rice vinegar**
- **1/4 cup soy sauce**
- **1/4 cup minced fresh cilantro**
- **2 tablespoons light brown sugar**
- **2 teaspoons minced fresh ginger**
- **1 garlic clove, minced**
- **1 pound extra-large shrimp (21 to 25 count), peeled and deveined**
- **1 pound sea scallops, tendons removed (see note above)**
- **Vegetable oil spray**
- **Salt and pepper**

1. Adjust oven rack 6 inches from broiler element and heat broiler. Line bottom of broiler pan with foil and fit with slotted broiler-pan top.

2. Combine hoisin sauce, vinegar, soy sauce, cilantro, brown sugar, ginger, and garlic in bowl. In separate bowl, toss shrimp and scallops with 1/4 cup hoisin mixture.

3. Thread shrimp and scallops onto skewers and arrange on broiler-pan top. Spray skewers with vegetable oil spray, then season with salt and pepper. Cover exposed end of skewers with sheet of aluminum foil and broil, flipping skewers halfway through cooking, until shrimp are pink and scallops are just cooked through, 4 to 6 minutes. Serve, passing remaining hoisin mixture at table.

BAKED CHICKEN BREASTS WITH PARMESAN-GARLIC CRUST SERVES 4

To make fresh bread crumbs, process 2 slices of hearty white sandwich bread in a food processor until coarsely ground.

- **1 cup bread crumbs, preferably fresh (see note above)**
- **1/2 cup grated Parmesan cheese**
- **3 garlic cloves, minced**
- **2 tablespoons extra-virgin olive oil**
- **1/2 teaspoon salt**
- **Pepper**
- **4 boneless, skinless chicken breasts (6 to 7 ounces each), trimmed**
- **1/4 cup minced fresh basil**
- **1/4 cup mayonnaise**
- **Lemon wedges for serving**

1. Adjust oven rack to upper-middle position and heat oven to 425 degrees. Combine bread crumbs, Parmesan, garlic, oil, salt, and pepper to taste in bowl.

2. Pat chicken dry with paper towels and transfer to 13 by 9-inch baking dish. Combine basil and mayonnaise in small bowl and spread mixture evenly over chicken. Sprinkle bread-crumb mixture over mayonnaise, pressing lightly to adhere.

3. Bake until crumbs are golden brown and instant-read thermometer inserted in thickest part of chicken registers 160 degrees, 18 to 22 minutes. Serve with lemon wedges.

HEARTY SCRAMBLED EGGS WITH TEXAS TOAST SERVES 4

Folding the eggs, instead of constantly stirring them, will result in very fluffy scrambled eggs.

- **8 large eggs**
- **1/4 cup half-and-half**
- **Salt and pepper**
- **6 tablespoons unsalted butter**
- **4 (1-inch-thick) slices Italian bread**
- **1 onion, chopped fine**
- **1 red bell pepper, seeded and chopped fine**
- **1/2 pound thick-cut deli ham, cut into 1/2-inch cubes**
- **1 cup shredded cheddar cheese**
- **2 scallions, sliced thin**

1. Whisk eggs, half-and-half, 3/4 teaspoon salt, and 1/4 teaspoon pepper in bowl.

2. Melt 4 tablespoons butter in large nonstick skillet over medium heat. Add bread and cook until golden on both sides, 2 to 3 minutes per side. Transfer to plate and tent with foil.

3. Melt 1 tablespoon butter in empty skillet over medium heat. Add onion, bell pepper, and ham and cook until lightly browned, 5 to 7 minutes. Transfer mixture to bowl.

4. Melt remaining tablespoon butter in empty skillet over medium heat. Add egg mixture and cook, using rubber spatula to stir and scrape bottom of skillet occasionally, until large curds begin to form, 3 to 5 minutes. Off heat, gently fold in onion mixture, cheddar, and scallions. Spoon eggs over toast. Serve.

SPAGHETTI WITH GARLIC, OLIVE OIL, AND SPICY BREAD CRUMBS SERVES 4

In step 2, be careful not to let the garlic get too brown or it will become bitter.

- **2 slices hearty white sandwich bread, torn into pieces**
- **6 tablespoons extra-virgin olive oil**
- **6 garlic cloves, minced**
- **3/4 teaspoon red pepper flakes**
- **Salt**
- **1 pound spaghetti**
- **1/2 cup grated Parmesan cheese**
- **1/4 cup chopped fresh parsley**

1. Bring 4 quarts water to boil in large pot. Meanwhile, process bread in food processor until coarsely ground. Heat 2 tablespoons oil in large skillet over medium-high heat until shimmering. Add bread crumbs and cook, stirring occasionally, until light golden, about 3 minutes. Add half of garlic and 1/4 teaspoon red pepper flakes and cook until fragrant, about 30 seconds. Transfer to bowl and season with salt.

2. Wipe out skillet and add remaining 4 tablespoons oil, remaining half of garlic, and remaining 1/2 teaspoon red pepper flakes. Cook over medium-low heat until garlic is just golden, 1 to 3 minutes. Remove pan from heat.

3. Add 1 tablespoon salt and spaghetti to boiling water. Cook until al dente. Reserve 1/4 cup cooking water, drain pasta, and return to pot along with reserved water. Stir in oil mixture, Parmesan, and parsley. Season with salt and sprinkle with bread crumbs. Serve.

Philly Cheesesteak

Cheesesteak is a way of life in Philadelphia. Could we develop a recipe that would work at home?

Our cheesesteak delivers tender "shaved" steak studded with onions and covered in melted cheese.

The Philly cheesesteak was born in 1930 at Pat's King of Steaks, located in an Italian-American neighborhood in South Philadelphia. Today you can find a cheesesteak joint on almost every corner in Philly—even in Chinatown—and just about every one has a devoted following. Some Philadelphians swear by Pat's, while others go for Geno's, Jim's, Steve's, D'Alessandro's, or Tony Luke's. Wanting to see what the fuss was all about, I hopped on a plane to Philadelphia and started eating. Could I find a way to make this iconic sandwich at home?

I took a cab from my hotel to Pat's, where I was lucky enough to get a grill-side demonstration from the man himself, Frank "Pat" Olivieri (Frank's uncle was the original Pat), as he heaped juicy, tender sliced rib-eye steak (most places use rib-eye or chopped round) on a soft, chewy sub roll and topped it with sweet fried onions and Cheez Whiz. Taking the advice of the experts, I assumed the stance known as the Philly lean to keep all the succulent juices from running down the front of my shirt. That was the first of more than a dozen cheesesteaks I tasted that day.

Now that I knew what the real McCoy tasted like, I was ready to try to re-create it in the test kitchen. My first challenge was finding a tender cut of meat that also had rich, beefy flavor. I sampled rib-eye, top sirloin, top round, blade, chuck, flank, and sirloin tips. Some cuts had good flavor but were too tough, some were nice and tender but lacking in flavor. Sirloin tips were perfect—tender, with big flavor—and they were half the price of rib-eye, which also worked quite well.

Unless you have the knife skills of a sushi chef, slicing meat paper-thin is impossible. I tried (and rejected) partially freezing the meat before slicing it as well as using the food processor to slice the meat. I had better luck cutting the room-temperature tips into small chunks and then pounding them with a mallet to produce thin, tender sheets of steak.

Aside from the beef, the most important element in a true Philly cheesesteak is the cheese, and my tasters had strong opinions on the subject. I fed them sandwiches made not only with the traditional Cheez Whiz but also with two other Philly favorites, provolone and American. In the end, the test kitchen voted for the provolone. But whichever cheese you end up using, don't go overboard—a real Philly cheesesteak is all about the beef. **–Katie Henderson**

(recipe on page 18)

Kitchen Know-How **THE SECRET TO PAPER-THIN SLICES**

Sirloin tips, tasty but much cheaper than the rib-eye steak used in Philly sandwich shops, are often sold in long strips, making slicing against the grain difficult. We found it much easier to cut the meat into cubes and then pound them into paper-thin pieces.

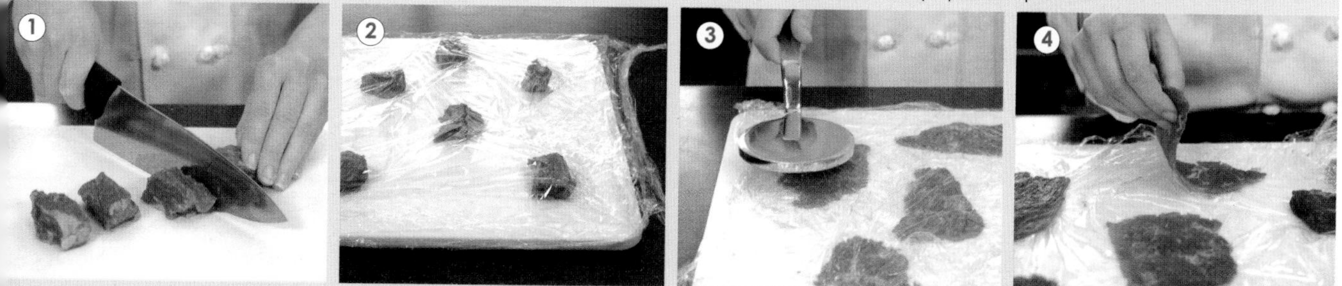

1. Cut each sirloin tip with the grain into 1-inch cubes. **2.** Stagger the beef cubes in a single layer 6 inches apart between two sheets of plastic wrap. **3.** Using a meat pounder, pound the cubes until paper-thin. **4.** When you're done, the slices of meat should be almost transparent.

ROAD TRIP:
Philly's Finest

My taxi ride from downtown to South Philly took me through a labyrinth of narrow one-way streets lined with crowded row houses. We drove past the Italian market, which spills out onto the street, and finally came to the tiny, bustling intersection where the cheesesteak got its start. The unassuming Pat's King of Steaks sits on one corner, the equally popular Geno's, with its bold, carnival-like neon signs, on the opposite corner.

At 10 A.M., long lines had already formed at both establishments. At Pat's, Frank "Pat" Olivieri showed off his custom-made German meat slicer as if it were a shiny new European sports car (the slicer, which cuts rib-eye steaks into those famously paper-thin slices, and the car would cost about the same). At Geno's, Geno himself (the son of Joey Vento, who founded Geno's in 1966) was equally generous with his time, showing me his sparkling kitchen, which was as clean as a hospital operating room. The cheesesteaks in both establishments were the best I've ever had. **–K.H.**

Philly Cheesesteak

continued from page 17

PHILLY CHEESESTEAKS

SERVES 4

We prefer thin slices of provolone cheese cut to order at the deli counter (packaged slices are too thick to melt quickly), but American cheese works well, too. If using Cheez Whiz, do not add it to the skillet; microwave 3/4 cup in a bowl until warmed through, then spoon it over the assembled sandwiches.

- **6 teaspoons vegetable oil**
- **2 small onions, chopped**
- **1 1/2 pounds sirloin tips, pounded until paper-thin (see photos on page 17)**
- **Salt and pepper**
- **8 thin slices provolone cheese, cut in half**
- **4 (6-inch) sub rolls, slit partially open lengthwise**

1. Heat 2 teaspoons oil in large nonstick skillet over medium-high heat until shimmering. Add onions and cook until softened and golden, about 5 minutes. Transfer to small bowl.

2. Heat additional 2 teaspoons oil in now-empty skillet over high heat until smoking. Place half of steak slices in skillet (don't worry if they overlap) and season with salt and pepper. Cook until meat is no longer pink, about 1 minute per side. Remove pan from heat, layer 4 half-slices of cheese over some meat, top with more with meat, and finally 4 more half-slices of cheese. Cover pan with lid to melt cheese, about 1 minute. Divide meat and cheese between 2 rolls, top with half of onions, and pour juices accumulated in skillet over meat. Wrap each sandwich tightly in foil and set aside while preparing remaining sandwiches.

3. Wipe skillet clean with paper towels and repeat step 2 with remaining 2 teaspoons oil, meat, cheese, and onions. Wrap sandwiches in foil and let sit for about 1 minute to let flavors come together. Serve.

Cranberry-Apple Crisp

My problem with cranberry-apple crisp is getting the right balance of flavors. When I add cranberries to the apples, the flavors don't come together—the cranberries taste too sour, even when I add extra sugar. Plus the apples bake unevenly, and my topping never lives up to the name "crisp." Please help. –Beth Haber, Providence, R.I.

Partially cooking the fruit filling before baking brings the flavors together and cuts the oven time by two-thirds.

Adding cranberries to a homespun apple crisp sounded pretty easy, but after a few initial tests I had my doubts. Like yours, my crisps had no balance of flavors; one bite tasted super-tart and overloaded with cranberries, while the next tasted of apples, with no cranberry flavor at all. To make matters worse, the soggy topping was a long way from crisp.

After several tests, I realized that tossing raw cranberries and apples together and then adding the topping was never going to work. The berries were too bitter, and their juices were making the topping soggy.

I ran across a crisp recipe that called for canned cranberry sauce. The idea of using canned cranberries when my supermarket was overflowing with bags of fresh berries seemed ridiculous, but what if I made my own cranberry sauce with fresh cranberries? That way I could get even cranberry distribution (a sauce would be easy to stir into the apples) and sweeten the cranberries before they met the apples.

I cooked fresh cranberries with sugar and a little water until they burst and thickened into a homemade sauce. I then added the mixture to diced Granny Smith apples (the test kitchen's favorite for baking) and topped the fruit with the classic combination of butter, flour, sugar, cinnamon, and oats.

After an hour and a half in the oven, when the fruit juices started to bubble up, I thought I had a winner. The scarlet filling looked like it was packed with cranberry flavor, but it actually tasted pretty dull and the consistency was soupy.

A colleague suggested that dried cranberries might be the answer to deeper cranberry flavor. Adding a cup of dried berries gave my crisp a one-two punch of concentrated cranberry flavor and added a welcome textural hit that my tasters loved. And as the dried berries rehydrated, they absorbed some of the excess juices, making for a drier topping. Adding some tapioca to the filling (better than either flour or cornstarch) also helped to thicken the fruit juices.

Now that I had the berries sorted out, I took another look at the apples. I liked the way Grannies held their shape in the oven, but they were awfully tart. To get a better balance of flavors, I tried combining the Grannies with sweeter apples like Gala, Golden Delicious, Red Delicious, and Braeburn. The Braeburns were my tasters' favorite, followed by Golden Delicious.

The crisp was taking nearly 90 minutes to bake. Any less time and the apples were too firm, but in 90 minutes the topping turned almost as hard as a stale granola bar. Since I was already dirtying a pot to make the cranberry sauce, I thought I'd use the same pot to jump-start the apples on the stovetop. Just five minutes of stovetop cooking was all it took to reduce the baking time from 90 to 30 minutes. The apples now cooked evenly in the baking dish, and the topping was no longer a dark, hard shell.

After peeling my way through bushels of apples (more than 150 pounds!) and puckering up to pounds of cranberries, I had finally found the path to perfect cranberry-apple crisp. **–Diane Unger**

Two Cranberries Are Better Than One

To pack cranberry flavor into our Cranberry-Apple Crisp, we cook fresh or frozen berries to a jammy consistency, then add chewy dried cranberries for texture and sweetness.

FRESH CRANBERRIES

DRIED CRANBERRIES

CRANBERRY-APPLE CRISP SERVES 8 TO 10

If you can't find Braeburn apples, Golden Delicious will work. Serve with vanilla ice cream or whipped cream.

Topping

- 3/4 cup all-purpose flour
- 1/2 cup packed light brown sugar
- 1/2 cup granulated sugar
- 1 teaspoon cinnamon
- 12 tablespoons (1 1/2 sticks) unsalted butter, cut into 1/2-inch pieces and chilled
- 3/4 cup old-fashioned oats

Filling

- 1 pound fresh or frozen cranberries (about 4 cups)
- 1 1/4 cups granulated sugar
- 1/4 cup water
- 2 1/2 pounds Granny Smith apples (6 to 8 apples), peeled, cored, and cut into 1/2-inch pieces
- 2 1/2 pounds Braeburn apples (6 to 8 apples), peeled, cored, and cut into 1/2-inch pieces
- 1 cup dried sweetened cranberries
- 3 tablespoons Minute Tapioca

1. For the topping: Adjust oven rack to middle position and heat oven to 400 degrees. Pulse flour, sugars, cinnamon, and butter in food processor until mixture has texture of coarse crumbs (some pea-sized pieces of butter will remain), about 12 one-second pulses. Transfer to medium bowl, stir in oats, and use fingers to pinch topping into peanut-sized clumps. Refrigerate while preparing filling.

2. For the filling: Bring fresh cranberries, 3/4 cup sugar, and water to simmer in Dutch oven over medium-high heat and cook until cranberries are completely softened and mixture is jam-like, about 10 minutes. Scrape mixture into bowl. Add apples, remaining 1/2 cup sugar, and dried cranberries to Dutch oven and cook over medium-high heat until apples begin to release their juices, about 5 minutes.

3. Off heat, stir cranberry mixture and tapioca into apple mixture. Pour into 13 by 9-inch baking dish set over rimmed baking sheet and smooth surface evenly with spatula.

4. To assemble: Scatter topping evenly over filling and bake until juices are bubbling and topping is deep golden brown, about 30 minutes. (If topping is browning too quickly, loosely cover with piece of aluminum foil.) Transfer to wire rack to cool. Serve warm.

Make Ahead

While this crisp is best eaten the day it is cooked, the topping and filling can be made ahead. After pinching the topping into small clumps in step 1, transfer the mixture to a zipper-lock bag and refrigerate for up to 5 days or freeze for up to 1 month. The cooked filling can be refrigerated for up to 2 days.

To bake, sprinkle the chilled topping evenly over the chilled filling, loosely cover with foil, and bake for 20 minutes. Uncover and bake until the juices are bubbling and the topping is deep golden brown, 15 to 20 minutes longer.

Kitchen Know-How CRISP ESSENTIALS

1. Cook the cranberries, sugar, and water until the mixture is thick and jammy. 2. Mound the topping in the center of the dish, then use your fingers to rake the topping out toward the edges of the dish.

Recipe Revival: Chicken Divan

A modern technique rescues this restaurant relic from the supermarket freezer case.

Despite its current reputation as a cheesy, creamy chicken and broccoli casserole you pick up in the frozen-food aisle and reheat in a microwave, chicken Divan has a long and elegant history. The original recipe from New York's famed (and now defunct) Divan Parisien restaurant dates back almost 100 years and required a whole poached chicken, boiled broccoli, and a sauce made with béchamel sauce, hollandaise sauce, Parmesan cheese, and whipped cream. The ingredients were combined "à la minute" (just before being plated) and broiled to perfection. Sounds good, but if I'm counting right, that's at least five pots, four recipes, and more time than I'd care to spend in the kitchen. No wonder most "modern" recipes rely on canned soup.

To bring Divan into the 21st century without compromising the flavors of the original dish, I turned to my trusty skillet. Batch-cooking was in order, and first up was the broccoli. It was easily sautéed and then steamed in a little chicken broth so it emerged flavorful, tender, and emerald green. Boneless, skinless chicken breasts got a similar treatment in the empty pan.

Mimicking the original sauce took some kitchen trickery. Simmering chicken broth with heavy cream (instead of folding in whipped cream at the end) gave the sauce a rich feel, and sherry, Worcestershire, and a full cup of grated Parmesan warmed up the flavors. My sauce was good, but without the hollandaise (and its decadent egg yolks and butter and bright lemon juice) it wasn't exactly right. Instead of preparing a separate hollandaise, could I just add these ingredients to my existing sauce? I whisked the yolks and lemon juice together, then tempered the mixture with a little of the hot pan sauce. Once returned to the pan (off the heat so as not to curdle the eggs), along with some butter, the sauce thickened to pure luxury.

I poured the sauce over the waiting chicken and broccoli, topped everything with more Parmesan, and slid the dish under the broiler for a few minutes. I now had chicken Divan that was as opulent as the original but didn't require anywhere near the effort.

–Bridget Lancaster

MODERN CHICKEN DIVAN SERVES 4

Use one small onion instead of the shallots, if desired.

- 3 tablespoons vegetable oil
- 1 1/2 pounds broccoli, stalks discarded, florets cut into bite-sized pieces
- 2 1/2 cups low-sodium chicken broth
- 1 1/2 pounds boneless, skinless chicken breasts
- Salt and pepper
- 1/4 cup all-purpose flour
- 2 medium shallots, minced
- 1 cup heavy cream
- 1/2 cup dry sherry
- 2 teaspoons Worcestershire sauce
- 1 1/2 cups grated Parmesan cheese
- 3 large egg yolks
- 1 tablespoon lemon juice
- 3 tablespoons unsalted butter

1. Adjust oven rack to lower-middle position and heat broiler. Heat 1 tablespoon oil in large skillet over medium-high heat until just smoking. Add broccoli and cook until spotty brown, about 1 minute. Add 1/2 cup broth, cover, and steam until just tender, about 1 1/2 minutes. Remove lid and cook until liquid has evaporated, about 1 minute. Transfer broccoli to plate lined with paper towels; rinse and wipe out skillet.

2. Heat remaining 2 tablespoons oil in now-empty skillet over medium-high heat until smoking. Meanwhile, season chicken with salt and pepper and dredge in flour to coat. Cook chicken until golden brown, 2 to 3 minutes per side. Transfer chicken to plate.

3. Off heat, add shallots to skillet and cook until just beginning to color, about 1 minute. Add remaining 2 cups broth and cream and scrape browned bits from bottom of pan. Return chicken to skillet and simmer over medium-high heat until cooked through, about 10 minutes. Transfer chicken to clean plate and continue to simmer sauce until reduced to 1 cup, about 10 minutes. Add sherry and Worcestershire and simmer until reduced again to 1 cup, about 3 minutes.

4. Stir in 1 cup Parmesan. Whisk yolks and lemon juice in small bowl, then whisk in about 1/4 cup sauce. Off heat, whisk egg yolk mixture into sauce in skillet, then whisk in butter.

5. Cut chicken into 1/2-inch-thick slices and arrange on broilersafe platter. Scatter broccoli over chicken and pour sauce over broccoli. Sprinkle with 1/2 cup Parmesan and broil until golden brown, 3 to 5 minutes. Serve.

30-Minute Meat Loaf

Meat loaf is my family's favorite, but it's not the best choice during the week. By the time I get home, it's really too late to start a meat loaf. Do you know any good shortcuts? –Theresa Clough, Bend, Ore.

Test Kitchen Tips

A BETTER MEAT LOAF

Thirty minutes or not, meat loaves suffer the same problems no matter their size—crumbly texture, pale exterior, and excessive greasiness. Here's how we eliminated these problems in our little loaves.

1. Pack the meat-loaf mixture tightly into compact loaves to make sure they don't fall apart.
2. Sear the top and bottom of the loaves to develop a crisp and flavorful exterior.
3. Bake the loaves on the top of a preheated broiler pan so excess fat can drip away.

Our single-serving meat loaves have a flavorful crust and a tender interior.

Most meat-loaf recipes call for an hour of baking time in an oven set to 350 or 375 degrees. Add another half-hour to cook some onions and garlic, measure other ingredients, and knead the meat mixture, and you're talking at least 90 minutes to get meat loaf on the table. Not bad considering that most of the time is hands-off, but not good if it's already 6 o'clock and everyone is hungry.

I decided to streamline the test kitchen's favorite recipe, which calls for meat-loaf mix (equal parts ground beef, pork, and veal sold in one package at most supermarkets), crushed saltines, a little milk, and a single egg. To speed up the process, I found that onion powder and garlic powder were decent substitutes for the real thing and saved 15 minutes of chopping and cooking. I tried to replace the fresh parsley with dried, but tasters objected to its stale flavor and dull color; I decided to take a couple of minutes to chop this one ingredient. Other seasonings—Worcestershire sauce, Dijon mustard, and cayenne pepper—required just a minute or two to assemble and measure.

With the ingredients set, I turned my focus to the cooking method. Based on my research, cranking up the oven temperature to 500 degrees seemed like the best option. The loaf was done in 30 minutes (rather than 60), but it was pale and greasy. (It wasn't in the oven long enough to render all the fat or to brown sufficiently.) Broiling was another common solution offered in "quick" cookbooks, but this method left the top half incinerated and the bottom half soggy and sitting in a puddle of grease. Then I found a recipe that called for dividing the meat-loaf mixture into smaller loaves. This was the quickest recipe yet, taking just 25 minutes to bake, but two problems remained: The loaves were swimming in their own grease, and they lacked a browned crust—the hallmark of any respectable meat loaf.

Searing the loaves in a skillet on the stovetop and then transferring them to the oven solved the browning issue and cut the total cooking time to just 15 minutes.

Even though much of the fat rendered in the skillet, some excess grease continued to pool around the loaves on the baking sheet. Baking the loaves on a slotted broiler pan solved this problem. Letting the broiler pan preheat in the oven shaved a few more minutes off the cooking time, leaving me with a recipe that could be prepped and cooked in less than 30 minutes.

Their size might be unconventional, but my little loaves are every bit as tasty as any big loaf, with an even better crust.

–Cali Rich

Make Ahead

The loaves can be formed, wrapped with plastic, and refrigerated overnight. Let the loaves sit at room temperature for 20 minutes before proceeding with step 3.

30-MINUTE MEAT LOAVES SERVES 4 TO 6

If meat-loaf mix is not available, substitute 3/4 pound each of ground pork and 85 percent lean ground beef.

Meat Loaves

- 17 saltines, crushed fine (about 2/3 cup)
- 1/4 cup milk
- 3 tablespoons Worcestershire sauce
- 1/3 cup minced fresh parsley
- 1 1/2 tablespoons Dijon mustard
- 1 large egg
- 1 teaspoon onion powder
- 1 teaspoon garlic powder
- 1/8 teaspoon cayenne pepper
- Salt and pepper
- 1 1/2 pounds meat-loaf mix
- 2 teaspoons vegetable oil

Glaze

- 1/2 cup ketchup
- 1/4 cup packed light brown sugar
- 4 teaspoons cider vinegar

1. For the meat loaves: Adjust oven rack to middle position, place broiler pan with slotted top on oven rack, and heat oven to 500 degrees.

2. Mix cracker crumbs, milk, Worcestershire, parsley, mustard, egg, onion powder, garlic powder, cayenne, ½ teaspoon salt, and ½ teaspoon pepper in large bowl. Add meat and mix with hands until evenly combined. Form into 4 tightly packed loaves, each measuring 4 by 3 inches.

3. Heat oil in large nonstick skillet over medium-high heat until just smoking. Cook loaves until well browned on top and bottom, 2 to 3 minutes per side.

4. For the glaze: While meat is browning, combine ketchup, brown sugar, and vinegar in bowl.

5. To finish: Carefully transfer loaves to slotted broiler-pan top and spoon 1 tablespoon glaze over each loaf. Bake until thermometer inserted in middle of loaf registers 160 degrees, 7 to 9 minutes. Let loaves rest on broiler pan for 3 minutes. Serve, passing remaining glaze separately.

Super-Creamy Mashed Potatoes

Do you have a way to make truly creamy mashed potatoes that aren't gluey? –Cynthia Kraft van Ermel, Roseville, Mich.

During the holiday season, I shelve my tried-and-true recipe for mashed otatoes in favor of a much nore luxurious mash, one that s silky smooth and loaded with ream and butter. But there's fine line between creamy and luey. Sometimes my potatoes re as good as any you might et in the finest restaurant. Other times, they closely esemble paste or Spackle. Why s this simple recipe (with just otatoes, cream, butter, and alt) so fickle?

The problem is the starch. Vhen the cooked potatoes re mashed, some starch is eleased, which helps to make he potatoes incredibly smooth nd creamy. But if you've ever nashed potatoes with an electric mixer, you've seen what appens when you get too nuch of a good thing: The nixer releases too much starch from the potatoes and turns them into a gluey mess.

Finding the right type of potato was my first challenge. Russets yielded a fluffy, relatively light mash. I wanted something a bit creamier and more substantial. Red potatoes were too dense and gluey. Yukon Golds were the perfect compromise—creamier than russets but not sticky and heavy, like the red potatoes.

Preparing potatoes for mashing is pretty straightforward. The potatoes are peeled, cut into chunks, boiled, drained, and mashed. Could I improve upon this method? I found a few recipes that suggested microwaving or baking the potatoes, but the results were grainy. I finally hit upon a simple refinement borrowed from classic french fry recipes, which call for rinsing the cut potatoes to wash away excess starch. What if I adapted this idea for mashed potatoes? Cutting the potatoes into round slices (rather than the usual chunks) would expose more surface area, so I ran a test with rinsed versus unrinsed rounds of potatoes. The differences were significant. The rinsed potatoes were much creamier (and not at all gluey) when mashed.

To remove any water still clinging to the potatoes, I returned them to the empty pot and set it over low heat (excess water reduces the amount of butter and cream the potatoes can hold).

As for the butter and cream, I've never understood cooks who add these ingredients cold to hot potatoes. Melting the butter and heating the cream ensure that the potatoes will arrive at the table hot.

Creamy potatoes demand a fair amount of butter and cream, but too much will turn them soupy. After testing various amounts of each, my tasters decided that 1½ sticks of butter and 1½ cups of cream gave 4 pounds of potatoes the best flavor and texture.

These rich potatoes are an indulgence, and I would never douse them with gravy (use a leaner recipe if that's your goal). Eat these mashed potatoes just as they are, so you can appreciate every drop of cream. **–Meredith Butcher**

Rinsing away excess starch and cooking off the extra water before mashing nsure a dense and creamy version of this holiday classic.

CREAMY MASHED POTATOES SERVES 8 TO 10

This recipe can be cut in half, if desired.

- **4 pounds Yukon Gold potatoes, peeled**
- **12 tablespoons (1½ sticks) unsalted butter, cut into 6 pieces**
- **1½ cups heavy cream**
- **2 teaspoons salt**

1. Cut potatoes into ¾-inch slices. Place potatoes in colander and rinse under running water, tossing with hands, for 30 seconds. Transfer potatoes to Dutch oven, add water to cover by 1 inch, and bring to boil over high heat. Reduce heat to medium and boil until potatoes are tender, 20 to 25 minutes.

2. Meanwhile, heat butter and heavy cream in small saucepan over medium heat until butter is melted, about 5 minutes. Keep warm.

3. Drain potatoes and return to Dutch oven. Stir over low heat until potatoes are thoroughly dried, 1 to 2 minutes. Set ricer or food mill (see box below) over large bowl and press or mill potatoes into bowl. Gently fold in warm cream mixture and salt with rubber spatula until cream is absorbed and potatoes are thick and creamy. Serve.

Kitchen Know-How
SECRET TO CREAMY POTATOES

These simple steps guarantee a luxuriously creamy—never gluey—texture every time.

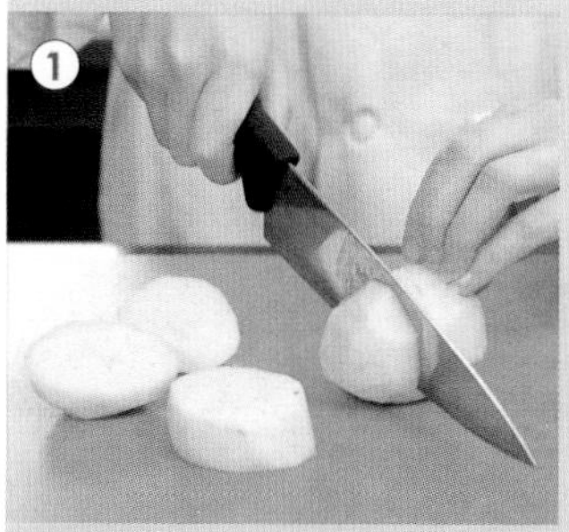

1. Cut the potatoes into 3/4-inch rounds (rather than the usual wedges or chunks) to expose the maximum amount of surface area.
2. Toss the potatoes in a colander under running water to rinse away as much starch as possible.
3. When the potatoes are tender, drain and then dry thoroughly in an empty pot over low heat.

Which Mashing Method Is Best?

The equipment you use to mash your potatoes will have a big effect on their texture. Here are the options, listed from least preferred to most preferred (left to right).

ELECTRIC MIXER
A real no-no, unless you like gluey potatoes.

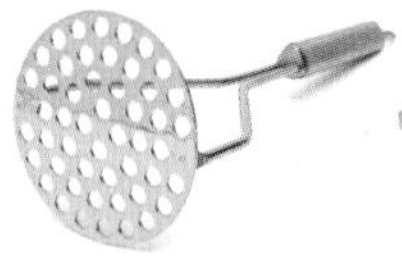

MASHER
Even with a good workout, some lumps are inevitable.

RICER
Almost perfect, with just the occasional lump.

FOOD MILL
Super-silky and smooth mashed potatoes without fail.

We take the guesswork out of this traditionally finicky recipe to bring you a perfectly wilted and dressed salad.

Spinach Salad with Hot Bacon Dressing

I love the idea of a warm spinach salad, but mine always ends up lifeless and limp. Do you have a recipe for me? –Jane Sullivan, Arvada, Colo.

In the salad world, not much satisfies like a wilted spinach salad—a hearty mix of earthy spinach, warm bacon-enriched dressing, and creamy hard-cooked eggs—at least as far as I've heard. I say "heard" because every spinach salad I've tasted fits your description. Not only are they lifeless and limp, but they're overdressed and greasy to boot.

The theory behind a wilted spinach salad is simple: The hot bacon dressing wilts the tough spinach leaves to an even tenderness. In practice, however, pouring hot dressing over spinach reduces some of the leaves to overcooked mush, while others remain raw. This is particularly true when using delicate baby spinach (as most modern recipes do), which wilts if you look at it crossly. The classic version of this salad relies on hearty, mature spinach (the kind with the curly leaves), which is much more forgiving. In fact, these leaves stand their ground to a fault—when doused with the hot vinaigrette, they wilt a bit, but not enough to become completely tender.

To help mature curly spinach wilt, most recipes take the low road and just increase the amount of dressing, leaving a sloppy pile of spinach swimming in a puddle of vinegar and bacon fat. I wondered if adding a bit of heft to the dressing (rather than increasing the volume) might weigh the spinach down and help it wilt.

My tasters liked a dressing with equal parts bacon drippings and cider vinegar. (I was surprised how much vinegar was needed to counter the richness of the bacon and eggs.) To add some heft, I sautéed red onion in the bacon drippings and added a dollop of Dijon mustard for heat and pungency. But even with the weight of additional ingredients, the spinach was still slightly underwilted. To achieve the ideal texture, one of my colleagues suggested partially cooking the spinach before tossing it with the hot dressing.

The microwave proved utterly disastrous, leaving me with rubbery, soggy spinach even before the dressing entered the equation. The sauté method was hard to manage and really clumsy. (You try fitting a whole bag of spinach in a 12-inch skillet.) Ultimately, steaming proved to be the ticket.

Trading in my skillet for a Dutch oven, I rendered the bacon, added the remaining dressing ingredients, took the pan off the heat, topped it all with the spinach, and put the lid on the pot. After only 15 seconds, I turned out the salad, dressing and all, into a mixing bowl for a quick toss. The steamy heat in the easy-to-handle Dutch oven had produced a perfect, evenly wilted salad. And with just a few wedges of hard-cooked egg, I finally had a wilted spinach salad that was worthy of its reputation. **–Jeremy Sauer**

Test Kitchen Technique
PERFECT HARD-COOKED EGGS

Cook: Place 6 eggs in a medium saucepan, cover with 1 inch of water, and bring to a boil over high heat. Remove pan from heat, cover, and let sit for 10 minutes.

Crack: Drain water from pan and carefully shake pan back and forth, cracking eggshells against each other and the side of the pan.

Cool: Transfer cracked eggs to ice-water bath to stop cooking. Let sit for 5 minutes; retrieve and peel.

SPINACH SALAD WITH HOT BACON DRESSING

SERVES 4 TO 6

Although most bagged spinach is supposedly washed before bagging, we have often found that some leaves remain gritty. Give the leaves a quick rinse and then dry them in a salad spinner before preparing the recipe.

- **8 slices thick-cut bacon, halved lengthwise and cut crosswise into 1/2-inch pieces**
- **1 (10-ounce) bag curly spinach, stemmed and torn into bite-sized pieces**
- **1/2 red onion, sliced thin**
- **2 garlic cloves, minced**
- **1/2 teaspoon salt**
- **1/2 teaspoon pepper**
- **2 teaspoons sugar**
- **1/4 cup cider vinegar**
- **1 tablespoon Dijon mustard**
- **3 hard-cooked eggs, peeled and quartered (optional)**

1. Fry bacon in Dutch oven over medium-high heat until crisp, about 7 minutes. Using slotted spoon, transfer bacon to paper-towel-lined plate and pour off all but ¼ cup bacon fat. Place spinach in large bowl next to stove.

2. Return pot to medium-high heat and cook onion, garlic, salt, pepper, and sugar until onion is softened, about 3 minutes. Working quickly, add vinegar and mustard and scrape bottom of pot with wooden spoon to loosen browned bits. Remove pot from heat, add spinach, and cover, allowing spinach to steam until just beginning to wilt, about 15 seconds.

3. Transfer steamed spinach and hot dressing to empty bowl and toss lightly with tongs. Divide salad among individual plates and garnish with reserved bacon and eggs (if using). Serve.

The Need for Speed

If you work too slowly during the final stages of this recipe, the spinach can go from raw to limp and lifeless very quickly. To ensure a perfectly wilted salad (as shown in the photo at left), make sure you have all your ingredients and equipment at hand. In step 2, when the onion is soft and it's time to add the vinegar and mustard, make sure the spinach, the Dutch oven lid, and your tongs are at the ready.

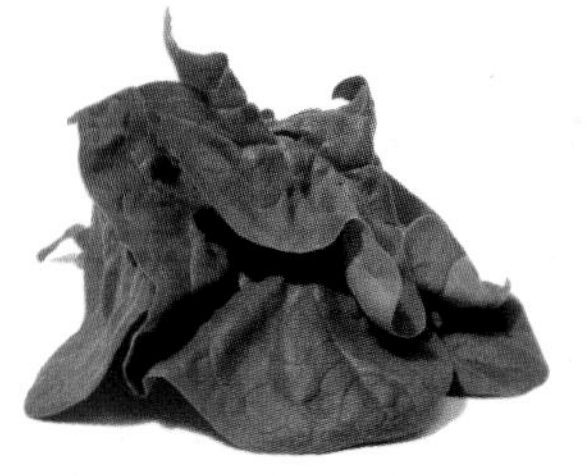

RAW SPINACH

OVER-WILTED

Getting to Know Hearty Greens

Vitamin-rich and flavorful, hearty greens are underappreciated. To see what we've been missing, we gathered 12 varieties and tasted them simply sautéed to compare their flavors. For more information about cooking hearty greens, see page 30.

Kale
GARNISHING GREEN
Sturdy kale tastes "cabbagey and musky," with "a touch of sweetness, like a big Brussels sprout." Discard thick stems and braise until tender. Good in soups and stews. Often used to garnish banquet platters.

Collards
SOUL FOOD'S FINEST
Synonymous with Southern cooking, collards have a "sweet, yeasty flavor" and a "pungent, slightly sulfurous aroma" that makes them a perfect match with pork or beans. Discard thick stems and boil or braise until tender.

Dandelion
LION'S TOOTH
The bane of gardeners everywhere, the dandelion (from the French *dent de lion*, or "lion's tooth") is in fact a pretty tasty weed. Its flavor is "grassy and acidic," with a "peppery edge." If picked when young and tender, dandelion leaves can be used in salads; the leaves from older, tougher plants are best braised.

Beet
SALT OF THE EARTH
Since beet greens are rarely sold in bulk, look for bunched beets with the fresh greens still attached. Beet greens have an "earthy, almost tobacco-like" flavor and a "natural salinity." Although the leaves are tender, the stems can be a bit fibrous. Best cooked quickly.

Tuscan Kale
ON THE DARK SIDE
Sometimes called black or dinosaur kale, this darkly colored Italian green has tightly curled leaves with a puckered appearance. More tender and flavorful than ordinary kale, the Tuscan variety has a mild, smoky" flavor that's "reminiscent of asparagus." Discard stems and use in sautés and braises.

Spinach
TENDER CLASSIC
Whether baby, curly, or flat (pictured), all three spinach varieties display a "nice mineral taste" and a "roasted peanut aroma." Because of its relatively tender texture, spinach is best used raw in salads or quickly sautéed.

Broccoli Rabe
ITALIAN FAVORITE
Although it resembles broccoli, this green is more closely related to the turnip. An Italian favorite, broccoli rabe has a "mustardy bitterness" that's balanced by a "smoky, floral" aftertaste. Discard the last inch or two of the stalks. It is best blanched before use to remove bitterness; can be sautéed or braised.

Chard
A RAINBOW OF CHOICES
Often called Swiss chard, this green looks a bit like rhubarb but is actually related to the beet. The crisp stalks come in a rainbow of colors (white, yellow, and red are the most common), but their flavor is consistent: "bitter and mineraly," with "notes of citrus." Like spinach, chard is "tender and very watery." Best cooked quickly.

Mustard
PUNGENT AND PEPPERY
This green, whose seeds are ground to make the popular condiment, is well liked in the South. The leaves are bright green and frilly around the edges. The flavor is "nutty and bitter," with a "peppery heat." Discard thick stems and braise until tender.

Turnip
GET THEM YOUNG
Turnip greens rival collards for the top spot in the Southern kitchen. We found them "firm, fibrous, and chewy," with a "buttery" flavor and "metallic aftertaste." Look for younger greens, which are much sweeter and more tender than older leaves. Discard thick stems and boil or braise until tender.

Kohlrabi
BROCCOLI WANNABE
Although kohlrabi is best known for its edible bulb, which looks like a turnip, the leafy greens are beginning to garner attention. Their flavor is similar to that of "steamed broccoli," with "a garlicky kick." Kohlrabi stems can be a bit tough, but the leaves are tender and are best quickly sautéed.

Stinging Nettles
ONE MEAN GREEN
This wild green is covered with hair-like spikes that irritate the skin. Thankfully, cooking destroys the compound responsible for this effect. Only young shoots and tops are eaten. Nettles taste "similar to mushrooms" and have a "briny flavor that's not unlike shellfish." Wear gloves whenever handling raw nettles. Discard thick stems and braise until tender.

Holiday Stuffed Turkey

Every year I stuff and roast a 22-pound turkey. It looks impressive, but the breast meat is really dry. And my homemade stuffing tastes like a boxed mix. Can you help? –Ted Washington, Fargo, N.D.

Kitchen Know-How
IT'S IN THE BAG

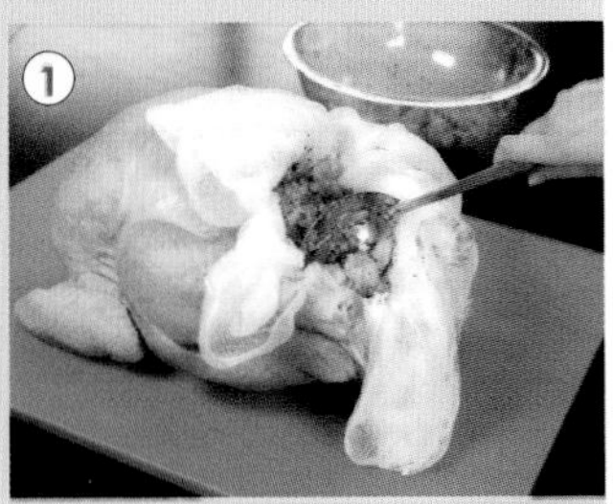

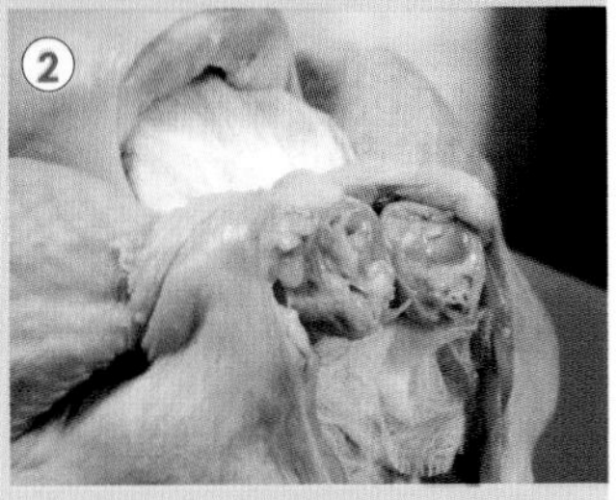

1. Line the empty cavity of the bird with a folded piece of cheesecloth, making sure that the cheesecloth reaches the end of the cavity. Loosely pack the stuffing into the cheesecloth "bag" (it should hold 10 to 12 cups of stuffing) and tie the bag securely with kitchen twine.
2. Secure the turkey's legs by tucking the ankles into the pocket of skin at the tail end.

Norman Rockwell's image of a giant, bronzed turkey packed with moist stuffing is the Thanksgiving ideal—beautiful to look at and ample enough to provide plenty of meat (both dark and white) for more than one trip to the kids' table and back. But stuffed turkeys, particularly those weighing 20 pounds or more, can be difficult to manage. It's not the huge turkey that gives us pause—it's a great way to feed a crowd—or even the stuffing, which sops up all those tasty turkey drippings; it's the combination of the two. By the time the stuffing reaches 165 degrees (the temperature recommended by the U.S. Department of Agriculture), the breast meat is pushing 190 degrees (25 degrees higher than ideal) and moist meat is a distant memory that no amount of gravy can recall.

In an attempt to keep the temperature of the stuffing closer to that of the turkey, I tried just about everything I could think of: stuffing a cold turkey with hot stuffing, cooking the stuffed turkey in an oven bag for more even heat, shielding the turkey breast with foil, and on and on. None of these tricks worked: The stuffing just wasn't coming up to temperature as soon as the meat.

The solution (and a forehead-slapping one at that) came from the mother of one of our test cooks. Just cook the stuffed turkey until the meat is at the appropriate temperature, then remove the stuffing and finish cooking it in the oven while the turkey rests. Finally, I could bring the stuffing up to a safe temperature without overcooking the white meat. A simple solution, indeed, and one with an unexpected benefit: Aside from perfectly cooked meat, this technique produced a nice crusty exterior on the stuffing.

Our recipe guarantees both hearty, savory stuffing *and* a perfectly cooked bird.

With the stuffing's temperature issues resolved, I turned my attention to texture. Most recipes fail on this front because they bake up wet and spongy inside the turkey—a direct byproduct of a heavy hand with the liquid ingredients. After much testing, I found that I needed only 3 cups of liquid (broth was preferred over milk, water, or wine) for almost 20 cups of cubed bread—less than half the liquid called for in some recipes. Tasters preferred the slight chew of a baguette to more delicate breads, especially when it was lightly toasted in a hot oven. A simple combination of vegetables (onion and celery), eggs, and fresh and dried herbs gave the stuffing a balanced flavor, while cooking it in a bag fashioned from cheesecloth made it both tidy and easy to remove from the turkey.

To make sure everyone got their share, I prepared almost double the amount of stuffing that would fit in the bird (the turkey's cavity held about 12 cups) and set the excess aside while the turkey roasted. Once the turkey was finished, I combined the reserved stuffing with the stuffing from the bird (along with a liberal saucing of turkey drippings to make up for any lost flavor) and transferred it all to the oven to heat through and crisp up. Finally, with the simplest of solutions, I had found a way to make a giant stuffed turkey that was good eating. **–Jeremy Sauer**

HOLIDAY STUFFED TURKEY **SERVES 15 TO 18**

Because large turkeys are prone to drying out in the oven, we highly recommend buying a frozen Butterball. These turkeys are injected with a salt solution that helps them stay moist during cooking. If you choose to roast a fresh bird, brining is the best option. To learn more about brining, see page 31, where you'll also find step-by-step photos that show you how to carve a turkey.

- **2 (24-inch) loaves French baguette, torn into 3/4-inch chunks (about 20 cups)**
- **12 tablespoons (1 1/2 sticks) unsalted butter, softened, plu[s] extra for greasing baking dis[h]**
- **2 onions, chopped fine**
- **4 celery ribs, chopped fine**
- **4 garlic cloves, minced**
- **1 teaspoon dried sage**
- **1 teaspoon dried thyme**
- **1/2 cup chopped fresh parsley**
- **Salt and pepper**
- **3 cups low-sodium chicken broth**
- **4 large eggs, lightly beaten**
- **1 (36-inch) square cheesecloth, folded into quarters (or store-bought stuffing bag)**
- **1 frozen Butterball turkey (18 to 22 pounds), thawed and patted dry with paper towels (neck and giblets reserved fo[r] gravy, if desired)**

1. Adjust oven racks to upper-middle and lower-middle positions and heat oven to 425 degrees. Divide bread chunks between two rimmed baking sheets and bake, tossing occasionally, until golden brown, about 15 minutes. Transfer to large bowl. (Do not turn off oven.)

2. Melt 8 tablespoons butter in large skillet over medium-high heat. Add onions and celery and cook until softened, about 8 minutes. Stir in garlic, herbs, 1½ teaspoons salt, and 1 teaspoon pepper and cook until fragrant, about 1 minute. Off heat, whisk in 2 cups broth, then eggs. Pour mixture over bread and toss until evenly coated.

3. Following photos on page 24, line turkey cavity with cheesecloth, pack with warm stuffing, tie ends of cheesecloth, and tuck turkey legs. Transfer remaining stuffing (8 to 12 cups) to large microwave-safe bowl. Pour remaining 1 cup broth over stuffing, cover with plastic wrap, and refrigerate.

4. Using oven mitts, adjust one oven rack to lowest position and remove other rack. Combine remaining 4 tablespoons softened butter, 1 teaspoon salt, and 1 teaspoon pepper in small bowl. Rub mixture all over turkey and position turkey breast side up on V-rack set in large disposable aluminum pan. Set pan on rimmed baking sheet and roast for 1 hour. Reduce oven temperature to 325 degrees and continue to roast until thickest part of breast registers 165 degrees and thickest part of thigh registers 175 degrees on instant-read thermometer (see photos at right), 2 to 3 hours longer. Transfer turkey to cutting board and let rest 30 minutes, reserving turkey drippings in roasting pan.

5. Remove stuffing bag from turkey and empty stuffing into 13 by 9-inch baking dish. Microwave reserved stuffing on high until hot, 5 to 7 minutes, then add to stuffing in baking dish. Pour ½ cup reserved drippings over stuffing, cover with foil, and bake until stuffing registers 165 degrees on instant-read thermometer, about 15 minutes. Remove foil and bake until top of stuffing is browned and crisp, 5 to 10 minutes longer. Transfer stuffing to platter and carve turkey. Serve.

Make Ahead

The stuffing can be prepared a day in advance and refrigerated. When ready to stuff the turkey, transfer 12 cups of stuffing to a microwave-safe bowl, cover with plastic wrap, and microwave on high, stirring once, until warm, about 5 minutes. Proceed as directed in step 3 of recipe.

How to TAKE THE TEMPERATURE OF TURKEY

Nothing ruins turkey timing like a faulty temperature reading, leaving the turkey unpalatably dry or, worse, undercooked. To be sure we've cooked our turkey correctly, we take the temperature in multiple spots. And forget about those pop-up timers. They are set to go off when the turkey is overcooked.

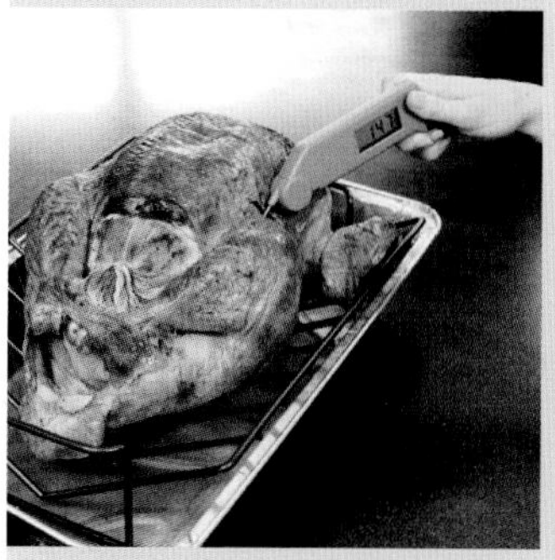

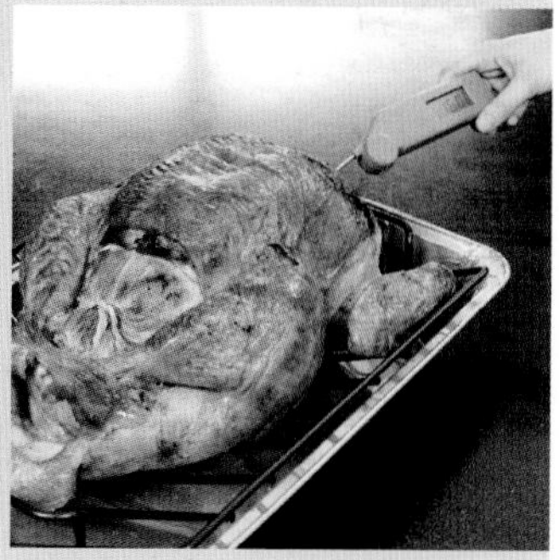

To take the temperature of the thigh: Insert an instant-read thermometer between the breast and drumstick and into the thickest part of the thigh, staying away from the bone. The thigh should reach 175 degrees. Confirm the temperature in the other thigh. **To take the temperature of the breast:** Insert the thermometer at the neck end, holding it parallel to the bird. Confirm the temperature in both sides of the bird. The breast should reach 165 degrees.

On the Side: Turkey Gravy

No more last-minute gravy headaches. Now you can have lump-free, flavorful gravy made before the turkey goes into the oven.

The pies are baked, the potatoes mashed, and every part of the Thanksgiving meal is going off without a hitch. And then—wham! As soon as the golden brown turkey emerges from the oven, it's time for the last-minute gravy scramble. This frantic dance of skimming hot fat from the turkey drippings, whisking in a thickener (usually flour or cornstarch), and getting the gravy to the table still warm is no small feat, and it's probably why most of us have had our fair share of greasy, lumpy, cold gravy. Our goal was to prepare a great gravy before the turkey went into the oven.

Good gravy starts with good turkey stock. After simmering the giblets with turkey parts (drumsticks, thighs, or wings, all sold separately at most markets), celery, onions, and carrots, we had pretty good stock. But when we roasted the turkey pieces and vegetables before simmering them together, we had great turkey stock—incredibly rich and flavorful.

Of course, gravy is more than just stock. It must be thickened. We had better results with a roux (fat and flour cooked together) than with cornstarch. Instead of the usual oil or butter for our roux, we used the turkey fat that had congealed on top of the cooled turkey stock. This ready-to-serve gravy could even be held in the fridge for a few days. Just reheat before serving and it will be absolutely perfect. **–Jeremy Sauer**

MAKE-AHEAD TURKEY GRAVY

MAKES ABOUT 2 QUARTS

For more flavor, after roasting the turkey you can skim the drippings from the pan and add them to the gravy just before serving. It's best to discard the strong-tasting liver before using the giblets; see page 30 for details. This recipe makes enough to accompany a large turkey and still have plenty for leftovers.

Reserved turkey giblets and neck
6 turkey drumsticks, thighs, or wings
2 carrots, chopped coarse
2 celery ribs, chopped coarse
2 onions, chopped coarse
1 head garlic, halved
Vegetable oil spray
10 cups low-sodium chicken broth
2 cups dry white wine
12 sprigs fresh thyme
1/2 cup all-purpose flour
Salt and pepper

1. Adjust oven rack to middle position and heat oven to 450 degrees. Place giblets, neck, drumsticks, carrots, celery, onions, and garlic in roasting pan, spray with vegetable oil, and toss well. Roast, stirring occasionally, until well browned, 1 to 1½ hours.

2. Transfer contents of roasting pan to Dutch oven. Add broth, wine, and thyme and bring to boil over high heat. Reduce heat to low and simmer until reduced by half, about 1½ hours. Pour through fine-mesh strainer into large container (discard solids), cover stock with plastic wrap, and refrigerate until fat congeals, at least 2 hours.

3. Using soup spoon, skim fat and reserve. Heat ½ cup fat in Dutch oven over medium-high heat until bubbling. Whisk in flour and cook, whisking constantly, until honey colored, about 2 minutes. Gradually whisk in stock, bring to boil, reduce heat to medium-low, and simmer until slightly thickened, about 10 minutes. Season with salt and pepper. (Gravy can be refrigerated for up to 3 days or frozen for up to 2 months.) Reheat gravy in saucepan over medium heat until bubbling.

Pumpkin-Praline Pie

Have you ever heard of pumpkin-praline pie? In my family, some people like pecan pie and others (myself included) like pumpkin. Could I make just one pie that would satisfy everyone?
–Janice Haughey, Camden, Maine

Steps to Success

PERFECT PUMPKIN-PRALINE PIE

1. Puree the pumpkin (with the brown sugar and spices) to break up any fibers.
2. Cook the pumpkin mixture to get rid of excess moisture.
3. Pour the hot filling into a hot pie crust to minimize baking time and promote even cooking.
4. Wait for the filling to crack on top. Usually the sign of a problem, in our recipe the cracking is the cue that tells you exactly when to add the praline topping.

What's not to like about a pie that combines the familiar spiced custard of a pumpkin pie with the praline-like chew of a pecan pie? Most recipes start out with pumpkin pie as the base and add a layer of pecan praline—in the crust, in the filling, or as a topping. I tried all three arrangements and arrived at a few conclusions. First, tasters preferred their praline crunchy, and that meant keeping it on top. Second, they preferred a lot of topping, and that meant the pumpkin custard base would have to be pretty sturdy. Third, some of the pies were so sweet they made my tasters' teeth ache, so I would have to watch my hand when it came to sweeteners.

To fortify the pumpkin base, I added three eggs (one more than usual) to a can of plain pumpkin puree. Tasters preferred the richness of evaporated milk to either heavy cream or milk and the caramel flavor of dark brown sugar to granulated sugar.

While the filling tasted good, it was too loose to support the praline, and I didn't care for the stringy pumpkin fibers. Getting rid of the stringiness was as easy as a whirl in the food processor, and cooking the pureed filling on the stovetop evaporated the excess moisture. (This last step had the added benefit of reducing the baking time by 30 minutes.)

The pie was now ready for the praline topping. Some recipes have the cook make authentic praline candy by boiling sugar, water, and pecans. This candy was good for snacking but much too complicated—and too sweet—for my pie. Other recipes made "shortcut" candy by boiling pecans in copious amounts of corn syrup. Sticky and insipid, this topping tasted nothing like rich praline.

I found a few recipes that didn't get into boiling sugar at all. Instead, they tossed chopped pecans with granulated sugar and a smidgen of corn syrup—just enough to make the topping clump like streusel—and scattered the uncooked mixture on top of the still-hot, baked pumpkin pie. Intrigued by the apparent ease of this method, I topped the pumpkin pie with the crumbly nut mixture and popped it back into the oven. Ten minutes later the kitchen was filled with the smells of toasty sugar and pecans, and the topping bubbled enticingly around the edges.

The topping was now nearly perfect. All I wanted was a little more praline flavor, and I got it by replacing the granulated sugar with dark brown (just as I'd done with the pumpkin filling). I reserved 2 teaspoons of granulated sugar for sprinkling on the top, as it helped to crisp the praline.

The last obstacle concerned timing: Exactly when should I add the topping? If added too early—a few minutes before the center was set (as other recipes suggested)—the topping caused the filling to buckle under its weight. I turned to a visual cue that is the bane of many pumpkin pie bakers: the notorious cracking on top of the pie. As the pie just began to crack, it was perfectly set and ready to receive the topping, which covered any trace of the cracks. This worked like a charm every single time, and I now had a pie that would satisfy everyone gathered around the holiday table. **–Bridget Lancaster**

An easy praline topping adds a "wow" factor to this rich pumpkin pie.

PUMPKIN-PRALINE PIE

SERVES 8 TO 10

Use your favorite pie dough or go to cookscountry.com for our recipe. For a convenient option, use one sheet of Pillsbury Just Unroll! Pie Crusts, available in the refrigerator biscuit section of your supermarket.

- 1 (9-inch) pie shell, chilled in pie plate for 30 minutes (see note above)

Pumpkin Filling

- 1 (15-ounce) can plain pumpkin puree
- 3/4 cup packed dark brown sugar
- 2 teaspoons cinnamon
- 1 teaspoon ginger
- 1/2 teaspoon allspice
- Pinch cloves
- 1/2 teaspoon salt
- 1 cup evaporated milk
- 3 large eggs
- 2 teaspoons vanilla extract

Praline Topping

- 1 cup pecans, chopped fine
- 1/2 cup packed dark brown sugar
- Pinch salt
- 2 teaspoons dark corn syrup
- 1 teaspoon vanilla extract
- 2 teaspoons granulated sugar

1. For the pie shell: Adjust oven rack to middle position and heat oven to 350 degrees. Line pie shell with foil, cover with 2 cups pie weights (pennies or dried beans are fine, too), and bake until dough under foil dries out, 20 to 25 minutes. Remove foil and weights, poke crust several times with fork, and continue to bake until firmly set and lightly browned, 10 to 15 minutes. Remove pie shell from oven (keep oven on) and set aside. (Shell can be cooled, wrapped tightly in plastic, and stored at room temperature for 1 day.)

2. For the filling: Puree pumpkin, brown sugar, spices, and salt in food processor until smooth, about 1 minute. Cook mixture in large saucepan over medium-high heat until sputtering and thickened, about 4 minutes, and remove from heat. Meanwhile, put pie shell back in oven to warm.

3. Whisk evaporated milk into pumpkin mixture, then whisk in eggs and vanilla. Pour filling into warmed pie shell and bake until filling is puffed and cracked around edges and center barely jiggles when pie is shaken, about 35 minutes.

4. For the topping: While pie is baking, toss pecans, brown sugar, and salt in bowl. Add corn syrup and vanilla, using fingers to ensure that ingredients are well blended.

5. Scatter topping evenly over puffed filling and sprinkle with granulated sugar. Bake until pecans are fragrant and topping is bubbling around edges, about 10 minutes. Cool pie completely on wire rack, at least 2 hours. (Pie can be refrigerated for up to 2 days.) Serve pie at room temperature.

Bake-Sale Favorites: Carrot Cupcakes

Moist and dense, carrot cake went from 1970s health food fad to seriously decadent dessert. But could it make the leap to cupcake?

All the spicy-sweet goodness of carrot cake, but in tidy cupcake form.

The very qualities that make carrot cake so appealing—the moist, dense texture that comes from the high amounts of carrots and oil—make it an unlikely candidate for cupcakes, which tend toward light and tender. But the richly spiced cake and sweet cream cheese frosting seem like an ideal pairing for a bake-sale cupcake—if I could make it work. I started by preparing some published recipes, but these were panned as excessively oily and overpoweringly spiced. Even the test kitchen's favorite carrot cake recipe had problems once baked in cupcake liners. The dense texture made the little cakes seem more like muffins than cupcakes.

For a less greasy texture, I turned to the obvious culprit and cut the amount of oil. This worked, but not completely; there was still an oily residue left behind and the texture was still undeniably dense. For a lighter, cakier texture, I tried swapping out the oil for butter, and the results were dramatic: The cupcakes were significantly more cakey and fluffy. There were two issues at play. First, butter contains water, while oil does not; when cooked, the water evaporates, releasing some of the excess moisture. Second, once the cupcakes return to room temperature, the butter solidifies, whereas the oil stays liquid; that difference translates into a cakey, rather than dense, texture.

Once I had the perfect cupcake, I turned to the frosting. The gooey cream cheese frosting that paired so well with the carrot cake overpowered my small cupcakes. Tasters wanted something lighter and fluffier to match the newfound delicate texture of the cupcake. I tried beating the cream cheese and butter in hopes of incorporating air, but this backfired, instead creating a soft, almost runny frosting. Instead I took a more restrained approach, first combining the butter and confectioners' sugar, then adding the cream cheese one piece at a time and finishing with a hit of vanilla. The light hand worked, and I had a fluffy frosting that was a perfect match for the cupcakes.

–Keri Fisher

CARROT CUPCAKES
MAKES 12 CUPCAKES

If you prefer, you can grind the carrots in a food processor rather than grate them by hand. If you add the optional currants and walnuts, the cupcakes will need to bake an additional 7 to 10 minutes. If you use walnuts, toast a few extra and use them as a garnish. This recipe and the frosting recipe are easily doubled.

- **8 tablespoons (1 stick) unsalted butter, melted and cooled**
- **3/4 cup granulated sugar**
- **1/4 cup packed dark brown sugar**
- **2 large eggs**
- **1 1/4 cups all-purpose flour**
- **1/2 teaspoon salt**
- **1/2 teaspoon cinnamon**
- **1/4 teaspoon nutmeg**
- **1/8 teaspoon cloves**
- **3/4 teaspoon baking powder**
- **1/2 teaspoon baking soda**
- **1/2 pound carrots, peeled and grated on small holes of box grater**
- **1/2 cup currants or chopped raisins (optional)**
- **1/2 cup chopped walnuts, toasted, plus extra for garnish (optional)**

1. Adjust oven rack to middle position and heat oven to 350 degrees. Line standard muffin tin with cupcake liners.

2. Whisk butter, granulated sugar, brown sugar, and eggs together in large bowl. Mix in remaining ingredients until thoroughly combined.

3. Divide batter evenly among cupcake liners. Bake until skewer or toothpick inserted in cupcake comes out clean, 15 to 18 minutes (25 minutes if using currants and walnuts). Cool cupcakes in muffin tin 5 minutes, then remove and cool completely on wire rack. Frost cupcakes with a thick and even layer of frosting.

FLUFFY CREAM CHEESE FROSTING
MAKES 1 1/2 CUPS, ENOUGH TO FROST 12 CUPCAKES

Soften the cream cheese at room temperature for at least 15 minutes. Do not soften in the microwave or the texture of the frosting will be runny.

- **4 tablespoons unsalted butter, softened but still cool**
- **1 cup confectioners' sugar**
- **4 ounces cream cheese, softened, cut into 4 pieces**
- **3/4 teaspoon vanilla extract**

With electric mixer on medium-high speed, beat butter and confectioners' sugar until light and fluffy, about 2 minutes. Add cream cheese one piece at a time, beating thoroughly after each addition. Add vanilla and mix until no lumps remain.

Make Ahead

Unfrosted cupcakes can be stored in an airtight container at room temperature for up to 3 days. (They can also be individually wrapped in plastic and frozen in a zipper-lock bag for up to 1 month.) The frosting can be refrigerated for up to 5 days; just allow it to soften at room temperature for 30 minutes before spreading on the cupcakes. Once frosted, the cupcakes are best eaten within 1 day, but leftovers will keep in the refrigerator for several days.

CREAMY PEANUT BUTTER: Are 'Natural' Brands Better?

The creamy, sweet peanut butter we enjoyed as kids now has plenty of competition at the supermarket. You now can buy low-sugar, no-sugar, and low-fat peanut butter. The latter isn't very good, but we wondered about the "natural" brands with less or no sugar. To find out how they stack up, we tasted nine brands of creamy peanut butter raw and in peanut butter cookies.

The results of the raw tasting were clear: Tasters liked sweet peanut butter. The big three winners were (in order) Skippy, Jif, and Reese's. Each of these brands has 3 grams of sugar per 2-tablespoon serving. Brands with just 1 or 2 grams of sugar per serving (including the natural options) landed at the bottom of the rankings.

The results from the cookie tasting mirrored those of the raw tasting, with one exception. Smucker's Natural, which finished last in the plain tasting, was the winner here, followed by Skippy. The complaints drawn by Smucker's in the raw tasting (not sweet enough, poor texture) didn't matter in a cookie recipe that called for both light and brown sugar—for cookies, all that matters is peanut flavor. Smucker's is darker (a result of longer roasting) and chunkier (yes, even with "creamy" on the label) than other brands, and these traits made cookies that were especially good.

Our conclusions? Natural peanut butter is fine for baking, but for sandwiches we'll stick with the sweet stuff. The peanut butters are listed in order of preference based on scores in the two tastings. **–Scott Kathan**

Our Favorites

1. **SKIPPY CREAMY PEANUT BUTTER $2.29 for 18 ounces**
Tasters loved Skippy (which also won a 2001 test kitchen tasting) for its "strong nuttiness" and "ideal texture," with one taster calling it "sweet, salty, creamy, and perfect" and another simply writing, "More, please." Skippy made "pleasantly soft and chewy" cookies with "distinct peanut flavor."

2. **JIF CREAMY PEANUT BUTTER $2.19 for 18 ounces**
Choosy tasters chose Jif for its "very robust" and "dark and rich" peanut flavor. Jif was a tad sugary for a small percentage of tasters, one of whom wrote, "The sweetness mutes the peanut flavor." The cookies made with Jif were "bland and too sweet," but tasters praised their "nice chewy texture."

3. **REESE'S CREAMY PEANUT BUTTER $2.29 for 18 ounces**
Overall, Reese's was praised for its good, "full-bodied" peanut flavor, described as pleasantly "sweet and salty." A few tasters were put off by its "stiff texture" and "strange color." The cookies made with Reese's tasted "well balanced" and "sugary" to most, "artificial" and "bitter" to a few.

Runners-Up

4. **PETER PAN CREAMY PEANUT BUTTER $2.49 for 18 ounces**
"Sweet and salty" was the prevailing sentiment for this "very thick, creamy, and viscous" brand, which many tasters thought had a "sugary aftertaste." The cookies were judged to be "light tasting" and "too crumbly."

5. **SIMPLY JIF CREAMY PEANUT BUTTER $2.29 for 17.3 ounces**
Simply Jif cuts back on the salt and sugar, and our tasters missed both. Many found the flavor "bland" and "not sweet enough." Better in cookies, where tasters liked the "subtle peanut flavor."

6. **SMUCKER'S NATURAL CREAMY PEANUT BUTTER $3.69 for 16 ounces**
Tasters complained about the "huge oil slick on top," the lack of sugar, and the "grainy and runny" texture. But they loved the cookies, with their "huge peanut flavor" and "nice balance of crunch and chew."

7. **PETER PAN NO SUGAR ADDED CREAMY PEANUT SPREAD $2.49 for 18 ounces**
This brand contains sucralose, better known by its trade name Splenda. Tasters noticed that something was amiss, commenting that it "tastes like peanut-butter-flavored something, not peanut butter."

8. **SKIPPY NATURAL CREAMY PEANUT BUTTER SPREAD $2.19 for 16.3 ounces**
With sugar as its second ingredient—and palm oil added—the "natural" on the label is somewhat misleading. Tasters found Skippy Natural to be "thick and salty" but "not very peanutty."

9. **TEDDIE SMOOTH OLD FASHIONED PEANUT BUTTER $2.49 for 16 ounces**
In the raw tasting, Teddie lost points for its "grainy" and "pasty" texture. The cookies were faulted for their lack of peanut punch: "Just not as much flavor as the others" was a common refrain.

Taste Test Mayonnaise

The rich, salty, bright taste of a good mayonnaise can awaken flavors in many foods, but it also adds a lot of fat—no surprise when you consider that mayo's main ingredients are oil and eggs.

Since our sister publication, *Cook's Illustrated,* held its first mayonnaise tasting almost a decade ago, Hellmann's Real Mayonnaise (known as Best Foods west of the Rockies) has been the test kitchen's favorite brand. But Hellmann's now makes a range of products, many with fewer calories and less fat. To find out how they measure up to the original, we tasted four types of Hellmann's plain and in macaroni salad. Each type is listed below in order of preference, with tasters' comments. **–S.K.**

Hellmann's Real Mayonnaise

90 calories, 10g fat,
1.5g saturated fat per serving
The gold standard for mayonnaise and the best choice for spreading on sandwiches. Tasters praised its "sweet tanginess," calling it "creamy and eggy" and "salty, vinegary, and fatty—just like mayo should be."

Hellmann's Canola Mayonnaise

90 calories, 10g fat,
1g saturated fat per serving
This mayo was called "well balanced," "mild and creamy," and "rich and lemony." Other than a modest drop in saturated fat, this product (which swaps out the soybean oil in the original for canola oil) is nutritionally almost identical to the original.

Hellmann's Light Mayonnaise

45 calories, 4.5g fat,
0.5g saturated fat per serving
This mayo won the macaroni salad portion of our tasting for having a "sweet, eggy flavor" and a thick texture that "coats the pasta perfectly." Slightly sweeter than the original Hellmann's but superior to other brands of light mayo we've tasted.

Hellmann's Reduced Fat Mayonnaise

20 calories, 2g fat,
no saturated fat
A disappointment, especially when tasted side by side with the other Hellmann's products. Its "fakely sweet" and "off-tasting" flavor couldn't compete with the real deal. In separate tests, this option tasted better in boldly flavored dips, where its creamy texture was more important than its flavor.

Equipment Roundup

RATINGS	
▯ ▯ ▯	Good
▯ ▯	Fair
▯	Poor
NA	Not included

INEXPENSIVE KNIFE SETS: Do They Make the Cut?

In the test kitchen, we've always advocated purchasing knives individually rather than in sets. That's because many sets include knives you'll never use—why pay for something you don't need? But when it comes to gift giving, a knife set (complete with a storage block) begins to make some sense. Could we find something we liked for $100 or less?

CONSTRUCTION DETAILS: Knives are either stamped (cut from a sheet of metal) or forged (molded from molten metal). Forged knives are generally heavier and more expensive and were for many years the standard of quality. In the past decade, however, stamped knives have gotten so much better that the test kitchen doesn't exclusively recommend forged over stamped. Four of the six sets we tested—including the top-rated set—were stamped; the forged sets finished second and fourth.

THE BIG THREE: We selected sets that contained 8-inch **chef's knives**, knowing from experience that anything shorter will not handle heavy jobs. We had testers with various hand sizes and levels of kitchen skills chop carrots, mince parsley, and quarter butternut squash with each chef's knife. The test kitchen prefers 3½-inch **paring knives**, which offer the most dexterity and can cut, peel, and pare with great precision. Our testers peeled apples and peeled and minced ginger with the paring knives. **Bread knives** should be long enough (ideally, 10 inches) to get through big loaves, and their serrated edge should glide through bread, making it almost effortless to cut thin slices. Our testers cut through both soft and crusty bread and also sliced tomatoes.

WHAT'S IN A SET? The elements common to every set we tested were the block itself (which manufacturers count as one piece), along with a chef's knife and at least one paring knife. Most sets included a slicing (also called carving) knife and kitchen shears, and every set (except the Culinart) came with a sharpening steel. Many sets included a utility knife (basically an oversized paring knife); we didn't find this knife very useful, except for slicing tomatoes. Remarkably, two sets did not include a bread knife.

SUMMING UP: These knives ranged from mediocre to just plain awful. Flimsy blades, clumsy handles, and dull edges were recurring complaints from testers. We did find a few good knives in these blocks, but each one came from a different set. The Wüsthof set had a nice paring knife, and the Chicago Cutlery Insignia set came with a decent chef's knife, but none of the other sets had a chef's or paring knife we'd recommend—and not one set came with a bread knife we'd want to own. In the end, we don't recommend any of these knife sets. (See the box, for a better alternative.) The knife sets are listed in order of preference (if you can call it that) at right. **–Scott Kathan**

The Best, If You Must
WÜSTHOF Silverpoint 10-Piece Block Set (#8338)

Price: $99.99
Contents: Chef's knife, 2 paring knives, bread knife, utility knife, slicing/carving knife, fork, shears, steel
Comments: Two testers had NASCAR on the brain when describing the paring knife, saying, "It's fast and handles well" and "Drives like a racecar." The chef's knife, however, was likened to "a toy," and several testers said that "it doesn't feel safe to use." The bread knife was sharp but flimsy and too short (just 8 inches).

Chef's Knife: ▯
Paring Knife: ▯ ▯ ▯
Bread Knife: ▯

Not Recommended
FARBERWARE Pro Forged 8-Piece Set in Hardwood Countertop Block (FPF8N)

Price: $39.99
Contents: Chef's knife, 2 paring knives, bread knife, slicing/carving knife, shears, steel
Comments: Testers disliked the "blocky" handles and "awkward" feel of these knives. One likened the chef's knife to "driving a truck," and another called it "beastly." The bread knife's blade was too short and too thick. The paring knife was described as dull and "blister inducing."

Chef's Knife: ▯
Paring Knife: ▯
Bread Knife: ▯

Not Recommended
CHICAGO CUTLERY Insignia Steel 8-Piece Block Set (1050102)

Price: $79.99
Contents: Chef's knife, 2 paring knives, 2 utility knives, slicing/carving knife, steel
Comments: This set contained a decent chef's knife that was sharp but "a little too light" to handle butternut squash. The paring knife received mixed reviews, with testers calling it "sharp, but not very nimble."

Chef's Knife: ▯ ▯
Paring Knife: ▯
Bread Knife: NA

Not Recommended
J.A. HENCKELS International Fine Edge Stainless 7-Piece Block Set (16027-100)

Price: $99.99
Contents: Chef's knife, paring knife, bread knife, utility knife, slicing/carving knife, steel
Comments: "Flimsy" was the word of choice to describe the chef's knife. Testers disliked the uncomfortable handle and thin, flexible blade. The bread knife had small teeth that required too much sawing to get through a loaf of bread but that cut right through a ripe tomato. The blade of the paring knife was deemed "too thick" and "not sharp enough" to easily perform the tasks at hand.

Chef's Knife: ▯
Paring Knife: ▯
Bread Knife: ▯

Not Recommended
J.A. HENCKELS Twin Signature 7-Piece Block Set (30707-000)

Price: $99.95
Contents: Chef's knife, 2 paring knives, serrated utility knife, shears, steel
Comments: Testers assessed the chef's knife as "nice and heavy, but awkward" and faulted its relatively flat (not curved) blade for not allowing it to rock properly. "It hits the board and stops," wrote one tester. The paring knife's long (4-inch) blade felt "dangerous."

Chef's Knife: ▯
Paring Knife: ▯
Bread Knife: NA

Not Recommended
CULINART 8-Piece Knife Set

Price: $49.99
Contents: Chef's knife, paring knife, bread knife, steak knife, utility knife, boning knife, slicing/carving knife
Comments: The bread knife had large teeth that shredded both bread and tomatoes. The chef's knife was "not curved enough to rock well," "very dull," and "took too much work to chop." The paring knife felt awkward, with one tester feeling that "it fought with the apple."

Chef's Knife: ▯
Paring Knife: ▯
Bread Knife: ▯

A Better Way to Build a Knife Set

If you want to put together an inexpensive knife set, we suggest that you buy an empty block and then add the following knives—all made by Forschner and winners of previous kitchen tests. These knives are available at cutleryandmore.com, where you can pick up an empty knife block for another $20 to $30. Total cost for three very good knives, a steel, and block—just about $100. Now that's a gift we'd be proud to give—and happy to receive. **–S.K.**

Chef's Knife
Forschner Fibrox
8-inch, $22.95

+

Paring Knife
Forschner Fibrox
3.25-inch, $4.95

+

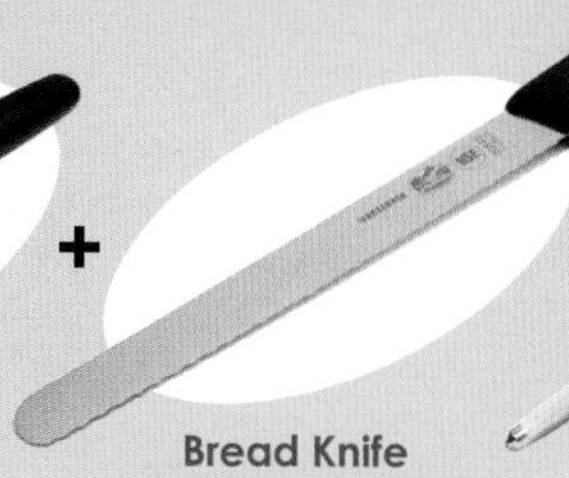

Bread Knife
Forschner Fibrox
10-inch, $22.95

+

Sharpening Steel
Forschner Fibrox
12-inch, $22.95

Notes from Our Test Kitchen

TIPS, TECHNIQUES, AND TOOLS FOR BETTER COOKING

Giblet Grab Bag

The bag of giblets hiding in the cavity of your turkey may look a bit intimidating, but to us this bag represents one thing: flavor. The giblet bag usually contains the neck, gizzard (a grinding organ from the bird's digestive tract), heart, and liver. When it's time to make gravy, we discard the soft, brownish liver (it tends to impart a strong flavor) but use all the other giblets to create a gravy with great turkey flavor.

We Love Cornstarch

Most of us have an open, mostly neglected box (or two) of cornstarch hiding in the back of our kitchen cabinets. Although it's occasionally used in baking recipes (it lends a delicate texture to some cakes and cookies), cornstarch is most often associated with Asian cuisine, where it is used to thicken sauces and soups. But lately we've been using it in some interesting applications. In our recipe for **Pecan-Crusted Chicken** (page 10), we found that a touch of cornstarch gave the coating a distinct crispness that bread crumbs alone could not provide. In our recipe for **Chocolate Blackout Cake** (page 7), cornstarch made the pudding filling smooth and silky, yet thick enough to cling to the exterior of the cake. Cornstarch is also a key ingredient in products like confectioner's sugar and pre-shredded cheeses! **–Jeremy Sauer**

Cracked Pepper

Many recipes (including the **Pepper-Crusted Steak** on one of our recipe cards) call for cracked—not ground—black pepper. To crack several tablespoons of peppercorns, spread them on a cutting board and place a heavy skillet on top. Pressing down firmly with both hands, use a rocking motion to crush the peppercorns beneath the "heel" of the skillet. Move the skillet back and forth, redistributing the peppercorns as needed. Repeat until the peppercorns are ground as desired.

–Diane Unger

Cook, Don't Kill, Your Greens

All of the hearty greens featured on page 23 are great on the plate—as long as you cook them correctly. Tender greens such as spinach and chard can be quickly sautéed, but the tougher types, like collard, turnip, and mustard greens, need a little more tender loving care. We blanch the washed and stemmed greens in salted water (1 tablespoon of salt per gallon of water) until they are just tender, about 7 minutes. We then drain the greens and rinse them with cold water to stop the cooking process. From here, squeeze the greens dry (by hand, in a salad spinner, or in a potato ricer) and chop them roughly. Now these once tough greens are ready to be sautéed, creamed, or eaten as is. **–Jeremy Sauer**

Pumpkin Cake Assembly

The **Pumpkin Patch Cake** on our inside back cover makes use of two Bundt cakes (for the pumpkin itself) and two cupcakes (for the stem) to create a pretty convincing, life-size pumpkin. Here's how to put it all together.

1. After placing one Bundt cake flat side up on a cake platter and covering the flat side with 1 cup orange frosting, place the second Bundt cake flat side down on top of the frosting, making sure the ridges on both cakes align. Then place one cupcake cut side up in the hole of the Bundt cake and spread 1 tablespoon orange frosting over the top of the cupcake.

2. Place the second cupcake cut side down on top of the frosting to create the stem. Completely cover the stem with green frosting.

3. Using a cake spatula, cover the entire cake with orange frosting.

4. Run the back of a small spoon up the sides of the orange frosting every few inches to create pumpkin "creases."

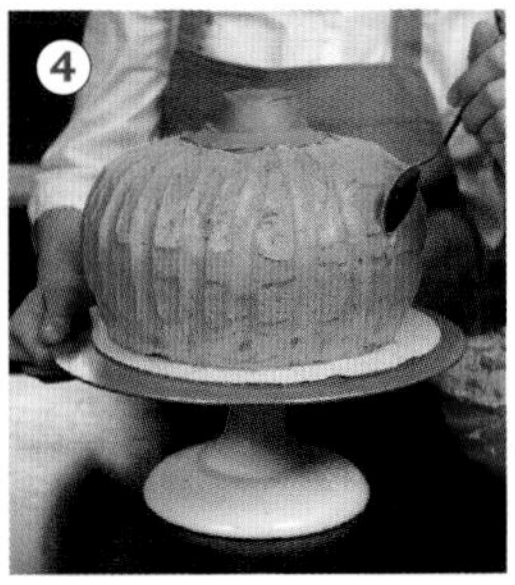

Which Rice Is Right?

In most recipes, long-grain rice and basmati rice can be used interchangeably, but not in our **Orange-Cranberry Rice Pilaf** (page 11). Basmati rice has more starch and is therefore less able to absorb water or broth—at least not without a little help. Typically, basmati rice is rinsed before cooking to slough off this excess starch, making it easier for liquid to penetrate. But the orange juice in our recipe creates a problem: The acid in the juice causes both the rice granules and any remaining exterior starch to toughen, making it very difficult for the rice to absorb liquid. We tried omitting the juice altogether (relying on just orange zest and chicken broth to flavor the pilaf), but tasters missed the full-bodied flavor of the rice cooked in juice. The solution was simple: When cooking rice in citrus juice, stick with regular long-grain rice.

–Stephanie Alleyne

The Root of the Matter

Celery root (or celeriac) is the swollen underground root of a plant similar to celery. We like its crisp, white flesh and clean celery-like flavor and find it ideal for roasting (see page 14), provided you know how to remove the tough skin. Celery root is also good braised, sautéed, or used raw in salads.

Trim a thick slice from both ends so that the celery root rests flat on the cutting board. Starting from the top, peel away the tough outer skin.

Shopping with the Test Kitchen

Butcher Shop

In Philadelphia, the rib-eye steak is the choice cut for a juicy and tender **Philly Cheesesteak** (page 18). But unless you're buying this meat by the truckload like the pros in Philadelphia, you'll be paying upward of $12.99 per pound at your local supermarket. After trying various cheaper cuts of beef for this sandwich, including round and blade steaks, we found that sirloin steak tips (called flap meat before being cut into tips) gave us plenty of beefy flavor and at $6 per pound, it's also a much more affordable choice.

RIB-EYE STEAK

If you've got money to burn, it's a great cut for a cheesesteak.

SIRLOIN TIPS

Big beefy flavor and, with a little strategic cutting and pounding, very tender.

Gadgets & Gear
Should You Own a Food Mill or Ricer?

To ensure a perfect, uniform mash, we recommend using a food mill or ricer for our **Creamy Mashed Potatoes** (page 21). But is it worth buying an extra piece of kitchen equipment just for mashed potatoes? Thankfully, both gadgets have many other uses. Food mills are perfect for pureeing fruits and vegetables, for making baby food, and especially for making applesauce and removing the skin and seeds from homemade tomato sauce. A ricer works well as a citrus juicer, a peeler/masher for roasted garlic, and a press for squeezing excess moisture out of spinach. Test kitchen favorites in each category are the R.S.V.P. Rotary Food Mill (cooking.com, $19.95) and the Cuisipro Potato Ricer (cooking.com, $29.95). **–Meredith Butcher**

Cleaning Scallops

You won't need to do much to prepare the scallops for our **Shrimp and Scallop Skewers** (see recipe card), but some scallops are sold with a small, crescent-shaped muscle attached to the side. Although this muscle is edible, we find that its rubbery texture detracts from the tender creaminess of the scallop. To remove this strip of muscle, just pull it off with your fingers.

This chewy strip of muscle should be removed before cooking scallops.

Pumpkin Pie Spice

With our **Pumpkin-Praline Pie** recipe (page 26) calling for four ground spices (cinnamon, ginger, allspice, and cloves), it might be tempting to buy just one jar of a spice blend instead of all four individual spices, especially when that blend is labeled "pumpkin pie spice." But don't be tempted. We found that the flavor varies greatly from brand to brand, and none had the right balance. In addition, all the brands we tested contained nutmeg, an aggressive spice that we'd rather leave out of our pumpkin pie. **–Bridget Lancaster**

Brining Basics

We recommend using an enhanced turkey (like a frozen Butterball) that has been injected with a salt solution for our **Holiday Stuffed Turkey** (page 24). If you prefer to use a fresh turkey, you should brine it before roasting. Brining is nothing more than soaking meat in a saltwater solution; the salt carries moisture into the bird, seasoning the meat and keeping it juicy. Here are three tips for brining success.

Make the Right Brine Our overnight brine (12 to 14 hours) uses ½ cup table salt per gallon of cold water. For a hurry-up brine (that will have the turkey ready to roast in 4 to 6 hours), use 1 cup table salt per gallon of water. For most birds, you'll need about 2 gallons of water. If using kosher salt, with its larger, airier crystals, the equation changes. Use 50 percent more Morton Kosher Salt or twice as much Diamond Crystal.

Keep It Cold The refrigerator is the best place to brine because the cold temperature ensures food safety. If your bird won't fit in the fridge, use a big cooler and ice packs.

Rinse and Dry Don't let the turkey brine beyond the recommended time or it will be overly salty. Once the turkey is ready to come out of the brine, rinse away excess salt and then pat it dry with paper towels.

Kitchen Technique Turkey Carving 101

Our recipe for **Holiday Stuffed Turkey** (page 24) won't do you any good if you don't know how to carve it. Here's our favorite (and the easiest) method.

1. Slice through the skin between the breast and leg and, using your hands, pull the leg quarters down until the joint between breast and leg is exposed. Remove the leg by cutting between the hip joint and any attached skin. Repeat with the opposite leg. Remove the wings by cutting through the wing joints. **2.** Separate the thighs from the drumsticks by cutting between the joint that connects the two. Leave the drumsticks whole and slice the thigh meat off the bone.

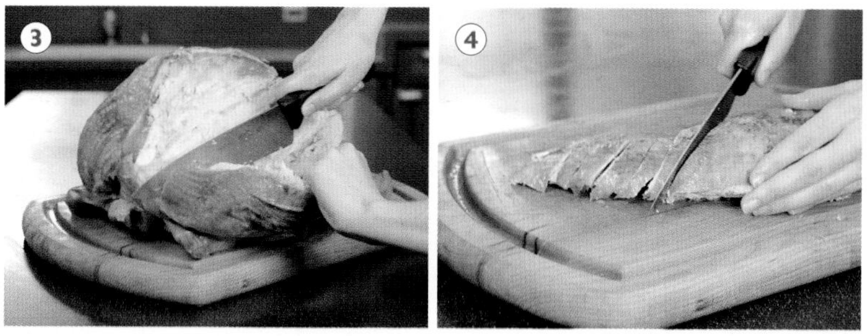

3. Remove the breast meat from the carcass by running the tip of the knife along the breastbone. Use your other hand to hold and pry meat from the bone as you cut. **4.** Slice the removed breast meat crosswise into thin slices. Repeat with the other breast.

Kitchen Creations
Flavored Croutons

Our **Spinach Salad** (page 22) doesn't really need additional toppings, but who can say no to croutons? We use a hearty white sandwich bread to make our croutons, but most any savory bread will work. Croutons can be stored in an airtight container for about a week.

GARLICKY CROUTONS
MAKES ABOUT 4 CUPS

- **3 tablespoons olive oil**
- **2 garlic cloves, minced**
- **1/4 teaspoon salt**
- **4 slices hearty white sandwich bread, cut into 1/2-inch cubes (about 4 cups)**

Adjust oven rack to middle position and heat oven to 350 degrees. Whisk oil, garlic, and salt in large bowl. Add bread cubes and toss until coated. Spread bread on baking sheet and bake until golden brown, 20 to 25 minutes. Cool before serving.

TEXAS CHILI CROUTONS
Follow Garlicky Croutons recipe, whisking 1 teaspoon chili powder, 1/4 teaspoon pepper, and 1/8 teaspoon cayenne into oil with garlic and salt.

BBQ CROUTONS
Follow Garlicky Croutons recipe, omitting garlic. Whisk 1/2 teaspoon cumin, 1/2 teaspoon coriander, 1/4 teaspoon paprika, and 1/2 teaspoon cayenne into oil with salt.

HERBED CROUTONS
Follow Garlicky Croutons recipe, whisking 2 teaspoons each minced fresh rosemary, thyme, and sage (or 1/2 teaspoon of each dried herb) and 1/4 teaspoon pepper into oil with garlic and salt.

CHEESY PARMESAN CROUTONS
Follow Garlicky Croutons recipe, increasing oil to 6 tablespoons and tossing 1 cup grated Parmesan cheese with oiled bread cubes before baking.

When Things Go Wrong in the Kitchen

READERS SHARE FUNNY STORIES ABOUT COOKING MISHAPS

ORANGE HAIR CAKE

Several years ago I was making an orange layer cake. I had just added the juice and zest from a freshly squeezed orange to the cake batter and was beating everything with my electric mixer. I just couldn't resist the urge to lean into the bowl and smell the refreshing orange scent. Unfortunately, as I was doing this, my shoulder-length hair fell forward and got caught up in the whirring beaters. Before I had a chance to shut off the mixer, my hair got wound in the beaters and caused them to lock up. I had quite a time unwinding my hair and then headed straight to the shower to wash off all the sticky cake batter. My oldest son, who was 5 years old at the time, was sitting at the kitchen table watching all of this silently. When I came back into the room he quietly said, "Mom, I don't think I'm going to eat any of that cake."

Anne Bowen Union, Ill.

PENNY PINCHER'S LASAGNA

After I graduated from college, I moved to the Boston area with two friends. We didn't have very much money during those first few months, so we stretched our food budget as far as it could go. One of the recipes that we made quite frequently was a spinach lasagna that used cottage cheese. After work one day, one of my roommates declared that she would make dinner for us. She clattered around the kitchen and soon the familiar smells of lasagna filled the apartment. As the lasagna baked, we suddenly heard an audible gasp come from the kitchen. During her trip to the grocery store, she had accidentally purchased pineapple-flavored cottage cheese. It was too late, however, and the pineapple-spinach lasagna was nearly done. We were too poor and hungry not to eat it, but I'd never tasted anything like it in my life—and I hope I never do again.

Meg Meffen Quincy, Mass.

THE TRIPLE-STUFFED TURKEY

My husband and I had been married for almost two years when he decided we should host his family for Thanksgiving dinner. As a fledgling cook, I was nervous and was up early on the big day to get the turkey stuffed and in the oven. I dug and dug around that bird for the giblets, but to no avail. I finally decided that my turkey didn't have any giblets and went on my merry way.

After about an hour, I peeked in the oven and noticed that the juices running out of my big, beautiful bird were awfully dark. I yelled for my husband to come help me, and we unstuffed the turkey. I fished around inside the hot turkey looking for those darn giblets. Still nothing. So I dutifully restuffed the bird and put it back in the oven. An hour later, I noticed that the drippings were looking downright bloody. I called for my husband and we went through the entire process again. Just before I was ready to stuff the turkey for the third time, I decided to try looking in the other end of the bird. Sure enough, there was the package of giblets, leaking dark red juice into my beautiful turkey! I yanked the soggy packet out and victoriously stuffed the bird for the third—and final—time.

Sara Suksdorf Spangle, Wash.

A HARD CHEESECAKE

I was making cheesecake for a dinner party, so I cut the cheesecake into squares and arranged them on a platter. On the way out the door, I looked down and saw a small black spot on one of the squares. I put the platter down to inspect the cheesecake, but as I tried to remove the spot it just kept getting larger until I uncovered a large, round black thing. Horrified, I realized that the black knob that screws onto the front of my KitchenAid mixer had somehow managed to fall off the mixer and into my cheesecake. I had actually cooked part of my mixer into my dessert. Just imagine if someone had bitten into that!

Julie Croft Butler, Pa.

AN UNUSUAL MARINADE

Fifty years ago, my mother was a newly arrived newlywed to the United States from Germany. While she spoke English rather well, she did have some difficulties understanding native speakers, especially those who spoke quickly. One day, as my great-grandmother was just getting ready to go out, she remembered she hadn't put the groceries away. Rather than walk all the way back to the house, she shouted to my mother, "Put the chicken and the milk in the refrigerator." What my mother heard was, "Put the chicken in the milk in the refrigerator." My mother thought this was a little odd, but she remembered that her mother would soak liver in milk before cooking it up, so she figured this was just the American way of making chicken. Needless to say, my great-grandmother was quite taken aback when she returned home to find a whole chicken resting in a big pot of milk in the refrigerator. The milk was sacrificed, but they say the chicken came out quite moist and tender.

Rita Warnock Via e-mail

STARVING ARTISTS

My friend and I, both poor newlyweds, wanted to cook an elaborate Thanksgiving dinner for our husbands. Fancying ourselves gourmet cooks, we decided that we would try a recipe for baker's clay roasted duck. The duck was encased in baker's clay that we had molded around the bird, and we painted the clay with mallard duck colors—teal, blue, green, and yellow. It was truly a work of art!

At the table, we tried to get the duck out of the clay by cracking it open with our little kitchen hammer, but pieces of clay flew all over the room, eventually covering the card table that was standing in as a dining table. While the wild rice and vegetable side dishes got cold, we attacked our bird with the gusto of true hunters. Our husbands covered their heads with their napkins to protect themselves from the shrapnel. After what seemed like hours, we finally got the duck out of the clay, but there was barely enough duck for two people, let alone for our party of four. We learned that rice and vegetables can make a delicious meal. At least we had a memorable Thanksgiving.

Ellie Schroeder Bellevue, Wash.

DECORATING WITH KETCHUP

One of my daughter's boyfriends was an engineer and a post-doctoral student at Caltech—about as brainy as it gets. Back in "prehistoric" times, when squeezable plastic ketchup bottles first came on the market, he was helping to serve some hamburgers and was admiring the new bottle. "See, unbreakable," he announced, as he demonstrated by throwing the bottle. He got to clean the ketchup off the ceiling, cabinets, walls, and floor. We had a good laugh.

Perle Sondergaard Via e-mail

Send us your funniest kitchen disaster stories. Please write to Kitchen Disasters, Cook's Country, P.O. Box 470739, Brookline, MA 02447. To send your story by e-mail, visit **cookscountry.com/emailus.** If we publish your story, you'll receive a complimentary one-year subscription to *Cook's Country*.

Pumpkin Patch Cake

Introduced in the 1950s, the Bundt pan has been used by inspired bakers to create cakes that look like mountains, cathedrals, flowers, and, yes, pumpkins. For this cake, you stack two Bundt cakes, making sure that the flat sides are sandwiched together and the ridges are aligned. Orange buttercream frosting and a cupcake 'stem' are the finishing touches.

To make this cake you'll need:

2 recipes spice or chocolate cake batter (enough to make 4 regular cake layers or 2 Bundt cakes)*

4 cups vanilla buttercream frosting*

Green, red, and yellow food coloring

To make the cakes and stem: Prepare first recipe cake batter. Scoop ½ cup batter in standard-sized muffin tin; pour remaining batter into greased and floured 12-cup Bundt pan. Bake both on middle rack in 350-degree oven until toothpick inserted in center of each comes out clean, 15 to 20 minutes for cupcake and 45 to 55 minutes for Bundt cake. Cool cupcake in pan 5 minutes, then turn out onto rack. Cool Bundt cake in pan 30 minutes, then turn out onto rack. Repeat with second recipe of cake batter. Let both cupcakes and both cakes cool completely.

To assemble and frost the pumpkin: Place ½ cup frosting in bowl and stir in two drops green food coloring to make frosting for stem. Stir two drops each red and yellow food coloring into remaining frosting, adding more until desired orange color is achieved. Use bread knife to level off domed top of cupcakes and even out bottoms of Bundt cakes. Assemble and frost cake as shown on page 30.

*Go to cookscountry.com for our spice cake, chocolate cake, and vanilla frosting recipes or use your own recipes.

Recipe Index

RC = Recipe Card

Cook's Country

DECEMBER/JANUARY 2007

Best Holiday Menu
Test Kitchen Favorites

Christmas Cookies
5 Prize-Winning Recipes

Dinner Party Beef Tenderloin
Fancy Herb & Cheese Crust

BOURBON BREAD PUDDING
Easy New Orleans Recipe

RATING ROASTING PANS
We Test 7 Models under $80

LITTLE ITALY MEATBALLS
Mamma Mia, They're Big!

FREEZER DINNER ROLLS
Ready Whenever You Are

CHICKEN MARSALA
Big Flavors in Just 20 Minutes

STUFFED MUSHROOMS
High-Roast for Perfect Texture

BEEF BURGUNDY
Best Slow-Cooker Recipe

CAKE MIX TASTE TEST
One Brand Ices Competition

Our $1,000 Contest Winner!
Jessie Apfel of Berkeley, Calif., won first place in our holiday cookie contest with a clever no-bake recipe. See page 4 for her **Crunchy Spiced Rum Balls.**

$4.95 U.S./$6.95 CANADA

Cook's Country

Dear Country Cook,

Years ago, I knew a woman who grew up in Germany right after World War II. Her family was poor, but, like most folks from simple backgrounds, she had rich memories. Her favorite time of year was Christmas Eve, when the doors to the living room were ceremoniously opened to unveil the simply decorated tree. Underneath it, each and every year, were new clothes for her one doll. She has gone on to lead a rewarding life filled with the jewels and trophies of modern times, yet no gift has ever touched her in the same way.

For my part, a bakery window at the holidays is my idea of Christmas. Like fantastic ornaments, each item is carefully displayed on a lace doily, and its secrets are hinted at but not fully revealed. How did they make that miniature chocolate cake filled with orange cream? Are those marzipan roses?

As my friend's Christmas story reveals, a gift is ultimately about the giver. It was her mother who made those clothes, even in their poverty, and that is why the memory is so fond, her voice so thick with emotion. As cooks, we know that a tart or cookie has something of the baker in it. The child at the window is in awe, not just of the treats beyond his reach, but of the baker who made them. It is the giving, from one to another, that makes the gift.

All of us at Cook's Country wish you the very best of holidays. Our gift to you is the food from our kitchen. We hope that you will share these gifts with others.

Christopher Kimball
Founder and Editor, Cook's Country Magazine

Longing for Cake, January 1945. A young boy stands with his face and hands pressed against the window of a bakery, which displays cookies and other pastries on lace doilies, at Berger Bakery, Ridgewood, New Jersey. © Hulton Archive/Getty Images

DECEMBER/JANUARY 2007

Cook's Country

features

departments

in every issue

Editorial Office: 17 Station Street, Brookline, MA 02445; 617-232-1000; fax 617-232-1572
Subscription Inquiries: Cook's Country, P.O. Box 8382, Red Oak, IA 51591-1382
800-526-8447

ON THE COVER: PHOTOGRAPHY: David Loftus/StockFood Munich/StockFood America. ILLUSTRATION: John Burgoyne.
IN THIS ISSUE: COLOR FOOD PHOTOGRAPHY: Keller + Keller. STYLING: Mary Jane Sawyer, Marie Piraino, Monica Mariano. ILLUSTRATION: Lisa Perrett.

Cook's Country magazine (ISSN 1552-1990), number 12, is published bimonthly by Boston Common Press Limited Partnership, 17 Station Street, Brookline, MA 02445. Application to mail at periodical postage rates pending at Boston, Mass., and additional mailing offices. POSTMASTER: Send address changes to Cook's Country, P.O. Box 8382, Red Oak, IA 51591-1382. For subscription and gift subscription orders, subscription inquiries, or change-of-address notices, call 800-526-8447 in the U.S. or 515-247-7571 from outside the U.S., or write us at Cook's Country, P.O. Box 8382, Red Oak, IA 51591-1382. PRINTED IN THE USA

Kitchen Shortcuts

READERS SHARE CLEVER TIPS FOR EVERYDAY COOKING CHALLENGES

Hot Idea

A Greenhouse for Butter

I'm one of those people who always forget to set the butter on the countertop to soften before I start baking. For recipes that only call for a few tablespoons of softened butter, I came up with this tip. Cut a piece of butter and set it on a small plate, fill a coffee mug with hot tap water and let it sit for a few seconds to warm up, pour out the water, then turn the mug upside down over the butter. In no time at all, the butter is nicely softened but not melted. It's like a little-bitty greenhouse for the butter!

Catherine Emery Marysville, Wash.

Buttermilk at the Ready

I rarely use buttermilk, so when a recipe calls for a cup or so, the rest of the container usually goes to waste. Now whenever I use buttermilk, I measure out the remainder of the carton into 1-cup portions, pour them into freezer bags, and freeze. This saves the buttermilk, and I don't have to measure it when I go to use it.

Ginger Garrett
Cumming, Ga.

A Cool Way to Crumble Cheese

To quickly crumble a large amount of soft cheese (such as blue cheese or goat cheese) for a salad, take the chilled block of cheese and gently push it through the metal grid of a cooling rack. Once pressed through the rack, the cheese will be perfectly crumbled.

Liza Tremblay
Sag Harbor, N.Y.

Take It to the Bank

SNOW BANKS COME IN HANDY

During the winter months, I've got a special way to cool down soups, stews, and stocks: Just cover the pot and put it in a snow bank. If there's one thing we've got plenty of in Ithaca, it's snow banks.

Johnny Mack Ithaca, N.Y.

AN UNLIKELY ORGANIZER

A wire potato masher can be used to keep other items in a drawer somewhat organized. Just lay the masher on its side and place spatulas, metal skewers, and knives in between the ridges of the masher. They stay put even when you slam the drawer shut.

Bob Johnson
Coupeville, Wash.

SAVE MONEY WITH SUPERMARKET BAGS

Every couple of years we purchase a roll of produce bags from our local supermarket. We use these instead of zip locks and they work fine—just twist the top for a tight seal. Cheeses, extra vegetables, clean lettuce, bacon, and sandwiches all stay just as fresh as with the other bags. I believe we paid $7 for the last roll, which must have had a thousand bags.

Mitchell R. Mosher
Newcastle, Calif.

CREDIT CARD IN THE KITCHEN

I use an old, washed credit card to loosen brownies from the edge of the pan and cut them into squares. The card cuts neatly and easily (you can push it through the brownies rather than dragging it, as you would a knife). And if you're using a nonstick pan, it saves the sides and bottom from scratching.

Marjorie Keeler
Harrington Park, N.J.

THINK SMALL

I hate opening a big bottle of wine when a recipe calls for just a cup or so. Instead, I pick up a four-pack of those small screw-top bottles and keep them on hand. The quality is decent, and you can buy white wine or red. No more wasted half-full bottles of wine!

Sarah Liebman
Berkeley, Calif.

CLEANING COFFEE GRINDERS

One of the easier ways to clean a coffee grinder is to run it with some uncooked white rice. Use 2 or 3 tablespoons, grind for a moment, then just wipe out the hopper. This dislodges all the old coffee grounds; works great for spice grinders as well.

Jim Pirotte
Prairie Village, Kan.

MAC 'N' FONDUE

We always make fondue on New Year's Day. I thought of a great idea for the leftovers. Cook a batch of macaroni, warm up the leftover fondue, and mix it with the macaroni, thinning the mixture with the macaroni cooking water, if necessary. Just as fast and a lot tastier than the boxed stuff.

Deborah Hoon
Crystal Lake, Ill.

MAKING USE OF BROWNIE CRUMBS

When the edges of brownies bake up hard, I cut them off and run them through the food processor to make chocolate crumbs. I freeze the crumbs in a freezer bag or container for later use on frosted cakes, ice cream, and other desserts.

Eileen Monturio
Weymouth, Mass.

UNLIKELY USE FOR UNUSED CHOPSTICKS

To protect my fingers from getting burned when trying to remove a piece of stuck or burnt toast or a bagel from the unplugged toaster, I use one of the chopsticks that come with Chinese takeout. I also use the chopstick to remove "stuck-on" waffles from the waffle iron.

Violet Dunlap
Orrs Island, Maine

MEASURING SCOOPS

I use spring-loaded ice cream scoops to measure my shortening and peanut butter. They come in different sizes that hold ¼, ⅓, and ½ cup. The scoops let me measure any amount I need, and filling them is a lot less messy than trying to fill regular measuring cups.

Marcia Blosser
Yates Center, Kan.

If you'd like to submit a tip, please send a letter to Kitchen Shortcuts, Cook's Country, P.O. Box 470739, Brookline, MA 02447. Or e-mail us by visiting **cookscountry.com/emailus.** Include your name, address, and phone number. If we publish your tip, you will receive a free one-year subscription to *Cook's Country*.

NO MORE WASTED PEPPER GRINDS

After several years of cleaning up under my pepper mill, I finally found a neat solution. I put a small, decorative dish underneath it. Not only does it look nice on my countertop, but when company comes over I fill the dish with olive oil and put it out on the table—people love dipping bread into the seasoned oil.

Evelyn Sukala
Haddonfield, N.J.

POWER UNDER THE HOOD

I have a range hood and I take a cutting board, lay it across the burners (generally on a kitchen towel to prevent sliding), and turn on the fan, then I start peeling and cutting my onions. Saves a lot of tearful times and eye irritation.

Dalen Mills
Southwest Harbor, Maine

LOOSEN UP LEFTOVER PASTA

I dread dry leftover pasta, but my Yankee sense of thrift requires that I dutifully save every morsel of uneaten food to serve at another meal. One day I thought to save some of the original pasta cooking water in addition to the pasta (I always reserve some for the fresh-cooked pasta anyway to add to the sauce if it's too thick). When I reheated pasta the next day, I stirred in a bit of the reserved pasta water. The result? Moist leftovers that were almost as good as the original.

Kimberly Burnett
Arlington, Mass.

HAIR BANDS COME IN HANDY

To keep open bags of frozen vegetables from getting freezer burn, we used to tie off the open end with a rubber band. The problem was that freezing made the rubber bands brittle; sometimes they broke and spilled the contents of the bag into the freezer. As a solution, we traded in the rubber bands for those bungee-like hair bands: They never get brittle and break in the freezer, and they're cheap (50 to a pack at our dollar store). They can also be used outside the freezer for anything from tying off bags of sandwich bread to holding together a pile of plastic utensils for a summertime picnic.

David and Sheri Knauth
Evanston, Ill.

COOKIE-CUTTER COOLING RACK

When I'm baking cookies, I tend to run out of wire cooling racks to hold the hot cookie sheets just out of the oven. I solved the problem by placing three metal cookie cutters in a triangle shape on the counter and carefully putting the hot cookie sheet on top. This lets the cookies rest in the pan for a bit before I transfer them to the racks to cool completely; it also frees up precious rack space, which I can use for more cookies instead of the pans. Cookie cutters can also be used to cool large and small baking dishes, round cake pans, lots of things.

Stephanie Wong
San Jose, Calif.

GRAB BAGGIE

Keep a clean plastic baggie handy when both hands are messy from cooking. If you get a call, just slip your hand into the bag and pick up the phone.

Elizabeth Zufelt
Logan, Utah

ALL-PURPOSE BAG CLIPS

I keep a package of large binder clips, bought at an office supply store, in my kitchen. I use the clips for bags of potato chips, confectioners' sugar, and even frozen vegetables.

Julia A. Manning
Montclair, Va.

CAREFUL CUSTARD POURING

I love crème brûlée, but on more than one occasion I have ruined it before it's even gone into the oven. My recipe calls for baking the custard in a water bath, and if I'm not careful when I move the pan—filled partway with water and with filled ramekins in place—the water splashes into the ramekins, leaving the crème brûlée a watery mess. To avoid this risky balancing act, I fill the pan less than halfway with water, place the ramekins—which are empty—in the pan, and place the pan on the oven rack. I then use a fat separator to pour the custard into the ramekins. The long spout of the fat separator makes pouring really easy. Now my crème brûlée is always perfect.

Isabel Lopes Clark
Boston, Mass.

Neat Trick

Thaw 'n' Drain Shrimp

To quickly thaw frozen shrimp, I place the shrimp in my salad spinner (without the top) and fill it with cold tap water. After a few minutes, the shrimp have thawed and I simply lift the colander out of the bowl, empty the water, and replace the colander in the bowl. When it's time to add the shrimp to my recipe, they're drained and ready!

Kristin Patterson Chambersburg, Pa.

Pitcher of Pancakes

To avoid messy drips, transfer pancake batter to a pitcher and pour it directly onto the hot griddle; any leftover batter can be covered with plastic wrap and refrigerated for an hour—perfect for late-risers.

Sharon Lehman
Newton, Kan.

Easy "Homemade" Pickles

Once the jar of bread-and-butter pickles is empty, don't throw out all that juice. Slice a regular cucumber thinly and throw the slices into the jar. After a day in the refrigerator, the pickles are ready to eat. These pickles are crisper than the kind you buy, taste great, and will keep for up to two weeks!

Cheryl Merser
Sag Harbor, N.Y.

One Big Crusher

RUN-OVER RUM BALLS

My recipe for rum balls—my favorite holiday treat—calls for finely crushed vanilla wafers, and crushing them by hand can be laborious. To the delight of my father-in-law, I found an easier way to crush the cookies. Take the whole, unopened box of wafers and use a skewer to poke a couple of small holes through the sealed end of the box (and the plastic bag on the inside) to release the pressure. Then drive your car right over the box and presto—instant crumbs.

Dave Branik Grosse Ile, Mich.

Safety Tip

Styrofoam Knife Rack

To protect my knives (and my kids' fingers), I cut a block of Styrofoam to fit inside my cookware drawer and insert the blades directly into the block. It holds the knives securely, and when the Styrofoam begins to wear down it's easy (and cheap) to replace. Now my knives stay sharp and my family stays safe.

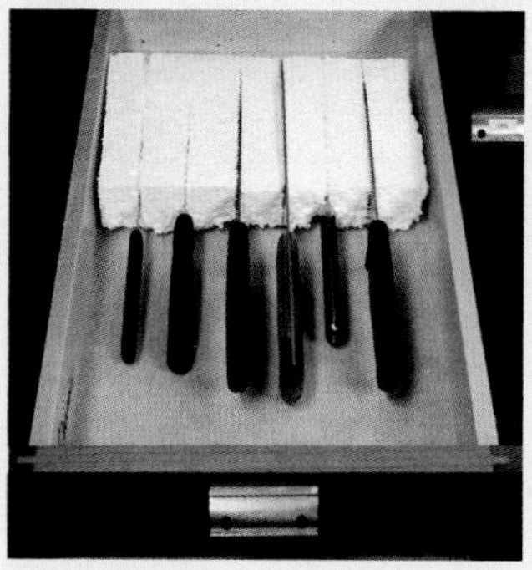

Rose Marr
San Francisco, Calif.

A No-Bake Cookie Gives the Baker Something to Celebrate

Our $1,000 Grand-Prize Winner!

Jessie Apfel
Berkeley, Calif.

Our winning Christmas cookie recipe seems pretty unlikely. No butter, no eggs, and no flour? No baking? Grand-prize winner Jessie Apfel created this recipe from pantry staples. She told us: "This recipe was a last-minute, mix-and-match experiment with ingredients I had on hand. Amazingly, everyone who tasted my first batch loved the unique and different tastes and textures of these rum balls. Sure enough, everyone kept coming back for more!" One taste and we understood why.

These elegant, festive holiday treats pack a grown-up rum punch.

CRUNCHY SPICED RUM BALLS

MAKES ABOUT 18

The unique flavor of spiced rum is perfect in these cookies, but regular rum will work, too.

- 1/2 cup raisins, chopped fine
- 1/4 cup spiced rum (such as Captain Morgan's)
- 1 cup confectioners' sugar
- 2 tablespoons cocoa powder
- 1 teaspoon cinnamon
- 1/4 teaspoon nutmeg
- 1/4 teaspoon salt
- 1/4 cup granulated sugar
- 3/4 cup cornflakes
- 12 vanilla wafers
- 3/4 cup whole almonds, toasted
- 1/2 cup sweetened, shredded coconut
- 2 tablespoons light corn syrup

1. Soak raisins and rum in small bowl until raisins plump, about 10 minutes. Whisk confectioners' sugar, cocoa powder, cinnamon, nutmeg, and salt in large bowl until combined. Place granulated sugar in shallow dish.

2. Process cornflakes, vanilla wafers, almonds, and coconut in food processor to fine crumbs and add to confectioners' sugar mixture. Mix in corn syrup, plumped raisins, and rum until mixture looks wet. Shape mixture into 1-inch balls, roll in granulated sugar, transfer to large plate, and refrigerate until firm, about 1 hour. (Rum balls can be refrigerated in airtight container for up to 1 week.)

Our Runners-Up

Susan Kramer
Jackson, Ga.

Mary P.G. Bilyeu
Ann Arbor, Mich.

Karen Bland
Gove, Kan.

Lee Fields
Avondale Estates, Ga.

POOR MAN'S TOFFEE

MAKES ABOUT 15 PIECES

Susan writes: "Forget buying expensive toffee. This recipe is so easy to make that everyone can afford to indulge!"

Toffee

- **24 saltines**
- **1 cup sugar**
- **1/2 cup light corn syrup**
- **1 1/2 cups roasted salted peanuts**
- **1 tablespoon unsalted butter**
- **1 teaspoon vanilla extract**
- **1 teaspoon baking powder**

Topping

- **1/2 cup semisweet chocolate chips**
- **4 tablespoons unsalted butter**
- **1 tablespoon light corn syrup**

1. For the toffee: Adjust oven rack to middle position and heat oven to 250 degrees. Line bottom of 13 by 9-inch baking dish with waxed paper and spray paper with cooking spray. Arrange crackers, in single layer, salt side down, on waxed paper.

2. Combine sugar, corn syrup, and peanuts in medium microwave-safe bowl. Microwave on highest power until sugar melts, about 2 minutes. Stir and microwave until mixture begins to boil, about 2 more minutes. Stir in butter and vanilla until butter melts. Microwave until liquid begins to brown, about 2 minutes. Stir in baking powder.

3. Working quickly, pour sugar mixture over saltines and spread evenly (if mixture hardens too quickly to spread, place baking dish in oven for 5 minutes). Refrigerate until firm, about 1 hour. Invert brittle onto cutting board, peel away waxed paper, and, using hands, break into large pieces. Return pieces, toffee side up, to baking dish.

4. For the topping: Melt chips and butter until smooth. Stir in corn syrup and, using spoon, drizzle mixture over brittle. Let harden for 1 hour. (Brittle can be stored in airtight container at room temperature for up to 4 days.)

MOJITO SHORTBREAD

MAKES 16 SQUARES

Mary writes: "My grandmothers, like so many in their generation, were instinctive cooks who never wrote down their recipes. So, I've spent my life trying to replicate their dishes. Shortbread cookies are a family favorite, but mojito flavors (lime and mint) are my twist on this classic recipe."

- **1/4 cup packed fresh mint leaves**
- **1/4 cup plus 1/3 cup granulated sugar**
- **2 cups all-purpose flour**
- **1/2 teaspoon salt**
- **1 tablespoon grated lemon zest**
- **1 tablespoon grated lime zest**
- **1/3 cup confectioners' sugar**
- **12 tablespoons (1 1/2 sticks) unsalted butter, cut into 1/2-inch cubes and chilled**

1. Adjust oven rack to middle position and heat oven to 325 degrees. Line 8-inch-square baking dish with foil, allowing excess to overhang pan edges. Spray foil with cooking spray. Pulse mint leaves and ¼ cup granulated sugar in food processor until well combined. Set aside.

2. With electric mixer at medium-low speed, beat 1¾ cups flour, salt, zests, confectioners' sugar, and remaining ⅓ cup granulated sugar until well combined. Using fork, cut butter into remaining ¼ cup flour in small bowl. Add butter mixture to sugar mixture and beat on low until damp, pale yellow crumbs form, about 4 minutes.

3. Firmly pack crumbs into pan and smooth top with back of spoon. Bake until shortbread is lightly golden, about 1 hour. Using foil overhang, lift from pan, transfer to cooling rack, and sprinkle with mint sugar. Cool completely, about 3 hours. Cut into 2-inch squares. (Shortbread actually improves over time and can be stored in airtight container at room temperature for up to 2 weeks.)

MARVELOUS CHOCOLATE MINT COOKIES

MAKES ABOUT 3 DOZEN

Karen writes: "The melted Andes candy on top makes perfect ready-to-go icing."

- **1 1/4 cups all-purpose flour**
- **1/2 teaspoon baking soda**
- **1/4 teaspoon salt**
- **6 tablespoons unsalted butter**
- **3/4 cup packed light brown sugar**
- **6 ounces bittersweet chocolate, chopped**
- **1 large egg**
- **36 pieces Andes chocolate mints (about 1/2 pound), unwrapped**

1. Adjust oven racks to upper-middle and lower-middle positions and heat oven to 350 degrees. Line 2 baking sheets with parchment paper.

2. Combine flour, baking soda, and salt in medium bowl. Melt butter and brown sugar in medium saucepan over low heat. Add chocolate, cover pan with lid, and let stand off heat until chocolate melts, about 4 minutes. Stir until smooth, transfer chocolate to bowl of electric mixer, and let cool, about 10 minutes.

3. With electric mixer on medium speed, beat egg into cooled chocolate mixture until thoroughly combined. Reduce speed to low and mix in flour mixture until just combined, about 1 minute. Cover dough with plastic wrap and refrigerate until firm, about 1 hour.

4. Roll 2 teaspoons dough into 1-inch balls and place 2 inches apart on prepared baking sheets. Bake until cookies are just set, 10 to 12 minutes, rotating and switching baking sheets halfway through baking time. Remove from oven, top each hot cookie with 1 mint, and allow chocolate to soften, about 1 minute. Using knife, spread softened mint over top of cookie and transfer to rack to cool completely, about 30 minutes. (Cookies can be stored in airtight container at room temperature for up to 1 week.)

OATMEAL LACE COOKIES

MAKES ABOUT 3 DOZEN

Lee writes: "This holiday cookie is the ultimate dress-up or dress-down treat. The best part about this recipe is how easy it is to make. I know when certain friends come around to have the butter already melting because they will always ask me to make a batch."

- **4 tablespoons unsalted butter**
- **6 tablespoons light brown sugar**
- **1/4 cup dark corn syrup**
- **2 teaspoons vanilla extract**
- **1/8 teaspoon salt**
- **1/4 cup all-purpose flour**
- **1 1/2 teaspoons heavy cream**
- **1/2 cup quick-cooking oats**

1. Adjust oven racks to upper-middle and lower-middle positions and heat oven to 350 degrees. Line 2 baking sheets with parchment paper.

2. Bring butter, brown sugar, and corn syrup to boil in medium saucepan over medium heat. Remove from heat and whisk in vanilla, salt, flour, cream, and oats until well combined.

3. Using 1-teaspoon measuring spoon, drop batter 3 inches apart on prepared baking sheets. Bake until cookies are golden and no longer bubbling, 6 to 8 minutes, rotating and switching baking sheets halfway through baking time. Cool cookies on parchment on wire rack, about 20 minutes. Repeat with remaining batter. Once cookies are cool, peel off parchment. (Cookies can be stored in airtight container at room temperature for up to 2 days.)

We want your best muffin recipes for an upcoming contest. Please submit entries by January 31, 2007. Write to us at Recipe Contest, Cook's Country, P.O. Box 470739, Brookline, MA 02447, or to contact us by e-mail, visit **cookscountry.com/emailus.** Include your name, address, and daytime phone number, and tell us what makes your recipe special. The grand-prize winner will receive $1,000. All entries become the property of *Cook's Country*. For more information on this and other contests, go to **cookscountry.com.**

Ask Cook's Country

WE'LL ANSWER ANY QUESTION YOU THROW AT US!

SMOKE POINTS OF OILS

I know that some oils have a higher smoke point than others, but I'm not sure which ones. And what happens if an oil smokes?

Maureen Connelly Cumberland Foreside, Maine

The smoke point of an oil refers to the temperature at which the fats in the oil break down into gaseous fumes—simply put, the temperature at which they start to smoke.

When we're cooking with a small amount of oil, as we do when pan-searing pork chops, we let the oil start to smoke—so we know it's hot—before adding the chops, and there is no adverse effect on flavor. But letting the oil smoke heavily, as can sometimes happen if you accidentally overheat frying oil, can negatively affect the oil. To demonstrate this, we fried several batches of onion rings in canola oil that had been smoking for 30 seconds (at a temperature of 500 degrees) and in canola oil that hadn't yet started smoking (at 375 degrees). Tasters had no trouble identifying the batches fried in the "smoked" oil, commenting that the rings had a "chemical," "petroleum," and "bitter" taste.

When frying, choose refined peanut, canola, and vegetable oils, which have the highest smoke points of all cooking oils, roughly 450 degrees and well above the usual frying temperatures of 350 to 375 degrees. These oils provide the most cushion should you accidentally overheat the oil. If your frying oil does smoke heavily, we suggest that you start over with fresh oil.

SHADES OF BROWN SUGAR

Some of my recipes specifically call for dark brown sugar, but I don't always have it on hand. Can I substitute light brown sugar when necessary?

Susan Feller West Tisbury, Mass.

According to experts at Domino Sugar, their dark brown sugar is made by stopping the refinement process (the boiling down of cane syrup) before the sugar becomes completely pure, leaving between 1.5 percent and 4 percent cane syrup present in the granules. The cane syrup adds moisture, color, and flavor. Light brown sugar has lower levels of this syrup, which produces a drier, more granulated texture and a sweeter, less complex flavor (as it more closely resembles pure white sugar). To see if they were interchangeable, we baked oatmeal cookies and pan-seared sugar-rubbed pork tenderloin with both dark and light brown sugars. As expected, the light brown sugar imparted a slightly sweeter, more one-dimensional flavor than the dark brown sugar in both applications. The cookies made with the dark brown sugar were noticeably softer, due to the higher moisture content of that sugar.

Interestingly when our blindfolded tasters sampled the sugars raw, most had difficulty distinguishing flavor differences. That being the case, you're safe using dark and light brown sugars interchangeably in recipes that call for only a little (¼ cup or less), but the differences will be more apparent—especially regarding moisture content and texture—when the brown sugar is a more substantial ingredient.

WHITE, LIGHT BROWN, AND DARK BROWN
Three stages of sugar refinement.

STOCK VERSUS BROTH

I see recipes that call for either stock or broth; I always thought they were the same thing. Can you clear up the confusion?

Lucy McDowell Athens, Ga.

If you read a classic cookbook, you will find that stock and broth are defined differently. Stock is a deeply rich liquid made from meat, vegetables, herbs, gelatin-rich bones, and sometimes wine and is most often used as a base for soups and sauces. Broths are made with just meat and vegetables and have lighter, fresher flavors.

At the supermarket, however, cartons and cans labeled "stock" and "broth" seldom adhere to those definitions. In fact, when we've tasted products labeled "broth" and "stock" side by side, we've been unable to detect huge differences. Unless you're working in a restaurant kitchen with classically trained chefs, you can use the terms stock and broth interchangeably. By the way, our favorite brands are Swanson's Organic Chicken Broth (Swanson's Natural Goodness is also quite good) and Pacific Beef Broth, both winners of test kitchen taste tests.

SEASONING CAST-IRON COOKWARE

Many recipes that call for cast iron specify that the pan should be "seasoned." What does this mean?

Kristina Katori New Paltz, N.Y.

Compared with other metals like stainless steel, cast iron is very porous and soft. Seasoning a cast-iron pan means saturating the cooking surface with enough oil to form a nonstick barrier.

If you're working with a new pan, heat it over high heat until a drop of water sizzles immediately upon contact. Remove the pan from the heat, then dunk a wad of paper towels in vegetable oil and wipe the entire inside of the pan with the oil. Then use another wad of paper towels to rub the oil into the metal and wipe out any excess. Use another wad of paper towels if needed. Repeat three or four times for a new pan, until it blackens. After each use, clean the cast-iron pan with hot water and a brush (soap or metal scrubbers can remove seasoning from the pan); thoroughly dry the pan and, while it is still warm, rub the inside of the pan with oil (the paper towel method works fine).

HEAVY DUTY
Proper seasoning makes a cast-iron skillet virtually nonstick.

FLOUR PRIMER

When I go to the supermarket, the baking aisle is lined with different kinds of flour to buy, but I'm never sure which one to use. Can you help?

Shannon Emerson Alexandria, Va.

The type of flour you choose should depend on how you plan to use it in the kitchen. Basic supermarket flours—bread, cake, and all-purpose—differ primarily in their protein levels (listed in grams of protein per serving on nutrition labels) and, subsequently, in their abilities to create gluten (the more protein in flour, the higher its capacity to produce gluten, which gives baked goods structure and chew).

For bread-baking, the high levels of protein in bread flour (13 to 14 percent) yield stronger gluten strands that help create a favorably chewy crumb. Alternatively, cake recipes often call for cake flour (8 percent protein) because its lower protein content helps limit the development of gluten and yields a softer, finer crumb.

If you bake a lot of cakes, you will want to keep cake flour on hand; likewise, bread bakers will want to stock bread flour. However, more than 90 percent of all baking recipes call for all-purpose flour (10 to 12 percent protein), and it should be your first choice when shopping. We have a slight preference for unbleached flour; bleached flour can impart a slight off-flavor to really simple, low-sugar baked goods such as biscuits, although the differences in most recipes will be impossible to detect. In the test kitchen, we use either Pillsbury or Gold Medal unbleached all-purpose flour.

To ask us a cooking question, write to Ask Cook's Country, P.O. Box 470739, Brookline, MA 02447. If you prefer e-mail, visit **cookscountry.com/emailus.** See if you can stump us!

Recipe Makeover MARBLE CHEESECAKE

Most low-fat marble cheesecakes don't have much chocolate flavor and, frankly, aren't worth eating.

A potent paste made from cocoa powder, sugar, and vanilla gives the chocolate swirls in this light cheesecake plenty of flavor.

The test kitchen spent months developing a recipe for low-fat New York–style cheesecake that tastes so good I can honestly say I will never go back to a full-fat version. Made with cottage cheese, light cream cheese, and drained yogurt, it is rich and creamy and contains half the calories and just one-third the fat of the original. I wondered if there was a way to incorporate chocolate into that recipe to make a marble cheesecake that was rich and chocolaty.

Using the existing recipe as a jumping-off point, I melted semisweet chocolate and swirled it into the cheesecake batter. The results weren't promising. The chocolate had a grainy texture and was so poorly integrated into the cake that as it cooled huge cracks appeared all over the top where the chocolate came together with the plain batter. Next I tried chocolate syrup, but it added too much moisture to the batter and made the cheesecake runny. Cocoa was an obvious test to run, but I needed to dissolve the powder first. I mixed ¼ cup of powder with ¼ cup of batter and swirled this chocolate batter back into the plain batter. What I ended up with were pockets of bitter, pasty cocoa and more nasty cracks on the top of the cheesecake. Could I dilute the intense bitterness of the cocoa and solve the appearance issues?

I decided to make a paste by mixing the cocoa with vanilla (so that it would really dissolve), and I added extra sugar to the paste to counteract the bitterness. Then, in an attempt to solve the texture issues, I added batter to the paste until it reached the same consistency as the plain batter (it took about 1 cup). I swirled the two together, baked the cake, and waited patiently for it to cool. The results were well worth the wait. I now had a creamy, crack-free cheesecake with deep chocolate flavor.

–Diane Unger

And the Numbers . . .

All nutritional information is for a single slice of marble cheesecake.

TRADITIONAL MARBLE CHEESECAKE
CALORIES: **670**
FAT: **49g**
SATURATED FAT: **30g**

COOK'S COUNTRY LOW-FAT MARBLE CHEESECAKE
CALORIES: **360**
FAT: **14g**
SATURATED FAT: **8g**

LOW-FAT CHOCOLATE MARBLE CHEESECAKE SERVES 12

Be sure to use light cream cheese (usually sold in tubs), not "1/3 less fat" cream cheese (commonly sold in blocks).

Crust

- 9 whole graham crackers, broken into rough pieces
- 4 tablespoons unsalted butter, melted
- 1 tablespoon sugar

Filling

- 1 pound 1 percent cottage cheese, drained 10 to 24 hours (see box on page 31)
- 1 pound low-fat plain yogurt, drained 10 to 24 hours (see box on page 31)
- 1 pound light cream cheese, at room temperature
- 1 1/2 cups plus 2 tablespoons sugar
- 2 tablespoons vanilla extract
- 1/4 teaspoon salt
- 3 large eggs, at room temperature
- 2 tablespoons Dutch-processed cocoa

1. For the crust: Adjust oven rack to middle position and heat oven to 325 degrees. Process crackers in food processor to fine crumbs. Combine crumbs with butter and sugar in small bowl. Transfer mixture to 9-inch springform pan and press evenly into pan bottom. Bake until fragrant and beginning to brown, 10 to 15 minutes. Cool on wire rack. Taking care not to disturb crust, coat inside of springform pan with cooking spray and set pan on rimmed baking sheet.

2. For the filling: Increase oven temperature to 500 degrees. Process drained cottage cheese in food processor until no visible lumps remain, about 1 minute, scraping down bowl as needed. Add drained yogurt and cream cheese and process until smooth, 1 to 2 minutes, scraping down bowl as needed. Add 1½ cups sugar, 1 tablespoon vanilla, and salt and process until smooth, about 1 minute, scraping down bowl as needed. With processor running, add eggs, one at a time, and process until smooth.

3. Combine remaining 2 tablespoons sugar and cocoa in medium bowl. Stir in 1 cup cheesecake batter and remaining 1 tablespoon vanilla until smooth.

4. Pour plain cheesecake batter into prepared pan. Following photos at right, spoon and swirl chocolate batter into cake. Bake for 10 minutes. Reduce oven temperature to 200 degrees (hold oven door open until oven thermometer reads 200 degrees) and bake until center of cheesecake registers 150 degrees, about 1 hour.

5. Transfer cake to wire rack and run paring knife around edge of cake to loosen. Cool completely, about 3 hours, then wrap pan tightly in plastic wrap and refrigerate until cold, at least 3 hours.

6. To unmold cheesecake, remove sides of pan and blot any excess moisture from top of cheesecake with paper towels. Let cheesecake stand at room temperature for 30 minutes before slicing.

Make Ahead: The pan with the cooled crust can be wrapped in plastic and kept at room temperature for up to 2 days. The baked cheesecake can be refrigerated for up to 3 days, although the crust will become progressively softer.

How to Make A MARBLE CHEESECAKE

1. Using a tablespoon, gently spoon the chocolate batter onto the plain batter around the edge and in the center of the cake, leaving about 1/2 inch between each spoonful. (If there's extra chocolate batter, add it to previous drops.)
2. Using the handle end of a wooden spoon or spatula, drag the handle back and forth through the batter to make a marbled pattern.

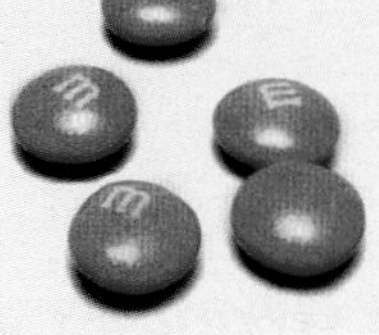

LOST AND FOUND Red velvet cake fell out of fashion in the 1970s amidst health scares relating to red dye #2 (a similar fate befell red M&Ms, even though the candies never contained the dye in question). Once consumers were convinced that other red dyes were safe, red candies made it back into the M&Ms assortment (in 1987) and red velvet cakes started a comeback in bakeries.

Frosted and uncut, it looks like any other cake. But cut—and bite—into our Red Velvet Cake, and you'll know you're experiencing something special.

Beyond its shocking color, there's something more to red velvet cake—an extra-tender cake and fluffy cream cheese frosting.

My introduction to red velvet cake happened 15 years ago when I was watching the movie *Steel Magnolias* with my mom. Besides having a good cry, I remember the wedding reception most vividly, especially the scene where Shelby (played by Julia Roberts) cuts into an armadillo-shaped cake that's bright red inside.

I finally got a chance to taste this cake during a recent visit to a trendy New York bakery, and I wasn't disappointed. The brilliant red cake was really tender (hence the "velvet" part of the name), and I loved the sweet-but-tangy cream cheese frosting. This cake was as delicious as it was eye-catching. I needed to create my own version.

Some research revealed that red cakes are actually nothing new. A faint red color is the by-product of a chemical reaction between vinegar and/or buttermilk and cocoa powder. Red cakes—with names like red devil cake and oxblood cake—date back to the late nineteenth century. Over time, the naturally occurring faint red color was augmented first by beets (a common ingredient during the sugar rations of World War II) and then by red food coloring (the standard choice in most recipes published since the 1950s).

The exact origins of red velvet cake are muddled. Most sources mention the Waldorf-Astoria hotel and the 1950s, but this history is most definitely false—the recipe did not start there. During the 1960s, the recipe appeared in countless newspapers, which sourced this cake in the Deep South, the Pacific Northwest, and even Canada. The best-known version of this recipe appeared in James Beard's 1972 classic *American Cookery*.

Although I wasn't able to figure out the precise origins of this cake, I had accumulated enough research to start baking. I tried a few recipes with beets, but no one liked their vegetal flavor. After several tests, I realized food coloring was a must and there was no use trying to skimp on it; any less than 2 tablespoons yielded a cake that was more pink than red. Despite the addition of cocoa, red velvet is not a chocolate cake—it's there for color. Some recipes contain as little as 1 tablespoon of cocoa. I found that 2 tablespoons produced the best color and gave the cake a pleasant (but mild) cocoa flavor.

Now the cake was definitely red, but it was also speckled with brown at the edges. I was mixing the cocoa powder in with the dry ingredients, yet it didn't seem to be evenly distributed in the cake. A few recipes suggested combining the cocoa powder with the red food coloring to make a paste before adding it to the batter, a step that had seemed fussy. It turns out that it was necessary; mixing the paste made the cakes uniformly red, even at the edges.

Now that I had the red part down, I turned to the velvet. After fiddling with the basic formula, I realized that a super-acidic batter (with both buttermilk and vinegar) was needed to react with the baking soda and create a fine, tender crumb. Thoroughly creaming the butter also helped create a velvety texture. To top it off, my tasters loved the contrast in color and flavor that a sweet, tangy, white cream cheese frosting gave the cake.

I now had a cake that lived up to both the "red" and the "velvet" in its name. Oh, and it tasted great, too.

–Keri Fisher

RED VELVET CAKE SERVES 12

This recipe must be prepared with natural cocoa powder. Dutch-processed cocoa will not yield the proper color or rise.

Cake

- 2 1/4 cups all-purpose flour
- 1 1/2 teaspoons baking soda
- Pinch salt
- 1 cup buttermilk
- 1 tablespoon white vinegar
- 1 teaspoon vanilla extract
- 2 large eggs
- 2 tablespoons natural cocoa powder
- 2 tablespoons (one 1-ounce bottle) red food coloring
- 12 tablespoons (1 1/2 sticks) unsalted butter, softened
- 1 1/2 cups granulated sugar

Frosting

- 16 tablespoons (2 sticks) unsalted butter, softened
- 4 cups confectioners' sugar
- 16 ounces cream cheese, cut into 8 pieces, softened
- 1 1/2 teaspoons vanilla extract
- Pinch salt

1. For the cake: Adjust oven rack to middle position and heat oven to 350 degrees. Grease and flour two 9-inch cake pans. Whisk flour, baking soda, and salt in medium bowl. Whisk buttermilk, vinegar, vanilla, and eggs in large measuring cup. Mix cocoa with food coloring in small bowl until a smooth paste forms.

2. With electric mixer on medium-high speed, beat butter and sugar together until fluffy, about 2 minutes, scraping down bowl as necessary. Add one-third of flour mixture and beat on medium-low speed until just incorporated, about 30 seconds. Add half of buttermilk mixture and beat on low speed until combined, about 30 seconds. Scrape down bowl as necessary and repeat with half of remaining flour mixture, remaining buttermilk mixture, and finally remaining flour mixture. Scrape down bowl, add cocoa mixture, and beat on medium speed until completely incorporated, about 30 seconds. Using rubber spatula, give batter final stir. Scrape into prepared pans and bake until toothpick inserted in center comes out clean, about 25 minutes. Cool cakes in pans 10 minutes then turn out onto rack to cool completely, at least 30 minutes.

3. For the frosting: With electric mixer, beat butter and sugar on medium-high speed until fluffy, about 2 minutes. Add cream cheese, one piece at a time, and beat until incorporated, about 30 seconds. Beat in vanilla and salt. Refrigerate until ready to use.

4. When cakes are cooled, spread about 2 cups frosting on one cake layer. Top with second cake layer and spread top and sides of cake with remaining frosting. Cover and refrigerate until ready to serve, up to 3 days.

To Dye For

We prefer liquid food coloring to gel or paste colors; it is much easier to incorporate and better distributes the cocoa powder. Look for the large bottle of McCormick Red Food Color (found with the vanilla extract) so you won't have to buy the multipack and be left, like we were, with dozens of bottles of blue, green, and yellow coloring.

BARELY RED
With just cocoa powder and no red food coloring, the cake has only a faint red hue.

REDDER
Adding a tablespoon of food coloring gives the cake muted red color.

REDDEST
With two tablespoons of food coloring, the cake has a deep, vibrant red color.

Slow Cooking BEEF BURGUNDY

Beef Burgundy from the slow cooker is terrific—if you can keep the wine tasting lively after 9 hours in the pot.

Our slow-cooked Beef Burgundy is based on refined wine flavor and a rich beefy sauce.

American-style beef stew is a perfect recipe for the slow cooker: The long, slow cooking tenderizes tough cuts of meat and creates a beefy sauce studded with soft vegetables. But beef Burgundy, a more refined beef stew built on a foundation of wine, doesn't fare so well in the slow cooker; the long hours in a covered cooker (with no evaporation or concentration of flavors) turn wine into sour, hot alcohol—not what I was looking for in this recipe.

What I *was* looking for was a rich, savory stew that was beefy, pleasantly winy, and a bit more sophisticated than regular beef stew. Starting with the beef, I knew from experience (and many prior tests) that chuck stew meat is best for long braises like beef Burgundy and that I needed to brown it first to develop a flavorful base for the dish. To save time, I used precut meat (instead of cutting up a whole roast myself) and browned it—along with carrots, onion, and garlic—in bacon drippings (the traditional fat in this recipe) before adding it to the slow cooker. Wanting to cut back on my prep time, I made a batch where I browned only half the meat, and my tasters couldn't tell the difference; half the work sounded good to me.

The slow cooker has a tendency to wash out the flavor of a stew. This led me to be aggressive with flavorful additions—my tasters preferred a lot of garlic and fresh thyme, half a can of tomato paste for sweetness and satiny texture, and a big hit of soy sauce to boost both flavor and color.

Now it was time to move on to the big challenge: the wine flavor. When I marinated the beef in wine, the resulting stew tasted (and smelled) sour. Adding all the wine at the onset produced an acrid and boozy sauce. I tried cutting the wine with chicken broth (the test kitchen generally prefers chicken broth to beef broth, even in beef recipes), and it was a step in the right direction—but the wine flavor was still underdeveloped and flat. I tried adding a few splashes of wine to the finished dish to reawaken the flavors, and although it did add brightness, my tasters found it too sharp and astringent. I was running out of options.

Most recipes that feature wine are cooked uncovered, allowing the alcohol time to cook out and giving the flavors a chance to reduce. Since my beef Burgundy was being slow-cooked under cover, I tried reducing the wine at the onset, before adding it to the pot, but that made the sauce too winy. I had better luck reducing the wine I was adding at the end. This time, the reduced wine, stirred in just before serving, brought the tired stew back to life. My humble slow cooker had finally produced a refined, full-bodied stew worthy of the best French restaurant.

–Stephanie Alleyne

BEEF BURGUNDY SERVES 6 TO 8

Make sure to use the low setting on your slow cooker; the stew will burn on the high setting. Serve with boiled potatoes (the traditional accompaniment), mashed potatoes, or buttered egg noodles.

- 8 ounces bacon, chopped
- 4 pounds stew beef (preferably chuck)
- Salt and pepper
- 1 large onion, chopped fine
- 2 carrots, peeled and chopped fine
- 8 garlic cloves, minced
- 2 teaspoons chopped fresh thyme
- 4 tablespoons tomato paste
- $2\frac{1}{2}$ cups Pinot Noir (see page 31)
- $1\frac{1}{2}$ cups low-sodium chicken broth
- $\frac{1}{3}$ cup soy sauce
- 3 bay leaves
- 3 tablespoons Minute tapioca
- 3 tablespoons minced fresh parsley

1. Cook bacon in large skillet over medium-high heat until crisp. Using slotted spoon, transfer bacon to paper towel–lined plate and refrigerate. Pour half of bacon fat into small bowl; set skillet with remaining bacon fat aside.

2. Dry beef thoroughly with paper towels. Season beef with salt and pepper; place half of beef in slow cooker insert. Heat skillet containing remaining bacon fat over medium-high heat until just smoking. Cook remaining beef in single layer until deep brown on all sides, about 8 minutes. Transfer browned beef to slow cooker insert.

3. Add reserved bacon fat to now-empty skillet and heat over medium-high heat until shimmering. Add onion, carrots, and $\frac{1}{4}$ teaspoon salt and cook until vegetables begin to brown, about 5 minutes. Add garlic and thyme and cook until fragrant, about 30 seconds. Add tomato paste and stir until beginning to brown, about 45 seconds. Transfer mixture to slow cooker insert.

4. Return now-empty skillet to high heat and add $1\frac{1}{2}$ cups wine, chicken broth, and soy sauce. Simmer, scraping up brown bits, until pan bottom is clean, about 1 minute. Transfer wine mixture to slow cooker insert.

5. Stir bay leaves and tapioca into slow cooker insert. Set slow cooker on low, cover, and cook until meat is fork-tender, about 9 hours.

6. When ready to serve, discard bay leaves and stir in reserved bacon. Bring remaining 1 cup wine to boil in large skillet over high heat and simmer until reduced by half, about 5 minutes. Stir reduced wine and parsley into stew and adjust seasonings. Serve.

Make Ahead: The recipe can be prepared through step 4 up to 2 days in advance. Refrigerate the bacon, browned beef, raw beef, vegetable mixture, and wine mixture separately. When ready to cook the stew, transfer these ingredients (except bacon) to the slow cooker and proceed with step 5.

Bigger Is Better

Not all packaged stew meat is created equal. Look for stew meat labeled "chuck," a flavorful cut that has enough fat to emerge silky and tender after withstanding hours in a slow cooker. Also, make sure to buy stew meat that has been cut into large pieces.

TOO SMALL

Small $\frac{1}{2}$-inch pieces of stew meat will disintegrate after 9 hours in a slow cooker.

JUST RIGHT

Meaty $1\frac{1}{2}$-inch chunks of stew meat will hold their shape in a slow cooker.

The Final Touch

In addition to the rich flavor of the wine, many people consider a garnish of sautéed onions and mushrooms one of the hallmarks of a great beef Burgundy. We think this little bit of last-minute kitchen work is worth the effort.

Instructions for the Garnish:
Before reducing wine in step 6, bring 2 cups frozen pearl onions, 5 tablespoons unsalted butter, 1 tablespoon sugar, and $\frac{1}{2}$ cup water to boil in large skillet over high heat. Cover and simmer over medium-low heat until onions are tender, about 5 minutes. Uncover, increase heat to high, and cook until liquid evaporates, about 3 minutes. Add 10 ounces white mushrooms, quartered, and $\frac{1}{4}$ teaspoon salt and cook until vegetables are browned and glazed, about 5 minutes. Stir onions and mushrooms into stew and proceed to reduce wine in now-empty skillet as directed in step 6.

Loaded Baked Potato Soup

Baked potato soups start with the hour-long process of baking potatoes. Could we find a way to avoid the baking but still load on the flavor?

Take a baked potato and pile it high with all of the fixin's: cheese, bacon, scallions, and sour cream. Now take that same loaded baked potato, buzz it in the blender with a little broth, and heat it on the stove—presto, loaded baked potato soup! That's exactly what I tasted when I ordered the "Loaded Baked Potato Soup" during a recent trip to a chain restaurant.

Most recipes for this type of soup start by baking the potatoes in the oven, which ensures that the soup tastes "baked" and more deeply flavored than potato soups that are boiled. But it takes over an hour to bake a potato, and that meant that from start to finish my soup was closing in on two hours to make. That seems too long for a simple soup.

A few recipes offered the microwave as a shortcut to cook the potatoes. Sure, the 10 minutes or so in the microwave was a big time-saver, but the potatoes felt mealy and tasted stale. Boiling the russet potatoes gave me my best results yet, at least in terms of texture. The potatoes were tender and moist, but because I had been peeling them (the skins were soggy when cooked in the soup), the baked flavor was gone. I hoped the other fixin' ingredients would help.

Starting by frying up bacon was mandatory. When the rendered fat was used to cook the other ingredients, the bacon flavor permeated the soup, and the crisped bacon pieces were ready to be used as a garnish. Scallions were another story; added to the soup at the onset, their delicate flavor and bright color were exhausted by the end of the cooking time. Instead, I cooked some chopped onion in the bacon fat and saved the scallions for garnish.

For more "loaded" flavor I whisked in some sour cream right before serving (being careful not to boil the soup to avoid curdling the sour cream), and this soup was bordering on just right.

The soup tasted like all the best parts of a loaded baked potato—plenty of smoky bacon, cheese, and sour cream—but one thing was missing; without the flavor from the potato skin, my soup didn't taste "baked." Luckily, a colleague happened to spy the discarded potato peelings in the trash and wondered if they could be fried in the bacon fat (like a fried potato skin) and used as a flavorful garnish. I gave the next batch a try, and the cooked skins added that exact "baked" flavor that had been lacking.

In half the time it takes to actually bake a potato, I had all the flavor of a loaded one—and I could eat it with a spoon.

–Bridget Lancaster

This potato soup is loaded with bacon, cheese, and sour cream.

LOADED BAKED POTATO SOUP SERVES 8

If you prefer, replace the thyme sprig with 1/4 teaspoon dried thyme (no need to remove it in step 3). Reserving some of the potatoes in step 3 results in a chunkier soup. For a smooth soup, puree all the potatoes.

- **8 ounces bacon, chopped**
- **3 pounds russet potatoes, scrubbed**
- **1 large onion, chopped**
- **2 garlic cloves, minced**
- **2 tablespoons all-purpose flour**
- **4 cups low-sodium chicken broth**
- **1 cup heavy cream**
- **1 sprig fresh thyme**
- **4 cups shredded sharp cheddar cheese, plus additional for garnish**
- **1 cup sour cream, plus additional for garnish**
- **Pepper**
- **3 scallions, sliced thin**

1. Cook bacon in Dutch oven over medium heat until crisp, about 8 minutes. While bacon is cooking, use vegetable peeler to remove wide strips of potato peel; reserve peels. Cut peeled potatoes into ¾-inch pieces. Using slotted spoon, transfer bacon to plate lined with paper towels. Add reserved potato skins to bacon fat in pot and cook until crisp, about 8 minutes. Using slotted spoon, transfer potato skins to plate with bacon.

2. Add onion to fat remaining in pot and cook over medium heat until golden, about 6 minutes. Stir in garlic and flour and cook until fragrant, about 1 minute. Gradually whisk in broth and cream, stir in thyme and potatoes, and bring to boil over high heat. Reduce heat to medium-low, cover pot, and cook until potatoes are tender, about 7 minutes.

3. Discard thyme and transfer 2 cups cooked potatoes to bowl. Puree remaining soup in batches in blender until smooth. Return to pot and warm over medium-high heat. Off heat, stir in cheese until melted, then whisk in sour cream. Return reserved potatoes to pot and season soup with pepper. Ladle soup into bowls, garnishing with bacon, fried potato skins, scallions, cheese, and sour cream.

Reheating Leftovers

To reheat leftover portions of our Loaded Baked Potato Soup, gently warm the soup in a saucepan over medium heat until steaming. Do not let the soup boil, which will cause the sour cream to separate.

Monte Cristo Sandwiches Come Home

This hybrid between a grilled ham and cheese sandwich and French toast gets soggy quickly, and you can make only two at a time. Is there a way to make a big batch so everyone can eat together?

By turns sweet and savory, crispy and tender, these Monte Cristos will satisfy the hungriest of crowds.

My first taste of a Monte Cristo is tied to memories of roller coasters, Cinderella, and Mickey Mouse. Like many Americans, I first tasted this exotically named sandwich at Disneyland (see American Table, below right). The Monte Cristo starts out like any other grilled Swiss cheese, ham, and turkey sandwich before it is dipped in an egg batter and cooked—only one or two at a time—in a skillet. This lunch favorite is then served with jam, sugar, and/or syrup to create a sweet and savory combination that's hard to beat.

Determined to produce a full batch of six piping-hot sandwiches, I abandoned the skillet and turned to oven-frying. For each sandwich, I layered a few slices of ham, turkey, and cheese between hearty sandwich bread (mushy, airy breads weren't sturdy enough), dipped the sandwich in a mixture of egg and cream, and placed it on a hot oiled baking sheet. After searing both sides for several minutes, my six Monte Cristos were only moderately crisp and browned. Still, the ease of this method made it worth pursuing.

Raising the oven temperature from 400 to 450 promoted browning, but the Monte Cristo's defining dunk in the egg mixture continued to impede crisping. Because French toast is often made with staled bread, I thought I'd try leaving the bread out all day to see if that would help. Sure enough, these sandwiches were crisper, though still not quite crisp enough. What if I toasted the bread before assembling and dunking the sandwiches? More progress. A light toasting dried the bread still more—enough so it could stand up to the egg mixture. Toasting also jump-started browning. Acting on the suggestion of another test cook, I added a few teaspoons of granulated sugar to the egg mixture. Now the bread browned and caramelized perfectly.

Monte Cristos are traditionally served with a sweet accompaniment, typically powdered sugar, chutney, maple syrup, or jam. After tasting Monte Cristos made with each, tasters preferred the flavor of strawberry jam, even though it was a little too sweet on its own. Mixing Dijon mustard into the jam balanced the flavors, creating a sweet and spicy mixture that tasters liked so much they wanted it spread on the bread and served on the side (which is traditional).

The perfect marriage of sweet and savory flavors with a no-fuss cooking method for a crowd, these Monte Cristos turned out even better than I remember. They've become a new brunch staple in my house. **–Cali Rich**

MONTE CRISTO SANDWICHES SERVES 6

Trim the slices of meat and cheese as necessary to fit neatly on the bread.

- **4 large eggs**
- **1/4 cup heavy cream**
- **2 teaspoons sugar**
- **1/2 teaspoon salt**
- **1/2 teaspoon dry mustard**
- **1/8 teaspoon cayenne pepper**
- **6 tablespoons strawberry or raspberry jam**
- **2 tablespoons Dijon mustard**
- **12 slices hearty white sandwich bread, lightly toasted**
- **18 thin slices deli Swiss or Gruyère cheese**
- **12 thin slices deli ham, preferably Black Forest**
- **12 thin slices deli turkey**
- **3 tablespoons vegetable oil**
- **Confectioners' sugar**

1. Adjust oven rack to upper-middle position and heat oven to 450 degrees. Whisk eggs, cream, sugar, salt, dry mustard, and cayenne in shallow dish until combined. Stir jam and Dijon mustard together in small bowl.

2. Spread 1 teaspoon jam mixture on one side of each slice of toast. Layer slices of cheese, ham, and turkey on 6 slices of toast. Repeat with second layer of cheese, ham, and turkey. Add final layer of cheese and top with remaining toast, with jam side facing cheese. Using hands, lightly press down on sandwiches.

3. Pour oil onto rimmed baking sheet and heat in oven until just smoking, about 7 minutes. Meanwhile, using 2 hands, coat each sandwich with egg mixture and transfer to large plate. Transfer sandwiches to preheated baking sheet and bake until golden brown on both sides, 4 to 5 minutes per side, using spatula to flip. Serve immediately with remaining jam mixture and sprinkling with confectioners' sugar.

Secrets to CRISP MONTE CRISTO SANDWICHES

Here's how we got crisp sandwiches without frying.

1. Toasted Bread: Toasting the bread jump-starts browning and helps keep it from turning soggy when coated with batter.

2. Sweet Batter: Coating the sandwiches in an egg batter that contains a bit of sugar encourages browning and crispness.

3. Hot Pan: Preheating the oil and baking sheet makes the sandwiches sizzle when they hit the pan; they begin to crisp right away.

The American Table: Disney Magic

It was the 1940s, but was it San Diego, San Francisco, or L.A.? It seems nearly every major city in California has been tagged as the birthplace of the Monte Cristo sandwich. It is widely assumed that it began as a variation of the French classic known as croque monsieur, a grilled ham and cheese sandwich that's sometimes dipped in batter before being cooked. The Monte Cristo achieved national recognition when it was added to the menus of the Blue Bayou and Tahitian Terrace restaurants at Disneyland in 1966. To this day, the Monte Cristo remains one of the most popular lunch items on the Blue Bayou menu.

Herb-Crusted Beef Tenderloin

A crusty, herb-flavored exterior is the perfect way to jazz up this mild, tender roast—but only if the crust sticks to the meat.

We pack the flavor onto this roast by incorporating fresh herbs, cheese, and bread crumbs into the crust.

For a cut of meat that costs about $75, a whole beef tenderloin sure presents a lot of problems for the home cook. Yes, the meat is very tender, but it's not very flavorful. In the test kitchen, we think a crusty, browned exterior is a must for this roast. It adds flavor and interest to a cut that can otherwise be mushy and boring.

If a thick seared crust is good, I figured that an additional herb crust would be even better. But this opened up another set of cooking problems: The herbs burn easily or just lose their flavor, and they aren't easily glued to the meat. I had my work cut out for me.

A hot oven can put a decent crust on the meat. I found that 400 degrees offered the best balance of nice browning and even cooking. (At higher temperatures, the interior overcooked very easily and the kitchen often filled with smoke.) Tucking the thinner, tapered end of the meat under itself and tying the roast at 1½-inch intervals created a regularly shaped roast and also promoted even cooking. Elevating the roast on a wire rack kept the bottom of the tenderloin from steaming in its own juices.

My roast was better, but still pretty soft. Could I make the crust thicker? Knowing that salting raw meat helps to draw out moisture, which results in a drier and crustier exterior, I tried rubbing the meat with salt while it was sitting on the counter losing its chill (bringing the roast to room temperature before cooking also aids even cooking). The salting did result in a firmer exterior, but the roast still lacked that deeply browned crust I was looking for. Adding sugar to the salt rub was a key discovery: A mere 2 teaspoons (along with 1 tablespoon of salt) was all that was needed to create a golden brown, perfectly caramelized crust about halfway through the cooking time.

Now I could introduce the herbs. (Added earlier in the roasting process, they burned.) After doing several tests, I found that tasters preferred the combination of parsley and thyme to the aggressive flavors of sage and rosemary. Dry herbs tasted stale, so I focused my tests on fresh. I worked out the right proportions and boosted the herb flavor with minced garlic, but I was having trouble keeping the herb paste on the roast. After some trial and error, I found a flavorful way to glue the herbs to the meat: grated Parmesan cheese.

My herb crust was flavorful, but could I make it crisper? I tried adding herbed bread crumbs and more Parmesan cheese (a topping that creates a nice crunchy crust on many foods) on top of my herb-

Secrets to HERB-CRUSTED BEEF TENDERLOIN

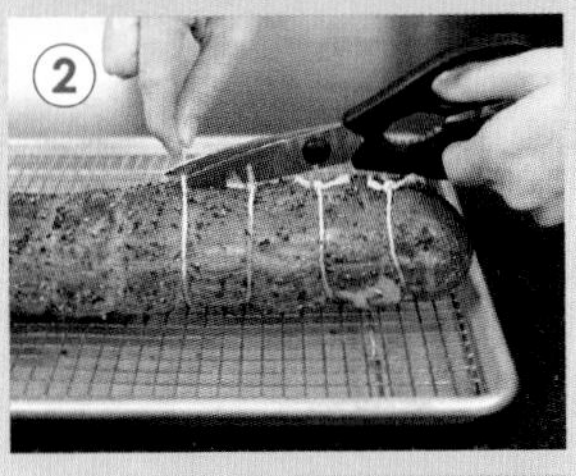

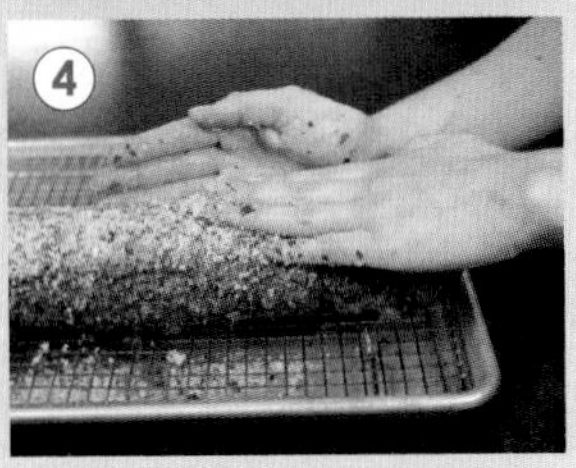

1. To ensure even cooking, fold the thin, tapered end under the roast, then tie the entire roast with kitchen twine every 1½ inches.
2. After the meat has cooked for 20 minutes, use scissors to snip the twine and carefully pull the strings away from the tenderloin.
3. Using a spatula, spread the herb paste evenly over the top and sides of the tenderloin.
4. Press the bread-crumb mixture evenly onto the roast, using the other hand to catch the crumbs and keep them from falling through the rack.

and-cheese paste. This extra crust was perfect, except for one small detail: When I went to remove the strings prior to carving, the bread crumbs came right off with it. Because I was already removing the half-cooked tenderloin from the oven to smear on the herb paste, I tried removing the strings and adding the bread crumbs at the same juncture. This method worked perfectly, as the shape of the tied meat had been set during the initial cooking. And the bread crumbs turned crisp and golden just as the tenderloin came up to temperature.

The three distinct crusts on this special holiday recipe—the oven-seared meat, the herb paste coating, and the herbed bread-crumb crown—make this premium roast something truly special. **–Cali Rich**

HERB-CRUSTED BEEF TENDERLOIN

SERVES 12 TO 16

Make sure to begin this recipe 2 hours before you plan to put the roast in the oven. The tenderloin can be trimmed, tied, rubbed with the salt mixture, and refrigerated up to 24 hours in advance; make sure to bring the roast back to room temperature before putting it into the oven.

- **1 whole beef tenderloin (5 to 6 pounds), trimmed (see page 31) and patted dry**
- **Kosher salt and cracked pepper**
- **2 teaspoons sugar**
- **2 slices hearty white sandwich bread, torn into pieces**
- **1/2 cup chopped fresh parsley**
- **2 teaspoons plus 2 tablespoons chopped fresh thyme**
- **1 1/4 cups grated Parmesan cheese**
- **6 tablespoons olive oil**
- **4 garlic cloves, minced**

1. Tuck tail of tenderloin under and tie roast (see photo 1 on page 12). Combine 1 tablespoon salt, 1 tablespoon pepper, and sugar in small bowl and rub all over tenderloin. Transfer tenderloin to wire rack set on rimmed baking sheet and let stand at room temperature for 2 hours.

2. Meanwhile, pulse bread in food processor to fine crumbs. Transfer bread crumbs to medium bowl and toss in 2 tablespoons parsley, 2 teaspoons thyme, 1/2 cup Parmesan, and 2 tablespoons oil until evenly combined. Wipe out food processor and process remaining 6 tablespoons parsley, 2 tablespoons thyme, 3/4 cup cheese, 4 tablespoons oil, and garlic until smooth paste forms. Transfer herb paste to small bowl.

3. Adjust oven rack to upper-middle position and heat oven to 400 degrees. Roast tenderloin 20 minutes and remove from oven. Using scissors, cut and remove twine (photo 2). Coat tenderloin with herb paste followed by bread-crumb topping (photos 3 and 4). Roast until thickest part of meat registers about 130 degrees (for medium-rare) and topping is golden brown, 20 to 25 minutes. (If topping browns before meat reaches preferred internal temperature, lightly cover with foil for balance of roasting time and remove while roast rests.) Let roast rest, uncovered, for 30 minutes on wire rack. Transfer to cutting board and carve. Serve.

Horseradish Cream Sauce

A horseradish cream sauce is no stranger to roast beef, but to pair it with our herbed beef tenderloin we wanted more tang and so added some Dijon mustard and sour cream. The sour cream also helps to "culture," or thicken, the heavy cream, yielding an especially rich (not to mention easy) sauce.

HORSERADISH CREAM SAUCE

MAKES ABOUT 1 CUP

This sauce can be refrigerated in an airtight container for up to 2 days.

- **1/2 cup sour cream**
- **1/2 cup heavy cream**
- **1/4 cup prepared horseradish, drained**
- **2 teaspoons Dijon mustard**
- **1 garlic clove, minced**
- **1/4 teaspoon sugar**
- **Salt and pepper**

Mix all ingredients, including salt and pepper to taste, in bowl. Cover and let stand at room temperature for 1 to 1 1/2 hours to thicken.

On the Side: Make-Ahead Garlic Green Beans

We've front-loaded most of the kitchen work for these garlicky beans.

Dry-toasting the garlic before mashing it with the softened butter gives us deep, nutty garlic flavor with no harsh burn.

Getting an entire holiday meal on the table requires precise timing. Side dishes get the least amount of attention and often end up overcooked or lukewarm. And do you really want to be cooking green beans in a pot of boiling water and then looking for space in the sink to drain them just five minutes before the big meal? To ease the last-minute kitchen frenzy, I decided to create a green bean dish, something fresher than a casserole, that could be simply reheated right before serving.

My plan was to cook the beans and then toss them with a garlic butter just before serving. Blanching the beans in salted boiling water and then shocking them in ice water (to immediately stop the cooking) proved to be the most foolproof and consistent method of evenly cooking the beans. After drying them off, I found that the beans could be held in the refrigerator for two days and then quickly reheated with a little water in a covered skillet when ready to use.

I wanted the same convenience with the garlic butter. Raw garlic was too harsh; it had to be cooked. Sautéing crushed and minced garlic cloves in butter led to burnt butter and bitter garlic. Boiling the cloves in water (with the green beans) dulled the garlic flavor, but toasting them (skins on) in a skillet was more successful. This dry-toasting method allowed the cloves to soften within their skins, producing a sweet and nutty garlic flavor. Once the cloves were cool, I removed their skins and mashed them with softened butter. Just like the beans, this garlic butter can be made two days in advance and simply tossed into the reheated beans for a no-stress side dish.

–Cali Rich

MAKE-AHEAD GARLIC GREEN BEANS

SERVES 8

The beans and garlic butter can be prepared up to 2 days in advance.

- **Salt**
- **2 pounds green beans, stem ends trimmed**
- **6 medium garlic cloves, unpeeled**
- **3 tablespoons unsalted butter, softened**
- **Pepper**

1. Bring 4 quarts water to boil in Dutch oven over high heat. Add 1 tablespoon salt and green beans, return to boil, and cook until beans are crisp-tender, 3 to 4 minutes. Meanwhile, fill large bowl with ice water. Drain beans in colander and immediately transfer to ice water. When beans no longer feel warm to touch, drain again and dry thoroughly with paper towels. Transfer beans to zipper-lock plastic bag and refrigerate for up to 2 days.

2. Meanwhile, toast garlic cloves in small skillet over medium-low heat, shaking pan occasionally, until fragrant and color of cloves deepens slightly, 5 to 8 minutes. Cool garlic. Peel and press (or mash) cloves, then, using dinner fork, mash garlic, butter, and 1/2 teaspoon salt in small bowl until combined. Cover with plastic wrap and refrigerate for up to 2 days.

3. When ready to serve, heat beans and 1/4 cup water in large skillet, covered, over high heat, 3 to 4 minutes. Remove lid and cook until moisture evaporates, about 30 seconds. Add garlic butter, toss to combine, and season with salt and pepper to taste. Serve.

FOOD FACT: *Although sweet potatoes are often referred to as yams, yams they are not. True yams are very starchy, rarely sweet, and are most commonly white-fleshed with a hairy exterior. Yams grow in Latin America and Africa and can weigh 100 pounds or more.*

Creamy Mashed Sweet Potatoes

What's the key to a creamy mash that actually tastes like sweet potatoes?

Kitchen Know-How
THE SLICE IS RIGHT

It is imperative to cut the sweet potato into thin, even slices to ensure perfect cooking.

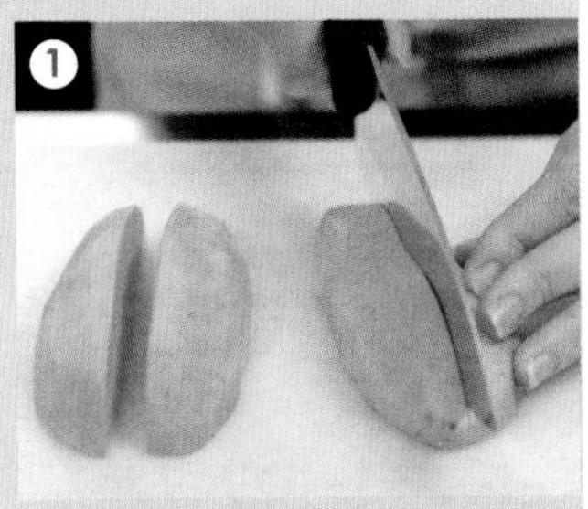

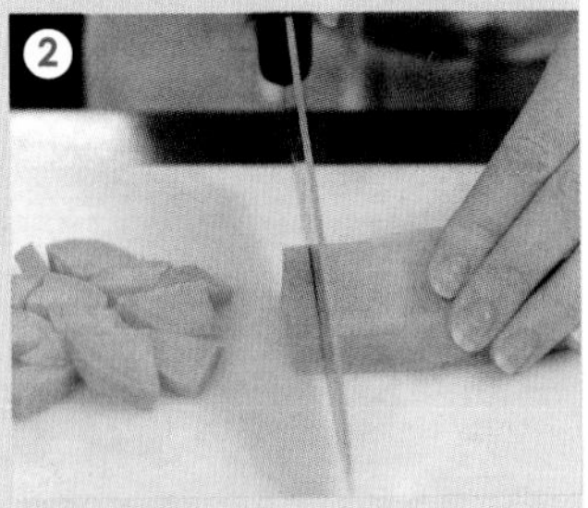

1. Quarter each peeled sweet potato lengthwise.
2. Cut each quarter into ¼-inch slices crosswise.

No-Boil Sweet Potatoes

Boiling sweet potatoes in lots of liquid—as you would regular potatoes—is not a good idea. Sweet potatoes will soak up too much water, and the resulting mash will be a soggy mess. Better to cook them in a small amount of liquid. Just 2 tablespoons of heavy cream (plus a little butter), along with the water released from the sweet potatoes as they cook, is enough to steam them to tenderness.

As a Southerner, I'm no stranger to candied sweet potatoes or even sweet potato pie, but I wanted to create a savory mash, rich with the earthy flavor of sweet potatoes—and save the marshmallows for dessert.

Baking, steaming, microwaving, and boiling are all methods used to cook sweet potatoes for mashing, but each has its problems. Baking whole sweet potatoes yields a full-flavored mash, but the lengthy baking time and the need to peel scalding-hot potatoes make this method a hassle. Steaming the potatoes leaves them tasteless, and cooking them in the microwave ruins their texture. Boiling the sweet potatoes, the most common method, produces the worst results: a waterlogged mush with washed-out flavor.

Years ago in the test kitchen, we found that the secret to getting silky and full-flavored mashed sweet potatoes was to thinly slice the potatoes and cook them covered, on the stovetop, over low heat in a small amount of liquid and sugar. When the sweet potatoes are fall-apart tender, they can be mashed right in the pot—no draining, no straining, no fuss.

This method works because the low heat allows the moisture-rich sweet potatoes to shed their liquid, which in turn produces steam that cooks them. By the time the sweet potatoes are tender, they have reabsorbed their natural juices, thus retaining all of their flavor. Although the sweet potatoes do shed a good amount of moisture during cooking, a small amount of starter liquid—my tasters preferred a combination of butter and cream—is needed to begin the process.

My basic mash recipe is rich in sweet potato flavor, but if you're looking for something a little more creative for the holidays, try one of the variations; they're quick and easy, and they won't leave you with a toothache. **–Cali Rich**

Our four simple recipes bring out the savory, earthy essence of sweet potatoes—without going overboard on the sweet stuff.

CREAMY MASHED SWEET POTATOES

SERVES 4 TO 6

This recipe can be doubled and prepared in a Dutch oven, but the cooking time will need to be doubled as well.

- **4 tablespoons unsalted butter, cut into 4 pieces**
- **3 tablespoons heavy cream**
- **Salt and pepper**
- **1 teaspoon sugar**
- **2 pounds sweet potatoes (2 large or 3 medium), peeled, quartered lengthwise, and cut into ¼-inch-thick slices**

1. Combine butter, 2 tablespoons cream, ½ teaspoon salt, ¼ teaspoon pepper, sugar, and sweet potatoes in large saucepan. Cook, covered, over low heat until potatoes are fall-apart tender, 35 to 40 minutes.

2. Off heat, add remaining tablespoon cream and mash sweet potatoes with potato masher. Serve.

SMOKEHOUSE MASHED SWEET POTATOES

Follow recipe for Creamy Mashed Sweet Potatoes, adding ⅛ teaspoon cayenne pepper to saucepan in step 1. In step 2, mash ½ cup shredded smoked Gouda cheese with sweet potatoes and cover with lid until cheese melts, about 1 minute. Sprinkle with 6 ounces chopped and cooked bacon and 1 thinly sliced scallion.

HERBED MASHED SWEET POTATOES WITH CARAMELIZED ONION

If you prefer, substitute ¼ teaspoon dried thyme for the thyme sprig (but do not remove in step 2).

Follow recipe for Creamy Mashed Sweet Potatoes, adding 1 sprig fresh thyme to saucepan in step 1. While sweet potatoes are cooking, melt 1 tablespoon butter in small nonstick skillet and add 1 small onion, chopped, ¼ teaspoon sugar, and ¼ teaspoon salt. Cook over low heat until onion is caramelized, about 15 minutes. Discard thyme and mash potatoes as directed in step 2. Stir in onion and 1 tablespoon sour cream.

FAR EAST MASHED SWEET POTATOES

Follow recipe for Creamy Mashed Sweet Potatoes, substituting 2 teaspoons soy sauce for salt and adding 1½ teaspoons minced fresh ginger and 1 minced garlic clove to saucepan in step 1. Follow recipe as directed, sprinkling mashed sweet potatoes with 2 tablespoons chopped fresh cilantro.

Make Ahead

These recipes can be prepared up to 2 days in advance. Mash the potatoes as directed in step 2, but hold off on adding the last tablespoon of cream. When you want to serve the potatoes, cover them with plastic wrap, microwave until hot, and then stir in the remaining cream and any last-minute flavorings, such as scallions, bacon, or herbs.

Fluffy Make-Ahead Dinner Rolls

Soft and pillowy dinner rolls are a holiday tradition—unfortunately, so is waking up early to bake them.

These rich, immense rolls freeze beautifully, making them perfect for the hectic holiday season.

For me, a holiday meal wouldn't be complete without a soft dinner roll teetering on the edge of my overflowing plate. My favorite kind are the ones that are oversized, slightly sweet, and fluffy enough to take a nap on. But turning out a batch of homemade dinner rolls when holiday stress is running high can be a daunting task. I was determined to figure out a way to serve my family fresh, homemade rolls that would require no more work than store-bought rolls (at least on the big day) but taste much, much better.

Baking the rolls ahead of time and freezing them seemed like a logical option, so I baked up a standard American dinner roll recipe for my first test. These buttery rolls (made with milk, sugar, flour, yeast, and salt) were fine fresh out of the oven, but they turned dry and stale-tasting in the freezer, no matter how carefully I wrapped them or at what stage of the process (unbaked, half-baked, or fully baked) I froze them. Simply put, these rolls were a disaster.

To figure out how to make rolls that would survive the drying environment of the freezer, I began tinkering with the amount of each ingredient. I theorized that the more moisture and fat I could add to the dough, the better chance I would have for successful freezing. I bumped up the butter from 4 to 7 tablespoons, and what I got was indeed a richer roll, but after freezing, it was still too dry. Next, I tried replacing some of the butter with shortening, hoping that the shortening would tenderize the dough and make for a softer crumb after freezing. I substituted 4 tablespoons of shortening for an equal amount of the butter, and my hunch turned out to be right. The rolls baked up higher and much more tender, with the fluffy texture I was looking for. It turns out the shortening coats the gluten strands in the flour more effectively than butter and keeps baked goods from drying out.

I added an egg for extra structure and richness and replaced the sugar with honey, which keeps the rolls moist and tender. Now these rolls withstood even a month in the deep freeze, baking up as soft and fluffy as the day they were made. And no one at my holiday table suspected they had been frozen. –Diane Unger

FLUFFY MAKE-AHEAD DINNER ROLLS

MAKES 15 LARGE ROLLS

Don't get the milk mixture too hot or the dough won't rise.

- **3 tablespoons unsalted butter, plus 2 tablespoons for bowl and baking dish**
- **1 1/2 cups whole milk**
- **1/3 cup honey**
- **4 tablespoons vegetable shortening**
- **5–5 1/2 cups all-purpose flour**
- **1 tablespoon rapid-rise or instant yeast**
- **2 teaspoons salt**
- **1 large egg, plus 1 large egg beaten with 1 tablespoon water**

1. Adjust oven rack to middle position and heat oven to 200 degrees. When oven reaches 200 degrees, shut oven off. Grease large bowl with 1 tablespoon butter. Line 13 by 9-inch baking dish with foil, leaving overhang on all sides. Grease foil with 1 tablespoon butter.

2. Place milk, honey, shortening, and remaining 3 tablespoons butter in large measuring cup. Microwave on high power until milk is warm (110 degrees) and butter and shortening begin to melt, 1 to 2 minutes. Stir well.

3. Mix 4½ cups flour, yeast, and salt in bowl of standing mixer fitted with dough hook. Turn mixer to low and slowly add milk mixture. After dough comes together, increase speed to medium, add 1 egg, and mix until dough is smooth, about 2 minutes. Add another ½ cup flour and knead until dough is shiny and smooth and comes away from sides of mixing bowl, 6 to 7 minutes (add up to ½ cup more flour if dough is too sticky). Turn dough onto unfloured surface and knead briefly to form smooth, cohesive ball. Transfer dough to buttered bowl and turn to coat. Cover bowl with plastic wrap and place in turned-off oven until dough has doubled in size, 50 to 60 minutes.

4. Punch down dough on floured surface and divide into 3 equal pieces. Roll each piece into thick cylinder and cut each cylinder into 5 equal pieces. Working one piece at a time (keep remaining pieces covered with plastic wrap) and following photos at right, form dough pieces into smooth, taut rounds and arrange in prepared baking dish. Lightly press on dough rounds so they just touch each other. Cover baking dish with plastic wrap and return to turned-off oven until dough rounds have doubled in size, 50 to 60 minutes.

5. Remove dish from oven and heat oven to 375 degrees. Unwrap baking dish and brush rolls with egg-water mixture. Bake until rolls are deep golden brown, 25 to 27 minutes. Remove from oven and cool on wire rack for 5 minutes. Using handles of foil sling, remove rolls from baking dish and cool on wire rack for 1 hour. Remove foil from rolls, return to rack, and cool completely, about 2 hours longer. Keeping rolls together, wrap tightly in plastic wrap, then in foil; freeze for up to 1 month.

6. To serve: Remove plastic wrap and foil (reserve foil) from rolls, wrap in reserved foil, and defrost at room temperature for 2 hours. Adjust oven rack to middle position and heat oven to 375 degrees. Bake foil-wrapped rolls on baking sheet until heated through, about 30 minutes. Serve.

Kitchen Know-How
SHAPING DINNER ROLLS

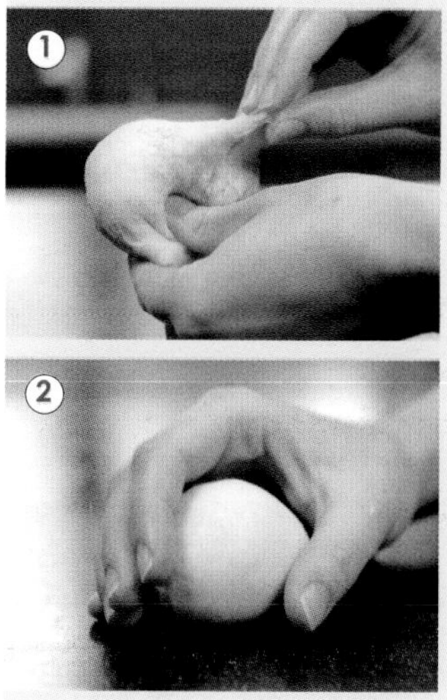

1. Form each piece of dough into a rough ball, pinching and pulling the edges under so that the top is smooth.
2. Cupping each dough round with the palm of your hand, move the dough in a circular motion on the unfloured work surface until a smooth ball forms.

Rolls without a Mixer

In step 3, mix 4 1/2 cups flour, yeast, and salt in large bowl. Make well in flour, then add milk mixture and egg to well. Stir with wooden spoon until dough becomes shaggy and difficult to stir. Turn dough out onto floured work surface and knead, adding remaining 1/2 cup flour (or more as needed), until dough forms smooth, cohesive ball, about 10 minutes. Proceed as directed.

I'm Looking for a Recipe

READERS HELP READERS FIND RECIPES

We've Got Mail

Several readers sent us recipes in response to Judy Wilde's request for baby food cake (June/July 2006 issue), including Judy herself. It turns out that Judy was contacted by a devoted reader of *Cook's Country* (see Judy's letter at right). To find dozens more recipes submitted by readers who responded to this page in other issues of *Cook's Country*, go to **cookscountry.com** and click on **Looking for a Recipe.**

BABY FOOD CAKE Beth Walentukonis

Yesterday afternoon, I received a phone call from a very sweet lady by the name of Beth Walentukonis. She had read my request in your magazine for a baby food cake recipe and called to give me her version of this easy, moist cake (printed here). When you said you'd publish my request I knew I'd get my answer, but finding out that someone would go to the trouble of looking me up and calling across the country just floored me. Everyone involved in publishing your magazine always struck me as "nice people," so I guess it comes through to everyone and you collect nice readers also. –Judy Wilde

- 1 **6-ounce jar fruit baby food, preferably plum or apricot**
- 2 **cups self-rising flour**
- 2 **cups sugar**
- 3 **eggs**
- 1 **teaspoon nutmeg**
- 1 **teaspoon cinnamon**
- 1 **cup oil**
- 1 **cup chopped pecans**

INSTRUCTIONS:

1. Preheat oven to 350 degrees. Grease and flour a Bundt pan.

2. Mix all ingredients together in large bowl and pour into prepared Bundt pan.

3. Bake until toothpick inserted in cake comes out with a few crumbs attached, about 50 minutes. After 30 minutes, invert cake onto wire rack to finish cooling.

Chock Full o' Nuts Doughnuts

Years ago, outside of Newark, N.J., there was a Chock Full o' Nuts diner that used to make the best doughnuts. My mom and I have tried to determine whether the doughnuts were made with whole grains, ground nuts, or both, but they had an almost cake-like texture and a wonderful nutty flavor. I'd love to try to make them but don't even know where to start.

Peg Gorman
Manassas, Va.

Betsy Ross Blueberry Cake

I used to own a cookbook that I had bought at a school fund-raiser. It was called the *Betsy Ross Cookbook*, and all the recipes had a colonial theme. There was a blueberry cake in the book that was wonderful. Unfortunately, in my hasty cleaning one day, the book got tossed. Everyone loved that cake, and every attempt I have made to duplicate it without the recipe has not been as successful. Does anyone have this recipe?

Kathy Byrne
Levittown, Pa.

Kahlúa Pie

Back in the 1980s we lived in Cortez, Colo., and we'd drive to Durango and dine at a Mexican Restaurant called Dos Juans'. Sometimes we could order a special dessert called Kahlúa pie. It was a cream pie with a hint of coconut. If anyone has the recipe, I would love to have it. Because we live in California now, it's a bit far to drive, but I sure do miss the restaurant's peach margaritas and that delicious Kahlúa pie.

Deborah Dunn
Antelope, Calif.

Great-Grandma's Molasses Cookies

My father and I have searched, in vain, through all of my great-grandmother's cookbooks for her molasses cookie recipe. Her cookies tasted like a very rich gingerbread. They were drop-style and spread out into chewy hand-sized cookies when baked. Most of the molasses cookie recipes we've found turn crispy when they cool, but these cookies remained chewy. I would love to give my dad some cookies like these as a present.

Elizabeth Rowley
Bethlehem, N.H.

Hawaiian Cheesecake

I am looking for a Hawaiian cheesecake recipe. The one I remember was baked in a spring-form pan and called for boxed pineapple cake mix to make the crust and the juice from a can of pineapple slices to make the glazed topping. The cake was decorated with pineapple slices and red and green maraschino cherries. I think the recipe appeared in a women's magazine about 12 to 15 years ago. This is a really great-tasting cheesecake, and I would love to find the recipe.

Robin Vizena
Oberlin, La.

Lemon Thins

When I was a little girl, my mother, grandmother, and I would have tea at 4 p.m. every day. We would always eat Lemon Thins, a packaged cookie from Nabisco. It was during the 1960s and 1970s that this cookie was in grocery stores, but now I can't find it anywhere. I was wondering if anyone has a recipe.

Karen Wheeler
Fremont, Calif.

Banana Bread in a Can

When I was a kid, my babysitter used to make a banana bread batter that she would pour into a clean can that was about the size of a big tomato sauce can. She would then cook it for several hours in a saucepan filled with water. It made the moistest banana bread ever. I've had no luck trying to find even a similar recipe.

Veronique Lamarche
Houston, Texas

Town Talk Cookies

I'm looking for a recipe for the Town Talk Cookies made at Braak's Bakery in Spring Lake, Mich. The bakery burned down in 1997, and that was the end of those yummy cookies. I can't stand the thought of never eating another Town Talk Cookie. Is there someone somewhere who may still be baking them?

Brenda Kling-Kella
via e-mail

Waldorf Astoria Chocolate Cake

I am looking for the original Waldorf-Astoria one-layer chocolate cake that had mayonnaise in the batter. It also had a chocolate frosting recipe that contained nuts.

Bobbe Weinig
Anchorage, Alaska

"San Antonio Light" Flank Steak

Back in 1974, when my husband and I were stationed in San Antonio, Texas, in the air force, a recipe for stuffed flank steak was published in the *San Antonio Light* newspaper (now out of business). We made this recipe several times and it was always wonderful. We've moved four times since then, and I cannot find the clipping. The flank steak was stuffed with a ground beef mixture and rolled and tied with string.

Beverly Link
Whitesburg, Ken.

Grapefruit Pie from the Valley

Many years ago, when I was in college in San Antonio, a friend took me down to the valley area of Texas. She told me about this place that was famous for its grapefruit pie, made with Ruby Red grapefruit and topped with meringue. It was an offbeat kind of place—I think it was a bowling alley of all things! Anyway, as odd as it sounds, the pie was delicious and it had big chunks of grapefruit. I have never had anything like it since, and my current friends think I made up this story. The friend who introduced me to the pie was from Mission, Texas, but I don't remember if that's where we actually got the pie. I have tried several recipes over the years, but none of them has come close. Can anyone help me?

Renee Brassard
Freihung, Germany

Pennsylvania Sugar Cookies

Back in the early 1970s, when I lived in Gettysburg, Pa., I used to buy packages of thick, soft, cake-like vanilla sugar cookies at the local grocery store. (I think they were made by a local baking company.) I recently tasted a very similar cookie at the food court at Hershey's Chocolate World in Hershey, Pa. They were very thick and soft and tasted almost like a cake. I have tried several recipes, but I can't duplicate them. Can anyone help?

Anne Hempfling
East Moriches, N.Y.

Are you looking for a special recipe? Or do you have a recipe a fellow *Cook's Country* reader is seeking? Post your requests and recipes by visiting **cookscountry.com** and clicking on **Looking For A Recipe.** We'll share recipe requests and found recipes on **cookscountry.com** and print as many as we can in the magazine. You may also write to us at Cook's Country, P.O. Box 470739, Brookline, MA 02447.

Find the Rooster!

A tiny version of this rooster has been hidden somewhere in the pages of this issue. If you find it, write to us with its location (plus your name and address) and you will be entered into a random drawing. The first winning entry will receive the Calphalon Contemporary Stainless Steel Roasting Pan (our test winner—see page 29), and the next five winners will each receive a complimentary one-year subscription to *Cook's Country*. To enter the contest, write to us at Rooster, Cook's Country, P.O. Box 470739, Brookline, MA 02447, or e-mail us by visiting **cookscountry.com.** Entries are due by January 31, 2007.

Did you find the rooster in the August/September 2006 issue? It was hidden in the stuffed pepper photo on page 24. Carol Suzuki of Dublin, Ohio, spotted it and won a Thermapen thermometer.

30-Minute Supper

EASY CHICKEN CORDON BLEU

30-Minute Supper

SKILLET CREOLE CHICKEN FRICASSEE

30-Minute Supper

CHINESE GLAZED PORK CHOPS

30-Minute Supper

RIGATONI WITH PORTOBELLOS
AND GORGONZOLA CREAM

SKILLET CREOLE CHICKEN FRICASSEE SERVES 4

Creole seasoning is a spicy blend of salt, paprika, cayenne, thyme, garlic, and other herbs and spices; we've had good results with Chachere's brand. Chorizo or kielbasa works well in place of andouille. Serve this quick chicken and sausage stew over rice.

4 boneless, skinless chicken breasts (about 1 1/2 pounds), halved crosswise
3 teaspoons Creole seasoning
8 ounces andouille sausage, cut into 1/2-inch rounds
3 tablespoons vegetable oil
1 onion, chopped
3 celery ribs, sliced thin
1 red bell pepper, seeded and chopped
4 garlic cloves, minced
1/4 cup all-purpose flour
2 cups low-sodium chicken broth

1. Pat chicken dry with paper towels and sprinkle with 2 teaspoons Creole seasoning. Cook sausage in large nonstick skillet over medium-high heat until browned, about 5 minutes. Transfer sausage to paper towel–lined plate, leaving fat in skillet. Cook chicken in sausage fat until browned, about 2 minutes per side. Transfer to plate with sausage.

2. Add oil, onion, celery, and pepper to now-empty skillet and cook until lightly browned, about 5 minutes. Add garlic and cook until fragrant, about 30 seconds. Stir in flour and remaining teaspoon Creole seasoning and cook until flour begins to brown, about 1 minute.

3. Slowly stir in broth until smooth. Return chicken and sausage to skillet. Cover and simmer until chicken registers 160 degrees, about 10 minutes. Serve.

EASY CHICKEN CORDON BLEU SERVES 4

Instead of trying to stuff chicken breasts with mustard, ham, and cheese, the chicken is topped with these ingredients, dusted with cracker crumbs, and baked. To save time, shred the cheese and crush the crackers while the chicken is browning.

4 boneless, skinless chicken breasts (about 1 1/2 pounds)
Salt and pepper
2 teaspoons vegetable oil
1 cup heavy cream
1/2 cup dry white wine
2 tablespoons Dijon mustard
1 tablespoon minced fresh tarragon (or 1 1/2 teaspoons dried)
4 slices baked deli ham
1 cup shredded Gruyère or Swiss cheese
16 Ritz crackers, crushed coarse

1. Adjust oven rack to lowest position and heat oven to 475 degrees. Pat chicken dry with paper towels and season with salt and pepper. Heat oil in large nonstick skillet over medium-high heat until just smoking. Brown chicken, about 3 minutes per side. Transfer chicken to 13 by 9-inch baking dish, smooth side up.

2. Add cream, wine, 2 teaspoons mustard, tarragon, and salt and pepper to taste to skillet and bring to simmer. Remove pan from heat.

3. Meanwhile, spread 1 teaspoon remaining mustard over each breast, lay 1 slice of ham on top, and mound each with 1/4 cup cheese. Sprinkle cracker crumbs over cheese, pressing to adhere. Pour sauce around chicken without disturbing crumbs. Bake until chicken registers 160 degrees, about 15 minutes. Serve.

COOK'S COUNTRY • DECEMBER/JANUARY 2007

RIGATONI WITH PORTOBELLOS AND GORGONZOLA CREAM SERVES 4

Any crumbly blue cheese can be substituted for the Gorgonzola.

2 tablespoons vegetable oil
4 large portobello mushroom caps, halved and sliced thin
4 garlic cloves, minced
1/2 cup dry white wine
1 cup heavy cream
1 cup crumbled Gorgonzola cheese
Salt
1 pound rigatoni
1 (5-ounce) bag baby spinach
Pepper

1. Bring 4 quarts water to boil in large pot. Meanwhile, heat 1 tablespoon oil in large nonstick skillet over medium-high heat until shimmering. Cook half of mushrooms and half of garlic until mushrooms are golden brown, about 4 minutes. Transfer to bowl and repeat with remaining oil, mushrooms, and garlic. Add wine to now-empty skillet and simmer until reduced by half, about 2 minutes. Add cream and 1/2 cup cheese and simmer until thickened, 3 to 5 minutes.

2. Meanwhile, add 1 tablespoon salt and pasta to boiling water and cook until al dente. Reserve 1/2 cup pasta cooking water, drain pasta, and return to pot. Add cooked mushrooms, spinach, and sauce to pot and stir until spinach is wilted, about 1 minute, adding reserved pasta water as needed. Add salt and pepper to taste and sprinkle with remaining 1/2 cup cheese. Serve.

COOK'S COUNTRY • DECEMBER/JANUARY 2007

CHINESE GLAZED PORK CHOPS SERVES 4

Chinese five-spice powder—a blend of ground star anise, cinnamon, fennel seed, clove, and peppercorns—can be found in the spice section of most supermarkets.

4 bone-in rib or center-cut pork chops, 3/4 to 1 inch thick
2 teaspoons vegetable oil
1/4 cup soy sauce
1/4 cup sugar
2 tablespoons orange juice
1 tablespoon grated fresh ginger
2 garlic cloves, minced
1/2 teaspoon cornstarch
1/4 teaspoon Chinese five-spice powder
1/8 teaspoon red pepper flakes

1. Pat pork chops dry with paper towels. Heat oil in large nonstick skillet over medium-high heat until just smoking. Add chops and cook until well browned, about 4 minutes per side. Transfer to plate.

2. Whisk remaining ingredients together in bowl. Pour off fat from skillet, add contents of bowl, and simmer until sauce thickens slightly, about 2 minutes.

3. Return chops and accumulated juices to skillet. Simmer, turning once or twice, until sauce glazes chops and meat registers 145 degrees, 3 to 5 minutes. Transfer chops and glaze to platter. Serve.

COOK'S COUNTRY • DECEMBER/JANUARY 2007

30-Minute Supper

FOIL-ROASTED COD WITH HERBED VEGETABLES

30-Minute Supper

POTATO AND ONION PIZZA WITH ROSEMARY AND GOAT CHEESE

30-Minute Supper

TUSCAN BREAD SOUP

30-Minute Supper

TOASTED TURKEY SUBS WITH SMOKED MOZZARELLA

POTATO AND ONION PIZZA WITH ROSEMARY AND GOAT CHEESE **SERVES 4**

A V-slicer or food processor fitted with the slicing disk will make quick work of the potatoes. You can find frozen pizza dough in many supermarkets or stop by your local pizzeria.

- **1 pound small red potatoes, sliced very thin**
- **6 tablespoons extra-virgin olive oil**
- **1/2 small red onion, sliced thin**
- **1/2 teaspoon minced fresh rosemary**
- **1 cup crumbled goat cheese**
- **Salt and pepper**
- **Flour for dusting**
- **1 (1-pound) ball ready-made pizza dough**

1. Adjust oven rack to upper-middle position and heat oven to 500 degrees. Toss potatoes with 1 tablespoon oil in large microwave-safe bowl. Cover tightly with plastic wrap and microwave on high power until potatoes are just tender, 3 to 7 minutes.

2. Meanwhile, combine 2 tablespoons oil, onion, rosemary, goat cheese, and salt and pepper to taste in bowl. Brush 2 tablespoons oil over rimmed baking sheet. On lightly floured work surface, roll dough into 16 by 9-inch oval (about 1/4 inch thick) and transfer to oiled baking sheet. Scatter potatoes in single layer over dough and top with onion mixture. Drizzle with remaining tablespoon oil and season with salt and pepper.

3. Bake until onions are soft and edges of pizza are well browned, about 15 minutes. Cut into wedges. Serve.

FOIL-ROASTED COD WITH HERBED VEGETABLES

SERVES 4

Haddock, halibut, or red snapper fillets are good alternatives for the cod.

- **1 medium zucchini, halved lengthwise and cut into thin half moons**
- **1 fennel bulb, trimmed, halved, cored, and sliced thin**
- **2 garlic cloves, minced**
- **6 scallions, sliced thin**
- **1/4 cup chopped fresh basil**
- **1 teaspoon dried thyme**
- **1/4 cup dry white wine or dry white vermouth**
- **Salt and pepper**
- **4 boneless, skinless cod fillets (about 2 pounds)**
- **4 tablespoons unsalted butter**

1. Adjust oven rack to lowest position and heat oven to 450 degrees. Combine zucchini, fennel, garlic, scallions, basil, thyme, wine, 1/4 teaspoon salt, and 1/8 teaspoon pepper in large bowl.

2. Lay four 14-inch-long pieces of foil on work surface. Place one fillet on lower half of each piece of foil and season with salt and pepper. Top each fillet with one-quarter of vegetable mixture and 1 tablespoon butter. Fold foil over fish and vegetables and crimp edges together to form 4 packets.

3. Arrange packets in single layer on rimmed baking sheet and cook until vegetables are tender and fish is just cooked through, 15 to 20 minutes. Transfer packets to individual plates and carefully cut open with scissors, being careful to avoid steam. Serve.

TOASTED TURKEY SUBS WITH SMOKED MOZZARELLA

SERVES 4

Store-bought pesto and a quick fresh tomato sauce enliven deli turkey in these Italian dinner sandwiches. Fresh mozzarella can be substituted for the smoked mozzarella.

- **3 tablespoons extra-virgin olive oil**
- **6 garlic cloves, minced**
- **1/2 teaspoon red pepper flakes**
- **2 (14.5-ounce) cans diced tomatoes, drained**
- **2/3 cup basil pesto**
- **Salt and pepper**
- **4 (6-inch) sub rolls, slit partially open lengthwise**
- **1 1/2 pounds thinly sliced deli turkey**
- **12 ounces smoked mozzarella, sliced into thin rounds**

1. Adjust oven rack to upper-middle position and heat oven to 500 degrees. Heat oil, garlic, and red pepper flakes in large skillet over medium-high heat until fragrant, about 1 minute. Add tomatoes and cook until mixture is dry, about 10 minutes. Off heat, stir in 2 tablespoons pesto and salt and pepper to taste.

2. Spread remaining pesto on insides of each roll and layer each roll with turkey, tomato mixture, and sliced cheese. Place sandwiches on baking sheet, with open sides facing up. Bake until edges of bread are golden and cheese begins to melt, about 5 minutes. Serve.

TUSCAN BREAD SOUP **SERVES 4 TO 6**

If you prefer, substitute 1/4 teaspoon minced fresh rosemary for the thyme.

- **4 slices crusty Italian bread, 1 1/2 inches thick**
- **4 tablespoons extra-virgin olive oil, plus extra for drizzling**
- **1 large onion, chopped**
- **6 garlic cloves, minced**
- **6 cups low-sodium chicken broth**
- **1/2 cup heavy cream**
- **1 teaspoon minced fresh thyme (or 1/2 teaspoon dried)**
- **Salt and pepper**
- **1/2 cup grated Parmesan cheese**

1. Adjust oven rack to middle position and heat oven to 475 degrees. Place bread slices on baking sheet, brush tops with 1 tablespoon oil, and bake until golden brown and crusty, 8 to 10 minutes.

2. Meanwhile, heat 3 tablespoons oil in Dutch oven over medium-high heat until shimmering. Add onion and cook until lightly browned, 8 to 10 minutes. Add garlic and cook until fragrant, about 30 seconds. Add broth, cream, and thyme and simmer until onions are softened, about 10 minutes. Season with salt and pepper to taste.

3. Cut bread into 1-inch chunks and place in soup bowls. Ladle soup over bread, sprinkle with Parmesan, and drizzle with olive oil. Serve.

"Little Italy" Meatballs

Mamma Mia! A novel cooking technique ensures rich and tender meatballs—even at this size.

How do you make great big meatballs that are moist and tender, not bready and dry?

Making big, "Little Italy"–sized meatballs is easy. Making big meatballs that are also tender and moist, with enough structure to hold their shape, is difficult. To keep the meatballs tender and moist, most recipes rely on two tricks: mixing the usual ground beef with ground pork (which has a higher fat content) and adding a panade, a paste made from bread and milk. The recipes I started testing made use of both tricks, but as soon as I made my first batch of meatballs I could see that I was in trouble. The moment the meatballs went into the pan, they collapsed under their own weight and spread out like soggy hamburger patties.

Most meatball recipes call for equal parts of pork and beef and use a soupy panade made with upward of 2 cups of liquid. I cut way back on both, using a 5-to-1 ratio of beef to pork and a stiff panade consisting of four slices of bread and only ¾ cup of milk. This drier, leaner mixture held its shape well and cooked up easily in the pan, but losing most of the fat meant I was also losing much of the flavor. Adding sautéed onion, garlic, red pepper flakes, dried oregano, and fresh parsley helped. A handful of Parmesan added richness. My meatballs were getting close, but there was still something missing. I tried different herbs and cheeses to no avail. Then a colleague suggested substituting raw Italian sausage for the ground pork. My tasters loved the flavor boost the sausage added.

When I started cooking the meatballs, my progress came to a grinding halt. Even in my largest pan, I could fry only five or six meatballs at a time. What's more, the meatballs were so big that they turned crusty and charred on the outside before they were cooked through. Getting frustrated, I turned to the oven. Lower temperatures produced flabby, gray meatballs; I turned up the heat and my luck began to change. At 475 degrees, the meatballs were baking to a nice golden brown. Now, without any babysitting or messy frying, I could focus on the marinara.

To build rich tomato flavor, I fried tomato paste along with the aromatics before adding crushed tomatoes and wine. The resulting sauce had a deep crimson color, a hearty texture, and a flavor that was deep and rich—all in just one hour.

Served over a bowl of steaming-hot spaghetti or eaten with a slice of crusty bread to sop up the sauce, these tender meatballs offer a big taste of Little Italy. **–Jeremy Sauer**

MEATBALLS AND MARINARA

SERVES 8 (MAKES ENOUGH TO COAT 2 POUNDS OF SPAGHETTI)

The meatballs and sauce both use the same onion mixture.

Onion Mixture

- 1/4 cup olive oil
- 3 onions, chopped fine
- 8 garlic cloves, minced
- 1 tablespoon dried oregano
- 3/4 teaspoon red pepper flakes

Easy Marinara

- 1 (6-ounce) can tomato paste
- 1 cup dry red wine
- 1 cup water
- 4 (28-ounce) cans crushed tomatoes
- 1/2 cup grated Parmesan cheese
- 1/4 cup chopped fresh basil
- Salt
- 1–2 teaspoons sugar, as needed

Meatballs

- 4 slices hearty white sandwich bread, torn into pieces
- 3/4 cup milk
- 1/2 pound sweet Italian sausage, casings removed
- 1 cup grated Parmesan cheese
- 1/2 cup chopped fresh parsley
- 2 large eggs
- 2 garlic cloves, minced
- 1 1/2 teaspoons salt
- 2 1/2 pounds (80 percent lean) ground chuck

1. For the onion mixture: Heat oil in Dutch oven over medium-high heat until shimmering. Cook onions until golden, 10 to 15 minutes. Add garlic, oregano, and pepper flakes and cook until fragrant, about 30 seconds. Transfer half of onion mixture to large bowl and set aside.

2. For the marinara: Add tomato paste to remaining onion mixture in pot and cook until fragrant, about 1 minute. Add wine and cook until slightly thickened, about 2 minutes. Stir in water and tomatoes and simmer over low heat until sauce is no longer watery, 45 to 60 minutes. Stir in cheese and basil and adjust seasonings with salt and sugar.

3. For the meatballs: Meanwhile, adjust oven rack to upper-middle position and heat oven to 475 degrees. Mash bread and milk in bowl with reserved onion mixture until smooth. Add remaining ingredients, except ground beef, to bowl and mash to combine. Add beef and knead with hands until well combined. Form mixture into 2½-inch meatballs (you should have about 16 meatballs), place on rimmed baking sheet, and bake until well browned, about 20 minutes.

4. Transfer meatballs to pot with sauce. Simmer for 15 minutes. Serve over pasta. (Meatballs and marinara can be frozen for up to 1 month.)

Kitchen Know-How
WHO'S FRYING NOW?

Not us, that's for sure. We found that a super-hot oven was all we needed to get a golden brown crust on these meatballs. Finally, a short dunk in the sauce allows the sauce to season the meat, and vice versa.

1. For a great crust without the hassle of frying, bake the meatballs in a very hot oven. **2.** For the best flavor, let the meatballs sit in the simmering sauce for at least 15 minutes before serving.

Taste Test: Pasta Sauces with Cheese

Jarred spaghetti sauce used to come in only one flavor—plain tomato—but now there are dozens of varieties on the market. Because most dishes made with red sauce also contain cheese, we thought cheesy tomato sauces sounded like a reasonable idea. But are these newfangled sauces any good? After tasting eight brands, we learned that the answer is "not really." Seven sauces were rejected by tasters for the "hard" and "stale" cheese bits they contain. Only one, Prego Ricotta Parmesan, made our "recommended" list (and just barely). Ricotta is the dominant cheese in this sauce, which was described by tasters as "nice and mild." **–Scott Kathan**

THE MILD ONE
We tasted eight jarred cheesy tomato sauces and found only one to be acceptable.

Best Stuffed Mushrooms

Stuffed mushrooms are often mushy and bland. Could we repair this recipe to produce an hors d'oeuvre that's the life of the party?

Warm, earthy mushroom caps stuffed with creamy cheese are pretty high up on my list of favorite party snacks. But mushrooms this good are elusive, and when it's my party, I wish they were easier to make. I set out to develop a recipe for great stuffed mushrooms that I could make ahead and quickly reheat when my guests arrived.

One of the biggest problems with stuffed mushrooms is sogginess. The only way to get water-laden button mushroom caps to shed their liquid is to roast them prior to stuffing. Using a common technique, I seasoned the mushrooms with olive oil, lemon juice, salt, and pepper before roasting them (gill side down, so the excess moisture could drain away) in a hot oven. These mushrooms were indeed dry, but the bottoms were so tough they were difficult to bite in half.

Thinking the hot baking sheet was to blame for the toughness, I roasted the caps on a wire rack so that air could circulate around them. This solved the problem of the leathery bottoms, but my tasters commented that there didn't seem to be a lot of mushroom flavor. Maybe I couldn't afford to waste the flavorful liquid the mushrooms were shedding. To keep that liquid, I roasted the mushrooms gill side up. Now the liquid pooled in the caps, infusing the mushrooms—not the pan—with flavor. A flip to gill side down for the final 10 minutes ensured that the caps shed any excess moisture.

Now I had firm-but-tender, flavorful mushroom caps; it was time to tackle the stuffing. I created four cheesy no-cook fillings, filled the mushrooms, and heated them for another 10 minutes. My recipe was very good, but tasters wanted something crunchy to contrast with the smooth filling. Dusting the stuffed mushrooms with fresh bread crumbs did the trick. The crumbs toasted in the hot oven, becoming golden and crunchy.

My stuffed mushrooms can be refrigerated for up to 3 days before serving. All you have to do is add the crumb topping and heat up the mushrooms as soon as the party starts.

–Stephanie Alleyne

We developed a recipe that takes the "mush" out of stuffed mushrooms. And they're easy to make in advance.

STUFFED MUSHROOMS

MAKES 24

Mushrooms shrink significantly as they cook, so choose large "stuffer mushrooms."

Topping

- 1 slice hearty white sandwich bread, quartered
- 1 tablespoon chopped fresh parsley
- 2 garlic cloves, minced
- 2 tablespoons olive oil

Mushrooms

- 24 large mushrooms, stems removed
- 1/4 cup olive oil
- 1 teaspoon lemon juice
- Salt and pepper
- 1 recipe stuffing (recipes follow)

1. For the topping: Pulse bread in food processor to coarse crumbs. Mix parsley, garlic, and oil in bowl. Stir crumbs into oil mixture to coat. Set aside.

2. For the mushrooms: Adjust oven rack to middle position and heat oven to 450 degrees. Line rimmed baking sheet with foil and set wire rack inside baking sheet. Toss mushrooms with oil, lemon juice, ¼ teaspoon salt, and ⅛ teaspoon pepper in bowl. Arrange mushrooms gill side up on rack and roast until juices are released, about 20 minutes. Turn caps over and roast until mushrooms are well browned, about 10 minutes.

3. Remove baking sheet from oven. Flip roasted mushrooms gill side up and cool slightly. Fill zipper-lock bag with stuffing and snip off one corner, then fill mushrooms (see photos on page 30). Press each cap (stuffing side down) into bread-crumb topping to coat and arrange (topping side up) on rack. Bake until filling is hot and topping is golden brown, about 10 minutes. Cool about 5 minutes before serving.

CHESAPEAKE SHRIMP STUFFING

MAKES ENOUGH TO STUFF 24 LARGE MUSHROOMS

If you prefer, substitute 1/2 cup lump crab meat for the shrimp.

- 1/4 pound cooked, peeled shrimp
- 1/2 cup shredded cheddar cheese
- 2 ounces cream cheese, softened
- 2 tablespoons chopped jarred roasted red peppers
- 3 scallions, sliced thin
- 1 garlic clove, minced
- 1 tablespoon lemon juice
- 1/2 teaspoon Old Bay seasoning
- 1/4 teaspoon salt
- 1/8 teaspoon pepper

Process all ingredients in food processor until smooth. Transfer to zipper-lock plastic bag until ready to use.

Visit us at cookscountry.com!
For a **Pepperoni Pizza Stuffing** for mushrooms, go to our website and click on **Cook's Country Extra.**

GOAT CHEESE AND HERB STUFFING

MAKES ENOUGH TO STUFF 24 LARGE MUSHROOMS

The herbs can be varied to include parsley, chives, or oregano.

- 4 ounces goat cheese, softened
- 2 ounces cream cheese, softened
- 1 tablespoon olive oil
- 1 garlic clove, minced
- 1 tablespoon chopped fresh basil
- 1 tablespoon chopped fresh tarragon
- 2 teaspoons chopped fresh thyme
- 1/4 teaspoon salt
- 1/8 teaspoon pepper

Process all ingredients in food processor until smooth. Transfer mixture to zipper-lock plastic bag until ready to use.

SPINACH AND LEMON STUFFING

MAKES ENOUGH TO STUFF 24 LARGE MUSHROOMS

To dry the spinach, see our shortcut on page 31.

- 1/2 cup frozen spinach, defrosted and squeezed dry
- 1/2 cup shredded cheddar cheese
- 2 ounces cream cheese, softened
- 2 tablespoons olive oil
- 1 garlic clove, minced
- 2 tablespoons lemon juice
- 3 scallions, sliced thin
- 1/2 teaspoon salt
- 1/8 teaspoon pepper

Process all ingredients in food processor until smooth. Transfer to zipper-lock plastic bag until ready to use.

Make Ahead: The mushrooms can be roasted and stuffed up to 3 days in advance, but don't top them with bread crumbs until you're ready to heat and serve the mushrooms. Store stuffed mushrooms, stuffing side up, on a paper towel–lined plate in the refrigerator, covered tightly with plastic wrap. The bread-crumb topping can be refrigerated separately for up to 3 days.

Easier Than You Think: Holiday Cheese Ball

How do you make a homemade version of the ubiquitous supermarket cheese ball—and make it taste good?

As soon as the holiday season arrives, so do the cheese balls. Stacked high in the refrigerator section of the supermarket, these almond-shingled spheres promise to be the perfect holiday hors d'oeuvre. But promises are made to be broken. With their straight-from-the-can texture, unnatural orange hue, and a flavor that's more Cheetos than cheddar, supermarket cheese balls make you wonder if there's any real cheese in them at all.

By using real cheese, I figured I was already well on my way to creating a superior recipe. For the optimal consistency—firm, yet spreadable—I used equal parts semisoft cheese (such as cheddar) and cream cheese. For a silky texture, I added a few tablespoons of mayonnaise and tossed everything into the food processor. I found that small amounts of assertive ingredients like Worcestershire, cayenne, and garlic enhanced the cheese flavor without compromising texture.

After a quick turn in the fridge to firm up, my cheese balls were almost ready to go, needing only a roll in toasted nuts, fresh herbs, or crushed tortilla chips before serving. Truly easy and really, really cheesy, these cheese balls are the right way to celebrate the holidays. **–Jeremy Sauer**

CLASSIC CHEDDAR CHEESE BALL SERVES 15 TO 20

- **2 cups shredded extra-sharp cheddar cheese**
- **8 ounces cream cheese, softened**
- **2 tablespoons mayonnaise**
- **1 tablespoon Worcestershire sauce**
- **1 garlic clove, minced**
- **1/4 teaspoon cayenne pepper**
- **1/2 cup sliced almonds, toasted**

Prepare according to directions at right.

ZESTY SMOKED SALMON CHEESE BALL SERVES 15 TO 20

- **2 cups shredded dill Havarti cheese**
- **8 ounces cream cheese, softened**
- **2 tablespoons mayonnaise**
- **4 ounces smoked salmon, chopped**
- **1 shallot, minced**
- **1 teaspoon lemon zest plus 1 tablespoon juice**
- **1/2 cup minced chives**

Prepare according to directions at right.

PORT WINE-BLUE CHEESE BALL SERVES 15 TO 20

- **1 cup crumbled blue cheese**
- **1 cup shredded mozzarella cheese**
- **8 ounces cream cheese, softened**
- **2 tablespoons mayonnaise**
- **1 tablespoon port wine**
- **1 garlic clove, minced**
- **1/2 cup pecans, toasted and chopped fine**

Prepare according to directions at right.

MEXICALI CHEESE BALL SERVES 15 TO 20

- **2 cups shredded pepper Jack cheese**
- **8 ounces cream cheese, softened**
- **3 tablespoons salsa**
- **2 tablespoons minced fresh cilantro**
- **1 garlic clove, minced**
- **1/2 cup blue corn tortilla chips, crushed**

Prepare according to directions at right.

How to MAKE A CHEESE BALL

1. Process all of the ingredients (except the nuts, chives, or tortilla chips) in a food processor until smooth, scraping down the sides as necessary, about 1 minute. Transfer the cheese mixture to the center of a large sheet of plastic wrap. **2.** Holding the corners of the wrap in one hand, twist the cheese with your other hand to seal the wrap and shape the cheese into a rough ball (mixture will be somewhat loose). Refrigerate until firm, about 3 hours. (The cheese ball can be refrigerated for up to 2 days.) Once the cheese ball is firm, reshape it as necessary into a smooth sphere. Unwrap the cheese ball and roll it in nuts, chives, or tortilla chips. Let it sit at room temperature for 15 minutes before serving.

Food Gift: Spiced Nuts

What's the best "glue" to attach sugar and spices to toasted nuts?

For me, the holidays officially begin once the house is perfumed with the heady smell of spiced nuts. Besides finding the right mix of spices, the key to this recipe is figuring out how to attach them to the nuts. I found that first tossing the nuts with melted butter yielded a spotty coating. Simmering the nuts in a spiced corn syrup glaze made the coating too candy-like and chewy. I had the best results when I mixed the nuts with egg whites, let the excess liquid drain away, and then tossed the nuts with the spice and sugar mixture. This technique created a cohesive, delicate shell around each nut. And toasting the nuts on a baking sheet in a relatively cool oven allowed plenty of time for the nuts and their coating to crisp up.

– Stephanie Alleyne

SPICED NUTS

MAKES ABOUT 10 CUPS

The nuts can be stored at room temperature in an airtight container for up to 3 weeks. Do not use salted nuts. Recipe can easily be halved.

- **2 large egg whites**
- **2 tablespoons water**
- **2 teaspoons salt**
- **2 pounds unsalted raw pecans, cashews, walnuts, or whole unblanched almonds**
- **1 1/3 cups sugar**
- **4 teaspoons cinnamon**
- **2 teaspoons ginger**
- **2 teaspoons coriander**

1. Adjust oven racks to upper-middle and lower-middle positions and heat oven to 300 degrees. Line 2 baking sheets with parchment paper. Whisk egg whites, water, and salt in large bowl. Add nuts and toss to coat. Drain in colander for 5 minutes.

2. Mix sugar, cinnamon, ginger, and coriander in large bowl. Add drained nuts and toss to coat. Spread nuts evenly on prepared baking sheets and bake until dry and crisp, 40 to 45 minutes, rotating and switching position of baking sheets halfway through baking time. Cool nuts completely. Break nuts apart and serve.

BARBECUED SPICED NUTS

Follow recipe for Spiced Nuts, adding 1/4 cup ketchup to egg white mixture in step 1 and replacing cinnamon, ginger, and coriander with 2 teaspoons chili powder, 2 teaspoons paprika, 1 teaspoon cumin, 1/4 teaspoon cayenne pepper, and 1/8 teaspoon cloves.

CURRIED SPICED NUTS

Follow recipe for Spiced Nuts, replacing cinnamon, ginger, and coriander with 2 teaspoons each curry powder, paprika, and cumin.

Test Kitchen's Holiday Menu

Everyone has favorite family holiday recipes, and our test kitchen staff is no different. We compiled a menu of our heirloom recipes—after extensively testing them, of course—for your family to enjoy.

Cook's Country Holiday Menu

First Course
Shrimp Cocktail Salad

Dinner
Pineapple Mustard Glazed Ham
Smoky Scalloped Potatoes
Apricot-Orange Gelatin Mold
Sweet & Sour Glazed Brussels Sprouts

Dessert
Cranberry-Raspberry Fools

SHRIMP COCKTAIL SALAD

SERVES 8

When I was a young girl, Mom would serve a special salad that she called "Shrimp Cocktail Salad" every Christmas Eve. It was a cross between a green salad (with iceberg lettuce, of course) and shrimp cocktail, with the most enormous shrimp I had ever seen. The tangy dressing was a mixture of French dressing and cocktail sauce. **–Diane Unger**

Dressing

- 1 cup ketchup
- 1 cup vegetable oil
- 3/4 cup white wine vinegar
- 2 teaspoons grated onion
- 1/2 cup extra-hot prepared horseradish
- Salt and pepper

Salad

- 2 cucumbers, peeled and diced
- 4 cups cherry tomatoes, quartered
- 2 small red onions, diced
- Salt and pepper
- 2 heads iceberg lettuce, outer leaves separated into 8-inch "cups"
- 2 pounds cooked and peeled jumbo shrimp

1. For the dressing: Combine all ingredients, including salt and pepper to taste, in blender until smooth, about 1 minute. Refrigerate until ready to use.

2. For the salad: Toss cucumbers, tomatoes, and red onion with 6 tablespoons dressing and salt and pepper to taste. Set iceberg cup in center of each plate and arrange shrimp over iceberg. Spoon cucumber salad over shrimp. Serve, passing remaining dressing separately.

Make Ahead: The dressing can be refrigerated for up to 2 days.

PINEAPPLE MUSTARD GLAZED HAM

SERVES 16 TO 20

My cousin Miranda cooks a glazed ham for her Christmas Eve party. Miranda's foolproof technique of keeping the ham tightly wrapped in the oven ensures that the meat remains succulent and juicy. The pineapple rings (minus the maraschino cherries) give it a very retro feel, and the classic pairing of mustard, brown sugar, and pineapple juice never gets old. I just wish I didn't have to wait all year to enjoy Miranda's next ham.

–Katie Henderson

- 2 (20-ounce) cans pineapple slices packed in juice
- 1 cup packed dark brown sugar
- 1/3 cup Dijon mustard
- 1/4 cup whole grain mustard
- 1 spiral-sliced, bone-in half ham (7 to 10 pounds), preferably shank end

We bring back the pineapple glazed ham—sans maraschino cherries—and it's better than ever.

1. Drain pineapple, reserving ¾ cup juice. Whisk juice, brown sugar, and mustards in bowl.

2. Remove ham from packaging and discard plastic disk that covers bone. Line 13 by 9-inch baking dish with two 24-inch-long pieces of foil. Place ham cut side down in lined baking dish and brush liberally with glaze. Using toothpicks, attach pineapple rings all over top and sides of ham. (Do not press toothpicks all the way into ham.) Brush with more glaze and wrap tightly in foil. Let stand at room temperature for 1½ hours.

3. Adjust oven rack to lowest position and heat oven to 300 degrees. Bake ham until center registers about 100 degrees on instant-read thermometer, 2 to 3 hours, depending on weight of ham (17 minutes per pound).

4. Remove ham from oven and roll back foil to expose ham. Increase oven temperature to 450 degrees. Brush ham liberally with more glaze and return to oven until glaze becomes golden brown and sticky, 30 to 40 minutes. Remove from oven, brush entire ham again with glaze, loosely cover with foil, and let rest for 30 to 40 minutes before carving, basting ham with juices once or twice. Serve.

Our scalloped potatoes (left) pack a spicy, smoky punch. This sweet and fruity gelatin mold (center) serves as a perfect foil for the salty ham and smoky potatoes. Brown sugar and cider vinegar bring out the sweetness in these Brussels sprouts (right).

SMOKY SCALLOPED POTATOES

SERVES 8, OR MORE

I come from a big family, so every year my brother and I were dragged all over creation on Christmas Eve to visit our relatives. That made for a long day for us kids, but our last stop—at Aunt Mitzi's house—always made it worthwhile. She was a heck of a cook, serving roast ham, sweet potato rolls, buttered sugar snap peas, and just about every kind of pie that I'd ever heard of, but my favorite was her scalloped potato casserole. It was tangy and smoky, and somehow the potatoes were always perfectly cooked. It took years before she would finally reveal the secrets behind this dish: The rich flavor came from buttermilk and smoked Gouda cheese, and a pinch of baking soda helped tenderize the potatoes.

–Jeremy Sauer

- **4 tablespoons unsalted butter**
- **1 large onion, minced**
- **4 garlic cloves, minced**
- **4 teaspoons dry mustard**
- **1 tablespoon minced fresh thyme**
- **2½ teaspoons salt**
- **½ teaspoon cayenne pepper**
- **5 pounds russet potatoes, peeled and sliced thin**
- **1½ cups heavy cream**
- **1½ cups buttermilk**
- **¼ teaspoon baking soda**
- **2 cups shredded smoked Gouda cheese**

1. Adjust oven rack to middle position and heat oven to 425 degrees. Melt butter in Dutch oven over medium-high heat. Add onion and cook until softened, about 5 minutes. Add garlic, mustard, thyme, salt, and cayenne and cook until fragrant, about 30 seconds. Stir in potatoes, cream, buttermilk, and baking soda and bring to simmer. Reduce heat to medium-low, cover, and cook until potatoes are almost tender, about 15 minutes. Stir in cheese and transfer mixture to 13 by 9-inch baking dish.

2. Bake until cream is bubbling around edges and top is golden brown, about 15 minutes. Cool 10 minutes before serving.

Make Ahead: The casserole can be prepared through step 1 and refrigerated for up to 24 hours. When ready to bake, cover with foil and bake in 400-degree oven until hot and bubbly, about 40 minutes. Remove foil and continue cooking until top is golden brown, about 30 minutes.

APRICOT-ORANGE GELATIN MOLD

SERVES 8, OR MORE

We fondly referred to my nana as the "Jell-O Mold Queen"—a title bestowed upon her one evening by my mother, through a fit of giggles, after Nana arrived at Sunday dinner with yet another one of her "famous" gelatin molds. This quickly became a loving family joke, but Nana would always retort: "Flowers can't be eaten, and chocolates spoil the appetite. If I am going to bring a hostess gift, it might as well make a useful and delicious contribution to the table." This dish has become such a tradition that it has replaced cranberry sauce on our family table. If you can't find apricot gelatin, use orange gelatin.

–Stephanie Alleyne

- **4 (3-ounce) boxes apricot-flavored gelatin**
- **2 cups boiling water**
- **2 cups apricot nectar, chilled**
- **2 cups orange sherbet, softened**
- **1 cup sour cream**
- **2 (15-ounce) cans mandarin oranges, drained and chilled**

1. Stir gelatin and boiling water in medium bowl until gelatin completely dissolves. Stir in chilled nectar. Refrigerate, uncovered, until slightly set (mixture should have consistency of egg whites), about 45 minutes.

2. Lightly coat 12-cup mold or nonstick Bundt pan with cooking spray. With electric mixer at medium-high speed, whip semi-set gelatin until foamy and well blended, about 1 minute. In separate bowl, whip sherbet and sour cream at medium-high until smooth. Combine sherbet mixture with gelatin and whip on medium-low until completely combined and free of streaks. Fold in oranges. Pour into prepared mold and refrigerate, uncovered, until set, about 4 hours. When ready to serve, invert onto large plate.

Make Ahead: The gelatin mold can be refrigerated in its pan for up to 2 days.

SWEET AND SOUR GLAZED BRUSSELS SPROUTS

SERVES 8

Every Christmas Eve my family abandons the formality of the dining room to dine, sitting on the floor, beside the living room fireplace. When I was a child, after enjoying our annual feast of barbecued pork shoulder, scalloped potatoes, Sister Schubert's rolls, and my mother's Brussels sprouts, we stayed by the fireside and listened to my uncle read *'Twas the Night before Christmas*. **–Cali Rich**

- **4 tablespoons unsalted butter**
- **1½ tablespoons light brown sugar**
- **2 pounds Brussels sprouts, trimmed and halved through core if large**
- **12 small shallots, halved lengthwise**
- **1 tablespoon cider vinegar**
- **Salt and pepper**

Adjust oven rack to middle position and heat oven to 400 degrees. Melt butter and sugar together in microwave. Toss Brussels sprouts, shallots, butter mixture, vinegar, ¾ teaspoon salt, and ½ teaspoon pepper in large bowl. Scatter on rimmed baking sheet and roast until golden brown, about 30 minutes, shaking pan every 10 minutes to redistribute vegetables. Serve.

CRANBERRY-RASPBERRY FOOLS

SERVES 8

Looking for a way to come up with a twist on the traditional cranberry-orange relish, my sister invented this light-as-a-feather dessert that's actually welcome at the end of the meal—just about the time that we're all adjusting our belts. Making it couldn't be easier, and because it requires no oven time (which is pretty hard to come by at this time of the year), it really is no-fuss. This dessert may be called a fool, but Mom sure didn't raise any. Serve with Christmas cookies.

–Bridget Lancaster

- **1 pound fresh or frozen cranberries**
- **2 cups fresh or frozen raspberries**
- **½ cup orange juice**
- **1 cup plus 2 tablespoons sugar**
- **Pinch salt**
- **3 cups heavy cream, chilled**

1. Bring cranberries, raspberries, orange juice, 1 cup sugar, and salt to boil in medium saucepan over medium-high heat. Reduce heat to medium and simmer until cranberries are softened and mixture becomes jammy, about 15 minutes. Puree in blender or food processor until smooth, then press through fine-mesh sieve into medium bowl. Set aside to cool to room temperature.

2. In electric mixer, beat 2 cups cream to stiff peaks. Gently fold into cooled cranberry mixture until no streaks remain. Spoon mixture into eight 6- to 8-ounce goblets or bowls.

3. When ready to serve, beat remaining 1 cup cream and remaining 2 tablespoons sugar to stiff peaks. Dollop cream onto fools. Serve.

Make Ahead: The fools can be refrigerated for up to 8 hours. Dollop whipped cream on top just before serving.

A no-bake, no-fuss holiday dessert? No foolin'.

An "Impossible" Breakfast Casserole

An Impossible Pie uses an eggy biscuit batter to create both a crust and filling for a quiche-like casserole. We retool this recipe with a crisper popover batter.

Our recipe puts a fresh spin on sausage, potato, and cheese breakfast casserole.

Impossible Pie was popularized back in the 1970s by the folks at Betty Crocker. The idea is to pour a thinned-out biscuit batter (made with Bisquick, milk, and eggs) on top of the filling ingredients in a pie plate; the batter sinks to the bottom of the dish and "impossibly" forms its own crust when baked. (The pies are also known as Impossibly Easy Pies.) During my research, I found almost every variation imaginable, from coconut cream (reportedly the first Impossible Pie) to asparagus to bacon. I was intrigued enough to try several recipes but found them impossibly heavy and dense. The edges were puffed and crisp, however, reminding everyone in the test kitchen of a super-sized popover and making us wonder if a popover batter would yield lighter results than a biscuit batter.

Popovers also seem to do the impossible, as the heat of the oven transforms their humble ingredients—eggs, milk, flour, salt, and butter—into the culinary equivalent of a hot air balloon. They are crisp and golden brown on the outside, tender and moist inside. Using the test kitchen's standard popover recipe (2 eggs, 1 cup each of milk and flour, and 1 tablespoon of melted butter), I traded in the popover pan for a pie plate and started incorporating some sausage and potatoes.

The sausage was easy: Tasters preferred ground, bulk sausage over diced links. The potatoes needed a bit more attention. Hoping to save time, I tested frozen hash browns, both shredded and diced. Even when precooked and crisped, the shredded hash browns were lost in the batter and didn't contribute anything. Diced hash browns had better texture, but they also had a stale freezer taste. Switching to freshly diced Yukon Gold potatoes was a big improvement. I precooked them in the microwave for three minutes before browning them quickly in a skillet. To make sure they didn't lose their crispness, I placed them on top of the popover batter.

Things were tasting good, but they still weren't looking quite right: The popover part of the casserole didn't have the dramatic rise I'd expected. Moreover, it was stubbornly sticking to the glass pie plate, and neither more butter nor more oil was helping. I knew that popovers need intense heat to turn the moisture in the batter to steam, which makes them rise and expand. Preheating the oven and the pan maximize this process. Preheating an empty glass pie plate is not safe, so I switched gears and tried a metal springform pan. The hot pan improved the rise and helped with the sticking issue. As an added bonus, I was able to remove the outer ring of the pan to reveal the visual glory of this puffy creation. **–Eva Katz**

Kitchen Know-How
DOUBLE UP ON THE NONSTICK

Even when we used a nonstick springform pan, we found that our breakfast casserole stubbornly stuck to the bottom of the pan, making it difficult to slice the casserole into wedges. Lining a springform pan (nonstick or regular) with foil (preferably nonstick) and then coating the foil with nonstick cooking spray ensured that our popover casserole released from the pan every time.

1. Line the bottom of a springform pan with aluminum foil (preferably nonstick), attach the sides of the pan, and tuck the foil underneath the pan bottom.
2. Coat the sides and bottom with cooking spray.

POTATO AND SAUSAGE BREAKFAST POPOVER CASSEROLE SERVES 6

This recipe requires careful timing. Once the batter is prepared and set aside to rest, the potatoes can be microwaved while the sausage is cooking. While the potatoes are pan-fried, the springform pan (with the cooked sausage) should be preheated in the oven.

- 2 large eggs
- 1 cup whole milk
- Salt
- 1 cup all-purpose flour
- 1 tablespoon unsalted butter, melted
- 2 scallions, chopped
- 3/4 pound Yukon Gold potatoes (about 2), peeled and cut into 1/4-inch dice
- 1 (12-ounce) package bulk sausage meat
- 2 tablespoons vegetable oil
- 1/2 cup grated Parmesan cheese

1. Adjust oven rack to upper-middle position and heat oven to 425 degrees. Prepare 9-inch springform pan as shown in photos, below left, and set aside on rimmed baking sheet.

2. Whisk eggs, milk, and ½ teaspoon salt in bowl until well combined. Stir in flour until just incorporated—the mixture will still be a bit lumpy. Whisk in butter until batter is smooth. Stir in scallions and set batter aside while preparing filling.

3. Toss potatoes with 1 tablespoon water in large microwave-safe bowl. Cover with plastic wrap, cut vent holes in plastic, and microwave on high power until potatoes just begin to soften, 3 to 4 minutes. Meanwhile, cook sausage in large nonstick skillet over medium heat, breaking up clumps, until meat has lost most of its pink color, about 4 minutes. Using slotted spoon, spread sausage evenly over bottom of prepared springform pan.

4. Heat oil in skillet with sausage fat over medium-high heat until shimmering. Add potatoes and ¼ teaspoon salt and cook until potatoes are golden and crisp, 8 to 10 minutes. Drain potatoes on paper towels.

5. While potatoes are cooking, place springform pan with sausage in oven for 10 minutes. Remove pan from oven and, working quickly, sprinkle ¼ cup cheese over sausage and pour batter evenly over filling. Scatter potatoes on top and sprinkle with remaining cheese. Bake until puffed and golden, 25 to 30 minutes. Remove pan from oven, run knife around edges of pan, and let cool 5 minutes. Release outer ring and, using spatula, transfer casserole to serving plate. Serve.

Almond Ring Coffee Cake

Don't be tempted by the saccharine boxed version at the supermarket. You can make a much better yeasted coffee cake at home—one with buttery, tender cake and a rich nut filling.

Most homemade coffee cakes combine plain yellow cake with brown sugar streusel. Although good, these cakes are pretty plain. When I want something fancier for the holidays, my thoughts turn to a yeasted coffee cake with buttery layers of rich dough, a sweet almond filling, and a flourish of sliced nuts and white icing. You can buy this kind of coffee cake at the supermarket (think Entenmann's), but most are made with shortening (not butter) and have an artificial flavor. My goal was to streamline the classic recipe and make it worth doing at home.

The method for making an almond ring coffee cake is pretty standard, and I didn't expect to deviate from the formula. An almond filling is placed on a rectangle of tender yeast dough, and the whole thing is rolled up, formed into a circle, and then cut to create a floral pattern that exposes some of the filling. The ingredients, however, required some testing. Some recipes produced rings that were too dry, while others were too sweet or lacked almond flavor.

I decided to start with the filling. Most recipes enrich cream cheese with ground almonds and sugar, but I found this combination problematic—the mixture was so soft it leaked out of the dough, and I could barely taste the almonds. I had better luck with almond paste (sold in tubes in the supermarket baking aisle). When mixed with a little cream cheese, it gave me the nutty flavor I was looking for, and it was thick enough to stay put inside the coffee cake.

Most yeasted coffee cakes rely on brioche, a rich dough made with milk, butter, and eggs. Because my almond filling was pretty rich, I found that a lighter dough (made with one stick of butter and not two, as many recipes directed) was better. Three egg yolks gave the dough good structure, and leaving out the whites made the dough easier to handle. (I saved the whites for gluing the garnish of sliced almonds onto the ring.)

After playing around with various amounts of granulated and brown sugar, I made the important discovery of using honey to sweeten the dough. My tasters loved its light caramel flavor; I liked the fact that honey made the dough moister and more tender.

By using a preheated and then turned-off oven as a proofing box, I was able to make my coffee cake in a couple of hours (not all day, as was the case with most recipes I tried). And my colleagues liked my coffee cake so much they suggested I "retest" it every morning in the test kitchen. My recipe was easy enough that I was willing to oblige. **–Katie Henderson**

We add flavor to—and remove mystery from—homemade yeasted coffee cake.

ALMOND RING COFFEE CAKES MAKES 2 RINGS, EACH SERVING 6

A single tube of almond paste makes enough filling for two coffee cakes; bake both at the same time or freeze one and bake it up to one month later (see page 30 for details).

Filling

- 1 (7-ounce) tube almond paste
- 1/2 cup confectioners' sugar
- 4 ounces cream cheese, softened

Dough

- 1 1/3 cups warm milk (110 degrees)
- 1/3 cup honey
- 8 tablespoons (1 stick) unsalted butter, melted
- 3 large egg yolks (reserve whites for topping)
- 2 teaspoons vanilla extract
- 4 1/2 cups all-purpose flour, plus extra for work surface
- 1 package rapid-rise or instant yeast
- 2 teaspoons salt

Topping

- 3 large egg whites
- 1/2 cup sliced almonds
- 1 1/2 cups confectioners' sugar
- 2 ounces cream cheese
- 2 tablespoons milk
- 1/2 teaspoon vanilla extract

1. For the filling: Fit standing mixer with paddle attachment and mix almond paste, confectioners' sugar, and cream cheese until smooth. Cover with plastic and refrigerate until ready to use.

2. For the dough: Adjust oven rack to upper-middle and lower-middle positions and heat oven to 200 degrees. When oven reaches 200 degrees, shut oven off. Lightly grease large bowl with nonstick cooking spray. Line 2 baking sheets with parchment paper and grease with cooking spray.

3. Mix milk, honey, melted butter, yolks, and vanilla in large measuring cup. Mix flour, yeast, and salt in bowl of

(continued on page 24)

How to MAKE A RING-SHAPED COFFEE CAKE

1. Spread a 1-inch-wide strip of filling about 1 inch above the bottom edge of the dough rectangle.
2. Using both hands, carefully roll the dough into an even cylinder and moisten the top 1/2 inch of the dough to seal.
3. Shape the dough into a ring. With a paring knife, make 11 cuts around the outside of the ring, spacing them about 1 1/2 inches apart.
4. Rotate each piece of dough cut side up.

Visit us at cookscountry.com! For **cinnamon**, **chocolate**, and **orange** variations on this coffee cake, go to our website and click on **Cook's Country Extra.**

Almond Ring Coffee Cake

continued from page 23

standing mixer fitted with dough hook. Turn mixer to low and slowly add milk mixture. After dough comes together, increase speed to medium and mix until shiny and smooth, 4 to 6 minutes. (Dough will be sticky.) Turn dough onto heavily floured work surface, shape into ball, and transfer to greased bowl. Cover bowl with plastic wrap and place in turned-off oven until dough is nearly doubled, about 20 minutes.

4. On lightly floured work surface, divide dough into 2 equal pieces. Working with one piece of dough at a time, roll dough into 18 by 9-inch rectangle with long side facing you. Following photos 1 and 2 on page 23, spread with half of filling and roll up dough. Brush top edge with water, then press to seal and transfer, seam side down, to parchment-lined baking sheet. Repeat with remaining dough and filling. Shape each cylinder into ring. Using paring knife, make cuts around outside of dough and shape as shown in photos 3 and 4.

5. Cover with plastic wrap coated with cooking spray and return to oven until rings have puffed slightly, 30 to 40 minutes. Remove from oven and heat oven to 375 degrees.

6. For the topping: Whisk reserved egg whites in small bowl, then brush rings with egg whites. Sprinkle with almonds and bake until deep brown, about 25 minutes, switching and rotating pans halfway through baking. While rings are baking or cooling, whisk confectioners' sugar, cream cheese, milk, and vanilla in small bowl until smooth. Drizzle icing over baked coffee cakes and serve warm.

Improving Chicken Marsala

Chicken Marsala seems like a simple dish, but a lot can—and does—go wrong. Could we develop a foolproof recipe that works every time?

Our Chicken Marsala succeeds because we used a few simple kitchen tricks—and a lot of restraint with the ingredient list.

Chicken Marsala is a well-loved Italian restaurant classic, traditionally made with sautéed chicken cutlets, browned mushrooms, and a rich Marsala pan sauce. But many recipes ruin this preparation with unnecessary ingredients and ill-advised techniques, which can leave you with chewy, dry, or slimy chicken in a sickeningly sweet sauce.

To make this recipe reliable, I started by cooking thin cutlets in a little oil over varying heat settings. Several sources indicated that thin, lean cutlets are best cooked over gentle heat, but this didn't prove true when I tried it. I found that I needed a hot skillet to achieve good color quickly; when cooked over medium-low heat the cutlets spent too much time in the pan and dried out. Some recipes direct the cook to dredge cutlets in flour before cooking them. This proved to be essential, as the unfloured cutlets turned out tough and stringy.

The first step in building the sauce was browning the mushrooms as well as some aromatic onions and garlic. Next, I deglazed the pan with Marsala and simmered the wine until it thickened slightly. Although either sweet or dry Marsala was acceptable, my tasters preferred the sweet variety, cut with a little chicken broth to yield a sauce that was moderately sweet but not saccharine.

My sauce was nearly perfect, except for the mushrooms. By the time the sauce reduced to the proper thickness, the mushrooms were limp and spongy, and they didn't taste very good—each bite of mushroom was like taking a swig of Marsala. Clearly, the mushrooms were absorbing too much liquid. Removing the browned mushrooms from the pan and simmering just the wine and broth solved the problem.

Some recipes simmer the cutlets in the sauce as it is being reduced, but my tasters thought the resulting cutlets were slimy. Adding the cutlets to the sauce at the last minute (with the mushrooms) gave the chicken enough time to absorb flavors and heat through without becoming slimy.

I now had a foolproof recipe for chicken Marsala—made in less time than it takes to flag down a waiter at a restaurant. **–Katie Henderson**

CHICKEN MARSALA

SERVES 4

Look for cutlets that are between 1/4 inch and 1/2 inch thick. See page 30 for more information about Marsala wine.

- **8 thin-cut boneless, skinless chicken cutlets (about 1 1/2 pounds)**
- **Salt and pepper**
- **1/4 cup all-purpose flour**
- **2 tablespoons vegetable oil**
- **3 tablespoons unsalted butter**
- **1/2 small onion, chopped fine**
- **8 ounces white mushrooms, trimmed and quartered**
- **1 large garlic clove, minced**
- **3/4 cup sweet Marsala**
- **1/2 cup low-sodium chicken broth**
- **2 teaspoons lemon juice**
- **1 tablespoon minced fresh parsley**

1. Pat cutlets dry with paper towels and season with salt and pepper. Dredge cutlets in flour to coat and shake to remove excess. Heat 1 tablespoon oil in large nonstick skillet over high heat until just smoking. Add 4 cutlets and cook until golden brown, 2 to 2½ minutes on each side. Transfer to large plate and cover with aluminum foil. Repeat with remaining oil and cutlets.

2. Heat 1 tablespoon butter in empty skillet over medium-high heat until foaming. Cook onion and mushrooms until browned, about 5 minutes. Add garlic and cook until fragrant, about 30 seconds. Transfer mushroom mixture to medium bowl and cover with foil.

3. Add Marsala and broth to empty skillet, bring to boil over high heat, and cook until reduced to ½ cup, about 5 minutes. Reduce heat to medium-low, return chicken and accumulated juices to skillet, and turn chicken to heat through, about 1 minute. Transfer chicken to serving platter. Off heat, whisk in remaining 2 tablespoons butter, lemon juice, parsley, and mushroom mixture. Pour sauce over chicken. Serve.

Getting to Know Mushrooms

We collected 12 varieties of edible mushrooms, some cultivated and some wild, and tasted them simply sautéed to best compare their flavors. For more information about storing and cleaning mushrooms, see page 30.

Portobello
GREAT FOR GRILLING

The heavyweights among cultivated mushrooms, portobellos can measure more than 6 inches across. When cooked, their "meaty, dense" flesh is often compared with steak. Their flavor is similarly robust, displaying a "pleasantly woody" taste and "port wine fruitiness." Discard stems and grill, sauté, or roast.

White Button
MOIST AND SPRINGY

The most common cultivated mushroom, the white button is recognizable for its pale color, broad cap, and stubby stem. Although they can differ greatly in size, their flavor is consistent: "mildly nutty," with a "springy, moist" texture. Trim stems and eat raw, sautéed, stuffed, roasted, or grilled.

Morel
SPRING'S TREASURE

Although they grow throughout the United States, morels are a favorite in the Midwest, where it is not uncommon to find them battered and fried. Morels have a "warm, smoky" flavor with a "bitter edge." Their "honeycombed" caps give them a "porous" texture that eagerly soaks up sauces. Sauté or roast.

Cremini
BABY BELLOS

Sometimes referred to as brown button mushrooms, cremini are simply tiny portobellos that are harvested before they mature. Their texture is firm ("almost crunchy") and their flavor is "sweet," "musty," and "slightly grassy." Trim stems and eat raw, sautéed, roasted, or grilled.

Shiitake
TASTE OF HONEY

Shiitakes are cultivated on inoculated oak logs. Although they can become very large, most caps are no more than 3 inches across when harvested. Their texture is "firm and chewy," their flavor often described as sweeter than that of other mushrooms. Our tasters detected honey. Discard stems and sauté or add to soups.

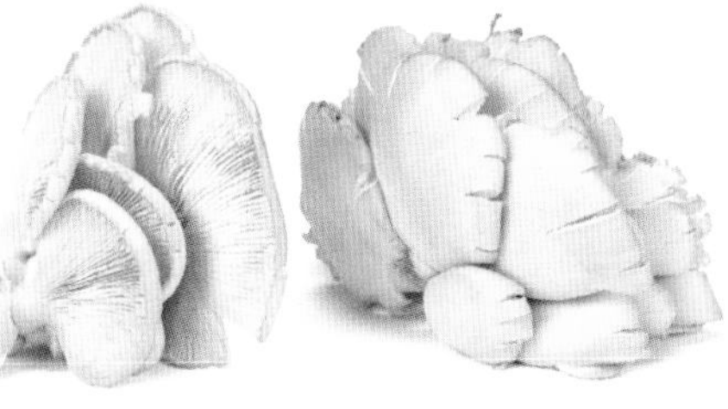

Oyster
FAN CLUB

These fan-shaped mushrooms, which grow in a range of colors and shapes, can be found both cultivated and wild. Their texture is "firm and springy" and their flavor at once "wheaty" and "briny," like a combination of "puffed rice" and "seaweed." Discard the base of stems, break up clusters, then roast, grill, or sauté.

Porcini
CROWNED HEADS

Considered the royalty of the mushroom world and often available only in dried form, when fresh these expensive wild mushrooms (also called cêpes) have bulbous caps and dense, spongy gills. Their texture is "meaty and crunchy," their flavor "complex, yeasty, almost bacon-like." Roast, sauté, or slice thinly and eat raw.

Enoki
SKINNY AND TINNY

These slender mushrooms are grown in narrow bottles to keep their skinny stems straight. A favorite in Asian cuisine, tender enoki mushrooms exhibit a "sweet, garlicky" flavor and a "tinny" aftertaste not unlike that of "canned bamboo shoots." Eat raw, quickly sauté, or add at the last minute to soups.

Maitake
FRILLY AND FRUITY

Also called "hen of the woods," this large, frilly mushroom is both cultivated and found wild. Similar in taste and texture to oyster mushrooms, maitakes are firm and "slightly chewy," with a "fruity, red wine–like complexity" and a "mossy" aftertaste. Discard the base of stems, break up clusters, and roast, grill, or sauté.

Chanterelle
YELLOW TRUMPET

Recognizable for both their color—ranging from pale yellow to deep orange—and their trumpet shape, chanterelles are favorites of mushroom hunters around the world. Their texture is "dense, almost crunchy" and their flavor "buttery and assertive," with a "fruity" aftertaste. Sauté or roast.

Lobster
PARASITE PARADISE

A lobster mushroom is not a true mushroom—it is a parasitic mold that infects mushrooms, turning their exterior a bright rusty-orange. This large, trumpet-shaped fungus is prized for its "dense, meaty" flesh. Its aroma is "musty and nutty," with a "buttery, shellfishy" taste. Trim stems and roast or sauté.

Black Trumpet
DARK AND DELICATE

Also known as the horn of plenty, this wild mushroom is a relative of the chanterelle. Recognizable for its imposing black hue, the black trumpet is "chewy," with a "rich, woodsy" flavor and subtle "apricot" aroma. Sauté quickly or add at the last minute to stews and rice dishes.

New Orleans Bourbon Bread Pudding

Toasting the bread makes it an equal partner to the rich custard in this rustic pudding served with a spoonful of potent bourbon sauce.

What's the secret to a creamy (not curdled) pudding with just the right mix of custard, bread, and bourbon?

The best bourbon bread pudding is a rich, scoopable custard that envelops the bread with a perfect balance of sweet spiciness and musky bourbon flavor. The history behind New Orleans's most famous dessert is as eclectic as the city itself. The basic custard and bread combination is of English origin. The bread—which in New Orleans is almost always a baguette—is from France. The addition of raisins to the custard can be credited to German settlers, while it was the Irish who infused the cream base with various liquors. The bourbon, of course, originally came from Kentucky traders.

I decided to stick to a custard-based recipe with raisins because it seemed both traditional and easy; unfortunately, the bread puddings I made in my initial test of five published recipes were awful. My tasters and I encountered a wide range of problems, from harsh bourbon flavor to curdled eggs to rock-hard raisins to slimy bread swimming in a river of custard. These bread puddings were nothing like my New Orleans ideal.

Some recipes cube the bread and stale it overnight, but these bread puddings looked more like the cobblestone streets in the French Quarter than something I'd like to eat for dessert. I wanted a more rustic look and had much better results tearing the baguette into ragged pieces. Toasting the torn pieces to a deep golden brown enriched their flavor and gave the bread a crispness that helped to prevent the finished dish from turning soggy.

The ratio of eggs to dairy (1 egg to ½ cup dairy) in the custard is time-tested, and I found that a mixture of 3 parts cream to 1 part milk was rich but not over the top. Tasters preferred the caramel flavor of brown sugar (rather than the usual white sugar) to sweeten the custard. Now it was time to tackle the most problematic aspect of this dish: the curdling custard.

Setting the baking dish with the pudding in a roasting pan filled with hot water (called a water bath) was one way to moderate the oven heat and keep the eggs from curdling, but this method is awfully cumbersome. I found that replacing the traditional whole eggs with just egg yolks helped stave off curdling. (I later found out that's because the whites set faster than the yolks.) Also helpful in curdle-proofing the pudding was lowering the oven temperature (to 300 degrees) and covering the baking dish with foil.

But with its foil cover, my pudding never formed much of a toasted top. Taking inspiration from pie recipes that sprinkle cinnamon and sugar on the dough to form a crunchy topping, I adapted this idea for my bread pudding. Once the custard had set up in the oven, I removed the foil, added the cinnamon, sugar, and some butter, and let it bake for another 30 minutes. The topping caramelized and formed a golden crust.

There's no doubt that bourbon bread pudding is an adult dessert. It should have enough robust bourbon flavor to warm you up, but not so much that it knocks you down. One-half cup to plump the raisins (which solved the rock-hard raisin problem from earlier tests) and another ¼ cup in the custard gave my bread pudding just enough bourbon punch. And for a real taste of New Orleans, I drizzle servings of the pudding with a warm bourbon-based cream sauce. **–Meredith Butcher**

Secrets to NEW ORLEANS BOURBON BREAD PUDDING

1. Toasting the torn French baguette enhances its flavor and texture.
2. Soaking the bread for 30 minutes in the custard softens the bread without turning it soggy.
3. Covering the bread pudding with foil allows the custard to set without drying out.
4. Sprinkling the half-baked pudding with a sugary topping adds a crisp crust. (To make the topping, use your hands to break butter into pea-size pieces and combine with the cinnamon and sugar.)

The American Table:
The History of Bourbon

How did Kentucky bourbon (the name given to whiskey distilled from at least 51 percent corn) end up playing such an important role in New Orleans's signature dessert? Right after the Revolutionary War, settlers in what eventually became Kentucky planted significant amounts of corn. Because there weren't many passable roads on which to transport this much grain back over the mountains to populated areas along the East Coast, many farmers distilled their crop to make whiskey. Bottles were packed in crates (stamped with the words "Old Bourbon," after the region of Kentucky where this liquor was produced) and shipped down the Ohio and Mississippi rivers to New Orleans and, eventually, the rest of the world. **–M.B.**

NEW ORLEANS BOURBON BREAD PUDDING SERVES 8 TO 10

This bread pudding is great on its own, but for a little more punch drizzle Bourbon Sauce over individual servings. A bakery-quality French baguette makes this dish even better.

- **1 (18- to 20-inch) French baguette, torn into 1-inch pieces (10 cups)**
- **1 cup golden raisins**
- **3/4 cup bourbon**
- **6 tablespoons unsalted butter, cubed and chilled, plus extra for baking dish**
- **8 large egg yolks**
- **1 1/2 cups packed light brown sugar**
- **3 cups heavy cream**
- **1 cup whole milk**
- **1 tablespoon vanilla extract**
- **1 1/2 teaspoons cinnamon**
- **1/4 teaspoon nutmeg**
- **1/4 teaspoon salt**
- **3 tablespoons granulated sugar**

1. Adjust oven rack to middle position and heat oven to 450 degrees. Arrange bread in single layer on baking sheet and bake until crisp and browned, about 12 minutes, turning pieces over halfway through drying time and rotating baking sheet front to back. Let bread cool. Reduce oven temperature to 300 degrees.

2. Meanwhile, heat raisins with ½ cup bourbon in small saucepan over medium-high heat until bourbon begins to simmer, 2 to 3 minutes. Strain mixture, reserving bourbon and raisins separately.

3. Butter 13 by 9-inch baking dish. Whisk yolks, brown sugar, cream, milk, vanilla, 1 teaspoon cinnamon, nutmeg, and salt in large bowl. Whisk in remaining ¼ cup bourbon plus bourbon used to plump raisins. Toss in toasted bread until evenly coated. Let mixture sit until bread begins to absorb custard, about 30 minutes, tossing occasionally. If majority of bread is still hard when squeezed, soak for another 15 to 20 minutes.

4. Pour half of bread mixture into prepared baking dish and sprinkle with half of raisins. Pour remaining bread mixture into dish and sprinkle with remaining raisins. Cover with foil and bake for 45 minutes.

5. Meanwhile, mix granulated sugar and remaining ½ teaspoon cinnamon in small bowl. Using fingers, cut 6 tablespoons butter into sugar mixture until size of small peas. Remove foil from pudding, sprinkle with butter mixture, and bake, uncovered, until custard is just set, 20 to 25 minutes. Increase oven temperature to 450 degrees and bake until top of pudding forms golden crust, about 2 minutes. Transfer to wire rack and cool at least 30 minutes or up to 2 hours. Serve. (Leftover bread pudding should be refrigerated; reheat individual portions in microwave.)

BOURBON SAUCE

MAKES ABOUT 1 CUP

Bourbon Sauce is traditionally drizzled over portions of bread pudding in New Orleans. It's potent stuff, so just a tablespoon per serving is enough. Leftover sauce is good over ice cream—but for adults only.

- **1 1/2 teaspoons cornstarch**
- **1/4 cup bourbon**
- **3/4 cup heavy cream**
- **2 tablespoons sugar**
- **Pinch salt**
- **2 teaspoons unsalted butter, cut into small pieces**

Whisk cornstarch and 2 tablespoons bourbon in small bowl until well combined. Heat cream and sugar in small saucepan over medium heat until sugar dissolves. Whisk in cornstarch mixture and bring to boil. Reduce heat to low and cook until sauce thickens, 3 to 5 minutes. Off heat, stir in salt, butter, and remaining 2 tablespoons bourbon. Drizzle warm sauce over cut bread pudding. (Sauce can be refrigerated in airtight container for up to 5 days; reheat on stovetop.)

Bake-Sale Favorites: Oatmeal Butterscotch Bars

We rethink this back-of-the-bag recipe and make it something special.

Studded with sweet, orange-hued butterscotch chips, "oatmeal scotchies" were my favorite cookies when I was a kid. The simplest recipes are oatmeal cookie dough with a bag of butterscotch morsels stirred in. Nostalgic for a taste of the past, I turned to the recipe my mother used—from the bag of Toll House butterscotch chips.

No wonder I had so many cavities as a kid. Tasters found the bars awfully sweet, and they felt the chips gave the bars an "unnatural taste." Instead of melting into the dough like chocolate chips, these chips turned hard and waxy. The "cakey and crumbly" texture of the bars was okay, but tasters wanted a chewier, moister version.

I hit the grocery store in search of better-tasting butterscotch products. I tried jarred butterscotch sauce, but it was too mild and the bars turned tough and taffy-like. Crushed butterscotch candies were even more artificial tasting than the chips. Having nowhere else to turn, I grudgingly reconsidered the butterscotch chips.

Reducing the amount of sugar solved the sweetness issue, and melting the chips eliminated their textural shortcoming. I found that melting the butter rather than creaming it gave the bars the chewy texture I wanted. Only one problem remained: Several tasters still complained about the "artificial" flavor of the chips.

Toasting the oatmeal didn't make much of a difference, but browning the butter (rather than just melting it) improved the bars tremendously, deepening their flavor and masking the unnatural taste of the chips. Substituting assertive dark brown sugar for light brown sugar created even more depth of flavor—and "scotchies" far better than the recipe on the bag. **–Cali Rich**

OATMEAL 'SCOTCH BARS MAKES 36 BARS

Old-fashioned oats will yield a chewier and less compact bar. Do not use instant oats.

Bars

- **1 1/4 cups all-purpose flour**
- **2 cups quick-cooking oats**
- **1/2 teaspoon baking soda**
- **1/2 teaspoon salt**
- **16 tablespoons (2 sticks) unsalted butter**
- **3/4 cup butterscotch chips**
- **1 cup packed dark brown sugar**
- **2 teaspoons vanilla extract**
- **1 large egg**

Glaze

- **2 tablespoons dark brown sugar**
- **1 tablespoon water**
- **1/8 teaspoon salt**
- **1/4 cup butterscotch chips**

1. For the bars: Adjust oven rack to middle position and heat oven to 350 degrees. Line 13 by 9-inch baking pan with aluminum foil, leaving overhang on all sides.

2. Mix flour, oats, baking soda, and salt in medium bowl until combined. Heat butter in small saucepan over medium-low heat until nutty brown in color, about 12 minutes. Pour hot butter over butterscotch chips in large bowl and whisk until smooth. Whisk in brown sugar until dissolved, then whisk in vanilla and egg until combined. Stir in flour mixture in two additions until combined.

3. Spread mixture into prepared pan and bake until edges are golden brown and toothpick inserted in center comes out with a few crumbs attached, 17 to 19 minutes. Transfer pan to wire rack.

4. For the glaze: Bring brown sugar, water, and salt to simmer in small saucepan. Pour hot sugar mixture over butterscotch chips in small bowl, whisking until smooth. Drizzle glaze over warm bars and cool on rack until warm to touch, about 1 1/2 hours.

5. Using foil overhang, lift bars from pan and cool completely on rack, about 30 minutes. Cut into bars and serve. (Bars will keep in airtight container at room temperature for up to 3 days.)

Don't overbake these chewy bars—they're done when a toothpick inserted in the center comes out with a few moist crumbs attached.

YELLOW CAKE MIXES: Can Any Come Close to Homemade?

While we here at *Cook's Country* prefer the rich flavor of a homemade cake, we know that many cooks invite Duncan Hines and Betty Crocker into their kitchens to help speed up the proceedings. But does it matter which cake mix you buy at the supermarket? Can any compete with homemade? We bought eight boxed yellow and gold cake mixes and headed into the test kitchen to find out. We served the plain, unfrosted cakes to 22 tasters, who rated each cake for flavor, texture, and overall appeal.

Our tasters weren't fooled by these mixes. All eight cakes had an unnaturally uniform crumb and extremely light, fluffy texture. Cake mixes are formulated to maximize the volume of air and moisture the batter can hold, which results in a very moist, tender, and delicate cake. Ingredients such as shortening, emulsifiers (mono- and diglycerides as well as lecithin), xanthan gum, and cellulose gum give cakes made from boxed mixes their distinctive texture.

Without these ingredients, a from-scratch cake doesn't rise as much and you end up with a tighter, more irregular crumb, which is able to withstand a heavy coating of frosting. Fluffy boxed cakes almost collapse under the weight of a rich frosting. Several of the cakes in our tasting were particularly fluffy (more like cotton candy than cake) and were downgraded by tasters.

The flavor of a boxed cake mix, even one that calls for the addition of butter, won't fool an observant taster, either—but some came surprisingly close. Tasters said that the cakes made from top-rated mixes tasted like butter and vanilla. Other mixes had an obvious artificial smell and flavor, which landed them at the bottom of our ratings.

The four top-rated cakes (three Betty Crocker mixes and one Pillsbury) all fall under the umbrella of General Mills; the two Duncan Hines mixes followed, with the two "independents," the Jiffy and King Arthur Flour mixes, bringing up the rear. Our conclusion: Betty Crocker knows how to make an appealing cake mix, Duncan Hines less so, and forget about the "alternative" brands you might find at the supermarket. The mixes are listed below, with tasters' comments, in order of preference. **–Scott Kathan**

① ② ③ ④ ⑤ ⑥ ⑦ ⑧

Recommended

1. **Betty Crocker Super Moist Butter Recipe Yellow Cake Mix $2.49**
This cake, which calls for a stick of butter, was praised for its "rich butter flavor" and "moist and tender" texture. Very "vanilla-y."

2. **Betty Crocker Super Moist Golden Vanilla Cake Mix $1.69**
Tasters appreciated the "very smooth," "nicely spongy" texture of this cake. Its flavor was deemed "mild but very good."

3. **Pillsbury Moist Supreme Classic Yellow Cake Mix $1.39**
This cake was "extremely tender and moist, with a very even crumb." So sweet "there's no need to add icing," quipped one taster.

4. **Betty Crocker Super Moist Yellow Cake Mix $1.69**
With its "nice flavors of butter and vanilla," this cake was deemed the best-tasting. However, some tasters complained about the "chalky," "mushy" texture.

5. **Duncan Hines Moist Deluxe Butter Recipe Golden Cake Mix $1.79**
Some tasters detected hints of "coconut and lemon," while others complained about a "chemical" aftertaste. This cake was substantially darker than the others.

Recommended with Reservations

6. **Duncan Hines Moist Deluxe Classic Yellow Cake Mix $1.69**
One taster likened this sample to a "spongy Twinkie," while other panelists were more generous and praised its "nice and light" crumb.

Not Recommended

7. **Jiffy Golden Yellow Cake Mix $.89 (makes only one 9" cake)**
"Tastes like the box it came from," said one taster. Overall, this cake mix was panned for its insipid, stale flavor and "dry and terrible" texture.

8. **King Arthur Flour Vanilla-Butter Cake Mix $4.95**
This mix contains fewer additives than the rest, but tasters were not impressed by the cake's "grainy," "crumbly" texture and strong "almond extract" aftertaste.

Taste Test Canned Tomato Products

Canned tomato products are a pantry staple, but which ones should you buy for which recipes? Whole, crushed, and diced tomatoes are fresher tasting, because they contain superior tomatoes and are cooked the least; tomato puree, sauce, and paste have less fresh tomato flavor, because they are cooked longer—but they do add more body. Here's how we use canned tomatoes in the test kitchen. **–S.K.**

Whole Tomatoes

Plum or round tomatoes that have been peeled and packed in juice or puree; those in juice have a livelier flavor. They are usually broken up before or during cooking. Use when freshness is key, like in a quick marinara sauce.

OUR FAVORITE: Progresso Italian-Style with Basil

Diced or Chopped Tomatoes

Sales of recipe-ready diced tomatoes dominate the canned tomato category. Look for diced tomatoes packed in juice; they have better flavor than those packed in puree. Diced tomatoes hold their shape fairly well, making them good choices for soups and chunky sauces.

OUR FAVORITE: Muir Glen

Crushed Tomatoes

Also known as ground tomatoes, these are whole peeled tomatoes that are crushed and enriched with tomato puree. Brands with less puree have better flavor. The texture of this product varies greatly among brands; some are chunky, others watery. Best used in stews and sauces.

OUR FAVORITE: Progresso

Tomato Puree

Made from cooked tomatoes that have been strained of seeds and skins. This product has weak tomato flavor and is little used in our test kitchen. Use in chilis, soups, and other long-cooked recipes where smooth, rich tomato texture is required.

OUR FAVORITE: Hunt's

Tomato Sauce

This product is cooked and strained like puree, but it is thinner and lightly seasoned; don't confuse with heat-and-serve jarred tomato sauces, which are much more flavorful. Use in dishes like chili and enchilada sauce, where a little extra spice and a more liquid texture is welcome.

OUR FAVORITE: Hunt's

Tomato Paste

Basically tomato puree with most of the moisture cooked out, tomato paste adds body, color, and intensity to many dishes. Stir into sautéed onions to build depth in stews, sauces, and braises. Tubes are more convenient than cans.

OUR FAVORITE: Amore

Equipment Roundup

INEXPENSIVE ROASTING PANS: Can They Stand the Heat?

How often do you use a roasting pan? Is it once or twice a year for a big holiday roast? A really nice roasting pan can easily retail for $200, and it doesn't make sense to spend so much money on a flashy pan that will sit in a cabinet most of the year. Could we find a more utilitarian pan?

Selecting which pans to test was easy. Since, to develop flavor, we often sear meat before roasting it, we chose pans that were flameproof and could be used on the stovetop; aluminum disposables, Pyrex, stoneware, and ceramic pans were out. We also wanted a pan that could accommodate a big holiday turkey with ease, so 15 by 11 inches was our minimum size. We wanted to be able to broil and roast at high heat, so we eliminated pans with nonstick finishes.

We found seven pans in the $20 to $80 range and headed into the test kitchen to put them through their paces. We also added the $100 Calphalon Contemporary Stainless roasting pan to the mix; this pan won a prior kitchen testing and has since become a favorite among our cooks. We used each pan to roast a 15-pound turkey and deglaze the drippings to make gravy, sear a 5-pound pork loin on the stovetop before roasting it, and roast 2 pounds of potatoes. The pans are listed at right in order of preference.

HANDLE WITH CARE: The best handles are sturdy and easy to grip with thick potholders and don't protrude far enough upward or outward to become a hazard. Our testers preferred the upright, riveted handles of the Calphalon, Cuisinart, and KitchenAid pans. Thick handles on the Anolon pan and hinged handles on the rectangular Metro pan were hard to grasp. The handles on the two oval pans were too small—especially when the pan was loaded with a heavy turkey.

HEFTY HEROES: The last thing you want to hear when you're working with a hot roasting pan—and its sizzling contents—on the stovetop is the "pop" of the pan buckling, which can send scalding-hot projectiles onto your arms. Buckling is also a telltale symptom of uneven heating, which leads to uneven cooking and browning. Most of the lighter pans buckled on the stovetop and produced food with spotty browning. The heaviest pans didn't buckle and were better at browning.

One surprising exception: The comparatively flimsy Granite Ware did a beautiful job browning the potatoes, because its black surface was a magnet for the oven's moderate heat. This benefit didn't carry over to the stovetop, however, where this thin pan scorched easily.

METAL MEDDLE: Stainless steel is attractive, nonreactive, lightweight, and relatively durable. It's also a poor conductor of heat, making it no surprise that our two top-performing pans featured an aluminum core inside the stainless steel. Aluminum is a superior metal for fast and even heat conductivity, which translates into no buckling and more responsive cooking—especially on the stovetop. The rest of the lineup was made of plain stainless steel or porcelain-enameled steel—fine materials for roasting a turkey in the oven (where the conductivity of the pan is not as important, as the food cooks mostly by radiant heat), but not well suited to the stovetop.

SUMMING UP: For cooks who do a lot of roasting, we recommend the Calphalon ($100) and Cuisinart ($80) pans—they are sturdy and excellent performers both in the oven and on the stovetop. Neither option is cheap, but both are solid values if you use a roasting pan often. The KitchenAid pan ($50) is the best bet for the occasional roaster. The once-a-year turkey roaster should be fine with the $22 Granite Ware.

–Scott Kathan

Recommended

CALPHALON Contemporary Stainless Steel Roasting Pan
Price: $99.99 at Cooking.com
Size: 16" x 13"
Weight: 5.2 lbs.
Materials: Stainless steel with aluminum core
Comments: This heavy, sturdy pan features good handles and an efficient, gently flared interior shape, making it especially easy to stir and deglaze. It was also the best at browning. Comes with sturdy nonstick U-rack.

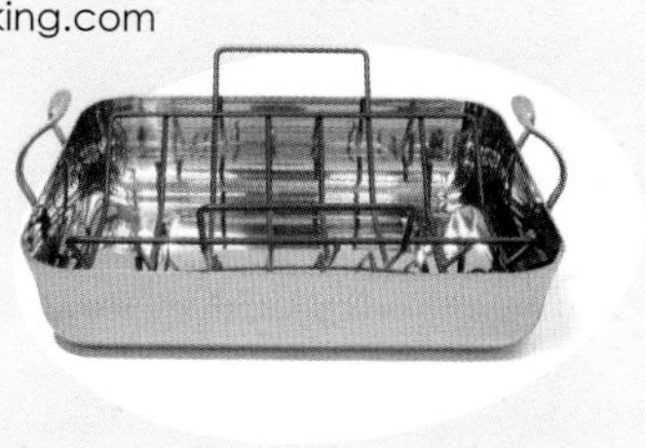

CUISINART Chef's Classic Roasting Pan
Price: $79.95 at Cooking.com
Size: 16" x 13"
Weight: 4.5 lbs.
Materials: Stainless steel with aluminum core
Comments: Very good on the stovetop, but testers saw some uneven browning in the pork loin test. Excellent handles, good heft, and an overall solid feel were more than enough to overcome that small demerit. Comes with useful V-rack.

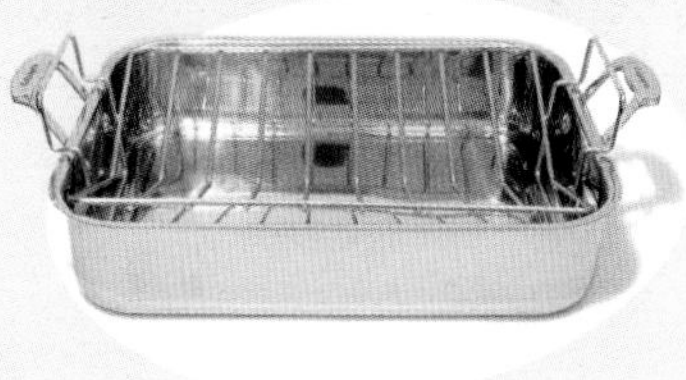

BEST BUY

KITCHENAID Gourmet Distinctions Roasting Pan
Price: $49.95 at Cooking.com
Size: 15" x 12"
Weight: 3.4 lbs.
Material: Stainless steel
Comments: This pan shined brightest in the potato test, but buckled a bit on the stovetop with both the turkey drippings and the pork loin. It has some of the winning attributes of two pans above, but wasn't quite in their class for heft and performance. Comes with U-rack that has awkward hinged handles.

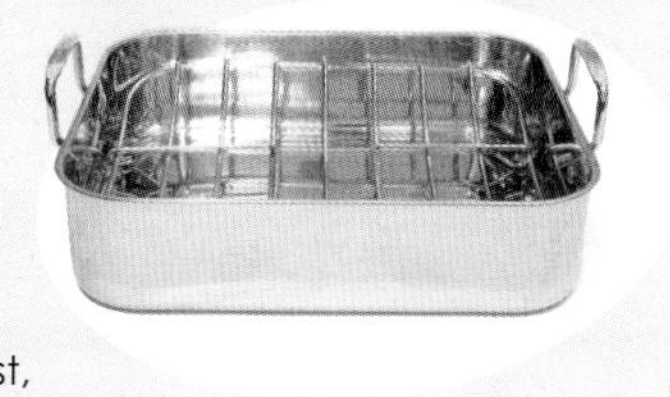

BEST BUY FOR INFREQUENT ROASTERS

GRANITE WARE Oval Roasting Pan
Price: $21.95 at Cooking.com
Size: 19" x 13.5"
Weight: 2.2 lbs.
Material: Porcelain-enameled steel
Comments: Very fast, even, deep browning on the potatoes, but this pan's thin bottom made it highly temperamental on the stovetop. Also, testers found the raised, patterned bottom to be problematic when deglazing. No rack included.

Recommended with Reservations

FARBERWARE Classic Accessories Large Roasting Pan
Price: $34.95
Size: 20" x 13"
Weight: 2.8 lbs.
Material: Stainless steel
Comments: This wide, shallow pan had acceptable performance, but felt flimsy and awkward. The rounded corners provided easy access for stirring and made pouring a breeze. Comes with flat rack that sits too low to be effective.

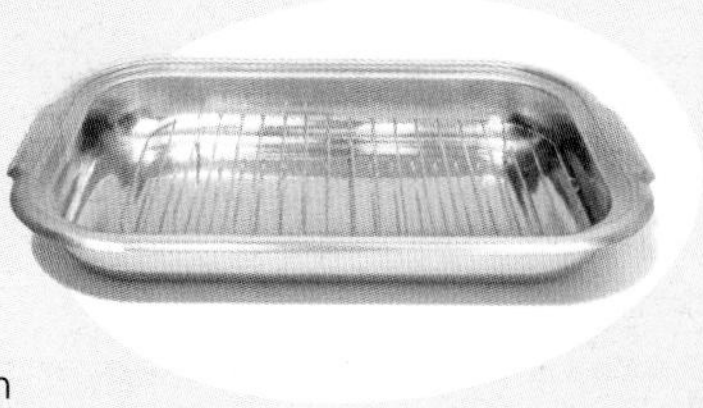

Not Recommended

METRO Roasting/Lasagna Pan
Price: $19.95
Size: 16" x 12"
Weight: 2.2 lbs.
Material: Stainless steel
Comments: The hinged handles were a big drawback, as they were very difficult to grab with potholders and felt perilously close to snapping under the weight of the turkey. Comes with flat rack that sits too low to be effective.

ANOLON Accessories Stainless Steel Roasting Pan
Price: $49.95
Size: 16" x 12"
Weight: 3.9 lbs.
Material: Stainless steel
Comments: This pan was noticeably hotter around the edges and cooler in the middle, resulting in very uneven browning, especially with the pork loin. Thick spots make handles hard to grip. Comes with U-rack that has awkward hinged handles.

METRO Stainless Steel Oval Roasting Pan with Domed Lid
Price: $29.95
Size: 15.5" x 11"
Weight: 2.4 lbs.
Material: Stainless steel
Comments: Deep sides on this oval pan make it hard to monitor browning, which was very uneven on both the potatoes and pork loin. Overall, performance just wasn't up to par. Comes with flat rack that sits too low to be effective.

Notes from Our Test Kitchen

TIPS, TECHNIQUES, AND TOOLS FOR BETTER COOKING

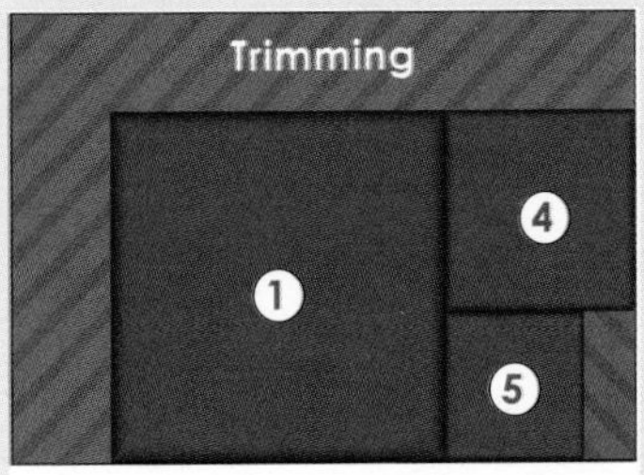

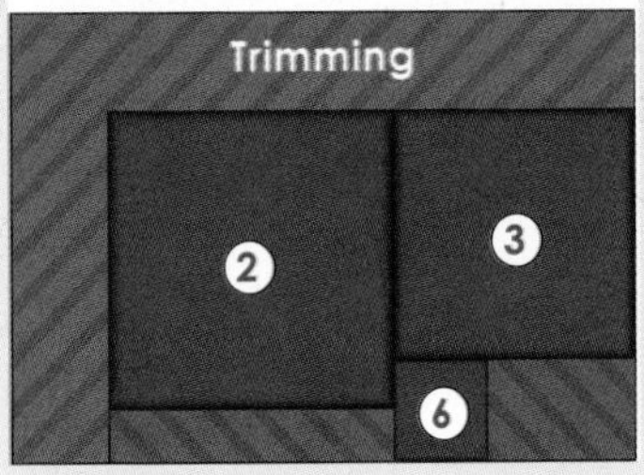

Kitchen Creations
Fancy Butters

Around the holidays, it's a nice idea to dress up plain vegetables with a quick flavored butter. The garlic butter on page 13 is one good example—but the possibilities are nearly endless. Here are a few butters we particularly like. These can be refrigerated for up to two days and will flavor two pounds of blanched or steamed vegetables. Try them with green beans, broccoli, carrots, cauliflower, or peas.

BLUE CHEESE BUTTER

- **3 tablespoons unsalted butter, softened**
- **1 1/2 tablespoons crumbled blue cheese**
- **1/4 teaspoon chopped fresh thyme**
- **Salt and pepper**

Combine all ingredients, including salt and pepper to taste, in small bowl.

DIJON TARRAGON BUTTER

- **3 tablespoons unsalted butter, softened**
- **1 1/2 tablespoons Dijon mustard**
- **1/2 teaspoon chopped fresh tarragon**
- **Salt and pepper**

Combine all ingredients, including salt and pepper to taste, in small bowl.

GINGER SESAME BUTTER

- **3 tablespoons unsalted butter, softened**
- **1/2 teaspoon finely grated ginger**
- **1/2 teaspoon toasted sesame oil**
- **Pepper**

Combine all ingredients, including pepper to taste, in small bowl.

Mushrooms 101

No matter their shape, size, or color, all mushrooms (see the photos on page 25) should be stored and cleaned the same way.

Storing Mushrooms
Mushrooms do best in a brown paper bag, but a zipper-lock bag with the zipper left partially open will suffice.

Cleaning Mushrooms
Even the button mushrooms sold in supermarkets should be cleaned before use. Use a brush or damp towel to remove any visible dirt. If mushrooms are particularly gritty, as many wild varieties can be, quickly rinse them under running water before drying them on a paper towel–lined plate. Don't wash mushrooms until you are ready to cook them, or the mushrooms will become slimy.

A Cake on Ice

Our **Almond Ring Coffee Cakes** (page 23) makes two cakes, which can be baked together or separately, with the second ring frozen for up to one month. Around the holidays, who wouldn't want an extra cake in the icebox? To freeze one coffee cake, transfer the ring (prepared through step 4) to a large plate and wrap in two layers of plastic and then foil. The night before baking, transfer the frozen ring to the refrigerator. The next day, unwrap the ring and transfer it to a baking sheet lined with parchment paper that has been greased with cooking spray. Proceed with step 5, letting the dough rise in an oven that has been heated to 200 degrees and then turned off. Brush with the egg wash, sprinkle with the almonds, bake (on the middle rack), cool, and ice as directed. **–Katie Henderson**

Cake Construction

Our Christmas Tree Cake (inside back cover) is made by cutting squares out of two separate 13 by 9-inch chocolate cakes and them stacking them to create the graduated tree shape. To cut the layers, first trim each 13 by 9-inch cake to measure 11 by 7 inches, then cut as follows:

From the first cake, cut out one 7 by 7-inch square (1), one 4 by 4-inch square (4), and one 3 by 3-inch square (5). From the second cake, cut one 6 by 6-inch square (2), one 5 by 5-inch square (3), and one 2 by 2-inch square (6). The trimmings from both cakes can be frozen and saved for another use.

The Cry to Fortify

Marsala is a fortified wine that originally hailed from Sicily. Like vermouth or sherry, Marsala starts with regular table wine that is then fortified with extra alcohol (often in the form of brandy) to increase its shelf life. An open bottle of fortified wine will keep in the pantry for several months (if not longer), making it the perfect choice for the cook who uses small quantities for recipes. Marsala comes in sweet and dry varieties. We like the sweet for Chicken Marsala (page 24). **–Katie Henderson**

SWEET STUFF
Sweet Marsala nicely balances the savory elements in pan sauces and is our first choice for cooking.

Kitchen Know-How SUCCESSFUL STUFFING

For mushroom caps that are roomy enough to accommodate the filling (see recipes on page 18), it's best to remove the stems with your fingers rather than a paring knife. For mess-free stuffing, use a zipper-lock storage bag, with one corner snipped off, to neatly squeeze the filling into each mushroom.

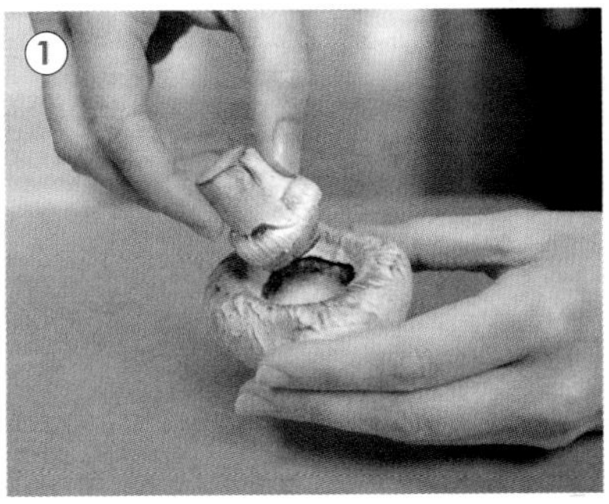

1. Grasp the stem where it joins the cap and gently wiggle the stem back and forth until it pops off in one solid piece. **2.** Press the filling down into one corner of a zipper-lock plastic bag, twist the bag to squeeze out excess air, then cut one corner off the bag with scissors. **3.** Gently squeeze some filling into each mushroom.

Kitchen Know-How DRAIN AWAY

Draining away the excess liquid from both the cottage cheese and the yogurt is an essential step when preparing our Marble Cheesecake (page 7). Don't be tempted to drain both in the same strainer—the drained cottage cheese needs to be pureed in a food processor until smooth. Be sure to use a brand of yogurt that doesn't contain modified food starch, gelatin, or gums—they prevent the yogurt from draining properly.

To drain the cottage cheese: Line a medium bowl with several layers of absorbent paper towels, spoon the cottage cheese into the bowl, cover with plastic wrap, and refrigerate overnight, at least 10 hours or up to 24 hours. Once drained, the cottage cheese can be used in the cheesecake recipe or transferred to a covered container and refrigerated for up to 1 week.

To drain the yogurt: Place a fine-mesh strainer over a medium bowl and line it with 3 to 4 paper coffee filters or a double layer of cheesecloth. Spoon the yogurt into the lined strainer, cover with plastic wrap, and refrigerate overnight, at least 10 hours or up to 24 hours. Once drained, the yogurt can be used in the cheesecake recipe or transferred to a covered container and refrigerated for up to 1 week.

A Rainbow of Sweet Potatoes

When developing our recipe for **Creamy Mashed Sweet Potatoes** (page 14), we used widely available Beauregards. How would the other varieties now popping up in markets fare in this recipe? Orange-fleshed Jewels and Garnets (both often sold as "yams") worked fine but were less sweet and a little wetter. The creamy texture and "buttery flavor" of white-fleshed Japanese and White Sweets were pleasing substitutes as well, but the purple-fleshed Okinawa and the pale yellow Batata were unacceptably dry. **–Cali Rich**

BEYOND ORANGE
The familiar orange variety has been joined by purple, yellow, and white varieties in many markets.

Cheaper Wine Is Just Fine

Beef Burgundy is a traditional French recipe made with red wine from the Burgundy region. But by the time these wines make it to our wine shops, they often cost $30 or more—a hefty investment for "cooking" wine. Since Burgundy is made with Pinot Noir grapes, we used inexpensive California Pinot Noirs—ranging in price from $6 to $20 a bottle—when developing our recipe on page 9. Even the cheapest Pinot Noir we tested delivered a richly flavored stew. **–Stephanie Alleyne**

A Bargain Beef Tenderloin

A warehouse club is a great place to find a quality beef tenderloin at a reasonable price. In fact, our tasters couldn't tell the difference between a $200 tenderloin we mail-ordered from a premier New York butcher and those we picked up for $50 to $60 at warehouse clubs. But expect to do some serious trimming at home—you might have to cut off 1½ pounds of fat and connective tissue from a 6-pound roast. Even so, a warehouse club roast is a great deal, as long as you have a sharp knife and 15 minutes. For a step-by-step look at cleaning up a whole beef tenderloin, go to **cookscountry.com.** Here are high points of the process.

Remove the Chain: The fatty chain runs along the entire length of the tenderloin. Gently pull and cut it away.

Trim the Silver Skin: A thin, translucent membrane covers much of the tenderloin. Remove the silver skin by inserting a knife just under the membrane and cutting away from you with a slightly upward angle. Take special care to remove the silver skin in the creases at the end of the tenderloin.

Trim the Fat: Remove all thick, hard pieces of fat.

Double Protection

We found it necessary to wrap our **Fluffy Make-Ahead Dinner Rolls** (page 15) in both plastic and aluminum foil to ensure their survival in the freezer. The plastic clings nicely to the rolls, while the sturdy foil keeps freezer burn at bay. Once the baked rolls have cooled, wrap them tightly in plastic and then foil. They will be fine for up to one month in the freezer. Another good idea: Keep the baked rolls together (the sides of the rolls will bake into each other) rather than wrapping the rolls individually. Wrapped as a single block, the rolls protect each other in the freezer.

–Diane Unger

A Cheesy Solution

The meatballs may get top billing in our recipe for **Meatballs and Marinara** (page 17), but the sauce is just as important. The ideal marinara sauce should be smooth, with just enough body to coat the meatballs and spaghetti. A good helping of tomato paste went a long way toward helping us achieve this texture, but the secret ingredient proved to be grated Parmesan cheese. When stirred into the sauce at the last minute, the cheese not only added a nutty flavor but also thickened the sauce, helping it cover the noodles and meatballs perfectly. **–Jeremy Sauer**

The Big Squeeze

Rather than spending time—and energy—wringing defrosted frozen spinach dry in a kitchen towel, try this trick. Place the defrosted spinach in a colander set over a bowl, press a layer of plastic wrap on top of the spinach, set a heavy can on top of the plastic, and let stand for about 10 minutes, pressing firmly on the can once or twice. The weight of the can will press out any liquid, freeing you up for other kitchen tasks. **–Stephanie Alleyne**

CAN DO
A quick press removes excess moisture from frozen spinach.

Gadgets & Gear: Springform Pan

Both our Marble Cheesecake (page 7) and Potato and Sausage Breakfast Casserole (page 22) recipes call for a springform pan. If you don't already own one, look for a model without a lip around the bottom edge (which we found can impede slicing and serving). When shopping, it can be hard to tell which models will leak and which ones won't. We've tested numerous models over the years and our favorite is the Frieling Handle-It ($31.95 at Cooking.com). The glass bottom makes it easy to judge browning on the bottom crust and the handles are helpful when maneuvering the pan in and out of the oven.

CLEARLY BETTER
A tempered glass bottom and nifty handles set this pan apart from the competition.

When Things Go Wrong in the Kitchen

READERS SHARE FUNNY STORIES ABOUT COOKING MISHAPS

ENVIRONMENTAL SAFETY

My wife loves spaghetti squash, and one day she decided it would be faster to cook it in our new microwave. She was standing there watching the carousel go around when she turned to ask me how long I thought it would take. I never got to reply, because at that very second the door flew open and a yellow projectile hurtled past her face and slammed against the refrigerator located across the narrow kitchen, splattering the boiling contents all over our appliances and kitchen floor. Fortunately, no one was hurt. We learned later that squash should be cut in half and seeded before cooking in the microwave.

Ted Sponsel Fairbanks, Alaska

CHEERIOS FOR CHRISTMAS

My husband and I had finally bought a house, and we were determined to make our first Christmas in it special. My entire family was visiting: my dad, my new stepmother, my three sisters, and their spouses. For Christmas Eve dinner we made a beautiful garlic rib roast. Later that evening, I made a large batch of cinnamon rolls, covered them with foil, and put them in the fridge to rise overnight. I popped them in the oven the next morning, and we all eagerly waited for our breakfast. What a disaster! I had covered my beautiful rolls with the same foil I had used to tent the garlic roast the night before. The rolls looked gorgeous, but the combined scents of cinnamon and garlic were not what we wanted to smell on Christmas morning. We tried cutting off the tops of the rolls, but the garlic taste had permeated the dough completely, so we all enjoyed a hearty breakfast of Cheerios instead.

Laura Bollard Seattle, Wash.

BREAD UNDER PRESSURE

When I was first married, my mother-in-law gave me a recipe for refrigerator bread. The recipe said to mix the dough up in the evening and refrigerate it overnight in a bowl with a tight lid so it could rise. The only large lidded "bowl" I had was my pressure cooker, so after mixing the dough, I put it in the pressure cooker pot, twisted the lid on firmly, and went to bed.

The next morning I was ready to use some dough for our breakfast, but when I opened the refrigerator it looked like cauliflower was oozing out of the spout of the pressure cooker. I pulled the dough out of the spout and tried to open the lid, but it wouldn't budge! Finally, my husband used a wrench to twist the pressure valve off, and I inserted a screwdriver in the spout to knead the bread and get the pressure down. When we finally got the lid off, I managed to make some bread for brunch.

Laurie Stone Friendswood, Texas

KENTUCKY BOURBON BALLS

I am from Northern California and my husband is from Kentucky. When we were first dating, we flew to Kentucky for Christmas so I could meet his family. I decided to make Kentucky bourbon balls as a gift for his parents. As I was preparing the recipe, I pictured their looks of delight and amazement as I, a Californian, unveiled their state's most beloved candy. The recipe I found online called for crushed crackers, but I didn't have any so I used crushed cornflakes instead. It seemed so logical, because cornflakes have roughly the same consistency as crackers.

After arriving in Kentucky, I noticed an unusually strong bourbon smell emanating from my bag. Opening the tin containing the bourbon balls, I was dismayed to find they had dissolved into a mushy puddle of brown goo. Apparently, the cereal had not absorbed the bourbon as well as cracker crumbs would have. I quickly tried to hide the tin under the bed, but at that moment my soon-to-be family walked into the room to invite me down for dinner. Noticing the strong reek of bourbon in the room, they asked me if I had been drinking. When forced to either admit my cooking gaffe or appear as if I'd been tippling, I decided to reveal the tin of goo, and my humiliation!

Amanda Bilby Moraga, Calif.

IT'S THE THOUGHT THAT COUNTS

When I was in college in the 1960s, I volunteered in a local elementary school. As a surprise for my 19th birthday, the kindergarten teacher I assisted had the kids make me a chocolate cake. To make sure there were no germs, she made all the kids scrub their hands with Phisohex, an antibacterial soap. The kids were very proud of their cake, and they loaded it up with birthday candles before singing "Happy Birthday" to me. They all had such bright smiles on their faces, but the cake was completely imbued with the chemical smell and taste of Phisohex. I had no choice but to gag it down with a big smile on my face to match the smiles on theirs. The kids clearly didn't care or notice the smell of the cake—to them it was chocolate and sugar! It was a long time before I ever ate chocolate cake again.

Suzanne Rampton Via e-mail

Send us your funniest kitchen disaster stories. Email us by visiting **cookscountry.com/emailus.** Or write to us at Kitchen Disasters, Cook's Country, P.O. Box 470739, Brookline, MA 02447. If we publish your story, you'll receive a complimentary one-year subscription to *Cook's Country*.

UNITED STATES POSTAL SERVICE

Statement of Ownership, Management, and Circulation (All Periodicals Publications Except Requester Publications)

1. Publication Title: Cook's Country	2. Publication Number: 1 5 5 2 - 1 9 9 0	3. Filing Date: 10-01-06
4. Issue Frequency: Bi-Monthly	5. Number of Issues Published Annually: 6 issues	6. Annual Subscription Price: $29.70
7. Complete Mailing Address of Known Office of Publication *(Not printer) (Street, city, county, state, and ZIP+4®)*: 17 Station Street, Brookline, MA 02445		Contact Person; Telephone *(Include area code)*: 617-232-1000

8. Complete Mailing Address of Headquarters or General Business Office of Publisher *(Not printer)*: same as publisher

9. Full Names and Complete Mailing Addresses of Publisher, Editor, and Managing Editor *(Do not leave blank)*

Publisher *(Name and complete mailing address)*: Christopher P. Kimball, Boston Common Press, 17 Station Street, Brookline, MA 02445

Editor *(Name and complete mailing address)*: same as publisher

Managing Editor *(Name and complete mailing address)*: Jack Bishop, Boston Common Press, 17 Station Street, Brookline, MA 02445

10. Owner *(Do not leave blank. If the publication is owned by a corporation, give the name and address of the corporation immediately followed by the names and addresses of all stockholders owning or holding 1 percent or more of the total amount of stock. If not owned by a corporation, give the names and addresses of the individual owners. If owned by a partnership or other unincorporated firm, give its name and address as well as those of each individual owner. If the publication is published by a nonprofit organization, give its name and address.)*

Full Name	Complete Mailing Address
Boston Common Press Limited Partnership	17 Station Street, Brookline, MA 02445
(Christopher P. Kimball)	

11. Known Bondholders, Mortgagees, and Other Security Holders Owning or Holding 1 Percent or More of Total Amount of Bonds, Mortgages, or Other Securities. If none, check box → ☐ None

Full Name	Complete Mailing Address
N/A	

12. Tax Status *(For completion by nonprofit organizations authorized to mail at nonprofit rates) (Check one)*
The purpose, function, and nonprofit status of this organization and the exempt status for federal income tax purposes:
☐ Has Not Changed During Preceding 12 Months
☐ Has Changed During Preceding 12 Months *(Publisher must submit explanation of change with this statement)*

PS Form 3526, September 2006 *(Page 1 of 3 (Instructions Page 3))* PSN 7530-01-000-9931 **PRIVACY NOTICE**: See our privacy policy on www.usps.com

13. Publication Title: Cook's Country

14. Issue Date for Circulation Data: October/November 2006

15. Extent and Nature of Circulation			Average No. Copies Each Issue During Preceding 12 Months	No. Copies of Single Issue Published Nearest to Filing Date
a. Total Number of Copies *(Net press run)*			385,771	392,793
b. Paid Circulation *(By Mail and Outside the Mail)*	(1)	Mailed Outside-County Paid Subscriptions Stated on PS Form 3541 *(Include paid distribution above nominal rate, advertiser's proof copies, and exchange copies)*	215,247	243,479
	(2)	Mailed In-County Paid Subscriptions Stated on PS Form 3541 *(Include paid distribution above nominal rate, advertiser's proof copies, and exchange copies)*	0	0
	(3)	Paid Distribution Outside the Mails Including Sales Through Dealers and Carriers, Street Vendors, Counter Sales, and Other Paid Distribution Outside USPS®	30,237	28,205
	(4)	Paid Distribution by Other Classes of Mail Through the USPS (e.g. First-Class Mail®)	0	0
c. Total Paid Distribution *(Sum of 15b (1), (2),(3), and (4))*			245,484	271,684
d. Free or Nominal Rate Distribution *(By Mail and Outside the Mail)*	(1)	Free or Nominal Rate Outside-County Copies Iincluded on PS Form 3541	1,096	945
	(2)	Free or Nominal Rate In-County Copies Included on PS Form 3541	0	0
	(3)	Free or Nominal Rate Copies Mailed at Other Classes Through the USPS (e.g. First-Class Mail)	0	0
	(4)	Free or Nominal Rate Distribution Outside the Mail *(Carriers or other means)*	2,955	2,895
e. Total Free or Nominal Rate Distribution *(Sum of 15d (1), (2), (3) and (4)*			4,051	3,840
f. Total Distribution *(Sum of 15c and 15e)* ▶			249,534	275,524
g. Copies not Distributed *(See Instructions to Publishers #4 (page #3))* ▶			136,237	117,269
h. Total *(Sum of 15f and g)* ▶			385,771	392,793
i. Percent Paid *(15c divided by 15f times 100)* ▶			98.38%	98.61%

16. Publication of Statement of Ownership
☒ If the publication is a general publication, publication of this statement is required. Will be printed in the Dec/Jan 2007 issue of this publication. ☐ Publication not required.

17. Signature and Title of Editor, Publisher, Business Manager, or Owner — Date 9/12/06

I certify that all information furnished on this form is true and complete. I understand that anyone who furnishes false or misleading information on this form or who omits material or information requested on the form may be subject to criminal sanctions (including fines and imprisonment) and/or civil sanctions (including civil penalties).

PS Form 3526, September 2006 *(Page 2 of 3)*

The Great American Cake

Christmas Tree Cake

Although this elegant cake looks hard to make, it actually starts with two regular chocolate sheet cakes, which are simply cut into squares of varying sizes and set atop one another. A bittersweet chocolate glaze and sugared cranberries complete the festive look.

To make this cake you'll need:

- **2 cups heavy cream**
- **16 ounces bittersweet chocolate**
- **2 (13 by 9-inch) baked chocolate sheet cakes***
- **3 cups chocolate buttercream***
- **1 cup fresh or frozen cranberries, picked through**
- **1 large egg white, beaten lightly**
- **1/2 cup sugar**

For the glaze: Boil cream, pour over chocolate, and let sit 5 minutes. Stir until smooth, then cool until just warm. Set aside.

For the cake: Trim each cake to measure 11 by 7 inches. Working with one cake, cut out one 7-inch square, one 4-inch square, and one 3-inch square. Working with second cake, cut out one 6-inch square, one 5-inch square, and one 2-inch square (see page 30).

To assemble: Use half of buttercream to frost each of the 6 layers separately; refrigerate until buttercream hardens (about 10 minutes). Refrost layers with half of remaining buttercream, smoothing as much as possible; refrigerate until hardened. Slowly pour and spread glaze over each layer, smoothing surface with spatula; refrigerate 10 minutes, then stack layers in order of descending size (starting with the 7-inch square on the bottom), off-setting each layer by 45 degrees.

To serve: Toss cranberries with egg white until well coated. (Use reconstituted powdered egg white if desired.) Using dinner fork, lift a few berries from white, allow excess to drain, then toss in sugar until coated. Repeat egg white dip and sugar coating with remaining berries. Using remaining buttercream in a pastry bag, pipe decorative border along base of each layer. Arrange cranberries on and around tree. Dust with powdered sugar if desired. To serve cake, remove layers and cut individual pieces.

*Visit **cookscountry.com** for our chocolate cake and chocolate buttercream recipes, or use your favorite.

Recipe Index

(RC) = Recipe Card